Java™

Software Solutions

Foundations of Program Design

Second Edition

Java™

Software Solutions

Foundations of Program Design

Second Edition

John Lewis
Villanova University

William Loftus
Breakaway Solutions, Inc.

ADDISON-WESLEY

An imprint of Addison Wesley Longman, Inc.

Reading, Massachusetts • Menlo Park, California • New York • Harlow, England
Don Mills, Ontario • Sydney • Mexico City • Madrid • Amsterdam

Senior Acquisitions Editor	Susan Hartman Sullivan
Assistant Editor	Lisa Kalner
Executive Marketing Manager	Michael Hirsch
Compositor	Michael and Sigrid Wile, Scott Silva, Sally Simpson
Technical Artist	Delgado Design, Inc.
Copyeditor	Roberta Lewis
Text Design	Delgado Design, Inc.
Proofreading	Trillium Project Management, Holly McLean-Aldis
Cover Designer	Night & Day Design, Joyce Cosentino

Cover image © Pedro Lobo/Photonica

Library of Congress Cataloging-in-Publication Data

Lewis, John, Ph.D.
Java software solutions : foundations of program design, 2 update / John Lewis, William Loftus.
p. cm.
ISBN 0-201-72597-5 (pbk.)
1. Java (Computer program language) 2. Object-oriented programming (Computer science) I. Loftus, William. II. Title.

QA76.73.J38 L49 2001
005.13´3--dc21 **00-064309**

Many of the designations used by manufacturers and sellers to distinguish their products are claimed as trademarks. Where those designations appear in this book, and Addison-Wesley was aware of a trademark claim, the designations have been printed in initial caps or all caps.

The programs and applications presented in this book have been included for their instructional value. They have been tested with care but are not guaranteed for any purpose. The publisher and author do not offer any warranties or representations, nor do they accept any liabilities with respect to the programs or applications.

Access the latest information about Addison-Wesley titles from our World Wide Web site: www.aw.com/cs

1 2 3 4 5 6 7 8 9 10–CRS–030201

This book has been developed to meet the needs of today's students and faculty. Let's hit the highlights. This book:

- is specifically designed for a first course in computing (traditionally called CS1 or introductory programming).
- uses Java 2 technology whenever appropriate, while still keeping an introductory perspective.
- has a state-of-the-art design with programs that are easy to read and main ideas that are clearly identified.
- includes hundreds of example programs, fully implemented for students and faculty to download and experiment with.
- is supplemented by many more fully implemented example programs on the textbook's Web site, as well as additional topic discussions that we call *web bonuses*.
- contains a large amount of reference material to support Java program development.

Cornerstones of the Text

This text is based on the following basic ideas that we believe make for a sound introductory text.

- **True object-orientation.** A text that really teaches a solid object-oriented approach must use what we call *object-speak*. That is, all processing should be discussed in object-oriented terms. That does not mean, however, that the first program a student sees must discuss the writing of multiple classes and methods. A student should learn to use objects before learning to write them. This text uses a natural progression that culminates in the ability to design real object-oriented solutions.
- **Sound programming practices.** Students should not be taught how to program; they should be taught how to write good software. There's a difference. Writing software is not a set of cookbook actions, and a good program is more than a collection of statements. This text integrates practices that serve as the foundation of good programming skills. These practices are used in all examples and are reinforced in the discussions. Students learn how to solve problems as well as how to implement solutions. We introduce and integrate basic software engineering techniques throughout the text and then devote a chapter to some more advanced software development activities.
- **Examples.** Students learn by example. This text is filled with fully-implemented examples that demonstrate specific concepts. We have intertwined small, readily understandable examples with larger, more realistic ones. There is a balance between graphics and nongraphical programs and between applets and applications. Additional examples can be found on the book's Web site.

Preface

Welcome to the Second Edition of ***Java Software Solutions, Foundations of Program Design.*** *We discovered after producing the first edition that the best part of textbook authorship is our interaction with you, the faculty and students using the book. We are pleased that the book serves your needs, and we are thrilled at the opportunity to revitalize and enhance it now.*

The first edition of this book was the first CS1/introductory programming text to be designed specifically with Java in mind. We were excited about Java's potential to serve as a pedagogical tool for demonstrating object-oriented concepts, and now we are delighted to see it become a realization. The success that Java has achieved commercially makes it an even more attractive tool for classroom use.

This second edition gives us the opportunity to enhance our approach, update the technical details, and provide new and improved examples. We've provided a `Keyboard` class to facilitate keyboard input for text-based applications, but have not complicated the model by adding any elements that seemed unnecessary. The new features of the Java 2 platform have been incorporated appropriately for an introductory programming course. We embrace the Swing graphical components without abandoning the underlying technology of the AWT on which Swing is based. Most importantly, we have significantly enhanced the examples throughout the book. Quoting from Albert Einstein:

> Example isn't another way to teach, it is the only way to teach.

We have a new Web site that supports the second edition of the text. The site is designed for both students and faculty. For students it contains extra examples, study aids, additional topics, and a few surprises. Faculty will find presentation slides, extra projects, problem solutions, and a detailed mapping between the first and second editions of the text, among other things. See the discussion about textbook supplements later in the preface for more details.

For our wives,
Sharon Lewis and
Veena Loftus

- **Appropriate Graphics and GUIs.** Graphics can be a great motivator for students, and their use can serve as excellent examples of object-orientation. As such, we use them throughout the text in a well-defined set of sections that we call the Graphics Track. This coverage includes the use of event processing and graphical user interfaces (GUIs). Students learn to build GUIs in the appropriate way by using a natural progression of topics. The Graphics Track can be avoided entirely for those who do not choose to use graphics.

Paths through the Text

This book is designed to be flexible, so that instructors can tailor its presentation to the needs of their students. Instructors can take a variety of paths through the text. The dependencies that exist between particular sections of the book are shown in the figure on the next page. Other than these dependencies, an instructor can vary the coverage as needed. Graphics can be emphasized or deemphasized as desired. Specific object-oriented issues can be covered at any point after Chapter 4.

Chapter Breakdown

Chapter 1 (Computer Systems) introduces computer systems in general, including basic architecture and hardware, networking, programming, and language translation. Java is introduced in this chapter, and the basics of program development are discussed. This chapter contains good introductory material that can be covered while students become familiar with their development environment.

Chapter 2 (Objects and Primitive Data) establishes the concept of an object and how they can be used. Many predefined classes from the Java standard library are explored and used, as well as the `Keyboard` class provided by the textbook authors. Primitive types, operators, and expressions are also explored.

Chapter 3 (Program Statements) covers most of the fundamental statements including conditionals and loops. Some additional operators are introduced at this point as well. Establishing key statements at this point allows the classes of the next chapter to be fully functional and realistic.

Chapter 4 (Writing Classes) explores issues related to writing classes and methods. Topics include instance data, visibility, scope, method parameters, and return types. Method overloading is covered as well. Some of the more involved topics are deferred to or revisited in Chapter 5. The key to Chapter 4 is the many fully implemented, realistic classes that are presented as examples of class design.

Chapter 5 (Enhancing Classes) covers additional issues related to class design and revisits topics that need further exploration. Object references are revisited and carefully explored, and their impact on parameter passing is discussed. Nested classes, interfaces, and their effect on design are also covered.

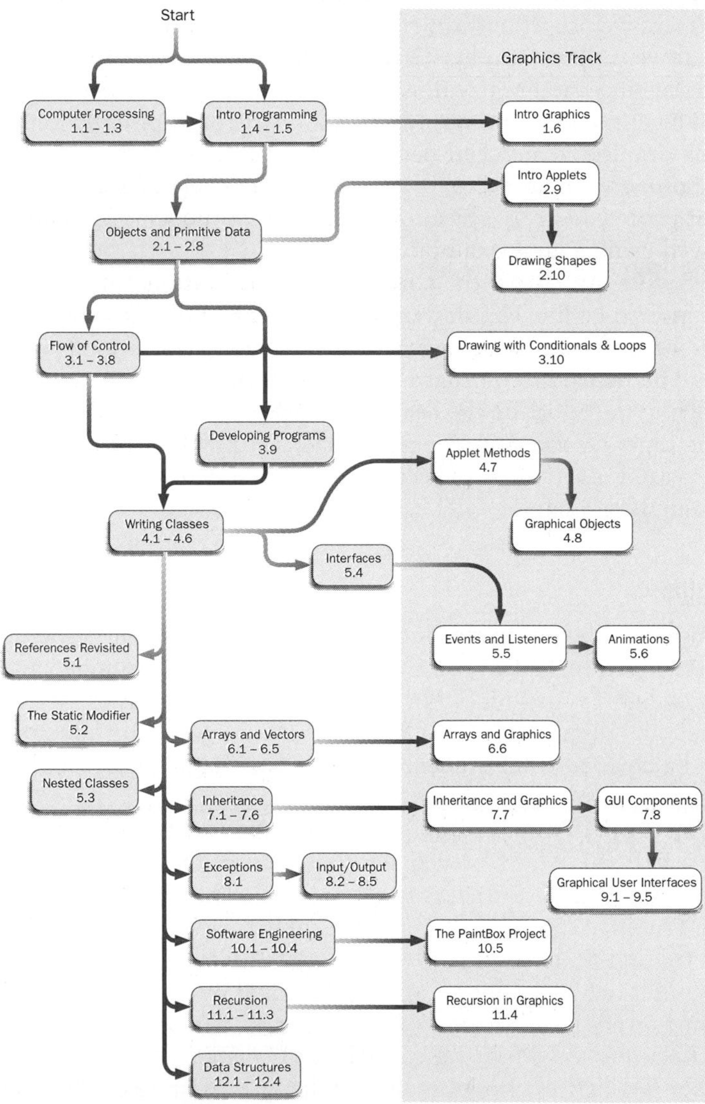

Chapter 6 (Arrays and Vectors) contains extensive coverage of arrays and array processing. Topics include multidimensional arrays and sorting. The `Vector` class is explored as well.

Chapter 7 (Inheritance) covers class derivations and associated concepts such as class hierarchies, overriding, and polymorphism. Emphasis is put on the proper use of inheritance and its role in software design.

Chapter 8 (Exceptions and I/O Streams) contains mostly new material covering the various Java I/O classes. The inner processing of the `Keyboard` class is unveiled. File I/O and object serialization are covered as well. All of the classes used in this chapter are clearly categorized to make sense out of the maze of Java I/O.

Chapter 9 (Graphical User Interfaces) introduces Swing components and covers various aspects of GUI construction and use. It includes a discussion of layout managers and special GUI features, then concludes with specific guidelines for the design of effective user interfaces.

Chapter 10 (Software Engineering) presents key issues related to the software development process. A truly object-oriented process model is presented, and then is followed using a large example.

Chapter 11 (Recursion) covers the concept, implementation, and proper use of recursion. Several examples from various domains are used to demonstrate how recursive techniques make certain types of processing elegant.

Chapter 12 (Data Structures) introduces the idea of a collection and its underlying data structure. Abstraction is revisited in this context and the classic data structures are explored. This chapter serves as a good introduction to a CS2 course.

Pedagogical Features

This text contains numerous pedagogical features that help make the material more accessible to students. Some of these features are listed below. See the Feature Walkthrough (at the end of the Preface) for examples of these elements.

- **Key Concepts.** Throughout the text, the Key Concept boxes highlight fundamental ideas and important guidelines. These concepts are summarized at the end of each chapter.
- **Listings.** All programming examples are presented in clearly labeled and screened listings, followed by the program's output, a sample run, or screen shot as appropriate. Comments in the programs are highlighted in color and provide additional insight into the program logic.
- **Keyboard Class.** Early programs use the author's `Keyboard` class to read information that the user enters on the keyboard. The `Keyboard` class keeps the student from getting bogged down in the complex declarations and conversions required in Java to perform keyboard input. It also serves as a good example of relying on predefined objects to abstract processing details. The details of the `Keyboard` class are discussed in the new chapter on Java I/O (Chapter 8).
- **Syntax Diagrams.** At appropriate points in the text, syntactic elements of the Java language are discussed in special highlighted sections with diagrams that clearly identify the valid forms for a statement or construct.

- **Graphics Track.** All processing that involves graphics and graphical user interfaces is discussed in one or two sections at the end of each chapter that we collectively refer to as the Graphics Track. This material can be skipped without loss of continuity or emphasized, as desired. The material in any graphics track section relates to the main topics of the chapter in which it is found.
- **Problem Sets.** Each chapter of the book concludes with a set of problems, separated into three categories:
  - *Self-Review Questions and Answers.* These short-answer questions review the fundamental ideas and terms established in the chapter. They are designed to allow students to asses their own basic grasp of the material. The answers to these questions can be found at the end of the problem sets.
  - *Exercises.* These intermediate problems require computations, the analysis or writing of code fragments, and often pose probing questions about the chapter content. While the exercises may deal with code, they do not require any online activity.
  - *Programming Projects.* These problems require the design and implementation of Java programs. They vary widely in level of difficulty.
- **Java reference material.** The text includes 13 appendices that contain a significant amount of language reference material, complementing the reference material presented in the text itself. Appendix M is particularly useful because it contains descriptions of many classes found in the Java standard class library.

Supplements

This book comes with a large variety of supplemental materials to assist in course preparation and execution. Links to the supplements can be found on the Addison Wesley Longman Web site for the text:

`www.awlonline.com/lewis`

Faculty and students should also visit the author's Web site for this text:

`jss.villanova.edu`

In addition, the authors can be contacted at the following email address:

`john.lewis@villanova.edu`

The following supplements are among those provided with this text. Visit the Web sites often to find updates and new materials. Faculty may want to direct students to particular examples and bonus discussions on the Web site. Material that is only for faculty use is password protected.

- **PowerPoint Slides.** A large collection of dynamic PowerPoint slides make it easy to present the book's material. Faculty are welcome to modify and augment the slides as they see fit.
- **Web Bonuses.** The textbook contains references to additional material discussed on the Web. These include topics from the book explored in more depth and advanced topics that are generally beyond the scope of a CS1 course. Additional Web Bonuses are added regularly.
- **Extra Examples and Projects.** The Web site contains many examples and project descriptions that are not found in the book. This searchable collection continues to grow.
- **Test Bank.** We also supply a set of problems that can be used as test questions or as additional homework exercises.
- **Exercise and Project Solutions.** Solutions for all exercises, test questions, and projects are provided for faculty.
- **Labs.** The lab materials, which integrate discussion and development activities, are designed for closed lab sessions, but can also be assigned as external projects.
- **Instructor's Manual.** This faculty-only resource contains chapter notes and teaching suggestions.
- **Java Development Environments.** The Web site contains instructions on the installation and use of several Java development environments.
- **Conversion Guide.** A detailed guide exists for instructors moving from the first edition of the text to the second edition.

Acknowledgments

As are most good things in life, the development of the second edition was a group effort. The success of this text is largely due to the support we received from many sources.

Since the first edition appeared, we have had the opportunity to talk to many faculty and students from around the world. Some of the best discussions we have ever had have come from the interaction with people who have used the book in their courses. We were pleased to see the depth of the faculty's concern for their students and the students' thirst for knowledge. You provided invaluable feedback concerning the best and less-than-best aspects of the first edition, and your constructive insight was fundamental in our development of the new edition. Thank you. Continued comments and questions are welcome.

Students at Villanova University were the first to see the new examples and materials, and they provided important feedback. They let us know what worked and what needed additional refinement. The special look that a student gets in his or her eyes when a concept clicks, which we like to call the "aha effect," was sometimes all that we needed to know that a particular example or explanation worked well.

Feature Walkthrough

Key Concepts. Throughout the text, the Key Concept boxes highlight fundamental ideas and important guidelines. These concepts are summarized at the end of each chapter.

value only needs to be changed where the constant is declared. For example, if capacity of the theatre changes (after a renovation) from 427 to 535, then we only have to change one declaration, and all uses of MAX_OCCUPANCY automatically reflect the change.

By convention, uppercase letters are used when naming constants to distinguish them from regular variables. Individual words are separated using the underscore character.

2.4 Primitive Data Types and Expressions

Key Concept

Each value in memory is associated with a specific data type. This data type determines what operations we can perform on the data.

There are eight primitive data types in Java: four variations of integers, two variations of floating point numbers, a boolean data type, and a character data type. Everything else is represented using objects. Let's examine the primitive data types in some detail.

Integers and Floating Points

Key Concept

Java has two kinds of numeric values—integers and floating point. There are four integer data types (`byte`, `short`, `int`, and `long`) and two floating point data types (`float` and `double`).

Java has two basic kinds of numeric values: integers, which have no fractional part, and floating points, which do. There are four integer data types (`byte`, `short`, `int`, and `long`) and two floating point data types (`float` and `double`). All of the numeric types differ by the amount of memory space used to store a value of that type, which determines the range of values that can be represented. The size of each data type is the same for all hardware platforms. All numeric types are *signed,* meaning that both positive and nega-

Listing 4.1

```
//********************************************************************
//  CountFlips.java       Author: Lewis and Loftus
//
//  Demonstrates the use of a programmer-defined class.
//********************************************************************

import Coin;

public class CountFlips
{
   //-----------------------------------------------------------------
   //  Flips a coin multiple times and counts the number of heads
   //  and tails that result.
   //-----------------------------------------------------------------
   public static void main (String[] args)
   {
      final int NUM_FLIPS = 1000;
      int heads = 0, tails = 0;

      Coin coin = new Coin();  // instantiate the Coin object

      for (int count=1; count <= NUM_FLIPS; count++)
      {
         coin.flip();

         if (coin.getFace() == coin.HEADS)
            heads++;
         else
            tails++;
```

Listings. All programming examples are presented in clearly labeled and screened listings, followed by the program output, a sample run, or screen shot as appropriate. Comments in the programs are highlighed in color and provide additional insight into the program logic.

Syntax Diagrams. At appropriate points in the text, syntactic elements of the Java language are discussed in special highlighted sections with diagrams that clearly identify the valid forms for a statement or construct. Syntax diagrams for the entire Java language are presented in Appendix L.

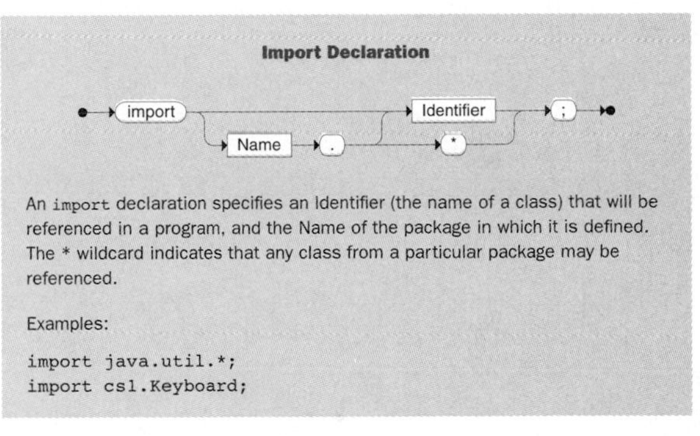
without the explicit package name. If only one class of a particular package will be used in a program, it is usually better to name the class specifically. However, if two or more will be used, the * notation is fine.

Import Declaration

An `import` declaration specifies an Identifier (the name of a class) that will be referenced in a program, and the Name of the package in which it is defined. The * wildcard indicates that any class from a particular package may be referenced.

Examples:

```
import java.util.*;
import cs1.Keyboard;
```

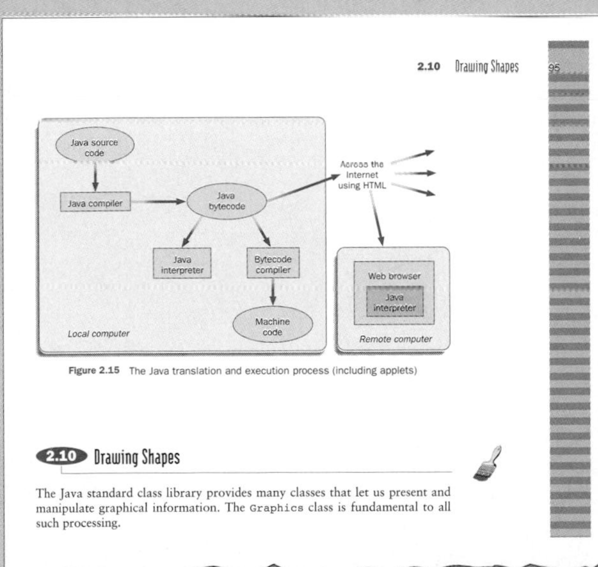
2.10 Drawing Shapes 95

Figure 2.15 The Java translation and execution process (including applets)

2.10 Drawing Shapes

The Java standard class library provides many classes that let us present and manipulate graphical information. The `Graphics` class is fundamental to all such processing.

Graphics Track. All processing that involves graphics and graphical user interfaces is discussed in one or two sections at the end of each chapter that we collectively refer to as the Graphics Track. This material can be skipped without loss of continuity, or focused on specifically as desired. The material in any Graphics Track section relates to the main topics of the chapter in which it is found. Graphics Track sections are indicated by a paintbrush icon and a patterned border on the edge of the page.

tive values can be stored in them. Figure 2.3 summarizes the numeric primitive types.

Remember from our discussion in Chapter 1 that a bit can either be a 1 or a 0. Because each bit can represent two different states, a string of n bits can be used to represent 2^n different values. Appendix B describes number systems and these kinds of relationships in more detail.

Web Bonus

The book's Web site includes a description of the internal storage representation of primitive data types.

When designing a program, you sometimes need to be careful about picking variables of appropriate size so that memory space is not wasted. For example, if a value will not vary outside of a range of 1 to 1000, then a two-byte integer (`short`) is large enough to accommodate it. On the other hand, when it's not clear what the range of a particular variable will be, you should provide a reasonable, even generous, amount of space. In most situations memory space is not a serious restriction and you can usually afford generous assumptions.

Web Bonus. The authors' web site contains additional examples and discussions. These are noted throughout the text as web bonuses.

Summary of Key Concepts

- The information we manage in a Java program is either represented as primitive data or as objects
- An abstraction hides details. A good abstraction hides the right details at the right time so that we can manage complexity.
- A variable is a name for a memory location used to hold a value of a particular data type.
- A variable can store only one value of its declared type.
- Java is a strongly typed language. Each variable is associated with a specific type for the duration of its existence, and you cannot assign a value of one type to a variable of an incompatible type.
- Constants are similar to variables, but they hold a particular value for the duration of their existence.
- Each value in memory is associated with a particular data type. This data type determines what operations we can perform on the data.
- Java has two kinds of numeric values—integers and floating point. There are four integer data types (`byte`, `short`, `int`, and `long`) and two floating point data types (`float` and `double`).
- Many programming statements involve expressions. Expressions are

Summary of Key Concepts. The Key Concepts presented throughout a chapter are summarized at the end of the chapter.

▶ **Self-Review Questions**

2.1 What is an object? Why is it abstract?

2.2 What is an escape sequence? Give some examples.

Self-Review Questions and Answers. These short-answer questions review the fundamental ideas and terms established in the chapter. They are designed to allow students to assess their own basic grasp of the material. The answers to these questions can be found at the end of the problem sets.

▶ **Answers to Self-Review Questions**

2.1 An object is a part of a program that provides services to another par of a program. These services are provided by the methods of the clas from which the object is instantiated. An object is considered to b abstract because the details of the object are hidden from the user of th object. Hidden details help us manage the complexity of software.

2.2 An escape sequence is a series of characters that begin with the back slash (\) and that imply that the following characters should be treate in some special way. Examples: \n represents the newline character, \

▸ **Exercises**

3.1 Using various relational and logical operators, give an equivalent expression for each of the following:

a. `total < sum`

b. `MAX <= highest`

c. `intensity > threshold`

3.2 What happens in the `MinOfThree` program if two or more of the values are equal? If exactly two of the values are equal, does it matter whether the equal values are lower or higher than the third?

3.3 Give four different statements that increment the value of an integer variable total.

3.4 Given the following declarations, trace the output of the listed conditional statements.

```
int i = 6;
int j = 9;

a. if (i < j)
      System.out.println ("Rapping");
```

Exercises. These intermediate problems require computations, the analysis or writing of code fragments, and probing questions about the chapter content. While the exercises may deal with code, they do not require any online activity.

Programming Projects

Programming Projects

2.1 Create a revised version of the `Lincoln` application from Chapter 1 such that quotes appear around the quotation.

2.2 Write an application that reads three integers and prints their average.

2.3 Write an application that reads two floating point numbers and prints their sum, difference, and product.

2.4 Create a revised version of the `TempConverter` application to convert from Fahrenheit to Celsius. Read the Fahrenheit temperature from the user.

2.5 Write an application that converts miles to kilometers. One mile equals 1.60935 kilometers. Read the miles value from the user as a floating point value.

2.6 Write an application that reads a value representing a number of seconds. Print the equivalent amount of time in hours, minutes, and seconds.

2.7 Create a revised version of the previous project to reverse the process. That is, read values representing a time duration in hours, minutes, and seconds, then print the equivalent total number of seconds.

2.8 Write an application that reads the `(x,y)` coordinates for two points. Compute the distance between the two points using the following for-

Programming Projects. These problems require the design and implementation of Java programs. They vary widely in level of difficulty.

Contents

1 Computer Systems

This book is about writing well-designed software. To understand software, we must first have a fundamental understanding of its role in a computer system. Hardware and software cooperate in a computer system to accomplish complex tasks. The nature of that cooperation and the purpose of various hardware components are important prerequisites to the study of software development. Furthermore, computer networks have revolutionized the manner in which computers are used, and they now play a key role in even basic software development. This chapter explores a broad range of computing issues, laying the foundation for the study of software development.

Chapter Objectives

- Describe the relationship between hardware and software.
- Define various types of software and how they are used.
- Identify the core hardware components of a computer and explain their purpose.
- Explain how the hardware components interact to execute programs and manage data.
- Describe how computers are connected together into networks to share information.
- Explain the impact and significance of the Internet and the World Wide Web.
- Introduce the Java programming language.
- Describe the steps involved in program compilation and execution.
- Introduce graphics and their representations.

1.1 Introduction

This section provides an overview of computers, defining some fundamental terminology and showing how the key pieces of a computer system interact.

Basic Computer Processing

A computer system is made up of hardware and software. The *hardware* components of a computer system are the physical, tangible pieces that support the computing effort. They include chips, boxes, wires, keyboards, speakers, disks, cables, plugs, printers, mice, monitors, and so on. If you can physically touch it and it can be considered part of a computer system, then it is computer hardware.

Key Concept

A computer system consists of hardware and software that work in concert to help us solve problems.

The hardware components of a computer are essentially useless without instructions to tell them what to do. A *program* is a series of instructions that the hardware executes one after another. *Software* consists of programs and the data those programs use. Software is the intangible counterpart to the physical hardware components. Together they form a tool that we can use to solve problems.

The key hardware components in a computer system are the following:

- central processing unit (CPU)
- main memory
- secondary memory devices
- input/output (I/O) devices

Each of these hardware components is described in detail in the next section. For now, let's simply examine their basic roles. The *central processing unit* (CPU) is the device that executes the individual commands of a program. *Input/output* (I/O) *devices,* such as the keyboard, mouse, and monitor, allow a human being to interact with the computer.

Programs and data are held in storage devices called memory, which fall into two categories: main memory and secondary memory. *Main memory* is the storage device that holds the software while it is being processed by the CPU. *Secondary memory* devices store software in a relatively permanent manner. Two common secondary memory devices are floppy disks and hard disks. A floppy disk cannot store as much information as a hard disk, but it can be moved from computer to computer. Figure 1.1 shows how information moves among the basic hardware components of a computer. Suppose you have an executable program you wish to run. The program is stored on some secondary memory device, such as a hard disk.

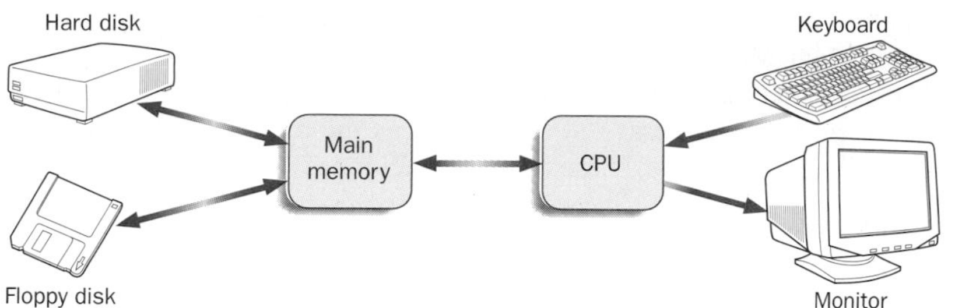

Figure 1.1 A simplified view of a computer system

When you instruct the computer to execute your program, a copy of the program is brought in from secondary memory and stored in main memory. The CPU reads the individual program instructions from main memory. Then the CPU executes the instructions one at a time until the program ends. The data that the instructions use, such as two numbers that will be added together, are also stored in main memory. They are either brought in from secondary memory or read from an input device such as the keyboard. During execution the program may display information to an output device such as a monitor.

Key Concept

To execute a program, the computer first copies the program from secondary memory to main memory. The CPU then reads the program instructions from main memory, executing them one at a time until the program ends.

The process of executing a program is fundamental to the operation of a computer. All computer systems basically work in the same way.

Software Categories

Software can be classified into many categories using various criteria. At this point we will simply differentiate between system programs and application programs.

The *operating system* is the core software of a computer. It performs two important functions. First, it provides a *user interface* so that the human user can interact with the machine. Second, the operating system manages computer resources such as the CPU and main memory. It determines when programs are allowed to run, where they are loaded into memory, and how hardware devices communicate. It is the job of the operating system to make the computer easy to use and ensure that it runs efficiently. Windows 98, Windows NT, Unix, Linux, and Mac OS are examples of popular operating systems.

Key Concept

The operating system provides a user interface and manages computer resources.

An *application* is a generic term for just about any software other than the operating system. Word processors, missile control systems, database managers, and games can all be considered application programs. Each application program has its own user interface that allows the user to interact with that particular program.

The user interface for most modern operating systems and applications are *graphical user interfaces* (GUIs), which, as the name implies, make use of graphical screen elements. These elements include:

- *windows,* used to separate the screen into distinct work areas
- *pull-down menus,* which provide the user with a list of options
- *icons,* which are small images that represent computer resources, such as a file
- *buttons,* which can be "pushed" with a mouse click to indicate a user selection

The mouse is the primary input device used with graphical user interfaces, and GUIs are sometimes called *point-and-click interfaces.* The screen shot in Figure 1.2 shows an example of a graphical user interface.

Key Concept

As far as the user is concerned, the interface *is* the program.

The interface to an application or operating system is an important part of the software because it is the only part of the program with which the user directly interacts. To the user, the interface *is* the program. Chapter 9 discusses the creation of graphical user interfaces.

The focus of this book is the development of high-quality application programs. We explore how to design and write software that will perform calcu-

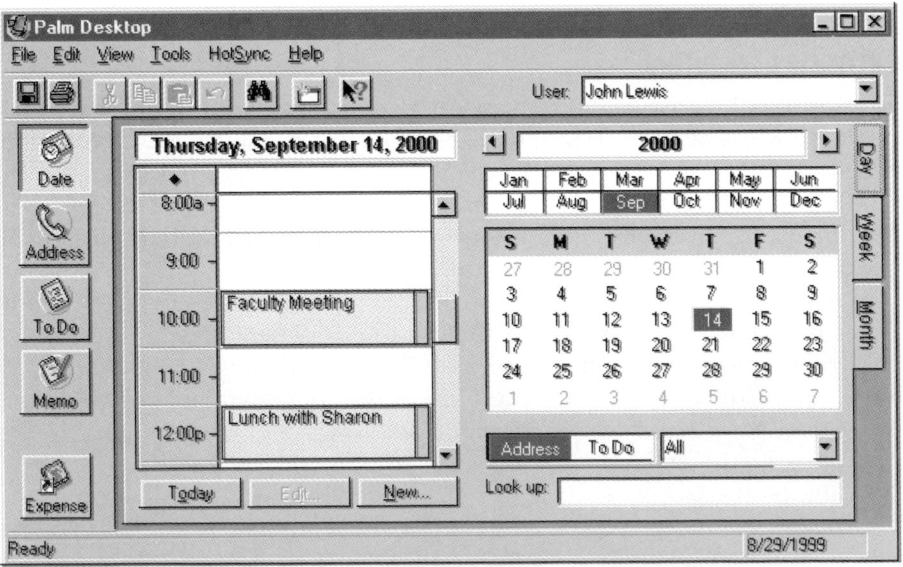

Figure 1.2 An example of a graphical user interface (GUI) (Palm Desktop™, courtesy of 3COM Corporation)

lations, make decisions, and control graphics. We use the Java programming language throughout the text to demonstrate various computing concepts.

Digital Computers

There are two fundamental techniques used to store and manage information: analog and digital. *Analog* information is continuous, in direct proportion to the source of the information. For example, a mercury thermometer is an analog device for measuring temperature. The mercury rises in a tube in direct proportion to the temperature outside the tube. Another example of analog information is an electronic signal used to represent the vibrations of a sound wave. The signal's voltage varies in direct proportion to the original sound wave. A stereo amplifier sends this kind of electronic signal to its speakers, which vibrate to reproduce the sound. We use the term analog because the signal is directly analogous to the information it represents. Figure 1.3 graphically depicts a sound wave captured by a microphone and represented as an electronic signal.

Digital technology breaks information down into discrete pieces and represents those pieces as numbers. The music on a compact disc is stored digitally, as a series of numbers. Each number represents the voltage level of one specific instance of the recording. Many of these measurements are taken in a short period of time, perhaps 40,000 measurements every second. The number of measurements per second is called the *sampling rate.* If samples are taken often enough, the discrete voltage measurements can be used to generate a continuous analog signal close enough to fool the human ear into thinking it is continuous sound.

Figure 1.4 shows the sampling of an analog signal. When analog information is converted to a digital format by breaking it into pieces, we say it has been *digitized.* Because the changes that occur in a signal between samples are lost, the sampling rate must be sufficiently fast.

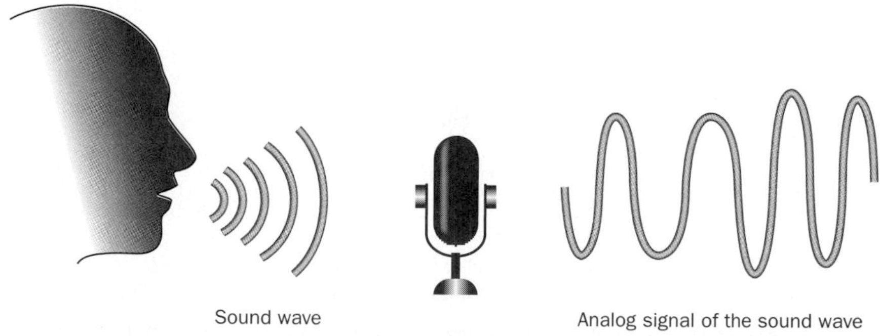

Figure 1.3 A sound wave and an electronic analog signal that represents the wave

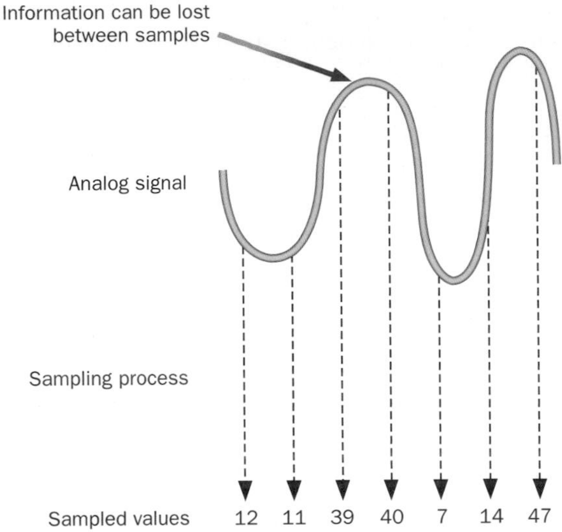

Figure 1.4 Digitizing an analog signal

Key Concept

Digital computers store information by breaking it down into pieces and representing each piece as a number.

Sampling is only one way to digitize information. For example, a sentence of text is stored on a computer as a series of numbers, where each number represents a single character in the sentence. Every letter, digit, and punctuation symbol has been assigned a number. Even the space character is assigned a number. Consider the following sentence:

```
Hi, Heather.
```

The characters of the sentence are represented as a series of twelve numbers, as shown in Figure 1.5. When a character is repeated, such as the uppercase 'H', the same representation number is used. Note that the uppercase version of a letter is stored as a different number than the lowercase version, such as the 'H' and 'h' in the word Heather. They are considered to be separate and distinct characters.

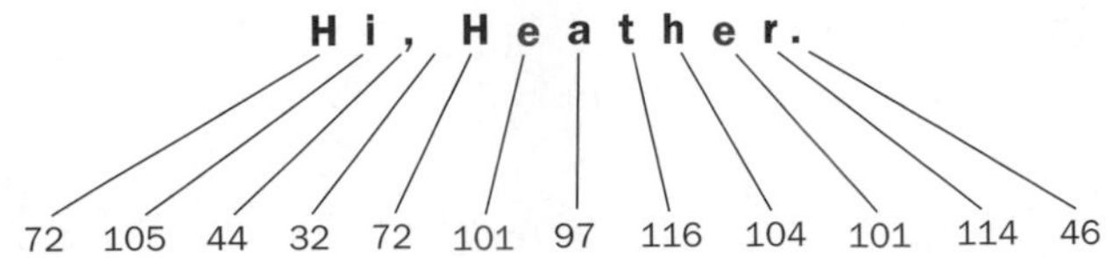

Figure 1.5 Text is stored by mapping each character to a number

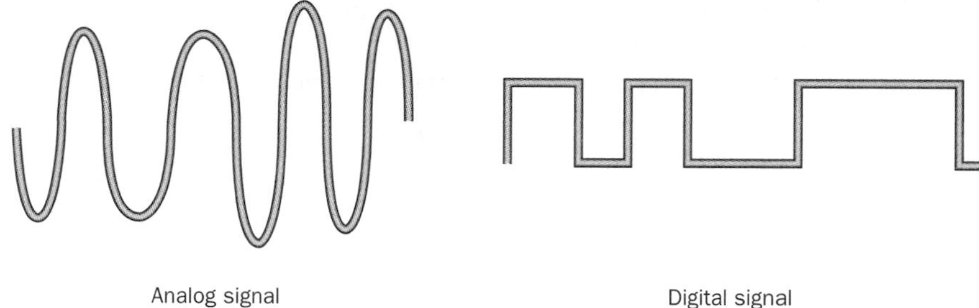

Figure 1.6 An analog signal vs. a digital signal

Modern electronic computers are digital. Every kind of information, including text, images, numbers, audio, video, and even program instructions, is broken down into pieces. Each piece is represented as a number. The information is stored by storing those numbers.

Another benefit of digital information is that it increases the distance that information can travel reliably across a wire. An analog signal has continuously varying voltage, but a digital signal is *discrete,* which means the digital voltage changes dramatically between one extreme and the other. At any point, the voltage of a digital signal is considered to be either "high" or "low." Figure 1.6 compares these two types of signals.

As a signal moves down a wire, it gets weaker. That is, its voltage drops. To make sure a signal gets to its destination, amplifiers can be placed along the line to reinforce the strength of the signal. The trouble with an analog signal is that as it loses strength, it loses information. Since the information is directly analogous to the signal, any change in the signal changes the information. An amplifier can reinforce the signal but it cannot recover the changes in the signal up to that point. A digital signal also degrades, but it can be reinforced before any information is lost because the original value was either at one extreme or the other.

Binary Numbers

A digital computer stores information as numbers, but those numbers are not stored as *decimal* values. All information in a computer is stored and managed as *binary* values. Unlike the decimal system, which has 10 digits (0 through 9), the binary number system has only two digits (0 and 1). A single binary digit is called a *bit.*

All number systems work according to the same rules. The *base value* of a number system dictates how many digits we have to work with and indicates the place value of each digit in a number. The decimal number system is base

10, and the binary number system is base 2. Appendix B contains a detailed discussion of number systems.

Key Concept

Binary values are used to store all information in a computer because the devices that store and move binary information are inexpensive and reliable.

Modern computers use binary numbers because the devices that store and move information are less expensive and more reliable if they only have to represent one of two possible values. Other than this characteristic, there is nothing special about the binary number system. Computers have been created that use other number systems to store information, but they aren't as convenient.

A single bit can represent two possible items or situations. The bit is either 1 or 0, similar to a light switch being either on or off. Two bits, taken together, can represent four possible items because there are exactly four combinations of two bits (00, 01, 10, and 11). Similarly, three bits can represent eight unique items, because there are eight combinations of three bits. Figure 1.7 shows the relationship between the number of bits used and the number of items they can represent. In general, *N* bits can represent 2^N unique items. For every bit added, the number of items that can be represented doubles.

Suppose you wanted to represent character strings in a language that contains 256 characters and symbols. You would need to use eight bits to store

1 bit 2 items	2 bits 4 items	3 bits 8 items	4 bits 16 items
0	00	000	0000
1	01	001	0001
	10	010	0010
	11	011	0011
		100	0100
		101	0101
		110	0110
		111	0111
			1000
			1001
			1010
			1011
			1100
			1101
			1110
			1111

Figure 1.7 The number of bits used determines the number of items that can be represented

each character because there are 256 unique combinations of eight bits (2^8 equals 256). Each combination represents a specific character.

All of the hardware components of a computer system store and move bits of data. A digital signal is well suited for transmitting binary data. If the voltage is high on a digital signal, it is interpreted as a binary 1. If the voltage is low, it is interpreted as a binary 0.

1.2 Hardware Components

Let's examine the hardware components of a computer system in more detail. Consider the computer described in Figure 1.8. What does it all mean? Is the system capable of running the software you want it to? How does it compare to other systems? These terms are explained throughout this section.

Computer Architecture

The architecture of a house defines its structure. Similarly, we use the term *computer architecture* to describe how the hardware components of a computer are put together. Figure 1.9 illustrates the basic architecture of a generic computer system. Information travels between components across a group of wires called a *bus*.

The CPU and the main memory make up the core of a computer. Main memory stores programs and data that are actively in use and the CPU methodically executes program instructions one at a time.

- 600 MHz Pentium III processor
- 256 MB RAM
- 16 GB Hard Disk
- 24x speed CD ROM drive
- 17" Video Display with 1280 x 1024 resolution
- 56 KB modem

Figure 1.8 The hardware specification of a particular computer

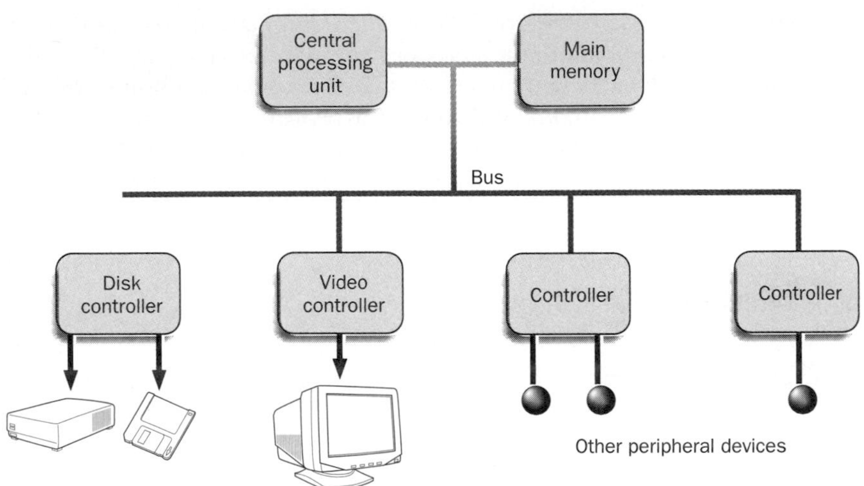

Figure 1.9 Basic computer architecture

Key Concept

The core of a computer is made up of the CPU and the main memory. Main memory is used to store programs and data, and the CPU executes a program's instructions one at a time.

Suppose we have a program that computes the average of a list of numbers. The program and the numbers must be stored in main memory while the program runs. The CPU reads one program instruction from main memory and executes it. If an instruction needs data to perform its task, such as a number in the list, the CPU reads that information as well. This process repeats until the program ends. The average, when computed, is stored in main memory to await further processing or long-term storage in secondary memory.

Almost all devices in a computer system other than the CPU and main memory are called *peripherals,* because they operate at the periphery, or outer edges, of the system (although they may be in the same box). Human beings don't directly interact with the CPU or main memory. Although they form the essence of the machine, the CPU and main memory would not be useful without peripheral devices.

Controllers are devices that coordinate the activities of specific peripherals. Every device has its own particular way of formatting and communicating data, and part of the controller's role is to handle these idiosyncrasies and isolate them from the rest of the computer hardware. Furthermore, the controller often handles much of the actual transmission of information, allowing the CPU to focus on other activities.

Input/Output (I/O) devices and secondary memory devices are considered peripherals. Another category of peripherals is *data transfer devices,* which allow information to be sent and received between computers. The computer specified in Figure 1.8 includes a data transfer device called a *modem,* which allows information to be sent across a telephone line. The modem in the example can transfer information at a rate of 56,000 *bits per second* (bps).

In some ways, secondary memory devices and data transfer devices can be thought of as I/O devices because they represent a source of information (input) and a place to send information (output). For our discussion, however, we define I/O devices as those that allow the human user to interact with the computer.

Input/Output Devices

Let's examine some I/O devices in more detail. The most common input devices are the keyboard and the mouse. Others include:

- *bar code readers,* such as the ones used at a grocery store checkout
- *light pens,* which can be touched to a monitor to indicate a user's action
- *microphones,* used by voice recognition systems that interpret simple voice commands
- *virtual reality devices,* such as gloves that interpret the movement of the user's hand
- *scanners,* which convert text, photographs, and graphics into machine-readable form

Monitors and printers are the most common output devices. Other examples are:

- *plotters,* which move pens across large sheets of paper
- *speakers,* for audio output
- *goggles,* for virtual reality display

Some devices can provide both input and output capabilities. A touch screen can detect the user touching the screen at a particular place. Software responding to the touch can use the screen to display text and graphics in response. Touch screens are particularly useful in situations where the interface to the machine must be simple, such as at an information booth.

The computer described in Figure 1.8 includes a monitor with a 17-inch diagonal display area. A picture is created by breaking it up into small pieces called *pixels,* a term that stands for picture elements. The monitor can display a grid of 1280 × 1024 pixels. The last section of this chapter explores the representation of graphics in more detail.

Main and Secondary Memory

Main memory is made up of a series of small, consecutive *memory locations* as shown in Figure 1.10. Associated with each memory location is a unique number called an *address.*

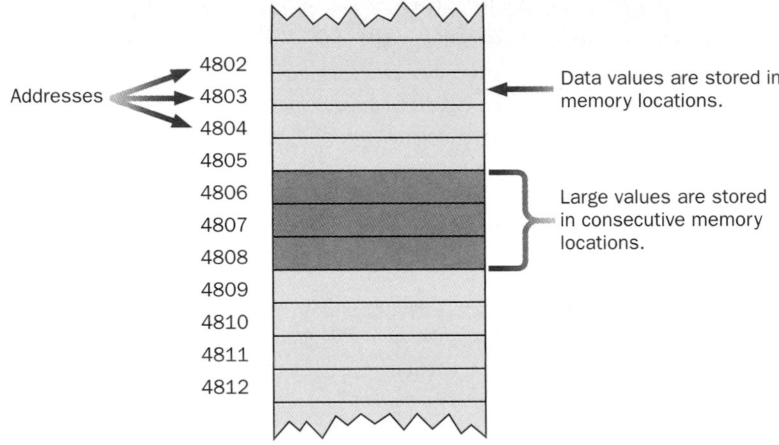

Figure 1.10 Memory locations

> **Key Concept**
> An address is a unique number associated with each memory location, used when storing and retrieving data from memory.

> **Key Concept**
> Data written to a memory location overwrites and destroys any information that was previously held in that location. Data read from a memory location leaves the value in memory unaffected.

When data is stored in a memory location, it overwrites and destroys any information that was previously held in that location. However, data is read from a memory location without affecting it.

On many computers, each memory location holds eight bits, or one *byte,* of information. If we need to store a value that cannot be represented in a single byte, such as a large number, then multiple, consecutive bytes are used to store the data.

The *storage capacity* of a device such as main memory is the total number of bytes it can hold. Because these devices can store thousands or millions of bytes, it is necessary to become familiar with larger units of measure. Because computer memory is based on the binary number system, all units of storage are powers of two. A *kilobyte* (KB) is 1,024, or 2^{10}, bytes. Some larger units of storage are a *megabyte* (MB), a *gigabyte* (GB), and a *terabyte* (TB), as listed in Figure 1.11. It's usually easier to think about these capacities by rounding them off. For example, most computer users think of a kilobyte as approximately one thousand bytes, a megabyte as approximately one million bytes, and so forth.

Many personal computers have 128 or 256 megabytes of main memory, such as the system described in Figure 1.8. A large main memory allows large programs, and multiple programs, to run efficiently, because they don't have to retrieve information from secondary memory as often.

Main memory is usually *volatile,* meaning that the information stored in it will be lost if its electric power supply is turned off. When you are working on a computer, you should often save your work onto a secondary memory

Unit	Symbol	Number of Bytes
byte		$2^0 = 1$
kilobyte	KB	$2^{10} = 1024$
megabyte	MB	$2^{20} = 1,048,576$
gigabyte	GB	$2^{30} = 1,073,741,824$
terabyte	TB	$2^{40} = 1,099,511,627,776$

Figure 1.11 Units of binary storage

device such as a disk in case the power goes out or a plug is pulled. Secondary memory devices are usually *nonvolatile;* the information is retained even if the power supply is turned off.

The most common secondary storage devices are hard disks and floppy disks. A high-density floppy disk can store 1.44 MB of information. The storage capacities of hard drives vary, but on personal computers, capacities typically range between 5 and 20 GB, such as in the system described in Figure 1.8.

Key Concept

Main memory is volatile, meaning the stored information is only maintained as long as electric power is supplied. Secondary memory devices are usually nonvolatile.

A disk is a magnetic medium, on which bits are represented as magnetized particles. A read/write head passes over the spinning disk, reading or writing information as appropriate. A hard disk drive might actually contain several disks with several read/write heads, such as the one shown in Figure 1.12.

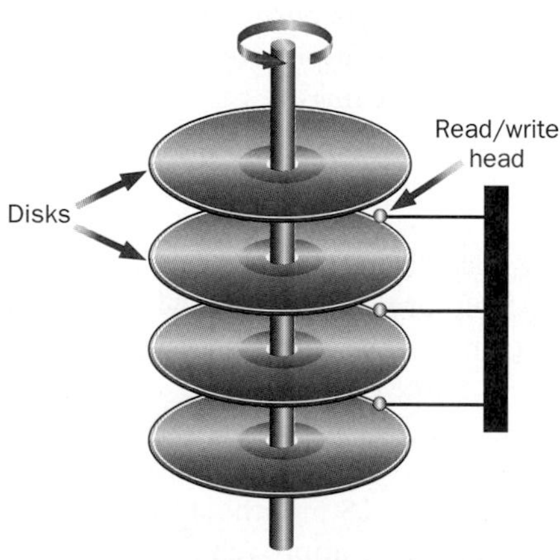

Figure 1.12 A hard disk drive with multiple disks and read/write heads

To get an intuitive feel for how much information these devices can store, consider that all the information in this book, including pictures and formatting, requires about 6 MB of storage.

Magnetic tapes are also used as secondary storage, but are considerably slower than disks because of the way information is accessed. A disk is a *direct access device* since the read/write head can move directly to the information needed. The terms direct access and *random access* are often used interchangeably. But information on a tape can be accessed only after first getting past the intervening data. A tape must be rewound or fast-forwarded to get to the appropriate position. A tape is therefore considered to be a *sequential access device.* Tapes are usually only used to store information when it is no longer often used, or to provide a backup copy of the information on a disk.

Two other terms are used to describe memory devices: *random access memory* (RAM) and *read only memory* (ROM). It's important to understand these terms because they are often used and because their names can be misleading. The terms RAM and main memory are basically interchangeable. When contrasted with ROM, however, the term RAM seems to imply something it shouldn't. Both RAM and ROM are direct (or random) access devices. RAM should probably be called read-write memory, since information can be both written to it and read from it. This feature distinguishes it from ROM. After information is stored on ROM, it cannot be altered (as the term read-only implies). ROM chips are often embedded into the main circuit board of a computer and used to provide the preliminary instructions needed when the computer is initially turned on.

A *CD ROM* is a portable secondary memory device. CD stands for compact disk. It is accurately called ROM because information is stored permanently when the CD is created and cannot be changed. Like its musical CD counterpart, a CD ROM stores information in binary format. When the CD is initially created, a microscopic pit is burned into the disk to represent a binary 1, and the disk is left smooth to represent a binary 0. The bits are read by shining a low-intensity laser beam on the spinning disk. The laser beam reflects strongly from a smooth area on the disk, but weakly from a pitted area. A sensor looking for the reflection determines if each bit is a 1 or 0 accordingly.

The CD ROM drive described in Figure 1.8 is characterized as having 24x speed, distinguishing it from previous CD ROM technologies (6x, 8x, and 12x for instance) relative to its data transfer rate. A typical CD ROM's storage capacity is approximately 630 MB.

The capacity of storage devices changes continually as technology improves. A general rule in the computer industry suggests that storage capacity doubles approximately every 18 months. However, this progress will eventually slow down as the capacities approach absolute physical limits.

The Central Processing Unit

The central processing unit (CPU) interacts closely with main memory to perform all fundamental processing in a computer. The CPU interprets and executes instructions, one after another, in a continuous cycle. It is made up of three important components as shown in Figure 1.13. The *control unit* coordinates the processing steps, the *registers* provide a small amount of storage space in the CPU itself, and the *arithmetic/logic unit* performs calculations and makes decisions.

The control unit coordinates the transfer of data and instructions between main memory and the registers in the CPU. It also coordinates the execution of the circuitry in the arithmetic/logic unit to perform a particular operation on data stored in particular registers.

In many computers, some registers are set aside for special purposes. For example, the *instruction register* holds the current instruction being executed. The *program counter* is a register that holds the address of the next instruction to be executed. In addition to these and other special-purpose registers, the CPU also contains a set of general-purpose registers that are used for temporary storage of values as needed.

The concept of storing both program instructions and data in main memory together is the underlying principle of the *von Neumann architecture* of computer design, named after John von Neumann who first advanced this programming concept in 1945. These computers continually follow the *fetch-decode-execute* cycle depicted in Figure 1.14. An instruction is fetched from main memory at the address stored in the program counter and put into the instruction register. The program counter is incremented at this point to prepare for the next cycle. Then the instruction is decoded

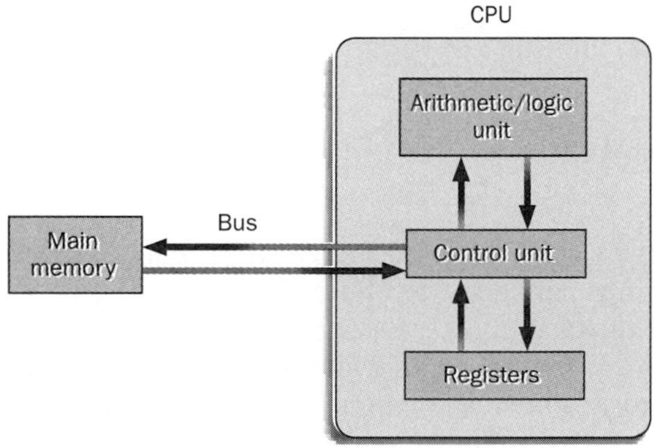

Figure 1.13 CPU components and main memory

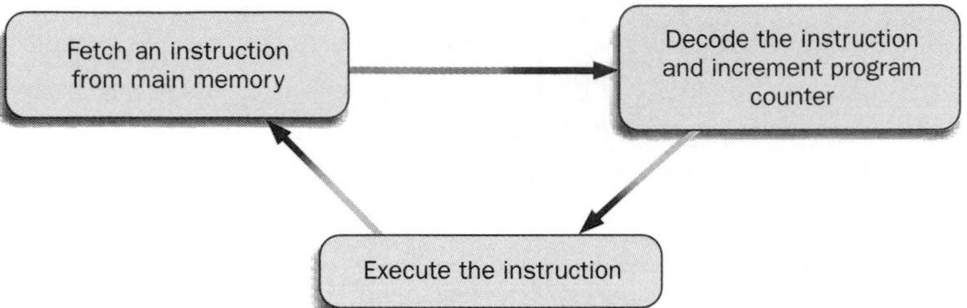

Figure 1.14 The continuous fetch-decode-execute cycle

electronically to determine which operation to carry out. Finally, the control unit activates the correct circuitry to carry out the instruction, which may load a data value into a register or add two values together, for example.

The CPU is constructed on a chip called a *microprocessor,* a device that is part of the main circuit board of the computer. This board also contains ROM chips and communication sockets to which device controllers, such as the controller that manages the video display, can be connected.

Another crucial component of the main circuit board is the *system clock.* The clock generates an electronic pulse at regular intervals, which synchronizes the events of the CPU. The rate at which the pulses occur is called the *clock speed,* and varies depending on the processor. The computer described in Figure 1.8 includes a Pentium III processor that runs at a clock speed of 600 megahertz (MHz), or approximately 600 million pulses per second. The speed of the system clock provides a rough measure of how fast the CPU executes instructions. Similar to storage capacities, the speed of processors is constantly increasing with advances in technology, approximately doubling every 18 months.

Key Concept

The speed of the system clock indicates how fast the CPU executes instructions.

1.3 Networks

A single computer can accomplish a great deal, but connecting several computers together into networks can dramatically increase productivity and the ability to share information. A *network* is two or more computers connected together so they can exchange information. Using networks has become the normal mode of commercial computer operation. New technologies are emerging every day to capitalize on the connected environments of modern computer systems.

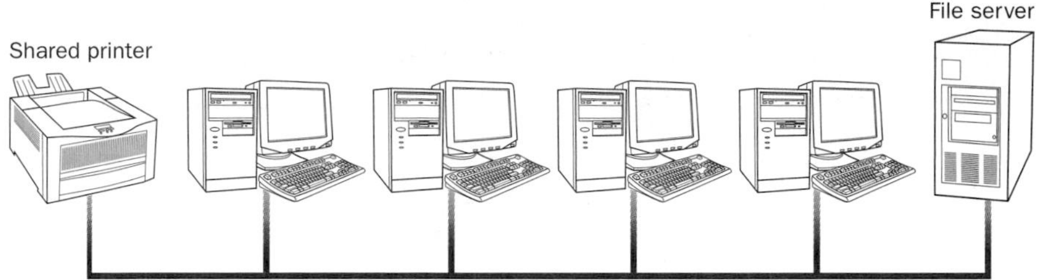

Figure 1.15 A simple network of computers

Figure 1.15 shows a simple computer network. One of the computers in the network has a printer connected to it. Because computers in a network can share information, any of these computers can print a document on that printer.

One of the computers in Figure 1.15 is designated as a *file server,* which is dedicated to storing programs and data that are needed by many network users. A file server usually has a large amount of secondary memory. When a network has a file server, each individual computer does not need its own copy of a program.

Key Concept

A network consists of two or more computers connected together so they can exchange information.

Network Connections

If two computers are directly connected, they can communicate in basically the same way that information moves across wires inside a single machine. When connecting two geographically close computers, this solution works well, and is called a *point-to-point connection.* But consider the task of connecting many computers together. If point-to-point connections are used, then every computer is directly connected by a wire to every other computer in the network. A separate wire for each connection is not a workable solution because every time a new computer is added to the network, a new communication line will have to be installed for each computer already in the network. Furthermore, a single computer can handle only a small number of direct connections.

Figure 1.16 shows multiple point-to-point connections. Consider the number of communication lines that would be needed if only two or three additional computers were added to the network.

Contrast the diagrams in Figure 1.15 and Figure 1.16. All of the computers shown in Figure 1.15 share a single communication line. Each computer on the network has its own *network address,* which uniquely identifies it.

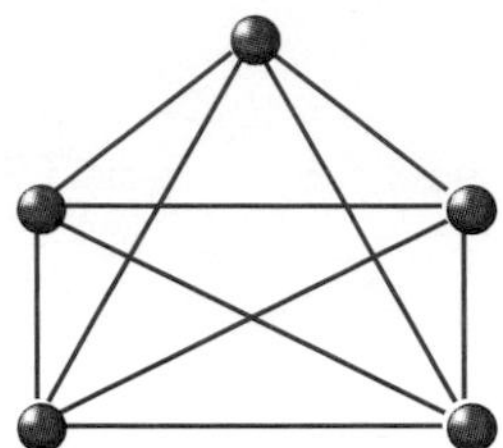

Figure 1.16 Point-to-point connections

These addresses are similar in concept to the addresses in main memory, except that they identify individual computers on a network instead of individual memory locations inside a single computer. A message is sent across the line from one computer to another by specifying the network address of the computer for which it is intended.

Sharing a communication line is cost-effective and makes adding new computers to the network relatively easy. However, a shared line introduces delays. The computers on the network cannot use the communication line at the same time. They have to take turns sending information, which means they have to wait when the line is busy.

Key Concept

Sharing a communication line is cost-effective and makes adding new computers to the network relatively easy.

One technique to improve network delays is to divide large messages into sections, called *packets,* then send the individual packets across the network intermixed with pieces of other messages sent by other users. The packets are collected at the destination and reassembled into the original message. This situation is similar to a group of people using a conveyor belt to move a set of boxes from one end to the other. If only one person were allowed to use the conveyor belt at a time, and that person had a large number of boxes to move, the others would be waiting a long time before they could use it. But by taking turns, each person can put one box on at a time, and they all can get their work done. It's not as fast as having a conveyor belt of your own, but it's not as slow as having to wait until everyone else is finished.

Local-Area and Wide-Area Networks

A *local-area network* (LAN) is a network designed to span short distances and a relatively small number of computers. Usually a LAN connects the machines in only one building, or in a single room. LANs are convenient to install and manage, and are highly reliable. As computers became increasingly small and versatile, LANs became an inexpensive way to share information throughout an organization. However, having a LAN is like having a tele-

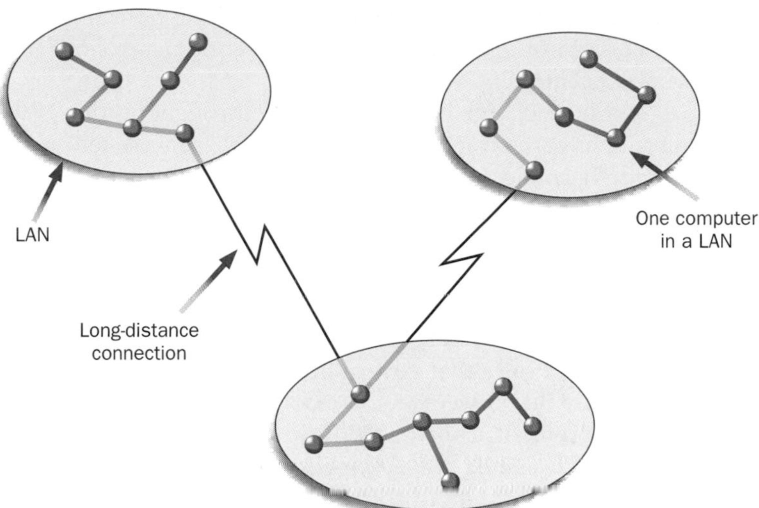

Figure 1.17 LANs connected into a wide-area network

phone system that allows you to call only the people in your own town. We need to be able to share information across longer distances.

A *wide-area network* (WAN) connects two or more LANs, often across long distances. Usually, one computer on each LAN is dedicated to handling the communication across a WAN. This technique relieves the other computers in a local-area network from having to perform the details of long-distance communication. Figure 1.17 shows several local area networks connected into a wide-area network. The LANs connected by a WAN are often owned by different companies or organizations, and might even be located in different countries.

Key Concept

A local-area network (LAN) is an inexpensive way to share information and resources throughout an organization.

The impact of networks on computer systems has been dramatic. Computing resources can now be shared among many users, and computer-based communication across the entire world is now possible. In fact, the use of networks is now so pervasive that some computers require network resources in order to operate.

The Internet

Throughout the 1970s, a United States government organization called the Advanced Research Projects Agency (ARPA) funded several projects to explore network technology. One result of these efforts was the ARPANET, a wide-area network that eventually was commercialized and became known as the Internet. The *Internet* is a network of networks. The term Internet comes from the WAN concept of *internetworking,* connecting many smaller heterogeneous networks together.

Key Concept

The Internet is a wide-area network that spans the globe.

In the mid and late 1980s, and throughout the 1990s, the Internet has grown incredibly. In 1983, there were fewer than 600 computers connected to the Internet. By the year 2000, that number will reach over 10 million. As more and more computers connect to the Internet, the ability to keep up with the larger number of users and heavier traffic has been difficult. New technologies have replaced the ARPANET several times since the initial development, each time providing more capacity and faster processing.

A *protocol* is a set of rules that govern how two things communicate. The software that controls the movement of messages across the Internet must conform to a set of protocols called TCP/IP (pronounced by spelling out the letters, T-C-P-I-P). TCP stands for *Transmission Control Protocol,* and IP stands for *Internet Protocol.* The IP software defines how information is formatted and transferred from the source to the destination. The TCP software handles problems such as pieces of information arriving out of their original order, or information getting lost, which can happen if too much information converges at one location at the same time.

Key Concept

TCP/IP is the set of software protocols that govern the movement of messages across the Internet.

Every computer connected to the Internet has an *IP address* that uniquely identifies it among all other computers on the Internet. An example of an IP address is `204.192.116.2`. Fortunately, the users of the Internet rarely have to deal with IP addresses. The Internet allows each computer to be given a name. Like IP addresses, the names must be unique. The Internet name of a computer is often referred to as its *Internet address.* Two examples of Internet addresses are `monet.villanova.edu` and `kant.breakaway.com`.

Key Concept

Every computer connected to the Internet has an IP address that uniquely identifies it.

The first part of an Internet address is the local name of a specific computer. The rest of the address is the *domain name,* which indicates the organization to which the computer belongs. For example, `villanova.edu` is the domain name for all computers at Villanova University, and `monet` is the name of a particular computer on that campus. Individual departments might add pieces to the name to uniquely distinguish their set of computers within the larger organization. A group called the Internet Naming Authority approves all domain names. Because the domain names are unique, many organizations can have a computer named `monet` without confusion.

The last part of each domain name usually indicates the type of organization to which the computer belongs. The suffix `edu` indicates an educational institution and the suffix `com` refers to a commercial business. For example, `breakaway.com` refers to Breakaway Solutions, Inc. Another common suffix is `org`, used by nonprofit organizations. Many computers, especially those outside of the United States, use a suffix that denotes the country of origin, such as `uk` for the United Kingdom.

When an Internet address is referenced, it gets translated to its corresponding IP address, which is used from that point on. The software that does this translation is called the *Domain Name System* (DNS). Each organization connected to the Internet operates a *domain server* that maintains a list of all computers at that organization and their IP address. It works somewhat like telephone directory assistance, in that you provide the name and the domain server gives back a number. If the local domain server does not have the IP address for the name, it contacts another domain server that does.

The Internet has revolutionized computer processing. Initially, the primary use of interconnected computers was to send electronic mail, but Internet capabilities continue to improve. One of the most significant uses of the Internet is the World Wide Web.

The World Wide Web

The Internet gives us the capability to exchange information. The *World Wide Web* (also known as WWW or simply the Web) makes the exchange of information easy. Web software provides a common user interface through which many different types of information can be accessed with the click of a mouse button.

The Web is based on the concepts of hypertext and hypermedia. The term *hypertext* was first used in 1965 to describe a way to organize information so that the flow of ideas was not constrained to a linear progression. In fact, that concept was entertained as a way to manage large amounts of information as early as the 1940s. Researchers on the Manhattan Project who were developing the first atomic bomb envisioned such an approach. The underlying idea is that documents can be linked at various points according to natural relationships so that the reader can jump from one document to another, following the appropriate path for that reader's needs. When other media components are incorporated, such as graphics, sound, and video, the resulting organization is called *hypermedia*.

> **Key Concept**
> The World Wide Web is software that makes sharing information across a network easy.

A *browser* is a software tool that loads and formats Web documents for viewing. *Mosaic,* the first graphical interface browser for the Web, was released in 1993. The designer of a web document defines *links* to other Web information that might be anywhere on the Internet. Some of the people who developed Mosaic went on to found the Netscape Communications Corporation and create the Netscape Navigator browser, which is shown in Figure 1.18. It is currently one of the most popular systems for accessing information on the Web. Microsoft's Internet Explorer is another popular browser.

> **Key Concept**
> A browser is a software tool that loads and formats Web documents for viewing. These documents are often written using the HyperText Markup Language (HTML).

Browsers load and interpret documents that have been formatted using the *HyperText Markup Language* (HTML). An overview of Web publishing using HTML is given in Appendix J. The Java programming language has an intimate relationship with Web processing since links to Java programs can be

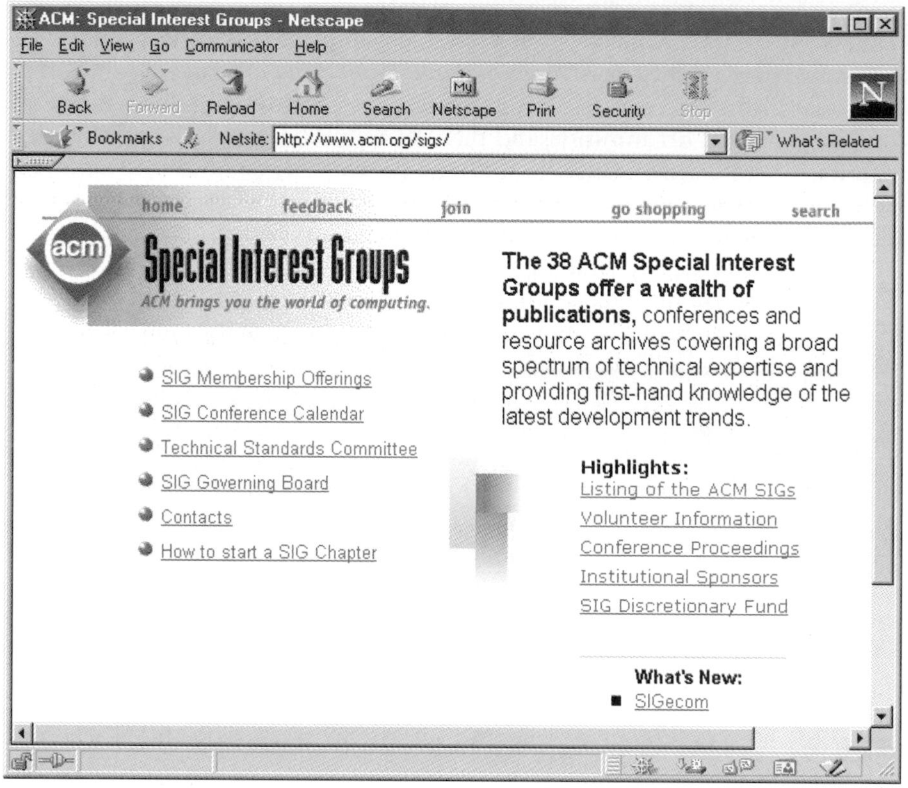

Figure 1.18 Netscape Navigator browsing an HTML document (used with permission of ACM)

embedded in HTML documents and executed through Web browsers. This relationship is explored in more detail in Chapter 2.

Uniform Resource Locators

Information on the Web is found by identifying a *Uniform Resource Locator* (URL). A URL uniquely specifies documents and other information for a browser to obtain and display. An example URL is:

```
http://www.yahoo.com
```

This particular URL will load a document that enables you to search the Web using particular words or phrases.

Key Concept

A URL specifies documents and other information on the World Wide Web for a browser to obtain and display.

A URL contains several pieces of information. The first piece is a protocol, which determines the way the browser should communicate. The second piece is the Internet address of the machine on which the document is stored. The third piece of information is the file name of interest. If no file name is given, as is the case with the

Yahoo URL, browsers make a default selection (such as `index.html`). Let's look at another example URL:

```
http://www.breakaway.com/vision.html
```

In this URL, the protocol is `http`, which stands for *HyperText Transfer Protocol*. The machine referenced is `www.breakaway.com`, and `vision.html` is a file to be transferred to the browser for viewing. There are many other forms for URLs, but this form is the most common.

The terms Internet and World Wide Web are sometimes used interchangeably, but there are important differences. The Web is essentially an information service including a set of software applications. It is not a network. Although it is used effectively with the Internet, it is not inherently bound to it. The Web can be used on a local area network that is not connected to any other network, or even on a single machine to display HTML documents.

The Internet makes communication via computers all across the world possible. The Web makes accessing information across the Internet a straightforward and enjoyable activity. The Java programming language is another important evolutionary step that allows software to be easily exchanged and executed via the Web. The rest of this book explores the process of creating programs using Java.

1.4 Programming

This textbook focuses on the development of high-quality programs. This section discusses the purpose of programming and introduces the Java programming language.

Problem Solving

The purpose of writing a program is to solve a problem. Problem solving, in general, consists of multiple steps:

1. Understand the problem.
2. Dissect the problem into manageable pieces.
3. Design a solution.
4. Consider alternatives to the solution and refine it.
5. Implement the solution.
6. Test the solution and fix any problems that exist.

Although this approach applies to any kind of problem solving, it works particularly well when developing software. We refine this series of activities and apply it to writing programs at various points throughout the text.

Key Concept
The purpose of writing a program is to solve a problem.

The first step, understanding the problem, may sound obvious, but a lack of attention to this step has been the cause of many misguided efforts. If we attempt to solve a problem we don't thoroughly understand, we often end up solving the wrong problem or at least going off on improper tangents. We must understand the needs of the people who will use the solution. These needs often include subtle nuances that will affect our overall approach to the solution.

After we thoroughly understand the problem, we then break the problem into manageable pieces and design a solution. These steps go hand in hand. A solution to any problem is rarely one big activity. Instead, it is a series of small cooperating tasks that interact to perform a larger task. When developing software, we don't write one big program. We design separate pieces that are responsible for certain parts of the solution.

Our first inclination toward a solution may not be the best one. We must always consider alternatives and refine the solution as necessary. The earlier we consider alternatives, the easier it is to modify our approach.

Implementing a solution is the act of taking the design and putting it in a usable form. When developing a software solution to a problem, the implementation stage is the process of actually writing the program. Too often this step is thought of as the act of programming. But to the extent that our programs are written to solve specific problems, the final implementation of the solution is one of the last steps. Throughout this text we explore programming techniques that allow us to elegantly design and implement solutions to problems. Although we will often delve into these specific techniques in detail, we should never forget that they are just tools to help us solve problems.

Key Concept
Specific programming techniques are the tools that help us solve problems.

The Java Programming Language

A program is written in a particular *programming language* that uses specific words and symbols to express a program. A programming language defines a set of rules that determines exactly how a programmer can combine the words and symbols of the language into *programming statements,* which are the instructions that are carried out when the program is executed.

Since the inception of computers, many programming languages have been created. We use the Java programming language in this book to demonstrate various concepts and techniques. Our overall goal is to learn these underlying software development concepts, but an important side-effect will be to become proficient in the development of Java programs.

Java is a relatively new programming language compared to others. It was developed by James Gosling at Sun Microsystems, initially as a tool to address problems that other languages didn't handle well. Java was introduced in 1995 and has gained tremendous popularity since then.

One reason Java got some initial attention was because it was the first programming language to deliberately embrace the concept of writing programs that can be executed using the World Wide Web. The original hype about Java's Web capabilities initially obscured the far more important features that make it a useful programming language.

Java is an *object-oriented programming language.* The principles of object-oriented software development are the cornerstone of this book and are discussed throughout the text. Objects are the fundamental pieces that make up a program. Other programming languages, such as C++, allow a programmer to use objects, but don't reinforce that approach, which can lead to confusing program designs.

Most importantly, Java is a good language to use to learn programming concepts. It is fairly elegant, in that it doesn't get bogged down in issues that other languages do. We are able to focus on important issues and not superfluous detail.

The Java language is accompanied by libraries of extra software that we can use when developing programs. These libraries include the ability to use graphics, communicate over networks, and interact with databases, among many other features. Although we won't be able to cover all aspects of the libraries, we will explore many of them. The set of supporting libraries is huge, and quite versatile.

Java is used in commercial environments all over the world. It is one of the fastest growing programming technologies of all time. So not only is it a good language in which to learn programming concepts, it is also a practical language that will serve you well in the future.

A Java Program

Let's take a look at a simple, but complete, Java program. The program in Listing 1.1 prints two sentences to the screen. This particular program prints a quote by Abraham Lincoln. The output is shown below the program listing.

All Java applications have a similar basic structure. Despite its small size and simple purpose, this program contains several important features. Let's carefully dissect it and examine its pieces.

The first few lines of the program are comments, which start with the `//` symbols and continue to the end of the line. Comments don't affect what the program does, but are included to make the program easier to understand by humans. Programmers can and should include comments throughout a program to clearly identify the purpose of the program and describe any special processing. Any written comments or documents, including a user's guide and technical references, are called *documentation.* Comments included in a program are called *inline documentation.*

> **Key Concept**
> Comments do not affect a program's processing, but are useful for human comprehension.

The rest of the program is a *class definition.* This class is called `Lincoln`, though we could have named it just about anything we wished. The class definition runs from the first opening brace (`{`) to the final closing brace (`}`) on the last line of the program. All Java programs are defined using class definitions.

Inside the class definition are some more comments describing the purpose of the `main` method, which is defined directly below the comments. A *method* is

Listing 1.1

```
//********************************************************************
//  Lincoln.java       Author: Lewis and Loftus
//
//  Demonstrates the basic structure of a Java application.
//********************************************************************

public class Lincoln
{
   //-----------------------------------------------------------------
   //  Prints a presidential quote.
   //-----------------------------------------------------------------
   public static void main (String[] args)
   {
      System.out.println ("A quote by Abraham Lincoln:");

      System.out.println ("Whatever you are, be a good one.");
   }
}
```

```
A quote by Abraham Lincoln:
Whatever you are, be a good one.
```

a group of programming statements that are given a name. In this case, the name of the method is `main` and it contains only two programming statements. Like a class definition, a method is also delimited by braces.

Key Concept

The `main` method must always be defined using the words `public`, `static`, and `void`.

All Java applications have a `main` method, which is where processing begins. Each programming statement in the `main` method is executed, one at a time in order, until the end of the method is reached. Then the program ends, or *terminates*. The `main` method definition in a Java program is always preceded by the words `public`, `static`, and `void`, which we examine later in the text. The use of `String` and `args` does not come into play in this particular program and is also described later.

The two lines of code in the `main` method invoke another method called `println` (pronounced print line). We *invoke* a method when we want it to execute. A method invocation is also referred to as a *call* to the method. The `println` method prints the specified characters to the screen. The characters to be printed are represented as a *character string*, enclosed in double quote characters ("). When the program is executed, it calls the `println` method to print the first statement, then calls it again to print the second statement, and because that is the last line in the program, the program then terminates.

The code executed when the `println` method is invoked is not defined in this program. The `println` method is part of the `System.out` object, which we explore in more detail in Chapter 2.

Comments

Let's examine comments in more detail. Comments are the only language feature that allows programmers to compose and communicate their thoughts independent of the code. Comments should provide insight to the author's intent when writing the program. A program is often used for many years, and it's likely that many modifications will be made to it over time. Often the original programmer will not remember the details of a particular program when, at some point in the future, modifications are required. Furthermore, it is often the case that the original programmer is not available to make the changes, and someone completely unfamiliar with the program needs to understand it. Therefore, good documentation is essential.

As far as the Java programming language is concerned, comments can be written with any content whatsoever. Comments are ignored by the computer; they do not affect how the program executes.

The comments in our `Lincoln` program represent one of two types of comments allowed in Java. The comments in `Lincoln` take the following form:

```
// This is a comment.
```

This type of comment begins with a double slash (`//`) and continues to the end of the line. You cannot have any characters between the two slashes. The computer ignores any text between the double slash and the end of the line. A comment can follow code on the same line to document that particular line, as in the following example:

```
System.out.println ("Monthly Report"); // always use this title
```

The second form of a Java comment is:

```
/*  This is another comment.  */
```

This comment type does not use the end of a line to indicate the end of the comment. Anything between the initiating slash-asterisk (`/*`) and the terminating asterisk-slash (`*/`) is part of the comment, including the invisible *newline* character that represents the end of a line. Therefore, this type of comment can extend over multiple lines. There cannot be any space between the slash and the asterisk.

If there is a second asterisk following the /* at the beginning of a comment, it can be used to automatically generate external documentation about your program using a tool called *javadoc*. This feature is not described in this book, but we do have a description and examples of this process on the Web site that supports this text. Throughout the book, we highlight additional information and examples that can be found on the Web site.

Web Bonus

The Web site supporting this text describes the ability to generate automatic program documentation using a special form of Java comments.

The two basic comment types can be used to create various documentation styles, such as:

```
// This is a comment on a single line.

//-------------------------------------------------------------
// Some comments deserve to be blocked off to focus special
// attention, such as above methods or classes.  Note that
// each of these lines is technically a separate comment.
//-------------------------------------------------------------

/*
   This is one comment
   that spans several lines.
*/
```

Programmers often concentrate so much on writing code, they focus too little on documentation. You should develop good commenting practices and follow them habitually. Comments should be well written, often in complete sentences. They should not belabor ideas that are obvious, but provide greater insight into the intent of the code. The following examples are *not* good comments:

```
System.out.println ("hello");  // prints hello
System.out.println ("test");   // change this later
```

The first comment paraphrases the obvious purpose of the line and does not add any value to the statement. It is better to have no comment than a useless one. The second comment is ambiguous. What should be changed later? When is later? Why should it be changed?

It is considered good programming style to use comments in a consistent way throughout an entire program. The guidelines in Appendix G suggest specific techniques for documenting programs.

Key Concept

Inline documentation should provide insight into your code. It should not be ambiguous or belabor the obvious.

Identifiers and Reserved Words

The various words used when writing programs are called *identifiers*. The identifiers in the `Lincoln` program are `class`, `Lincoln`, `public`, `static`, `void`, `main`, `String`, `args`, `System`, `out`, and `println`. These fall into three categories:

- words that we make up (`Lincoln` and `args`)
- words that another programmer chose (`String`, `System`, `out`, `println`, and `main`)
- words that are reserved for special purposes in the language (`class`, `public`, `static`, `void`)

We simply chose to name the class `Lincoln`, but could have used many other possibilities. The identifier `args` (short for arguments) is often used in the way we use it in `Lincoln`, but we could have used just about any identifier in its place.

The identifiers `String` , `System`, `out`, and `println` were chosen by other programmers. These words are not part of the Java language. They are part of a huge set of predefined code, a set of classes and methods that someone has already written for us. The authors of that code chose the identifiers. We're just making use of them. This set of predefined code is discussed in more detail in Chapter 2.

Reserved words are identifiers that have a special meaning in a programming language and can only be used in predefined ways. In the `Lincoln` program, the reserved words used are `class`, `public`, `static`, and `void`. All of the Java reserved words are listed in Figure 1.19, in alphabetical order. The words marked with an asterisk are reserved for possible future use in later versions of the language, but currently have no meaning in Java. A reserved word cannot be used for any other purpose, such as naming a class or method.

An identifier that we make up for use in a program can be composed of any combination of letters, digits, the underscore character (_), and the dollar sign (`$`), but it cannot begin with a digit. Identifiers may be of any length. Therefore, `total`, `label7`, `nextStockItem`, `NUM_BOXES`, and `$amount` are all valid identifiers, but `4th_word` and `coin#value` are not valid.

Both uppercase and lowercase letters can be used in an identifier, and the difference is important. Java is *case sensitive,* which means that two identifier names that differ only by the case of their letters are considered to be different identifiers. Therefore `total`, `Total`, `ToTaL`, and `TOTAL` are all different identifiers. As you can imagine, it is not a good idea to use multiple identifiers that differ only by their case because they can be easily confused.

```
abstract    default     goto*        operator*   synchronized
boolean     do          if           outer*      this
break       double      implements   package     throw
byte        else        import       private     throws
byvalue*    extends     inner*       protected   transient
case        false       instanceof   public      true
cast*       final       int          rest*       try
catch       finally     interface    return      var*
char        float       long         short       void
class       for         native       static      volatile
const*      future*     new          super       while
continue    generic*    null         switch
```

Figure 1.19 Java reserved words

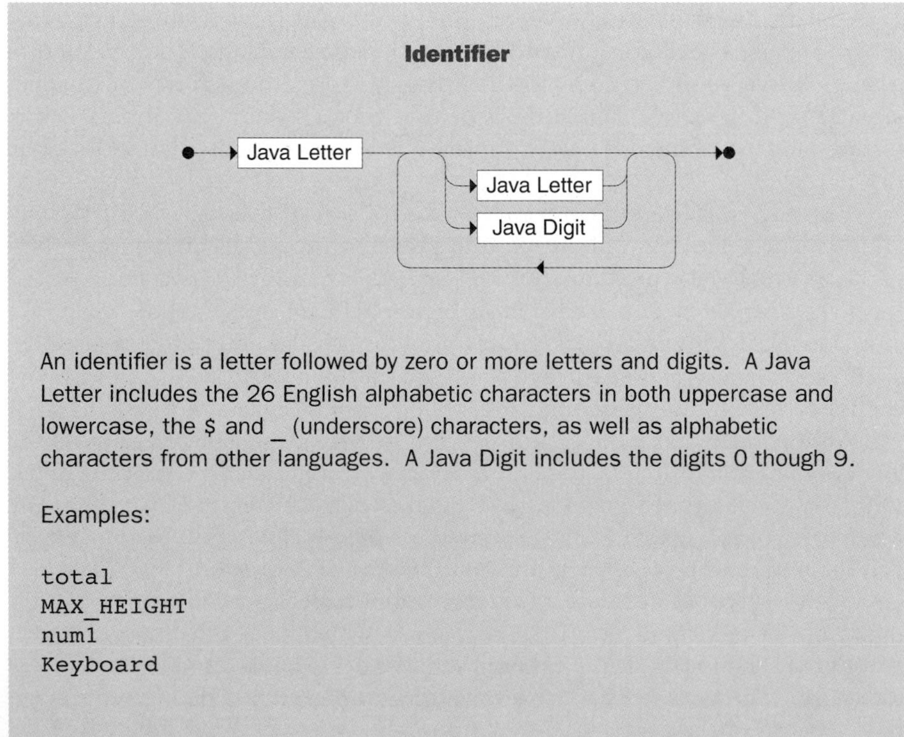

An identifier is a letter followed by zero or more letters and digits. A Java Letter includes the 26 English alphabetic characters in both uppercase and lowercase, the $ and _ (underscore) characters, as well as alphabetic characters from other languages. A Java Digit includes the digits 0 though 9.

Examples:

```
total
MAX_HEIGHT
num1
Keyboard
```

The appropriate use of uppercase and lowercase letters in identifiers makes your code more readable. Although the Java language doesn't require it, using a consistent case format for each kind of identifier makes your identifiers easier to understand. For example, we use *title case* (uppercase for the first letter of each word) for class names. That is a Java convention, although it does not technically have to be followed. Throughout the text, we describe the preferred case style for each type of identifier as it is encountered, and guidelines for naming identifiers are collectively presented in Appendix G.

Key Concept

Java is case sensitive. The uppercase and lowercase versions of a letter are distinct. You should use a consistent case convention for different types of identifiers.

An identifier can be of any length, but you should choose your names carefully. They should be descriptive but not overly verbose. You should avoid meaningless names such as `a` or `x`. An exception to this rule can be made if the short name is actually descriptive, such as using `x` and `y` to represent an (x, y) coordinate on a two-dimensional grid. Likewise, you should not use unnecessarily long names, such as the identifier `theCurrentItemBeingProcessed`. The name `currentItem` would serve just as well.

As you might imagine, the use of identifiers that are too verbose is a much less prevalent problem than the use of names that are not descriptive. We should try to err on the side of readability, but a reasonable balance can almost always be found. Also, we should always be careful when abbreviating words. You might think `curStVal` is a good name to represent the current stock value, but another person trying to understand the code is likely to have trouble figuring out what you meant. It might not even be clear to you two months after writing it.

A *name* in Java is a series of identifiers separated by the dot (period) character. The name `System.out` is the way we designate the object through which we invoked the `println` method. Names appear quite regularly in Java programs.

Key Concept

Identifier names should be descriptive and readable.

White Space

All Java programs use *white space* to separate the words and symbols used in a program. White space consists of blanks, tabs, and newline characters. The phrase white space refers to the fact that, on a white sheet of paper with black printing, the space between the words and symbols is white. The way a programmer uses white space is important because it can be used to emphasize parts of the code and can make a program easier to read.

Key Concept

Appropriate use of white space makes a program easier to read and understand.

Except when it's used to separate words, the computer ignores white space. It does not affect the execution of a program. This fact gives programmers a great deal of flexibility in how they format a

Listing 1.2

```
//********************************************************************
//  Lincoln2.java       Author: Lewis and Loftus
//
//  Demonstrates a poorly formatted, though valid, program.
//********************************************************************

public class Lincoln2{public static void main(String[]args){
System.out.println("A quote by Abraham Lincoln:");
System.out.println("Whatever you are, be a good one.");}}
```

```
A quote by Abraham Lincoln:
Whatever you are, be a good one.
```

program. The lines of a program should be divided in logical places and certain lines should be indented and aligned so that the program's underlying structure is clear.

Because white space is ignored, we can write a program in many different ways. For example, taking white space to one extreme, we could put as many words as possible on each line. The code in Listing 1.2, the `Lincoln2` program, is formatted quite differently than `Lincoln` but prints the same message.

Taking white space to the other extreme, we could write almost every word and symbol on a different line, such as `Lincoln3`, shown in Listing 1.3.

All three versions of `Lincoln` are technically valid and will execute in the same way, but they are radically different from a reader's point of view. Both of the latter examples show poor style and make the program difficult to understand. Appendix G contains guidelines for writing Java programs, including the appropriate use of white space. You may be asked to adhere to these or similar guidelines. In any case, you should adopt and consistently use a set of style guidelines in order to increase the readability of your code.

Key Concept

You should always adhere to a set of guidelines that establish the way you format and document your programs.

1.5 Programming Languages

Suppose a particular person is giving travel directions to a friend. That person might explain those directions in any one of several languages, such as English, French, or Italian. The directions are the same no matter which lan-

Listing 1.3

```
//********************************************************************
//  Lincoln3.java       Author: Lewis and Loftus
//
//  Demonstrates another valid program that is poorly formatted.
//********************************************************************

          public       class
     Lincoln3
   {
                 public
   static
        void
  main
        (
String
           []
    args                          )
  {
  System.out.println        (
"A quote by Abraham Lincoln:"          )
  ;        System.out.println
           (
      "Whatever you are, be a good one."
     )
  ;
}
         }
```

```
A quote by Abraham Lincoln:
Whatever you are, be a good one.
```

guage is used to explain them, but the manner in which the directions are expressed is different. Furthermore, the friend must be able understand the language being used in order to follow the directions.

Similarly, a problem can be solved by writing a program in one of many programming languages, such as Java, Ada, C, C++, Pascal, and Smalltalk. The purpose of the program is essentially the same no matter which language is used, but the particular statements used to express the instructions vary with each language. A computer must be able to understand the instructions in order to carry them out.

This section explores various categories of programming languages and describes the special programs used to prepare and execute them.

Programming Language Levels

Programming languages are often categorized into the following four groups. These groups basically reflect the historical development of computer languages:

- machine language
- assembly language
- high-level languages
- fourth-generation languages

In order for a program to run on a computer, it must be expressed in that computer's *machine language*. Each type of CPU has its own language. For that reason, we can't run a program specifically written for a Sun Workstation, with its Sparc processor, on an IBM PC, with its Intel processor.

Key Concept

All programs must be translated to a particular CPU's machine language in order to be executed.

Each machine language instruction can only accomplish a simple task. For example, a single instruction might only copy a value into a register or compare a value to zero. It might take four separate machine language instructions to add two numbers together and store the result. However, a computer can do millions of these instructions in a second, and therefore many simple commands can be quickly executed to accomplish complex tasks.

Machine language code is expressed as a series of binary digits and is extremely difficult for humans to read and write. Originally, programs were entered into the computer using switches or some similarly tedious method. Early programmers found these techniques to be time consuming and error prone.

These problems gave rise to the use of *assembly language,* which replaced binary digits with *mnemonics,* short English-like words that represent commands or data. It is much easier for programmers to deal with words than with binary digits. However, an assembly language program cannot be executed directly on a computer. It must first be translated into machine language.

Generally, each assembly language instruction corresponds to an equivalent machine language instruction. Therefore, similar to machine language, each assembly language instruction only accomplishes a simple operation. Although assembly language is an improvement over machine code from a programmer's perspective, it is still tedious to use. Both assembly language and machine language are considered to be *low-level languages.*

High-Level Language	Assembly Language	Machine Language

`a + b`	`ld [%fp-20], %o0`
	`ld [%fp-24], %o1`
	`add %o0, %o1, %o0`
		`...`
		`1101 0000 0000 0111`
		`1011 1111 1110 1000`
		`1101 0010 0000 0111`
		`1011 1111 1110 1000`
		`1001 0000 0000 0000`
		`...`

Figure 1.20 A high-level expression and its machine language equivalent

Today, most programmers use a *high-level language* to write software. A high-level language is expressed in English-like phrases, and thus is easier for programmers to read and write. A single high-level language programming statement can accomplish the equivalent of many, perhaps hundreds, of machine language instructions. The term high-level refers to the fact that the programming statements are expressed in a form that is far removed from the machine language that is ultimately executed. Java is a high-level language, as are Ada, C, C++, Pascal, and Smalltalk.

Figure 1.20 shows equivalent expressions in a high-level language, assembly language, and machine language. The expressions add two numbers together. The assembly language and machine language in this example are specific to a Sparc processor.

The high-level language expression in Figure 1.20 is readable and intuitive for programmers. It is similar to an algebraic expression. The equivalent assembly language code is somewhat readable but it is more verbose and less intuitive. The machine language is basically unreadable and much longer. In fact, only a small portion of the binary machine code to add two numbers together is shown in Figure 1.20. The complete machine language code for this particular expression is over 400 bits long.

High-level language code must be translated into machine language in order to be executed. A high-level language insulates programmers from needing to know the underlying machine language for the processor on which they are working.

Key Concept

Working with high-level languages allows the programmer to ignore the underlying details of machine language.

Some programming languages are considered to operate at an even higher level than high-level languages. They might include special facilities for automatic report generation or interaction with a database. These languages are called *fourth-generation languages,* or simply 4GLs, because they followed the first three generations of computer programming: machine, assembly, and high-level.

Compilers and Interpreters

Several special-purpose programs are needed to help with the process of developing new programs. They are sometimes called software tools, since they are used to build programs. Examples of basic software tools include an editor, a compiler, and an interpreter.

Initially, you use an *editor* to type a program into a computer and store it in a file. There are many different editors with many different features. You should become familiar with the editor you will use regularly, since it can dramatically affect the speed at which you enter and modify your programs.

Once the source code is stored, it must be translated into machine language before it can be executed. This translation process can occur in a variety of ways. A *compiler* is a program that translates code in one language to equivalent code in another language. The original code is called *source code,* and the language into which it is translated is called the *target language.* For many traditional compilers, the source code is translated directly into a particular machine language. The translation process occurs once, and the resulting executable version of the program can be run whenever needed.

An *interpreter* is similar to a compiler but has an important difference. An interpreter interweaves the translation and execution activities. A small part of the source code, such as one statement, is translated and executed. Then another statement is translated and executed, and so on. One advantage of this technique is that it eliminates the need for a separate compilation phase, but the program generally runs more slowly because the translation process occurs during each execution.

Key Concept

A Java compiler translates Java source code into Java bytecode. A Java interpreter translates and executes the bytecode.

The process often used to translate and execute Java programs combines the use of a compiler and an interpreter. This process is pictured in Figure 1.21. The Java compiler translates Java source code into Java *bytecode,* which is a representation of the program in a low-level form similar to machine language code. The Java interpreter reads Java bytecode and executes it on a specific machine. Another compiler could translate the bytecode into a particular machine language for efficient execution on that machine.

Key Concept

Java is architecture neutral because Java bytecode is not associated with any particular hardware platform.

The difference between Java bytecode and true machine language code is that Java bytecode is not tied to any particular processor type. This approach has the distinct advantage of making Java *architecture neutral,* and therefore easily portable from one machine type to another. The only restriction is that there must be a Java interpreter or a bytecode compiler for each processor type on which you want to execute Java bytecode.

Since the compilation process translates the high-level Java source code into a low-level representation, the interpretation process is more efficient than interpreting high-level code directly. Executing a program by interpreting its bytecode is still slower than executing machine code directly, but it is fast

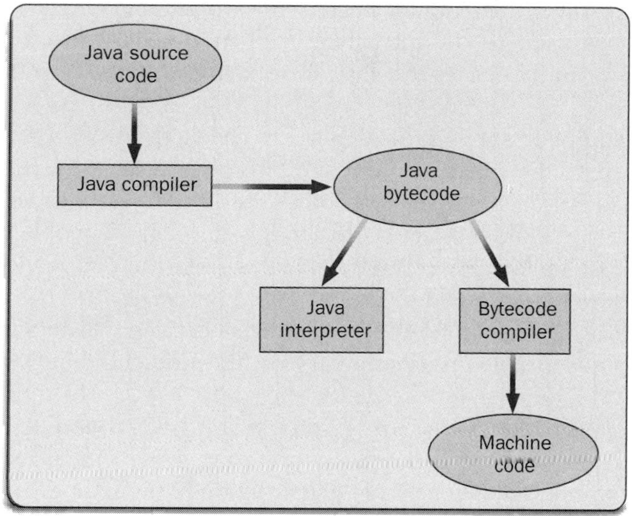

Figure 1.21 The Java translation and execution process

enough for most applications. Note that for efficiency, Java bytecode could be compiled into machine code.

The Java compiler and interpreter are part of the Java *Software Development Kit* (SDK), which also contains several other software tools that may be useful to a programmer. Similar tools have been developed as part of an *Integrated Development Environment* (IDE), which combines an editor, compiler, and other Java support tools into a single application. The specific tools you will use to develop your programs depend on your environment.

Web Bonus

The text Web site contains information about several specific development environments for Java programs.

Syntax and Semantics

Each programming language has its own unique *syntax*. The syntax rules of a language dictate exactly how the vocabulary elements of the language can be put together to form statements. These rules must be followed in order to create a program. We've already discussed several Java syntax rules. For instance, the fact that an identifier cannot begin with a digit is a syntax rule. The fact that braces are used to delimit classes and methods is also a syntax rule. Appendix L formally defines the basic syntax rules for the Java programming language.

During compilation, all syntax rules are checked. If a program is not syntactically correct, the compiler will issue error messages and will not produce bytecode. Java has a similar syntax to the programming languages C and C++, and therefore the look and feel of the code is familiar to people with a background in those languages. Because of these similarities, some people tend to think of Java as a variant of C and C++. However, beyond the basic syntax issues, there are many important differences between Java and these languages. Appendix I contains a summary of the differences between Java and C++.

Key Concept

The syntax rules of a programming language dictate the form of a program. The semantics dictate the meaning of the program statements.

The *semantics* of a statement in a programming language define what will happen when that statement is executed. Programming languages are generally unambiguous, which means the semantics of a program are well defined. That is, there is one and only one interpretation for each statement. On the other hand, the natural languages that humans use to communicate, such as English and French, are full of ambiguities. A sentence can often have two or more different meanings. For example, consider the following sentence:

Time flies like an arrow.

We might interpret this to mean that time moves quickly in the same way that an arrow moves quickly. However, if we interpret the word *time* as a verb (as in "run the 50-yard dash and I'll time you") and the word *flies* as a noun (plural of fly), the interpretation changes completely. We know that arrows don't time things, so humans wouldn't normally interpret the sentence that way, but it is a valid interpretation of the words in the sentence. A computer would have a difficult time trying to determine which meaning is intended. Moreover, this statement could describe the preferences of an unusual insect known as a "time fly." After all, fruit flies like a banana.

The point is that the same exact English sentence can have multiple, valid meanings. A computer language cannot allow such ambiguities to exist. If a programming language instruction could have two different meanings, a computer would not be able to determine which one to follow.

Errors

Several different kinds of problems can occur in software, particularly during program development. The term computer error is often misused and varies in meaning depending on the person using it. From a user's point of view, anything that goes awry when interacting with a machine is often called computer error. For example, suppose you charged a $23 item to your credit card, but when you received the bill the item was listed at $230 dollars. After you have the problem fixed, the credit card company apologizes for the "computer error." Did the computer arbitrarily add a zero to the end of the number, or perhaps multiply the value by 10? Of course not. A computer follows the commands we give it and operates on the data we provide. If our programs are wrong or our data inaccurate, then we cannot expect the results to be correct. A common phrase used to describe this situation is "garbage in, garbage out."

Key Concept

A computer follows our instructions exactly. The programmer is responsible for the accuracy and reliability of a program.

There are three kinds of errors that you will encounter while developing programs:

- compile-time error
- run-time error
- logical error

The compiler checks to make sure you are using the correct syntax. If you have any statements that do not conform to the syntactic rules of the language, the compiler will produce a *syntax error.* The compiler also tries to find other problems, such as the use of incompatible types of data. The syntax might be technically correct, but you are still attempting to do something that the language doesn't semantically allow. Any error identified by the compiler is called a *compile-time error.* If a compile-time error occurs, an executable version of the program is not created.

Key Concept

A program must be syntactically correct or the compiler will not produce bytecode.

The second kind of problem occurs during program execution. It is called a *run-time error,* and causes the program to terminate abnormally. For example, if we attempt to divide by zero, the program will "blow up" and halt execution at that point. Because the requested operation is undefined, the system simply abandons its attempt to continue processing your program. The best programs are *robust;* that is, they avoid as many run-time errors as possible. For example, the program code could guard against the possibility of dividing by zero and handle the situation appropriately if it arises. In Java, many run-time errors are represented as *exceptions* that can be caught and dealt with accordingly. Exceptions are discussed in Chapter 8.

The third kind of software problem is a *logical error.* In this case, the software compiles and executes without complaint, but it produces incorrect results. For example, a logical error occurs when a value is calculated incorrectly or when a graphical button does not appear in the correct place. A programmer must test the program thoroughly, comparing the expected results to those that actually occur. When defects are found, they must be traced back to the source of the problem in the code and corrected. The process of finding and correcting defects in a program is called *debugging.* Logical errors can manifest themselves in many ways, and the actual root cause might be quite difficult to discover.

Language Evolution

As computer technology evolves, so must the languages we use to program them. The Java programming language has undergone various changes since its initial creation. This text uses the most recent Java technology.

Specifically, this book uses the *Java 2 platform,* which simply refers to the most advanced collection of Java language features, software libraries, and tools. Several important advances have been made since its previous version, Java 1.1.

The Java Software Development Kit (SDK), sometimes called the *Java Development Kit* (JDK), is the set of software tools provided by Sun Microsystems that can be used for creating Java software. These tools include a compiler and interpreter, among others. The Java SDK version 1.2 is a part of the Java 2 platform. You might be using the Java SDK to develop your programs, or you may use some other development environment.

Some parts of early Java technologies have been *deprecated,* which means they are considered old-fashioned and should not be used. When it is important, we will point out deprecated elements and discuss their state-of-the-art alternatives.

One particular area in which Java has changed is in the software libraries that support the development of graphical user interfaces. Specifically, earlier releases of Java used the *Abstract Windowing Toolkit* (AWT). Included with the Java 2 platform is a software library called *Swing,* which builds on the AWT and extends its capabilities. The Swing library contains many elements that replace older, less useful AWT elements. Whenever appropriate, we use Swing technology in this text.

1.6 Graphics

Graphics play a crucial role in computer systems. Throughout this book we explore various aspects of graphics and discuss how they are accomplished. In fact, the last one or two sections of each chapter are devoted to graphics topics. If desired, they can be skipped without loss of continuity through the rest of the text. In this section we explore the basic concepts of representing a picture in a computer and displaying it on a screen.

A picture, like all other information stored on a computer, must be digitized by breaking the information down into pieces and representing those pieces as numbers. In the case of pictures, we break the picture down into *pixels* (picture elements), as we mentioned when discussing the quality of a

Figure 1.22 A digitized picture, with a small portion magnified

computer system's monitor screen. A pixel is a tiny dot that represents a very small piece of the picture. The color of each pixel is stored separately.

A black and white picture can be stored by representing each pixel using a single bit. If the bit is zero, that pixel is white; if the bit is 1, it is black. The picture can be reproduced when needed by reassembling the pixels that make it up. The more pixels used to represent a picture, the more realistic it looks when reproduced. Figure 1.22 shows a black and white picture that has been stored digitally and an enlargement of a portion of that picture, which shows the individual pixels.

Key Concept

The pixels of a black and white picture can be represented using a single bit each, mapping 0 to white and 1 to black.

Coordinate Systems

When drawn, each pixel of the picture is somehow mapped to a pixel on the screen. Each computer system and programming language defines a coordinate system so that we can refer to particular pixels.

A traditional two-dimensional coordinate system has two axes that meet at the origin. Values on either axis can be negative or positive. The Java programming language has a relatively simple coordinate system, in which the visible coordinates are positive. A traditional coordinate system and the Java coordinate system are shown in Figure 1.23.

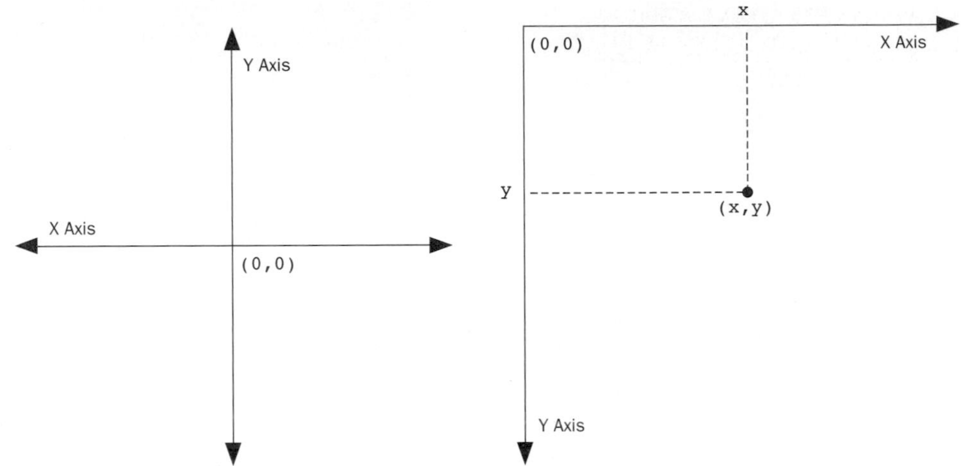

Figure 1.23 A traditional coordinate system and the Java coordinate system

Each point in the Java coordinate system is represented using an (*x*, *y*) pair of values. The top-left corner of any Java drawing area is coordinate (0, 0). The *x*-axis coordinates get larger as you move to the right and the *y*-axis coordinates get larger as you move down.

Representing Color

Color pictures are divided into pixels, just as black and white pictures are. However, since each pixel can be one of many possible colors, it is not sufficient to represent each pixel using only one bit. There are various ways to represent the color of a pixel. This section explores one popular technique.

Every color can be represented as a mix of three *primary colors:* red, green, and blue. In Java, as in many other computer languages, colors are specified by three numbers that are collectively referred to as an *RGB value.* RGB stands for Red-Green-Blue. Each number represents the contribution of a primary color. Using one byte (8 bits) to store each of the three numbers, the numbers can range from 0 to 255. The level of each primary color determines the overall color. For example, high values of red and green combined with a low level of blue results in a shade of yellow.

Key Concept

The pixels of a color picture can be represented using three numbers, collectively called the RGB value, which represent the relative contributions of three primary colors: red, green, and blue.

In the graphics sections of other chapters we explore the use of color and how to control it in a Java program.

Summary of Key Concepts

- A computer system consists of hardware and software that work in concert to help us solve problems.
- To execute a program, the computer first copies the program from secondary memory to main memory. The CPU then reads the program instructions from main memory, executing them one at a time until the program ends.
- The operating system provides a user interface and manages computer resources.
- As far as the user is concerned, the interface *is* the program.
- Digital computers store information by breaking it down into pieces and representing each piece as a number.
- Binary values are used to store all information in a computer because the devices that store and move binary information are inexpensive and reliable.
- The core of a computer is made up of the CPU and the main memory. Main memory is used to store programs and data, and the CPU executes a program's instructions one at a time.
- An address is a unique number associated with each memory location, used when storing and retrieving data from memory.
- Data written to a memory location overwrites and destroys any information that was previously held in that location. Data read from a memory location leaves the value in memory unaffected.
- Main memory is volatile, meaning the stored information is only maintained as long as electric power is supplied. Secondary memory devices are usually nonvolatile.
- The speed of the system clock indicates how fast the CPU executes instructions.
- A network consists of two or more computers connected together so they can exchange information.
- Sharing a communication line is cost-effective and makes adding new computers to the network relatively easy.
- A local-area network (LAN) is an inexpensive way to share information and resources throughout an organization.
- The Internet is a wide-area network that spans the globe.
- TCP/IP is the set of software protocols that govern the movement of messages across the Internet.

- Every computer connected to the Internet has an IP address that uniquely identifies it.
- The World Wide Web is software that makes sharing information across a network easy.
- A browser is a software tool that loads and formats Web documents for viewing. These documents are often written using the HyperText Markup Language (HTML).
- A URL uniquely specifies documents and other information found on the World Wide Web for a browser to obtain and display.
- The purpose of writing a program is to solve a problem.
- Specific programming techniques are the tools that help us solve problems.
- Comments do not affect a program's processing, but are useful for human comprehension.
- The `main` method must always be defined using the words `public`, `static`, and `void`.
- Inline documentation should provide insight into your code. It should not be ambiguous or belabor the obvious.
- Java is case sensitive. The uppercase and lowercase versions of a letter are distinct. You should use a consistent case convention for different types of identifiers.
- Identifier names should be descriptive and readable.
- Appropriate use of white space makes a program easier to read and understand.
- You should always adhere to a set of guidelines that establish the way you format and document your programs.
- All programs must be translated to a particular CPU's machine language in order to be executed.
- Working with high-level languages allows the programmer to ignore the underlying details of machine language.
- A Java compiler translates Java source code into Java bytecode. A Java interpreter translates and executes the bytecode.
- Java is architecture neutral because Java bytecode is not associated with any particular hardware platform.
- The syntax rules of a programming language dictate the form of a program. The semantics dictate the meaning of the program statements.
- A computer follows our instructions exactly. The programmer is responsible for the accuracy and reliability of a program.

- A program must be syntactically correct or the compiler will not produce bytecode.
- The pixels of a black and white picture can be represented using a single bit each, mapping 0 to white and 1 to black.
- The pixels of a color picture can be represented using three numbers, collectively called the RGB value, which represent the relative contributions of three primary colors: red, green, and blue.

Self-Review Questions

1.1 What is hardware? What is software?

1.2 What are the two primary functions of an operating system?

1.3 What happens to information when it is stored digitally?

1.4 How many unique items can be represented with:

a. 2 bits?

b. 4 bits?

c. 5 bits?

1.5 What are the two primary hardware components in a computer? How do they interact?

1.6 What is a memory address?

1.7 What does volatile mean? Which memory devices are volatile and which are nonvolatile?

1.8 What is a file server?

1.9 What is the origin of the word Internet?

1.10 What is the relationship between a high-level language and machine language?

1.11 What is Java bytecode?

1.12 What is white space? How does it affect program execution? How does it affect program readability?

1.13 What do we mean by the syntax and semantics of a programming language?

1.14 Why can a black and white picture be represented using 1s and 0s?

▶ Exercises

1.1 If a picture was made up of 64 possible colors, how many bits would be needed to store each pixel of the picture? Why?

1.2 Determine the storage capacity of main memory and secondary memory on your computer or on a computer in a lab to which you have access. Explain how you determined your answer.

1.3 How many bits are there in:

a. 12 KB?

b. 5 MB?

c. 1 GB?

1.4 Explain the difference between random-access memory (RAM) and read-only memory (ROM).

1.5 A disk is a random-access device, but it is not RAM (random-access memory). Explain why and give an example of each.

1.6 Determine how your computer, or a computer in a lab to which you have access, is connected to others across a network. Is it linked to the Internet? Draw a diagram to show the basic connections in your environment.

1.7 Explain the differences between a local-area network (LAN) and a wide-area network (WAN). What is the relationship between them?

1.8 What is the total number of communication lines needed for a fully connected point-to-point network of eight computers? Nine computers? Ten computers? What is a general formula for determining this result?

1.9 Explain the difference between the Internet and the World Wide Web.

1.10 List and explain the parts of the URL for:

a. your school.

b. the Computer Science department of your school.

c. your professor's Web page.

1.11 Use a Web browser to access information through the World Wide Web about the following topics. For each one, explain the process you used to find the information and record the specific URLs found.

a. The Philadelphia Phillies baseball team

b. Wine production in California

c. The subway systems in four major cities throughout the world

d. Vacation opportunities in the Caribbean

1.12 How many bits are needed to store a color picture that is 400 pixels wide and 250 pixels high? Assume color is represented using the RGB technique described in this chapter and that no special compression is done.

1.13 Give examples of the two types of Java comments. Explain the differences between them.

1.14 Which of the following are not valid Java identifiers? Why?

a. `Factorial`

b. `anExtremelyLongIdentifierIfYouAskMe`

c. `2ndLevel`

d. `level2`

e. `highest$`

f. `hook&ladder`

1.15 Why are the following valid Java identifiers not considered to be good identifiers?

a. `i`

b. `totVal`

c. `theNextValueInTheList`

1.16 Java is case sensitive. What does that mean?

1.17 Categorize each of the following situations as a compile-time error, run-time error, or logical error.

a. Multiplying two numbers when you meant to add them

b. Dividing by zero

c. Spelling a word wrong in the output

d. Producing inaccurate results

e. Typing a `{` when you should have typed `(`

1.18 Why is the English language ambiguous? Give two examples of English ambiguity (other than the example used in this chapter). Why is ambiguity a problem for programming languages?

Programming Projects

1.1 Enter, compile, and run the following application:

```
public class Test
{
   public static void main (String[] args)
   {
      System.out.println ("An Emergency Broadcast");
   }
}
```

1.2 Introduce the following errors, one at a time, to the program in Programming Project 1.19. Record any error messages that the compiler produces. Fix the previous error each time before you introduce a new one. If no error messages are produced, explain why.

a. Change `Test` to `test`.

b. Change `Emergency` to `emergency`.

c. Remove the first quotation mark in the string literal.

d. Remove the last quotation mark in the string literal.

e. Change `main` to `man`.

f. Change `println` to `bogus`.

g. Change `Broadcast` to `Brxoadxcaxst`.

h. Remove the semicolon at the end of the `println` statement.

i. Remove the last brace in the program.

1.3 Write an application that prints `Knowledge is Power`:

a. on one line.

b. centered on three lines.

c. inside a box made up of the characters = and |.

1.4 Write an application that displays your initials in large block letters. Make each large letter out of the corresponding regular character.

Answers to Self-Review Questions

1.1 The hardware of a computer system are its physical components such as a circuit board, monitor, or keyboard. Computer software are programs that are executed by the hardware, and the data that those programs use. Hardware is tangible but software is intangible. In order to be useful, hardware requires software and software requires hardware.

1.2 The operating system provides a user interface and efficiently coordinates the use of resources such as main memory and the CPU.

1.3 The information is broken down into pieces, and those pieces are represented as numbers.

1.4 a. 2 bits can represent four items because $2^2 = 4$.

b. 4 bits can represent 16 items because $2^4 = 16$.

c. 5 bits can represent 32 items because $2^5 = 32$.

1.5 The two primary hardware components are main memory and the CPU. Main memory holds the currently active programs and data. The CPU retrieves individual program instructions from main memory, one at a time, and executes them.

1.6 A memory address is a number that uniquely identifies a particular memory location in which a value is stored.

1.7 Main memory is volatile, which means the information that is stored in it will be lost if the power supply to the computer is turned off. Secondary memory devices are nonvolatile; therefore, the information that is stored on them is retained even if the power goes off.

1.8 A file server is a network computer that is dedicated to storing and providing programs and data that are needed by many network users.

1.9 The word Internet comes from the word internetworking, a concept related to wide-area networks (WANs). An internetwork connects one network to another. The Internet is a WAN.

1.10 High-level languages allow a programmer to express a series of program instructions in English-like terms that are relatively easy to read and use. However, in order to execute, a program must be expressed in a particular computer's machine language, which consists of a series of bits basically unreadable by humans. A high-level language program must be translated into machine language before it can be run.

1.11 Java bytecode is a low-level representation of a Java source code program. The Java compiler translates the source code into bytecode, which can then be executed using the Java interpreter. The bytecode might be transported across the Web prior to being executed by a Java interpreter that is part of a Web browser.

1.12 White space is a term that includes the spaces, tabs, and newline characters that separate words and symbols in a program. The compiler ignores extra white space; therefore, it doesn't affect execution. However, it is crucial to use white space appropriately to make a program readable to humans.

1.13 Syntax rules define how the symbols and words of a programming language can be put together. The semantics of a programming language instruction determines what will happen when that instruction is executed.

1.14 A black and white picture can be drawn using a series of dots, represented as pixels. Pixels that contain a value of 0 are drawn in white and pixels that contain a value of 1 are drawn in black. By using thousands of pixels with values of 0 or 1, a realistic black and white photo can be produced on a computer screen.

2 Objects and Primitive Data

This chapter explores the key elements that we use in a program: primitive data and objects. We will develop the ability to create and use objects for the services they provide. This ability is fundamental to the process of writing any program in an object-oriented language such as Java. We use objects to manipulate character strings, obtain information from the user, perform complex calculations, and format output. In the Graphics Track of this chapter we explore the relationship between Java and the World Wide Web, and delve into Java's abilities to manipulate color and draw shapes.

Chapter Objectives

- Establish the difference between primitive data and objects.
- Declare and use variables.
- Perform mathematical computations.
- Create objects and use them for the services they provide.
- Explore the difference between a Java application and a Java applet.
- Create graphical programs that draw shapes.

2.1 Introduction to Objects

A Java program manages two general types of information: primitive data and objects. *Primitive data* are common, fundamental values such as numbers and characters. An object usually represents something more specialized or complex, such as a bank account.

Key Concept

The information we manage in a Java program is either represented as primitive data or as objects.

A *data type* defines a set of values and the operations that can be performed on those values. We perform operations on primitive types using *operators* that are built into the programming language. For example, the addition symbol (+) is used to add two numbers together. Section 2.4 discusses primitive data types and their operators in detail.

An object is defined by a *class,* which can be thought of as the data type of the object. A class contains methods that generally represent the operations that can be performed on objects created from that class. As we discussed in Chapter 1, a method is a collection of programming statements that is given a specific name so that we can invoke the method as needed.

This chapter focuses on the use of primitive data and objects. We explore how to define our own objects, by writing our own classes and methods, in Chapter 4.

The `print` and `println` Methods

In the `Lincoln` program in Chapter 1, we invoked a method through an object:

```
System.out.println ("Whatever you are, be a good one.");
```

The `System.out` object represents an output device or file, which by default is the monitor screen. To be more precise, the object's name is `out` and it is stored in the `System` class. We will explore that relationship in more detail at the appropriate point in the text.

The `println` method is part of the `System.out` object. We can think of the `println` method as an operation that we perform on the `System.out` object. Alternatively, we can think of `println` as a service that the `System.out` object performs for us. The act of invoking a method on an object is sometimes referred to as sending a *message* to the object, requesting that the service be performed. Therefore, we can say that we send the `println` message to the `System.out` object to request that some text be printed.

The `System.out` object provides another service we can use: the `print` method. The difference between `print` and `println` is small but important. The `println` method prints the information sent to it, then moves to the next line. The `print` method is similar to `println`, but does not advance to the next line when completed.

Listing 2.1

```
//********************************************************************
//  Countdown.java        Author: Lewis and Loftus
//
//  Demonstrates the difference between print and println.
//********************************************************************

public class Countdown
{
   //-----------------------------------------------------------------
   //  Prints two lines of output representing a rocket countdown.
   //-----------------------------------------------------------------
   public static void main (String[] args)
   {
      System.out.print ("Three... ");
      System.out.print ("Two... ");
      System.out.print ("One... ");
      System.out.print ("Zero... ");

      System.out.println ("Liftoff!"); // appears on first output line
      System.out.println ("Houston, we have a problem.");
   }
}
```

```
Three . . . Two . . . One . . . Zero . . . Liftoff!
Houston, we have a problem.
```

The program shown in Listing 2.1 is called `Countdown`, and it invokes both the `print` and `println` methods.

Carefully compare the output of the `Countdown` program to the program code. Note that the word `Liftoff` is printed on the same line as the first few words, even though it is printed using the `println` method. Remember that the `println` method moves to the next line *after* the information passed to it is printed.

We can use an *object diagram* to show how objects and classes interact. Figure 2.1 shows the object diagram representing the interaction of the `Countdown` program. The `Countdown` class, which contains the `main` method, is shown to invoke the `print` and `println` methods of the `System.out` object.

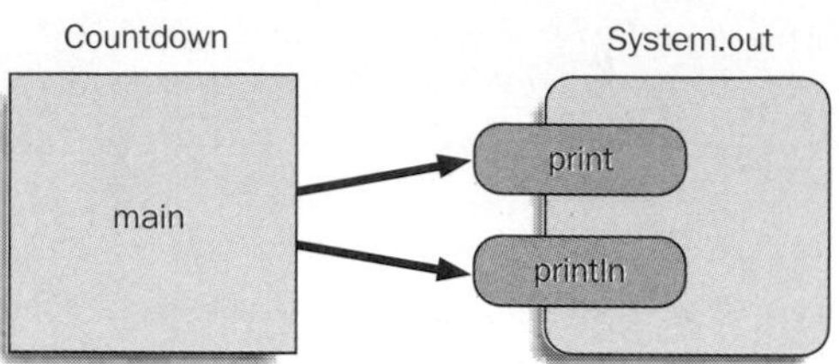

Figure 2.1 An object diagram for `Countdown`

Classes are shown in an object diagram using rectangles with square corners, and objects are shown as rectangles with rounded corners. The name of the class or object is written above the rectangle. Inside the rectangle we list the important data and methods contained in the classes and objects, superimposing invoked methods as shown. The `System.out` object contains other methods, but they are not relevant to this program so we don't bother showing them.

Object diagrams can be useful in capturing the way objects and classes communicate. We will use them occasionally to highlight the processing of a program.

Sometimes the act of invoking a method through an object is referred to as sending a *message* to the object. That terminology is consistent with the idea that the object is performing a service that we are requesting.

Abstraction

An object is an *abstraction,* meaning that the precise details of how it works are irrelevant from the point of view of the user of the object. We don't really need to know how the `println` method prints characters to the screen, as long as we can count on it to do its job. Of course, there are times when it is helpful to understand such information, but it is not necessary in order to *use* the object.

Sometimes it is important to hide or ignore certain details. A human being is capable of mentally managing around seven (plus or minus two) pieces of information in short-term memory. Beyond that, we start to lose track of some of the pieces. However, if we group pieces of information together, then those pieces can be managed as one "chunk" in our minds. We don't actively deal with all of the details in the chunk but can still manage it as a single entity. We, therefore, can deal with large quantities of information by organizing them into chunks. An object is a construct that organizes information and allows us to hide the details inside. An object is therefore a wonderful abstraction.

We use abstractions every day. Think about a car for a moment. You don't necessarily need to know how a four-cycle combustion engine works in order to drive a car. You just need to know some basic operations: how to turn it on, how to put it in gear, how to make it move with the pedals and steering wheel, and how to stop it. These operations define the way a person interacts with the car.

These operations mask the details of what is happening inside the car that allow it to function. When you're driving a car, you're not usually thinking about the spark plugs igniting the gasoline that drives the piston that turns the crankshaft that turns the axle that turns the wheel. If we had to worry about all of these underlying details, we'd never be able to operate something as complicated as a car.

Initially, all cars had manual transmissions. The driver had to understand and deal with the details of changing gears with the stick shift. Eventually, automatic transmissions were developed, and the driver no longer had to worry about shifting gears. Those details were hidden by raising the *level of abstraction*.

Key Concept

An abstraction hides details. A good abstraction hides the right details at the right time so that we can manage complexity.

Of course, someone has to deal with the details. The car manufacturer has to know the details in order to design the car together in the first place. A car mechanic relies on the fact that most people don't have the expertise or tools necessary to fix a car when it breaks. The level of abstraction must be appropriate for the situation. Some people prefer to drive a manual transmission car. A race car driver, for instance, needs to control the shifting manually for optimum performance.

Likewise, someone has to write the code for the objects we use. Soon we will define our own objects and use them. For now, we can make use of objects that have already been defined for us. Abstraction makes that possible.

2.2 String Literals

A character string is an object in Java, defined by the class `String`. Because strings are so fundamental in computer programming, Java provides the ability to use a *string literal*, delimited by double quotation marks, as we've seen in previous examples. We explore the `String` class and its methods in more detail in Section 2.5. For now, let's explore two other useful details about strings: concatenation and escape sequences.

String Concatenation

The program called `Facts` shown in Listing 2.2 contains several `println` statements. The first one prints a sentence that is somewhat long and will not fit on one line of the program. A character string, delimited by the double quote characters, cannot be split between two lines of code. One way to get around this problem is to use the *string concatenation* operator, the plus sign (+). String concatenation produces one string in which the second string is

Listing 2.2

```
//********************************************************************
//  Facts.java       Author: Lewis and Loftus
//
//  Demonstrates the use of the string concatenation operator and the
//  automatic conversion of an integer to a string.
//********************************************************************

public class Facts
{
   //-----------------------------------------------------------------
   //  Prints various facts.
   //-----------------------------------------------------------------
   public static void main (String[] args)
   {
      // Strings can be concatenated into one long string
      System.out.println ("We present the following facts for your "
                          + "extracurricular edification:");

      System.out.println ();

      // A string can contain numeric digits
      System.out.println ("Letters in the Hawaiian alphabet: 12");

      // A numeric value can be concatenated to a string
      System.out.println ("International dialing code for Antarctica: "
                          + 672);

      System.out.println ("Year in which Leonardo da Vinci invented "
                          + "the parachute: " + 1515);

      System.out.println ("Speed of ketchup: " + 40 + " km per year");
   }
}
```

```
We present the following facts for your extracurricular edification:

Letters in the Hawaiian alphabet: 12
International dialing code for Antarctica: 672
Year in which Leonardo da Vinci invented the parachute: 1515
Speed of ketchup: 40 km per year
```

appended to the first. The string concatenation operation in the first `println` statement results in one large string that is passed to the method and printed.

Note that we don't have to pass any information to the `println` method, as shown in the second line of the `Facts` program. This call has the effect of printing a blank line.

The rest of the calls to `println` in the `Facts` program demonstrate another interesting thing about string concatenation: strings can be concatenated with numbers. Note that the numbers in those lines are not enclosed in double quotes, and are therefore not character strings. In these cases, the number is automatically converted to a string, then the two strings are concatenated.

Because we are printing particular values, we could have simply included the numeric values as part of the preceding string literal. We separate them in this program to demonstrate the ability to concatenate a string and a number. This technique will be useful in upcoming examples.

As you might imagine, the + operator is also used for arithmetic addition. Therefore, what the + operator does depends on the types of data on which it operates. If either or both of the operands of the + operator are strings, then string concatenation is performed.

The `Addition` program shown in Listing 2.3 demonstrates the distinction between string concatenation and arithmetic addition. The `Addition` program uses the + operator four times. In the first call to `println`, both + operations perform string concatenation. This is because the operators execute left to right. The first operator concatenates the string with the first number (`24`), creating a larger string. Then that string is concatenated with the second number (`45`), creating an even larger string which gets printed.

In the second call to `println`, parentheses are used to group the + operation with the two numbers. This forces that operation to happen first. Because both operands are numbers, the numbers are added in the arithmetic sense, producing the result `69`. That number is then concatenated to the string, producing a larger string that gets printed.

We revisit this type of situation later in this chapter when we formalize the rules that define the order in which operators get evaluated.

Escape Sequences

Because the double quotation character (`"`) is used in the Java language to indicate the end of a string, we must use a special technique to print the quotation mark. If we try to just put it in a string (`"""`), the compiler gets confused because it thinks the second quotation character is the end of the string, and doesn't know what to do with the third one. This results in a compile-time error.

To overcome this problem, Java defines several *escape sequences* to represent special characters. An escape sequence begins with the backslash character (`\`), and indicates that the character or characters that follow should be interpreted in a special way. The Java escape sequences are listed in Figure 2.2.

Listing 2.3

```
//********************************************************************
//  Addition.java       Author: Lewis and Loftus
//
//  Demonstrates the difference between the addition and string
//  concatenation operators.
//********************************************************************

public class Addition
{
   //-----------------------------------------------------------------
   //  Concatenates and adds two numbers and prints the results.
   //-----------------------------------------------------------------
   public static void main (String[] args)
   {
      System.out.println ("24 and 45 concatenated: " + 24 + 45);

      System.out.println ("24 and 45 added: " + (24 + 45));
   }
}
```

```
24 and 45 concatenated: 2445
24 and 45 added: 69
```

Escape Sequence	Meaning
`\b`	backspace
`\t`	tab
`\n`	newline
`\r`	carriage return
`\"`	double quote
`\'`	single quote
`\\`	backslash

Figure 2.2 Java escape sequences

Listing 2.4

```
//********************************************************************
//  Roses.java       Author: Lewis and Loftus
//
//  Demonstrates the use of escape sequences.
//********************************************************************

public class Roses
{
   //-----------------------------------------------------------------
   //  Prints a poem (of sorts) on multiple lines.
   //-----------------------------------------------------------------
   public static void main (String[] args)
   {
      System.out.println ("Roses are red,\n\tViolets are blue,\n" +
         "Sugar is sweet,\n\tBut I have \"commitment issues\",\n\t" +
         "So I'd rather just be friends\n\tAt this point in our " +
         "relationship.");
   }
}
```

```
Roses are red,
        Violets are blue,
Sugar is sweet,
        But I have "commitment issues",
        So I'd rather just be friends
        At this point in our relationship.
```

The program in Listing 2.4, called `Roses`, prints some text resembling a poem to the screen. It uses only one `println` statement to do it, despite the fact that the poem is several lines long. Note the escape sequences used throughout the string. The `\n` escape sequence forces the output to a new line, and the `\t` escape sequence represents a tab character. The `\"` escape sequence ensures that that quote character is treated as part of the string, not the termination of it, which enables it to be printed as part of the output.

2.3 Variables and Assignment

Most of the information we manage in a program is represented by a variable. Let's examine how we declare and use them in a program.

Variables

A *variable* is a name for a location in memory used to hold a data value. When you declare a variable, you are instructing the compiler to reserve a portion of main memory space large enough to hold a particular type of value and indicating the name by which you will refer to that location. Consider the program `PianoKeys`, shown in Listing 2.5.

Listing 2.5

```
//********************************************************************
//  PianoKeys.java       Author: Lewis and Loftus
//
//  Demonstrates the declaration, initialization, and use of an
//  integer variable.
//********************************************************************

public class PianoKeys
{
   //-----------------------------------------------------------------
   //  Prints the number of keys on a piano.
   //-----------------------------------------------------------------
   public static void main (String[] args)
   {
      int keys = 88;

      System.out.println ("A piano has " + keys + " keys.");
   }
}
```

```
A piano has 88 keys.
```

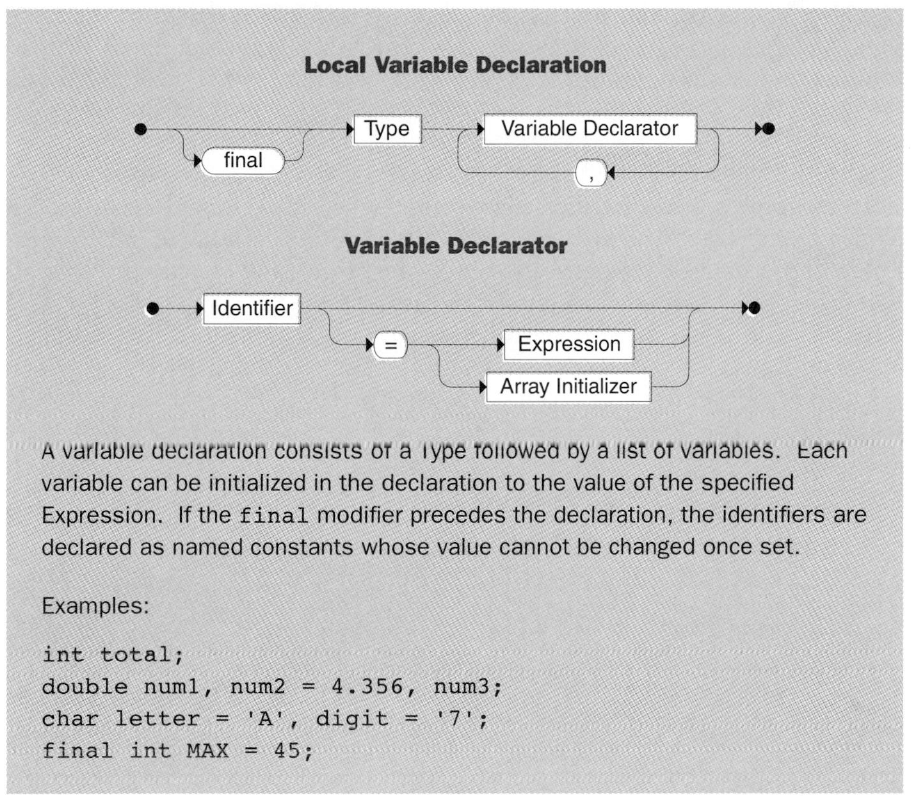

A variable declaration consists of a Type followed by a list of variables. Each variable can be initialized in the declaration to the value of the specified Expression. If the `final` modifier precedes the declaration, the identifiers are declared as named constants whose value cannot be changed once set.

Examples:

```
int total;
double num1, num2 = 4.356, num3;
char letter = 'A', digit = '7';
final int MAX = 45;
```

The first line of the `main` method is the declaration of a variable named `keys` that holds an integer (`int`) value. The declaration also gives `keys` an initial value of `88`. If an initial value is not specified for a variable, the value is undefined. In fact, most Java compilers give errors or warnings if you attempt to use a variable before you've explicitly given it a value.

Key Concept

A variable is a name for a memory location used to hold a value of a particular data type.

In the `PianoKeys` program, two pieces of information are provided in the call to the `println` method. The first is a string, and the second is the variable `keys`. When a variable is referenced, the value currently stored in it is used. Therefore, when the call to `println` is executed, the value of `keys` is obtained. Because that value is an integer, it is automatically converted to a string so it can be concatenated with the initial string. The concatenated string is passed to `println` and printed.

Note that a variable declaration can have multiple variables of the same type declared on one line. Each variable on the line can be declared with or without an initializing value.

The Assignment Statement

Let's examine a program that changes the value of a variable. Listing 2.6 shows a program called `Geometry`. This program first declares an integer variable called `sides` and initializes it to `7`. It then prints out the current value of `sides`.

Listing 2.6

```
//********************************************************************
//  Geometry.java       Author: Lewis and Loftus
//
//  Demonstrates the use of an assignment statement to change the
//  value stored in a variable.
//********************************************************************

public class Geometry
{
   //-----------------------------------------------------------------
   //  Prints the number of sides of several geometric shapes.
   //-----------------------------------------------------------------
   public static void main (String[] args)
   {
      int sides = 7;  // declaration with initialization
      System.out.println ("A heptagon has " + sides + " sides.");

      sides = 10;  // assignment statement
      System.out.println ("A decagon has " + sides + " sides.");

      sides = 12;
      System.out.println ("A dodecagon has " + sides + " sides.");
   }
}
```

```
A heptagon has 7 sides.
A decagon has 10 sides.
A dodecagon has 12 sides.
```

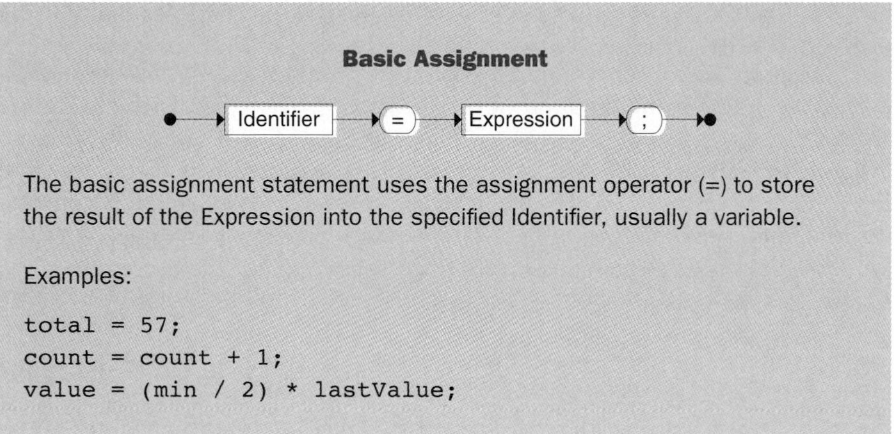

The basic assignment statement uses the assignment operator (=) to store the result of the Expression into the specified Identifier, usually a variable.

Examples:

```
total = 57;
count = count + 1;
value = (min / 2) * lastValue;
```

The next line in `main` changes the value stored in the variable `sides`:

```
sides = 10;
```

This is called an *assignment statement* because it assigns a value to a variable. When executed, the expression on the right-hand side of the assignment operator (=) is evaluated, and the result is stored in the memory location indicated by the variable on the left-hand side. In this example, the expression is simply a number, `10`. More involved expressions are described in the next section.

A variable can only store one value of its declared type, and the new value overwrites the old one. In this case, when the value `10` is assigned to `sides`, the original value `7` is overwritten and lost forever. However, when a reference is made to a variable, such as when it is printed, the value of the variable is not changed.

> **Key Concept**
> A variable can store only one value of its declared type.

The Java language is *strongly typed,* meaning that we are not allowed to assign a value to a variable that is inconsistent with its declared type. Trying to combine incompatible types will generate an error when you attempt to compile the program. Therefore, the expression on the right-hand side of an assignment statement must evaluate to a value compatible with the type of the variable on the left-hand side.

> **Key Concept**
> Java is a strongly typed language. Each variable is associated with a specific type for the duration of its existence, and you cannot assign a value of one type to a variable of an incompatible type.

Constants

Sometimes we use data that is constant throughout a program. For instance, you might write a program that deals with a theatre that can hold no more than 427 people. It is often helpful to give a constant value a name, such as

MAX_OCCUPANCY, instead of using a literal value, such as 427, throughout the code.

Constants are identifiers and are similar to variables except that they hold a particular value for the duration of their existence. The compiler will produce an error message if you attempt to change the value of a constant using an assignment statement. In Java, if you precede a declaration with the reserved word `final`, the identifier is made a constant. For example, the constant describing the maximum occupancy of a theatre could be declared as follows:

```
final int MAX_OCCUPANCY = 427;
```

Key Concept

Constants are similar to variables, but they hold a particular value for the duration of their existence.

It is good practice to use constants instead of literal values in a program because they prevent inadvertent errors by not allowing their value to change. They also make code more readable by giving meaning to a possibly unclear value. Furthermore, if a value is used throughout a program and it needs to be modified, then the value only needs to be changed where the constant is declared. For example, if capacity of the theatre changes (after a renovation) from 427 to 535, then we only have to change one declaration, and all uses of `MAX_OCCUPANCY` automatically reflect the change.

By convention, uppercase letters are used when naming constants to distinguish them from regular variables. Individual words are separated using the underscore character.

2.4 Primitive Data Types and Expressions

Key Concept

Each value in memory is associated with a specific data type. This data type determines what operations we can perform on the data.

There are eight primitive data types in Java: four variations of integers, two variations of floating point numbers, a boolean data type, and a character data type. Everything else is represented using objects. Let's examine the primitive data types in some detail.

Integers and Floating Points

Key Concept

Java has two kinds of numeric values—integers and floating point. There are four integer data types (`byte`, `short`, `int`, and `long`) and two floating point data types (`float` and `double`).

Java has two basic kinds of numeric values: integers, which have no fractional part, and floating points, which do. There are four integer data types (`byte`, `short`, `int`, and `long`) and two floating point data types (`float` and `double`). All of the numeric types differ by the amount of memory space used to store a value of that type, which determines the range of values that can be represented. The size of each data type is the same for all hardware platforms.

Type	Storage	Min Value	Max Value
`byte`	8 bits	–128	127
`short`	16 bits	–32,768	32,767
`int`	32 bits	–2,147,483,648	2,147,483,647
`long`	64 bits	–9,223,372,036,854,775,808	9,223,372,036,854,775,807
`float`	32 bits	Approximately –3.4E+38 with 7 significant digits	Approximately 3.4E+38 with 7 significant digits
`double`	64 bits	Approximately –1.7E+308 with 15 significant digits	Approximately 1.7E+308 with 15 significant digits

Figure 2.3 The Java numeric primitive types

All numeric types are *signed,* meaning that both positive and negative values can be stored in them. Figure 2.3 summarizes the numeric primitive types.

Remember from our discussion in Chapter 1 that a bit can either be a 1 or a 0. Because each bit can represent two different states, a string of n bits can be used to represent 2^n different values. Appendix B describes number systems and these kinds of relationships in more detail.

Web Bonus

The book's Web site includes a description of the internal storage representation of primitive data types.

When designing a program, you sometimes need to be careful about picking variables of appropriate size so that memory space is not wasted. For example, if a value will not vary outside of a range of 1 to 1000, then a two-byte integer (`short`) is large enough to accommodate it. On the other hand, when it's not clear what the range of a particular variable will be, you should provide a reasonable, even generous, amount of space. In most situations memory space is not a serious restriction and you can usually afford generous assumptions.

Note that even though a regular floating point value supports very large (and very small) numbers, it only has seven significant digits. Therefore if it is important to accurately maintain a value such as 50341.2077, you need to use a double.

A *literal* is an explicit data value used in a program. The various numbers used in programs such as `Facts` and `Addition` and `PianoKeys` are all *integer*

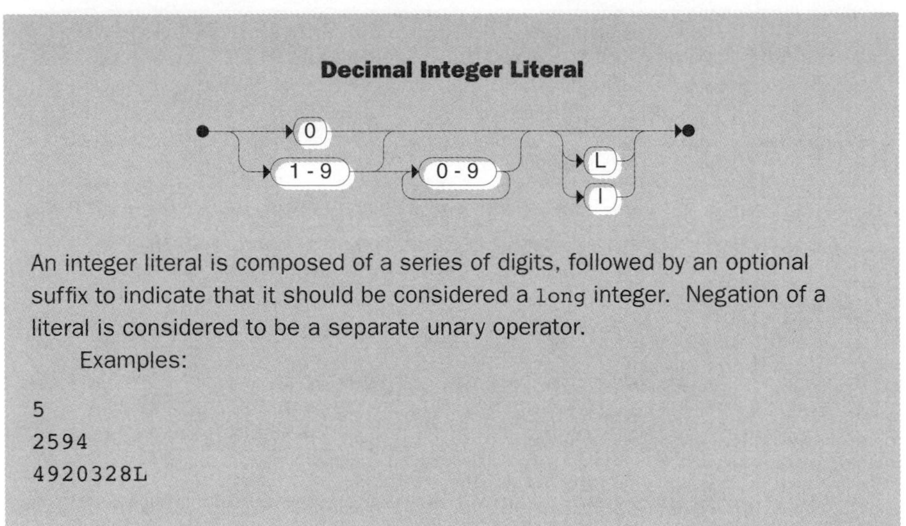
Decimal Integer Literal
0
1 - 9
0 - 9
L
l
An integer literal is composed of a series of digits, followed by an optional suffix to indicate that it should be considered a long integer. Negation of a literal is considered to be a separate unary operator.
Examples:
5
2594
4920328L

literals. Java assumes all integer literals are of type `int`, unless an `L` or `l` is appended to the end of the value to indicate that it should be considered to be a literal of type `long`, such as `45L`.

Likewise, Java assumes that all *floating point literals* are of type `double`. If you require that a floating point literal be treated as a `float`, then append an `F` or `f` to the end of the value, as in `2.718F` or `123.45f`. Numeric literals of type `double` can be followed by a `D` or `d` if desired.

Characters

Characters are another fundamental type of data used and managed on a computer. A *character set* is a list of characters in a particular order. Each programming language supports a particular character set that defines the valid values for a character variable in that language. Several character sets have been proposed, but only a few have been used over the years. The *ASCII character set* is a popular choice. ASCII stands for the American Standard Code for Information Interchange. The basic ASCII set uses seven bits per character, providing room to support 128 different characters, including:

- uppercase letters (A, B, C, etc.)
- lowercase letters (a, b, c, etc.)
- punctuation (period, semicolon, comma, etc.)
- digits (0 through 9)
- special symbols (such as ampersand, vertical bar, backslash)
- control characters (such as carriage return, null, end-of-text)

The *control characters* are sometimes called nonprintable or invisible characters because they do not have a specific symbol that represents them. Yet they are as valid as any other character and can be stored and used in the same ways. Many control characters have special meaning to certain software applications.

As computing became a worldwide endeavor, users demanded a more flexible character set to reflect other language alphabets. ASCII was extended to use eight bits per character and the number of characters in the set doubled to 256. The extended ASCII contains many accented and diacritical characters not used in English.

However, even with 256 characters, the ASCII character set cannot represent the world's languages, especially given the various Asian languages and their many thousands of ideograms. Therefore the developers of the Java programming language chose the *Unicode character set,* which uses 16 bits per character, supporting 65,536 unique characters. The characters and symbols from many languages are included in the Unicode definition. ASCII is essentially a subset of the Unicode character set. Portions of the Unicode character set are presented in Appendix C.

A *character literal* is expressed in a Java program with single quotes, such as `'b'` or `'J'` or `';'`. *String literals* are delineated using double quotes, as we've seen in several example programs. The `String` type is not a primitive data type in Java and is discussed in detail later in this chapter.

Booleans

The `boolean` data type has only two valid values: `true` and `false`. A `boolean` variable is usually used to indicate if a particular condition is true or not, but it can also be used to represent any situation that has two states, such as a light bulb being on or off. A `boolean` value cannot be converted to any other data type, nor can any other data type be converted to a `boolean` value. The words `true` and `false` are reserved in Java as *boolean literals* and cannot be used outside of this context.

Arithmetic Expressions

Programming statements often involve *expressions,* which are combinations of operators and operands used to perform a calculation. The value calculated does not have to be a number, but it often is. The operands used in the operations might be literals, constants, variables, or other sources of data. The way we evaluate and use expressions is fundamental to programming.

> **Key Concept**
> Many programming statements involve expressions. Expressions are combinations of operators and operands used to perform a calculation.

The usual arithmetic operations are defined for both integer and floating point numeric types, including addition (+), subtraction (-), multiplication (*), and division (/). The *remainder operator* (%)

returns the remainder after dividing the second operand into the first. The sign of the result of a remainder operation is the sign of the numerator.

As you might expect, if either or both operands to any numeric operator are floating point values, the result is a floating point value. However, the division operator produces results that are not always intuitive, depending on the types of the operands. If both operands are integers, the / operator performs *integer division,* meaning that any fractional part of the result is truncated and discarded. If one or the other or both operands are floating point values, it performs *floating point division,* and the fractional part of the result is kept.

Operator Precedence

Operators can be combined into even more complicated expressions. For example, consider the following assignment statement:

```
result  =  14 + 8 / 2;
```

What is the result? It is `11` if the addition is performed first, or it is `18` if the division is performed first. The order of operator evaluation makes a big difference. In this case, the division is performed before the addition, yielding a result of `18`. You should note that in this and subsequent examples we have used literal values rather than variables to simplify the expression. The order of operator evaluation is the same even if the operands are variables.

All expressions are evaluated according to an *operator precedence hierarchy* that establishes the rules that govern the order in which operations are evaluated. In the case of arithmetic operators, multiplication, division, and the remainder operator all have equal precedence and are performed before addition and subtraction. Any arithmetic operators at the same level of precedence are performed left to right. Therefore, we say the arithmetic operators have a *left-to-right association.*

Precedence, however, can be forced in an expression by using parentheses. For instance, if we really wanted the addition to be performed first in the previous example, we could write the expression as follows:

```
result  =  (14 + 8) / 2;
```

Key Concept

Java follows a well-defined set of rules that govern the order in which operators will be evaluated in an expression. These rules form an operator precedence hierarchy.

Any expression in parentheses is evaluated first. In complicated expressions, it is good practice to use parentheses even when it is not strictly necessary in order to make it clear how the expression is evaluated.

Parentheses can be nested, and the innermost nested expressions are evaluated first. Consider the expression:

```
result  =  3 * ((18 - 4) / 2);
```

Precedence Level	Operator	Operation	Associates
1	+	unary plus	R to L
	–	unary minus	
2	*	multiplication	L to R
	/	division	
	%	remainder	
3	+	addition	L to R
	–	subtraction	
	+	string concatenation	
4	=	assignment	R to L

Figure 2.4 Precedence among some of the Java operators

In this example, the result is `21`. First, the subtraction is evaluated, forced by the inner parentheses. Then, even though multiplication and division are at the same level of precedence and would be evaluated left to right, the division is evaluated first because of the outer parentheses. Finally, the multiplication is performed.

After the arithmetic operations are complete, then the computed result is stored in the variable on the left-hand side of the assignment operator (=). In other words, the assignment operator has a lower precedence than any of the arithmetic operators.

A precedence table, showing the relationships between the arithmetic operators, parentheses, and the assignment operator is shown in Figure 2.4. A full precedence table showing all Java operators is given in Appendix D.

A *unary operator* has only one operand, while a *binary operator* has two. The + and - arithmetic operators can be both unary and binary. The binary versions accomplish addition and subtraction, and the unary versions represent positive and negative numbers. For example, −1 is an example of using the unary minus operator to make the value negative.

For an expression to be syntactically correct, the number of left parentheses must match the number of right parentheses and they must be properly nested. The following examples are *not* valid expressions:

```
result  =  ((19 + 8) % 3) - 4);    // not valid
result  =  (19 (+ 8 %) 3 - 4);     // not valid
```

The program in Listing 2.7, called `TempConverter`, converts a Celsius temperature value to its equivalent Fahrenheit value. Note that the operands to the

Listing 2.7

```
//********************************************************************
//  TempConverter.java       Author: Lewis and Loftus
//
//  Demonstrates the use of primitive data types and arithmetic
//  expressions.
//********************************************************************

public class TempConverter
{
   //-----------------------------------------------------------------
   //  Computes the Fahrenheit equivalent of a specific Celsius
   //  value using the formula F = (9/5)C + 32.
   //-----------------------------------------------------------------
   public static void main (String[] args)
   {
      final int BASE = 32;
      final double CONVERSION_FACTOR = 9.0 / 5.0;

      int celsiusTemp = 24;  // value to convert
      double fahrenheitTemp;

      fahrenheitTemp = celsiusTemp * CONVERSION_FACTOR + BASE;

      System.out.println ("Celsius Temperature: " + celsiusTemp);
      System.out.println ("Fahrenheit Equivalent: " + fahrenheitTemp);
   }
}
```

```
Celsius Temperature: 24
Fahrenheit Equivalent: 75.2
```

division operation are double to ensure that the fractional part of the number is kept. The precedence rules dictate that the multiplication happens before the addition in the final conversion computation, which is what we want.

Data Conversion

Because Java is a strongly typed language, each data value is associated with a particular type. Sometimes it is helpful or necessary to convert a data value of one type to another type, but we must be careful that we don't lose important information in the process. For example, suppose a `short` variable that holds the number 1000 is converted to a `byte` value. Because a `byte` does not store enough bits to represent the value 1000, some bits would be lost in the conversion and the number represented in the `byte` would not keep its original value.

A conversion between one primitive type and another falls into one of two categories: widening conversions and narrowing conversions. *Widening conversions* are the safest because they usually do not lose information. They are called widening conversions because they go from one data type to another type that uses an equal or greater amount of space to store the value. Figure 2.5 lists the Java widening conversions.

For example, it is safe to convert from a `byte` to a `short` because a `byte` is stored in 8 bits and a `short` is stored in 16 bits. There is no loss of information. All widening conversions that go from an integer type to another integer type, or from a floating point type to another floating point type, preserve the numeric value exactly.

Although widening conversions do not lose any information concerning the magnitude of a value, the widening conversions that result in a floating point value can lose precision. When converting from an `int` or a `long` to a `float`, or from a `long` to a `double`, some of the least significant digits may be lost. In this case, the resulting floating point value will be a rounded version of the integer value, following the rounding techniques defined in the IEEE 754 floating point standard.

Narrowing conversions are more likely to lose information than widening conversions. They often go from one type to a type that uses less space to store a value, and therefore some of the information may be compromised. Narrowing conversions can lose both numeric magnitude and precision. Therefore, in general, they should be avoided. Figure 2.6 lists the Java narrowing conversions.

From	To
`byte`	`short`, `int`, `long`, `float`, or `double`
`short`	`int`, `long`, `float`, or `double`
`char`	`int`, `long`, `float`, or `double`
`int`	`long`, `float`, or `double`
`long`	`float` or `double`
`float`	`double`

Figure 2.5 Java widening conversions

From	To
`byte`	`char`
`short`	`byte` or `char`
`char`	`byte` or `short`
`int`	`byte`, `short`, or `char`
`long`	`byte`, `short`, `char`, or `int`
`float`	`byte`, `short`, `char`, `int`, or `long`
`double`	`byte`, `short`, `char`, `int`, `long`, or `float`

Figure 2.6 Java narrowing conversions

An exception to the space-shrinking situation in narrowing conversions is when we convert a `byte` (8 bits) or `short` (16 bits) to a `char` (16 bits). These are still considered narrowing conversions because the sign bit is incorporated into the new character value. Since a character value is unsigned, a negative integer will be converted into a character that has no particular relationship to the numeric value of the original integer.

Key Concept
Avoid narrowing conversions because they can lose information.

Note that `boolean` values are not mentioned in either widening or narrowing conversions. A `boolean` value cannot be converted to any other primitive type and vice versa.

In Java, conversions can occur in three ways:

- assignment conversion
- arithmetic promotion
- casting

Assignment conversion occurs when a value of one type is assigned to a variable of another type, during which the value is converted to the new type. Only widening conversions can be accomplished through assignment. For example, if `money` is a `float` variable and `dollars` is an `int` variable, then the assignment statement

```
money = dollars;
```

would automatically convert the value in `dollars` to a `float`. Therefore, if `dollars` contained the value `25`, after the assignment, money would contain

25.0. However, if you attempted to assign money to dollars, the compiler would issue an error message alerting you to the fact that you are attempting a narrowing conversion that could lose information. If you really want to do this assignment, you would have to make the conversion explicit using a cast (explained below).

Arithmetic promotion occurs automatically when certain arithmetic operators need to modify their operands in order to perform the operation. For example, when a floating point value called sum is divided by an integer value called count, the value of count is promoted to a floating point value automatically before the division takes place, producing a floating point result:

```
result = sum / count;
```

Casting is the most general form of conversion in Java. If a conversion can be accomplished at all in a Java program, it can be accomplished using a cast. A cast is a Java operator that is specified by a type name in parentheses. It is placed in front of the value to be converted. For example, to convert money to an integer value, we could put a cast in front of it:

```
dollars = (int) money;
```

The cast returns the value in money, truncating any fractional part. If money contained the value 84.69, then after the assignment, dollars would contain the value 84. Note, however, that the cast does not change the value in money.

Casts are helpful in many situations where we temporarily need to treat a value as another type. For example, if we want to divide the integer value total by the integer value count and get a floating point result, we could do it as follows:

```
result = (float) total / count;
```

First, the cast operator returns a floating point version of the value in total. This operation does not change the value in total. Then, count is treated as a floating point value via arithmetic promotion. Now the division operator will perform floating point division and produce the intended result. If the cast had not been included, the operation would have performed integer division and truncated the answer prior to assigning it to result. Also note that because the cast operator has a higher precedence than the division operator, the cast operates on the value of total, not on the result of the division.

2.5 Creating Objects

A variable holds either a primitive value or a *reference to an object.* Like variables that hold primitive types, a variable that serves as an object reference must be declared. A class is used to define an object, and the class name can be thought of as the type of an object. The declarations of object references have a similar structure to the declarations of primitive variables.

The following declaration creates a reference to a `String` object:

```
String name;
```

That declaration is not unlike the declaration of an integer, in that the type is followed by the variable name we want to use. However, no string object actually exists yet. To create an object, we use the `new` operator:

```
name = new String ("James Gosling");
```

Key Concept

The `new` operator returns a reference to a newly created object.

The act of creating an object using the `new` operator is called *instantiation.* An object is said to be an *instance* of a particular class. The `new` operator calls a *constructor,* which is similar to a method that has the same name as the class. A constructor is used to help set up the object initially. In this example, the constructor is passed a string literal that specifies the characters that the string object will hold.

The act of declaring the object reference variable and creating the object itself can be combined into one step by initializing the variable in the declaration, just as we do with primitive types:

```
String name = new String ("James Gosling");
```

After an object has been instantiated, we use the *dot operator* to access its methods. We've used the dot operator many times in previous programs, such as in calls to `System.out.println`. The dot operator is appended directly after the object reference name, followed by the method being invoked. For example, to invoke the `toLowerCase` method defined in the `String` class, we would use the dot operator on the `name` reference as follows:

```
name.toLowerCase()
```

An object reference variable actually stores the address where the object is stored in memory. We will explore the nuances of object references, instantiation, and constructors later in the book. Initially, though, we will use the ability to instantiate objects to create even more interesting programs.

The `String` Class

Let's examine the `String` class in more detail. Strings in Java are objects, represented by the `String` class. Figure 2.7 lists some of the more useful methods of the `String` class. The method headers are listed and they indicate the type of information that must be passed to the method. The type in front of the

`String (String str)`
Constructor: creates a new string object with the same characters as `str`.

`char charAt (int index)`
Returns the character at the specified `index`.

`int compareTo (String str)`
Returns an integer indicating if this string is lexically before (a negative return value), equal to (a zero return value), or lexically after (a positive return value), the string `str`.

`String concat (String str)`
Returns a new string consisting of this string concatenated with `str`.

`boolean equals (String str)`
Returns true if this string contains the same characters as `str` (including case) and false otherwise.

`boolean equalsIgnoreCase (String str)`
Returns true if this string contains the same characters as `str` (without regard to case) and false otherwise.

`int length ()`
Returns the number of characters in this string.

`String replace (char oldChar, char newChar)`
Returns a new string that is identical with this string except that every occurrence of `oldChar` is replaced by `newChar`.

`String substring (int offset, int endIndex)`
Returns a new string that is a subset of this string starting at index `offset` and extending through `endIndex-1`.

`String toLowerCase ()`
Returns a new string identical to this string except all upper case letters are converted to their lower case equivalent.

`String toUpperCase ()`
Returns a new string identical to this string except all lower case letters are converted to their upper case equivalent.

Figure 2.7 Some methods of the `String` class

method name indicates the information that will be *returned,* if anything. A return type of `void` indicates that the method does not return a value. The returned value can be used in the calling method as needed.

Once a `String` object is created, its value cannot be lengthened, shortened, nor can any of its characters change. Thus we say that a string object is *immutable*. However, several methods in the `String` class return new `String` objects that are often the result of modifying the original string's value.

Note also that some of the `String` methods refer to the *index* of a particular character. A character in a string can be specified by its position, or index, in the string. The index of the first character in a string is zero, the second character is one, and so on. Therefore, in the string `"Hello"`, the index of the character `'H'` is zero and the character at index four is `'o'`.

Several `String` methods are exercised in the program called `StringMutation`, shown in Listing 2.8.

An object diagram for `StringMutation` is shown in Figure 2.8. It shows two of the `String` objects that are managed by the program and indicates the methods that are invoked on them. The other `String` objects could be shown in a similar manner. The data held by each object is also indicated, which is helpful in this case, though not always necessary. We should use object diagrams as needed to convey the important interactions between the elements of a program.

Even though they are not primitive types, strings are so fundamental and frequently used that Java defines string literals delimited by double quotation

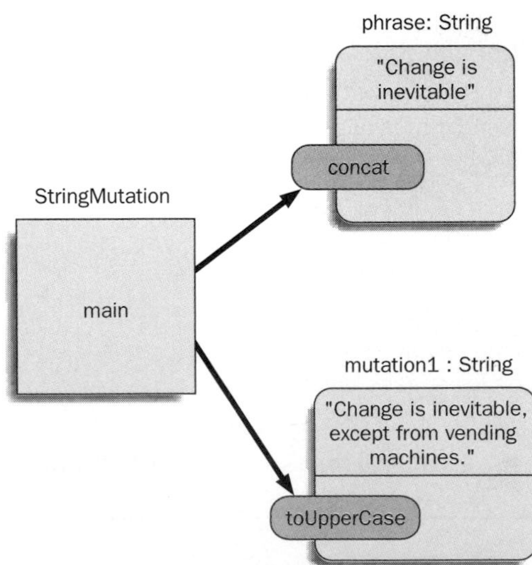

Figure 2.8 An object diagram for `StringMutation`

Listing 2.8

```
//********************************************************************
//  StringMutation.java       Author: Lewis and Loftus
//
//  Demonstrates the use of the String class and its methods.
//********************************************************************

public class StringMutation
{
   //-----------------------------------------------------------------
   //  Prints a string and various mutations of it.
   //-----------------------------------------------------------------
   public static void main (String[] args)
   {
      String phrase = new String ("Change is inevitable");
      String mutation1, mutation2, mutation3, mutation4;

      System.out.println ("Original string: \"" + phrase + "\"");
      System.out.println ("Length of string: " + phrase.length());

      mutation1 = phrase.concat (", except from vending machines.");
      mutation2 = mutation1.toUpperCase();
      mutation3 = mutation2.replace ('E', 'X');
      mutation4 = mutation3.substring (3, 30);

      // Print each mutated string
      System.out.println ("Mutation #1: " + mutation1);
      System.out.println ("Mutation #2: " + mutation2);
      System.out.println ("Mutation #3: " + mutation3);
      System.out.println ("Mutation #4: " + mutation4);

      System.out.println ("Mutated length: " + mutation4.length());
   }
}
```

```
Original string: "Change is inevitable"
Length of string: 20
Mutation #1: Change is inevitable, except from vending machines.
Mutation #2: CHANGE IS INEVITABLE, EXCEPT FROM VENDING MACHINES.
Mutation #3: CHANGX IS INXVITABLX, XXCXPT FROM VXNDING MACHINXS.
Mutation #4: NGX IS INXVITABLX, XXCXPT F
Mutated length: 27
```

marks, as we've seen in various examples. This is a shortcut notation. Whenever a string literal appears, a `String` object is created. Therefore, the following declaration is valid:

```
String name = "James Gosling";
```

That is, for `String` objects, the explicit use of the `new` operator and the call to the constructor can be eliminated. In most cases we will use this simplified syntax.

2.6 Class Libraries and Packages

A *class library* is a set of classes that support the development of programs. A compiler often comes with a class library, and class libraries can also be obtained separately through third-party vendors. The classes in a class library contain methods that are often invaluable to a programmer because of the special functionality they offer. In fact, programmers often become dependent on the methods in a class library and begin to think of them as part of the language. But, technically, they are not in the language definition.

The `String` class, for instance, is not an inherent part of the Java language. It is part of the Java *standard class library* that can be found in any Java development environment. The classes that make up the library were written by employees at Sun Microsystems, the people who created the Java language.

The class library is made up of several clusters of related classes, which are sometimes called Java APIs. API stands for *Application Programmer Interface*. For example, we may refer to the Java Database API when we're talking about the set of classes that help us write programs that interact with a database. Another example of an API is the Java Swing API, which refers to a set of classes that define special graphical components used in a graphical user interface.

Key Concept

The Java standard class library is a useful set of classes that anyone can use when writing Java programs.

The classes of the Java standard class library are also grouped into *packages*, which like the APIs, let us group related classes by one name. Each class is part of a particular package. The `String` class, for example, is part of the `java.lang` package. The `System` class is part of the `java.lang` package as well. The package organization is more fundamental and language-based than the esoteric API names. We therefore will primarily refer to classes via their package organization in this text.

Key Concept

A package is a Java language element used to group related classes under a common name.

Package	Provides support to
`java.applet`	Create programs (applets) that are easily transported across the Web.
`java.awt`	Draw graphics and create graphical user interfaces; AWT stands for Abstract Windowing Toolkit.
`java.beans`	Define software components that can be easily combined into applications.
`java.io`	Perform a wide variety of input and output functions.
`java.lang`	General support; it is automatically imported into all Java programs.
`java.math`	Perform calculations with arbitrarily high precision.
`java.net`	Communicate across a network.
`java.rmi`	Create programs that can be distributed across multiple computers; RMI stands for Remote Method Invocation
`java.security`	Enforce security restrictions.
`java.sql`	Interact with databases; SQL stands for Structured Query Language.
`java.text`	Format text for output.
`java.util`	General utilities.

Figure 2.9 Some packages in the Java standard class library

Figure 2.9 describes some of the packages that are part of the Java standard class library. These packages are available on any platform that supports Java software development. Many of these packages support highly specific programming techniques and will not come into play in the development of basic programs. Many classes of the Java API are discussed throughout this book. Appendix M serves as a general reference for many of the classes in the Java class library.

The `import` Declaration

The classes of the package `java.lang` are automatically available for use when writing a program. To use classes from any other package, however, we must either *fully qualify* the reference, or use an *import declaration.*

When you want to use a class from a class library in a program, you could use its fully qualified name, including the package name, every time it is referenced. For example, every time you want to refer to the `Random` class that is defined in the `java.util` package, you can write `java.util.Random`. However, completely specifying the package and class name every time it is needed quickly becomes monotonous. Java provides the import declaration to simplify these references.

The import declaration identifies the packages and classes that will be used in a program, so that the fully qualified name is not necessary on each reference. The following is an example of an import declaration:

```
import java.util.Random;
```

This declaration asserts that the `Random` class of the `java.util` package may be used in the program. Once this import declaration is made, it is sufficient to use the simple name `Random` whenever referring to that class in the program.

Another form of the import declaration uses the asterisk (`*`) to indicate that any class inside the package might be used in the program. Therefore, the declaration

```
import java.util.*;
```

allows all classes in the `java.util` package to be referenced in the program without the explicit package name. If only one class of a particular package will be used in a program, it is usually better to name the class specifically. However, if two or more will be used, the `*` notation is fine.

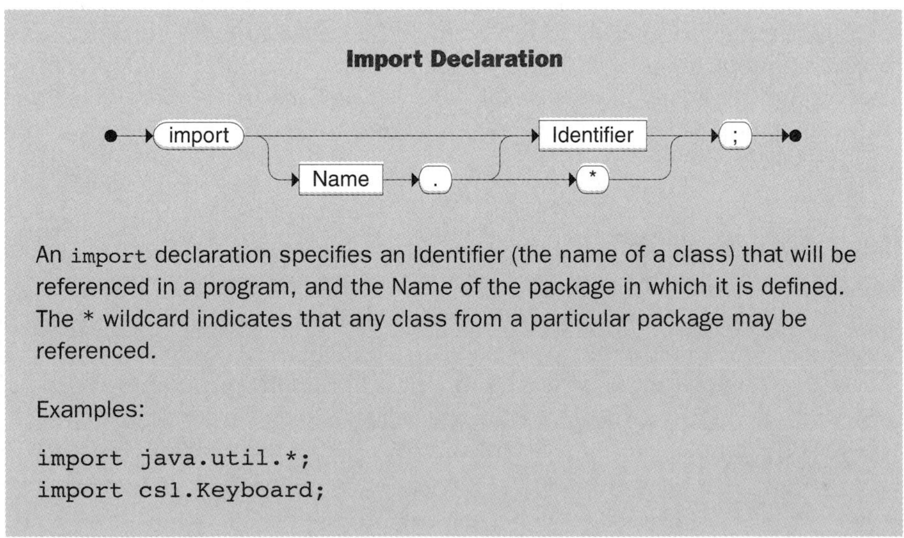

An `import` declaration specifies an Identifier (the name of a class) that will be referenced in a program, and the Name of the package in which it is defined. The * wildcard indicates that any class from a particular package may be referenced.

Examples:

```
import java.util.*;
import cs1.Keyboard;
```

The classes of the `java.lang` package are automatically imported because they are fundamental and can be thought of as basic extensions to the language. Therefore, any class in the `java.lang` package, such as `String`, can be used without an explicit import statement. It is as if all programs contain the following statement:

```
import java.lang.*;
```

The `Random` Class

The need for random numbers occurs frequently when writing software. Games often use a random number to represent the roll of a die or to shuffle a deck of cards. A flight simulator may use random numbers to determine how often a simulated flight has engine trouble. A program designed to help a high school student prepare for the SATs may use random numbers to choose the next question to ask.

The `Random` class implements a *pseudorandom number generator.* A random number generator picks a number at random out of a range of values. A program that serves this role is technically pseudorandom, because a program has no means to actually pick a number randomly. A pseudorandom number generator performs a series of complicated calculations, starting with an initial *seed value,* and produces a number. Though they are technically not random (because they are calculated), the values produced by a pseudorandom number generator usually appear random, at least random enough for most situations. Figure 2.10 lists some of the methods of the `Random` class.

The need to *scale* and *shift* a random number into an appropriate range is a common programming activity. The program shown in Listing 2.9 produces several random numbers in various ranges.

`Random ()`
Constructor: creates a new pseudorandom number generator.

`float nextFloat ()`
Returns a random number between 0.0 (inclusive) and 1.0 (exclusive).

`int nextInt ()`
Returns a random number that ranges over all possible int values (positive and negative).

Figure 2.10 Some methods of the `Random` class

Listing 2.9

```
//********************************************************************
//  RandomNumbers.java       Author: Lewis and Loftus
//
//  Demonstrates the import statement, and the creation of pseudo-
//  random numbers using the Random class.
//********************************************************************

import java.util.Random;

public class RandomNumbers
{
   //-----------------------------------------------------------------
   //  Generates random numbers in various ranges.
   //-----------------------------------------------------------------
   public static void main (String[] args)
   {
      Random generator = new Random();
      int num1;
      float num2;

      num1 = generator.nextInt();
      System.out.println ("A random integer: " + num1);

      num1 = Math.abs (generator.nextInt()) % 10;
      System.out.println ("0 to 9: " + num1);

      num1 = Math.abs (generator.nextInt()) % 10 + 1;
      System.out.println ("1 to 10: " + num1);

      num1 = Math.abs (generator.nextInt()) % 20 + 10;
      System.out.println ("10 to 29: " + num1);

      num2 = generator.nextFloat();
      System.out.println ("A random float [between 0-1]: " + num2);

      num2 = generator.nextFloat() * 6;  // 0.0 to 5.999999
      num1 = (int) num2 + 1;
      System.out.println ("1 to 6: " + num1);
   }
}
```

```
A random integer: -889285970
0 to 9: 6
1 to 10: 9
10 to 29: 18
A random float [between 0-1] : 0.8815305
1 to 6: 2
```

Note that using N as the denominator of remainder division (%) will always result in a value in the range 0 to $N-1$, thereby scaling the value as needed. Then shifting the value by adding or subtracting a particular value will produce a final pseudorandom number in a particular range. The method `Math.abs` returns the absolute value of a number. The `Math` class is discussed in the next section.

When a floating point value is generated, we can use multiplication to scale it, casting the result into an `int` value, then shifting as before.

2.7 Invoking Class Methods

Some methods can be invoked through the class name in which they are defined, without having to instantiate an object of the class first. These are called *class methods* or *static methods*. Let's look at some examples.

The `Math` Class

The `Math` class provides a large number of basic mathematical functions. The `Math` class is part of the Java standard class library, defined in the `java.lang` package. Several of its methods are listed in Figure 2.11. The reserved word `static` indicates that the method can be invoked through the name of the class.

Note that one of the methods, `random`, produces a pseudorandom floating point number in the range 0.0 to 1.0. This method is essentially equivalent to the `nextFloat` method of the `Random` class. We will use this method for random number generation in the future because there is no need to create an object first.

We'll make use of some `Math` methods in examples after examining the `Keyboard` class.

The `Keyboard` Class

The `Keyboard` class contains methods that help us obtain information that the user types on the keyboard. The methods of the `Keyboard` class are static and are therefore invoked through the `Keyboard` class name, just as we do with the methods of the `Math` class.

However, there is one very important characteristic of the `Keyboard` class to point out. The `Keyboard` class is *not* part of the Java standard class library.

```
static int abs (int num)
```
Returns the absolute value of num.

```
static double acos (double num)

static double asin (double num)

static double atan (double num)
```
Returns the arc cosine, arc sine, or arc tangent of num.

```
static double cos (double angle)

static double sin (double angle)

static double tan (double angle)
```
Returns the cosine, sine, or tangent of angle, which is measured in radians.

```
static double ceil (double num)
```
Returns the ceiling of num, which is the smallest whole number greater than or equal to num.

```
static double exp (double power)
```
Returns the value e raised to the specified power.

```
static double floor (double num)
```
Returns the floor of num, which is the largest whole number less than or equal to num.

```
static double pow (double num, double power)
```
Returns the value num raised to the specified power.

```
static double random ()
```
Returns a random number between 0.0 (inclusive) and 1.0 (exclusive).

```
static double sqrt (double num)
```
Returns the square root of num, which must be positive.

Figure 2.11 Some methods of the `Math` class

It has been written by the authors of this book to help you in the process of reading user input. It is defined as part of a package called `cs1`.

The process of reading input from the user in Java can get somewhat involved. These issues are explored in Chapter 8, in which the details of the `Keyboard` class are explored. For now, we will use the `Keyboard` class for the services it provides, just as we do any other class.

Key Concept

The `Keyboard` class is not part of the Java standard class library. It will therefore not be available on all Java development platforms.

The `Keyboard` class exemplifies one of the nice things about object-oriented software that we discussed earlier in this chapter: classes and objects simply provide services that we can use. We interact with them in the same way, no matter whether they are part of a library, written by a third party, or we write them ourselves. Figure 2.12 lists the input methods of the `Keyboard` class.

Let's look at some examples that use the `Keyboard` class. The program shown in Listing 2.10, called `Echo`, simply reads a string that is typed by the user and echoes it back to the screen.

The `Quadratic` program, shown in Listing 2.11, reads values that represent the coefficients in a quadratic equation, then evaluates the quadratic formula.

```
static boolean readBoolean ()

static char readChar ()

static double readDouble ()

static float readFloat ()

static int readInt ()

static long readLong ()

static String readString ()
```

Returns a value of the indicated type obtained from user keyboard input.

Figure 2.12 Some methods of the `Keyboard` class

Listing 2.10

```
//********************************************************************
//  Echo.java       Author: Lewis and Loftus
//
//  Demonstrates the use of the readString method of the Keyboard
//  class.
//********************************************************************

import cs1.Keyboard;

public class Echo
{
   //-----------------------------------------------------------------
   //  Reads a character string from the user and prints it.
   //-----------------------------------------------------------------
   public static void main (String[] args)
   {
      String message;

      System.out.println ("Enter a line of text:");

      message = Keyboard.readString();

      System.out.println ("You entered: \"" + message + "\"");
   }
}
```

```
Enter a line of text:
Set your laser printer on stun!
You entered: "Set your laser printer on stun!"
```

Listing 2.11

```
//********************************************************************
//  Quadratic.java       Author: Lewis and Loftus
//
//  Demonstrates a calculation based on user input.
//********************************************************************

import cs1.Keyboard;

public class Quadratic
{
   //-----------------------------------------------------------------
   //  Determines the roots of a quadratic equation.
   //-----------------------------------------------------------------
   public static void main (String[] args)
   {
      int a, b, c;  // ax^2 + bx + c

      System.out.print ("Enter the coefficient of x squared: ");
      a = Keyboard.readInt();

      System.out.print ("Enter the coefficient of x: ");
      b = Keyboard.readInt();

      System.out.print ("Enter the constant: ");
      c = Keyboard.readInt();

      // Use the quadratic formula to compute the roots.
      // Assumes a positive discriminant.

      double discriminant = Math.pow(b, 2) - (4 * a * c);
      double root1 = ((-1 * b) + Math.sqrt(discriminant)) / (2 * a);
      double root2 = ((-1 * b) - Math.sqrt(discriminant)) / (2 * a);

      System.out.println ("Root #1: " + root1);
      System.out.println ("Root #2: " + root2);
   }
}
```

```
Enter the coefficient of x squared: 3
Enter the coefficient of x: 8
Enter the constant: 4
Root #1: -0.6666666666666666
Root #2: -2.0
```

2.8 Formatting Output

The `NumberFormat` class and the `DecimalFormat` class are used to format information so that it looks appropriate when printed or displayed. They are both part of the Java standard class library, and are defined in the `java.text` package.

The `NumberFormat` Class

The `NumberFormat` class provides generic formatting capabilities for numbers. You don't instantiate a `NumberFormat` object using the `new` operator. Instead, you request an object from one of the methods that you can invoke through the class itself. The reasons for this approach involve issues that we haven't covered yet, and are explained in due course. Some of the methods of the `NumberFormat` class are listed in Figure 2.13.

Two of the methods in the `NumberFormat` class, `getCurrencyInstance` and `getPercentInstance`, return an object that is used to format numbers. The `getCurrencyInstance` method returns a formatter for monetary values, and the `getPercentInstance` method returns an object that formats a percentage. The `format` method is invoked through a formatter object and returns a `String` that contains the number formatted in the appropriate manner.

The `Price` program shown in Listing 2.12 uses both types of formatters. It reads in a sales transaction and computes the final price, including tax.

`String format (double number)`
Returns a string containing the specified number formatted according to this object's pattern.

`static NumberFormat getCurrencyInstance()`
Returns a NumberFormat object that represents a currency format for the current locale.

`static NumberFormat getPercentInstance()`
Returns a NumberFormat object that represents a percentage format for the current locale.

Figure 2.13 Some methods of the `NumberFormat` class

Listing 2.12

```
//********************************************************************
//  Price.java       Author: Lewis and Loftus
//
//  Demonstrates the use of various Keyboard and NumberFormat
//  methods.
//********************************************************************

import cs1.Keyboard;
import java.text.NumberFormat;

public class Price
{
   //-----------------------------------------------------------------
   //  Calculates the final price of a purchased item using values
   //  entered by the user.
   //-----------------------------------------------------------------
   public static void main (String[] args)
   {
      final double TAX_RATE = 0.06;  // 6% sales tax

      int quantity;
      double subtotal, tax, totalCost, unitPrice;

      System.out.print ("Enter the quantity: ");
      quantity = Keyboard.readInt();

      System.out.print ("Enter the unit price: ");
      unitPrice = Keyboard.readDouble();

      subtotal = quantity * unitPrice;
      tax = subtotal * TAX_RATE;
      totalCost = subtotal + tax;

      // Print output with appropriate formatting
      NumberFormat money = NumberFormat.getCurrencyInstance();
      NumberFormat percent = NumberFormat.getPercentInstance();

      System.out.println ("Subtotal: " + money.format(subtotal));
      System.out.println ("Tax: " + money.format(tax) + " at "
                          + percent.format(TAX_RATE));
      System.out.println ("Total: " + money.format(totalCost));
   }
}
```

```
Enter the quantity: 5
Enter the unit price: 3.87
Subtotal: $19.35
Tax: $1.16 at 6%
Total: $20.51
```

The `DecimalFormat` Class

Unlike the `NumberFormat` class, the `DecimalFormat` class is instantiated in the traditional way using the `new` operator. Its constructor takes a string that represents the pattern that will guide the formatting process. We can then use the `format` method to format a particular value. At a later point, if we want to change the pattern that the formatter object uses, we can invoke the `applyPattern` method. These methods are described in Figure 2.14.

The pattern defined by the string that is passed to the `DecimalFormat` constructor gets fairly elaborate. Various symbols are used to represent particular formatting guidelines.

The book's Web site contains additional information about techniques for formatting information, including a discussion of the various patterns that can be defined for the `DecimalFormat` class.

The pattern defined by the string "`0.###`", for example, indicates that at least one digit should be printed to the left of the decimal point, and should be a zero if the integer portion of the value is zero. It also indicates that the fractional portion of the value should be rounded to three digits. This pattern is used in the `CircleStats` program shown in Listing 2.13, which reads the radius of a circle from the user and computes its area and circumference. Trailing zeros, such as in the circle's area of 78.540, are not printed.

`DecimalFormat (String pattern)`
Constructor: creates a new DecimalFormat object with the specified pattern.

`void applyPattern (String pattern)`
Applies the specified pattern to this DecimalFormat object.

`String format (double number)`
Returns a string containing the specified number formatted according to the current pattern.

Figure 2.14 Some methods of the `DecimalFormat` class

Listing 2.13

```
//********************************************************************
//  CircleStats.java       Author: Lewis and Loftus
//
//  Demonstrates the formatting of decimal values using the
//  DecimalFormat class.
//********************************************************************

import cs1.Keyboard;
import java.text.DecimalFormat;

public class CircleStats
{
   //-----------------------------------------------------------------
   //  Calculates the area and circumference of a circle given its
   //  radius.
   //-----------------------------------------------------------------
   public static void main (String[] args)
   {
      int radius;
      double area, circumference;

      System.out.print ("Enter the circle's radius: ");
      radius = Keyboard.readInt();

      area = Math.PI * Math.pow(radius, 2);
      circumference = 2 * Math.PI * radius;

      // Round the output to three decimal places
      DecimalFormat fmt = new DecimalFormat ("0.###");

      System.out.println ("The circle's area: " + fmt.format(area));
      System.out.println ("The circle's circumference: "
                          + fmt.format(circumference));
   }
}
```

```
Enter the circle's radius: 5
The circle's area: 78.54
The circle's circumference: 31.416
```

2.9 An Introduction to Applets

There are two kinds of Java programs: Java applets and Java applications. A Java *applet* is a Java program that is intended to be embedded into an HTML document, transported across a network, and executed using a Web browser. A Java *application* is a stand-alone program that can be executed using the Java interpreter. All programs seen so far in this book are Java applications.

Key Concept

Applets are Java programs that are usually transported across a network and executed using a Web browser. Java applications are stand-alone programs that can be executed using the Java interpreter.

The Web enables users to send and receive various types of media, such as text, graphics, and sound, using a point-and-click interface that is extremely convenient and easy to use. A Java applet was the first kind of executable program that could be retrieved using World Wide Web software. Java applets are considered to be just another type of media that can be exchanged across the Web.

Though Java applets are generally intended to be transported across a network, they don't have to be. They can be viewed locally using a Web browser. For that matter, they don't even have to be executed through a Web browser at all. A tool in Sun's Java Software Development Kit called *appletviewer* can be used to interpret and execute an applet. We use appletviewer to display most of the applets in the book. However, usually the point of making a Java applet is to provide a link to it on a Web page and allow it to be retrieved and executed by World Wide Web users anywhere in the world.

Java bytecode (not Java source code) is linked to an HTML document and sent across the Web. A version of the Java interpreter embedded in a Web browser is used to execute the applet once it reaches its destination. A Java applet must be compiled into bytecode format before it can be used with the Web.

There are some important differences between the structure of a Java applet and the structure of a Java application. Because the Web browser that executes an applet is already running, applets can be thought of as a part of a larger program. As such they do not have a `main` method where execution starts. The `paint` method in an applet is automatically invoked by the applet. Consider the program in Listing 2.14, in which the `paint` method is used to draw a few shapes and write a quotation by Albert Einstein to the screen.

The two import statements at the beginning of the program explicitly indicate the packages that are used in the program. In this example, we need the `Applet` class, which is part of the `java.applet` package, and various graphics capabilities defined in the `java.awt` package.

A class that defines an applet *extends* the `Applet` class, as indicated in the header line of the class declaration. This process is making use of the

Listing 2.14

```
//********************************************************************
//  Einstein.java       Author: Lewis and Loftus
//
//  Demonstrates a simple applet.
//********************************************************************

import java.applet.Applet;
import java.awt.*;

public class Einstein extends Applet
{
   //-----------------------------------------------------------------
   //  Draws a quotation by Albert Einstein among some shapes.
   //-----------------------------------------------------------------
   public void paint (Graphics page)
   {
      page.drawRect (50, 50, 40, 40);    // square
      page.drawRect (60, 80, 225, 30);   // rectangle
      page.drawOval (75, 65, 20, 20);    // circle
      page.drawLine (35, 60, 100, 120);  // line

      page.drawString ("Out of clutter, find simplicity.", 110, 70);
      page.drawString ("-- Albert Einstein", 130, 100);
   }
}
```

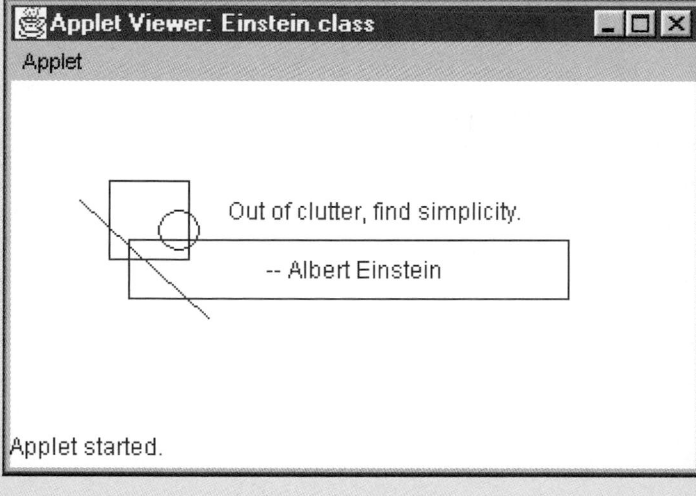

object-oriented concept of *inheritance,* which is explored in more detail in Chapter 7. Applet classes must also be declared as `public`.

The `paint` method is one of several applet methods that have particular significance. It is called when the graphic elements of the applet need to be painted to the screen. The `paint` method is automatically called. It takes a parameter of a `Graphics` object, which allows us to draw various shapes using methods such as `drawRect`, `drawOval`, `drawLine`, and `drawString`.

A `Graphics` object defines a particular *graphics context* with which we can interact. The graphics context referred to in the `Einstein` program represents the entire applet window. Each graphics context has its own coordinate system. In later examples we will have multiple components that each have their own graphic context.

The information passed to the drawing methods indicate the coordinates and sizes of the shapes to be drawn. These and other methods that draw shapes are explored further in the next section.

Executing Applets using the Web

In order for the applet to be transmitted over the Web and executed by a browser, it must be referenced in a HyperText Markup Language (HTML) document. An HTML document contains *tags* that specify formatting instructions and identify the special types of media that are to be included in a document. A Java program is considered to be a specific media type, just as text, graphics, and sound are.

An HTML tag is enclosed in angle brackets. Appendix J contains a tutorial on HTML that explores various tag types. Below is an example of an applet tag:

```
<applet code="Einstein.class" width=350 height=175>
</applet>
```

This tag dictates that the bytecode stored in the file `Einstein.class` should be transported over the network and executed on the machine that wants to view this particular HTML document. The applet tag also indicates the width and height of the applet.

Note that the applet tag refers to the bytecode file of the Einstein applet, not to the source code. Before an applet can be transported using the Web, it must be compiled into its bytecode format. Then, as shown in Figure 2.15, the document can be loaded using a Web browser, which will automatically interpret and execute the applet.

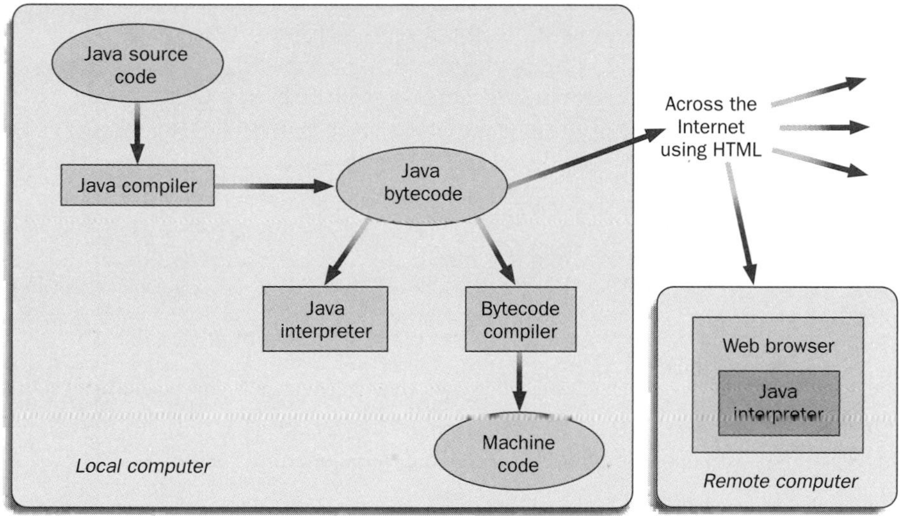

Figure 2.15 The Java translation and execution process (including applets)

2.10 Drawing Shapes

The Java standard class library provides many classes that let us present and manipulate graphical information. The `Graphics` class is fundamental to all such processing.

The `Graphics` Class

The `Graphics` class is defined in the `java.awt` package. It contains various methods that allow us to draw shapes, including lines, rectangles, and ovals. Figure 2.16 lists some of the fundamental drawing methods of the `Graphics` class. Note that these methods also let us draw circles and squares, which are just specific types of ovals and rectangles, respectively. The `drawPolyline` and `drawPolygon` methods are explained in Chapter 6 after we explore arrays, but we can make use of the rest immediately.

Key Concept

Most shapes can be drawn filled (opaque) or unfilled (as an outline).

The methods of the `Graphics` class allow us to specify whether we want a shape filled or not. An unfilled shape shows only the outline of the shape, and is otherwise transparent (you can see any underlying graphics). A filled shape is solid between its edges, and it covers any underlying graphics.

```
void drawArc (int x, int y, int width, int height, int
startAngle, int arcAngle)
```
Paints an arc along the oval bounded by the rectangle defined by x, y, width, and height. The arc starts at startAngle and extends for a distance defined by arcAngle.

```
void drawLine (int x1, int y1, int x2, int y2)
```
Paints a line from point (x1, y1) to point (x2, y2).

```
void drawOval (int x, int y, int width, int height)
```
Paints an oval bounded by the rectangle with an upper left corner of (x, y) and dimensions width and height.

```
void drawRect (int x, int y, int width, int height)
```
Paints a rectangle with upper left corner (x, y) and dimensions width and height.

```
void drawString (String str, int x, int y)
```
Paints the character string str at point (x, y), extending to the right.

```
void fillArc (int x, int y, int width, int height,
int startAngle, int arcAngle)

void fillOval (int x, int y, int width, int height)

void fillRect (int x, int y, int width, int height)
```
Same as their draw counterparts, but filled with the current foreground color.

```
Color getColor ()
```
Returns this graphics context's foreground color.

```
void setColor (Color color)
```
Sets this graphics context's foreground color to the specified color.

Figure 2.16 Some methods of the `Graphics` class

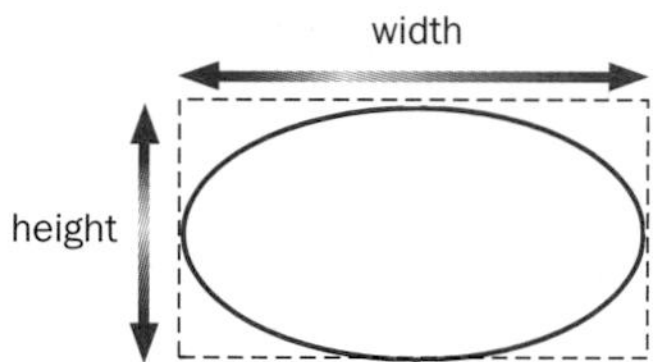

Figure 2.17 An oval and its bounding rectangle

All of these methods rely on the Java coordinate system, which was discussed in Chapter 1. Recall that point `(0,0)` is in the upper left corner, X values get larger as we move to the right, and Y values get larger as we move down. Any shapes drawn at coordinates that are outside of the visible area will not be seen.

Many of the `Graphics` drawing methods are self explanatory, but some require a little more discussion. Note, for instance, that an oval drawn by the `drawOval` method is defined by the coordinate of the upper-left corner and dimensions that specify the width and height of a *bounding rectangle*. Shapes with curves such as ovals are often defined by a rectangle that encompasses their boundaries. A bounding rectangle for an oval is depicted in Figure 2.17.

Key Concept

A bounding rectangle is often used to define the position and size of curved shapes such as an oval.

An arc can be thought of as a segment of an oval. To draw an arc, we specify the oval of which the arc is a part and the portion of the oval in which we're interested. The starting point of the arc is defined by the *start angle* and the ending point of the arc is defined by the *arc angle*. The arc angle does not indicate where the arc ends, but rather its range. The start angle and the arc angle are measured in degrees. The origin for the start angle is an imaginary horizontal line passing through the center of the oval and can be referred to as 0°. See Figure 2.18.

Key Concept

An arc is a segment of an oval; the segment begins at a specific start angle and extends for a distance specified by the arc angle.

Web Bonus

The book's Web site contains additional information and examples about drawing shapes.

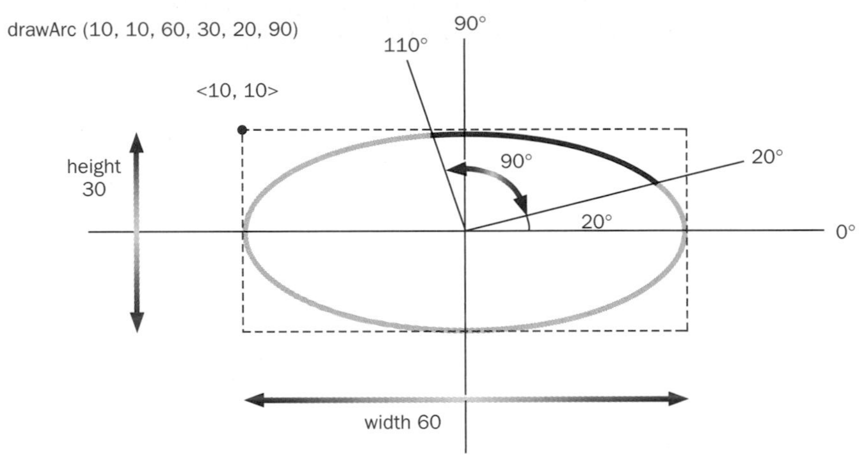

Figure 2.18 An arc defined by an oval, a start angle, and an arc angle

The `Color` Class

In Java, a programmer uses the `Color` class, which is part of the `java.awt` package, to define and manage colors. Each object of the `Color` class represents a single color, and the class contains several instances of itself to provide a basic set of predefined colors. The predefined colors of the `Color` class are listed in Figure 2.19.

> **Key Concept**
> The `Color` class contains several common colors predefined.

It also contains methods to define and manage many other colors. Recall from Chapter 1 that colors can be defined using the RGB technique for specifying the contributions of three primary colors: red, green, and blue.

Every graphics context has a current *foreground color* that is used whenever shapes or strings are drawn. Every surface that can be drawn on has a *background color*. The foreground color is set using the `setColor` method of the `Graphics` class, and the background color is set using the `setBackground` method of the component on which we are drawing, such as the applet.

An applet called `Snowman` is shown in Listing 2.15. It uses various drawing and color methods to draw a winter scene featuring a snowman. Review the code carefully to note how each shape is drawn to create the overall picture.

Note that the snowman figure is based on two constant values called `MID` and `TOP`, which define the midpoint of the snowman (left to right) and the top of the snowman's head. The entire snowman figure is drawn relative to these values. Using constants like these make it easier to make modifications later. For example, to shift the snowman to the right or left in our picture, only one constant declaration would have to change.

Color	Object	RGB Value
black	`Color.black`	0, 0, 0
blue	`Color.blue`	0, 0, 255
cyan	`Color.cyan`	0, 255, 255
gray	`Color.gray`	128, 128, 128
dark gray	`Color.darkGray`	64, 64, 64
light gray	`Color.lightGray`	192, 192, 192
green	`Color.green`	0, 255, 0
magenta	`Color.magenta`	255, 0, 255
orange	`Color.orange`	255, 200, 0
pink	`Color.pink`	255, 175, 175
red	`Color.red`	255, 0, 0
white	`Color.white`	255, 255, 255
yellow	`Color.yellow`	255, 255, 0

Figure 2.19 Predefined colors in the `Color` class

Listing 2.15

```
//********************************************************************
//  Snowman.java       Author: Lewis and Loftus
//
//  Demonstrates basic drawing methods and the use of color.
//********************************************************************

import java.applet.Applet;
import java.awt.*;

public class Snowman extends Applet
{
   //-----------------------------------------------------------------
   //  Draws a snowman.
   //-----------------------------------------------------------------
   public void paint (Graphics page)
   {
      final int MID = 150;
      final int TOP = 50;
```

Listing 2.14 (continued)

```
      setBackground (Color.cyan);

      page.setColor (Color.blue);
      page.fillRect (0, 175, 300, 50);  // ground

      page.setColor (Color.yellow);
      page.fillOval (-40, -40, 80, 80);  // sun

      page.setColor (Color.white);
      page.fillOval (MID-20, TOP, 40, 40);      // head
      page.fillOval (MID-35, TOP+35, 70, 50);   // upper torso
      page.fillOval (MID-50, TOP+80, 100, 60);  // lower torso

      page.setColor (Color.black);
      page.fillOval (MID-10, TOP+10, 5, 5);   // left eye
      page.fillOval (MID+5, TOP+10, 5, 5);    // right eye

      page.drawArc (MID-10, TOP+20, 20, 10, 190, 160);   // smile

      page.drawLine (MID-25, TOP+60, MID-50, TOP+40);  // left arm
      page.drawLine (MID+25, TOP+60, MID+55, TOP+60);  // right arm

      page.drawLine (MID-20, TOP+5, MID+20, TOP+5);  // brim of hat
      page.fillRect (MID-15, TOP-20, 30, 25);        // top of hat
   }
}
```

Summary of Key Concepts

- The information we manage in a Java program is either represented as primitive data or as objects
- An abstraction hides details. A good abstraction hides the right details at the right time so that we can manage complexity.
- A variable is a name for a memory location used to hold a value of a particular data type.
- A variable can store only one value of its declared type.
- Java is a strongly typed language. Each variable is associated with a specific type for the duration of its existence, and you cannot assign a value of one type to a variable of an incompatible type.
- Constants are similar to variables, but they hold a particular value for the duration of their existence.
- Each value in memory is associated with a particular data type. This data type determines what operations we can perform on the data.
- Java has two kinds of numeric values—integers and floating point. There are four integer data types (`byte`, `short`, `int`, and `long`) and two floating point data types (`float` and `double`).
- Many programming statements involve expressions. Expressions are combinations of operators and operands used to perform a calculation.
- Java follows a well-defined set of rules that govern the order in which operators will be evaluated in an expression. These rules form an operator precedence hierarchy.
- Avoid narrowing conversions because they can lose information.
- The `new` operator returns a reference to a newly created object.
- The Java standard class library is a useful set of classes that anyone can use when writing Java programs.
- A package is a Java language element used to group related classes under a common name.
- The `Keyboard` class is not part of the Java standard library. It will therefore not be available on all Java development platforms.
- Applets are Java programs that are usually transported across a network and executed using a Web browser. Java applications are standalone programs that can be executed using the Java interpreter.
- Most shapes can be drawn filled (opaque) or unfilled (as an outline).
- A bounding rectangle is often used to define the position and size of curved shapes such as an oval.

- An arc is a segment of an oval; the segment begins at a specific start angle and extends for a distance specified by the arc angle.
- The `Color` class contains several common colors predefined.

▶ Self-Review Questions

2.1 What is an object? Why is it abstract?

2.2 What is an escape sequence? Give some examples.

2.3 How many values can be stored in an integer variable?

2.4 What is operator precedence?

2.5 Why are widening conversions safer than narrowing conversions?

2.6 What does the `new` operator accomplish?

2.7 Why doesn't the `String` class have to be specifically imported into our programs?

2.8 What is the difference between a Java application and a Java applet?

▶ Exercises

2.1 How might the World Wide Web be involved in the translation and execution of a Java program?

2.2 Given the following declarations, what is the result of each of the listed expressions?

```
int w = 2;
int y = 7;
int z = 12;
```

a. `w * z`

b. `w + z`

c. `w * z + y`

d. `y + w * z`

e. `w + z * y`

f. `w + z - y`

g. `w - y + z`

h. `w - z + y`

i. `(w + z) * y`

j. `w + (z * y)`

k. `y / w`

l. `w / y`

2.3 Given the following declarations, what is the result of each of the listed expressions?

```
double w = 12.9;
double y = 3.2;
double z = 12.2;
```

a. `w / z`

b. `w - z`

c. `w / z - y`

d. `y - w / z`

e. `w - z * y`

f. `(w - z) * y`

g. `w - (z * y)`

h. `z / w`

i. `z / y / w`

j. `z / w / y`

k. `z / (w / y)`

2.4 Given the following declarations, what is the result of each of the listed expressions?

```
double w = 69.9;
int y = 3;
double z = 23.2;
```

a. `w / z`

b. `w - z`

c. `w / z - y`

d. `y - w / z`

e. `w - z * y`

f. `(w - z) * y`

g. `w - (z * y)`

2.5 Given the following declarations, what is the result of each of the listed expressions?

```
double w = 10.0;
double y = 3.0;
```

a. `w / y`

b. `y / w`

2.6 Given the following declarations, what is the result of each of the listed expressions?

```
int w = 10;
int y = 3;
```

a. `w % y`

b. `y % w`

2.7 Given the following declarations, what is the result of each of the listed expressions?

```
int w = -10;
int y = 3;
```

a. `w % y`

b. `y % w`

2.8 The following lines of code draw the eyes of the snowman in the `Snowman` applet. The eyes seem centered on the face when drawn, yet the first parameters of each call are not equally offset from the midpoint. Explain.

```
page.fillOval (MID-10, TOP+10, 5, 5);
page.fillOval (MID+5, TOP+10, 5, 5);
```

Programming Projects

2.1 Create a revised version of the `Lincoln` application from Chapter 1 such that quotes appear around the quotation.

2.2 Write an application that reads three integers and prints their average.

2.3 Write an application that reads two floating point numbers and prints their sum, difference, and product.

2.4 Create a revised version of the `TempConverter` application to convert from Fahrenheit to Celsius. Read the Fahrenheit temperature from the user.

2.5 Write an application that converts miles to kilometers. One mile equals 1.60935 kilometers. Read the miles value from the user as a floating point value.

2.6 Write an application that reads a value representing a number of seconds. Print the equivalent amount of time in hours, minutes, and seconds.

2.7 Create a revised version of the previous project to reverse the process. That is, read values representing a time duration in hours, minutes, and seconds, then print the equivalent total number of seconds.

2.8 Write an application that reads the `(x,y)` coordinates for two points. Compute the distance between the two points using the following formula:

$$\text{Distance} = \sqrt{(x_2 - x_1)^2 + (y_2 - y_1)^2}$$

2.9 Write an application that reads the radius of a sphere and prints its volume and surface area. Use the following formulas. Print the output to four decimal places. r represents the radius.

$$\text{Volume} = \frac{4}{3}\pi r^3$$

$$\text{Surface area} = 4\pi r^2$$

2.10 Write an application that reads the lengths of the sides of a triangle from the user. Compute the area of the triangle using Heron's formula, in which s represents half of the perimeter of the triangle, and a, b, and c represent the lengths of the three sides. Print the area to three decimal places.

$$\text{Area} = \sqrt{s(s-a)(s-b)(s-c)}$$

2.11 Write an application that computes the number of miles per gallon (MPG) of gas for a trip. Accept as input a floating point number that represents the total amount of gas used. Also accept two integers representing the odometer readings at the start and end of the trip. Compute the number of kilometers per liter if you prefer.

2.12 Write an application that determines the value of a jar of coins and prints the total in dollars and cents. Read integer values that represent the number of quarters, dimes, nickels, and pennies. Use a currency formatter to print the output.

2.13 Write an application that creates and prints a random phone number of the form `XXX-XXX-XXXX`. Include the dashes in the output. Do not let the first three digits contain an 8 or 9, and make sure that the second set of three digits are not, collectively, greater than 742. *Hint:* Think through the easiest way to construct the phone number. Each digit does not have to be determined separately.

2.14 Create a personal Web page using HTML (see Appendix J).

2.15 Create a revised version of the `Snowman` applet with the following modifications:

a. Add two red buttons to the upper torso.

b. Make the snowman frown instead of smile.

c. Move the sun to the upper-right corner of the picture.

d. Draw your name in the upper-left corner of the picture.

e. Shift the entire snowman figure 20 pixels to the right.

2.16 Write an applet that writes your name using the `drawString` method. Embed a link to your applet in an HTML document and view it using a Web browser.

2.17 Write an applet that draws a smiling face. Give the face eyes with pupils, ears, a nose, and a mouth.

2.18 Write an applet that draws the Big Dipper. Add some extra stars in the night sky.

2.19 Write an applet that draws some balloons tied to strings. Make the balloons various colors.

2.20 Write an applet that draws the olympic logo. The circles in the logo should be colored, from left to right, blue, yellow, black, green, and red.

2.21 Write an applet that draws a house with a door (and doorknob), windows, and a chimney. Add some smoke coming out of the chimney and some clouds in the sky.

2.22 Write an applet that displays a business card of your own design. Include both graphics and text.

2.23 Write an applet that displays your name in shadow text by drawing your name in black, then drawing it again slightly offset in a lighter color.

2.24 Write an applet the shows a pie chart with eight equal slices, all colored differently.

► Answers to Self-Review Questions

2.1 An object is a part of a program that provides services to another part of a program. These services are provided by the methods of the class from which the object is instantiated. An object is considered to be abstract because the details of the object are hidden from the user of the object. Hidden details help us manage the complexity of software.

2.2 An escape sequence is a series of characters that begin with the backslash (`\`) and that imply that the following characters should be treated in some special way. Examples: `\n` represents the newline character, `\t` represents the tab character, and `\"` represents the quotation character (as opposed to using it to terminate a string).

2.3 An integer variable can only store one value at a time. When a new value is assigned to it, the old one is overwritten and lost.

2.4 Operator precedence is the set of rules that dictate the order in which operators are evaluated in an expression.

2.5 A widening conversion tends to go from a small data value, in terms of the amount of space used to store it, to a larger one, while a narrowing conversion does the opposite. Information is more likely to be lost in a narrowing conversion, which is why narrowing conversions are considered to be less safe than a widening one.

2.6 The `new` operator creates a new instance of an object. A class can be thought of as the type of the object, and the constructor of the class is used to help set up the newly created object.

2.7 The `String` class is part of the `java.lang` package, which is automatically imported into any Java program. Therefore, no separate import declaration is needed.

2.8 A Java applet is a Java program that is executed using a Web browser. Usually, the bytecode form of the Java applet is pulled across the Internet from another computer and executed locally. A Java application is a Java program that can stand alone. It does not require a Web browser in order to execute.

3 Program Statements

All programming languages have specific statements that allow you to perform basic operations. These statements accomplish all programming activity, including our interaction with objects and the definition of the services those objects provide. This chapter examines several of these programming statements, as well as some additional operators. It also explores the basic activities that a programmer should go through when developing software. These activities form the cornerstone of high-quality software development and represent the first step toward a disciplined development process. Finally, we use the statements we examine in this chapter to augment our ability to produce graphical output.

Chapter Objectives

- Define the flow of control through a program.
- Perform decision-making using `if` and `switch` statements.
- Define expressions that let us make complex decisions.
- Perform statements repetitively using `while`, `do`, and `for` statements.
- Explore the fundamental stages of software development.
- Draw with the aid of conditionals and loops.

3.1 Control Flow

The order that statements are executed in a running program is called the *flow of control*. Unless otherwise specified, the execution of a program proceeds in a linear fashion. That is, it starts at the first programming statement and moves down one statement at a time until the program is complete. A Java application begins executing with the first line of the `main` method and proceeds step by step until it gets to the end of the `main` method.

Invoking a method alters the flow of control. When a method is called, control jumps to the code defined for that method. When the method completes, control returns to the place in the calling method where the invocation was made and processing continues from there. In our examples thus far, we've invoked methods in classes and objects using the Java libraries, and we haven't been concerned about the code that defines those methods. We discuss how to write our own separate classes and methods in Chapter 4.

Within a given method, we can alter the flow of control through the code by using certain types of programming statements. In particular, statements that control the flow of execution through a method fall into two categories: conditionals and loops.

Key Concept

Conditionals and loops allow us to control the flow of execution through a method.

A *conditional statement* is sometimes called a *selection statement* because it allows us to choose which statement will be executed next. The conditional statements in Java are the `if` statement, the `if-else` statement, and the `switch` statement. These statements allow us to make fundamental decisions.

The decisions are based on a *boolean expression* (also called a *condition*), which is an expression that evaluates to either true or false. The result of the expression determines what statement is executed next.

For example, we may want to compute a person's taxes one way if their income is under a certain level, and calculate it another way if it is above that level. The role of a conditional statement is to evaluate a boolean condition that determines if the income falls above or below the threshold level, then execute the proper calculation accordingly.

A *loop*, or *repetition statement*, allows us to execute a statement over and over again. Like a conditional, a loop is based on a boolean expression that determines how many times the statement is executed.

For example, suppose we wanted to calculate the grade point average of every student in a class. The calculation is the same for each student; it is just performed on different data. We would set up a loop that repeats the calculation for each student until there are no more students to process.

There are three types of loop statements in Java: the `while` statement, the `do` statement, and the `for` statement. Each type of repetition statement has unique characteristics that distinguish it from the others.

Conditionals and loops are fundamental to controlling the flow through a method and are necessary in many situations. This chapter explores various conditional and loop statements, as well as some additional operators.

3.2 The `if` Statement

The *`if` statement* is a conditional statement found in many programming languages, including Java. The following is an example of an `if` statement:

```
if (total > amount)
   total = total + (amount + 1);
```

An `if` statement consists of the reserved word `if` followed by a boolean expression, or condition. The condition is enclosed in parentheses and must evaluate to `true` or `false`. If the condition is true, then the statement is executed and processing continues with the next statement. If the condition is false, the statement is skipped, and processing continues immediately with the next statement. In this example, if the value in `total` is greater than the value in `amount`, then the assignment statement is executed; otherwise, the assignment statement is skipped. This processing is shown in Figure 3.1.

Key Concept

An `if` statement allows a program to choose whether or not to execute a particular statement.

Note that the assignment statement is indented under the header line of the `if` statement. This indicates that the assignment statement is part of the `if` statement; it shows that the `if` statement somehow governs

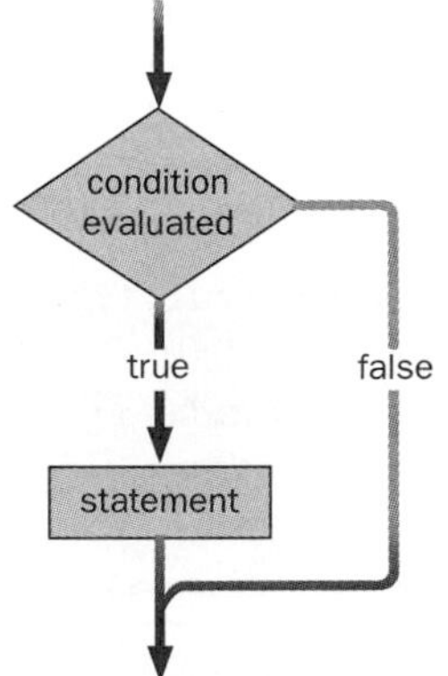

Figure 3.1 The logic of an `if` statement

Key Concept

Even though the compiler does not care about indentation, proper indentation is essential for human readability.

whether or not the assignment statement will be executed. This indentation is extremely important for the human reader.

The example in Listing 3.1 reads the age of the user, then makes a decision whether or not to print a particular sentence based on the age that is entered.

The `Age` program echoes the age value that is entered in all cases. Then, if the age is less than the value of the constant `MINOR`,

Listing 3.1

```
//********************************************************************
//  Age.java       Author: Lewis and Loftus
//
//  Demonstrates the use of an if statement.
//********************************************************************

import cs1.Keyboard;

public class Age
{
   //-----------------------------------------------------------------
   //  Reads the user's age and prints comments accordingly.
   //-----------------------------------------------------------------
   public static void main (String[] args)
   {
      final int MINOR = 21;

      System.out.print ("Enter your age: ");
      int age = Keyboard.readInt();

      System.out.println ("You entered: " + age);

      if (age < MINOR)
         System.out.println ("Youth is a wonderful thing. Enjoy.");

      System.out.println ("Age is a state of mind.");
   }
}
```

```
Enter your age: 35
You entered: 35
Age is a state of mind.
```

the statement about youth is printed. If the age is equal to or greater than the value of `MINOR`, the `println` statement will be skipped and therefore the sentence will not be printed. In either case, the final sentence about age being a state of mind will be printed.

Equality and Relational Operators

Boolean expressions evaluate to either `true` or `false` and are fundamental to our ability to make decisions. Java has several operators that produce a `true` or `false` result. The `==` and `!=` operators are called *equality operators;* they test if two values are equal or not equal, respectively. Note that the equality operator consists of two equal signs side by side and should not be mistaken for the assignment operator that uses only one equal sign.

The following `if` statement prints a sentence only if the variables `total` and `sum` contain the same value:

```
if (total == sum)
   System.out.println ("total equals sum");
```

Likewise, the following `if` statement prints a sentence only if the variables `total` and `sum` do *not* contain the same value:

```
if (total != sum)
   System.out.println ("total does NOT equal sum");
```

In the `Age` program we used the < operator to decide if one value was less than another. The less than operator is one of several *relational operators* that let us decide the relationships between values. The equality and relational operators are listed in Figure 3.2.

The equality and relational operators have precedence lower than the arithmetic operators. Therefore, arithmetic operations are evaluated first, then

Operator	Meaning
==	equal to
!=	not equal to
<	less than
<=	less than or equal to
>	greater than
>=	greater than or equal to

Figure 3.2 Java equality and relational operators

equality and relational operations are evaluated. As always, parentheses can be used to explicitly specify the order of evaluation.

The `if-else` Statement

Sometimes we want to do one thing if a condition is true and a different thing if that condition is false. We can add an *`else` clause* to an `if` statement, making it an *`if-else` statement,* to handle this kind of situation.

The following is an example of an `if-else` statement:

```
if (height <= MAX)
   adjustment = 0;
else
   adjustment = MAX - height;
```

Key Concept

An `if-else` statement allows a program to do one thing if a condition is true and a different thing if the condition is false.

If the condition is true, then the first assignment statement is executed; but if the condition is false, then the second assignment statement is executed. Only one or the other will be executed, because all boolean conditions will evaluate to either true or false. Note that proper indentation is used again to indicate that the statements are part of the governing `if` statement.

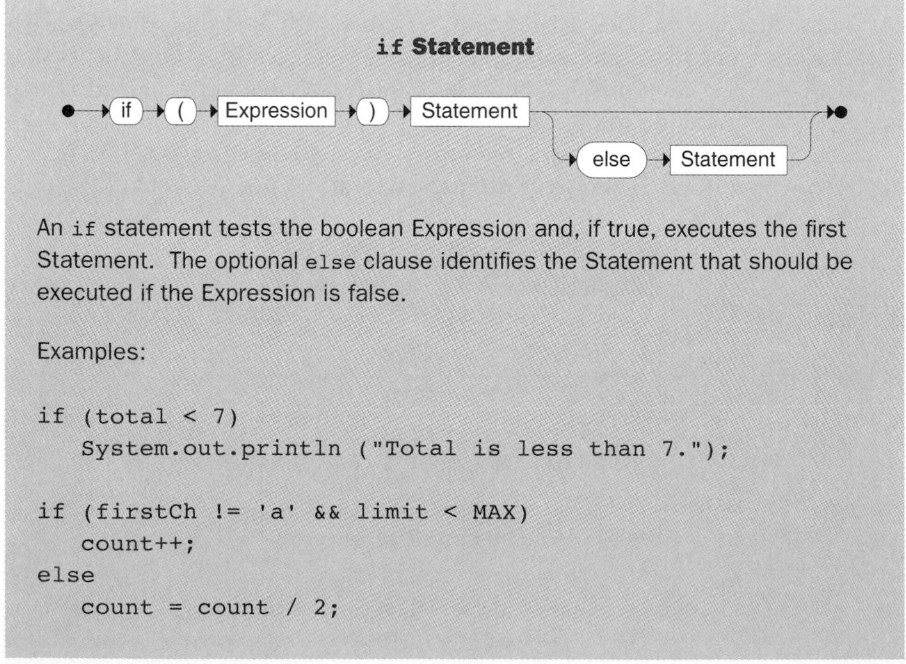

`if` Statement

An `if` statement tests the boolean Expression and, if true, executes the first Statement. The optional `else` clause identifies the Statement that should be executed if the Expression is false.

Examples:

```
if (total < 7)
   System.out.println ("Total is less than 7.");

if (firstCh != 'a' && limit < MAX)
   count++;
else
   count = count / 2;
```

The `Wages` program shown in Listing 3.2 uses an `if-else` statement to compute the proper payment amount for an employee.

In the `Wages` program, if an employee works over 40 hours in a week, the payment amount takes into account the overtime hours. An `if-else` statement is used to determine if the number of hours entered by the user is greater than forty. If it is, the extra hours are paid at a rate one and a half times the normal rate. If there are no overtime hours, the total payment is based solely on the number of hours worked.

Using Block Statements

We may want to do more than one thing as the result of evaluating a boolean condition. In Java, we can replace any single statement with a *block statement*. A block is a list of statements enclosed in braces. We've already seen these braces used to delimit the `main` method and a class definition. The program called `Guessing`, shown in Listing 3.3, uses an `if-else` statement in which the statement of the `else` clause is a block.

If the guess entered by the user equals the randomly chosen answer, a correct acknowledgment is printed. However, if the answer is incorrect, two statements are printed, one that states that the guess is wrong and one that prints the actual answer.

Note that if the block braces were not used, the sentence `"That is not correct, sorry."` would be printed if the answer was wrong, and the sentence stating the correct answer would be printed in all cases. That is, only the first one would be considered to be part of the `else` clause. Remember that indentation means nothing except to the human reader. Statements that are not aligned or blocked properly can lead to the programmer making improper assumptions about how the code will execute.

A block statement can be used anywhere a single statement is called for in Java syntax. In the `Guessing` program, we use a block statement only in the `else` clause. However, we could have used a block in the `if` portion if we desired. How you use blocks depends on what you want to accomplish in each situation.

Nested `if` Statements

The statement executed as the result of an `if` statement could be another `if` statement. This situation is called a *nested* `if`. It allows us to make a decision after already determining the results of a previous decision. The program in Listing 3.4, called `MinOfThree`, uses nested `if` statements to determine the smallest of three integer values entered by the user.

Carefully trace the logic of the `MinOfThree` program, using various input sets with the minimum value in all three positions, to see how it determines the lowest value.

An important situation arises due to nested `if` statements. It may seem that an `else` clause after a nested `if` could apply to either `if` statement. The

Listing 3.2

```
//********************************************************************
//  Wages.java       Author: Lewis and Loftus
//
//  Demonstrates the use of an if-else statement.
//********************************************************************

import java.text.NumberFormat;
import cs1.Keyboard;

public class Wages
{
   //-----------------------------------------------------------------
   //  Reads the number of hours worked and calculates wages.
   //-----------------------------------------------------------------
   public static void main (String[] args)
   {
      final double RATE = 8.25;  // regular pay rate
      final int STANDARD = 40;   // standard hours in a work week

      double pay = 0.0;

      System.out.print ("Enter the number of hours worked: ");
      int hours = Keyboard.readInt();

      System.out.println ();

      // Pay overtime at "time and a half"
      if (hours > STANDARD)
         pay = STANDARD * RATE + (hours-STANDARD) * (RATE * 1.5);
      else
         pay = hours * RATE;

      NumberFormat fmt = NumberFormat.getCurrencyInstance();
      System.out.println ("Gross earnings: " + fmt.format(pay));
   }
}
```

```
Enter the number of hours worked: 46

Gross earnings: $404.25
```

Listing 3.3

```
//********************************************************************
//  Guessing.java       Author: Lewis and Loftus
//
//  Demonstrates the use of a block statement in an if-else.
//********************************************************************

import cs1.Keyboard;

public class Guessing
{
   //-----------------------------------------------------------------
   //  Plays a simple guessing game with the user.
   //-----------------------------------------------------------------
   public static void main (String[] args)
   {
      final int MAX = 10;
      int answer, guess;

      answer = (int) (Math.random() * MAX) + 1;

      System.out.print ("I'm thinking of a number between 1 and "
                        + MAX + ". Guess what it is: ");
      guess = Keyboard.readInt();

      if (guess == answer)
         System.out.println ("You got it! Good guessing!");
      else
      {
         System.out.println ("That is not correct, sorry.");
         System.out.println ("The number was " + answer);
      }
   }
}
```

```
I'm thinking of a number between 1 and 10. Guess what it is: 7
That is not correct, sorry.
The number was 4
```

Listing 3.4

```
//********************************************************************
//  MinOfThree.java       Author: Lewis and Loftus
//
//  Demonstrates the use of nested if statements.
//********************************************************************

import cs1.Keyboard;

public class MinOfThree
{
   //-----------------------------------------------------------------
   //  Reads three integers from the user and determines the smallest
   //  value.
   //-----------------------------------------------------------------
   public static void main (String[] args)
   {
      int num1, num2, num3, min = 0;

      System.out.println ("Enter three integers: ");
      num1 = Keyboard.readInt();
      num2 = Keyboard.readInt();
      num3 = Keyboard.readInt();

      if (num1 < num2)
         if (num1 < num3)
            min = num1;
         else
            min = num3;
      else
         if (num2 < num3)
            min = num2;
         else
            min = num3;

      System.out.println ("Minimum value: " + min);
   }
}
```

```
Enter three integers:
45   22   69
Minimum value: 22
```

semantics of the `if-else` statement is that an `else` clause is always matched to the closest unmatched `if` that came before it. However, if you're not careful you can easily mismatch it in your mind. This is another reason why appropriate, consistent indentation is crucial. Braces can be used to specify the `if` statement to which an `else` clause belongs.

Key Concept

In a nested `if` statement, an `else` clause is matched to the closest unmatched `if`.

3.3 The `switch` Statement

Another conditional statement in Java is called the ***switch statement***, which directs the executing program to follow one of several paths based on a single value. We also discuss the ***break statement*** in this section because it is usually used with a `switch` statement.

The `switch` statement evaluates an expression to determine a value, then matches that value with one of several possible *cases*. Each case has statements associated with it. After evaluating the expression, control jumps to the statement associated with the first case that matches the value. Consider the following example:

```
switch (idChar)
{
   case 'A':
      aCount = aCount + 1;
      break;
   case 'B':
      bCount = bCount + 1;
      break;
   case 'C':
      cCount = cCount + 1;
      break;
   default:
      System.out.println ("Error in Identification Character.");
}
```

First, the expression is evaluated. In this example, the expression is a simple `char` variable. Execution then transfers to the first statement identified by the case value that matches the result of the expression. Therefore, if `idChar` contains an `'A'`, then the variable `aCount` is incremented. If it contains a `'B'`, the case for `'A'` is skipped and processing continues where `bCount` is incremented.

If no case value matches that of the expression, then execution continues with the optional *default case,* indicated by the reserved word `default`. If no default case exists, then no statements in the switch statement are executed,

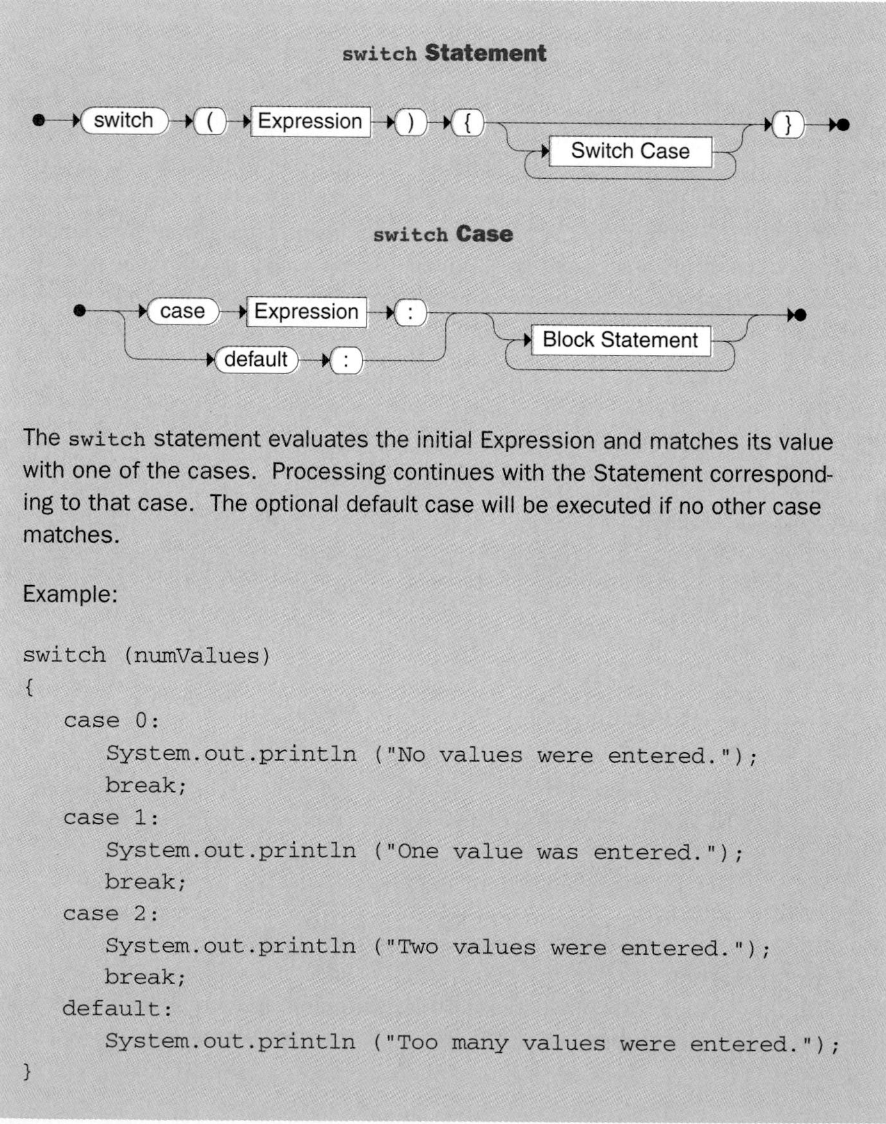

The `switch` statement evaluates the initial Expression and matches its value with one of the cases. Processing continues with the Statement corresponding to that case. The optional default case will be executed if no other case matches.

Example:

```
switch (numValues)
{
   case 0:
      System.out.println ("No values were entered.");
      break;
   case 1:
      System.out.println ("One value was entered.");
      break;
   case 2:
      System.out.println ("Two values were entered.");
      break;
   default:
      System.out.println ("Too many values were entered.");
}
```

and processing continues with the statement after the switch. It is often a good idea to include a default case, even if you don't expect it to be executed.

When a ***break statement*** is encountered, processing jumps to the statement following the `switch` statement. A `break` statement is usually used to break out of each case of a `switch` statement. Without a `break` statement, processing continues into the next case of the `switch`. If the `break` statement at the end of the `'A'` case in the previous example was not there, both the `aCount` and `bCount` variables would be incremented when the `idChar` contains an `'A'`. Usually we only want to perform one and only one case, so a `break` statement is almost always used. Occasionally, though, the "pass through" feature comes in handy.

Key Concept

A `break` statement is usually used at the end of each case alternative of a `switch` statement to jump to the end of the `switch`.

The expression evaluated at the beginning of a `switch` statement must be an *integral data type,* such as an integer or a character. It cannot evaluate to a boolean or floating point value. Furthermore, each case value associated must be a constant; it cannot be a variable or other expression.

Note that the implicit boolean condition of a `switch` statement is based on equality. The expression at the beginning of the statement is compared to each case value to determine which one it equals. A `switch` statement cannot be used to determine other relational operations (such as less than), unless some clever processing is done along the way. For example, the `GradeReport` program in Listing 3.5 prints comments relative to a numeric grade that is entered by the user.

Listing 3.5

```
//********************************************************************
//  GradeReport.java       Author: Lewis and Loftus
//
//  Demonstrates the use of a switch statement.
//********************************************************************

import cs1.Keyboard;

public class GradeReport
{
   //-----------------------------------------------------------------
   //  Reads a grade from the user and prints comments accordingly.
   //-----------------------------------------------------------------
   public static void main (String[] args)
   {
      int grade, category;
```

Listing 3.5 *(continued)*

```
      System.out.print ("Enter a numeric grade (0 to 100): ");
      grade = Keyboard.readInt();

      category = grade / 10;

      System.out.print ("That grade is ");

      switch (category)
      {
         case 10:
            System.out.println ("a perfect score. Well done.");
            break;
         case 9:
            System.out.println ("well above average. Excellent.");
            break;
         case 8:
            System.out.println ("above average. Nice job.");
            break;
         case 7:
            System.out.println ("average.");
            break;
         case 6:
            System.out.println ("below average. You should see the");
            System.out.println ("instructor to clarify the material "
                                + "presented in class.");
            break;
         default:
            System.out.println ("not passing.");
      }
   }
}
```

```
Enter a numeric grade (0 to 100): 86
That grade is above average. Nice job.
```

In `GradeReport`, the category of the grade is determined by dividing the grade by 10 using integer division, resulting in an integer value between 0 and 10 (assuming a valid grade is entered). This is used as the expression of the `switch`, printing a different sentence for grades 60 or higher, and a default sentence for all other values.

Note that any `switch` statement could be implemented as a set of nested `if` statements. However, nested `if` statements quickly become difficult for a human reader to understand, and are error-prone to implement and debug. But because a `switch` can only determine equality, sometimes nested `if` statements are the correct choice. It all depends on the situation.

> **Key Concept**
> A `switch` statement could be implemented as a series of `if-else` statements, but the `switch` is often a more convenient and readable construct.

3.4 Boolean Expressions Revisited

Let's examine a few more options concerning the use of boolean expressions.

Logical Operators

In addition to the equality and relational operators, Java has three *logical operators* that produce boolean results. They also take boolean operands. The logical operators are listed and described in Figure 3.3.

The `!` operator is used to perform the *logical NOT* operation, which is also called the *logical complement*. The logical complement of a boolean value yields its opposite value. That is, if a boolean variable called `found` has the value false, then `!found` is true. Likewise, if `found` is true, then `!found` is false. The logical NOT does not change the value stored in `found`.

A logical operation can be described by a *truth table* that lists all possible combinations of values for the variables involved in an expression. Because the logical NOT operator is unary, there are only two possible values for its one operand, true or false. A truth table that describes the `!` operator is shown in Figure 3.4.

Operator	Description	Example	Result
!	logical NOT	! a	true if a is false and false if a is true
&&	logical AND	a && b	true if a and b are both true and false otherwise
||	logical OR	a || b	true if a or b or both are true and false otherwise

Figure 3.3 Java logical operators

a	!a
false	true
true	false

Figure 3.4 Truth table describing the logical NOT operator

The `&&` operator performs a *logical AND*. The result is true if both operands are true, but false otherwise. Since it is a binary operator and each operand has two possible values, there are four combinations to consider.

The result of the *logical OR* operator (`||`) is true if one or the other or both operands are true, but false otherwise (if they are both false). It is also a binary operator. A truth table that show both the `&&` and `||` operators is shown in Figure 3.5.

The logical NOT has the highest precedence of the three logical operators, followed by logical AND, then logical OR.

Logical operators are often used as part of a condition for a selection or repetition statement. For example, consider the following `if` statement:

```
if ( !done && (count > MAX) )
   System.out.println ("logical operators");
```

Key Concept

Logical operators return a boolean value and are often used to construct sophisticated conditions.

Under what conditions would the `println` statement be executed? The value of the boolean variable `done` is either true or false, and the NOT operator reverses that value. The value of `count` is either greater than `MAX` or it isn't. The truth table in Figure 3.6 breaks down all of the possibilities.

An important characteristic of the `&&` and `||` operators is that they are "short-circuited." That is, if their left operand is sufficient to decide

a	b	a && b	a || b
false	false	false	false
false	true	false	true
true	false	false	true
true	true	true	true

Figure 3.5 Truth table describing the logical AND and OR operators

done	count > MAX	!done	!done && (count > MAX)
false	false	true	false
false	true	true	true
true	false	false	false
true	true	false	false

Figure 3.6 A truth table for a specific condition

the boolean result of the operation, then the right operand is not evaluated. This situation can occur with both operators but for different reasons. If the left operand of the `&&` operator is false, then the result of the operation will be false, no matter what the value of the right operand. Likewise, if the left operand of the `||` is true, then the result of the operation is true, no matter what the value of the right operand.

Sometimes you can capitalize on the fact that the operation is short-circuited. For example, the condition in the following `if` statement will not attempt to divide by zero if the left operand is false. If `count` has the value zero, then the left side of the `&&` operation is false, therefore the whole expression is false, and the right side is not evaluated.

```
if ( count != 0 && total / count > MAX )
   System.out.println ("testing");
```

Be careful when you count on these kinds of subtle programming language characteristics. Not all programming languages work the same way. As we have mentioned several times, you should always strive to make it extremely clear to the reader exactly how the logic of your program works.

Comparing Characters and Strings

We know what it means when we say that one number is less than another, but what does it mean to say one character is less than another? As we discussed Chapter 2, characters in Java are based on the Unicode character set, which defines an ordering of all possible characters that can be used. Because the character `'a'` comes before the character `'b'` in the character set, we can say that `'a'` is less than `'b'`.

We can use the equality and relational operators on character data. For example, if two character variables `ch1` and `ch2` hold the values of two characters, we might determine their relative ordering in the Unicode character set with an `if` statement:

```
if (ch1 > ch2)
   System.out.println (ch1 + " is greater than " + ch2);
else
   System.out.println (ch1 + " is NOT greater than " + ch2);
```

The Unicode character set is structured so that all lowercase alphabetic characters (`'a'` through `'z'`) are continuous and in alphabetical order. The same is true of the uppercase alphabetic characters (`'A'` through `'Z'`) and the characters that represent digits (`'0'` through `'9'`).

These relationships make it easy to sort characters and strings of characters. If you have a list of names, for instance, you can put them in alphabetical order based on the inherent relationships among characters in the character set.

However, you should not use the equality or relational operators to compare `String` objects. The `String` class contains a method called `equals` that returns a boolean value that is true if the two strings being compared contain exactly the same characters, and false otherwise. To determine the relative alphabetical ordering of two strings, use the `compareTo` method of the `String` class.

Comparing Floats

Another interesting situation occurs when comparing floating point data. Specifically, you should rarely use the equality operator (==) when comparing floating point values. Two floating point values are equal, according to the == operator, only if every binary digit of their underlying representation is the same. If the values you are comparing are the results of computation, it may be unlikely that they are exactly equal even if they are close enough for the specific situation.

Therefore, a better way to check for floating point equality is to compute the absolute value of the difference between the two values and compare the result to some tolerance level. For example, we may choose a tolerance level of 0.00001. If the two floating point values are so close that their difference is less than the tolerance, then we are willing to consider them equal. Comparing two floating point values `f1` and `f2` could be accomplished as follows:

```
if (Math.abs(f1 - f2) < TOLERANCE)
   System.out.println ("Essentially equal.");
```

The value of the constant `TOLERANCE` should be appropriate for the situation.

3.5 More Operators

Before moving on to repetition statements, let's examine a few more Java operators to give us even more flexibility in the way we express our program commands. Some of these are commonly used in loop processing.

Increment and Decrement Operators

The *increment operator* (++) adds 1 to any integer or floating point value. The two plus signs that make up the operator cannot be separated by white space. The *decrement operator* (--) is similar except that it subtracts 1 from the value. They are both unary operators because they operate on only one operand. The statement

```
count++;
```

causes the value of count to be incremented, and the result stored back into the variable count. Therefore, it is basically equivalent to the following statement:

```
count = count + 1;
```

The increment and decrement operators can be applied after the variable (such as count++), creating what is called the *postfix form* of the operator. The increment and decrement operators can also be applied before the variable (such as ++count), in what is called the *prefix form*. When used alone in a statement, the prefix and postfix forms are basically equivalent. That is, it doesn't matter if you write

```
count++;
```

or

```
++count;
```

although when such a form is written as a statement by itself, it is usually written in its postfix form.

However, when the increment or decrement operator is used in a larger expression, it can yield different results depending on the form used. For example, if the variable count currently contains the value 15, then the statement

```
total = count++;
```

assigns the value 15 to total and the value 16 to count. Whereas the statement

```
total = ++count;
```

assigns the value 16 to both total and count. The value of count is incremented in both situations, but the value used in the larger expression depends on whether a prefix or postfix form of the increment operator is used, as described in Figure 3.7.

Let's look at another example. Consider the following statement, assuming the current value of the integer variable sum is 25.

```
System.out.println(sum++ + "   " + ++sum + "   " + sum + "   "
                   + sum--);
```

The first increment operator increases sum to 26 but sends the original value 25 to the println method. The second increment is a prefix form, which changes sum to 27 and sends 27 to the println method. Then the current value of sum, which is 27, is printed. Finally, sum is decremented back to 26, but the original value of 27 is sent to the println method. So the output of that statement is

Key Concept

The prefix and postfix increment and decrement operators have subtle effects on programs because of differences in when they are evaluated.

```
25 27 27 27
```

and the value of sum is 26 after that line is complete.

Because of the subtle differences between the prefix and postfix forms of the increment and decrement operators, they should be used with care. As always, favor the side of readability.

Assignment Operators

As a convenience, several operators have been defined in Java that combine a basic operation with assignment. For example, the += operator can be used as follows

```
total += 5;
```

Expression	Operation	Value of Expression
count++	add 1 to count	the original value of count
++count	add 1 to count	the new value of count
count—	subtract 1 from count	the original value of count
—count	subtract 1 from count	the new value of count

Figure 3.7 Prefix and postfix forms of the increment and decrement operators

It performs the same activity as the statement

```
total = total + 5;
```

The right-hand side of the assignment operator can be a full expression. The expression on the right-hand side of the operator is evaluated, then that result is added to the current value of the variable on the left-hand side, and that value is stored in the variable. Therefore, the statement

```
total += (sum - 12) / count;
```

is equivalent to

```
total = total + ((sum - 12) / count);
```

Many similar assignment operators are defined in Java. They are listed in Figure 3.8. Additional operators are discussed in Appendix E.

Operator	Description	Example	Equivalent Expression
=	assignment	x = y	x = y
+=	addition, then assignment	x += y	x = x + y
+=	string concatenation, then assignment	x += y	x = x + y
-=	subtraction, then assignment	x -= y	x = x - y
*=	multiplication, then assignment	x *= y	x = x * y
/=	division, then assignment	x /= y	x = x / y
%=	remainder, then assignment	x %= y	x = x % y
<<=	left shift, then assignment	x <<= y	x = x << y
>>=	right shift with sign, then assignment	x >>= y	x = x >> y
>>>=	right shift with zero, then assignment	x >>>= y	x = x >>> y
&=	bitwise AND, then assignment	x &= y	x = x & y
&=	boolean AND, then assignment	x &= y	x = x & y
^=	bitwise XOR, then assignment	x ^= y	x = x ^ y
^=	boolean XOR, then assignment	x ^= y	x = x ^ y
|=	bitwise OR, then assignment	x |= y	x = x | y
|=	boolean OR, then assignment	x |= y	x = x | y

Figure 3.8 Java assignment operators

All of the assignment operators evaluate the entire expression on the right-hand side first, then use the result as the right operand of the other operation. Therefore, the statement

```
result *= count1 + count2;
```

is equivalent to

```
result = result * (count1 + count2);
```

and the statement

```
result %= (highest - 40) / 2;
```

is equivalent to

```
result = result % ((highest - 40) / 2);
```

Some assignment operators perform particular functions depending on the types of the operands, just as their corresponding regular operators do. For example, if the operands to the += operator are strings, then the assignment operator performs string concatenation.

The Conditional Operator

The Java *conditional operator* is a *ternary operator* because it requires three operands. The symbol for the conditional operator is usually written `? :`, but it is not like other operators in that the two symbols that make it up are always separated. Below is an example of an expression that contains the conditional operator:

```
(total > MAX) ? total + 1 : total * 2;
```

Preceding the `?` is a boolean condition. Following the `?` are two expressions separated by the `:` symbol. The complete conditional expression returns the value of the first expression if the condition is true, and the value of the second expression if the condition is false. Keep in mind that this is an expression that returns a value, and usually we would want to do something with that value, such as assign it to a variable:

```
total = (total > MAX) ? total + 1 : total * 2;
```

In many ways, the `? :` operator serves like an abbreviated `if-else` statement. Therefore, the previous statement is basically equivalent to the following:

```
if (total > MAX)
   total = total + 1;
else
   total = total * 2;
```

The two expressions that define the larger conditional expression must evaluate to the same type. Consider the following declaration:

```
int larger = (num1 > num2) ? num1 : num2;
```

If `num1` is greater than `num2`, then the value of `num1` is returned and used to initialize the variable larger. If not, the value of `num2` is returned and used. Similarly, the following statement prints the smaller of the two values:

```
System.out.println ("Smaller: " + ((num1 < num2) ? num1 : num2));
```

The conditional operator is occasionally helpful to evaluate a short condition and return a result. It is not a replacement for an `if-else` statement, however, because the operands to the `? :` operator are expressions, not necessarily full statements. Even when the conditional operator is a viable alternative, you should use it sparingly because it is often not as readable as an `if-else` statement.

3.6 The `while` Statement

As we discussed in Section 3.1, a repetition statement (or loop) allows us to execute another statement multiple times. A ***`while`* statement** is a loop that evaluates a boolean condition, just like an `if` statement does, and executes a statement if the condition is true. However, unlike the `if` statement, after the statement is executed, the condition is evaluated again. If it is still true, the statement is executed again. This repetition continues until the condition eventually becomes false; then processing continues with the statement after the body of the while loop. This processing is shown in Figure 3.9.

Key Concept

A `while` statement allows a program to execute the same statement multiple times.

The `Counter` program shown in Listing 3.6 simply prints the values from 1 to 5. Each iteration through the loop prints one

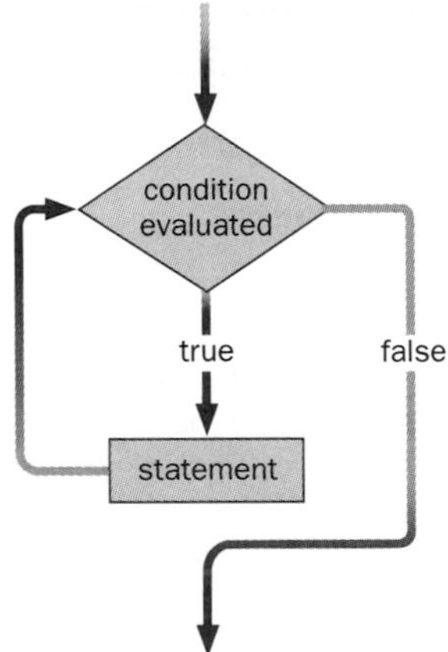

Figure 3.9 The logic of a `while` loop

value, then increments the counter. A constant called `LIMIT` is used to hold the maximum value that `count` is allowed to reach.

Note that the body of the `while` loop is a block containing two statements. Because the value of `count` is incremented each time, we are guaranteed that `count` will eventually reach the value of `LIMIT`.

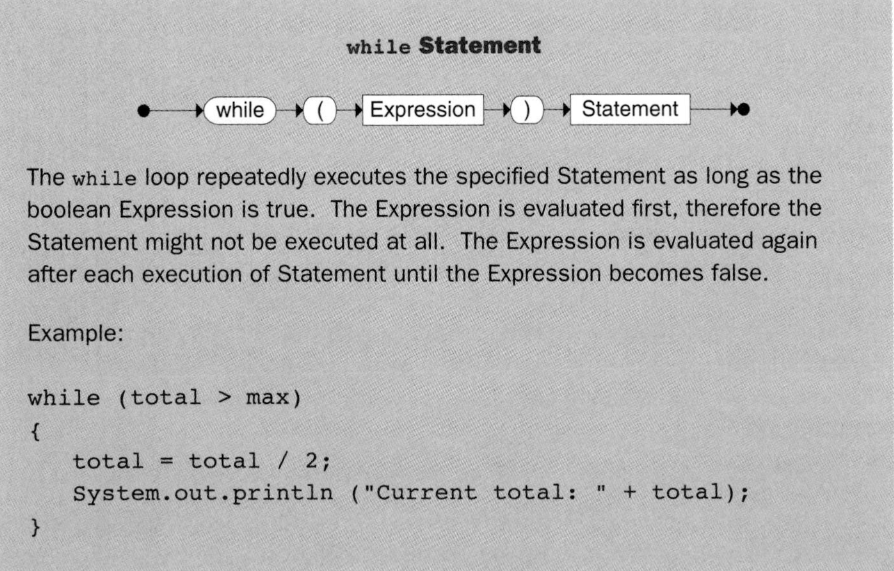

`while` Statement

The `while` loop repeatedly executes the specified Statement as long as the boolean Expression is true. The Expression is evaluated first, therefore the Statement might not be executed at all. The Expression is evaluated again after each execution of Statement until the Expression becomes false.

Example:

```
while (total > max)
{
   total = total / 2;
   System.out.println ("Current total: " + total);
}
```

Listing 3.6

```
//********************************************************************
//  Counter.java       Author: Lewis and Loftus
//
//  Demonstrates the use of a while loop.
//********************************************************************

public class Counter
{
   //-----------------------------------------------------------------
   //  Prints integer values from 1 to a specific limit.
   //-----------------------------------------------------------------
   public static void main (String[] args)
   {
      final int LIMIT = 5;
      int count = 1;

      while (count <= LIMIT)
      {
         System.out.println (count);
         count = count + 1;
      }

      System.out.println ("Done");
   }
}
```

```
1
2
3
4
5
Done
```

Let's look at another program that uses a `while` loop. The `Average` program shown in Listing 3.7 reads a series of integer values from the user, sums them up, and computes their average.

Listing 3.7

```
//********************************************************************
//  Average.java       Author: Lewis and Loftus
//
//  Demonstrates the use of a while loop, a sentinel value, and a
//  running sum.
//********************************************************************

import java.text.DecimalFormat;
import cs1.Keyboard;

public class Average
{
   //-----------------------------------------------------------------
   //  Computes the average of a set of values entered by the user.
   //  The running sum is printed as the numbers are entered.
   //-----------------------------------------------------------------
   public static void main (String[] args)
   {
      int sum = 0, value, count = 0;
      double average;

      System.out.print ("Enter an integer (0 to quit): ");
      value = Keyboard.readInt();

      while (value != 0)  // sentinel value of 0 to terminate loop
      {
         count++;

         sum += value;
         System.out.println ("The sum so far is " + sum);

         System.out.print ("Enter an integer (0 to quit): ");
         value = Keyboard.readInt();
      }

      System.out.println ();
      System.out.println ("Number of values entered: " + count);

      average = (double)sum / count;

      DecimalFormat fmt = new DecimalFormat ("0.###");
      System.out.println ("The average is " + fmt.format(average));
   }
}
```

Listing 3.7 *(continued)*

```
Enter an integer (0 to quit): 25
The sum so far is 25
Enter an integer (0 to quit): 164
The sum so far is 189
Enter an integer (0 to quit): -14
The sum so far is 175
Enter an integer (0 to quit): 84
The sum so far is 259
Enter an integer (0 to quit): 12
The sum so far is 271
Enter an integer (0 to quit): -35
The sum so far is 236
Enter an integer (0 to quit): 0

Number of values entered: 6
The average is 39.333
```

We don't know how many values the user may enter, so we have to have a way to indicate that the user is done entering numbers. In this program we designate zero to be a *sentinel value* that indicates the end of the input. The `while` loop, therefore, continues to process input values until the user enters zero. This assumes that zero is not one of the valid numbers that should contribute to the average. A sentinel value must always be outside the normal range of values entered.

Note that in the `Average` program, a variable called `sum` is used to maintain a *running sum,* which means it is the sum of the values entered thus far. The variable `sum` is initialized to zero, and each value read is added to and stored back into `sum`.

We also have to count the number of values that are entered so that after the loop concludes we can divide by the appropriate value to compute the average. Note that the sentinel value is not counted.

Let's examine yet another program that uses a `while` loop. The `WinPercentage` program shown in Listing 3.8 computes the winning percentage of a sports team based on the number of games won.

We use a `while` loop in the `WinPercentage` program to *validate the input,* meaning we guarantee that the user enters a value that we consider to be valid. In this example, that means that the number of games won must be zero or greater, and less than or equal to the total number of games played. The `while` loop continues to execute, reprompting the user for valid input, until the entered number is indeed valid.

Listing 3.8

```
//********************************************************************
//  WinPercentage.java       Author: Lewis and Loftus
//
//  Demonstrates the use of a while loop for input validation.
//********************************************************************

import java.text.NumberFormat;
import cs1.Keyboard;

public class WinPercentage
{
   //-----------------------------------------------------------------
   //  Computes the percentage of games won by a team.
   //-----------------------------------------------------------------
   public static void main (String[] args)
   {
      final int NUM_GAMES = 12;
      int won;
      double ratio;

      System.out.print ("Enter the number of games won (0 to "
                        + NUM_GAMES + "): ");
      won = Keyboard.readInt();

      while (won < 0 || won > NUM_GAMES)
      {
         System.out.print ("Invalid input. Please reenter: ");
         won = Keyboard.readInt();
      }

      ratio = (double)won / NUM_GAMES;

      NumberFormat fmt = NumberFormat.getPercentInstance();

      System.out.println ();
      System.out.println ("Winning percentage: " + fmt.format(ratio));
   }
}
```

```
Enter the number of games won (0 to 12): -5
Invalid input. Please reenter: 13
Invalid input. Please reenter: 7

Winning percentage: 58%
```

Input validation and other actions that guarantee the validity of the data we use in our programs is an important issue. We want our programs to be *robust,* which means that they handle erroneous data as elegantly as possible.

Infinite Loops

It is the programmer's responsibility to ensure that the condition of a loop will eventually become false. If it doesn't, the loop body will execute forever, or at least until the program is interrupted by the user. This situation, called an *infinite loop,* is a common mistake inadvertently created by programmers.

The program shown in Listing 3.9 demonstrates an infinite loop. Be prepared to interrupt this program if you execute it. On most systems, pressing the Control-C keyboard combination (hold down the Control key and press C) terminates a running program.

Key Concept

Design your programs carefully to avoid infinite loops. The body of the loop should eventually make the loop condition false.

In the `Forever` program, the initial value of `count` is `1` and it is decremented in the loop body. The `while` loop will continue as long as `count` is less than or equal to `25`. Because `count` gets smaller with each iteration, the condition will always be true.

Nested Loops

The body of a loop can contain another loop. This situation is called a *nested loop.* Keep in mind that for each iteration of the outer loop, the inner loop executes completely.

Consider the program `PalindromeTester` shown in Listing 3.10. A *palindrome* is a string of characters that reads the same forwards or backwards. This program tests to see if a string is a palindrome. The user may test as many strings as desired.

The code for `PalindromeTester` contains two loops, one inside the other. The outer loop controls how many strings are tested, and the inner loop scans through each string, character by character, until it determines that the string is or is not a palindrome.

The variables `left` and `right` store the indexes of two characters. They initially indicate the characters on either end of the string. Each iteration of the inner loop compares the two characters indicated by `left` and `right`. We fall out of the inner loop when either the characters don't match, meaning the string is not a palindrome, or when the value of `left` becomes equal to or greater than the value of `right`, which means the entire string has been tested and it is a palindrome.

Other Loop Controls

We've seen how the `break` statement can be used to break out of the cases of a `switch` statement. The `break` statement can also be used in the body of any

Listing 3.9

```
//********************************************************************
//  Forever.java       Author: Lewis and Loftus
//
//  Demonstrates an INFINITE LOOP.  WARNING!!
//********************************************************************

public class Forever
{
   //-----------------------------------------------------------------
   //  Prints ever-decreasing integers in an INFINITE LOOP!
   //-----------------------------------------------------------------
   public static void main (String[] args)
   {
      int count = 1;

      while (count <= 25)
      {
         System.out.println (count);
         count = count - 1;
      }

      System.out.println ("Done");  // this statement is never reached
   }
}
```

```
1
0
-1
-2
-3
-4
-5
-6
-7
-8
-9
```

and so on until interrupted

Listing 3.10

```
//********************************************************************
//  PalindromeTester.java       Author: Lewis and Loftus
//
//  Demonstrates the use of nested while loops.
//********************************************************************

import cs1.Keyboard;

public class PalindromeTester
{
   //-----------------------------------------------------------------
   //  Tests strings to see if they are palindromes.
   //-----------------------------------------------------------------
   public static void main (String[] args)
   {
      String str, another = "y";
      int left, right;

      while (another.equalsIgnoreCase("y")) // allows y or Y
      {
         System.out.println ("Enter a potential palindrome:");
         str = Keyboard.readString();

         left = 0;
         right = str.length() - 1;

         while (str.charAt(left) == str.charAt(right) && left < right)
         {
            left++;
            right--;
         }

         System.out.println();

         if (left < right)
            System.out.println ("That string is NOT a palindrome.");
         else
            System.out.println ("That string IS a palindrome.");

         System.out.println();
         System.out.print ("Test another palindrome (y/n)? ");
         another = Keyboard.readString();
      }
   }
}
```

Listing 3.10 *(continued)*

```
Enter a potential palindrome:
radar

That string IS a palindrome.

Test another palindrome (y/n)? y
Enter a potential palindrome:
able was I ere I saw elba

That string IS a palindrome.

Test another palindrome (y/n)? y
Enter a potential palindrome:
abcddcba

That string IS a palindrome.

Test another palindrome (y/n)? y
Enter a potential palindrome:
abracadabra

That string is NOT a palindrome.

Test another palindrome (y/n)? n
```

loop. Its effect on a loop is similar to its effect on a `switch` statement. The execution of the loop is stopped, and the statement following the loop is executed.

It is never necessary to use a `break` statement in a loop. An equivalent loop can always be written without it. Because the `break` statement causes program flow to jump from one place to another, using a `break` in a loop is not good practice. Its use is tolerated in a `switch` statement because an equivalent `switch` statement cannot be written without it. But you can and should avoid it in a loop.

A `continue` *statement* has a similar effect on loop processing. The `continue` statement is similar to a break, but the loop condition is evaluated again, and the loop body is executed again if it is still true. Like the `break` statement, the `continue` statement can always be avoided in a loop, and for the same reasons, it should be.

The book's Web site contains a detailed discussion of the `break` and `continue` statements, but their use should be avoided in general.

3.7 The `do` Statement

The *do statement* is similar to the `while` statement, except that its termination condition is at the end of the body of the loop. Like the `while` loop, the `do` loop executes the statement in the loop body until the condition becomes false. The condition is written at the end of the loop to indicate that it is not evaluated until the body of the loop is executed. Therefore, the body of a `do` loop is always executed at least once. This processing is shown in Figure 3.10.

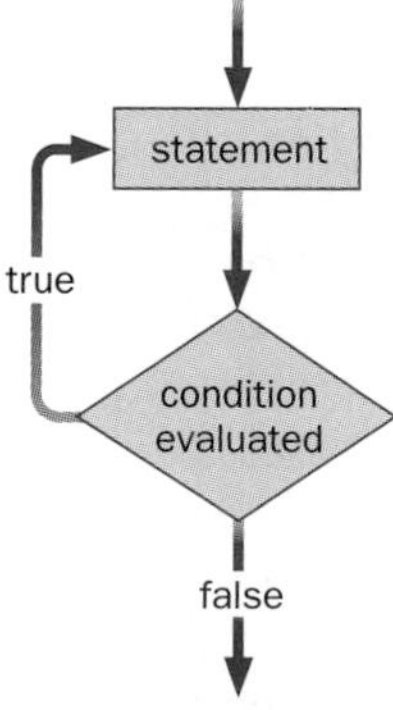

Figure 3.10 The logic of a `do` loop

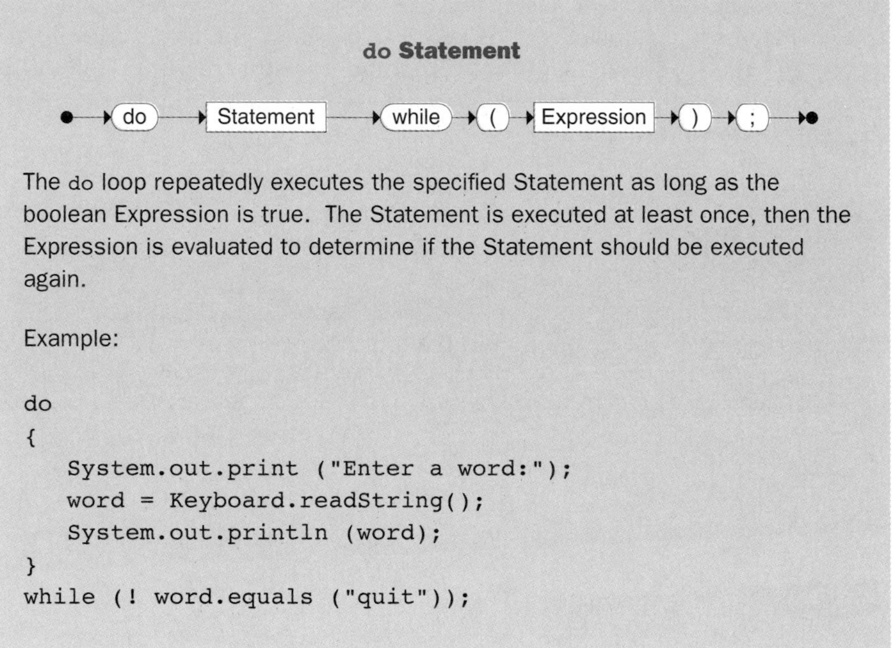

do Statement
do
Statement
while
(
Expression
)
;
The do loop repeatedly executes the specified Statement as long as the boolean Expression is true. The Statement is executed at least once, then the Expression is evaluated to determine if the Statement should be executed again.
Example:
do
{
System.out.print ("Enter a word:");
word = Keyboard.readString();
System.out.println (word);
}
while (! word.equals ("quit"));

Key Concept

A `do` statement executes its loop body at least once.

The program `Counter2` shown in Listing 3.11 uses a `do` loop to print the numbers 1 to 5, just as we did in an earlier version of this program with a `while` loop.

Note that the `do` loop begins simply with the reserved word `do`. The body of the `do` loop continues until the *`while` clause* that expresses the boolean condition that determines if the loop body will be executed again. Sometimes it is difficult to determine if a line of code that begins with the reserved word `while` is the beginning of a `while` loop or the end of a `do` loop.

Let's look at another example of the `do` loop. The program called `ReverseNumber`, shown in Listing 3.12, reads an integer from the user and reverses its digits mathematically.

The `do` loop in the `ReverseNumber` program uses the remainder operation to determine the digit in the one's position, then adds it into the reversed number, then truncates that digit from the original using integer division. The `do` loop terminates when we run out of digits to process, which corresponds to the point when the variable `number` reaches the value zero. Carefully trace the logic of this program with several examples to see how it works.

If you know you want to perform the body of a loop at least once, then you probably want to use a `do` statement. A `do` loop has essentially the same properties as a `while` statement, so it must also be checked for termination conditions to avoid infinite loops.

Listing 3.11

```
//********************************************************************
//  Counter2.java       Author: Lewis and Loftus
//
//  Demonstrates the use of a do loop.
//********************************************************************

public class Counter2
{
   //-----------------------------------------------------------------
   //  Prints integer values from 1 to a specific limit.
   //-----------------------------------------------------------------
   public static void main (String[] args)
   {
      final int LIMIT = 5;
      int count = 0;

      do
      {
         count = count + 1;
         System.out.println (count);
      }
      while (count < LIMIT);

      System.out.println ("Done");
   }
}
```

```
1
2
3
4
5
Done
```

Listing 3.12

```
//********************************************************************
//  ReverseNumber.java       Author: Lewis and Loftus
//
//  Demonstrates the use of a do loop.
//********************************************************************

import cs1.Keyboard;

public class ReverseNumber
{
   //-----------------------------------------------------------------
   //  Reverses the digits of an integer mathematically.
   //-----------------------------------------------------------------
   public static void main (String[] args)
   {
      int number, lastDigit, reverse = 0;

      System.out.print ("Enter a positive integer: ");
      number = Keyboard.readInt();

      do
      {
         lastDigit = number % 10;
         reverse = (reverse * 10) + lastDigit;
         number = number / 10;
      }
      while (number > 0);

      System.out.println ("That number reversed is " + reverse);
   }
}
```

```
Enter a positive integer: 2846
That number reversed is 6482
```

3.8 The `for` Statement

The `while` and the `do` statements are good to use when you don't initially know how many times you want to execute the loop body. The *`for` statement* is another repetition statement that is particularly well suited for executing the body of a loop a specific number of times.

Key Concept

A `for` statement is usually used when a loop will be executed a set number of times.

The `Counter3` program, shown in Listing 3.13, once again prints the numbers 1 through 5, except this time we use a `for` loop to do it.

The header of a `for` loop contains three parts separated by semicolons. Before the loop begins, the first part of the header, called the *initialization*, is

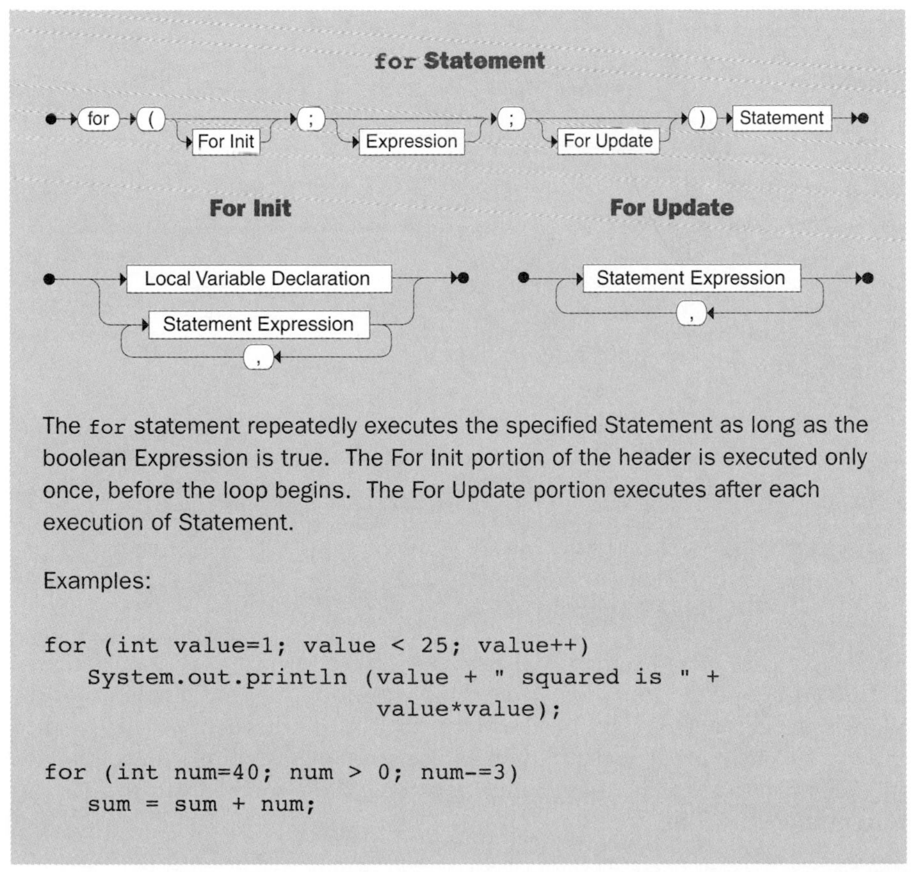

The `for` statement repeatedly executes the specified Statement as long as the boolean Expression is true. The For Init portion of the header is executed only once, before the loop begins. The For Update portion executes after each execution of Statement.

Examples:

```
for (int value=1; value < 25; value++)
   System.out.println (value + " squared is " +
                       value*value);

for (int num=40; num > 0; num-=3)
   sum = sum + num;
```

Listing 3.13

```
//********************************************************************
//  Counter3.java       Author: Lewis and Loftus
//
//  Demonstrates the use of a for loop.
//********************************************************************

public class Counter3
{
   //-----------------------------------------------------------------
   //  Prints integer values from 1 to a specific limit.
   //-----------------------------------------------------------------
   public static void main (String[] args)
   {
      final int LIMIT = 5;

      for (int count=1; count <= LIMIT; count++)
         System.out.println (count);

      System.out.println ("Done");
   }
}
```

```
1
2
3
4
5
Done
```

executed. The second part of the header is the boolean condition, which is evaluated before the loop body (like the `while` loop). If true, the body of the loop is executed, followed by the third part of the header, which is called the *increment*. Note that the initialization part is executed only once, but the increment part is executed after each iteration of the loop. This processing is shown in Figure 3.11.

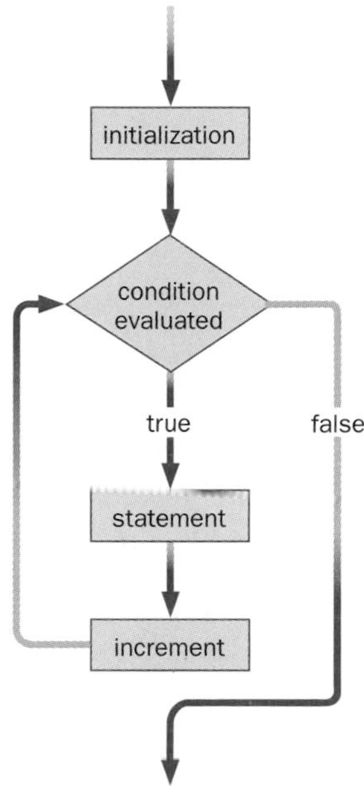

Figure 3.11 The logic of a `for` loop

Note how the three parts of the `for` loop header map to the equivalent parts of the original `Counter` program that uses a `while` loop. The initialization portion of the `for` loop header is used to declare the variable `count` as well as give it an initial value. We are not required to declare a variable there, but it is common practice in situations where the variable is not needed outside of the loop. Because `count` is declared in the `for` loop header, it only exists inside the loop body and cannot be referenced elsewhere. The loop control variable is set up, checked, and modified by the actions in the loop header. It can be referenced inside the loop body, but should not be modified.

The three loop statements (`while`, `do`, and `for`) are essentially equivalent. Any particular loop written using one statement type can be written in using either of the other two loop types. Which one we use depends on the situation. Figure 3.12 shows the general structure of equivalent `for` and `while` loops.

The increment portion of the `for` loop does not have to perform a simple increment. Consider the program shown in Listing 3.14, which prints multiples of a particular value up to a particular limit.

The increment portion of the `Multiples` program adds the value entered by the user after each iteration. The number of values printed per

for (*initialization*; *condition*; *increment*)
   statement;
	initialization;
	while (*condition*)
	{
	   statement;
	   increment;
	}

Figure 3.12 The general structure of equivalent `for` and `while` loops

Listing 3.14

```
//********************************************************************
//  Multiples.java       Author: Lewis and Loftus
//
//  Demonstrates the use of a for loop.
//********************************************************************

import cs1.Keyboard;

public class Multiples
{
   //-----------------------------------------------------------------
   //  Prints multiples of a user-specified number up to a user-
   //  specified limit.
   //-----------------------------------------------------------------
   public static void main (String[] args)
   {
      final int PER_LINE = 5;
      int value, limit, mult, count = 0;

      System.out.print ("Enter a positive value: ");
      value = Keyboard.readInt();

      System.out.print ("Enter an upper limit: ");
      limit = Keyboard.readInt();
```

Listing 3.14 ***(continued)***

```
      System.out.println ();
      System.out.println ("The multiples of " + value + " between " +
                          value + " and " + limit + " (inclusive) are:");

      for (mult = value; mult <= limit; mult += value)
      {
         System.out.print (mult + "\t");

         // Print a specific number of values per line of output
         count++;
         if (count % PER_LINE == 0)
            System.out.println();
      }
   }
}
```

```
Enter a positive value: 7
Enter an upper limit: 400

The multiples of 7 between 7 and 400 (inclusive) are:
7       14      21      28      35
42      49      56      63      70
77      84      91      98      105
112     119     126     133     140
147     154     161     168     175
182     189     196     203     210
217     224     231     238     245
252     259     266     273     280
287     294     301     308     315
322     329     336     343     350
357     364     371     378     385
392     399
```

line is controlled by counting the values printed and then moving to the next line whenever `count` is evenly divisible by the `PER_LINE` constant.

The `Stars` program in Listing 3.15 shows the use of nested `for` loops. The output is a triangle shape made of asterisk characters. The outer loop executes exactly 10 times. Each iteration of the outer loop prints one line of the

Listing 3.15

```
//********************************************************************
//  Stars.java       Author: Lewis and Loftus
//
//  Demonstrates the use of nested for loops.
//********************************************************************

public class Stars
{
   //-----------------------------------------------------------------
   //  Prints a triangle shape using asterisk (star) characters.
   //-----------------------------------------------------------------
   public static void main (String[] args)
   {
      final int MAX_ROWS = 10;

      for (int row = 1; row <= MAX_ROWS; row++)
      {
         for (int star = 1; star <= row; star++)
            System.out.print ("*");

         System.out.println();
      }
   }
}
```

```
*
**
***
****
*****
******
*******
********
*********
**********
```

output. The inner loop performs a different number of iterations depending on the line value controlled by the outer loop. Each iteration of the inner loop prints one star on the current line.

3.9 Developing Programs

Creating software involves much more than just writing code. This section introduces some of the basic programming activities necessary for developing software.

Development Stages

There are four basic *development activities* that are a part of any software development effort:

- establishing the requirements
- creating a design
- implementing the code
- testing the implementation

It would be nice if these activities, in this order, defined a step-by-step approach for developing software. However, although they may seem to be sequential, they almost never are in reality. These activities overlap and interact. They are often integrated into a repetitive development strategy. Let's briefly discuss each development stage.

Software requirements specify *what* a program must accomplish. They indicate the tasks that a program should perform, but not how to perform them. Requirements often address user interface issues such as screen layouts, buttons, and menus. Essentially, requirements establish the characteristics that make the program useful for the end user. They also may apply constraints to your program, such as how fast tasks must be performed, and impose restrictions such as deadlines on the developer.

Key Concept

Software requirements specify what a program must accomplish.

The person or group who wants a software product developed (the *client*) will often provide an initial set of requirements. However, these initial requirements are often incomplete or ambiguous. The software developer must work to refine the requirements until all key decisions have been addressed.

A *software design* specifies *how* a program will accomplish its requirements. The design lays out the classes and objects needed in a program and defines how they interact. A detailed design might even specify the individual steps that the code will follow.

Key Concept

A software design specifies how a program will accomplish its requirements.

A civil engineer would never consider building a bridge without designing it first. The design of software is no less essential.

Many problems in software are directly attributable to a lack of good design effort. Alternatives need to be considered and explored. Often the first attempt at a design is not the best.

Key Concept

An algorithm is a step-by-step process for solving a problem.

One of the most fundamental design issues is defining the *algorithm* to be used in the program. An algorithm is a step-by-step process for solving a problem. A recipe is an algorithm. Travel directions are an algorithm. Every program implements an algorithm. Every software developer should spend time thinking about the algorithm before writing any code. An algorithm is often described using *pseudocode,* which is a mixture of code statements and English phrases.

When developing an algorithm, you should first analyze all of the requirements involved with that part of the problem. This step is necessary to ensure that the algorithm takes into account all aspects of the problem. Similar to writing an essay, the design of a program is often revised many times. After the design has been developed and refined, we can focus on the implementation stage.

Key Concept

Implementation is the process of writing source code, based on the design.

Implementation is the process of writing source code. More precisely, implementation is the act of translating the design into a particular programming language. Too many programmers focus on implementation exclusively when it actually should be the least creative of all development activities. The important decisions should be made when establishing the requirements and creating the design.

Key Concept

Testing a program involves running it multiple times with various input and observing the results; the goal is to find errors.

Testing a program involves running it multiple times with various input and observing the results. The goal of testing is to find errors. Running a program with specific input and producing the correct results only establishes that your program works for that particular input. It is important to repetitively test your program with various kinds of input.

By finding and fixing errors, we increase the reliability of the program. As more test cases execute without finding errors, our confidence in the program rises. Test cases should be created to ensure that a program accomplishes its intended purpose and fulfills its requirements.

Let's apply the basic program development activities to a particular problem. Suppose an instructor wants a program that will analyze exam scores. The initial requirements are given as follows. The program will

- Accept a series of test scores
- Compute the average test score
- Determine the highest and lowest test score
- Display the average, highest, and lowest score

These requirements raise questions that need to be answered before we can design a suitable solution. Clarifying requirements often involves an extended dialog with the client. The client may very well have a clear vision about what the program should do, but this list of requirements does not specify enough detail.

For example, how many test scores should be processed? Is this program intended to handle a particular class size, or should it handle varying size classes? Is the input stored in a data file, or should it be read interactively? Should the average be computed to a specific degree of accuracy? Should the output be presented in any particular format?

After conferring with the client, we establish that the program needs to handle a varying number of test scores each time it is run and that the input should be read interactively. Furthermore, the client wants the average computed to two decimal places, and allows the developer to specify the details of the output format.

Now that we have enough detail about the requirements, let's consider some design questions. Because there is no limit to the number of grades that can be entered, how should the user indicate that there are no more grades? We can address this situation in several possible ways. The program could prompt the user after each grade is entered, asking if there are more grades to process. Or, the program could prompt the user initially for the total number of grades that will be entered, then allow exactly that many grades to be entered. A third option: When prompted for a grade, the instructor could enter a sentinel value that indicates that there are no more grades to be entered.

The first option requires a lot more input from the user and therefore is too cumbersome a solution. The second option seems reasonable, but it forces the user to have an exact count of the number of grades to enter and therefore may not be convenient.

The third option is reasonable, but before we can pick an appropriate value to end the input, we must ask additional questions. What is the range of valid grades? What would be an appropriate value to use as a sentinel value? After conferring with the client again, we establish that a student cannot receive a negative grade, therefore the use of −1 as a sentinel value in this situation will work.

Let's sketch out the design of this program. The pseudocode for a program that reads in a list of grades and computes their average might be expressed as follows:

```
prompt for and read the first grade.
while (grade does not equal -1)
{
    increment count.
    sum = sum + grade;
    prompt for and read another grade.
}
average = sum / count;
print average
```

This algorithm only addresses the calculation of the average grade. Now we must augment the algorithm to compute the highest and lowest grade. We can use two variables, `max` and `min`, to keep track of the highest and lowest scores. The augmented pseudocode is now:

```
prompt for and read the first grade.
max = min = grade;
while (grade does not equal -1)
{
   increment count.
   sum = sum + grade;
   if (grade > max)
      max = grade;
   if (grade < min)
      min = grade;
   prompt for and read another grade.
}
average = sum / count;
print average, highest, and lowest grades
```

Having planned out an initial algorithm for the program, the implementation can proceed. Consider the solution to this problem shown in Listing 3.16.

Let's examine how this program accomplishes the stated requirements and critique the implementation. After the variable declarations in the main method, we prompt the user to enter the value of the first grade. Prompts should provide information about any special input requirements. In this case, we inform the user that entering a value of −1 will indicate the end of the input.

The variables `max` and `min` are initially set to the first value entered. Note that this is accomplished using *chained assignments*. An assignment statement returns a value and can be used as an expression. The value returned by an assignment statement is the value that gets assigned. Therefore, the value of `grade` is first assigned to `min`, then that value is assigned to `max`. In the unusual case that no larger or smaller grade is ever entered, the initial values of `max` and `min` will not change.

The `while` loop condition specifies that the loop body will be executed as long as the current grade being processed is greater than zero. Therefore, in this implementation, any negative value will indicate the end of the input, even though the prompt suggests a specific value. This change is a slight variation on the original design and ensures that no negative values will be counted as grades.

The implementation uses a nested `if` structure to determine if the new grade is a candidate for the highest or lowest grade. It cannot be both, so using an `else` statement is slightly more efficient. There is no need to ask if the grade is a minimum if we already know it was a maximum.

Listing 3.16

```
//********************************************************************
//  ExamGrades.java       Author: Lewis and Loftus
//
//  Demonstrates the use of various control structures.
//********************************************************************

import java.text.DecimalFormat;
import cs1.Keyboard;

public class ExamGrades
{
   //-----------------------------------------------------------------
   //  Computes the average, minimum, and maximum of a set of exam
   //  scores entered by the user.
   //-----------------------------------------------------------------
   public static void main (String[] args)
   {
      int grade, count = 0, sum = 0, max, min;
      double average;

      //  Get the first grade and give max and min that initial value
      System.out.print ("Enter the first grade (-1 to quit): ");
      grade = Keyboard.readInt();

      max = min = grade;

      //  Read and process the rest of the grades
      while (grade >= 0)
      {
         count++;
         sum += grade;

         if (grade > max)
            max = grade;
         else
            if (grade < min)
               min = grade;

         System.out.print ("Enter the next grade (-1 to quit): ");
         grade = Keyboard.readInt ();
      }
```

Listing 3.16 ***(continued)***

```
      //  Produce the final results
      if (count == 0)
         System.out.println ("No valid grades were entered.");
      else
      {
         DecimalFormat fmt = new DecimalFormat ("0.##");
         average = (double)sum / count;
         System.out.println();
         System.out.println ("Total number of students: " + count);
         System.out.println ("Average grade: " + fmt.format(average));
         System.out.println ("Highest grade: " + max);
         System.out.println ("Lowest grade: " + min);
      }
   }
}
```

```
Enter the first grade (-1 to quit): 89
Enter the next grade (-1 to quit): 95
Enter the next grade (-1 to quit): 82
Enter the next grade (-1 to quit): 70
Enter the next grade (-1 to quit): 98
Enter the next grade (-1 to quit): 85
Enter the next grade (-1 to quit): 81
Enter the next grade (-1 to quit): 73
Enter the next grade (-1 to quit): 69
Enter the next grade (-1 to quit): 77
Enter the next grade (-1 to quit): 84
Enter the next grade (-1 to quit): 82
Enter the next grade (-1 to quit): -1

Total number of students: 12
Average grade: 82.08
Highest grade: 98
Lowest grade: 69
```

If at least one positive grade was entered, then `count` is not equal to zero after the loop, and the `else` portion of the `if` statement is executed. The average is computed by dividing the sum of the grades by the number of grades. Note that the `if` statement prevents us from attempting to divide by zero in situations where no valid grades are entered. We want to design robust programs that handle unexpected or erroneous input without a run-time error. This solution is robust up to a point because it processes any numeric input without a problem but would fail if a nonnumeric, like a word, is entered at the grade prompt.

3.10 Drawing using Conditionals and Loops

Although they are not specifically related to graphics, the use of conditionals and loops greatly enhance our ability to generate interesting graphics.

The program called `Bullseye`, which is shown in Listing 3.17, uses a loop to draw a specific number of rings of a target.

Listing 3.17

```
//********************************************************************
//  Bullseye.java       Author: Lewis and Loftus
//
//  Demonstrates the use of conditionals and loops to guide drawing.
//********************************************************************

import java.applet.Applet;
import java.awt.*;

public class Bullseye extends Applet
{
   private final int MAX_WIDTH = 300;
   private final int NUM_RINGS = 5;
   private final int RING_WIDTH = 25;

   //-----------------------------------------------------------------
   //  Paints a bullseye target.
   //-----------------------------------------------------------------
   public void paint (Graphics page)
   {
      int x = 0, y = 0, diameter;
```

Listing 3.17 ***(continued)***

```
      setBackground (Color.cyan);

      diameter = MAX_WIDTH;
      page.setColor (Color.white);

      for (int count = 0; count < NUM_RINGS; count++)
      {
         if (page.getColor() == Color.black)  // alternate colors
            page.setColor (Color.white);
         else
            page.setColor (Color.black);

         page.fillOval (x, y, diameter, diameter);

         diameter -= (2 * RING_WIDTH);
         x += RING_WIDTH;
         y += RING_WIDTH;
      }

      // Draw the red bullseye in the center
      page.setColor (Color.red);
      page.fillOval (x, y, diameter, diameter);
   }
}
```

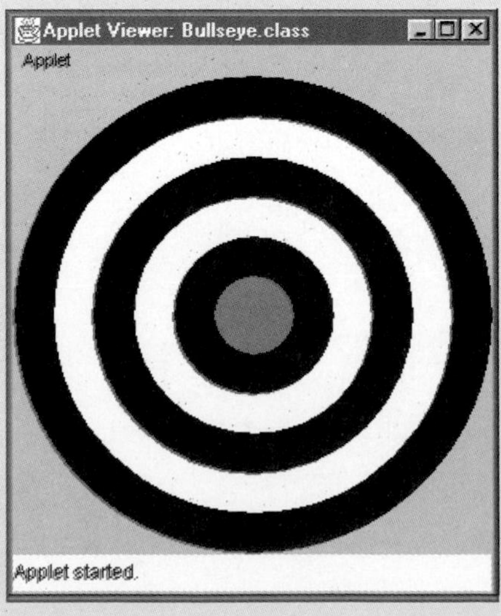

The `Bullseye` program uses an `if` statement to alternate the colors between black and white. Note that each ring is actually drawn as a filled circle (an oval of equal width and length). Because we draw each circle on top of each other, the inner circles "cover" the inner part of the larger circles, creating the ring effect. At the end, a final red circle is drawn for the bullseye.

Listing 3.18 shows the `Boxes` applet, in which several randomly sized rectangles are drawn in random locations. If the width of a rectangle is below a certain thickness (5 pixels), that box is filled with the color yellow. If the height is less than the same thickness, the box is filled with the color green. Otherwise, the box is drawn, unfilled, in white.

Listing 3.18

```
//********************************************************************
//  Boxes.java       Author: Lewis and Loftus
//
//  Demonstrates the use of conditionals and loops to guide drawing.
//********************************************************************

import java.applet.Applet;
import java.awt.*;

public class Boxes extends Applet
{
   private final int NUM_BOXES = 50;
   private final int THICKNESS = 5;
   private final int MAX_SIDE = 50;
   private final int MAX_X = 350;
   private final int MAX_Y = 250;

   //-----------------------------------------------------------------
   //  Paints boxes of random width and height in a random location.
   //  Narrow or short boxes are highlighted with a fill color.
   //-----------------------------------------------------------------
   public void paint(Graphics page)
   {
      int x, y, width, height;

      setBackground (Color.black);
```

Listing 3.18 ***(continued)***

```
      for (int count = 0; count < NUM_BOXES; count++)
      {
         x = (int) (Math.random() * MAX_X);
         y = (int) (Math.random() * MAX_Y);

         width = (int) (Math.random() * MAX_SIDE);
         height = (int) (Math.random() * MAX_SIDE);

         if (width <= THICKNESS)  // check for narrow box
         {
            page.setColor (Color.yellow);
            page.fillRect (x, y, width, height);
         }
         else
            if (height <= THICKNESS)  // check for short box
            {
               page.setColor (Color.green);
               page.fillRect (x, y, width, height);
            }
            else
            {
               page.setColor (Color.white);
               page.drawRect (x, y, width, height);
            }
      }
   }
}
```

Listing 3.18 ***(continued)***

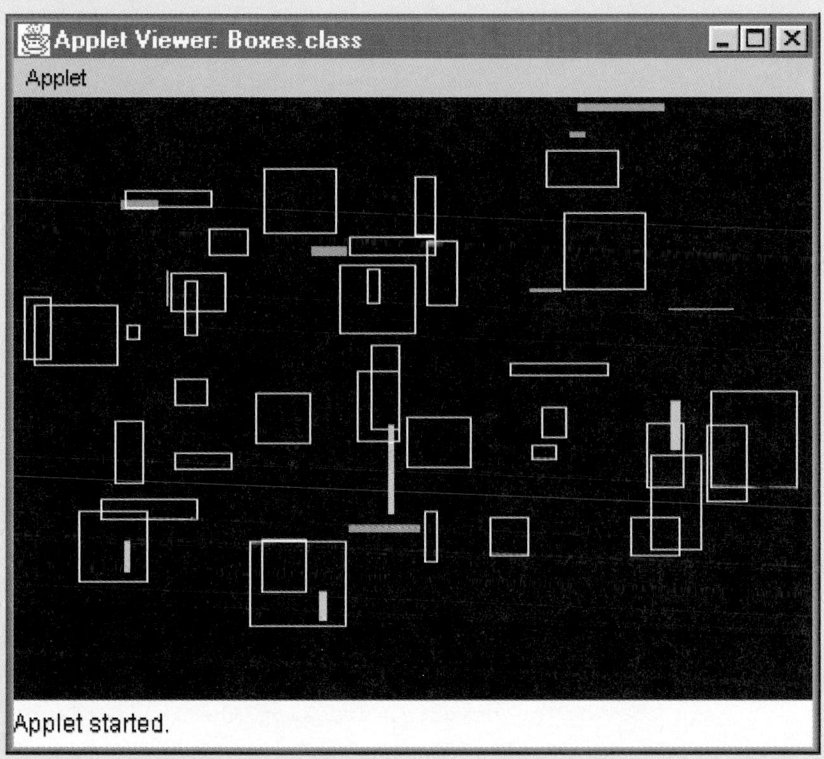

Note that in the `Boxes` program, the color is decided before each rectangle is drawn. In the `BarHeights` applet, shown in Listing 3.19, we handle the situation differently. The goal of `BarHeights` is to draw 10 vertical bars of random heights, coloring the tallest bar in red and the shortest bar in yellow.

Listing 3.19

```
//********************************************************************
//  BarHeights.java       Author: Lewis and Loftus
//
//  Demonstrates the use of conditionals and loops to guide drawing.
//********************************************************************

import java.applet.Applet;
import java.awt.*;

public class BarHeights extends Applet
{
   private final int NUM_BARS = 10;
   private final int BAR_WIDTH = 30;
   private final int MAX_HEIGHT = 300;
   private final int GAP = 9;

   //-----------------------------------------------------------------
   //  Paints bars of varying heights, tracking the tallest and
   //  shortest bars, which are redrawn in color at the end.
   //-----------------------------------------------------------------
   public void paint (Graphics page)
   {
      int x, height;
      int tallX = 0, tallest = 0, shortX = 0, shortest = MAX_HEIGHT;

      setBackground (Color.black);

      page.setColor (Color.blue);
      x = GAP;

      for (int count = 0; count < NUM_BARS; count++)
      {
         height = (int) (Math.random() * MAX_HEIGHT);
         page.fillRect (x, MAX_HEIGHT-height, BAR_WIDTH, height);
```

Listing 3.19 ***(continued)***

```
         // Keep track of the tallest and shortest bars
         if (height > tallest)
         {
            tallX = x;
            tallest = height;
         }

         if (height < shortest)
         {
            shortX = x;
            shortest = height;
         }

         x = x + BAR_WIDTH + GAP;
      }

      // Redraw the tallest bar in red
      page.setColor (Color.red);
      page.fillRect (tallX, MAX_HEIGHT-tallest, BAR_WIDTH, tallest);

      // Redraw the shortest bar in yellow
      page.setColor (Color.yellow);
      page.fillRect (shortX, MAX_HEIGHT-shortest, BAR_WIDTH, shortest);
   }
}
```

Listing 3.19 ***(continued)***

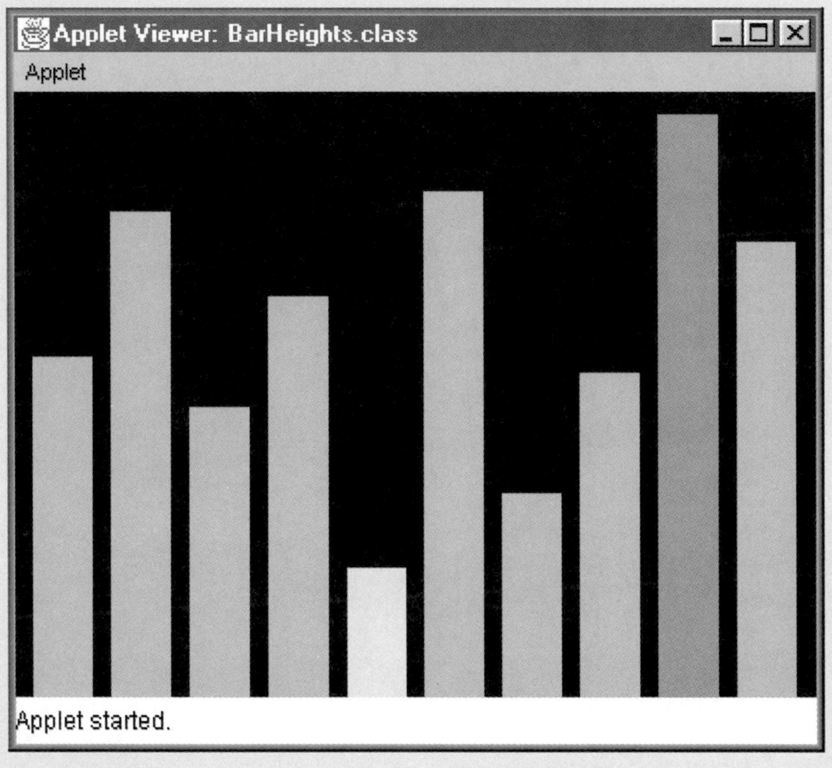

In the `BarHeights` program, we don't know if the bar we are about to draw is either the highest or the shortest, because we haven't created them all yet. Therefore, we keep track of the position of both the highest and shortest as they are drawn, then after they are all drawn, go back and redraw these two in the appropriate color.

Summary of Key Concepts

- Conditionals and loops allow us to control the flow of execution through a method.
- An `if` statement allows a program to choose whether or not to execute a particular statement.
- Even though the compiler does not care about indentation, proper indentation is essential for human readability; it shows the relationship between one statement and another.
- An `if-else` statement allows a program to do one thing if a condition is true and a different thing if the condition is false.
- In a nested `if` statement, an `else` clause is matched to the closest unmatched `if`.
- A `break` statement is usually used at the end of each case alternative of a `switch` statement to jump to the end of the switch.
- A `switch` statement could be implemented as a series of `if-else` statements, but the `switch` is often a more convenient and readable construct.
- Logical operators return a boolean value and are often used to construct sophisticated conditions.
- The prefix and postfix increment and decrement operators have subtle effects on programs because of differences in when they are evaluated.
- A `while` statement allows a program to execute the same statement multiple times.
- Design your programs carefully to avoid infinite loops. The body of the loop must eventually make the loop condition false.
- A `do` statement executes its loop body at least once.
- A `for` statement is usually used when a loop will be executed a set number of times.
- Software requirements specify what a program must accomplish.
- A software design specifies how a program will accomplish its requirements.
- An algorithm is a step-by-step process for solving a problem.
- Implementation is the process of writing source code, based on the design.
- Testing a program involves running it multiple times with various input and observing the results; the goal is to find errors.

▶ Self-Review Questions

3.1 What type of conditions are conditionals and loops based on?

3.2 What is a nested `if`? A nested loop?

3.3 How do block statements help us in the construction of conditionals and loops?

3.4 What happens if a case in a `switch` does not end with a `break` statement?

3.5 What is a truth table?

3.6 What is an infinite loop? Specifically, what causes it?

3.7 Why would we use a `for` loop instead of a `while` loop?

3.8 Name the four basic activities that are involved in a software development process.

3.9 What is an algorithm? What is pseudocode?

▶ Exercises

3.1 Using various relational and logical operators, give an equivalent expression for each of the following:

a. `total < sum`

b. `MAX <= highest`

c. `intensity > threshold`

3.2 What happens in the `MinOfThree` program if two or more of the values are equal? If exactly two of the values are equal, does it matter whether the equal values are lower or higher than the third?

3.3 Give four different statements that increment the value of an integer variable total.

3.4 Given the following declarations, trace the output of the listed conditional statements.

```
int i = 6;
int j = 9;
```

a.
```
if (i < j)
     System.out.println ("Rapping");
```

b.
```
if (i < j/2)
   System.out.println ("Rapping");
else
   System.out.println ("Ravin");
```

c.
```
if (i < j)
   System.out.println ("Rapping");
   if (j > 7)
      System.out.println ("Chamber Door");
else
   System.out.println ("Ravin");
```

d.
```
if (i < j)
   System.out.println ("Rapping");
   if (j < i * 2)
      System.out.println ("Chamber Door");
   else
      System.out.println ("Ravin");
```

e.
```
if (i > j)
   System.out.println ("Rapping");
```

3.5 What is wrong with the following code fragment? Rewrite it so that it produces correct output.

```
if (total == MAX)
   if (total < sum)
      System.out.println ("total equals MAX and is less than sum.");
else
   System.out.println ("total is not equal to MAX");
```

3.6 What is wrong with the following code fragment? Will this code compile if it is part of a valid program? Explain completely.

```
if (length = MIN_LENGTH)
   System.out.println ("The length cannot be reduced.");
```

3.7 Trace the execution of the following loops.

a.
```
int i = 1;
while (i < 10)
{
   System.out.println ("Nevermore");
   i++;
}
```

b.
```
int i = 2;
while (i < 10)
{
   System.out.println ("Nevermore");
   i++;
}
```

c.
```
int i = 1;
while (i <= 10)
{
   System.out.println ("Nevermore");
   i = i + 2;
}
```

d.
```
int i = 10;
while (i > 1)
{
   System.out.println ("Nevermore");
   i--;
}
```

e.
```
int i = 1;
while (i > 10)
{
   System.out.println ("Nevermore");
}
```

3.8 Trace the execution of the following loops.

a.
```
for (int i = 1; i < 10; i++)
   System.out.println (i);
```

b.
```
for (int i = 1; i <= 10; i++)
   System.out.println (i);
```

c.
```
for (int i = 1; i < 10 * 2; i++)
   System.out.println (i);
```

d.
```
for (int i = 10; i > 10; i--)
   System.out.println (i);
```

e.
```
for (int i = -2; i < 10; i++)
   System.out.println (i);
```

f.
```
for (int i = 1; i < 10; i = i * 2)
   System.out.println (i);
```

g.
```
for (int i = 11; i < 10; i++)
   System.out.println (i);
```

3.9 Trace the execution of the following loops.

a.
```
int i = 1;
do
{
   System.out.println (i);
   i++;
}
while (i < 10);
```

b.
```
int i = 1;
do
{
   i++;
   System.out.println (i);
}
while (i < 10);
```

c.
```
int i = 10;
do
{
   i--;
   System.out.println (i);
}
while (i < 10);
```

3.10 Transform the following `while` loop into a `for` loop and a `do` loop.

```
int i = 1;
while (i < 20)
{
   i++;
   System.out.println (i);
}
```

3.11 What is wrong with the following code fragment? What are three distinct ways it could be changed to remove the flaw?

```
count = 50;
while (count >= 0)
{
   System.out.println (count);
   count = count + 1;
}
```

Programming Projects

3.1 Design and implement an application that reads an integer value and prints the sum of all even integers between 2 and the input value, inclusive. Print an error message if the input value is less than 2. Prompt accordingly.

3.2 Design and implement an application that reads a string from the user and prints it one character per line.

3.3 Design and implement an application that determines and prints the number of odd, even, and zero digits in an integer value read from the user.

3.4 Design and implement an application that produces a multiplication table, showing the results of multiplying the integers 1 through 12 by themselves.

3.5 Create a revised version of the `Counter2` program such that the `println` statement comes before the counter increment in the body of the loop. Make sure the program still produces the same output.

3.6 Design and implement an application that prints the first few verses of the traveling song "One Hundred Bottles of Beer." Use a loop such that each iteration prints one verse. Read the number of verses to print from the user. Validate the input. The following are the first two verses of the song:

```
100 bottles of beer on the wall
100 bottles of beer
If one of those bottles should happen to fall
99 bottles of beer on the wall

99 bottles of beer on the wall
99 bottles of beer
If one of those bottles should happen to fall
98 bottles of beer on the wall
```

3.7 Design and implement an application that plays the HI-LO guessing game with numbers. The program should pick a random number between 1 and 100 (inclusive), then repeatedly prompt the user to guess the number. On each guess, report to the user that they are correct, or whether the guess was high or low. Continue accepting guesses until the user guesses correctly or chooses to quit. Use a sentinel value to determine if the user wants to quit. Count the number of guesses and report that value when the user guesses correctly. At the end of each game (by quitting or correct guess), prompt to see if the user wants to play again. Continue playing games until the user chooses to stop.

3.8 Create modified versions of the `Stars` program to print the following patterns. Create a separate program to produce each pattern. *Hint:* Parts b, c, and d require several loops, some of which print a specific number of spaces.

```
a. **********    b.          *    c. **********    d.     *
   *********              **        *********          ***
   ********              ***         ********         *****
   *******              ****          *******        *******
   ******              *****           ******       *********
   *****              ******            *****       *********
   ****              *******             ****        *******
   ***              ********              ***         *****
   **              *********               **          ***
   *              **********                *           *
```

3.9 Design and implement an application that prints a table showing a subset of the Unicode characters and their numeric values. Print five number/character pairs per line, separated by tab characters. Print the table for numeric values from 32 (the space character) to 126 (the ~ character), which corresponds to the printable ASCII subset of the Unicode character set. Compare your output to the table in Appendix C. Unlike the table in Appendix C, the values in your table can increase as they go across a row.

3.10 Design and implement an application that reads a string from the user, then determines and prints how many of each vowel (a, e, i, o, and u) appear in the string. Have a separate counter for each vowel. Also count and print the number of nonvowel characters.

3.11 Design and implement an application that plays the Rock-Paper-Scissors game against the computer. When played between two people, each person picks one of the three options (usually shown by a hand gesture) at the same time and a winner is determined. In the game, Rock beats Scissors, Scissors beats Paper, and Paper beats Rock. The program should randomly choose one of the three options (without revealing it), then prompt for the user's selection. At that point the program reveals both choices and prints a statement indicating if the user won, the computer won, or if it was a tie. Continue playing until the user chooses to stop; then print the number of user wins, losses, and ties.

3.12 Design and implement an application that prints the verses of the song "The Twelve Days of Christmas," in which each verse adds one line. The first two verses of the song are:

```
On the 1st day of Christmas my true love gave to me
A partridge in a pear tree.

On the 2nd day of Christmas my true love gave to me
Two turtle doves, and
A partridge in a pear tree.
```

Use a `switch` statement in a loop to control which lines get printed. *Hint:* Order the cases carefully and avoid the `break` statement. Use a separate `switch` statement to put the appropriate suffix on the day number (1st, 2nd, 3rd, etc.) The final verse of the song involves all twelve days, as follows:

```
On the 12th day of Christmas, my true love gave to me
Twelve drummers drumming,
Eleven pipers piping,
Ten lords a leaping,
Nine ladies dancing,
Eight maids a milking,
Seven swans a swimming,
Six geese a laying,
Five golden rings,
Four calling birds,
Three French hens,
Two turtle doves, and
A partridge in a pear tree.
```

3.13 Design and implement an application that simulates a simple slot machine in which three numbers between 0 and 9 are randomly selected and printed side by side. Print an appropriate statement if all three of the numbers are the same. Continue playing until the user chooses to stop.

3.14 Create a modified version of the `ExamGrades` program to validate the grades entered to make sure they are in the range 0 to 100, inclusive. Print an error message if a grade is not valid; then continue to collect grades. Continue to use the sentinel value to indicate the end of the input, but do not print an error message when it is entered. Do not count an invalid grade or include it as part of the running sum.

3.15 Design and implement an applet that draws 20 horizontal, evenly spaced, parallel lines of random length.

3.16 Design and implement an applet that draws the side view of stair steps from the lower left to the upper right.

3.17 Design and implement an applet that draws 100 circles of random color and random diameter in random locations. Ensure that in each case the entire circle appears in the visible area of the applet.

3.18 Design and implement an applet that draws 10 concentric circles of random radius.

3.19 Design and implement an applet that draws a brick wall pattern in which each row of bricks is off center from the row above and below it.

3.20 Design and implement an applet that draws a quilt in which a simple pattern is repeated in a grid of squares.

3.21 Design and implement an applet that draws a simple fence with vertical, equally spaced boards backed by two horizontal support boards. Behind the fence show a simple house in the background. Make sure the house is visible through the open slats in the fence.

3.22 Design and implement an applet that draws a rainbow. Use tightly spaced, concentric arcs to draw each part of the rainbow in a particular color.

3.23 Design and implement an applet that draws 20,000 points in random locations within the visible area of the applet. Make the points on the left half of the applet appear in red and the points on the right half of the applet appear in green. Draw a point by drawing a line with a length of only one pixel.

3.24 Design and implement an applet that draws 10 circles of random radius in random locations. Fill in the largest circle in red.

▶ Answers to Self-Review Questions

3.1 Conditionals and loops are based on a boolean condition that evaluates to either true or false.

3.2 A nested `if` occurs when the statement inside an `if` or `else` clause is an `if` statement. A nested `if` lets us make a series of multiple decisions. Likewise, a nested loop is a loop within a loop.

3.3 A block statement groups several statements together. We use them to define the body of an `if` statement or loop when we want to do multiple things based on the boolean condition.

3.4 If a case does not end with a `break` statement, processing continues into the next case. We usually want the `break` statements in order to jump to the end of the `switch`.

3.5 A truth table is a table that shows all possible results of a boolean expression, given all possible combinations of variables and subconditions.

3.6 An infinite loop is a repetition statement that never terminates. Specifically, the body of the loop never causes the condition to become false.

3.7 A `for` loop is usually used when we know how many times we want to iterate through the loop body and a `while` sets up a more generic situation.

3.8 Software development consists of requirements analysis, design, implementation, and testing.

3.9 An algorithm is a step-by-step process that describes the solution to a problem. Every program can be described in algorithmic terms. An algorithm is often expressed in pseudocode, a loose combination of English and code-like terms used to capture the basic processing steps informally.

Writing Classes

In Chapters 2 and 3 we used objects and classes for the various services they provide, and explored several fundamental programming statements. With that experience as a foundation, we are now ready to design more complex software. In particular, in this chapter we turn our attention to writing our own classes to define our own objects to perform whatever services we choose.

Chapter Objectives

- Define classes that serve as blueprints for new objects, composed of variables and methods.
- Explain the advantages of encapsulation and the use of Java modifiers to accomplish it.
- Explore the details of method declarations.
- Revisit the concepts of method invocation and parameter passing.
- Describe various relationships between objects.
- Explain and use method overloading to create versatile classes.
- Demonstrate the usefulness of method decomposition with respect to object abstraction.
- Create graphics-based objects.

4.1 Objects Revisited

We've used objects in previous examples for their particular services, and in this chapter we will define our own objects to serve specific needs. Before we do, however, it's important for us to revisit the concept of an object and think about it in more detail.

What is an object? Think about objects in the world around you. How would you describe them? Let's use a ball as an example. A ball has particular characteristics such as its diameter, color, and elasticity. Formally, we say these characteristics contribute to the ball's *state of being*. We also describe a ball by what it does, such as the fact that it can be thrown, bounced, or rolled. These activities define the ball's *behavior.*

Key Concept

An object contains variables and methods. The values of the variables define the state of the object and the methods define the behaviors of the object.

All objects, including software objects, have a state and a set of behaviors. These correspond to the object's variables and methods. The values of the variables describe the object's state, and the methods define the object's behaviors.

Consider a computer game that plays baseball. The baseball could be represented as an object. It would have variables to store its size and location, and methods that draw it on the screen and calculate how it moves when hit. The variables and methods defined in the ball object establish the state and behavior that are relevant to the ball's use in the computerized baseball game.

Each object has its own state. Each ball object has a particular location and size, which is often different from another ball's state. Behaviors, though, tend to apply to all objects of a particular type. For instance, in general, any ball can be thrown, bounced, or rolled. The act of rolling a ball is generally the same for any kind of ball.

The state of an object and its behaviors work together. How high a ball bounces depends on its elasticity. The action is the same, but the specific result depends on that particular object's state. An object's behavior often modifies its state. For example, when a ball is rolled, its position changes.

Any object can generally be described in terms of state and behavior. Let's consider another example. In software used to manage a university, a student could be represented as an object. The collection of all such objects represents the entire student body. Each student has a state. That is, each object would contain the variables that store information about a particular student, such as name, address, major, courses taken, grades, and grade point average. The student object also has behaviors. For example, the student object may contain a method to add a new course.

Although software objects often represent tangible items, they don't have to. An error message can be an object, for instance. A common mistake is to limit the possibilities to tangible entities.

Classes

Objects are defined by classes. A class is the model, or pattern, or blueprint, from which an object is created.

Consider the blueprint created by an architect when designing a house. The blueprint defines the important characteristics of the house: walls, windows, doors, electrical outlets, and so forth. Once the blueprints are created, several houses can be built using the same blueprint, as depicted in Figure 4.1. In one sense, the houses built from the blueprint are different. They are physically in different places, have different addresses, different furniture, and different people live in them. Yet, in many ways they are the "same" house. The layout of the rooms and other crucial characteristics are the same in each. To create a completely different house, we would need a different blueprint.

A class is a blueprint of an object. It defines the types of data that will be held in an object, and defines the code for the methods. But a class is not an object any more than a blueprint is a house. Generally, no data space is reserved in a class. We have to instantiate one or more objects from the class. Each object will have its own space for data, which is why each object can have its own state.

Key Concept

A class is a blueprint of an object; it reserves no memory space for data. Each object has its own data space; an object is an instance of a class.

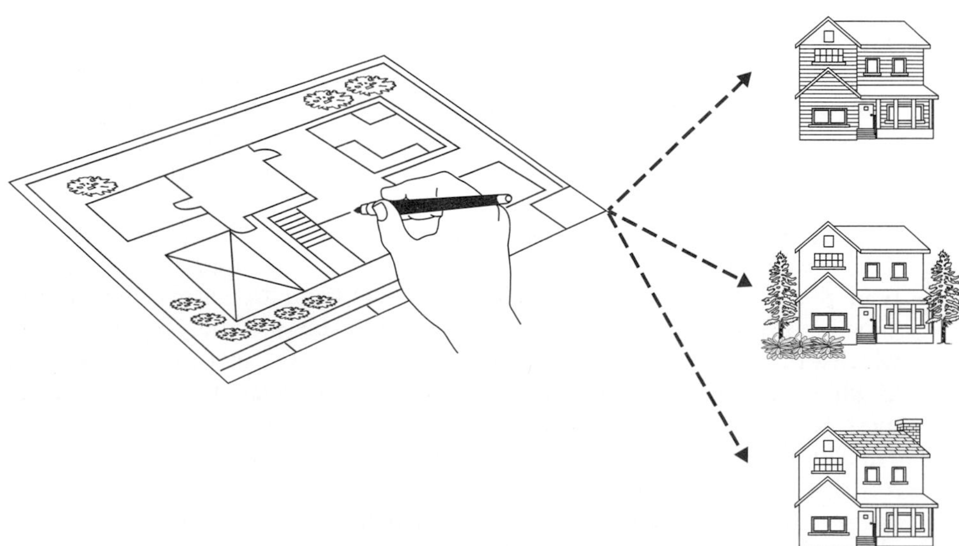

Figure 4.1 A house blueprint and three houses created from it

4.2 Anatomy of a Class

A class can contain any number of data declarations and methods, which are collectively called the *members* of a class.

Consider the `CountFlips` program, shown in Listing 4.1. It uses an object that represents a coin that you can flip to get a random result of "heads" or "tails." The `CountFlips` program simulates the flipping of a coin 1,000 times to see how often it comes up heads or tails. The coin object is instantiated from a class called `Coin`.

The `Coin` class used by the `CountFlips` program is shown in Listing 4.2. A class, and therefore any object created from it, is composed of data values (variables and constants) and methods. In the `Coin` class, we have two integer constants, `HEADS` and `TAILS`, and one integer variable, `face`. The rest of the `Coin` class is composed of four methods: `Coin`, `flip`, `getFace`, and `toString`.

The first method, `Coin`, defines a constructor for the class, which is why it has the same name as the class. This is the method that gets called when the `new` operator creates a new instance of the `Coin` class. The rest of the methods define the various services provided by `Coin` objects.

Note that a header block of documentation is used to explain the purpose of each method in the class. This practice is not only crucial for anyone trying to understand the software, it also separates the code visually so that it's easier to jump from one method to the next while reading. The definitions of these methods have various parts and are dissected in later sections of this chapter.

The services defined in the `Coin` class are listed in Figure 4.2. From this point of view, it looks no different than any other class that we've used in previous examples. The only important difference is that the `Coin` class was not provided for us by some third-party class library. We had to write it ourselves.

Instance Data

Note that in the `Coin` class, the constants `HEADS` and `TAILS` and the variable `face` are declared inside the class, but not inside any method. The location at which a variable is declared defines its *scope*, which is the area within a program in which that variable can be referenced. By being declared at the class level, these variables and constants can be referred to in any method of the class.

This data is also called *instance data*, because its memory space is created for each instance of the class that is created. Each coin object, for example, has its own `face` variable with its own data space. Therefore, two `Coin` objects can have a different state relative to the face that is showing at any point in time.

Listing 4.1

```
//********************************************************************
//  CountFlips.java       Author: Lewis and Loftus
//
//  Demonstrates the use of a programmer-defined class.
//********************************************************************

import Coin;

public class CountFlips
{
   //-----------------------------------------------------------------
   //  Flips a coin multiple times and counts the number of heads
   //  and tails that result.
   //-----------------------------------------------------------------
   public static void main (String[] args)
   {
      final int NUM_FLIPS = 1000;
      int headCount = 0, tailCount = 0;

      Coin myCoin = new Coin();  // instantiate a Coin object

      for (int count=1; count <= NUM_FLIPS; count++)
      {
         myCoin.flip();

         if (myCoin.getFace() == myCoin.HEADS)
            headCount++;
         else
            tailCount++;
      }

      System.out.println ("The number flips: " + NUM_FLIPS);
      System.out.println ("The number of heads: " + headCount);
      System.out.println ("The number of tails: " + tailCount);
   }
}
```

```
The number flips: 1000
The number of heads: 486
The number of tails: 514
```

Listing 4.2

```
//********************************************************************
//  Coin.java       Author: Lewis and Loftus
//
//  Represents a coin with two sides that can be flipped.
//********************************************************************

public class Coin
{
   public final int HEADS = 0;
   public final int TAILS = 1;

   private int face;

   //-----------------------------------------------------------------
   //  Sets up the coin by flipping it initially.
   //-----------------------------------------------------------------
   public Coin ()
   {
      flip();
   }

   //-----------------------------------------------------------------
   //  Flips the coin by randomly choosing a face.
   //-----------------------------------------------------------------
   public void flip ()
   {
      face = (int) (Math.random() * 2);
   }

   //-----------------------------------------------------------------
   //  Returns the current face of the coin as an integer.
   //-----------------------------------------------------------------
   public int getFace ()
   {
      return face;
   }
```

Listing 4.2 *(continued)*

```
   //-----------------------------------------------------------------
   //  Returns the current face of the coin as a string.
   //-----------------------------------------------------------------
   public String toString()
   {
      String faceName;

      if (face == HEADS)
         faceName = "Heads";
      else
         faceName = "Tails";

      return faceName;
   }
}
```

`Coin ()`
Constructor: creates a new `Coin` object with a random initial face.

`void flip ()`
Flips the coin.

`int getFace ()`
Returns an integer indicating the current face of the coin.

`String toString ()`
Returns a string describing the current face of the coin.

Figure 4.2 Some methods of the `Coin` class

The program `FlipRace`, shown in Listing 4.3, declares two `Coin` objects. They are used in a race to see which coin will flip to three heads in a row first.

Note that at any point during the race, `coin1` has a particular face showing, which may or may not be the same as the face showing on `coin2`. Each

Listing 4.3

```
//********************************************************************
//  FlipRace.java       Author: Lewis and Loftus
//
//  Demonstrates the existence of separate data space in multiple
//  instantiations of a programmer-defined class.
//********************************************************************

import Coin;

public class FlipRace
{
   //-----------------------------------------------------------------
   //  Flips two coins until one of them comes up heads a set number
   //  of times in a row.
   //-----------------------------------------------------------------
   public static void main (String[] args)
   {
      final int GOAL = 3;
      int count1 = 0, count2 = 0;

      // Create two separate coin objects
      Coin coin1 = new Coin();
      Coin coin2 = new Coin();

      while (count1 < GOAL && count2 < GOAL)
      {
         coin1.flip();
         coin2.flip();

         // Print the flip results (uses Coin's toString method)
         System.out.print ("Coin 1: " + coin1);
         System.out.println ("   Coin 2: " + coin2);

         // Increment or reset the counters
         count1 = (coin1.getFace() == coin1.HEADS) ? count1+1 : 0;
         count2 = (coin2.getFace() == coin2.HEADS) ? count2+1 : 0;
      }
```

Listing 4.3 ***(continued)***

```
      // Determine the winner
      if (count1 < GOAL)
         System.out.println ("Coin 2 Wins!");
      else
         if (count2 < GOAL)
            System.out.println ("Coin 1 Wins!");
         else
            System.out.println ("It's a TIE!");
   }
}
```

```
Coin 1: Heads   Coin 2: Tails
Coin 1: Heads   Coin 2: Tails
Coin 1: Tails   Coin 2: Heads
Coin 1: Tails   Coin 2: Heads
Coin 1: Heads   Coin 2: Tails
Coin 1: Tails   Coin 2: Heads
Coin 1: Heads   Coin 2: Tails
Coin 1: Heads   Coin 2: Heads
Coin 1: Heads   Coin 2: Tails
Coin 1 Wins!
```

coin object has a variable called `face` that represents a unique place in memory to store a value.

Key Concept

Classes define the variables for an object, but reserve no memory space for them. Each object, when instantiated, has a unique storage space for variables, and therefore their values can be different. Methods, however, are shared among all objects of a class.

The output of the `FlipRace` program shows the results of each coin flip on each turn. The object reference variables, `coin1` and `coin2`, are used in the `println` statement. When an object is used as an operand of the string concatenation operator (+), that object's `toString` method is automatically called to get a string representation of the object. The `toString` method is also called if an object is sent to a `print` or `println` method by itself. If no `toString` method is defined for a particular class, a default version is called that returns a string that contains the name of the class. It is usually a good idea to define a `toString` method for classes whose objects may be printed.

Note also, by the way, that we've used the same class, `Coin`, to create objects in two separate programs (`CountFlips` and `FlipRace`). This is no different than using the `String` class in whatever program we need it. When designing a class, it is always good to look to the future and try to give the class behaviors that will be beneficial in other programs, not just fit the specific purpose for which you are creating it at the moment.

Encapsulation and Visibility Modifiers

We can think about an object in one of two ways. The view we take depends on what we are trying to accomplish at the moment. First, when we are designing and implementing an object, we need to think about the details of how an object works. That is, we have to design the class; we have to define the variables that will be held in the object and write the methods that make the object useful.

However, when we are designing a solution to a larger problem, we have to think in terms of how the objects in the program interact. At that level, we only have to think about the services that an object provides, not on the details of how those services are accomplished. As we discussed in Chapter 2, an object provides a level of abstraction that allows us to focus on the larger picture when we need to.

This abstraction works only if we are careful to respect its boundaries. An object should be *self governing,* which means that the variables contained in an object should only be modified within the object. Only the methods within an object should have access to the variables in that object. For example, the methods of the `Coin` class should be solely responsible for changing the value of the `face` variable. We should make it difficult, if not impossible, for code outside of the `Coin` class to "reach in" and change the value of a variable in the class.

The object-oriented term for this characteristic is *encapsulation.* An object should be encapsulated from the rest of the system. It should interact with other parts of a program only through the specific set of methods that define the services that that object provides. These methods define the *interface* between that object and the program that uses it.

Key Concept

Objects should be encapsulated. The rest of a program should interact with an object only through a well-defined interface.

Encapsulation is depicted graphically in Figure 4.3. The code that uses an object, sometimes called the *client* of an object, should not be allowed to access variables directly. The client should interact with the object's methods, and those methods interact with the data encapsulated within the object. For example, the `main` method in the `CountFlips` program calls the `flip` and `getFace` methods of the `coin` object. It should not (and in fact cannot) access the `face` variable directly.

In Java, we accomplish object encapsulation using *modifiers.* A modifier is a Java reserved word that is used to specify particular characteristics of a programming language construct. We've already seen one in use, `final`, which we used to declare a constant. Java has several modifiers that can be used in various ways. Some modifiers can be used together, whereas other combinations are invalid. All of the Java modifiers are discussed in Appendix F.

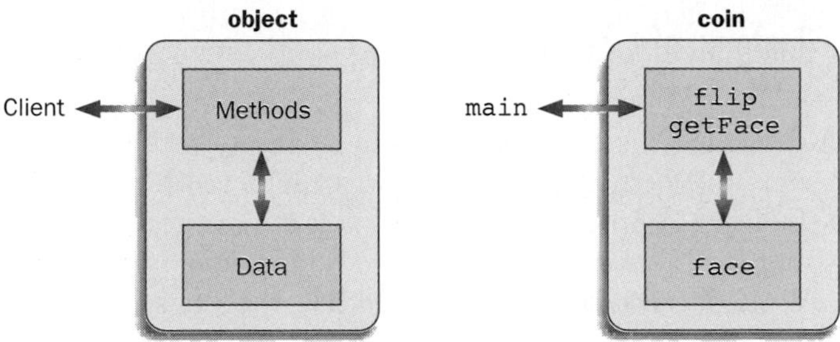

Figure 4.3 A client interacting with the methods of an object

Some Java modifiers are called *visibility modifiers* because they control the extent to which a member of a class can be accessed and referenced. The reserved words `public` and `private` are visibility modifiers that can be applied to the variables and methods of a class. If a variable or method has *public visibility,* then it can be directly referenced from outside of the object. If a member of a class has *private visibility,* it cannot be referenced externally but still can be used anywhere inside the class definition.

In general, if a method provides a service of the class, it should be declared with public visibility. In the `Coin` class, all of the methods are declared with public visibility because we want any part of a program that uses a coin object to be able to invoke the methods. If we had declared `flip` to be `private`, for example, the `main` method in `CountFlips` would not have been able to invoke it. The compiler would have generated an error indicating that the `CountFlips` class did not have the ability to invoke a private method of the `Coin` class.

On the other hand, to promote encapsulation, we declare the variable `face` to be `private`. Therefore the `main` method cannot reference the `face` variable directly without the compiler generating an error message. This is what we want, because a `coin` object should be self-governing, and the `main` method, or any other part of the software, should not be allowed to reach in and change the value of `face`. That control is the responsibility of the methods in the class. Note, though, that the `main` method can call `flip` to change the face of the coin. It can therefore affect the value of `face` indirectly, but not directly.

However, note that the constants `HEADS` and `TAILS` are declared with public visibility. Giving constants public visibility is generally considered acceptable because although their values can be accessed directly, they cannot be changed because they were declared as `final`. Keep in mind that encapsulation means that values should not be changed by another part of the code. We can access the value of `coin.HEADS` in the `CountFlips` class, but we cannot set that constant to another value.

4.3 Anatomy of a Method

We've seen that a class is composed of data declarations and method declarations. Let's examine method declarations in more detail.

As we stated in Chapter 1, a method is a group of programming language statements that are given a name. Every method in Java is part of a particular class. A *method declaration* specifies the code that gets executed when the method is invoked.

When a method is called, the flow of control transfers to that method. One by one, the statements of that method are executed. When that method is done, control returns to the location where the call was made and execution continues. This process is pictured in Figure 4.4.

We've defined the `main` method of a program many times. Its definition follows the same syntax as all methods. The header of a method includes the type of the return value, the method name, and a list of parameters that the method accepts. The statements that make up the body of the method are defined in a block delimited by braces.

Let's look at another example as we explore method declarations. The `BankAccounts` class shown in Listing 4.4 contains a `main` method that creates a few `Account` objects and invokes their services. The `BankAccounts` program doesn't really do anything useful except demonstrate how to interact with `Account` objects. Such programs are often called *driver programs* because all they do is drive the use of other, more interesting, parts of our program. They are often used for testing purposes.

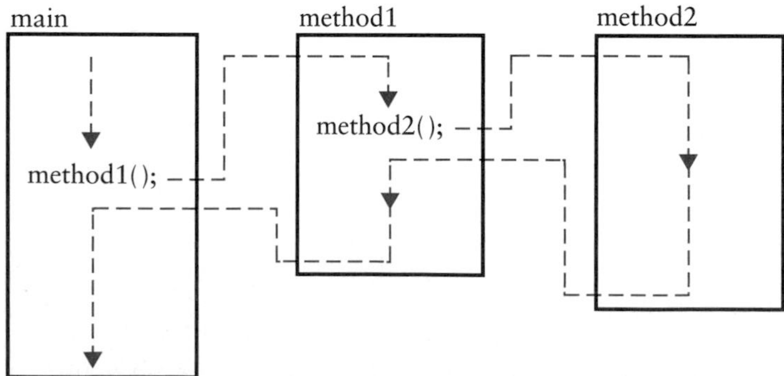

Figure 4.4 The flow of control following method invocations

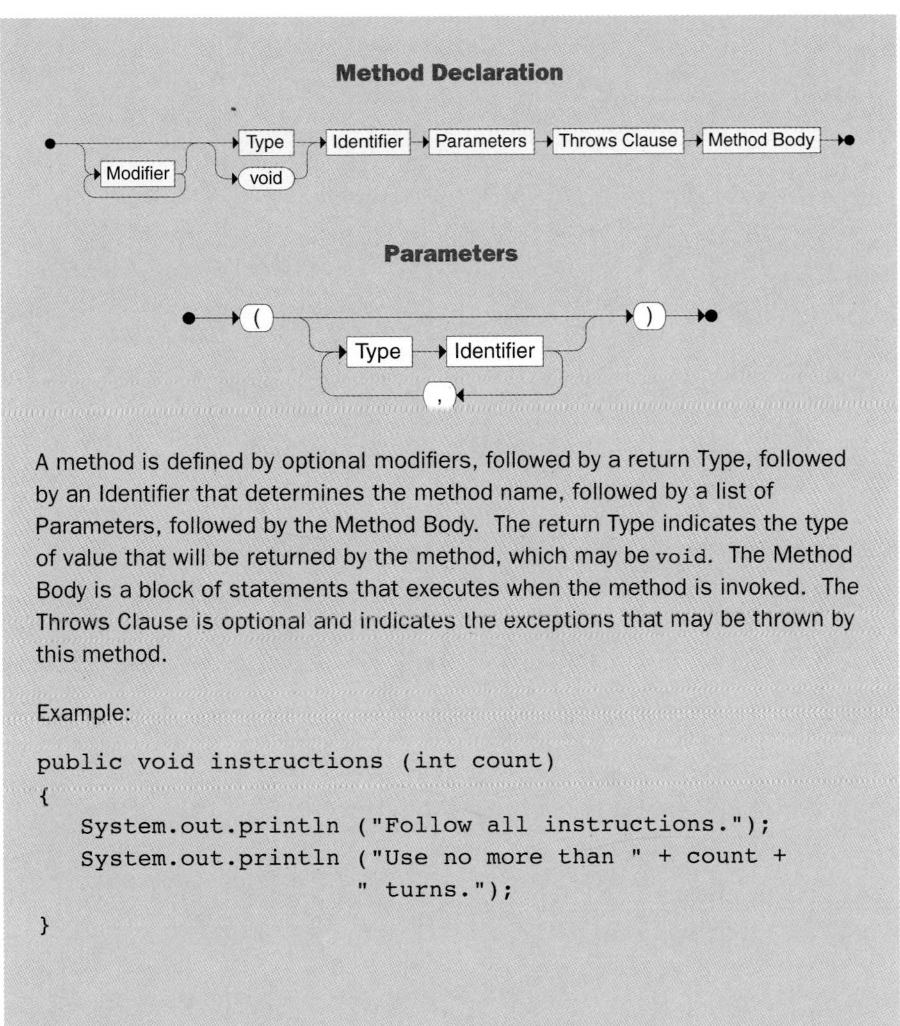

A method is defined by optional modifiers, followed by a return Type, followed by an Identifier that determines the method name, followed by a list of Parameters, followed by the Method Body. The return Type indicates the type of value that will be returned by the method, which may be `void`. The Method Body is a block of statements that executes when the method is invoked. The Throws Clause is optional and indicates the exceptions that may be thrown by this method.

Example:

```
public void instructions (int count)
{
   System.out.println ("Follow all instructions.");
   System.out.println ("Use no more than " + count +
                       " turns.");
}
```

The `Account` class is shown in Listing 4.5. It contains data values important to a bank account: the account number, the balance, and the name of the account's owner. The interest rate for an account is stored as a constant. The methods of the `Account` class perform various services on a bank account, such as making deposits and withdrawals. The methods of the `Account` class are explored in detail in the following sections.

Listing 4.4

```
//********************************************************************
//  BankAccounts.java       Author: Lewis and Loftus
//
//  Driver to exercise the use of multiple Account objects.
//********************************************************************

import Account;

public class BankAccounts
{
   //-----------------------------------------------------------------
   //  Creates some bank accounts and requests various services.
   //-----------------------------------------------------------------
   public static void main (String[] args)
   {
      Account acct1 = new Account ("Ted Murphy", 72354, 102.56);
      Account acct2 = new Account ("Jane Smith", 69713, 40.00);
      Account acct3 = new Account ("Edward Demsey", 93757, 759.32);

      acct1.deposit (25.85);

      double smithBalance = acct2.deposit (500.00);
      System.out.println ("Smith balance after deposit: " +
                          smithBalance);

      System.out.println ("Smith balance after withdrawal: " +
                          acct2.withdraw (430.75, 1.50));

      acct3.withdraw (800.00, 0.0);  // exceeds balance

      acct1.addInterest();
      acct2.addInterest();
      acct3.addInterest();

      System.out.println ();
      System.out.println (acct1);
      System.out.println (acct2);
      System.out.println (acct3);
   }
}
```

Listing 4.4 ***(continued)***

```
Smith balance after deposit: 540.0
Smith balance after withdrawal: 107.75

Error: Insufficient funds.
Account: 93757
Requested: $800.00
Available: $759.32

72354   Ted Murphy       $134.19
69713   Jane Smith       $112.60
93757   Edward Demsey    $793.49
```

Listing 4.5

```
//********************************************************************
//  Account.java       Author: Lewis and Loftus
//
//  Represents a bank account with basic services such as deposit
//  and withdrawal.
//********************************************************************

import java.text.NumberFormat;

public class Account
{
   private NumberFormat fmt = NumberFormat.getCurrencyInstance();

   private final double RATE = 0.045;  // interest rate of 4.5%

   private long acctNumber;
   private double balance;
   private String name;
```

Listing 4.5 ***(continued)***

```
   //-----------------------------------------------------------------
   //  Sets up the account by defining its owner, account number,
   //  and initial balance.
   //-----------------------------------------------------------------
   public Account (String owner, long account, double initial)
   {
      name = owner;
      acctNumber = account;
      balance = initial;
   }

   //-----------------------------------------------------------------
   //  Validates the transaction, then deposits the specified amount
   //  into the account. Returns the new balance.
   //-----------------------------------------------------------------
   public double deposit (double amount)
   {
      if (amount < 0)  // deposit value is negative
      {
         System.out.println ();
         System.out.println ("Error: Deposit amount is invalid.");
         System.out.println (acctNumber + "  " + fmt.format(amount));
      }
      else
         balance = balance + amount;

      return balance;
   }

   //-----------------------------------------------------------------
   //  Validates the transaction, then withdraws the specified amount
   //  from the account. Returns the new balance.
   //-----------------------------------------------------------------
   public double withdraw (double amount, double fee)
   {
      amount += fee;

      if (amount < 0)  // withdraw value is negative
```

Listing 4.5 ***(continued)***

```
      {
         System.out.println ();
         System.out.println ("Error: Withdraw amount is invalid.");
         System.out.println ("Account: " + acctNumber);
         System.out.println ("Requested: " + fmt.format(amount));
      }
      else
         if (amount > balance)  // withdraw value exceeds balance
         {
            System.out.println ();
            System.out.println ("Error: Insufficient funds.");
            System.out.println ("Account: " + acctNumber);
            System.out.println ("Requested: " + fmt.format(amount));
            System.out.println ("Available: " + fmt.format(balance));
         }
         else
            balance = balance - amount;

      return balance;
   }

   //-----------------------------------------------------------------
   //  Adds interest to the account and returns the new balance.
   //-----------------------------------------------------------------
   public double addInterest ()
   {
      balance += (balance * RATE);
      return balance;
   }

   //-----------------------------------------------------------------
   //  Returns the current balance of the account.
   //-----------------------------------------------------------------
   public double getBalance ()
   {
      return balance;
   }
```

Listing 4.5 ***(continued)***

```
   //-----------------------------------------------------------------
   //  Returns the account number.
   //-----------------------------------------------------------------
   public long getAccountNumber ()
   {
      return acctNumber;
   }

   //-----------------------------------------------------------------
   //  Returns a one-line description of the account as a string.
   //-----------------------------------------------------------------
   public String toString ()
   {
      return (acctNumber + "\t" + name + "\t" + fmt.format(balance));
   }
}
```

The `return` Statement

The return type specified in the method header can be a primitive type, class name, or the reserved word `void`. When a method does not return any value, `void` is used as the return type, as is always done with the `main` method.

Key Concept

A method must return a value consistent with the return type specified in the method header.

A method that returns a value must have a *return statement.* When executed, control is immediately returned to the statement in the calling method and processing continues there. A `return` statement consists of the reserved word `return` followed by an expression that dictates the value that gets returned. The expression must be consistent with the return type in the method header.

A method that does not return a value does not usually contain a `return` statement. The method automatically returns to the calling method when the end of the method is reached. A `void` method may, however, contain a `return` statement without an expression.

It is usually not good practice to use more than one `return` statement in a method even though it is possible to do so. In general, a method should have one `return` statement as the last line of the method body, unless that makes the method overly complex.

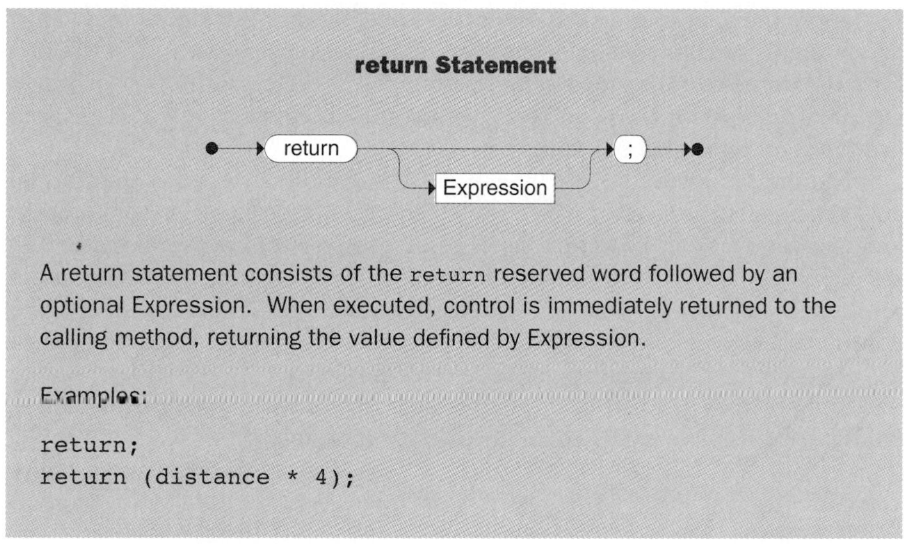

return Statement
return
Expression
;
A return statement consists of the return reserved word followed by an optional Expression. When executed, control is immediately returned to the calling method, returning the value defined by Expression.
Examples:
return;
return (distance * 4);

Many of the methods of the `Account` class return a double that represents the balance of the account. Constructors do not have a return type at all (not even `void`), and therefore cannot have a `return` statement. Constructors are discussed in more detail in a later section.

Note that a return value can be ignored when the invocation is made. In the `main` method of the `BankAccounts` class, sometimes the value that is returned by a method is used in some way, and in other cases the value that gets returned is simply ignored.

Parameters

A *parameter* is a value that is passed into a method when it is invoked. The *parameter list* in the header of a method specifies the types of the values that are passed and the names by which the called method will refer to the parameters.

In the method declaration, the names of the accepted parameters are called *formal parameters*. In an invocation, the values passed into a method are called *actual parameters*. A method invocation and definition always give the parameter list in parentheses after the method name. If there are no parameters, an empty set of parentheses is used.

The formal parameters are identifiers that serve as variables inside the method and whose initial values come from the actual parameters in the invocation. Actual parameters can be literals, variables, or full expressions that are evaluated and the result passed as the parameter.

The parameter lists in the invocation and the method declaration must match up. That is, the value of the first actual parameter is stored in the first formal parameter, the second actual parameter in the second formal parameter, etc. The types of the actual parameters must be consistent with the specified types of the formal parameters.

The deposit method of the `Account` class, for instance, takes one formal parameter called `amount` of type `double` representing the amount to be deposited into the account. Each time the method is invoked in the `main` method of the `BankAccounts` class, one literal value of type `double` is passed as an actual parameter. In the case of the withdraw method, two parameters of type `double` are expected and passed. The types and number of parameters must be consistent or the compiler will issue error messages.

Constructors can also take parameters, as discussed in the next section. Parameter passing is discussed in more detail in Chapter 5.

Constructors

As we stated in Chapter 2, a constructor is similar to a method that is invoked when an object is instantiated. When we define a class, we usually define a constructor that helps us set up the class initially.

A constructor is differentiated from a regular method in two ways. First, the name of a constructor is the same name as the class. Therefore, the name of the constructor in the `Coin` class is `Coin`, and the name of the constructor of the `Account` class is `Account`. Second, a constructor cannot return a value and does not have a return type specified in the method header.

A constructor is generally used to initialize the object in some way. For instance, the constructor of the `Coin` class calls the `flip` method initially to determine the face value of the coin. The constructor of the `Account` class explicitly sets the values of the instance variables to the values passed in as parameters to the constructor.

We don't have to define a constructor for every class. Each class has a *default constructor* that takes no parameters and is used if we don't provide our own.

Local Data and Scope

The *scope* of a variable (or constant) is the part of a program in which that variable can validly be referenced. A variable or constant can be declared inside a method, making it *local data* as opposed to instance data, which (as mentioned earlier) is declared in a class but not inside any particular method. Local data has scope limited to only the method in which it is declared. The `faceName` variable declared in the `toString` method of the `Coin` class is local data. Any reference to `faceName` in any other method of the `Coin` class would cause the compiler to issue an error message. A local variable simply does not exist outside of the method in

> **Key Concept**
> A variable declared in a method is local to that method and cannot be used outside of it.

which it is declared. Instance data, declared at the class level, has a scope of the entire class. Any method of the class can refer to it.

Formal parameter names serve as local data of that method. They don't exist until that method is called, and cease to exist when the method is exited. For example, although `amount` is the name of the formal parameter in both the `deposit` and `withdraw` method of the `Account` class, they are two separate pieces of local data that don't exist until the method is invoked.

4.4 Object Relationships

Objects can have particular types of relationships to other objects. This section examines two common relationships, which are established by the way we define the classes of the objects.

The `has-a` Relationship

Some objects are essentially composed of other objects. For example, an `Account` object contains, among other things, a `String` object that represents the name of the account owner. We sometimes tend to forget that strings are objects.

Let's consider another example. Suppose a class called `House` represents a family home. Suppose that an address, with a street name, town, etc. is also represented as an object defined by a class called `Address`. The address of a house would be represented as an `Address` object, which would be created and stored in a `House` object.

This situation is an example of a *has-a relationship*. An *aggregate object* is one that is made up of other objects. A house is an aggregate object because it is made up, in part, of an address. The more complex an object, the more likely it will need to be represented as an aggregate object.

Interaction Between Objects of the Same Class

The methods of the `Account` class used various primitive types of information as parameters. However, methods of a class often have objects as parameters. In fact, one common situation is for an object of one type to perform services using another object of the same type.

The `concat` method of the `String` class is an example of this situation. The method is executed through one `String` object, and is passed another `String` object. The `String` object executing the method appends its characters to those of the `String` passed as a parameter, and a new `String` object is returned as a result.

The `RationalNumbers` program shown in Listing 4.6 demonstrates a similar situation. It creates two objects representing rational numbers, then performs various operations on them to produce new rational numbers.

Listing 4.6

```
//********************************************************************
//  RationalNumbers.java       Author: Lewis and Loftus
//
//  Driver to exercise the use of multiple Rational objects.
//********************************************************************

import Rational;

public class RationalNumbers
{
   //-----------------------------------------------------------------
   //  Creates some rational number objects and performs various
   //  operations on them.
   //-----------------------------------------------------------------
   public static void main (String[] args)
   {
      Rational r1 = new Rational (6, 8);
      Rational r2 = new Rational (1, 3);

      System.out.println ("First rational number: " + r1);
      System.out.println ("Second rational number: " + r2);

      if (r1.equals(r2))
         System.out.println ("r1 and r2 are equal.");
      else
         System.out.println ("r1 and r2 are NOT equal.");

      Rational r3 = r1.add(r2);
      Rational r4 = r1.subtract(r2);
      Rational r5 = r1.multiply(r2);
      Rational r6 = r1.divide(r2);

      System.out.println ("r1 + r2: " + r3);
      System.out.println ("r1 - r2: " + r4);
      System.out.println ("r1 * r2: " + r5);
      System.out.println ("r1 / r2: " + r6);
   }
}
```

```
First rational number: 3/4
Second rational number: 1/3
r1 and r2 are NOT equal.
r1 + r2: 13/12
r1 - r2: 5/12
r1 * r2: 1/4
r1 / r2: 9/4
```

The `Rational` class is shown in Listing 4.7. Each object of type `Rational` represents one rational number. The `Rational` class contains various operations on rational numbers, such as the ability to add or subtract them.

The methods of the `Rational` class, such as `add`, `subtract`, `multiply`, and `divide`, use the `Rational` object that is executing the method as the first

Listing 4.7

```
//********************************************************************
//  Rational.java        Author: Lewis and Loftus
//
//  Represents one rational number with a numerator and denominator.
//********************************************************************

public class Rational
{
   private int numerator, denominator;

   //-----------------------------------------------------------------
   //  Sets up the rational number by ensuring a nonzero denominator
   //  and making only the numerator signed.
   //-----------------------------------------------------------------
   public Rational (int numer, int denom)
   {
      if (denom == 0)
         denom = 1;

      // Make the numerator "store" the sign
      if (denom < 0)
      {
         numer = numer * -1;
         denom = denom * -1;
      }

      numerator = numer;
      denominator = denom;

      reduce();
   }
```

Listing 4.7 *(continued)*

```
//-----------------------------------------------------------------
//  Adds this rational number to the one passed as a parameter.
//  A common denominator is found by multiplying the individual
//  denominators.
//-----------------------------------------------------------------
public Rational add (Rational op2)
{
   int commonDenominator = denominator * op2.getDenominator();
   int numerator1 = numerator * op2.getDenominator();
   int numerator2 = op2.getNumerator() * denominator;
   int sum = numerator1 + numerator2;

   return new Rational (sum, commonDenominator);
}

//-----------------------------------------------------------------
//  Subtracts the rational number passed as a parameter from this
//  rational number.
//-----------------------------------------------------------------
public Rational subtract (Rational op2)
{
   int commonDenominator = denominator * op2.getDenominator();
   int numerator1 = numerator * op2.getDenominator();
   int numerator2 = op2.getNumerator() * denominator;
   int difference = numerator1 - numerator2;

   return new Rational (difference, commonDenominator);
}

//-----------------------------------------------------------------
//  Multiplies this rational number by the one passed as a
//  parameter.
//-----------------------------------------------------------------
public Rational multiply (Rational op2)
{
   int numer = numerator * op2.getNumerator();
   int denom = denominator * op2.getDenominator();

   return new Rational (numer, denom);
}
```

Listing 4.7 *(continued)*

```
   //-----------------------------------------------------------------
   //  Divides this rational number by the one passed as a parameter
   //  by multiplying by the reciprocal of the second rational.
   //-----------------------------------------------------------------
   public Rational divide (Rational op2)
   {
      return multiply (op2.reciprocal());
   }

   //-----------------------------------------------------------------
   //  Returns the reciprocal of this rational number.
   //-----------------------------------------------------------------
   public Rational reciprocal ()
   {
      return new Rational (denominator, numerator);
   }

   //-----------------------------------------------------------------
   //  Returns the numerator of this rational number.
   //-----------------------------------------------------------------
   public int getNumerator ()
   {
      return numerator;
   }

   //-----------------------------------------------------------------
   //  Returns the denominator of this rational number.
   //-----------------------------------------------------------------
   public int getDenominator ()
   {
      return denominator;
   }

   //-----------------------------------------------------------------
   //  Determines if this rational number is equal to the one passed
   //  as a parameter.  Assumes they are both reduced.
   //-----------------------------------------------------------------
   public boolean equals (Rational op2)
   {
      return ( numerator == op2.getNumerator() &&
               denominator == op2.getDenominator() );
   }
```

Listing 4.7 *(continued)*

```
   //-----------------------------------------------------------------
   //  Returns this rational number as a string.
   //-----------------------------------------------------------------
   public String toString ()
   {
      String result;

      if (numerator == 0)
         result = "0";
      else
         if (denominator == 1)
            result = numerator + "";
         else
            result = numerator + "/" + denominator;

      return result;
   }

   //-----------------------------------------------------------------
   //  Reduces this rational number by dividing both the numerator
   //  and the denominator by their greatest common divisor.
   //-----------------------------------------------------------------
   private void reduce ()
   {
      if (numerator != 0)
      {
         int common = gcd (Math.abs(numerator), denominator);

         numerator = numerator / common;
         denominator = denominator / common;
      }
   }
```

Listing 4.7 ***(continued)***

```
   //-----------------------------------------------------------------
   //  Computes and returns the greatest common divisor of the two
   //  positive parameters. Uses Euclid's algorithm.
   //-----------------------------------------------------------------
   private int gcd (int num1, int num2)
   {
      while (num1 != num2)
         if (num1 > num2)
            num1 = num1 - num2;
         else
            num2 = num2 - num1;

      return num1;
   }
}
```

(left) operand and use the `Rational` object passed as a parameter as the second (right) operand.

Note that some of the methods in the `Rational` class are declared with private visibility, such as `reduce` and `gcd`. These methods are private because we don't want them executed directly from outside a `Rational` object. They exist only to support the other services of the object.

4.5 Method Overloading

When a program is compiled, a method invocation is bound to the appropriate definition. That is, code is inserted at the location of the method call to shift processing to the location of the method definition. After the method's code has been executed, control returns to the location of the call and processing continues.

The method name is often sufficient to indicate which method definition is being referenced by a given invocation. But in Java, as in other object-oriented languages, you can use the same method name for multiple methods. This technique is called *method overloading*. It is useful when you need to perform similar methods on different types of data.

The compiler must still be able to bind an invocation to a specific method declaration. If the method name for two or more definitions is the same, then additional information is used to uniquely identify the definition that is being referenced by a particular invocation. In Java, a method name can be used for multiple methods as long as some combination of the number of parameters, the types of those parameters, and the order of the types of parameters is distinct. A method's name along with the number, type, and order of its parameters is called the *method signature*. The compiler uses the complete method signature to *bind* a method invocation to the appropriate definition.

Key Concept

The different versions of an overloaded method are distinguished by their signature, which is the number, type, and order of the parameters.

The compiler must be able to examine a method invocation, including the parameter list, and determine which specific definition is being referenced. If you attempt to specify two method names with the same signature, the compiler will issue an appropriate error message and will not create an executable program. There can be no ambiguity.

The `println` method is an example of a method that is overloaded several times, each accepting a single type. A partial list of its various signatures is given below:

- `println (String s)`
- `println (int i)`
- `println (double d)`
- `println (char c)`
- `println (boolean b)`

The following two lines of code actually invoke different methods that have the same name:

```
System.out.println ("The total number of students is: ");
System.out.println (count);
```

The first line invokes the `println` that accepts a string and the second, assuming `count` is an integer variable, invokes the `println` that accepts an integer. We often use a `println` statement that prints several distinct types, such as:

```
System.out.println ("The total number of students is: " +
                    count);
```

In this case, the plus sign is the string concatenation operator. First, the value in the variable `count` is converted to a string representation, then the two strings are concatenated into one longer string, and the definition of `println` that accepts a single string is invoked.

Constructors are a primary candidate for overloading. By providing multiple versions of a constructor, you have a variety of ways to create and initialize an object. For example, the `SnakeEyes` program shown in Listing 4.8 refers to two `Die` objects. The purpose of the program is to roll the dice and

Listing 4.8

```
//********************************************************************
//  SnakeEyes.java       Author: Lewis and Loftus
//
//  Demonstrates the use of a class with overloaded constructors.
//********************************************************************

import Die;

public class SnakeEyes
{
   //-----------------------------------------------------------------
   //  Creates two die objects, then rolls both dice a set number of
   //  times, counting the number of snake eyes that occur.
   //-----------------------------------------------------------------
   public static void main (String[] args)
   {
      final int ROLLS = 500;
      int snakeEyes = 0, num1, num2;

      Die die1 = new Die();     // creates a six-sided die
      Die die2 = new Die(20);   // creates a twenty-sided die

      for (int roll = 1; roll <= ROLLS; roll++)
      {
         num1 = die1.roll();
         num2 = die2.roll();

         if (num1 == 1 && num2 == 1)  // check for snake eyes
            snakeEyes++;
      }

      System.out.println ("Number of rolls: " + ROLLS);
      System.out.println ("Number of snake eyes: " + snakeEyes);
      System.out.println ("Ratio: " + (float)snakeEyes/ROLLS);
   }
}
```

Listing 4.8 *(continued)*

```
Number of rolls: 500
Number of snake eyes: 6
Ratio: 0.012
```

count the number of times both dice show a one on the same throw (snake eyes).

In this case, however, one die has six sides and the other has 20 sides. Each `Die` object was created using two different constructors of the `Die` class. The `Die` class is shown in Listing 4.9.

Listing 4.9

```
//********************************************************************
//  Die.java       Author: Lewis and Loftus
//
//  Represents one die (singular of dice) with faces showing values
//  between 1 and the number of faces on the die.
//********************************************************************

public class Die
{
   private final int MIN_FACES = 4;

   private int numFaces;   // number of sides on the die
   private int faceValue;  // current value showing on the die

   //-----------------------------------------------------------------
   //  Defaults to a six-sided die, initially showing 1.
   //-----------------------------------------------------------------
   public Die ()
   {
      numFaces = 6;
      faceValue = 1;
   }
```

Listing 4.9 ***(continued)***

```
   //-----------------------------------------------------------------
   //  Explicitly sets the size of the die. Defaults to a size of
   //  six if the parameter is invalid.  Initial face is 1.
   //-----------------------------------------------------------------
   public Die (int faces)
   {
      if (faces < MIN_FACES)
         numFaces = 6;
      else
         numFaces = faces;

      faceValue = 1;
   }

   //-----------------------------------------------------------------
   //  Rolls the die and returns the result.
   //-----------------------------------------------------------------
   public int roll ()
   {
      faceValue = (int) (Math.random() * numFaces) + 1;
      return faceValue;
   }

   //-----------------------------------------------------------------
   //  Returns the current die value.
   //-----------------------------------------------------------------
   public int getFaceValue ()
   {
      return faceValue;
   }
}
```

Both `Die` constructors have the same name, but one takes no parameters and the other takes an integer as a parameter. The compiler can examine the invocation and determine which version of the method is intended.

4.6 Method Decomposition

Sometimes a service that an object provides is so complicated it cannot reasonably be handled using one method. We often will decompose a method into multiple methods to create a cleaner design. As an example, we will examine a program that translates English sentences into Pig Latin. This example uses another class provided by the Java standard class library, called `StringTokenizer`.

The `StringTokenizer` Class

Often the characters in a string can be grouped into meaningful pieces. For example, the characters in a sentence can be grouped into individual words. The characters in the string `"75 69 81"` can be thought of as a series of integers separated by white space. To the Java compiler, a string is just a series of characters, but we can identify separate, possibly important, components within a string. Extracting and processing the data contained in a string is a common programming activity.

The `java.util` package provides the `StringTokenizer` class to aid programmers in this task. The purpose of the `StringTokenizer` class is to break a string up into pieces, called *tokens,* based on a set of delimiters. The default delimiters used by the `StringTokenizer` class are the space, tab, carriage return, and newline characters. Figure 4.5 lists some methods of the `StringTokenizer` class.

The `StringTokenizer` class will allow us to solve a problem whose main driver is shown in Listing 4.10. The `PigLatin` program repeatedly

`StringTokenizer (String str)`
Constructor: creates a new `StringTokenizer` object to parse the specified string `str` based on white space.

`StringTokenizer (String str, String delimiters)`
Constructor: creates a new `StringTokenizer` object to parse the specified string `str` based on the specified set of `delimiters`.

`int countTokens ()`
Returns the number of tokens still left to be processed in the string.

`boolean hasMoreTokens ()`
Returns true if there are tokens still left to be processed in the string.

`String nextToken ()`
Returns the next token in the string.

Figure 4.5 Some methods of the `StringTokenizer` class

Listing 4.10

```
//********************************************************************
//  PigLatin.java       Author: Lewis and Loftus
//
//  Driver to exercise the PigLatinTranslator class.
//********************************************************************

import PigLatinTranslator;
import cs1.Keyboard;

public class PigLatin
{
   //-----------------------------------------------------------------
   //  Reads sentences and translates them into Pig Latin.
   //-----------------------------------------------------------------
   public static void main (String[] args)
   {
      String sentence, result, another;
      PigLatinTranslator translator = new PigLatinTranslator();

      do
      {
         System.out.println ();
         System.out.println ("Enter a sentence (no punctuation):");
         sentence = Keyboard.readString();

         System.out.println ();
         result = translator.translate (sentence);
         System.out.println ("That sentence in Pig Latin is:");
         System.out.println (result);

         System.out.println ();
         System.out.print ("Translate another sentence (y/n)? ");
         another = Keyboard.readString();
      }
      while (another.equalsIgnoreCase("y"));
   }
}
```

Listing 4.10 ***(continued)***

```
Enter a sentence (no punctuation):
Do you speak Pig Latin

That sentence in Pig Latin is:
oday ouyay eakspay igpay atinlay

Translate another sentence (y/n)? y

Enter a sentence (no punctuation):
Play it again Sam

That sentence in Pig Latin is:
ayplay ityay againyay amsay

Translate another sentence (y/n)? n
```

accepts a string from the user and translates the sentence, word by word, into Pig Latin.

The workhorse behind the `PigLatin` program is the `PigLatinTranslator` class, shown in Listing 4.11. An object of type `PigLatinTranslator` provides one fundamental service, a method called `translate`, which accepts a string and translates it into Pig Latin. Note that the `PigLatinTranslator` class does not contain a constructor because none is needed.

The act of translating an entire string to Pig Latin is not trivial. If written all in one big method, it would be very long and difficult to follow. A better solution, as implemented in the `PigLatinTranslator` class, is to decompose the translate method and use several other support methods to help with the work.

The `translate` method first uses a `StringTokenizer` object to separate the string into words. Then it translates each word using a separate call to `translateWord`, which is a private support method of the class. Its sole role is to translate the one word it is passed. But even that is a big job, so we farm out some of the work to other private methods called `beginsWithVowel` and `beginsWithPrefix`.

Listing 4.11

```
//********************************************************************
//  PigLatinTranslator.java       Author: Lewis and Loftus
//
//  Represents a translation system from English to Pig Latin.
//  Demonstrates method decomposition and the use of StringTokenizer.
//********************************************************************

import java.util.StringTokenizer;

public class PigLatinTranslator
{
   //-----------------------------------------------------------------
   //  Translates a sentence of words into Pig Latin.
   //-----------------------------------------------------------------
   public String translate (String sentence)
   {
      String result = "";

      sentence = sentence.toLowerCase();
      StringTokenizer tokenizer = new StringTokenizer (sentence);

      while (tokenizer.hasMoreTokens())
      {
         result += translateWord (tokenizer.nextToken());
         result += " ";
      }

      return result;
   }

   //-----------------------------------------------------------------
   //  Translates one word into Pig Latin. If the word begins with a
   //  vowel, the suffix "yay" is appended to the word.  Otherwise,
   //  the first letter or two are moved to the end of the word,
   //  and "ay" is appended.
   //-----------------------------------------------------------------
   private String translateWord (String word)
   {
      String result = "";

      if (beginsWithVowel(word))
         result = word + "yay";
      else
         if (beginsWithPrefix(word))
            result = word.substring(2) + word.substring(0,2) + "ay";
         else
            result = word.substring(1) + word.charAt(0) + "ay";

      return result;
   }
```

Listing 4.11 ***(continued)***

```
   //-----------------------------------------------------------------
   //  Determines if the specified word begins with a vowel.
   //-----------------------------------------------------------------
   private boolean beginsWithVowel (String word)
   {
      String vowels = "aeiouAEIOU";

      char letter = word.charAt(0);

      return (vowels.indexOf(letter) != -1);
   }

   //-----------------------------------------------------------------
   //  Determines if the specified word begins with a particular
   //  two-character prefix.
   //-----------------------------------------------------------------
   private boolean beginsWithPrefix (String str)
   {
      return ( str.startsWith ("bl") || str.startsWith ("pl") ||
               str.startsWith ("br") || str.startsWith ("pr") ||
               str.startsWith ("ch") || str.startsWith ("sh") ||
               str.startsWith ("cl") || str.startsWith ("sl") ||
               str.startsWith ("cr") || str.startsWith ("sp") ||
               str.startsWith ("dr") || str.startsWith ("sr") ||
               str.startsWith ("fl") || str.startsWith ("st") ||
               str.startsWith ("fr") || str.startsWith ("th") ||
               str.startsWith ("gl") || str.startsWith ("tr") ||
               str.startsWith ("gr") || str.startsWith ("wh") ||
               str.startsWith ("kl") || str.startsWith ("wr") ||
               str.startsWith ("ph") );
   }
}
```

Whenever a method becomes large or complex, consider decomposing it into multiple methods to create a cleaner class design. First, however, consider how other objects can be defined to create better overall system design.

4.7 Applet Methods

In earlier applets we've seen the use of the `paint` method to draw the contents of the applet on the screen. An applet has several other methods that perform specific duties. Because an applet is designed to work with Web pages, some applet methods are particular designed around that concept. Several applet methods are listed in Figure 4.6.

The `init` method is executed once when the applet is first loaded, such as when the browser or appletviewer initially view the applet. Therefore the `init` method is the place to initialize the applet's environment and permanent data.

The `start` and `stop` methods of an applet are called when the applet becomes active or inactive, respectively. For example, after we use a browser to initially load an applet, the applet's `start` method is called. We may then leave that page to visit another one, at which point the applet becomes

`public void init ()`
Initializes the applet. Called just after the applet is loaded.

`public void start ()`
Starts the applet. Called just after the applet is made active.

`public void stop ()`
Stops the applet. Called just after the applet is made inactive.

`public void destroy ()`
Destroys the applet. Called when the browser is exited.

`public URL getCodeBase ()`
Returns the URL at which this applet's bytecode is located.

`public URL getDocumentBase ()`
Returns the URL at which the HTML document containing this applet is located.

`public AudioClip getAudioClip (URL url, String name)`
Retrieves an audio clip from the specified URL.

`public Image getImage (URL url, String name)`
Retrieves an image from the specified URL.

Figure 4.6 Some methods of the `Applet` class

inactive and the stop method is called. If we return to the applet's page, the applet becomes active again and the start method is called again. Note that the init method is called once when the applet is loaded, but start may be called several times as the page is revisited. It is good practice to implement start and stop when the applet is actively using CPU time, such as when it is showing an animation, so that CPU time is not wasted on an applet that is not visible.

Note that reloading the Web page in the browser does not necessarily reload the applet. To force the applet to reload, most browsers provide some key combination for that purpose. For example, in Netscape Navigator, holding down the shift key while pressing the reload button with the mouse will not only reload the Web page, but will reload (and reinitialize) all applets linked to that page as well.

The getCodeBase and getDocumentBase methods are useful to determine where the applet bytecode or its HTML document reside. Once we have the desired URL on the original Web server, we may use it to retrieve an image or audio clip using the applet methods getImage or getAudioClip.

The various applet methods are used as needed throughout the text.

4.8 Graphical Objects

Often an object has a graphical representation. Consider the LineUp applet, shown in Listing 4.12. It creates several StickFigure objects, of varying color and random height. The StickFigure objects are instantiated in the init method of the applet, so they are created once when the applet is loaded.

The paint method of LineUp simply requests that the stick figures redraw themselves whenever it gets called. The paint method gets called whenever an event occurs that might influence the graphic representation of

Listing 4.12

```
//********************************************************************
//  LineUp.java       Author: Lewis and Loftus
//
//  Demonstrates the use of a graphical object.
//********************************************************************

import StickFigure;
import java.applet.Applet;
import java.awt.*;
```

Listing 4.12 ***(continued)***

```
public class LineUp extends Applet
{
   private final int APPLET_WIDTH = 400;
   private final int APPLET_HEIGHT = 150;
   private final int HEIGHT_MIN = 100;
   private final int VARIANCE = 30;

   private StickFigure figure1, figure2, figure3, figure4;

   //-----------------------------------------------------------------
   //  Creates several stick figures with varying characteristics.
   //-----------------------------------------------------------------
   public void init ()
   {
      int h1, h2, h3, h4;  // heights of stick figures

      h1 = (int) (Math.random() * VARIANCE) + HEIGHT_MIN;
      h2 = (int) (Math.random() * VARIANCE) + HEIGHT_MIN;
      h3 = (int) (Math.random() * VARIANCE) + HEIGHT_MIN;
      h4 = (int) (Math.random() * VARIANCE) + HEIGHT_MIN;

      figure1 = new StickFigure (100, 150, Color.red, h1);
      figure2 = new StickFigure (150, 150, Color.cyan, h2);
      figure3 = new StickFigure (200, 150, Color.green, h3);
      figure4 = new StickFigure (250, 150, Color.yellow, h4);

      setBackground (Color.black);
      setSize (APPLET_WIDTH, APPLET_HEIGHT);
   }

   //-----------------------------------------------------------------
   //  Paints the stick figures on the applet.
   //-----------------------------------------------------------------
   public void paint (Graphics page)
   {
      figure1.draw (page);
      figure2.draw (page);
      figure3.draw (page);
      figure4.draw (page);
   }
}
```

Listing 4.12 ***(continued)***

the applet itself. For instance, when the window that the applet is displayed in is moved, `paint` is called to redraw the applet contents.

The `StickFigure` class is shown in Listing 4.13. Like any other object, a `StickFigure` object contains data that defines its state, such as the position, color, and height of the figure. The `draw` method contains the individual commands that draw the figure itself, relative to the position and height.

Listing 4.13

```
//********************************************************************
//  StickFigure.java       Author: Lewis and Loftus
//
//  Represents a graphical stick figure.
//********************************************************************

import java.awt.*;

public class StickFigure
{
   private int baseX;     // center of figure
   private int baseY;     // floor (bottom of feet)
   private Color color;   // color of stick figure
   private int height;    // height of stick figure

   //-----------------------------------------------------------------
   //  Sets up the stick figure's primary attributes.
   //-----------------------------------------------------------------
   public StickFigure (int center, int bottom, Color shade, int size)
   {
      baseX = center;
      baseY = bottom;
      color = shade;
      height = size;
   }

   //-----------------------------------------------------------------
   //  Draws this figure relative to baseX, baseY, and height.
   //-----------------------------------------------------------------
   public void draw (Graphics page)
   {
      int top = baseY - height;  // top of head

      page.setColor (color);

      page.drawOval (baseX-10, top, 20, 20);  // head

      page.drawLine (baseX, top+20, baseX, baseY-30);  // trunk

      page.drawLine (baseX, baseY-30, baseX-15, baseY);  // legs
      page.drawLine (baseX, baseY-30, baseX+15, baseY);

      page.drawLine (baseX, baseY-70, baseX-25, baseY-70);  // arms
      page.drawLine (baseX, baseY-70, baseX+20, baseY-85);
   }
}
```

Summary of Key Concepts

- An object contains variables and methods. The values of the variables define the state of the object and the methods define the behaviors of the object.
- A class is a blueprint of an object; it reserves no memory space for data. Each object has its own data space; an object is an instance of a class.
- Classes define the variables for an object, but reserve no memory space for them. Each object, when instantiated, has a unique storage space for variables, and therefore their values can be different. Methods, however, are shared among all objects of a class.
- Objects should be encapsulated. The rest of a program should interact with an object only through a well-defined interface.
- A method must return a value consistent with the return type specified in the method header.
- A variable declared in a method is local to that method and cannot be used outside of it.
- The different versions of an overloaded method are distinguished by their signature, which is the number, type, and order of the parameters.

Self-Review Questions

4.1 What is the difference between an object and a class?

4.2 What are constructors used for? How are they defined?

4.3 Explain the difference between an actual parameter and a formal parameter.

4.4 How is information passed back from a method?

4.5 What is a modifier?

4.6 Describe the following:

a. public method

b. private method

c. public variable

4.7 How are overloaded methods distinguished from each other?

▶ Exercises

4.1 Explain why encapsulation is an abstraction and give a specific example.

4.2 Explain the difference between a method and a class.

4.3 Think about representing an alarm clock as a software object. Then:

a. list some characteristics of the object that represent its state and behavior.

b. list the primary data and methods of the object.

4.4 Repeat the steps in Exercise 4.3, representing a basketball stadium scoreboard.

4.5 Repeat the steps in Exercise 4.3, representing a daily schedule planner.

4.6 Repeat Exercise 4.3, using an object you come up with yourself. Describe a program that might make use of the class you define.

Programming Projects

4.1 Design and implement a class called `PairOfDice`, composed of two six-sided `Die` objects. Create a driver class with a `main` method that rolls a `PairOfDice` object multiple times, counting the number of box cars (two sixes) that occur.

4.2 Using the `PairOfDice` class from the previous question, design and implement a class to play a game in which the user plays the computer in a game called Pig. On each turn, the player rolls a pair of dice and accumulates points. The goal is to reach 100 points before your opponent does. If, on any turn, the player rolls one 1, all points accumulated for that round are forfeited and control of the dice moves to the other player. If the player rolls two 1s in one turn, the player looses all points accumulated thus far in the game and looses control of the dice. The player may voluntarily turn over the dice at any point. Therefore, on each roll, the player must decide to either roll again (be a pig) and risk loosing points, or relinquish control of the dice, possibly allowing the other player to win. Implement the computer player such that it always relinquishes the dice after accumulating 20 or more points in any given round.

4.3 Design and implement a class called `Card` that represents a standard playing card. Each card has a suit and a face value. Create a program that deals 50 random cards.

4.4 Design and implement a class called `Building` that represents a graphical depiction of a building. Allow the parameters to the constructor to specify the building's width and height. Each building should be colored black, with a few random windows of yellow. Create an applet that draws a random skyline of buildings.

4.5 Project 3.20 in Chapter 3 describes an applet that draws a quilt with a repeating pattern. Design and implement an applet that draws a quilt using a separate class called `Pattern` that represents a particular pattern. Allow the constructor of the `Pattern` class to vary some characteristics of the pattern, such as its color scheme. Instantiate two separate `Pattern` objects and incorporate them in a checkerboard layout in the quilt.

4.6 Write an applet that displays a graphical seating chart for a dinner party. Create a class called `Diner` (as in one who dines) that stores the person's name, gender, and location at the dinner table. A diner is graphically represented as a circle, color coded by gender, with the person's name printed in the circle.

4.7 Create a class called `Crayon` that represents one crayon of a particular color and length (height). Design and implement an applet that draws a box of crayons.

4.8 Create a class called `Star` that represents a graphical depiction of a star. Let the constructor of the star accept the number of points in the star (4, 5, or 6), and the radius of the star. Write an applet that draws a sky full of various types of stars.

4.9 Enhance the concept of the `LineUp` program to create a `PoliceLineUp` class. Instead of a stick figure, create a class called `Thug` that has a more realistic graphical representation. In addition to varying the person's height, vary the clothes and shoes by color, and add a hat or necktie for some thugs.

▶ Answers to Self-Review Questions

4.1 A class is the blueprint of an object. It defines the variables and methods that will be a part of every object that is instantiated from it. But a class reserves no memory space for variables. Each object has its own data space, and therefore its own state.

4.2 Constructors are special methods in an object that are used to initialize the object when it is instantiated. A constructor has the same name as its class, and it does not return a value.

4.3 An actual parameter is the value or variable sent to a method when it is invoked. A formal parameter is the corresponding variable in the definition of the method; it takes on the value of the actual parameter so that it can be used inside the method.

4.4 An explicit `return` statement can be used to define the value that is returned from a method. The type of the return value must match the type specified in the method definition.

4.5 A modifier is a Java reserved word that can be used in the definition of a variable or method and that specifically defines certain characteristics of its use. For example, by declaring a variable with private visibility, the variable cannot be directly accessed outside of the object in which it is defined.

4.6 The modifiers affect the methods and variables in the following ways:

a. A public method is called a service method for an object because it defines a service that the object provides.

b. A private method is called a support method. It cannot be invoked from outside the object and is used to support the activities of other methods in the class.

c. A public variable is a variable that can be directly accessed and modified by a client. This explicitly violates the concept of encapsulation and therefore should be avoided.

4.7 Overloaded methods are distinguished by having their own signature, which includes the number, order, and type of the parameters. The return type is not part of the distinguishing signature.

Enhancing Classes

This chapter explores a variety of issues related to the design and implementation of classes. First, we revisit the concept of an object reference to explore what it really is and how it affects our processing. Then we examine the `static` *modifier to see how it can be applied to variables, methods, and classes. We also explore the ability to nest one class definition within another. We then examine the use of an interface construct to formalize the interaction between classes. Interfaces are important to a graphical topic in this chapter, events and event listeners, which allow us to acknowledge user interaction such as mouse clicks.*

Chapter Objectives

- Define reference aliases and explore Java garbage collection.
- Explore the effects of passing object references as parameters.
- Define the use and effects of the `static` modifier.
- Define nested and inner classes and explore their appropriate use.
- Define formal interfaces and their class implementations.
- Determine how to capture and respond to mouse and keyboard events.

5.1 References Revisited

In previous examples, we've declared many *object reference variables* through which we access particular objects. We need to examine this relationship in more detail. Object references play an important role in a program, and we need a careful understanding of how they work in order to write sophisticated object-oriented software.

An object reference variable and an object are two separate things. Remember that the declaration of the reference variable and the creation of the object that it refers to are two separate steps. We often declare the reference variable and create an object for it to refer to on the same line, but keep in mind that we don't have to do so. In fact, in many cases, we won't want to.

Key Concept

An object reference variable stores the address of an object.

The reference variable holds the address of an object. When we use the dot operator to invoke an object's method, we are actually using the address in the reference variable to locate the representation of the object in memory, look up the appropriate method, and invoke it.

The `null` Reference

A reference variable that does not currently point to an object is called a *null reference*. When a reference variable is initially declared, it is a null reference. If we tried to follow that reference, a `NullPointerException` would be thrown, indicating that there is no object to reference. For example, consider the following two lines of code:

```
String name;
System.out.println (name.length());
```

The first line declares the variable `name` to be a reference to a `String` object, but doesn't create any `String` object for it to refer to. The variable `name`, therefore, contains a null reference. When the second line attempts to invoke the `length` method of the object to which `name` refers, an exception is thrown because no object exists to execute the method.

The identifier `null` is a reserved word in Java, and represents a null reference. We can explicitly set a reference to `null` to make sure it doesn't point to any object. We can also use it to check to see if a reference currently points to an object:

```
if (name != null)
   System.out.println (name.length());
```

Aliases

The semantics of an assignment statement for primitive types and for objects is different. Consider the following declarations of primitive data:

```
int num1 = 5;
int num2 = 12;
```

In the following assignment statement, a copy of the value that is stored in num1 is stored in num2:

```
num2 = num1;
```

The original value of 12 in num2 is overwritten by the new value 5. The variables num1 and num2 still refer to different locations in memory, and both of those locations now contain the value 5. This situation is pictured in Figure 5.1.

Now consider the following object declarations:

```
ChessPiece bishop1 = new ChessPiece();
ChessPiece bishop2 = new ChessPiece();
```

Initially, the references bishop1 and bishop2 refer to two different ChessPiece objects. The following assignment statement, because it works on references instead of primitive data, has a different effect than the assignment of integer values:

```
bishop2 = bishop1;
```

The assignment copies the value of the reference from bishop1 to bishop2. The two references originally referred to different objects. After the assignment, both bishop1 and bishop2 refer to the same object (the one that bishop1 originally referred to) as shown in Figure 5.2.

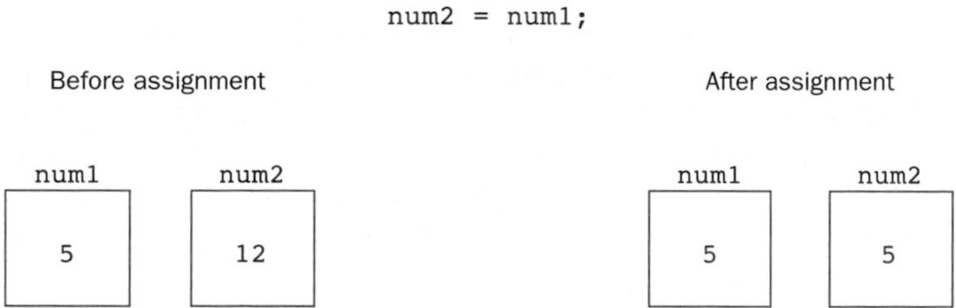

Figure 5.1 Primitive data assignment

Figure 5.2 Reference assignment

> **Key Concept**
> Several references can refer to the same object. These references are aliases of each other.

The `bishop1` and `bishop2` references are now *aliases* of each other because they are two names that refer to the same object. All references to the object that was originally referenced by `bishop2` are now gone and that object cannot be used again in the program.

One important implication of aliases is that when we use one reference to change the state of the object, it is also changed for the other because there is really only one object. If you change the state of `bishop1`, for instance, you change the state of `bishop2` because they both refer to the same object. Aliases can be confusing unless they are managed carefully.

> **Key Concept**
> The == operator compares object references for equality, returning true if the references are aliases of each other.

Another important aspect of references is the way they affect how we determine if two objects are equal. The == operator that we use for primitive data can be used with object references, but it returns true only if the two references being compared are aliases of each other. That is, the following expression is true only if `bishop1` and `bishop2` currently refer to the same object:

```
bishop1 == bishop2
```

> **Key Concept**
> The `equals` method can be defined to determine equality between objects in any way we think is appropriate.

A method called `equals` is defined for all objects, but unless we give it a specific definition when we write a class, it has the same semantics as the == operator. The `equals` method returns a `boolean` value that, by default, will be true if the two objects being compared are aliases of each other. The `equals` method is invoked through one object, and takes the other one as a parameter. Therefore, the expression

```
bishop1.equals(bishop2)
```

will return true if both references refer to the same object. We could define the `equals` method in the `ChessPiece` class to define equality for `ChessPiece` objects any way we would like. That is, we could define the `equals` method to return true under whatever conditions we think are appropriate to mean that one `ChessPiece` is equal to another.

As we discussed in Chapter 2, the `equals` method has been given an appropriate definition in the `String` class. When comparing two `String` objects, the `equals` method returns true only if both strings contain the same characters. A common mistake is to use the == operator to compare strings, which compares the references for equality, when most of the time we want to compare the characters in the strings for equality. The `equals` method is discussed further in Chapter 7.

Garbage Collection

All interaction with an object occurs through a reference variable, so we can only use an object if we have a reference to it. When all references to an object are lost (perhaps by reassignment), that object can no longer contribute to the program. The program can no longer invoke its methods or use its variables. At this point the object is called *garbage* because it serves no useful purpose.

Java performs *automatic garbage collection*. When the last reference to an object is lost, the object becomes a candidate for garbage collection. Occasionally, the Java runtime executes a method that "collects" all of the objects marked for garbage collection and returns their allocated memory to the system for future use. The programmer does not have to worry about explicitly returning allocated memory.

Key Concept

If an object has no references to it, a program cannot use it. Java performs automatic garbage collection by periodically reclaiming the memory space used by these objects.

If there is an activity that a programmer wants to accomplish in conjunction with the object being destroyed, the programmer can define a method called `finalize` in the object's class. The `finalize` method takes no parameters and uses a `void` return type. It will be executed by the Java runtime after the object is marked for garbage collection and before it is actually destroyed. The `finalize` method is not often used because the garbage collector performs most normal cleanup operations. However, it is useful for performing activities that the garbage collector does not address, such as closing files.

Web Bonus

The Web site of the text contains a detailed discussion of the `finalize` method.

Passing Objects as Parameters

Java passes all parameters to a method *by value*. That is, the current value of the actual parameter is copied into the formal parameter in the method header. Parameter passing is essentially like an assignment statement, assigning to the formal parameter the value of the actual parameter.

This issue is important when you consider making changes to a formal parameter inside a method. The formal parameter is a separate copy of the value that is passed in, so any changes made to it have no effect on the actual parameter. After control returns to the calling method, the actual parameter will have the same value as it did before the method was called.

Key Concept

When an object is passed to a method, the actual and formal parameters become aliases of each other. Changes to the object through the reference will be reflected in the calling method.

However, when an object is passed to a method, we are actually passing a reference to that object. The value that gets copied is the address of the object. Therefore, the formal parameter and the actual parameter become aliases of each other. If we change the state of the object through the formal parameter reference inside the method, we are changing the object referenced by the actual parameter; they refer to the same object. If we change the formal parameter reference itself (to make it point to a new object, for instance), we have not changed the fact that the actual parameter still refers to the original object.

The nuances of parameter passing are demonstrated in the program in Listing 5.1. Carefully trace the processing of this program and note the values that are output. The `ParameterPassing` class contains a `main` method that calls the `changeValues` method in a `ParameterTester` object. Two of the parameters to `changeValues` are `Num` objects, each of which simply stores an integer value. The other parameter is a primitive integer value.

Listing 5.1

```
//********************************************************************
//  ParameterPassing.java       Author: Lewis and Loftus
//
//  Demonstrates the effects of passing various types of parameters.
//********************************************************************

import ParameterTester;
import Num;

public class ParameterPassing
{
   //-----------------------------------------------------------------
   //  Sets up three variables (one primitive and two objects) to
   //  serve as actual parameters to the changeValues method. Prints
   //  their values before and after calling the method.
   //-----------------------------------------------------------------
```

Listing 5.1 ***(continued)***

```
    public static void main (String[] args)
    {
        ParameterTester tester = new ParameterTester();

        int a1 = 111;
        Num a2 = new Num (222);
        Num a3 = new Num (333);

        System.out.println ("Before calling changeValues:");
        System.out.println ("a1\ta2\ta3");
        System.out.println (a1 + "\t" + a2 + "\t" + a3 + "\n");

        tester.changeValues (a1, a2, a3);

        System.out.println ("After calling changeValues:");
        System.out.println ("a1\ta2\ta3");
        System.out.println (a1 + "\t" + a2 + "\t" + a3 + "\n");
    }
}
```

```
Before calling changeValues:
a1      a2      a3
111     222     333

Before changing the values:
f1      f2      f3
111     222     333

After changing the values:
f1      f2      f3
999     888     777

After calling changeValues:
a1      a2      a3
111     888     333
```

The `ParameterTester` class is shown in Listing 5.2, and the `Num` class is shown in Listing 5.3. Inside the `changeValues` method, a modification is made to each of the three formal parameters: the integer parameter is set to a different value, the value stored in the first `Num` parameter is changed using its `setValue` method, and a new `Num` object is created and assigned to the second `Num` parameter. These changes are reflected in the output printed at the end of the `changeValues` method.

However, note the final values printed after returning from the method. The primitive integer was not changed from its original value because the change was done to a copy inside the method. Likewise, the last parameter still refers to its original object with its original value. That's because the new

Listing 5.2

```
//********************************************************************
//  ParameterTester.java       Author: Lewis and Loftus
//
//  Demonstrates the effects of passing various types of parameters.
//********************************************************************

import Num;

public class ParameterTester
{
   //-----------------------------------------------------------------
   //  Modifies the parameters, printing their values before and
   //  after making the changes.
   //-----------------------------------------------------------------
   public void changeValues (int f1, Num f2, Num f3)
   {
      System.out.println ("Before changing the values:");
      System.out.println ("f1\tf2\tf3");
      System.out.println (f1 + "\t" + f2 + "\t" + f3 + "\n");

      f1 = 999;
      f2.setValue (888);
      f3 = new Num (777);

      System.out.println ("After changing the values:");
      System.out.println ("f1\tf2\tf3");
      System.out.println (f1 + "\t" + f2 + "\t" + f3 + "\n");
   }
}
```

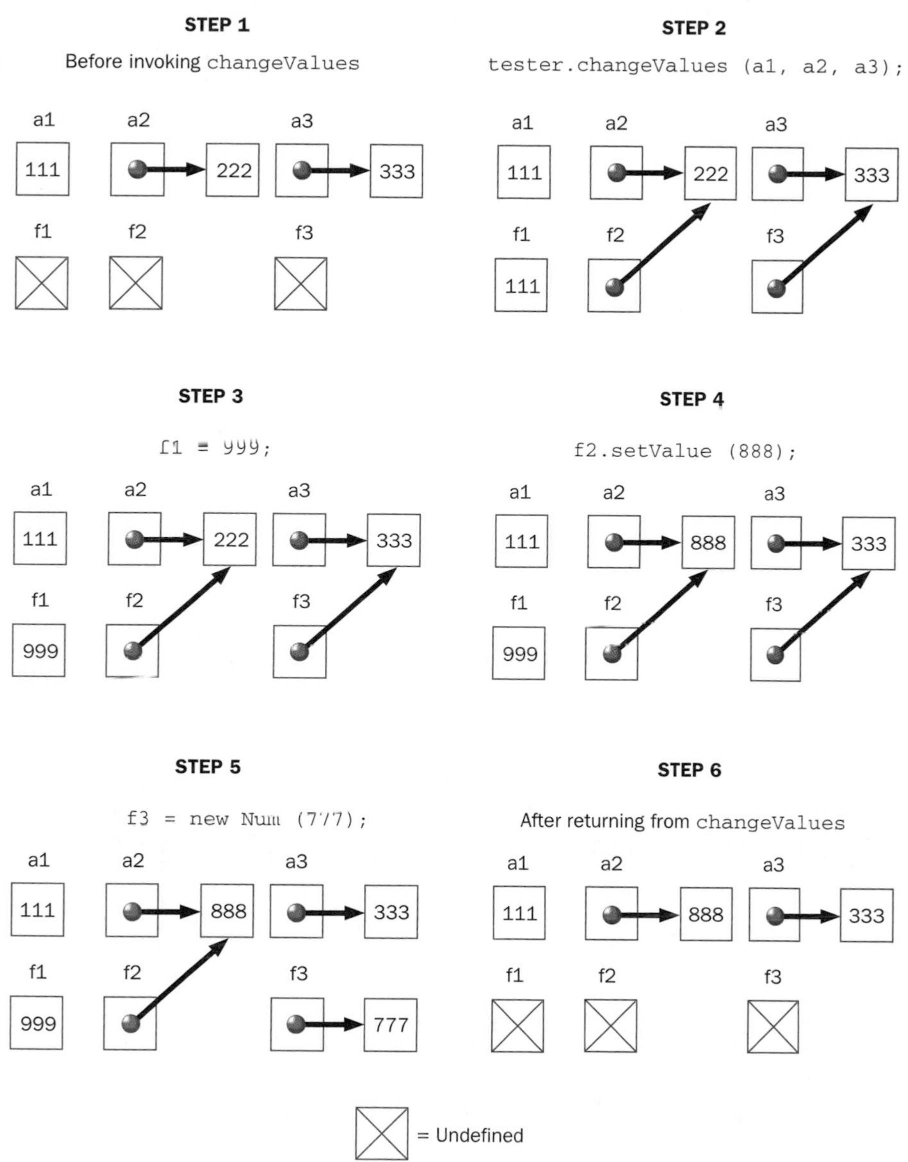

Figure 5.3 Tracing parameters in the `ParameterPassing` program

`Num` object created in the method was only referred to by the formal parameter. The only change that was "permanent" is the change made to the state of the second parameter. The processing of this program is shown step by step in Figure 5.3.

Listing 5.3

```
//********************************************************************
//  Num.java       Author: Lewis and Loftus
//
//  Represents a single integer as an object.
//********************************************************************

public class Num
{
   private int value;

   //-----------------------------------------------------------------
   //  Sets up the new Num object, storing an initial value.
   //-----------------------------------------------------------------
   public Num (int update)
   {
      value = update;
   }

   //-----------------------------------------------------------------
   //  Sets the stored value to the newly specified value.
   //-----------------------------------------------------------------
   public void setValue (int update)
   {
      value = update;
   }

   //-----------------------------------------------------------------
   //  Returns the stored integer value as a string.
   //-----------------------------------------------------------------
   public String toString ()
   {
      return value + "";
   }
}
```

The `this` Reference

Another special reference for Java objects is called the `this` reference. The word `this` is a reserved word in Java, and it allows an object to refer to itself. As we have discussed, a method is always invoked through (or by) a particular object or class. Inside that method, the `this` reference can be used to refer to the currently executing object.

For example, in the `ChessPiece` class there could be a method called move, which could contain the line

```
if (this.position == piece2.position)
   result = false;
```

The `this` reference is being used to clarify which position is being referred to. The `this` reference refers to the object through which the method was invoked. So when the following line is used to invoke the method, the `this` reference refers to `bishop1`:

```
bishop1.move();
```

But when another object is used to invoke the method, the `this` reference refers to it. Therefore, when the following invocation is used, the `this` reference in the `move` method refers to `bishop2`:

```
bishop2.move();
```

The `this` reference is handy in some cases when it is necessary to specifically use the executing object. We will use it throughout the rest of the text as appropriate.

5.2 The `static` Modifier

We've seen how visibility modifiers allow us to specify the encapsulation characteristics of variables and methods in a class. Java has several other modifiers that determine other characteristics. For example, the `static` modifier associates a variable or method with its class rather than with an object of the class.

Static Variables

So far, we've seen two categories of variables: local variables that are declared inside a method, and instance variables that are declared in a class but not inside a method. The term *instance variable* is used because an instance variable is accessed through a particular instance (an object) of a class. In general, each object has distinct memory space for each variable, so that each object can have a distinct value for that variable.

Another kind of variable, called a *static variable* or *class variable,* is shared among all instances of a class. There is only one copy of a static variable for all objects of a class. Therefore, changing the value of a static variable in one object changes it for all of the others. The reserved word `static` is used as a modifier to declare a static variable:

```
private static int count = 0;
```

Memory space for a static variable is established when the class that contains it is referenced for the first time in a program. A local variable cannot be static.

Key Concept

A static variable is shared among all instances of a class. A static method can be called through the class in which it is defined.

Constants, which are declared using the `final` modifier, are also often declared using the `static` modifier. Because the value of constants cannot be changed, there might as well be only one copy of the value across all objects of the class.

Static Methods

Methods can also be declared using the `static` modifier. This kind of method is referred to as a *static method* or *class method.* A static method can be invoked through the class itself. You don't have to instantiate an object of the class to invoke a static method.

We've seen the use of static methods in previous examples. The `main` method of a Java program must be declared with the `static` modifier so that `main` can be executed by the interpreter without instantiating an object from the class that contains `main`.

In Chapter 2 we established that the methods of the `Math` class are invoked using class name, such as:

```
System.out.println ("Square root of 27: " + Math.sqrt(27));
```

All of the methods in the `Math` class are declared as `static`. These methods perform basic computations based on values passed as parameters. There is no object state to maintain in these situations; therefore there is no good reason to force us to create an object in order to request these services.

The `Keyboard` class, which was written by the authors of this text to simplify keyboard input, contains static methods. Note that these methods are always invoked through the `Keyboard` class name. The details of these methods are discussed in Chapter 8.

Because static methods do not operate in the context of a particular object, they cannot reference instance variables, which only exist in an instance of a class. The compiler will issue an error if a static method attempts

Listing 5.4

```
//********************************************************************
//  CountInstances.java       Author: Lewis and Loftus
//
//  Demonstrates the use of the static modifier.
//********************************************************************

import MyClass;

public class CountInstances
{
   //-----------------------------------------------------------------
   //  Creates several MyClass objects and prints the number of
   //  objects that were created.
   //-----------------------------------------------------------------
   public static void main (String[] args)
   {
      MyClass obj;

      for (int scan=1; scan <= 10; scan++)
         obj = new MyClass();

      System.out.println ("Objects created: " + MyClass.getCount());
   }
}
```

```
Objects created: 10
```

to use a nonstatic variable. They can, however, reference static variables, because static variables exist independent of specific objects. Therefore, the `main` method can access only static or local variables.

The program in Listing 5.4 uses a loop to instantiate several objects of the `MyClass` class. The constructor of `MyClass` increments a static variable called `count`, which is initialized to zero when it is declared. Therefore, `count` serves to keep track of the number of instances of `MyClass` that are created.

The `getCount` method of `MyClass`, shown in Listing 5.5, is also declared as `static`, which allows it to be invoked through the class name in the `main` method. It did not have to be declared as `static`, but it might as well be because the instance through which it would be called is irrelevant.

Listing 5.5

```
//********************************************************************
//  MyClass.java       Author: Lewis and Loftus
//
//  Demonstrates the use of the static modifier.
//********************************************************************

public class MyClass
{
   private static int count = 0;

   //-----------------------------------------------------------------
   //  Counts the number of instances created.
   //-----------------------------------------------------------------
   public MyClass ()
   {
      count++;
   }

   //-----------------------------------------------------------------
   //  Returns the number of instances of this class that have been
   //  created.
   //-----------------------------------------------------------------
   public static int getCount ()
   {
      return count;
   }
}
```

5.3 Nested Classes

A class can be declared inside another class. Just as a loop written inside another loop is called a nested loop, a class written inside another class is called a *nested class*. The nested class is considered to be a member of the enclosing class, just like a variable or method.

Because it is a member of the enclosing class, a nested class has access to the enclosing class's variables and methods, even if they are declared with private visibility. Such a privileged relationship should be reserved for appropriate situations. A class should be nested inside another only if it makes sense in the context of the enclosing class. Then the nesting reinforces that relationship and simplifies the implementation.

Just like any other class, a nested class produces a separate bytecode file. The name of the bytecode file is the name of the enclosing class followed by the `$` character followed by the name of the nested class. Like any other bytecode file, it has an extension of `.class`. A class called `Nested` that is declared inside a class called `Outer` will result in a compiled bytecode file called `Outer$Nested.class`.

The `static` modifier can be applied to a class, as long as that class is nested inside another. Like static methods, a static nested class cannot reference instance variables or methods defined in its enclosing class.

Inner Classes

A nonstatic, nested class is called an *inner class*. Because it is not static, an inner class is associated with each instance of the enclosing class. Therefore, no member inside an inner class can be declared `static`. An instance of an inner class can exist only within an instance of the enclosing class. An inner class is depicted in Figure 5.4.

The nuances of nested and inner classes go beyond the scope of this textbook, but their basic concepts will prove useful in certain examples.

The textbook Web site contains a detailed discussion of nested and inner classes.

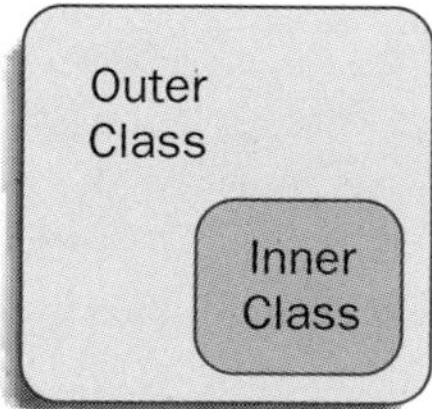

Figure 5.4 One class defined within another

5.4 Interfaces

We've used the term interface to mean the public methods through which we can interact with an object. That definition is consistent with our use of it in this section, but we are now going to formalize the concept of an interface using a particular language construct in Java.

A Java *interface* is a collection of constants and abstract methods. An *abstract method* is a method that does not have an implementation. That is, there is no body of code defined for an abstract method. The header of the method, including its parameter list, is simply followed by a semicolon. An interface cannot be instantiated. An interface called `Speaker` is shown in Listing 5.6. It contains two abstract methods: `speak` and `announce`.

An abstract method can be preceded by the reserved word `abstract`, though in interfaces it usually is not. Methods in interfaces also have public visibility by default.

Key Concept

An interface is a collection of abstract methods that are defined by all classes that implement the interface.

A class *implements* an interface by providing method implementations for each of the abstract methods defined in the interface. A class that implements an interface uses the reserved word `implements` followed by the interface name in the class header. If a class asserts that it implements a particular interface, it must provide a definition for all methods in the interface. The compiler will produce errors if any of the methods in the interface are not given a definition in the class.

The `Philosopher` class, shown in Listing 5.7, implements the `Speaker` interface. Both the `speak` and `announce` methods are implemented. They must be declared with the same signatures as their abstract counterparts have

Listing 5.6

```
//********************************************************************
//  Speaker.java       Author: Lewis and Loftus
//
//  Demonstrates the declaration of an interface.
//********************************************************************

public interface Speaker
{
   public void speak ();
   public void announce (String str);
}
```

Listing 5.7

```
//********************************************************************
//  Philosopher.java       Author: Lewis and Loftus
//
//  Demonstrates the implementation of an interface.
//********************************************************************

public class Philosopher implements Speaker
{
   private String philosophy;

   //-----------------------------------------------------------------
   //  Establishes this philosopher's philosophy.
   //-----------------------------------------------------------------
   public Philosopher (String thoughts)
   {
      philosophy = thoughts;
   }

   //-----------------------------------------------------------------
   //  Prints this philosopher's philosophy.
   //-----------------------------------------------------------------
   public void speak ()
   {
      System.out.println (philosophy);
   }

   //-----------------------------------------------------------------
   //  Prints the specified announcement.
   //-----------------------------------------------------------------
   public void announce (String announcement)
   {
      System.out.println (announcement);
   }

   //-----------------------------------------------------------------
   //  Prints this philosopher's philosophy multiple times.
   //-----------------------------------------------------------------
   public void pontificate ()
   {
      for (int count=1; count <= 5; count++)
         System.out.println (philosophy);
   }
}
```

in the interface. In the Philosopher class, the methods are defined so that they produce some printed output.

Note that the Philosopher class also implements a method called pontificate, which has nothing to do with the interface. The interface guarantees that the class implements certain methods, but does not restrict it from having others. It is not uncommon for a class that implements an interface to have other responsibilities.

Multiple classes can implement the same interface, providing alternative definitions for the methods. For example, the Dog class, shown in Listing 5.8, also implements the Speaker interface. The designer of a class may implement the methods in any way he or she chooses, though usually an interface represents a general goal that should guide the implementation of the methods.

Listing 5.8

```
//********************************************************************
//  Dog.java       Author: Lewis and Loftus
//
//  Demonstrates the implementation of an interface.
//********************************************************************

public class Dog implements Speaker
{
   //-----------------------------------------------------------------
   //  Prints this dog's philosophy.
   //-----------------------------------------------------------------
   public void speak ()
   {
      System.out.println ("woof");
   }

   //-----------------------------------------------------------------
   //  Prints this dog's philosophy and the specified announcement.
   //-----------------------------------------------------------------
   public void announce (String announcement)
   {
      System.out.println ("woof: " + announcement);
   }
}
```

An interface establishes a guarantee regarding the services that can be requested of a given object. In our example, all philosophers, because they are speakers, can speak and announce. Philosophers can also pontificate, though not all speakers can. Similarly, all dogs are speakers, but all speakers are not dogs.

A class may implement more than one interface. In these cases, all of the interfaces implemented by the class are listed in the implements clause, separated by commas. The class must provide an implementation for all methods in all interfaces listed.

An interface may contain constants, defined using the `final` modifier. When a class implements an interface, it gains access to all of the constants defined in it. This mechanism allows multiple classes to share a set of constants that are defined in a single location.

Not only does the interface construct formally define the ways in which we can interact with a class, it also serves as the basis for a powerful programming technique called polymorphism. This concept is explained in the next section.

Polymorphism via Interfaces

Just as a class name is used to declare the type of an object reference variable, an interface name can be used to declare a reference variable as well. An interface reference variable can be used to refer to any object of any class that implements that interface.

Key Concept

An interface name can be used to declare an object reference variable. An interface reference can refer to any object of any class that implements the interface.

Consider the following declaration:

```
Speaker current;
```

The reference variable `current` can be used to refer to any object of any class that implements the `Speaker` interface. The program shown in Listing 5.9 demonstrates the use of an interface reference to refer to different object types at different times.

The variable `current` is initially set to refer to a new `Dog` object. This assignment is valid because a dog is a speaker. That is, the `Dog` class implements the `Speaker` interface. Later, `current` is assigned to reference a `Philosopher` object, which is also valid because a philosopher is a speaker. In general, an object of one class cannot be assigned to a reference of another class, but interfaces give us more freedom in that regard.

Note that when `current` refers to the `Dog` object, and the `speak` method is invoked, it is the version of `speak` found in the `Dog` class that is invoked. When `current` refers to a `Philosopher` object, the version found in the `Philosopher` class is invoked. This situation demonstrates an important rule: it is the type of the object, not the type of the reference, that determines which method is invoked.

Listing 5.9

```
//********************************************************************
//  Talking.java       Author: Lewis and Loftus
//
//  Demonstrates the use of an interface for polymorphic references.
//********************************************************************

import Dog;
import Philosopher;

public class Talking
{
   //-----------------------------------------------------------------
   //  Instantiates two objects using an interface reference and
   //  invokes one of the common methods. Then casts the interface
   //  reference into a class reference to invoke its unique method.
   //-----------------------------------------------------------------
   public static void main (String[] args)
   {
      Speaker current;

      current = new Dog();
      current.speak();

      current = new Philosopher ("I think, therefore I am.");
      current.speak();

      ((Philosopher) current).pontificate();
   }
}
```

```
woof
I think, therefore I am.
I think, therefore I am.
I think, therefore I am.
I think, therefore I am.
I think, therefore I am.
I think, therefore I am.
```

The term *polymorphism* can be defined as "having many forms." A polymorphic reference is one that can refer to different types of objects at different times. Interfaces provide one way to create a polymorphic reference. In Chapter 7 we explore another way to create them.

Consider the following polymorphic reference:

```
current.speak();
```

Because `current` is defined to be a reference to a `Speaker`, it is impossible to know, looking at that line in isolation, which version of the `speak` method will be invoked. It depends on the type of the object that `current` is referencing. In fact, if that line were in a loop, that specific line of code could invoke different methods each time it is executed. Polymorphic references are powerful, but must be designed with care.

At some point, the commitment is made to execute certain code when a method invocation is carried out. This commitment is referred to as binding a method invocation to a method definition. For some situations, the binding of a method invocation to a method definition can occur at compile time. For polymorphic references, however, the decision cannot be made until run time. In fact, the decision cannot be made until the moment that the method invocation is executed, because the method definition that is used is based on the object that is being referred to by the reference variable at that moment. This deferred commitment is called *late binding* or *dynamic binding*. It is less efficient than binding at compile time because the decision has to be made during the execution of the program, but the flexibility that a polymorphic reference gives us is far more important.

Key Concept

Interfaces allow us to make polymorphic references, in which the method that is invoked is based on the particular object being referenced at the time.

Note that the last line of the `Talking` program is used to invoke the `pontificate` method of the `Philosopher` class. We cannot simply invoke `pontificate` through the `current` reference because `current` is declared to be of type `Speaker`. Using the `current` reference directly, we are only able to request services (invoke methods) that are guaranteed to exist in the object by the `Speaker` interface. Therefore, even though we know that the `pontificate` method exists in the object, we must first cast the `Speaker` reference into a `Philosopher` reference, through which the `pontificate` method is valid.

Another way interfaces are used to create polymorphic references is by using the interface name as the type of a parameter to a method. Therefore, any object of any class that implements the interface can be passed into the method. For example, the following method takes a `Speaker` object as a parameter. Therefore, both a `Dog` object and a `Philosopher` object could be passed into it in separate invocations.

```
public void sayIt (Speaker current)
{
      current.speak();
}
```

The `Comparable` Interface

The `Comparable` interface is part of the Java standard class library. It contains only one method, `compareTo`, which takes an object as a parameter and returns an integer. This method is listed in Figure 5.5.

The intention of this interface is to provide a common mechanism for comparing one object to another. One object calls the method, and passes another as a parameter:

```
if (obj1.compareTo(obj2) < 0)
   System.out.println ("obj1 is less than obj2");
```

The integer that is returned from the `compareTo` method should be negative if the executing object is less than the parameter, 0 if they are equal, and positive if the parameter is greater. It is up to the designer of each class to decide what it means for one object of that class to be less than another.

The `String` class implements the `Comparable` interface. Therefore, we can call the `compareTo` method through one string object, passing it to another, to decide which one is "greater." In this case, the comparison is based on the order of characters as defined by the Unicode character set. This method could be used, for instance, to decide which of two names comes first alphabetically.

The `Iterator` Interface

The `Iterator` interface is another interface defined as part of the Java standard class library. It is used by classes that represent a collection of objects, providing a means to move through that group one object at a time.

The two primary methods in the interface are `hasNext`, which returns a boolean result, and `next`, which returns an object. Neither of these methods takes any parameters. The `hasNext` method returns true if there are items left to process, and `next` returns the next object. It is up to the designer of the class that implements the `Iterator` interface to decide the order in which

```
int compareTo (Object obj)
```
Compares the executing object to the parameter to determine their relative ordering. Returns an integer that is less than, equal to, or greater than zero if the executing object is less than, equal to, or greater than the parameter, respectively.

Figure 5.5 The methods of the `Comparable` interface

```
boolean hasNext ()
```
Returns true if the executing object contains one or more objects that have not been returned by the `next` method.

```
Object next ()
```
Returns a reference to the next object in the iterator.

```
void remove ()
```
Removes the item most recently returned by the `next` method from the underlying collection.

Figure 5.6 The methods of the `Iterator` interface

objects will be delivered by the `next` method. The methods of the `Iterator` interface are listed in Figure 5.6.

Note that the `next` method does not remove the object from the underlying collection, it simply returns a reference to it. The `Iterator` interface also has a method called `remove`, which takes no parameters and has a void return type. A call to the `remove` method removes the object that was most recently returned by the `next` method from the underlying collection.

The `Iterator` interface is an improved version of an older interface called `Enumeration`, which is still part of the Java standard class library. The `Enumeration` interface does not have a `remove` method. Generally, the `Iterator` interface is the preferred choice between the two.

We explore an example that uses the `Iterator` interface in Chapter 6.

5.5 Events and Listeners

Events and listeners are two important categories of objects that are key to the implementation of graphical user interfaces. They allow us to acknowledge and respond to user actions.

Events

An *event* is an object that represents some occurrence in which we may be interested. Often, events correspond to user actions, such as pressing a mouse button or typing a key on the keyboard. Events are also generated by GUI components such as graphical buttons or sliders. The Java standard class library contains classes that represent the events we will most often want to capture.

Key Concept

An event is an object that usually represents a user action, such as a mouse click. A program can be designed to recognize and respond to events.

Let's examine the events that are generated by the use of the mouse. Java divides these events into two categories: *mouse events* and *mouse motion events*. Mouse events are defined to be:

- *mouse pressed*—the mouse button is pressed down.
- *mouse released*—the mouse button is released.
- *mouse clicked*—the mouse button is pressed down and released without moving the mouse in between.
- *mouse entered*—the mouse pointer is moved over a particular component.
- *mouse exited*—the mouse pointer is moved off of a particular component.

Note that when you click a mouse, three events are generated: one when the mouse button is pushed down and two when it is let up, indicating that both a mouse release and a mouse click has occurred. We may only listen for one mouse event, or perhaps a few, in a particular program. What we listen for depends on what we are trying to accomplish.

A component such as an applet will generate a mouse entered event when the mouse pointer passes into its graphical space. Likewise, it generates a mouse exited event when it leaves.

The mouse motion events are:

- *mouse moved*—the mouse is moved.
- *mouse dragged*—the mouse is moved while the mouse button is pressed down.

These events are continually generated as the mouse is moved. They give us a way to keep track of a constantly moving mouse.

To respond to an event, the program must first recognize that it has occurred. That is the role of an event listener, as described in the next section.

Listener Interfaces

A *listener* is an object that is waiting for an event to occur and will generally respond in some way when it does. To respond to an event, we must do two things: create a listener object for the event of interest and add that listener to the graphical component that may generate the event.

A common method for creating a listener object is to define a class that implements a *listener interface*. The Java standard class library contains a set of interfaces for various event categories. For example, the `MouseListener` interface contains methods that correspond to mouse events. The methods of this interface are listed in Figure 5.7.

When an event occurs, the appropriate method of the listener is called automatically. Each method receives an object as a parameter that represents

```
void mousePressed (MouseEvent event)
```
Called when the mouse button is pressed down.

```
void mouseReleased (MouseEvent event)
```
Called when the mouse button is released.

```
void mouseClicked (MouseEvent event)
```
Called when the mouse button is pressed and released at the same location.

```
void mouseEntered (MouseEvent event)
```
Called when the mouse pointer passes into (over) a component.

```
void mouseExited (MouseEvent event)
```
Called when the mouse pointer passes out of a component.

Figure 5.7 The methods of the `MouseListener` interface

the event. This object contains information about the event that may be useful. For example, we can invoke a service of a `MouseEvent` object to find out the coordinates at which the mouse was clicked. Figure 5.8 lists some methods of the `MouseEvent` class.

Key Concept

A listener object has methods that are automatically called when an event occurs.

Components that can generate certain events have methods that we can call to add a listener of the appropriate type. For example, an applet can generate mouse events, so an applet has a method called `addMouseListener` that takes a `MouseListener` object as a parameter. When we call this method, we are establishing the relationship between the component that generates the event and the listener that listens for it.

```
Point getPoint ()
```
Returns the location of this mouse event.

```
int getX ()
```
Returns the *x* coordinate of the location of this mouse event.

```
int getY ()
```
Returns the *y* coordinate of the location of this mouse event.

```
int getClickCount ()
```
Returns the number of quick, consecutive clicks represented by this mouse event.

Figure 5.8 Some methods of the `MouseEvent` class

The `Dots` program, shown in Listing 5.10, responds to mouse events. Specifically, it draws a green dot at the location of the mouse pointer whenever the mouse button is clicked. The coordinates at which the mouse is clicked are stored in the applet as a `Point` object. When the applet's `paint` method is called, a filled oval is drawn at that location.

The `init` method of the applet instantiates a new listener object that is defined by the `DotsMouseListener` class, shown in Listing 5.11. A reference to the applet is passed as a parameter to the constructor of the `DotsMouseListener` class using the `this` reference, so that the listener object

Listing 5.10

```
//********************************************************************
//  Dots.java       Author: Lewis and Loftus
//
//  Demonstrates events and listeners.
//********************************************************************

import java.applet.Applet;
import java.awt.*;

public class Dots extends Applet
{
   private final int APPLET_WIDTH = 200;
   private final int APPLET_HEIGHT = 100;
   private final int RADIUS = 6;

   private Point clickPoint = null;

   //-----------------------------------------------------------------
   //  Creates a listener for mouse events for this applet.
   //-----------------------------------------------------------------
   public void init()
   {
      DotsMouseListener listener = new DotsMouseListener(this);
      addMouseListener(listener);

      setBackground (Color.black);
      setSize (APPLET_WIDTH, APPLET_HEIGHT);
   }
```

Listing 5.10 ***(continued)***

```
   //-----------------------------------------------------------------
   //  Draws the dot at the appropriate location.
   //-----------------------------------------------------------------
   public void paint (Graphics page)
   {
      page.setColor (Color.green);
      if (clickPoint != null)
         page.fillOval (clickPoint.x - RADIUS, clickPoint.y - RADIUS,
                        RADIUS * 2, RADIUS * 2);
   }

   //-----------------------------------------------------------------
   //  Sets the point at which to draw the next dot.
   //-----------------------------------------------------------------
   public void setPoint (Point point)
   {
      clickPoint = point;
   }
}
```

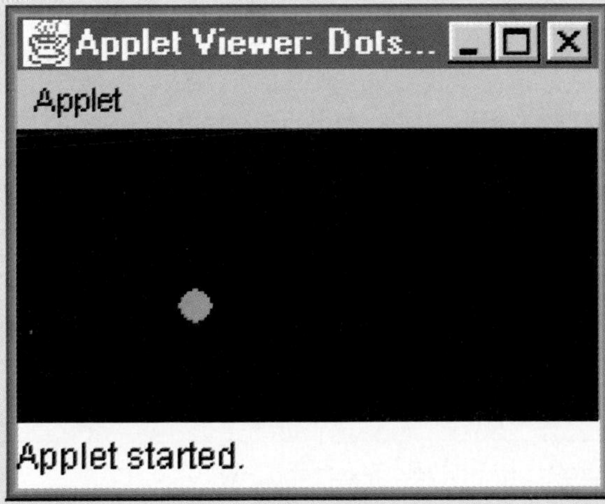

Listing 5.11

```
//********************************************************************
//  DotsMouseListener.java       Author: Lewis and Loftus
//
//  Represents a listener object for mouse events.
//********************************************************************

import java.applet.Applet;
import java.awt.*;
import java.awt.event.*;

public class DotsMouseListener implements MouseListener
{
   private Dots applet;

   //-----------------------------------------------------------------
   //  Stores a reference to the applet.
   //-----------------------------------------------------------------
   public DotsMouseListener (Dots theApplet)
   {
      applet = theApplet;
   }

   //-----------------------------------------------------------------
   //  Determines the point at which the mouse is clicked, sets the
   //  point in the applet, then forces the applet to repaint.
   //-----------------------------------------------------------------
   public void mouseClicked (MouseEvent event)
   {
      Point clickPoint = event.getPoint();
      applet.setPoint (clickPoint);
      applet.repaint();
   }

   //-----------------------------------------------------------------
   //  Provides empty definitions for unused event methods.
   //-----------------------------------------------------------------
   public void mousePressed (MouseEvent event) {}
   public void mouseReleased (MouseEvent event) {}
   public void mouseEntered (MouseEvent event) {}
   public void mouseExited (MouseEvent event) {}
}
```

can invoke methods of the applet. After creating the listener object, it is added to the applet using the `addMouseListener` method.

The `DotsMouseListener` class implements the `MouseListener` interface. One of the methods from that interface that it implements is `mouseClicked`, which will be called whenever the mouse button is clicked. The `getPoint` method of the `MouseEvent` object is called to get the location at which the mouse was clicked. That point is stored in the applet by calling the `setPoint` method, then the applet is repainted. Note that because the repaint method is called, the applet is cleared before the dot is drawn, so that only one dot at a time appears on the applet. In Chapter 6 we discuss a way to maintain the original state of the drawing.

Because the `DotsMouseListener` class implements the `MouseListener` interface, all methods of the interface must be defined, even those corresponding to events we don't care about. Therefore the `DotsMouseListener` class contains empty methods for `mousePressed`, `mouseReleased`, `mouseEntered`, and `mouseExited`. These events occur, and the corresponding methods are called, but do nothing. In Chapter 7 we discuss another technique for creating listener objects, allowing us to avoid declaring these empty methods.

Let's look at an example that responds to two events. The `RubberLines` program, shown in Listing 5.12, draws a line between two points. The first

Listing 5.12

```
//********************************************************************
//  RubberLines.java       Author: Lewis and Loftus
//
//  Demonstrates events, listeners, and rubberbanding.
//********************************************************************

import java.applet.Applet;
import java.awt.*;
import java.awt.event.*;

public class RubberLines extends Applet implements MouseListener,
                                             MouseMotionListener
{
   private final int APPLET_WIDTH = 200;
   private final int APPLET_HEIGHT = 200;

   private Point point1 = null;
   private Point point2 = null;
```

Listing 5.12 (continued)

```
   //-----------------------------------------------------------------
   //  Adds this class as a listener for all mouse-related events.
   //-----------------------------------------------------------------
   public void init()
   {
      addMouseListener (this);
      addMouseMotionListener (this);

      setBackground (Color.black);
      setSize (APPLET_WIDTH, APPLET_HEIGHT);
   }

   //-----------------------------------------------------------------
   //  Draws the current line from the intial mouse down point to
   //  the current position of the mouse.
   //-----------------------------------------------------------------
   public void paint (Graphics page)
   {
      page.setColor (Color.green);
      if (point1 != null && point2 != null)
         page.drawLine (point1.x, point1.y, point2.x, point2.y);
   }

   //-----------------------------------------------------------------
   //  Captures the position at which the mouse is initially pushed.
   //-----------------------------------------------------------------
   public void mousePressed (MouseEvent event)
   {
      point1 = event.getPoint();
   }

   //-----------------------------------------------------------------
   //  Gets the current position of the mouse as it is dragged and
   //  draws the line to create the rubberband effect.
   //-----------------------------------------------------------------
   public void mouseDragged (MouseEvent event)
   {
      point2 = event.getPoint();
      repaint();
   }
```

Listing 5.12 (continued)

```
   //-----------------------------------------------------------------
   //  Provides empty definitions for unused event methods.
   //-----------------------------------------------------------------
   public void mouseClicked (MouseEvent event) {}
   public void mouseReleased (MouseEvent event) {}
   public void mouseEntered (MouseEvent event) {}
   public void mouseExited (MouseEvent event) {}
   public void mouseMoved (MouseEvent event) {}
}
```

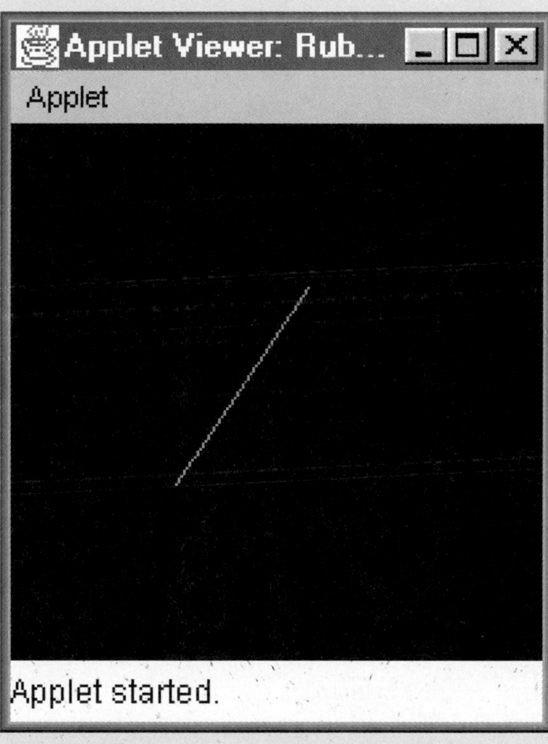

point is determined by the location at which the mouse is first pressed down. The second point changes as the mouse is dragged while the mouse button is held down. When the button is released, the line is finished. When the mouse button is pressed again, a new line is started.

Key Concept

Rubberbanding is the visual effect created when a graphical shape seems to expand and contract as the mouse is dragged.

When the `mousePressed` method is called, the variable `point1` is set. Then as the mouse is dragged, the variable `point2` is continually being reset and the applet repainted. Therefore, the line is constantly being redrawn as the mouse is dragged, giving the appearance that one line is being drawn, or stretched, to the position where it belongs. This effect is called *rubberbanding,* and is common among graphical programs.

Because we need to listen for both a mouse pressed event and a mouse dragged event, we need a listener that responds to both mouse events and mouse motion events. Instead of creating a separate listener object for this program, we allow the applet itself to serve as the listener. Note that the `RubberLines` class implements both the `MouseListener` and `MouseMotionListener` interfaces. Then a reference to the applet, using the `this` reference, is passed to `addMouseListener` and `addMouseMotionListener` methods. So not only does the applet generate the mouse events, it also listens for them to occur and responds appropriately.

Having the applet serve as the listener simplifies the program somewhat. Note that we no longer need to have methods dedicated to communicating information between the listener and the applet, as we did in the `Dots` program. However, putting too much responsibility on one class is not always a good idea. For larger programs, it is often better to carefully distribute the responsibilities.

Not only could we have had a separate listener object for the events, we could have had two: one listening for mouse events and one listening for mouse motion events. A component can have multiple listeners for various event categories. For that matter, a single listener object can serve multiple components, if appropriate.

The `Direction` program, shown in Listing 5.13, is another example of an applet that uses events and listeners. The purpose of this program is to move an image of an arrow around the screen as the user presses the directional arrow keys on the keyboard.

In fact, the `Direction` applet loads four separate images of arrows pointing in the four primary directions (up, down, right, and left). When the user presses an arrow key, the corresponding image is displayed. If that arrow key is continually pressed, the image moves in that direction. The user can hold down an arrow key and watch the image move across the applet window. When the arrow reaches a boundary of the window, it moves no further.

To respond to the user pressing keys on the keyboard, we listen for *key events.* The `KeyListener` interface defines three methods that we can use to respond to keyboard activity. These methods are listed in Figure 5.9.

Listing 5.13

```
//********************************************************************
//  Direction.java       Author: Lewis and Loftus
//
//  Demonstrates key events and the use of inner classes for event
//  listeners.
//********************************************************************

import java.applet.*;
import java.awt.*;
import java.awt.event.*;

public class Direction extends Applet
{
   private final int APPLET_WIDTH = 200;
   private final int APPLET_HEIGHT = 200;
   private final int JUMP = 5;  // increment for image movement

   private final int IMAGE_SIZE = 31;

   private Image up, down, right, left, currentImage;
   private AudioClip bonk;
   private int x, y;

   //-----------------------------------------------------------------
   //  Sets up the applet by creating listeners, loading images, etc.
   //-----------------------------------------------------------------
   public void init()
   {
      requestFocus();  // make sure the applet has the keyboard focus

      addKeyListener (new DirectionKeyListener());

      x = y = 0;

      up = getImage (getCodeBase(), "cyanUp.gif");
      down = getImage (getCodeBase(), "cyanDown.gif");
      left = getImage (getCodeBase(), "cyanLeft.gif");
      right = getImage (getCodeBase(), "cyanRight.gif");

      currentImage = right;

      bonk = getAudioClip (getCodeBase(), "bonk.au");

      setBackground (Color.black);
      setSize (APPLET_WIDTH, APPLET_HEIGHT);
   }
```

Listing 5.13 ***(continued)***

```
   //-----------------------------------------------------------------
   //  Paints the current image in the current location.
   //-----------------------------------------------------------------
   public void paint (Graphics page)
   {
      page.drawImage (currentImage, x, y, this);
   }

   //*****************************************************************
   //  Represents a listener for keyboard activity.
   //*****************************************************************
   private class DirectionKeyListener implements KeyListener
   {
      //--------------------------------------------------------------
      //  Responds to the user pressing arrow keys by adjusting the
      //  image location accordingly.
      //--------------------------------------------------------------
      public void keyPressed (KeyEvent event)
      {
         switch (event.getKeyCode())
         {
            case KeyEvent.VK_UP:
               currentImage = up;
               if (y > 0)
                  y -= JUMP;
               break;
            case KeyEvent.VK_DOWN:
               currentImage = down;
               if (y < APPLET_HEIGHT-IMAGE_SIZE)
                  y += JUMP;
               break;
            case KeyEvent.VK_LEFT:
               currentImage = left;
               if (x > 0)
                  x -= JUMP;
               break;
            case KeyEvent.VK_RIGHT:
               currentImage = right;
               if (x < APPLET_WIDTH-IMAGE_SIZE)
                  x += JUMP;
               break;
            default:
               bonk.play();
         }

         repaint();
      }
```

Listing 5.13 ***(continued)***

```
      //-----------------------------------------------------------------
      //  Provides empty definitions for unused event methods.
      //-----------------------------------------------------------------
      public void keyTyped (KeyEvent event) {}
      public void keyReleased (KeyEvent event) {}
   }
}
```

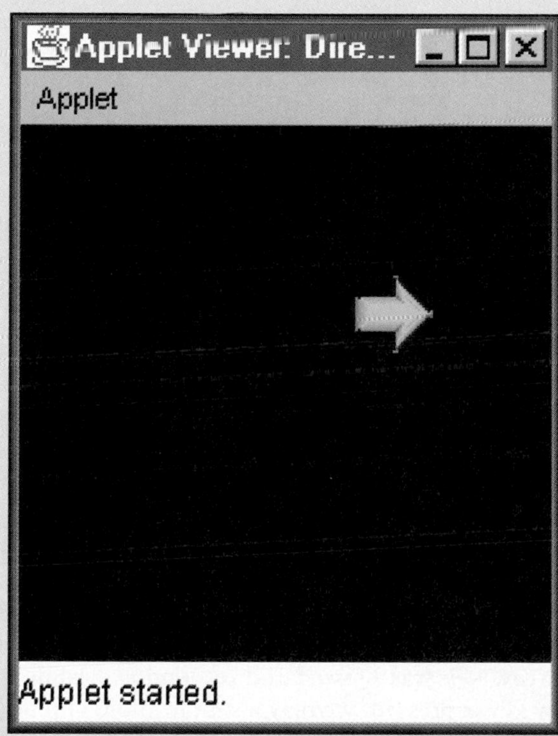

```
void keyPressed (KeyEvent event)
   Called when a key is pressed.

void keyReleased (KeyEvent event)
   Called when a key is released.

void keyTyped (KeyEvent event)
   Called when a pressed key or key combination produces a key character.
```

Figure 5.9 The methods of the `KeyListener` interface

In the `Direction` program, we handle events using a separate listener class that is implemented as an inner class, as described in Section 5.3. That is, the listener class is completely defined within the scope of an outer class, which usually represents the component with which the listener interacts. This is an excellent use of a nested class, because there is a natural relationship between the listener and the outer class, and the communication between the two classes is simplified. Note that the inner class can make use of the data defined in the outer class (such as the `currentImage` variable) simply because the scope allows it. This way we avoid the clumsy communication that we had to set up in the `Dots` program, and we have avoided putting too much responsibility in one place, as we did in the `RubberLines` program. Using inner classes to define listeners is generally considered to be the preferred technique, and we will use it in all future event-driven examples.

Key Concept

Inner classes are often used to define listener objects.

The `KeyEvent` object passed to the `keyPressed` method of the listener can be used to determine which key was pressed. In the `Direction` example, we call the `getKeyCode` method of the event object to get a numeric code that represents the key that was pressed. We use a `switch` statement to determine which arrow key was pressed and respond accordingly. If any key other than an arrow key is pressed, we play a simple audio clip to indicate that an invalid key was used.

5.6 Animations

An *animation* is an image or drawing, or a series of images or drawings, that give the appearance of movement on the screen. A cartoon is animated by drawing several images that are similar such that, when shown in progression at an appropriate speed, they fool the human eye into thinking there is one image in continuous motion.

We can create animations in a Java program in a similar way. For example, we can make it seem that a single image is moving across the screen. This is similar to the effect in the `Direction` program seen in the previous section, except that in that case, the user controlled the movement of the image by pressing an arrow key. In animations, the program will control the speed at which the scene changes. We draw an image in one location, wait long enough for the human eye to see it, then redraw it in a slightly different location.

To create the necessary pause during our animation, we use a *timer* object created from the `Timer` class.

The `Timer` Class

A timer object generates *action events* at regular intervals. An action event is used to represent a general action. We set up an action event listener to catch and handle the action events as they occur, just as we do for any other kind of event. An action listener requires that we define a method called `actionPerformed`. To perform an animation, we set up a timer to generate an action event periodically, then update the animation graphics in the action listener. The methods of the `Timer` class are shown in Figure 5.10.

The `Rebound` applet, shown in Listing 5.14, displays the image of a smiling face that seems to glide across the applet window at an angle, bouncing off of the window edges.

The timer is created in the `init` method of the applet so that its events are handled by a listener defined by the `ReboundActionListener` class. An inner

`Timer (int delay, ActionListener listener)`
Constructor: creates a timer that generates an action event at regular intervals, specified by the delay. The event will be handled by the specified listener.

`void addActionListener (ActionListener listener)`
Adds an action listener to the timer.

`boolean isRunning ()`
Returns true if the timer is running.

`void setDelay (int delay)`
Sets the delay of the timer.

`void start ()`
Starts the timer, causing it to generate action events.

`void stop ()`
Stops the timer, causing it to stop generating action events.

Figure 5.10 Some methods of the `Timer` class

Listing 5.14

```
//********************************************************************
//  Rebound.java       Author: Lewis and Loftus
//
//  Demonstrates an animation and the use of the Timer class.
//********************************************************************

import java.applet.Applet;
import java.awt.*;
import java.awt.event.*;
import javax.swing.Timer;

public class Rebound extends Applet
{
   private final int APPLET_WIDTH = 200;
   private final int APPLET_HEIGHT = 100;

   private final int IMAGE_SIZE = 35;
   private final int DELAY = 20;

   private Timer timer;
   private Image image;
   private int x, y, moveX, moveY;

   //-----------------------------------------------------------------
   //  Sets up the applet, including the timer for the animation.
   //-----------------------------------------------------------------
   public void init()
   {
      addMouseListener (new ReboundMouseListener());

      timer = new Timer (DELAY, new ReboundActionListener());
      timer.start();

      x = 0;
      y = 40;
      moveX = moveY = 3;

      image = getImage (getCodeBase(), "happyFace.gif");

      setBackground (Color.black);
      setSize (APPLET_WIDTH, APPLET_HEIGHT);
   }
```

Listing 5.14 ***(continued)***

```
   //-----------------------------------------------------------------
   //  Draws the image in the current location.
   //-----------------------------------------------------------------
   public void paint (Graphics page)
   {
      page.drawImage (image, x, y, this);
   }


   //*****************************************************************
   //  Represents the mouse listner for the applet.
   //*****************************************************************
   private class ReboundMouseListener implements MouseListener
   {
      //--------------------------------------------------------------
      //  Stops or starts the timer (and therefore the animation)
      //  when the mouse button is clicked.
      //--------------------------------------------------------------
      public void mouseClicked (MouseEvent event)
      {
         if (timer.isRunning())
            timer.stop();
         else
            timer.start();
      }

      //--------------------------------------------------------------
      //  Provide empty definitions for unused event methods.
      //--------------------------------------------------------------
      public void mouseEntered (MouseEvent event) {}
      public void mouseExited (MouseEvent event) {}
      public void mousePressed (MouseEvent event) {}
      public void mouseReleased (MouseEvent event) {}
   }
```

Listing 5.14 ***(continued)***

```
   //*****************************************************************
   //  Represents the action listener for the timer.
   //*****************************************************************
   private class ReboundActionListener implements ActionListener
   {
      //--------------------------------------------------------------
      //  Updates the position of the image and possibly the direction
      //  of movement whenever the timer fires an action event.
      //--------------------------------------------------------------
      public void actionPerformed (ActionEvent event)
      {
         x += moveX;
         y += moveY;
         if (x <= 0 || x >= APPLET_WIDTH-IMAGE_SIZE)
            moveX = moveX * -1;

         if (y <= 0 || y >= APPLET_HEIGHT-IMAGE_SIZE)
            moveY = moveY * -1;

         repaint();
      }
   }
}
```

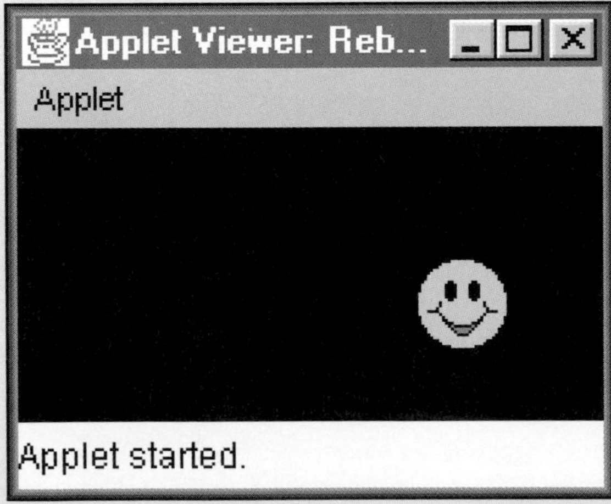

class defines a mouse listener. The user can press the mouse button to pause and resume the animation.

The methods `start` and `stop` are implemented in the applet to start and stop the timer, respectively. This causes the animation to pause or resume as appropriate. It is always appropriate to implement the `stop` method of an applet when it performs continuous processing, such as an animation. Recall from Chapter 4 that the `stop` method of an applet is called automatically when the user leaves the browser page of the applet. Therefore the animation is automatically paused when the user can't see it. This is considered to be the polite way to implement an applet, so that the user's machine isn't wasting CPU time on unproductive activity.

Note that the `Timer` class is part of the `javax.swing` package. Using the `Timer` class is the preferred technique for performing animations in Java, but will only work in a browser that is set up to execute applets that use Java 2 technology (as discussed in Chapter 1). The JDK 1.2 appletviewer will execute these applets correctly without any special setup. Other Swing classes are explored in Chapter 9.

Web Bonus

The text Web site contains instructions on how to set up a browser to use Java 2 classes such as the Swing classes.

The speed of the animation in the `Rebound` applet is a function of two factors: the pause between the action events and the distance the image is shifted each time. In this example, the timer is set to generate an action event every 20 milliseconds, and the image is shifted 3 pixels each time it is updated. Experiment with these values to change the speed of the animation. The goal should be to create the illusion of movement that is pleasing to the eye.

Summary of Key Concepts

- An object reference variable stores the address of an object.
- Several references can refer to the same object. These references are aliases of each other.
- The == operator compares object references for equality, returning true if the references are aliases of each other.
- The `equals` method can be defined to determine equality between objects in any way we think is appropriate.
- If an object has no references to it, a program cannot use it. Java performs automatic garbage collection by periodically reclaiming the memory space used by these objects.
- When an object is passed to a method, the actual and formal parameters become aliases of each other. Changes to the object through the reference will be reflected in the calling method.
- A static variable is shared among all instances of a class. A static method can be called through the class in which it is defined.
- An interface is a collection of abstract methods that are defined by all classes that implement the interface.
- An interface name can be used to declare an object reference variable. An interface reference can refer to any object of any class that implements the interface.
- Interfaces allow us to make polymorphic references, in which the method that is invoked is based on the particular object being referenced at the time.
- An event is an object that usually represents a user action, such as a mouse click. A program can be designed to recognize and respond to events.
- A listener object has methods that are automatically called when an event occurs.
- Rubberbanding is the visual effect created when a graphical shape seems to expand and contract as the mouse is dragged.
- Inner classes are often used to define listener objects.

▶ Self-Review Questions

5.1 What is an alias?

5.2 What is the difference between a static variable and an instance variable?

5.3 What is the difference between a class and an interface?

5.4 What is a polymorphic reference? How do interfaces allow us to create them?

5.5 What is the relationship between an event and a listener?

Exercises

5.1 Discuss the manner in which Java passes parameters to a method. Include in your discussion the ways that different types of information are affected by this policy.

5.2 Explain why a static method cannot refer to an instance variable.

5.3 Explain how polymorphic references seem to relax the type compatibility rules regarding assignment. Explain why this extension is reasonable.

5.4 Can a class implement two interfaces that each contain the same method signature? Explain.

5.5 Explain how a call to the `addMouseListener` method represents a polymorphic situation.

Programming Projects

5.1 Modify the `PigLatinTranslator` class from Chapter 4 so that its `translate` method is static. Modify the `PigLatin` class so that it invokes the method correctly.

5.2 Modify the `Rational` class from Chapter 4 so that it implements the `Comparable` interface. To perform the comparison, compute an equivalent floating point value from the numerator and denominator for both `Rational` objects, then compare them using a tolerance value of 0.0001. Write a main driver to test your modifications.

5.3 Design and implement an applet that counts the number of times the mouse has been clicked and display that number in the center of the applet window.

5.4 Design and implement an applet that draws a circle using a rubberbanding technique. The circle size is determined by a mouse drag. Expand the circle using the original mouse click location as a fixed center point. Compute the distance between the current location of the mouse pointer and the center point to determine the current radius of the circle.

5.5 Design and implement an applet that serves as a mouse odometer, continually displaying how far the mouse has moved (while it is over the applet). Use the mouse movement event to determine the current position and compare it to the last position of the mouse. Use the distance formula to see how far the mouse has traveled, and add that to a running total distance. Display the value in the middle of the applet window.

5.6 Design and implement an applet that changes color depending on where the mouse pointer is currently located. If the mouse pointer is on the left half of the applet window, display green; if it is on the right half, display cyan. Do not repaint the applet unless the color actually changes.

5.7 Design and implement a class that represents a space ship, which can be drawn (side view) in any particular location. Create an applet that displays the spaceship so that it follows the movement of the mouse. When the mouse button is pressed down, have a laser beam shoot out of the front of the spaceship (one continuous beam, not a moving projectile) until the mouse button is released. Have a laser sound continually play as long as the laser is "firing."

5.8 Design and implement an applet that plays a game called Catch the Creature. Create a class that represents a creature that can be drawn on the screen at any particular location. Have the creature appear at a random location on the applet window for a random duration, then disappear and reappear somewhere else. The goal is to "catch" the creature by pressing the mouse button while the mouse pointer is on the creature image. Include in the creature class a method that determines if the location of the mouse click corresponds to the current location of the creature. Display an updated count of the number of times the creature is caught. Play an appropriate audio clip whenever the creature pops into another location.

5.9 Modify the `Direction` program from this chapter to respond to keyclicks to move the image in diagonal directions. When the character 't' is pressed, move the image up and to the left. Likewise, use 'u' to move up and right, 'g' to move down and left, and 'j' to move down and right. Do not move the image if it has reached a window boundary. Retain the ability to move the image in the primary directions using the arrow keys.

5.10 Modify the `StickFigure` class from Chapter 4 to include methods `setX` and `setY` to set the x and y coordinate of the figure. Use the `Timer` class to create an animation that lets a stick figure glide across the floor from left to right. When the figure reaches the right edge of the window, have it reappear on the left side again. Implement the start and stop methods for polite browsing.

5.11 Design and implement an animation applet that shows a horizontal line moving across the screen, eventually passing across a vertical line. As the vertical line is passed, the horizontal line should change color. The change of color should occur while the horizontal line crosses the vertical one; therefore, while crossing, the horizontal line will be two different colors.

5.12 Design and implement an animation applet that shows a car driving across the screen from right to left. Create a `Car` class that represents the car.

▶ Answers to Self-Review Questions

5.1 Two references are aliases of each other if they refer to the same object. Changing the state of the object through one reference changes it for the other because there is actually only one object.

5.2 Memory space for an instance variable is created for each object that is instantiated from a class. A static variable is shared among all objects of a class.

5.3 A class can be instantiated; an interface cannot. An interface contains a set of abstract methods for which a class provides the implementation.

5.4 A polymorphic reference is one that can be used to refer to objects of various types at different times. An interface name can be used to declare a reference, and that reference can be used to refer to any object of any class that has implemented the method.

5.5 Events are separated into various categories, such as mouse events, mouse motion events, keyboard events, and so on. A listener is set up to listen for a certain category of events to be generated from a particular component.

Arrays and Vectors

In our programming efforts, we often want to gather objects or primitive data in a form that is easy to access and modify. This chapter introduces arrays, which are programming constructs that group data into lists. They are a fundamental component of most high-level languages. We then explore the `Vector` *class in the Java standard class library, which provides capabilities similar to arrays and with additional features.*

Chapter Objectives

- Define and use arrays for basic data organization.
- Describe how arrays and array elements are passed as parameters.
- Explore how arrays and other objects can be combined to manage complex information.
- Describe the use of multidimensional arrays.
- Examine the `Vector` class and the costs of its versatility.

6.1 Arrays

An *array* is a simple but powerful programming language construct used to group and organize data. When writing a program that manages a large amount of information, such as a list of 100 names, it is not feasible to declare separate variables for each piece of data. Arrays solve this problem by letting us declare one variable that can hold multiple values.

Array Indexing

An array is a list of values. Each value is stored at a specific, numbered position in the array. The number corresponding to each position is called an *index* or a *subscript*. Figure 6.1 shows an array of integers and the indexes that correspond to each position. The array is called `height` and it contains integers that represent several people's heights in inches.

In Java, array indexes always begin at zero. Therefore, the value stored at index 5 is actually the sixth value in the array. The array shown in Figure 6.1 has 11 values, indexed from 0 to 10.

To access a value in an array, you use the name of the array followed by the index in square brackets. For example, the following expression refers to the ninth value in the array `height`:

```
height[8]
```

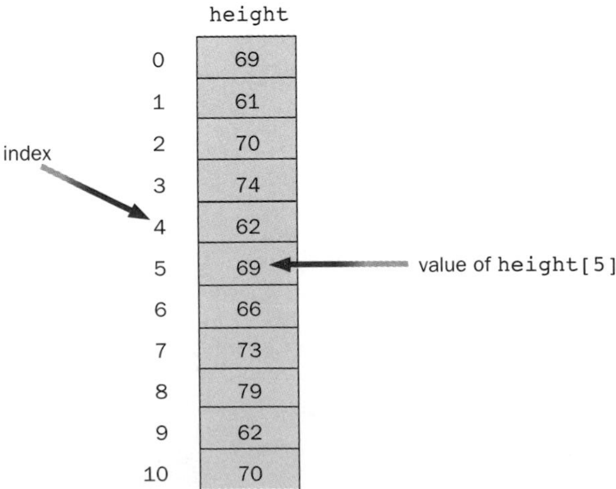

Figure 6.1 An array called `height` containing integer values

According to Figure 6.1, `height[8]` (pronounced height-sub-eight) contains the value 79. Don't confuse the value of the index, in this case 8, with the value stored in the array at that index, in this case 79.

> **Key Concept**
> A Java array of size N is indexed from 0 to $N - 1$.

The expression `height[8]` refers to a single integer stored at a particular memory location. It can be used wherever an integer variable can be used. Therefore, you can assign a value to it, use it in calculations, print its value, and so on. Furthermore, because array indexes are integers, you can use integer expressions to determine the index into an array. These concepts are demonstrated in the following lines of code:

```
height[2] = 72;
height[count] = feet * 12;
average = (height[0] + height[1] + height[2]) / 3;
System.out.println ("The middle value is " + height[MAX/2]);
pick = height[(int)Math.random()*11];
```

Declaring and Using Arrays

In Java, arrays are objects. To create an array, the reference to the array must be declared. The array can then be instantiated using the `new` operator, which allocates memory space to store values. The following code represents the declaration for the array shown in Figure 6.1:

```
int[] height = new int[11];
```

The variable `height` is declared to be an array of integers whose type is written as `int[]`. An array contains multiple values all having the same type. For example, we can create an array that can hold integers or an array that can hold strings, but not an array that can hold both integers and strings. Note that the type of the variable (`int[]`) does not include the size of the array. The instantiation of `height`, using the `new` operator, reserves the memory space to store 11 integers indexed from 0 to 10. Once an array is declared to be a certain size, the number of values it can hold cannot be changed.

> **Key Concept**
> A Java array is an object. Memory space for the array elements are reserved by instantiating the array using the `new` operator.

The example shown in Listing 6.1 creates an array called list that can hold 15 integers, and loads it with successive increments of 10. It then changes the value of the sixth element in the array (at index 5). Finally, it prints all values stored in the array.

Figure 6.2 shows the array as it changes during program execution. It is often convenient to use `for` loops when handling arrays because the number of positions in the array is constant. Note that a constant called `LIMIT` is used in several places in the `BasicArray` program. This constant is used to declare the size of the array, to control the `for` loop that initializes the array values,

Listing 6.1

```
//********************************************************************
//  BasicArray.java       Author: Lewis and Loftus
//
//  Demonstrates basic array declaration and use.
//********************************************************************

public class BasicArray
{
   //-----------------------------------------------------------------
   //  Creates an array, fills it with various integer values,
   //  modifies one value, then prints them out.
   //-----------------------------------------------------------------
   public static void main (String[] args)
   {
      final int LIMIT = 15;
      final int MULTIPLE = 10;

      int[] list = new int[LIMIT];

      //  Initialize array values
      for (int index = 0; index < LIMIT; index++)
         list[index] = index * MULTIPLE;

      list[5] = 999;  // change one array value

      for (int index = 0; index < LIMIT; index++)
         System.out.print (list[index] + "  ");

      System.out.println ();
   }
}
```

```
0  10  20  30  40  999  60  70  80  90  100  110  120  130  140
```

and to control the `for` loop that prints the values. The use of constants in this way is a good practice. It makes your program more readable and easier to modify. For instance, if the size of the array needed to change, only one line of code (the constant declaration) would need to be modified.

The square brackets used to indicate the index of an array are treated as an operator in Java. Therefore, just like the + operator or the <= operator, the

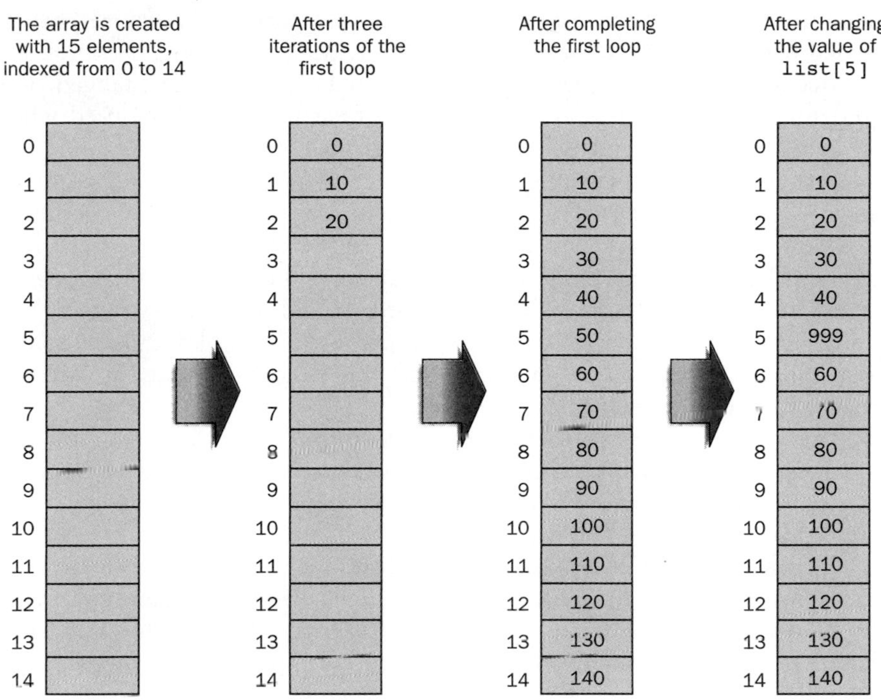

Figure 6.2 The array `list` as it changes in the `BasicArray` program

index operator (`[]`) has a precedence relative to the other Java operators that determines when it is executed. It has the highest precedence of all Java operators.

The index operator performs *automatic bounds checking*. Bounds checking ensures that the index is in range for the array being referenced. Whenever a reference to an array element is made, the index must be greater than or equal to zero and less than the size of the array. For example, suppose an array called `prices` is created with 25 elements. The valid indexes for the array are from 0 to 24. Whenever a reference is made to a particular element in the array (such as `prices[count]`), the value of the index is checked. If it is in the valid range of indexes for the array (0 to 24), the reference is carried out. If the index is not valid, an exception called `ArrayIndexOutOfBoundsException` is thrown.

> **Key Concept**
>
> Bounds checking ensures that an index used to refer to an array element is in range. The Java index operator performs automatic bounds checking.

Because array indexes begin at zero and go up to one less than the size of the array, it is easy to inadvertently create *off-by-one errors* in a program. When referencing array elements, be careful to ensure that the index stays within the array bounds.

Another important characteristic of Java arrays is that their size is held in a constant called `length` in the array object. It is a public constant, and therefore can be referenced directly. For example, after the array `prices` is created with 25 elements, the constant `prices.length` contains the value 25. Its value is set once when the array is first created and cannot be changed. The `length` constant, which is an integral part of each array, can be used when the array size is needed instead of using a separate constant.

Let's look at another example. The program shown in Listing 6.2 reads 10 integers into an array called numbers, and then prints them in reverse order.

Note that in the `ReverseNumbers` program the array numbers is declared to have 10 elements and therefore is indexed from 0 to 9. The index range is controlled in the `for` loops by using the `length` field of the array object. You should carefully set the initial value of loop control variables and the conditions that terminate loops to guarantee that only valid indexes are used to reference an array element.

The `LetterCount` example, shown in Listing 6.3, uses two arrays and a `String` object. The array called `upper` is used to store the number of times each uppercase alphabetic letter is found in the string. The array called `lower` serves the same purpose for lowercase letters.

Because there are 26 letters in the English alphabet, both the `upper` and `lower` arrays are declared with 26 elements. Each element contains an integer that is initially zero by default. The `for` loop scans through the string one character at a time. The appropriate counter in the appropriate array is incremented for each character found in the string.

Both of the counter arrays are indexed from 0 to 25. We have to map each character to a counter. A logical way to do this is to use `upper[0]` to count the number of `'A'` characters found, `upper[1]` to count the number of `'B'` characters, etc. Likewise, `lower[0]` is used to count `'a'` characters, `lower[1]` to count `'b'` characters, etc. A separate variable called `other` is used to count any nonalphabetic characters that are encountered.

Listing 6.2

```
//********************************************************************
//  ReverseNumbers.java       Author: Lewis and Loftus
//
//  Demonstrates array index processing.
//********************************************************************
```

Listing 6.2 ***(continued)***

```
import cs1.Keyboard;

public class ReverseNumbers
{
   //-----------------------------------------------------------------
   //  Reads a list of numbers from the user, storing them in an
   //  array, then prints them in the opposite order.
   //-----------------------------------------------------------------
   public static void main (String[] args)
   {
      double[] numbers = new double[10];

      System.out.println ("The size of the array: " + numbers.length);

      for (int index = 0; index < numbers.length; index++)
      {
         System.out.print ("Enter number " + (index+1) + ": ");
         numbers[index] = Keyboard.readDouble();
      }

      System.out.println ("The numbers in reverse:");

      for (int index = numbers.length-1; index >= 0; index--)
         System.out.print (numbers[index] + "  ");

      System.out.println ();
   }
}
```

```
The size of the array: 10
Enter number 1: 45.7
Enter number 2: 17.25
Enter number 3: 29.03
Enter number 4: 55.2
Enter number 5: 91.404
Enter number 6: 34.6
Enter number 7: 28.38
Enter number 8: 86.55
Enter number 9: 69.0
Enter number 10: 72.91
The numbers in reverse:
72.91  69.0  86.55  28.38  34.6  91.404  55.2  29.03  17.25  45.7
```

Listing 6.3

```
//********************************************************************
//  LetterCount.java       Author: Lewis and Loftus
//
//  Demonstrates the relationship between arrays and strings.
//********************************************************************

import cs1.Keyboard;

public class LetterCount
{
   //-----------------------------------------------------------------
   //  Reads a sentence from the user and counts the number of
   //  uppercase and lowercase letters contained in it.
   //-----------------------------------------------------------------
   public static void main (String[] args)
   {
      final int NUMCHARS = 26;

      int[] upper = new int[NUMCHARS];
      int[] lower = new int[NUMCHARS];

      char current;   // the current character being processed
      int other = 0;  // counter for non-alphabetics

      System.out.println ("Enter a sentence:");
      String line = Keyboard.readString();

      //  Count the number of each letter occurance
      for (int ch = 0; ch < line.length(); ch++)
      {
         current = line.charAt(ch);
         if (current >= 'A' && current <= 'Z')
            upper[current-'A']++;
         else
            if (current >= 'a' && current <= 'z')
               lower[current-'a']++;
            else
               other++;
      }
```

Listing 6.3 (continued)

```
      //  Print the results
      System.out.println ();
      for (int letter=0; letter < upper.length; letter++)
      {
         System.out.print ( (char) (letter + 'A') );
         System.out.print (": " + upper[letter]);
         System.out.print ("\t\t" + (char) (letter + 'a') );
         System.out.println (": " + lower[letter]);
      }

      System.out.println ();
      System.out.println ("Non-alphabetic characters: " + other);
   }
}
```

```
Enter a sentence:
In Casablanca, Humphrey Bogart never says "Play it again, Sam."
A: 0            a: 10
B: 1            b: 1
C: 1            c: 1
D: 0            d: 0
E: 0            e: 3
F: 0            f: 0
G: 0            g: 2
H: 1            h: 1
I: 1            i: 2
J: 0            j: 0
K: 0            k: 0
L: 0            l: 2
M: 0            m: 2
N: 0            n: 4
O: 0            o: 1
P: 1            p: 1
Q: 0            q: 0
R: 0            r: 3
S: 1            s: 3
T: 0            t: 2
U: 0            u: 1
V: 0            v: 1
W: 0            w: 0
X: 0            x: 0
Y: 0            y: 3
Z: 0            z: 0

Non-alphabetic characters: 14
```

We use the current character to calculate which index in the array to reference. Remember that each character has a numeric value based on the Unicode character set, and that the uppercase and lowercase alphabetic letters are continuous and in order (see Appendix C). Therefore, taking the numeric value of an uppercase letter such as `'E'` (which is 69) and subtracting the numeric value of the character `'A'` (which is 65) yields 4, which is the correct index for the counter of the character `'E'`. Note that nowhere in the program do we actually have to know what the specific numeric values are.

Alternate Array Syntax

Syntactically, there are two ways to declare an array reference in Java. The first, which is used in the previous examples and throughout this book, is by associating the brackets with the type of the values stored in the array. The second technique is to associate the brackets with the name of the array. Therefore, the following two declarations are equivalent:

```
int[] grades;
int grades[];
```

Although there is no difference between these declaration techniques as far as the compiler is concerned, the first is consistent with other types of declarations. Consider the following declarations:

```
int total, sum, result;
int[] grade1, grade2, grade3;
```

In the first declaration, the type of the three variables, `int`, is given at the beginning of the line. Similarly, in the second declaration, the type of the three variables, `int[]`, is also given at the beginning. In both cases, the type applies to all variables in that particular declaration.

When the alternative form of array declaration is used, it can lead to confusing situations, such as the following:

```
int grade1[], grade2, grade3[];
```

The variables `grade1` and `grade3` are declared to be arrays of integers, but `grade2` is a single integer. Although most declarations declare variables of the same type, this example declares variables of two different types. Why did the programmer write a declaration this way? Is it a mistake? Should `grade2` be an array? This confusion is eliminated if the array brackets are associated with the element's type. Therefore, we associate the brackets with the element's type throughout this book.

Initializer Lists

An important alternative technique for instantiating arrays is the use of an *initializer list* that lists the initial values for the elements of the array. It is essentially the same idea as initializing a variable of a primitive data type in its declaration, except that an array requires several values. The items in an initializer list are separated by commas and delimited by braces ({}). When an initializer list is used, the new operator is not used. The size of the array is determined by the number of items in the initializer list. For example:

```
int[] scores = {87, 98, 69, 54, 65, 76, 87, 99};
```

Key Concept
An initializer list can be used to instantiate an array object instead of using the new operator. The size of the array and its initial values are determined by the initializer list.

This declaration instantiates the array scores as an array of eight integers, indexed from 0 to 7. An initializer list can only be used when an array is first declared.

The type of each value in an initializer list must match the type of the array elements. Let's look at another example:

```
char[] letterGrades = {'A', 'B', 'C', 'D', 'F'};
```

In this case, the variable letterGrades is declared to be an array of five characters, and the initializer list contains character literals. The program shown in Listing 6.4 demonstrates the use of an initializer list to instantiate an array.

Arrays as Parameters

An entire array can be passed as a parameter to a method. Because an array is an object, when an entire array is passed as a parameter, a copy of the reference to the original array is passed. The method can change an element of the array permanently because it is referring to the original element value. The method cannot permanently change the reference itself because a copy of the original reference is sent to the method. These rules are consistent with the rules that govern any object type.

Key Concept
An entire array can be passed as a parameter, making the formal parameter an alias to the original.

An element of an array can be passed to a method as well. If the type of the element is a primitive type, a copy of the value is passed. If that element is a reference to an object, a copy of the object reference is passed. Arrays of objects are discussed further in the next section. As always, the impact of changes made to a parameter inside the method depends on the type of the parameter.

Listing 6.4

```
//********************************************************************
//  Primes.java       Author: Lewis and Loftus
//
//  Demonstrates the use of an initializer list for an array.
//********************************************************************

public class Primes
{
   //-----------------------------------------------------------------
   //  Stores some prime numbers in an array and prints them.
   //-----------------------------------------------------------------
   public static void main (String[] args)
   {
      int[] primes = {2, 3, 5, 7, 11, 13, 17, 19};

      System.out.println ("Array length: " + primes.length);

      System.out.println ("The first few prime numbers are:");

      for (int prime = 0; prime < primes.length; prime++)
         System.out.print (primes[prime] + "  ");

      System.out.println ();
   }
}
```

```
Array length: 8
The first few prime numbers are:
2  3  5  7  11  13  17  19
```

6.2 Arrays of Objects

In previous examples, the arrays stored primitive types, such as integers and characters. Arrays can also have references to objects as elements. Fairly complex information management structures can be created using only arrays and other objects. For example, an array could contain objects, and each of those objects could contain several variables and the methods that use them. Those variables could themselves be arrays, and so on. The design of a program should capitalize on the ability to combine these constructs to create the most appropriate representation for all information.

Arrays of String Objects

Consider the following declaration:

```
String[] words = new String[25];
```

The variable words is an array of references to String objects. The new operator in the declaration instantiates the array and reserves space for 25 String references. Note that this declaration does not create any String objects; it merely creates an array that holds references to String objects.

The program called GradeRange, shown in Listing 6.5, creates an array of String objects called grades, which stores letter grades for a course. The String objects are created using string literals in the initialization list. Note that this array could not have been declared as an array of characters because the plus and minus grades create two-character strings.

The output for the GradeRange program lists various letter grades and their corresponding lower numeric cutoff values, which have been stored in a corresponding array of integers.

Command-Line Arguments

The formal parameter to the main method is always an array of String objects. We've ignored that parameter in previous examples, but now we can discuss how that parameter might occasionally be useful.

The Java runtime environment invokes the main method when an application is submitted to the interpreter. The String[] parameter, which we typically call args, represents *command-line arguments* that are provided when the interpreter is invoked. Any extra information on the command line when the interpreter is invoked is stored in the args array for use by the program. This technique is another way to provide input to a program.

> **Key Concept**
> Command-line arguments are stored in an array of String objects and are passed to the main method.

The program shown in Listing 6.6 uses command-line arguments to print a name tag. It assumes the first argument represents some type of greeting and the second argument represents a person's name.

If two strings are not provided on the command line for the NameTag program, the args array will not contain any elements and the references in the program will cause an ArrayIndexOutOfBoundsException to be thrown. Extra information could be included on the command line, and it would be stored in the args array, but ignored by the program.

Listing 6.5

```
//********************************************************************
//  GradeRange.java       Author: Lewis and Loftus
//
//  Demonstrates the use of an array of String objects.
//********************************************************************

public class GradeRange
{
   //-----------------------------------------------------------------
   //  Stores the possible grades and their numeric lowest value,
   //  then prints them out.
   //-----------------------------------------------------------------
   public static void main (String[] args)
   {
      String[] grades = {"A", "A-", "B+", "B", "B-", "C+", "C", "C-",
                         "D+", "D", "D-", "F"};

      int[] cutoff = {95, 90, 87, 83, 80, 77, 73, 70, 67, 63, 60, 0};

      for (int level = 0; level < cutoff.length; level++)
         System.out.println (grades[level] + "\t" + cutoff[level]);
   }
}
```

```
A       95
A-      90
B+      87
B       83
B-      80
C+      77
C       73
C-      70
D+      67
D       63
D-      60
F       0
```

Listing 6.6

```
//********************************************************************
//  NameTag.java       Author: Lewis and Loftus
//
//  Demonstrates the use of command-line arguments.
//********************************************************************

public class NameTag
{
   //-----------------------------------------------------------------
   //  Prints a simple name tag using a greeting and a name that is
   //  specified by the user.
   //-----------------------------------------------------------------
   public static void main (String[] args)
   {
      System.out.println ();
      System.out.println ("     " + args[0]);
      System.out.println ("My name is " + args[1]);
      System.out.println ();
   }
}
```

```
>java NameTag Howdy John

     Howdy
My name is John

>java NameTag Hello William

     Hello
My name is William
```

Remember that the parameter to the `main` method is always an array of `String` objects. If you want numeric information, for instance, to be input as a command-line argument, the program will have to convert it from its string representation. Also note that in some program development environments in which a command line is not actually typed in to submit an application to the interpreter, the command-line information is specified in some other way. Consult the documentation for these specifics if necessary.

Creating Object-Array Elements

We must always take into account an important characteristic of object arrays, because the creation of the array and the creation of the objects that we store in the array are two separate things. When we declare an array of `String` objects, for example, we create an array that holds `String` references. The `String` objects themselves must be created separately. In previous examples, the `String` objects were created using `String` literals in an initializer list, or, in the case of command-line arguments, they were created by the Java runtime environment.

Key Concept

Instantiating an array of objects reserves room to store references only. The objects that are stored in each element must be instantiated separately.

This issue is demonstrated in the `Tunes` program and its accompanying classes. Listing 6.7 shows the `Tunes` class, which contains a `main` method that creates, modifies, and examines a compact disc (CD) col-

Listing 6.7

```
//********************************************************************
//  Tunes.java       Author: Lewis and Loftus
//
//  Driver for demonstrating the use of an array of objects.
//********************************************************************

import CDCollection

public class Tunes
{
   //-----------------------------------------------------------------
   //  Creates a CDCollection object and adds some CDs to it. Prints
   //  reports on the status of the collection.
   //-----------------------------------------------------------------
   public static void main (String[] args)
   {
      CDCollection music = new CDCollection ();

      music.addCD ("Storm Front", "Billy Joel", 14.95, 10);
      music.addCD ("Come On Over", "Shania Twain", 14.95, 16);
      music.addCD ("Soundtrack", "Les Miserables", 17.95, 33);
      music.addCD ("Graceland", "Paul Simon", 13.90, 11);

      System.out.println (music);

      music.addCD ("Double Live", "Garth Brooks", 19.99, 26);
      music.addCD ("Greatest Hits", "Jimmy Buffet", 15.95, 13);

      System.out.println (music);
   }
}
```

Listing 6.7 (continued)

```
******************************************
My CD Collection

Number of CDs: 4
Total value: $61.75
Average cost: $15.44

CD List:

$14.95   10      Storm Front       Billy Joel
$14.95   16      Come On Over      Shania Twain
$17.95   33      Soundtrack        Les Miserables
$13.90   11      Graceland         Paul Simon

******************************************
My CD Collection

Number of CDs: 6
Total value: $97.69
Average cost: $16.28

CD List:

$14.95   10      Storm Front       Billy Joel
$14.95   16      Come On Over      Shania Twain
$17.95   33      Soundtrack        Les Miserables
$13.90   11      Graceland         Paul Simon
$19.99   26      Double Live       Garth Brooks
$15.95   13      Greatest Hits     Jimmy Buffet
```

lection. Each CD added to the collection is specified by its title, artist, purchase price, and the number of tracks on the CD.

The `CDCollection` class is shown in Listing 6.8. It contains an array of `CD` objects representing the collection. It maintains a count of the CDs in the collection and their combined value. It also keeps track of the current size of the collection array, so that it can be increased if too many CDs are added to the collection.

Listing 6.8

```
//********************************************************************
//  CDCollection.java       Author: Lewis and Loftus
//
//  Represents a collection of compact discs.
//********************************************************************

import CD;
import java.text.NumberFormat;

public class CDCollection
{
   private CD[] collection;
   private int count;
   private double totalValue;
   private int currentSize;

   //-----------------------------------------------------------------
   //  Creates an initially empty collection.
   //-----------------------------------------------------------------
   public CDCollection ()
   {
      currentSize = 100;
      collection = new CD[currentSize];
      count = 0;
      totalValue = 0.0;
   }

   //-----------------------------------------------------------------
   //  Adds a CD to the collection, increasing the size of the
   //  collection if necessary.
   //-----------------------------------------------------------------
   public void addCD (String title, String artist, double value,
                      int tracks)
   {
      if (count == currentSize)
         increaseSize();

      collection[count] = new CD (title, artist, value, tracks);
      totalValue += value;
      count++;
   }
```

Listing 6.8 ***(continued)***

```
   //-----------------------------------------------------------------
   //  Returns a report describing the CD collection.
   //-----------------------------------------------------------------
   public String toString()
   {
      NumberFormat fmt = NumberFormat.getCurrencyInstance();

      String report = "******************************************\n";
      report += "My CD Collection\n\n";

      report += "Number of CDs: " + count + "\n";
      report += "Total value: " + fmt.format(totalValue) + "\n";
      report += "Average cost: " + fmt.format(totalValue/count);

      report += "\n\nCD List:\n\n";


      for (int cd = 0; cd < count; cd++)
         report += collection[cd].toString() + "\n";

      return report;
   }

   //-----------------------------------------------------------------
   //  Doubles the size of the collection by creating a larger array
   //  and copying into it the existing collection.
   //-----------------------------------------------------------------
   private void increaseSize ()
   {
      currentSize *= 2;

      CD[] temp = new CD[currentSize];

      for (int cd = 0; cd < collection.length; cd++)
         temp[cd] = collection[cd];

      collection = temp;
   }
}
```

The collection array is instantiated in the CDCollection constructor. Every time a CD is added to the collection (using the addCD method) a new CD object is created and a reference to it is stored in the collection array.

Each time a CD is added to the collection, we check to see if we have reached the current capacity of the collection array. If we didn't perform this check, an exception would be thrown eventually when we try to store a new CD object at an invalid index. If the current capacity has been reached, the private increaseSize method is invoked, which first creates an array that is twice as big as the current collection array. Then each CD in the existing collection is copied into the new array. Finally, the collection reference is set to the larger array. Using this technique, we theoretically never run out of room in our CD collection. The user of the CDCollection object (the main method) never has to worry about running out of space because it's all handled internally.

The toString method of the CDCollection class returns an entire report summarizing the collection. The report is created, in part, using calls to the toString method of each CD object stored in the collection. The CD class is shown in Listing 6.9.

Listing 6.9

```
//********************************************************************
//  CD.java       Author: Lewis and Loftus
//
//  Represents a compact disc.
//********************************************************************

import java.text.NumberFormat;

public class CD
{
   private String title, artist;
   private double value;
   private int tracks;

   //-----------------------------------------------------------------
   //  Creates a new CD with the specified information.
   //-----------------------------------------------------------------
   public CD (String name, String singer, double cost, int numTracks)
   {
      title = name;
      artist = singer;
      value = cost;
      tracks = numTracks;
   }
```

Listing 6.9 (continued)

```
   //-----------------------------------------------------------------
   //  Returns a description of this CD.
   //-----------------------------------------------------------------
   public String toString()
   {
      NumberFormat fmt = NumberFormat.getCurrencyInstance();

      String description;

      description = fmt.format(value) + "\t" + tracks + "\t";
      description += title + "\t" + artist;

      return description;
   }
}
```

6.3 Sorting

Sorting is the process of arranging a list of items into a well-defined order. For example, you may want to alphabetize a list of names or put a list of survey results into descending numeric order. Many sorting algorithms have been developed and critiqued over the years. In fact, sorting is considered to be a classic area of study in computer science.

This section examines two relatively simple sorting algorithms: selection sort and insertion sort. Complete coverage of various sorting techniques is beyond the scope of this book. Instead we want to introduce the topic and establish some of the fundamental ideas involved. We do not delve into a detailed analysis of the algorithms, but instead focus on the strategies involved and general characteristics.

Key Concept

Selection sort and insertion sort are two sorting algorithms that define the processing steps for putting a list of values into a well-defined order.

Selection Sort

Key Concept

Selection sort works by putting each value into its final position, one at a time.

The *selection sort* algorithm sorts a list of values by repetitively putting a particular value into its final, sorted, position. In other words, for each position in the list, the algorithm selects the value that should go in that position and puts it there. Consider the problem of putting a list of numeric values into ascending order.

The general strategy of selection sort is: Scan the entire list to find the smallest value. Exchange that value with the value in the first position of the list. Scan the rest of the list (all but the first value) to find the smallest value, then exchange it with the value in the second position of the list. Scan the rest of the list (all but the first two values) to find the smallest value, then exchange it with the value in the third position of the list. Continue this process for each position in the list. When complete, the list is sorted. Figure 6.3 demonstrates the use of the selection sort algorithm.

The program shown in Listing 6.10 uses a selection sort to arrange a list of values into ascending order. The `SortGrades` class contains a `main` method that creates an array of integers. It calls the `static` method `selectionSort` in the `Sorts` class to put them in ascending order.

The `Sorts` class is shown in Listing 6.11. It contains three static sorting algorithms. The `SortGrades` program uses only the `selectionSort` method. The other methods are discussed later in this section.

Key Concept

Swapping is the process of exchanging two values. Swapping requires three assignment statements.

The implementation of the `selectionSort` method uses two loops to sort an array of integers. The outer loop controls the position in the array where the next smallest value will be stored. The inner loop finds the smallest value in the rest of the list by scanning all positions greater than or equal to the index specified by the outer loop. When the smallest value is determined, it is exchanged

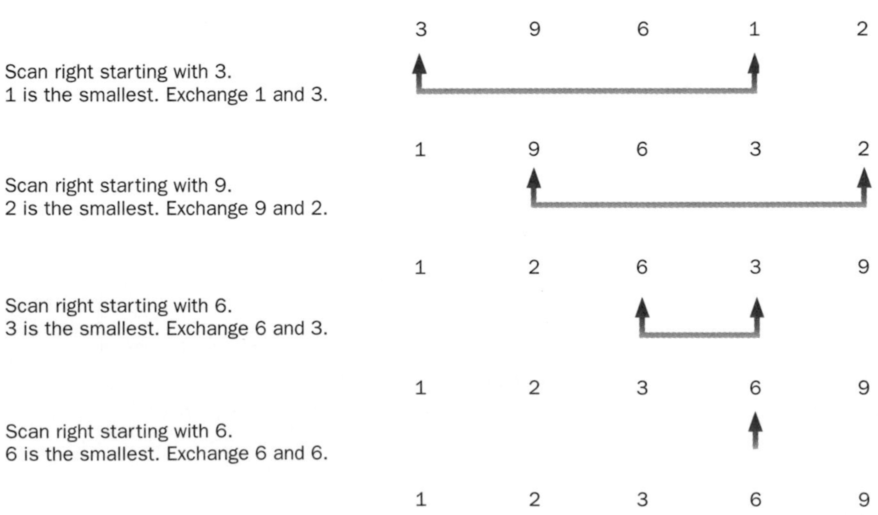

Figure 6.3 Selection sort processing

Listing 6.10

```
//********************************************************************
//  SortGrades.java       Author: Lewis and Loftus
//
//  Driver for testing a numeric selection sort.
//********************************************************************

import Sorts;

public class SortGrades
{
   //-----------------------------------------------------------------
   //  Creates an array of grades, sorts them, then prints them.
   //-----------------------------------------------------------------
   public static void main (String[] args)
   {
      int[] grades = {89, 94, 69, 80, 97, 85, 73, 91, 77, 85, 93};

      Sorts.selectionSort (grades);

      for (int index = 0; index < grades.length; index++)
         System.out.print (grades[index] + "   ");
   }
}
```

```
69   73   77   80   85   85   89   91   93   94   97
```

Listing 6.11

```
//********************************************************************
//  Sorts.java       Author: Lewis and Loftus
//
//  Demonstrates the selection sort and insertion sort algorithms,
//  as well as a generic object sort.
//********************************************************************

public class Sorts
{
   //-----------------------------------------------------------------
   //  Sorts the specified array of integers using the selection
   //  sort algorithm.
   //-----------------------------------------------------------------
   public static void selectionSort (int[] numbers)
   {
      int min, temp;

      for (int index = 0; index < numbers.length-1; index++)
      {
         min = index;
         for (int scan = index+1; scan < numbers.length; scan++)
            if (numbers[scan] < numbers[min])
               min = scan;

         // Swap the values
         temp = numbers[min];
         numbers[min] = numbers[index];
         numbers[index] = temp;
      }
   }
```

Listing 6.11 ***(continued)***

```
   //-----------------------------------------------------------------
   //  Sorts the specified array of integers using the insertion
   //  sort algorithm.
   //-----------------------------------------------------------------
   public static void insertionSort (int[] numbers)
   {
      for (int index = 1; index < numbers.length; index++)
      {
         int key = numbers[index];
         int position = index;
         // Shift larger values to the right
         while (position > 0 && numbers[position-1] > key)
         {
            numbers[position] = numbers[position-1];
            position--;
         }

         numbers[position] = key;
      }
   }

   //-----------------------------------------------------------------
   //  Sorts the specified array of objects using the insertion
   //  sort algorithm.
   //-----------------------------------------------------------------
   public static void insertionSort (Comparable[] objects)
   {
      for (int index = 1; index < objects.length; index++)
      {
         Comparable key = objects[index];
         int position = index;
```

Listing 6.11 ***(continued)***

```
         // Shift larger values to the right
         while (position > 0 && objects[position-1].compareTo(key) > 0)
         {
            objects[position] = objects[position-1];
            position--;
         }

         objects[position] = key;
      }
   }
}
```

with the value stored at index. This exchange is done in three assignment statements by using an extra variable called `temp`. This type of exchange is often called *swapping*.

Note that because this algorithm finds the smallest value during each iteration, the result is an array sorted in ascending order (i.e., smallest to largest). The algorithm can easily be changed to put values in descending order by finding the largest value each time.

Insertion Sort

The `Sorts` class also contains a method that performs an insertion sort on an array of integers. If used to sort the array of grades in the `SortGrades` program, it would produce the same results as the selection sort did. However, the processing to put the numbers in order is different.

Key Concept

Insertion sort works by inserting each value into a previously sorted subset of the list.

The *insertion sort* algorithm sorts a list of values by repetitively inserting a particular value into a subset of the list that has already been sorted. One at a time, each unsorted element is inserted at the appropriate position in that sorted subset until the entire list is in order.

The general strategy of insertion sort is: Sort the first two values in the list relative to each other by exchanging them if necessary. Insert the list's third value into the appropriate position relative to the first two (sorted) values. Then insert the fourth value into its proper position relative to the first three values in the list. Each time an insertion is made, the number of values in the sorted subset increases by one. Continue this process until all values in the list are completely sorted.

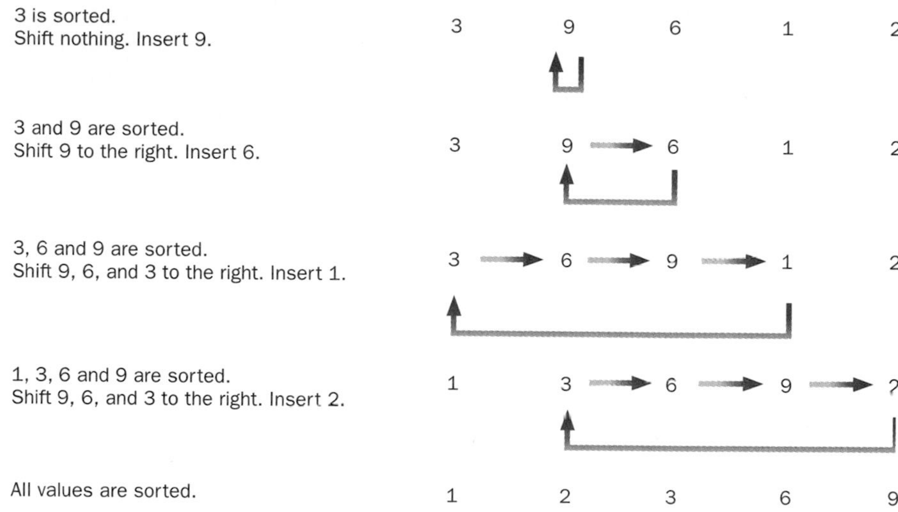
3 is sorted.
Shift nothing. Insert 9.
3 9 6 1 2
3 and 9 are sorted.
Shift 9 to the right. Insert 6.
3 9 6 1 2
3, 6 and 9 are sorted.
Shift 9, 6, and 3 to the right. Insert 1.
3 6 9 1 2
1, 3, 6 and 9 are sorted.
Shift 9, 6, and 3 to the right. Insert 2.
1 3 6 9 2
All values are sorted.
1 2 3 6 9

Figure 6.4 Insertion sort processing

The insertion process requires that the other values in the array shift to make room for the inserted element. Figure 6.4 demonstrates the use of the insertion sort algorithm.

Similar to the selection sort implementation, this `insertionSort` method uses two loops to sort an array of integers. In the insertion sort, however, the outer loop controls the index in the array of the next value to be inserted. The inner loop compares the current insert value with values stored at lower indexes (which make up a sorted subset of the entire list). If the current insert value is less than the value at `position`, then that value is shifted to the right. Shifting continues until the proper position is opened to accept the insert value. Each iteration of the outer loop adds one more value to the sorted subset of the list, until the entire list is sorted.

Sorting an Array of Objects

The `Sorts` class contains an overloaded version of the `insertionSort` method. This version of the method accepts an array of `Comparable` objects and uses the insertion sort algorithm to put the objects in sorted order. Note the similarities in the general logic of both versions of the `insertionSort` method.

The main difference between the two methods is that one sorts an array of integers and the other sorts an array of objects. We know what it means for one integer to be less than another integer, but what does it mean for one object to be less than another object? Basically, that decision is left up to the objects being sorted to determine.

The key is that the parameter to the method is an array of `Comparable` objects. That is, the array is filled with objects that have implemented the `Comparable` interface, which was discussed in Chapter 5. Recall that the `Comparable` interface contains one method, `compareTo`, which is designed to return an integer that is less than zero, equal to zero, or greater than zero (respectively) if the object is less than, equal to, or greater than the object to which it is being compared.

Let's look at an example. The `SortPhoneList` program, shown in Listing 6.12, creates an array of `Contact` objects, sorts these objects using a call to the `insertionSort` method, then prints the sorted list.

Listing 6.12

```
//********************************************************************
//  SortPhoneList.java       Author: Lewis and Loftus
//
//  Driver for testing an object selection sort.
//********************************************************************

import Sorts;

public class SortPhoneList
{
   //-----------------------------------------------------------------
   //  Creates an array of Contact objects, sorts them, then prints
   //  them.
   //-----------------------------------------------------------------
   public static void main (String[] args)
   {
      Contact[] friends = new Contact[7];

      friends[0] = new Contact ("John", "Smith", "610-555-7384");
      friends[1] = new Contact ("Sarah", "Barnes", "215-555-3827");
      friends[2] = new Contact ("Mark", "Riley", "733-555-2969");
      friends[3] = new Contact ("Laura", "Getz", "663-555-3984");
      friends[4] = new Contact ("Larry", "Smith", "464-555-3489");
      friends[5] = new Contact ("Frank", "Phelps", "322-555-2284");
      friends[6] = new Contact ("Marsha", "Grant", "243-555-2837");

      Sorts.insertionSort(friends);

      for (int index = 0; index < friends.length; index++)
         System.out.println (friends[index]);
   }
}
```

Listing 6.12 ***(continued)***

```
Barnes, Sarah    215-555-3827
Getz, Laura      663-555-3984
Grant, Marsha    243-555-2837
Phelps, Frank    322-555-2284
Riley, Mark      733-555-2969
Smith, John      610-555-7384
Smith, Larry     464-555-3489
```

Each `Contact` object represents a person with a last name, a first name, and a phone number. The `Contact` class is shown in Listing 6.13. It implements the `Comparable` interface and therefore provides a definition of the `compareTo` method. In this case, the contacts are sorted by last name; if two contacts have the same last name, their first names are used.

Listing 6.13

```
//********************************************************************
//  Contact.java       Author: Lewis and Loftus
//
//  Represents a phone contact.
//********************************************************************

public class Contact implements Comparable
{
   private String firstName, lastName, phone;

   //-----------------------------------------------------------------
   //  Sets up this contact with the specified information.
   //-----------------------------------------------------------------
   public Contact (String first, String last, String telephone)
   {
      firstName = first;
      lastName = last;
      phone = telephone;
   }
```

Listing 6.13 (continued)

```
   //-----------------------------------------------------------------
   //  Returns a description of this contact as a string.
   //-----------------------------------------------------------------
   public String toString ()
   {
      return lastName + ", " + firstName + "\t" + phone;
   }

   //-----------------------------------------------------------------
   //  Uses both last and first names to determine lexical ordering.
   //-----------------------------------------------------------------
   public int compareTo (Object other)
   {
      int result;

      if (lastName.equals(((Contact)other).lastName))
         result = firstName.compareTo(((Contact)other).firstName);
      else
         result = lastName.compareTo(((Contact)other).lastName);

      return result;
   }
}
```

When the `insertionSort` method executes, it relies on the `compareTo` method of each object to determine the order. We are guaranteed that the objects in the array have implemented the `compareTo` method because they are all `Comparable` objects (according to the parameter type). The compiler will issue an error message if we attempt to pass an array to this method that does not contain `Comparable` objects. Therefore, this version of the `insertionSort` method can be used to sort any array of objects, as long as the objects have implemented the `Comparable` interface. This example demonstrates a classic and powerful use of interfaces to create generic algorithms that work on a variety of data.

Comparing Sorts

There are a variety of reasons for choosing one sorting algorithm over another, including the algorithm's simplicity, its level of efficiency, the amount of memory it uses, and the type of data being sorted. An algorithm that is easier to understand is also easier to implement and debug. However, often the simplest sorts are the most inefficient ones. Efficiency is usually considered to be the primary criteria when comparing sorting algorithms. In general, one sorting algorithm is less efficient than another if it performs more comparisons than the other. There are several algorithms that are more efficient than the two we examined, but they are also more complex.

Key Concept

Sorting algorithms are ranked according to their efficiency, which is usually defined as the number of comparisons required to perform the sort.

Both selection sort and insertion sort have essentially the same level of efficiency. Both have an outer loop and an inner loop with similar properties, if not purposes. The outer loop is executed once for each value in the list, and the inner loop compares the value in the outer loop with most, if not all, of the values in the rest of the list. Therefore, both algorithms perform approximately n^2 number of comparisons, where n is the number of values in the list. We say that both selection sort and insertion sort are algorithms of *order* n^2. More efficient sorts perform fewer comparisons and are of a smaller order, such as $n \log_2 n$.

Key Concept

Both selection sort and insertion sort algorithms are of order n^2. Other sorts are more efficient.

Because both selection sort and insertion sort have the same general efficiency, the choice is fairly arbitrary. Selection sort is usually easy to understand and will often suffice in many situations. Some people find insertion sort to be a good choice when they are continually adding values to a list while keeping the list in sorted order, because that process is essentially the strategy that the insertion sort technique uses anyway.

Web Bonus

The textbook's Web site contains a discussion and examples of additional sorting algorithms.

6.4 Two-Dimensional Arrays

The arrays we've examined so far have all been *one-dimensional arrays* in the sense that they represent a simple list of values. As the name implies, a *two-dimensional* (2D) array has values in two dimensions, which are often thought of as the rows and columns of a table. Figure 6.5 graphically compares a one-dimensional array with a two-dimensional array. We must use two indexes to refer to a value in a two-dimensional array, one specifying the row and another the column.

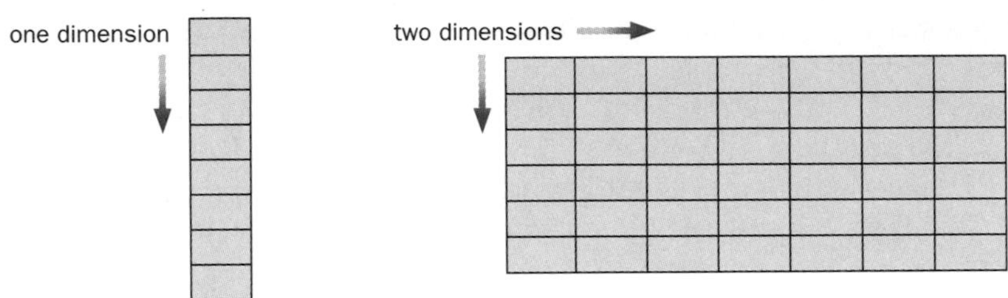

Figure 6.5 A one-dimensional array and a two-dimensional array

Brackets are used to represent each dimension in the array. Therefore, the type of a two-dimensional array that stores integers is `int[][]`. Technically, Java represents two-dimensional arrays as an array of arrays. A two-dimensional integer array is really a one-dimensional array of references to one-dimensional integer arrays.

The `TwoDArray` program, shown in Listing 6.14, instantiates a two-dimensional array of integers. As with one-dimensional arrays, the size of the dimensions are specified when the array is created. The size of the dimensions can be different.

Nested `for` loops are used in the `TwoDArray` program to load the array with values and also to print those values in a table format. Carefully trace the processing to see how the nested loops eventually visit each element in the two-dimensional array. Note that the outer loops are governed by `table.length`, which represents the number of rows, and the inner loops are governed by `table[row].length`, which represents the number of columns in that row.

As with one-dimensional arrays, an initializer list can be used to instantiate a two-dimensional array, where each element is itself an array initializer list. This technique is shown in the program, which is shown in Listing 6.15.

Suppose a soda manufacturer held a taste test for four new flavors to see how people liked them. The company got 10 people to try each new flavor and give it a score from 1 to 5, where 1 means poor and 5 means excellent. The two-dimensional array called `scores` in the `SodaSurvey` program stores the results of that survey. Each row corresponds to a soda and each column corresponds to the person who tasted it. That is, each row holds the responses that all testers gave for one particular soda flavor, and each column holds the responses of one person for all sodas.

The `SodaSurvey` program computes and prints the average responses for each soda and for each respondent. The sums of each soda and person are first stored in one-dimensional arrays of integers, then the averages are computed and printed.

Listing 6.14

```
//********************************************************************
//  TwoDArray.java       Author: Lewis and Loftus
//
//  Demonstrates the use of a two-dimensional array.
//********************************************************************

public class TwoDArray
{
   //-----------------------------------------------------------------
   //  Creates a 2D array of integers, fills it with increasing
   //  integer values, then prints them out.
   //-----------------------------------------------------------------
   public static void main (String[] args)
   {
      int[][] table = new int[5][10];

      // Load the table with values
      for (int row=0; row < table.length; row++)
         for (int col=0; col < table[row].length; col++)
            table[row][col] = row * 10 + col;

      // Print the table
      for (int row=0; row < table.length; row++)
      {
         for (int col=0; col < table[row].length; col++)
            System.out.print (table[row][col] + "\t");
         System.out.println();
      }
   }
}
```

```
0       1       2       3       4       5       6       7       8       9
10      11      12      13      14      15      16      17      18      19
20      21      22      23      24      25      26      27      28      29
30      31      32      33      34      35      36      37      38      39
40      41      42      43      44      45      46      47      48      49
```

Listing 6.15

```
//********************************************************************
//  SodaSurvey.java       Author: Lewis and Loftus
//
//  Demonstrates the use of a two-dimensional array.
//********************************************************************

import java.text.DecimalFormat;

public class SodaSurvey
{
   //-----------------------------------------------------------------
   //  Determines and prints the average of each row (soda) and each
   //  column (respondent) of the survey scores.
   //-----------------------------------------------------------------
   public static void main (String[] args)
   {
      int[][] scores = { {3, 4, 5, 2, 1, 4, 3, 2, 4, 4},
                         {2, 4, 3, 4, 3, 3, 2, 1, 2, 2},
                         {3, 5, 4, 5, 5, 3, 2, 5, 5, 5},
                         {1, 1, 1, 3, 1, 2, 1, 3, 2, 4} };

      final int SODAS = scores.length;
      final int PEOPLE = scores[0].length;

      int[] sodaSum = new int[SODAS];
      int[] personSum = new int[PEOPLE];

      for (int soda=0; soda < SODAS; soda++)
         for (int person=0; person < PEOPLE; person++)
         {
            sodaSum[soda] += scores[soda][person];
            personSum[person] += scores[soda][person];
         }

      DecimalFormat fmt = new DecimalFormat ("0.#");
      System.out.println ("Averages:\n");

      for (int soda=0; soda < SODAS; soda++)
         System.out.println ("Soda #" + (soda+1) + ": " +
                   fmt.format ((float)sodaSum[soda]/PEOPLE));
```

Listing 6.15 *(continued)*

```
      System.out.println ();
      for (int person =0; person < PEOPLE; person++)
         System.out.println ("Person #" + (person+1) + ": " +
                    fmt.format ((float)personSum[person]/SODAS));
   }
}
```

```
Averages:

Soda #1: 3.2
Soda #2: 2.6
Soda #3: 4.2
Soda #4: 1.9

Person #1: 2.2
Person #2: 3.5
Person #3: 3.2
Person #4: 3.5
Person #5: 2.5
Person #6: 3
Person #7: 2
Person #8: 2.8
Person #9: 3.2
Person #10: 3.8
```

Multidimensional Arrays

An array can have two, three, or even more dimensions. Any array with more than one dimension is called a *multidimensional array.*

Its fairly easy to picture a two-dimensional array as a table. A three-dimensional array could be drawn as a cube. But once you are past three dimensions, multidimensional arrays might seem to be hard to visualize. However, you can consider that each subsequent dimension is simply a subdivision of the previous one, and it is often best to think of larger multidimensional arrays in this way.

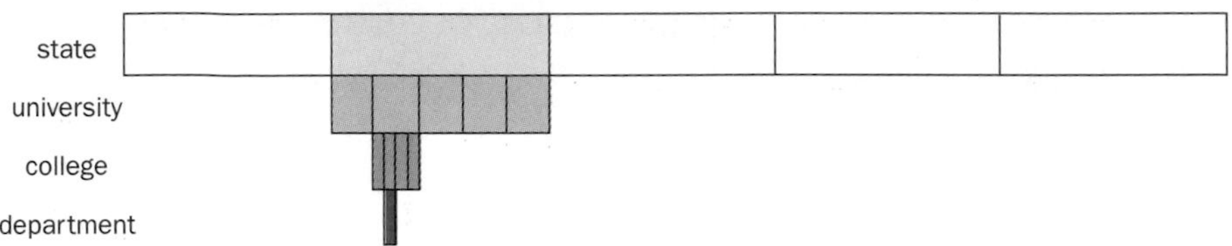

Figure 6.6 Visualization of a four-dimensional array

For example, suppose we wanted to store the number of students attending universities across the country, broken down in a meaningful way. We might represent it as a four-dimensional array of integers. The first dimension is an array of states. Each state contains an array of the universities in that state. Each university contains an array of the colleges in that university. Each college contains an array of departments, which stores the number of students in that department. These subdivisions can be pictured as shown in Figure 6.6.

Key Concept

Using an array with more than two dimensions is rare in an object-oriented system because intermediate levels are usually represented as separate objects.

Two-dimensional arrays are fairly common. However, care should be taken when deciding to create multidimensional arrays in a program. When dealing with large amounts of data that are managed at multiple levels, other information and the methods to manage that information will probably be required. It is far more likely, for instance, that each state would be represented by an object, which may contain, among other things, an array to store information about each university, and so on.

There is one other important characteristic of Java arrays to consider. As we established previously, Java does not directly support multidimensional arrays. Instead, they are represented as arrays of references to array objects. Those arrays could themselves contain references to other arrays. This layering continues for as many dimensions as required. Because of this technique for representing each dimension, the arrays in any one dimension could be of different lengths. These are sometimes called *ragged arrays*. For example, the number of elements in each row of a two-dimensional array may not be the same.

Key Concept

Each array in a given dimension of a multidimensional array could have a different length.

6.5 The `Vector` Class

The `Vector` class is part of the `java.util` package of the Java standard class library. It provides a service similar to an array in that it can store a list of values and reference them by an index. But whereas an array remains a fixed size throughout its existence, a `Vector` object can dynamically grow and shrink as needed. A data element can be inserted into or removed from any location of a vector with a single method invocation.

Key Concept

A `Vector` object is similar to an array, but it dynamically changes size as needed and elements can be inserted and removed

Unlike an array, a vector is not declared to store a particular type. A `Vector` object manages a list of references to the `Object` class. A reference to any type of object can be added to a vector. Because vectors store references, a primitive type must be stored in an appropriate wrapper class in order to be stored in a vector. Several methods of the `Vector` class are listed in Figure 6.7.

The program shown in Listing 6.16 instantiates a `Vector` called `band`. The method `addElement` is used to add several `String` objects to the vector,

`Vector ()`
Constructor: creates a vector that is initially empty.

`void addElement (Object obj)`
Adds the specified object to the end of this vector.

`void insertElementAt (Object obj, int index)`
Inserts the specified object into this vector at the specified index.

`void setElementAt (Object obj, int index)`
Sets the vector element at the specified index to the specified object.

`Object remove (int index)`
Removes the object at the specified index from this vector and returns it.

`boolean removeElement (Object obj)`
Removes the first occurance of the specified object from this vector.

`void removeElementAt (int index)`
Removes the object at the specified index from this vector.

`void clear ()`
Removes all of the elements from this vector.

`boolean contains (Object obj)`
Returns true if the specified object is contained in this vector.

`int indexOf (object obj)`
Returns the index of the specified object. Returns –1 if the object is not found.

`Object elementAt (int index)`
Returns the component at the specified index.

`boolean isEmpty ()`
Returns true if this vector contains no elements.

`int size ()`
Returns the number of elements in this vector.

Figure 6.7 Some methods of the `Vector` class

Listing 6.16

```
//********************************************************************
//  Beatles.java       Author: Lewis and Loftus
//
//  Demonstrates the use of a Vector object.
//********************************************************************

import java.util.Vector;

public class Beatles
{
   //-----------------------------------------------------------------
   //  Stores and modifies a list of band members.
   //-----------------------------------------------------------------
   public static void main (String[] args)
   {
      Vector band = new Vector();

      band.addElement ("Paul");
      band.addElement ("Pete");
      band.addElement ("John");
      band.addElement ("George");

      System.out.println (band);

      band.removeElement ("Pete");

      System.out.println (band);
      System.out.println ("At index 1: " + band.elementAt(1));

      band.insertElementAt ("Ringo", 2);

      System.out.println ("Size of the band: " + band.size());
   }
}
```

```
[Paul, Pete, John, George]
[Paul, John, George]
At index 1: John
Size of the band: 4
```

in a specific order. Then one particular string is deleted, and another is inserted at a particular index. As with any other object, the vector's `toString` method is automatically called whenever it is sent to the `println` method.

Note that when an element from a vector is deleted, the list of elements "collapses" so that the indexes are continuous for the remaining elements. Likewise, when an element is inserted at a particular point, the indexes of the other elements are adjusted accordingly.

The objects stored in a `Vector` object can be of different reference types. The methods of the `Vector` class are designed to accept references to the `Object` class as parameters, thus allowing a reference to any kind of object to be passed to it. Note that an implication of this implementation is that the `elementAt` method's return type is an `Object` reference. In order to retrieve a specific object from the `Vector` class, the returned object must be cast to its original class. The `Object` class and its relationship to other classes is explained further in Chapter 7.

Vector Efficiency

The `Vector` class is implemented using arrays. When a `Vector` object is instantiated, it is created with an initial capacity that defines the number of references it can currently handle. Elements can be added to the vector without needing to allocate more memory until it reaches this capacity. When required, the capacity is expanded to accommodate the new need. We performed a similar operation in the `Tunes` program earlier in this chapter.

When an element is inserted into the middle of a vector, all of the elements at higher indexes are copied into their new locations in the vector. This process is illustrated in Figure 6.8. If several elements are inserted, this copying is repeated many times over.

The processing of an array is significantly slowed down when capacity is enlarged and when insertions are made that cause a great deal of element copying. A `Vector`, with its dynamic characteristics, is a useful abstraction of an array but the abstraction masks some underlying activity that can be fairly inefficient depending on how it is used.

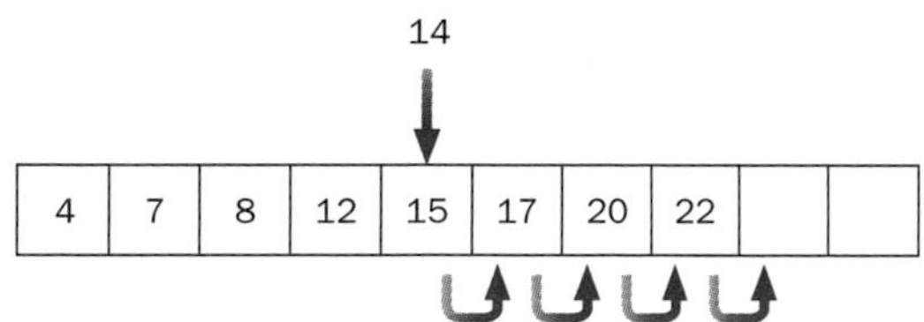

Figure 6.8 Inserting an element into a `Vector` object

6.6 Arrays and Graphics

Arrays can be quite helpful in conjunction with graphical processing. Polygons and polylines are two types of shapes that are defined using arrays. We can also use arrays to store the state of a drawing so that it can be redrawn as necessary. These issues are explored in this section.

Polygons and Polylines

A polygon is a multisided shape. In Java, it is defined using a series of <*x*, *y*> points that indicate the end points of the line segments of the polygon sides. Like several other shapes, a polygon can be drawn filled or unfilled. The methods used to draw a polygon are called `drawPolygon` and `fillPolygon`. They are part of the `Graphics` class, along with the other drawing methods such as `drawRect` and `fillRect`.

Both `drawPolygon` and `fillPolygon` are overloaded. One version uses arrays of integers to define the polygon, and the other uses an object of the `Polygon` class to define the polygon. The `Polygon` class is discussed later in this section.

In the version that uses arrays, the `drawPolygon` and `fillPolygon` methods take three parameters. The first is an array of integers representing the *x* coordinates of the points in the polygon, the second is an array of integers representing the *y* coordinates of those same points, and the third is an integer that indicates how many points are in the array. Taken together, the first two parameters represent the <*x*, *y*> coordinates of the end points of the line segments of the polygon sides.

Key Concept

A polygon is always a closed shape. The last point is automatically connected back to the first one.

A polygon is always closed. If the last <*x*, *y*> coordinate pair in the coordinate list is not the same as the first coordinate pair in the list, the shape that is drawn is automatically closed by connecting the last point to the first point.

Similar to a polygon, a *polyline* contains a series of points connected by line segments. Polylines differ from polygons in that the first and last coordinates are not connected when it is drawn. Since a polyline is not closed, it cannot be filled. Therefore, there is only one method, called `drawPolyline` used to draw a polyline.

Key Concept

A polyline is similar to a polygon except that a polyline is not a closed shape.

As with the `drawPolygon` method, the first two parameters of the `drawPolyline` method are both arrays of integers. Taken together, the first two parameters represent the <*x*, *y*> coordinates of the end points of the line segments of the polyline. The third parameter is the number of points in the coordinate list.

The program shown in Listing 6.17 uses polygons to draw a rocket. The arrays called `xRocket` and `yRocket` define the points of the polygon that make up the main body of the rocket. The first point in the arrays is the upper tip of the rocket, and they progress clockwise from there. The `xWindow` and `yWindow` arrays specify the points for the polygon that forms the window in the rocket. Both the rocket and the window are drawn as filled polygons.

Listing 6.17

```
//********************************************************************
//  Rocket.java       Author: Lewis and Loftus
//
//  Demonstrates the use of polygons and polylines.
//********************************************************************

import java.applet.Applet;
import java.awt.*;

public class Rocket extends Applet
{
   private final int APPLET_WIDTH = 200;
   private final int APPLET_HEIGHT = 200;

   private int[] xRocket = {100, 120, 120, 130, 130, 70, 70, 80, 80};
   private int[] yRocket = {15, 40, 115, 125, 150, 150, 125, 115, 40};

   private int[] xWindow = {95, 105, 110, 90};
   private int[] yWindow = {45, 45, 70, 70};

   private int[] xFlame = {70, 70, 75, 80, 90, 100, 110, 115, 120,
                           130, 130};
   private int[] yFlame = {155, 170, 165, 190, 170, 175, 160, 185,
                           160, 175, 155};

   //-----------------------------------------------------------------
   //  Sets up the basic applet environment.
   //-----------------------------------------------------------------
   public void init()
   {
      setBackground (Color.black);
      setSize (APPLET_WIDTH, APPLET_HEIGHT);
   }
```

Listing 6.17 (continued)

```
   //-----------------------------------------------------------------
   //  Draws a rocket using polygons.
   //-----------------------------------------------------------------
   public void paint (Graphics page)
   {
      page.setColor (Color.cyan);
      page.fillPolygon (xRocket, yRocket, xRocket.length);

      page.setColor (Color.gray);
      page.fillPolygon (xWindow, yWindow, xWindow.length);

      page.setColor (Color.red);
      page.drawPolyline (xFlame, yFlame, xFlame.length);
   }
}
```

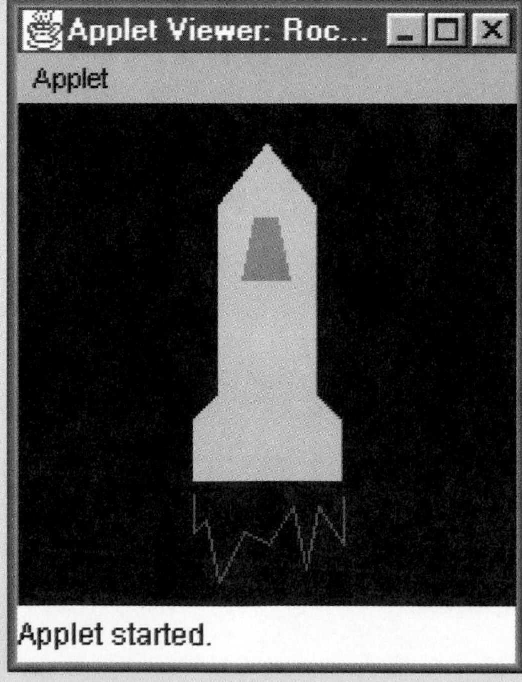

The `xFlame` and `yFlame` arrays define the points of a polyline that are used to create the image of flame shooting out of the end of the rocket. Because it is drawn as a polyline, and not a polygon, the shape is not closed or filled.

The `Polygon` Class

A polygon can also be defined explicitly using an object of the `Polygon` class, which is defined in the `java.awt` package of the Java standard class library. Two overloaded versions of the `drawPolygon` and `fillPolygon` methods take a single `Polygon` object as a parameter.

A `Polygon` object encapsulates the coordinates of the polygon sides. The constructors of the `Polygon` class allow the creation of an initially empty polygon, or one defined by arrays of integers representing the point coordinates. The `Polygon` class contains methods to add points to the polygon, and to determine whether a given point is contained within the polygon shape. It also contains methods to get a representation of a bounding rectangle for the polygon, and one to translate all of the points in the polygon to another position. These methods are listed in Figure 6.9.

`Polygon ()`
Constructor: creates an empty polygon.

`Polygon (int[] xpoints, int[] ypoints, int npoints)`
Constructor: creates a polygon using the <x, y> coordinate pairs in corresponding entries of xpoints and ypoints.

`void addPoint (int x, int y)`
Appends the specified point to this polygon.

`boolean contains (int x, int y)`
Returns true if the specified point is contained in this polygon.

`boolean contains (Point p)`
Returns true if the specified point is contained in this polygon.

`Rectangle getBounds ()`
Gets the bounding rectangle for this polygon.

`void translate (int deltaX, int deltaY)`
Translates the vertices of this polygon by deltaX along the x axis and deltaY along the y axis.

Figure 6.9 Some methods of the `Polygon` class

Saving the State of a Drawing

Recall that, when the `repaint` method is called for an applet, the applet window is cleared and the `paint` method is called. Therefore, in past examples the existing state of the drawing was lost when the applet was repainted. For example, in the case of the `Dots` program in Chapter 5, each dot was erased when the newest dot was drawn.

There are various ways of addressing this problem. One way is to use a structure like an array or vector to keep track of all the information necessary to completely redraw the picture whenever the `paint` method is called. The `Dots2` program, shown in Listing 6.18, is a redesign of the `Dots` program so that the dots do not disappear as new dots are drawn.

Listing 6.18

```
//********************************************************************
//  Dots2.java       Author: Lewis and Loftus
//
//  Demonstrates the use of a Vector to store the state of a drawing.
//********************************************************************

import java.applet.Applet;
import java.awt.*;
import java.awt.event.*;
import java.util.*;

public class Dots2 extends Applet implements MouseListener
{
   private final int APPLET_WIDTH = 200;
   private final int APPLET_HEIGHT = 100;
   private final int RADIUS = 6;

   private Vector pointList;
   private int count;
```

Listing 6.18 (continued)

```
   //-----------------------------------------------------------------
   //  Creates a Vector object to store the points.
   //-----------------------------------------------------------------
   public void init()
   {
      pointList = new Vector();
      count = 0;

      addMouseListener(this);

      setBackground (Color.black);
      setSize (APPLET_WIDTH, APPLET_HEIGHT);
   }

   //-----------------------------------------------------------------
   //  Draws all of the dots stored in the Vector.
   //-----------------------------------------------------------------
   public void paint (Graphics page)
   {
      page.setColor (Color.green);

      Iterator pointIterator = pointList.iterator();

      while (pointIterator.hasNext())
      {
         Point drawPoint = (Point) pointIterator.next();
         page.fillOval (drawPoint.x - RADIUS, drawPoint.y - RADIUS,
                        RADIUS * 2, RADIUS * 2);
      }

      page.drawString ("Count: " + count, 5, 15);
   }

   //-----------------------------------------------------------------
   //  Adds the current point to the list of points and redraws the
   //  applet whenever the mouse is pressed.
   //-----------------------------------------------------------------
   public void mousePressed (MouseEvent event)
   {
      pointList.addElement (event.getPoint());
      count++;
      repaint();
   }
```

Listing 6.18 (continued)

```
   //-----------------------------------------------------------------
   //  Provide empty definitions for unused event methods.
   //-----------------------------------------------------------------
   public void mouseClicked (MouseEvent event) {}
   public void mouseReleased (MouseEvent event) {}
   public void mouseEntered (MouseEvent event) {}
   public void mouseExited (MouseEvent event) {}
}
```

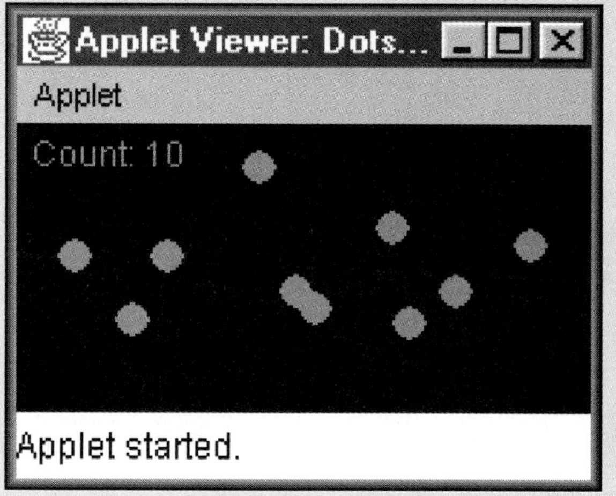

Applet Viewer: Dots...

Applet

Count: 10

Applet started.

A `Vector` object is created in the `init` method of the `Dots2` applet. It is used to store all of the `Point` objects that are obtained from the mouse event whenever the user presses the mouse button. Each time the `paint` method is called, we scan through the entire list of points and redraw the dots that they represent. We scan through the `Vector` using an `Iterator` object that the `Vector` provides via the `iterator` method. Recall that `Iterator` is an interface that allows us to scan through a collection of objects. In this case, the collection is the `Vector` object and the items we are scanning through are the `Point` objects that we stored in the vector. Note that the object returned by the `next` method of the iterator must be cast into a `Point` reference in order to access its *x* and *y* coordinate values.

Summary of Key Concepts

- A Java array of size N is indexed from 0 to $N - 1$.
- A Java array is an object. Memory space for the array elements are reserved by instantiating the array using the `new` operator.
- Bounds checking ensures that an index used to refer to an array element is in range. The Java index operator performs automatic bounds checking.
- An initializer list can be used to instantiate an array object instead of using the `new` operator. The size of the array and its initial values are determined by the initializer list.
- An entire array can be passed as a parameter, making the formal parameter an alias to the original.
- Command-line arguments are stored in an array of `String` objects and are passed to the `main` method.
- Instantiating an array of objects reserves room to store references only. The objects that are stored in each element must be instantiated separately.
- Selection sort and insertion sort are two sorting algorithms that define the processing steps for putting a list of values into a well-defined order.
- Selection sort works by putting each value into its final position, one at a time.
- Swapping is the process of exchanging two values. Swapping requires three assignment statements.
- Insertion sort works by inserting each value into a previously sorted subset of the list.
- Sorting algorithms are ranked according to their efficiency, which is usually defined as the number of comparisons required to perform the sort.
- Both selection sort and insertion sort algorithms are of order n^2. Other sorts are more efficient.
- Using an array with more than two dimensions is rare in an object-oriented system because intermediate levels are usually represented as separate objects.
- Each array in a given dimension of a multidimensional array could have a different length.
- A `Vector` object is similar to an array, but it dynamically changes size as needed and elements can be inserted and removed.

- A polygon is always a closed shape. The last point is automatically connected back to the first one.
- A polyline is similar to a polygon except that a polyline is not a closed shape.

Self-Review Questions

6.1 Explain the concept of array bounds checking. What happens when a Java array is indexed with an invalid value?

6.2 Describe the process of creating an array. When is memory allocated for the array?

6.3 What is an off-by-one error? How does it relate to arrays?

6.4 What does an array initializer list accomplish?

6.5 Can an entire array be passed as a parameter? How is this accomplished?

6.6 How is an array of objects created?

6.7 Which is better: selection sort or insertion sort?

6.8 How are multidimensional arrays implemented in Java?

6.9 What are the advantages of using a `Vector` as opposed to an array? What are the disadvantages?

6.10 What is a polyline? How do we specify its shape?

Exercises

6.1 Which of the following are valid declarations? Which instantiate an array object? Explain your answers.

a. `int primes = {2, 3, 4, 5, 7, 11};`

b. `float elapsedTimes[] = {11.47, 12.04, 11.72, 13.88};`

c. `int[] scores = int[30];`

d. `int[] primes = new {2,3,5,7,11};`

e. `int[] scores = new int[30];`

f. `char grades[] = {'a', 'b', 'c', 'd', 'f'};`

g. `char [] grades = new char[];`

6.2 Describe five programs that are difficult to implement without using arrays.

6.3 Describe what occurs in the following code. What modifications should be made to it?

```
int[] numbers = {3, 2, 3, 6, 9, 10, 12, 32, 3, 12, 6};
for (int count = 1; count <= numbers.length; count++)
{
   System.out.println (numbers[count]);
}
```

6.4 Write an array declaration with any necessary supporting classes to represent the following statements:

a. Students' names for a class of 25 students

b. Students' test grades for a class of 40 students

c. Credit-card transactions that contain a transaction number, a merchant name, and a charge

d. Students' names for a class and homework grades for each student

e. For each employee of the L&L International Corporation: the employee number, hire date, and the amount of the last five raises

6.5 Write a method that accepts an array of integers and sums the values stored in the array.

6.6 Write a method that accepts two array parameters and switches the contents of the arrays. What happens when the arrays are different sizes? What happens when one of the arrays is null?

6.7 Describe a program for which you would use the `Vector` class instead of arrays to implement choices. Describe a program for which you would use an array instead of the `Vector` class. Explain your choices.

Programming Projects

6.1 Design and implement an application that reads an arbitrary number of integers that are in the range 0 to 50 inclusive and counts how many occurrences of each are entered. After all input has been processed, print all of the values (with the number of occurrences) that were entered one or more times.

6.2 Modify the program from the previous problem so that it works for numbers in the range between −25 and 25.

6.3 Rewrite the `Sorts` class so that both sorting algorithms put the values in descending order. Create a driver class with a `main` method to exercise the modifications.

6.4 Design and implement an application that creates a histogram that allows you to visually inspect the frequency distribution of a set of values. The program should read in an arbitrary number of integers that are in the range 1 to 100 inclusive; then produce a chart similar to the one below that indicates how many input values fell in the range 1–10, 11–20, and so on. Print one asterisk for each value entered.

```
1  - 10  | *****
11 - 20  | **
21 - 30  | ******************
31 - 40  |
41 - 50  | ***
51 - 60  | ********
61 - 70  | **
71 - 80  | *****
81 - 90  | *******
91 - 100 | *********
```

6.5 The lines in the histogram in the previous problem will be too long if a large number of values are entered. Modify the program so that it prints an asterisk for every five values in each category. Ignore leftovers. For example, if a category had 17 values, print three asterisks in that row. If a category had 4 values, do not print any asterisks in that row.

6.6 Design and implement an application that computes and prints the mean and standard deviation of a list of integers. Assume that there will be no more than 50 input values. Compute both the mean and standard deviation as floating point values.

6.7 The L&L Bank can handle up to 30 customers who have savings accounts. Design and implement a program that manages the accounts. Each customer has a name, phone number, and an account balance. Allow each customer to make deposits and withdrawals. Produce appropriate error messages for invalid transactions. Also provide a method to add 3 percent interest to all accounts whenever the method is invoked.

6.8 The programming projects of Chapter 4 discussed a `Card` class that represents a standard playing card. Create a class called `DeckOfCards` that stores 52 objects of the `Card` class. Include methods to shuffle the deck, deal a card, and report the number of cards left in the deck. The `shuffle` method should assume that all cards are recollected. Create a driver class with a `main` method that deals each card from a shuffled deck, printing each card as it is dealt.

6.9 Modify the `Tunes` program so that it keeps the CDs sorted by title. Use the general object sort defined in the `Sorts` class from this chapter.

6.10 Modify the `Sorts` class to include an overloaded version of the `selectionSort` method that performs a general object sort. Modify the `SortPhoneList` program to test the new sort.

6.11 Design and implement an applet that graphically displays the processing of a selection sort. Use bars of various heights to represent the values being sorted. Display the set of bars after each swap. Put a delay in the processing of the sort to give the human observer a chance to see how the order of the values changes. Start the sort when the mouse button is clicked.

6.12 Repeat the previous problem using an insertion sort.

6.13 Modify the `RubberLines` program from Chapter 5 so that previous lines are not erased when a new line is drawn. Create a representation of the line as a class and store the lines in a `Vector`.

6.14 Design a class that represents a star with a specified radius and color. Use a filled polygon to draw the star. Design and implement an applet that draws 10 stars of random radius in random locations.

6.15 Design and implement an applet to create a polyline shape dynamically using mouse clicks. Each mouse click adds a new line from the last point. Store the points in an array.

6.16 Design and implement an applet that performs an animation of a car driving across the screen. Represent the car as an object and use polygons to draw the shape of the car. Use the array versions of the polygon drawing methods.

6.17 Redesign the program from the previous problem so that the polygons used to draw the car are represented using objects of the `Polygon` class. Use the `translate` method to help reposition the car as it moves.

6.18 Design and implement an applet that draws 20 circles, with the radius and location of each circle determined at random. If a circle does not overlap any other circle, draw that circle in black. If a circle overlaps one or more other circles, draw it in cyan. Use an array to store a representation of each circle, then determine the color of each circle. Two circles overlap if the distance between their center points is less than the sum of their radii.

6.19 Design and implement an applet that draws a checkerboard with five red and eight black checkers on it in various locations. Store the checkerboard as a two-dimensional array.

6.20 Modify the applet from the previous problem so that the program determines if any black checkers can jump any red checkers. Under the checkerboard, print the position (row, column) of all black checkers that have possible jumps.

Answers to Self-Review Questions

6.1 Whenever a reference is made to a particular array element, the index operator ensures that the value of the index is greater than or equal to zero and less than the size of the array. If it is not within the valid range, an `ArrayIndexOutOfBoundsException` is thrown.

6.2 Arrays are objects. Therefore, as with all objects, to create an array we first create a reference to the array (its name). Then we instantiate the array itself, which reserves memory space to store the array elements. The only difference between a regular object instantiation and an array instantiation is the bracket syntax.

6.3 An off-by-one error occurs when a program's logic misses the boundary of an array (or similar structure) by one. These errors include forgetting to process a boundary element and attempting to process a nonexistent element. Array processing is susceptible to off-by-one errors because their indexes begin at zero and run to one less than the size of the array.

6.4 An array initializer list is used in the declaration of an array to set up the initial values of its elements. An initializer list instantiates the array object, so no `new` operator is needed.

6.5 An entire array can be passed as a parameter. Specifically, because an array is an object, a reference to the array is passed to the method. Any changes made to the array elements will be reflected outside of the method.

6.6 An array of objects is really an array of object references. The array itself must be instantiated, and the objects that are stored in the array must be referenced separately.

6.7 Selection sort and insertion sort are generally equal in efficiency, because they both take about n^2 number of comparisons to sort a list of n numbers. Therefore it is really a matter of which algorithm is more easily understood and implemented. There are several sorting algorithms that are more efficient than either of these.

6.8 A multidimensional array is implemented in Java as an array of array objects. The arrays that are elements of the outer array could also contain arrays as elements. This nesting process could continue for several levels.

6.9 One advantage of using a `Vector` is that it stores references to the `Object` class, which allows any object to be stored in it. In addition, a `Vector` object can dynamically grow and shrink as needed. A disadvantage of the `Vector` class is that it copies a significant amount of data in order to insert and delete elements, and this process is inefficient.

6.10 A polyline is defined by a series of points that represent the end points for the line segments that make up the polyline. The `drawPolyline` method takes three parameters to specify its shape. The first is an array of integers that represent the x coordinates of the points. The second is an array of integers that represent the y coordinates of the points. The third parameter is a single integer that indicates the number of points in the arrays.

Inheritance

This chapter explains inheritance, a fundamental technique for organizing and creating classes. It is a simple but powerful idea that influences the way we design an object-oriented software system. Furthermore, inheritance enhances our ability to reuse classes in multiple situations and programs. We explore how classes can be related to form inheritance hierarchies and how these relationships allow us to create polymorphic references. Finally, we discuss how inheritance affects various issues related to graphics in Java, and we introduce the concept of a graphical user interface (GUI) component.

Chapter Objectives

- Derive new classes from existing ones.
- Explain how inheritance supports software reuse.
- Add and modify methods in child classes.
- Extend simple class derivations into well-designed class hierarchies.
- Explore how inheritance can be used to create polymorphic references.
- Examine inheritance hierarchies for interfaces.
- Discuss the use of inheritance in Java graphics frameworks.
- Examine and use the GUI component class hierarchy.

7.1 Creating Subclasses

We discussed in Chapter 4 the idea that we can use an analogy to explain the relationship of a class to an object: A class is to an object as a blueprint is to a house. A class establishes the structure and purpose of an object, but reserves no memory space for variables (unless those variables are declared as `static`). Classes are the plan, and objects are the embodiment of that plan.

Many houses can be created from the same blueprint, and they are essentially the same house in different locations with different people living in them. But suppose you want a house that was similar to another, but having some fundamentally different characteristics. You want to start with the same basic blueprint but need to modify it to suit your needs. Many housing developments are created this way. The houses in the development have the same core layout, but they can have unique features. For instance, they might all be split-level homes with the same bedroom, kitchen, and living-room configuration, but some have attached garages, or fireplaces, or full basements, while others do not.

It's likely that the housing developer commissioned a master architect to create a single blueprint establishing the basic design of all houses in the development. Then a series of new blueprints were created, starting with the original layout but including variations designed to please different buyers. The act of creating the series of blueprints was simplified since they all begin with the same underlying structure, yet the variations give them unique characteristics that may be very important to the owners.

Key Concept

Inheritance is the act of deriving a new class from an existing one. It is analogous to creating a new house blueprint from an existing blueprint with similar characteristics.

Creating one blueprint based on a similar one that already exists is analogous to the object-oriented concept of *inheritance*, which allows a software designer to derive a new class from an existing one. It is a powerful software development technique and a defining characteristic of object-oriented programming.

Derived Classes

Through inheritance, a new class is derived from an existing one. The new class automatically contains some or all of the variables and methods in the original class. The software designer can then add new variables and methods to the newly derived class, or modify the inherited ones to define the class appropriately.

Key Concept

A primary purpose of inheritance is to reuse existing software.

New classes can be created via inheritance faster, easier, and cheaper than by writing them from scratch. At the heart of inheritance is the idea of *software reuse*. By using existing software components to create new ones, we capitalize on all of the effort that went into the design, implementation, and testing of the existing software.

Keep in mind that the word class comes from the idea of classifying groups of objects with similar characteristics. Classification schemes often use levels of classes that relate to each other. For example, all mammals share certain characteristics: they are warm-blooded, have hair, and bear live offspring. Now consider a subset of mammals, such as horses. All horses are mammals, and have all of the characteristics of mammals. But they also have unique features that make them different from other mammals.

If we map this idea into software terms, an existing `Mammal` class would have certain variables and methods that describe the state and behavior of mammals. A `Horse` class could be derived from the existing `Mammal` class, automatically inheriting the variables and methods contained in `Mammal`. The `Horse` class can refer to the inherited variables and methods as if they had been declared locally in that class. New variables and methods can then be added to the derived class, to distinctly define a horse. Inheritance nicely models many situations found in the natural world.

> **Key Concept**
> Inherited variables and methods can be used in the derived class as if they had been declared locally.

The original class that is used to derive a new one is called the *parent class,* or *superclass,* or *base class.* The derived class is called a *child class,* or *subclass.* Java uses the reserved word `extends` to indicate that a new class is being derived from another.

The derivation process should establish a specific kind of relationship between two classes: an *is-a relationship.* This type of relationship means that the derived class should be a more specific version of the original. For example, a horse is-a mammal. Not all mammals are horses, but all horses are mammals.

> **Key Concept**
> You should maintain the is-a relationship between all derived classes in a class hierarchy.

Let's look at an example. The program shown in Listing 7.1 instantiates an object of class `Dictionary`, which is derived from a class called `Book`. Two methods are invoked through the `Dictionary` object, one that was declared locally in the `Dictionary` class, and one that was inherited from `Book`.

The `Book` class (Listing 7.2) is used to derive the `Dictionary` class (Listing 7.3) using the reserved word `extends` in the header of `Dictionary`. The `Dictionary` class automatically inherits the definition of the `pageMessage` method and the `pages` variable. Therefore, it is as if the `pageMessage` method and the `pages` variable were declared inside the `Dictionary` class. Note that the `definitionMessage` method refers to the `pages` variable explicitly.

Also, note that although the `Book` class is necessary to create the definition of `Dictionary`, no `Book` object is ever instantiated in the program. An instance of a child class does not rely on an instance of the parent class.

Inheritance is a one-way street. No new variables or methods declared in the `Dictionary` class can be used by the `Book` class. For instance, if we created an object from the `Book` class, it could not be used to invoke the

Listing 7.1

```
//********************************************************************
//  Words.java       Author: Lewis and Loftus
//
//  Demonstrates the use of an inherited method.
//********************************************************************

import Dictionary;

public class Words
{
   //-----------------------------------------------------------------
   //  Instantiates a derived class and invokes its inherited and
   //  local methods.
   //-----------------------------------------------------------------
   public static void main (String[] args)
   {
      Dictionary webster = new Dictionary ();

      webster.pageMessage();
      webster.definitionMessage();
   }
}
```

```
Number of pages: 1500
Number of definitions: 52500
Definitions per page: 35
```

`definitionMessage` method. This restriction makes sense in that a child class is a more specific version of the parent. A dictionary has pages, because all books have pages; but although a dictionary has definitions, not all books do.

Inheritance relationships are often depicted graphically. Figure 7.1 depicts a *class diagram,* which shows the inheritance relationship between the two classes. The arrow points from the child class to the parent class. Class diagrams can be used to show many types of relationships, such as the *has-a relationship* discussed in Chapter 4, though at this point we are primarily concerned with inheritance.

Listing 7.2

```
//********************************************************************
//  Book.java       Author: Lewis and Loftus
//
//  Represents a book.
//********************************************************************

public class Book
{
   protected int pages = 1500;

   //----------------------------------------------------------------
   //  Prints a message concerning the pages of this book.
   //----------------------------------------------------------------
   public void pageMessage ()
   {
      System.out.println ("Number of pages: " + pages);
   }
}
```

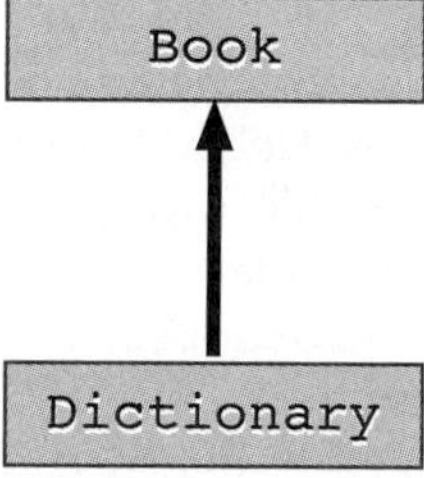

Figure 7.1 A class diagram showing an inheritance relationship

Listing 7.3

```
//********************************************************************
//  Dictionary.java       Author: Lewis and Loftus
//
//  Represents a dictionary, which is a book.
//********************************************************************

import Book;

public class Dictionary extends Book
{
   private int definitions = 52500;

   //-----------------------------------------------------------------
   //  Prints a message using both local and inherited values.
   //-----------------------------------------------------------------
   public void definitionMessage ()
   {
      System.out.println ("Number of definitions: " + definitions);

      System.out.println ("Definitions per page: " + definitions/pages);
   }
}
```

The `protected` Modifier

Not all variables and methods are inherited in a derivation. The visibility modifiers used to declare them determine which variables and methods get inherited and which do not. Specifically, the child class inherits variables and methods that are declared `public`, and does not inherit those that are declared `private`. The `pageMessage` method was inherited by `Dictionary` in the `Words` program because it is declared `public`.

However, if we declare a variable with public visibility so that a derived class inherits it, we violate the principle of encapsulation. Therefore, Java provides a third visibility modifier: `protected`. Note that the variable `pages` is declared with protected visibility in the `Words` program. When a variable or method is declared with protected visibility, it retains some of its encapsulation properties and a derived class will inherit it. The encapsulation with protected visibility is not as tight as it would be if the variable or method was declared `private`, but it is better than if it were declared `public`. Specifically, a variable or method declared with protected visibility may be accessed by a class in the same package. The relationships among all Java modifiers are explained completely in Appendix F.

Key Concept

Visibility modifiers determine which variables and methods are inherited. Protected visibility provides the best encapsulation while still permitting inheritance.

Inherited variables and methods retain the effect of their original visibility modifier. For example, the `pageMessage` method is still considered to be public in its inherited form.

The `super` Reference

Constructors are not inherited in a derived class, even though they have public visibility. This is an exception to the rule about public members being inherited. Constructors are special methods that are used to set up a particular type of object, so it wouldn't make sense for a class called `Dictionary` to have a constructor called `Book`.

Java does provide, however, a mechanism by which the parent's constructor can be accessed. The reserved word `super` can be used in a class to refer to its parent class. Like the `this` reference, what the word `super` refers to depends on where it is used. However, unlike the `this` reference, which refers to a particular instance of a class, `super` is a general reference to the parent class.

Key Concept

The parent's constructor can be invoked using the `super` reference.

Listing 7.4 shows a modification of the original `Words` program. Similar to the earlier version, we use a class called `Book2` (Listing 7.5) as the parent of `Dictionary2` (Listing 7.6). Unlike earlier versions of these classes, `Book2` and `Dictionary2` have explicit constructors used to initialize their instance variables. The output of the `Words2` program is the same as it is for the original `Words` program.

The `Dictionary2` constructor takes two integer values as parameters, representing the number of pages and definitions in the book. Because the `Book2` class already has a constructor that performs the work to set up the parts of the dictionary that were inherited, we will rely on that constructor to do that work. But since the constructor is not inherited, we cannot invoke it directly, and so we use the `super` reference to get to it in the parent class. The `Dictionary2` constructor then proceeds to initialize its own `definitions` variable.

In this case, it would have been just as easy to set the `pages` variable explicitly in the `Dictionary2` constructor, instead of using `super` to call the `Book2` constructor. However, it is good practice to let each class "take care" of itself. If we choose to change the way that the `Book2` constructor set up its `pages` variable, we would also have to remember to make that change in `Dictionary2`. By using the `super` reference, a change made in `Book2` is automatically reflected in `Dictionary2`.

Listing 7.4

```
//********************************************************************
//  Words2.java       Author: Lewis and Loftus
//
//  Demonstrates the use of the super reference.
//********************************************************************

import Dictionary2;

public class Words2
{
   //-----------------------------------------------------------------
   //  Instantiates a derived class and invokes its inherited and
   //  local methods.
   //-----------------------------------------------------------------
   public static void main (String[] args)
   {
      Dictionary2 webster = new Dictionary2 (1500, 52500);

      webster.pageMessage();
      webster.definitionMessage();
   }
}
```

```
Number of pages: 1500
Number of definitions: 52500
Definitions per page: 35
```

A child's constructor is responsible for calling the parent's constructor. Generally, the first line of a constructor should use the `super` reference call to a constructor of the parent class. If no such call exists, Java will automatically make a call to `super()` at the beginning of the constructor. This rule ensures that all data of a parent class are initialized before the child class constructor

Listing 7.5

```
//********************************************************************
//  Book2.java       Author: Lewis and Loftus
//
//  Represents a book.
//********************************************************************

public class Book2
{
   protected int pages;

   //-----------------------------------------------------------------
   //  Sets up the book with the specified number of pages.
   //-----------------------------------------------------------------
   public Book2 (int numPages)
   {
      pages = numPages;
   }

   //-----------------------------------------------------------------
   //  Prints a message concerning the pages of this book.
   //-----------------------------------------------------------------
   public void pageMessage ()
   {
      System.out.println ("Number of pages: " + pages);
   }
}
```

begins to execute. Using the super reference to invoke a parent's constructor can only be done in the child's constructor, and if included it must be the first line of the constructor.

The super reference can also be used to reference other variables and methods defined in the parent's class. This technique is discussed later in this chapter.

Listing 7.6

```
//********************************************************************
//  Dictionary2.java       Author: Lewis and Loftus
//
//  Represents a dictionary, which is a book.
//********************************************************************

import Book2;

public class Dictionary2 extends Book2
{
   private int definitions;

   //-----------------------------------------------------------------
   //  Sets up the dictionary with the specified number of pages
   //  (maintained by the Book parent class) and defintions.
   //-----------------------------------------------------------------
   public Dictionary2 (int numPages, int numDefinitions)
   {
      super (numPages);

      definitions = numDefinitions;
   }

   //-----------------------------------------------------------------
   //  Prints a message using both local and inherited values.
   //-----------------------------------------------------------------
   public void definitionMessage ()
   {
      System.out.println ("Number of definitions: " + definitions);

      System.out.println ("Definitions per page: " + definitions/pages);
   }
}
```

Multiple Inheritance

Java's approach to inheritance is called *single inheritance*. This term means that a derived class can only have one parent. Some object-oriented languages allow a child class to have multiple parents. This approach is called *multiple inheritance;* this approach is useful for describing objects that are in between

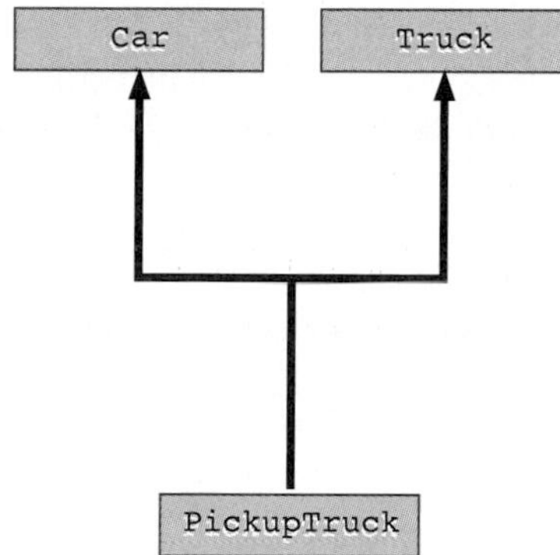

Figure 7.2 A class diagram showing multiple inheritance

two categories or classes. For example, suppose we had a class `Car` and a class `Truck`, and we wanted to create a new class called `PickupTruck`. A pickup truck is somewhat like a car and somewhat like a truck. With single inheritance, we have to decide whether it is better to derive the new class from `Car` or `Truck`. With multiple inheritance, it can be derived from both, as shown in Figure 7.2.

Multiple inheritance is nice in some situations, but it comes with a price. What if both `Truck` and `Car` have methods with the same name? Which method would `PickupTruck` inherit? The answer to this question is complex, and it depends on the rules of the language that supports multiple inheritance.

Java does not support multiple inheritance, but the use of interfaces provides the some of the abilities that multiple inheritance gives us. Although a Java class can be derived from only one parent class, it can implement many different interfaces. Therefore, we can guarantee that we can interact with a particular class in particular ways while inheriting the most crucial information from one particular parent.

7.2 Overriding Methods

When a child class defines a method with the same name and signature as a method in the parent, we say that the child's version *overrides* the parent's version in favor of its own. The need for overriding occurs often in inheritance situations.

> **Key Concept**
> A child class can override (redefine) the parent's definition of an inherited method.

The program in Listing 7.7 provides a simple demonstration of method overriding in Java. The `Messages` class contains a `main` method that instantiates two objects, one from class `Thought` and one from class `Advice`. The `Thought` class is the parent of `Advice`.

Listing 7.7

```
//********************************************************************
//  Messages.java        Author: Lewis and Loftus
//
//  Demonstrates the use of an overridden method.
//********************************************************************

import Thought;
import Advice;

public class Messages
{
   //-----------------------------------------------------------------
   //  Instatiates two objects and invokes the message method in each.
   //-----------------------------------------------------------------
   public static void main (String[] args)
   {
      Thought parked = new Thought();
      Advice dates = new Advice();

      parked.message ();

      dates.message ();  // overridden
   }
}
```

```
I feel like I'm diagonally parked in a parallel universe.

Warning: Dates in calendar are closer than they appear.

I feel like I'm diagonally parked in a parallel universe.
```

Both the `Thought` class (Listing 7.8) and the `Advice` class (Listing 7.9) contain a definition for a method called `message`. The version of `message` from `Thought` is inherited by `Advice`, but `Advice` overrides it with an alternative definition. The new version of the method prints out an entirely different message, then invokes the parent's version of the `message` method using the `super` reference.

The object that is used to invoke a method determines which version of the method is actually executed. When `message` is invoked using the `parked`

Listing 7.8

```
//********************************************************************
//  Thought.java       Author: Lewis and Loftus
//
//  Represents a stray thought.
//********************************************************************

public class Thought
{
   //-----------------------------------------------------------------
   //  Prints a message.
   //-----------------------------------------------------------------
   public void message()
   {
      System.out.println ("I feel like I'm diagonally parked in a " +
                          "parallel universe.");

      System.out.println();
   }
}
```

object in the `main` method, the `Thought` version of `message` is executed. When `message` is invoked using the `dates` object, the `Advice` version of `message` is executed. This flexibility allows two objects that are related by inheritance to use the same naming conventions for methods that accomplish the same general task in different ways.

A method can be defined with the `final` modifier. A child class cannot override a final method. This technique is used to ensure that a derived class uses a particular definition for a method.

The concept of method overriding is important to several issues related to inheritance. These issues are explored throughout the rest of this chapter.

Shadowing Variables

It is possible for a child class to redefine variables that were inherited from the parent. This technique is called *shadowing variables*. It is similar to the process of overriding methods, but creates some confusing subtleties. Note the

Listing 7.9

```
//********************************************************************
//  Advice.java       Author: Lewis and Loftus
//
//  Represents a hopefully helpful piece of advice.
//********************************************************************

import Thought;

public class Advice extends Thought
{
   //-----------------------------------------------------------------
   //  Prints a message. This method overrides the parent's version.
   //  It also invokes the parent's version explicitly using super.
   //-----------------------------------------------------------------
   public void message()
   {
      System.out.println ("Warning: Dates in calendar are closer " +
                          "than they appear.");

      System.out.println();

      super.message();
   }
}
```

distinction between redeclaring a variable and simply giving an inherited variable a particular value.

Because an inherited variable is already available to the child class, there is usually no good reason to redeclare it. Someone reading code with a shadowed variable will find two different declarations that seem to apply to a variable used in the child class. That confusion causes problems and serves no purpose. A redeclaration of a particular variable name could change its type, though that is usually unnecessary. In general, shadowing variables should be avoided.

7.3 Class Hierarchies

A child class derived from one parent can be the parent of its own child class. Furthermore, multiple classes can be derived from a single parent. Therefore, inheritance relationships often develop into *class hierarchies*. Figure 7.3 shows a class hierarchy that incorporates the inheritance relationship between classes `Mammal` and `Horse`.

Key Concept

The child of one class can be the parent of one or more other classes, creating a class hierarchy.

There is no limit to the number of children a class can have, or to the number of levels to which a class hierarchy can extend. Two children of the same parent are called *siblings*. Although siblings share the characteristics passed on by their parent, they are not related by inheritance because one is not used to derive the other.

In class hierarchies, common features should be kept as high in the hierarchy as reasonably possible. That way, only specific differences are established in a child class, which explicitly identifies the characteristics that make the class unique from its parent. Common traits are established high in the hierarchy for the child classes to use. This approach maximizes the ability to reuse classes. It also facilitates maintenance activities, because when changes are made to the parent, they are automatically reflected in the descendents. Always remember to maintain the is-a relationship when building class hierarchies.

Key Concept

Common features should be located as high in a class hierarchy as is reasonable, maximizing reuse potential and minimizing maintenance efforts.

The inheritance mechanism is transitive. That is, a parent passes along a trait to a child class, and that child class passes it along to its children, and so

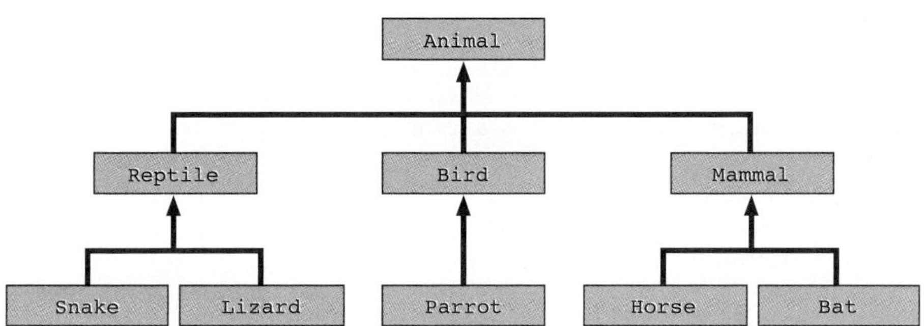

Figure 7.3 A class hierarchy

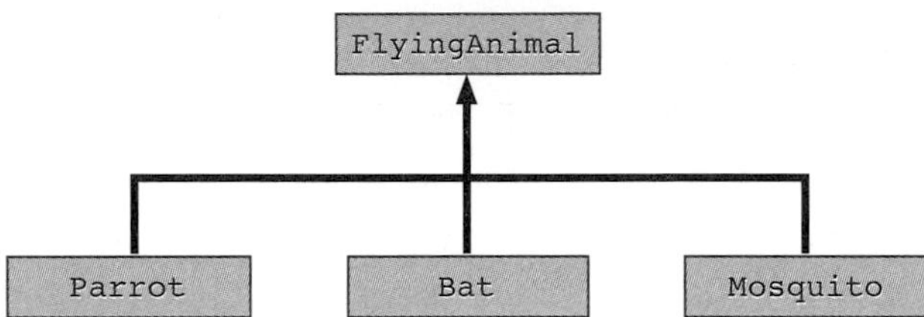

Figure 7.4 An alternative hierarchy for organizing animals

on. An inherited feature might have originated in the immediate parent, or possibly from several levels higher from a more distant ancestor class.

There is no single best hierarchy organization for all situations. The decisions made when designing a class hierarchy restrict and guide more detailed design decisions and implementation options, and they must be made carefully.

Earlier in this chapter we discussed a class hierarchy that organized animals by their major biological classifications, such as `Mammal`, `Bird`, and `Reptile`. However, in a different situation, the same animals might logically be organized in a different way. For example, as shown in Figure 7.4, the class hierarchy may be organized around a function of the animals, such as their ability to fly. In this case, a `Parrot` class and a `Bat` class would be siblings derived from a general `FlyingAnimal` class. This class hierarchy is as valid and reasonable as the original one. It depends on the need of the programs that use the hierarchies.

The `Object` Class

In Java, all classes are derived ultimately from the `Object` class. If a class definition doesn't use the `extends` clause to explicitly derive itself from another class, then that class is automatically derived from the `Object` class by default. Therefore, the following two class definitions are equivalent:

```
class Thing
{
   // whatever
}
```

```
boolean equals (Object obj)
   Returns true if this object is an alias of the specified object.

String toString ()
   Returns a string representation of this object.

Object clone ()
   Creates and returns a copy of this object.
```

Figure 7.5 Some methods of the `Object` class

and

```
class Thing extends Object
{
   // whatever
}
```

Because all classes are derived from `Object`, any public method of `Object` can be invoked on any object created in any Java program. Figure 7.5 lists some of the methods of the `Object` class.

Key Concept
All Java classes are derived, directly or indirectly, from the `Object` class.

As it turns out, we've been using `Object` methods quite often in our examples. The `toString` method, for instance, is originally defined in the `Object` class, so the `toString` method can be called for any object. As we've seen several times, when a `println` method is called with an object parameter, `toString` is called to determine what to print. The definition for `toString` that is provided by the `Object` class returns a string containing the object's class name followed by a numeric hash value that is unique for that object. Usually, we override the `Object` version of `toString` to fit our own needs. The `String` class has overridden the `toString` method so that it returns its stored string value.

The `equals` method of the `Object` class is also useful. In general, its purpose is to determine if two objects are equal. The original definition of the `equals` method in the `Object` class returns `true` if the two object references actually refer to the same object (that is, if they are aliases). Classes often override the definition of the `equals` method in favor of a more appropriate

> **Key Concept**
>
> The `toString` and `equals` methods are defined in the `Object` class and therefore are inherited by every class in every Java program.

version. For instance, the `String` class overrides `equals` so that it returns `true` only if both strings contain the same characters in the same order.

The program called `Academia` is shown in Listing 7.10. In this program, a `Student` object and a `GradStudent` object are instantiated. The `Student` class (Listing 7.11) is the parent of `GradStudent` (Listing 7.12). A graduate student is a student that has a potential source of income, such as being a graduate teaching assistant (GTA).

The `GradStudent` class inherits the variables `name` and `numCourses`, as well as the method `toString` that was defined in `Student` (overriding the version from `Object`). The `GradStudent` constructor uses the `super` reference to invoke the constructor of `Student`, then initializes its own variables.

The `GradStudent` class augments its inherited definition with variables concerning financial support, and overrides `toString` (yet again) to print additional information. Note that in the `GradStudent` version of `toString`, the `Student` version of `toString` is explicitly invoked using the `super` reference.

Abstract Classes

An *abstract class* represents a generic concept in a class hierarchy. An abstract class cannot be instantiated, and usually contains one or more abstract methods, which have no definition. In this sense, an abstract class is similar to an interface. Unlike interfaces, however, an abstract class can contain methods that are not abstract, and can contain data declarations other than constants.

A class is declared as abstract by including the `abstract` modifier in the class header. Any class that contains one or more abstract methods must be declared as `abstract`. In abstract classes (unlike interfaces) the `abstract` modifier must be applied to each abstract method. A class declared as `abstract` does not have to contain abstract methods.

> **Key Concept**
>
> An abstract class cannot be instantiated. It represents a concept on which other classes can build their definitions.

Abstract classes serve as placeholders in a class hierarchy. As the name implies, an abstract class represents an abstract entity that is usually too ill defined to be useful by itself. Instead, an abstract class may contain a partial description that is inherited by all of its descendants in the class hierarchy. Its children, which are more specific, fill in the gaps.

Consider the class hierarchy shown in Figure 7.6. The `Vehicle` class at the top of the hierarchy may be too generic for a particular application. Therefore, we may choose to implement it as an abstract class. Concepts that apply to all vehicles can be represented in the `Vehicle` class and are inherited by its descendants. That way each of its children doesn't have to define the same concept redundantly, and perhaps inconsistently.

Listing 7.10

```
//********************************************************************
//  Academia.java       Author: Lewis and Loftus
//
//  Demonstrates inheritance from the Object class.
//********************************************************************

import Student;
import GradStudent;

public class Academia
{
   //-----------------------------------------------------------------
   //  Creates objects of two student types, prints some information
   //  about them, then checks them for equality.
   //-----------------------------------------------------------------
   public static void main (String[] args)
   {
      Student susan = new Student ("Susan", 5);
      GradStudent frank = new GradStudent ("Frank", 3, "GTA", 8.75);

      System.out.println (susan);

      System.out.println ();

      System.out.println (frank);

      System.out.println ();

      if (! susan.equals(frank))
         System.out.println ("These are two different students.");
   }
}
```

```
Student name: Susan
Number of courses: 5

Student name: Frank
Number of courses: 3
Support source: GTA
Hourly pay rate: 8.75

These are two different students.
```

Listing 7.11

```
//********************************************************************
//  Student.java       Author: Lewis and Loftus
//
//  Represents a student.
//********************************************************************

public class Student
{
   protected String name;
   protected int courses;

   //-----------------------------------------------------------------
   //  Sets up a student with the specified name and number of
   //  courses.
   //-----------------------------------------------------------------
   public Student (String StuName, int numCourses)
   {
      name = StuName;
      courses = numCourses;
   }

   //-----------------------------------------------------------------
   //  Returns information about this student as a string.
   //-----------------------------------------------------------------
   public String toString ()
   {
      String result = "Student name: " + name + "\n";

      result += "Number of courses: " + courses;

      return result;
   }
}
```

Listing 7.12

```
//********************************************************************
//  GradStudent.java          Author: Lewis and Loftus
//
//  Represents a graduate student with financial support.
//********************************************************************

import Student;

public class GradStudent extends Student
{
   private String source;
   private double rate;

   //-----------------------------------------------------------------
   //  Sets up the graduate student using the specified information.
   //-----------------------------------------------------------------
   public GradStudent (String StuName, int numCourses, String funds,
                       double pay)
   {
      super (StuName, numCourses);

      source = funds;
      rate = pay;
   }

   //-----------------------------------------------------------------
   //  Returns a description of this graduate student as a string.
   //-----------------------------------------------------------------
   public String toString ()
   {
      String result = super.toString();

      result += "\nSupport source: " + source + "\n";
      result += "Hourly pay rate: " + rate;

      return result;
   }
}
```

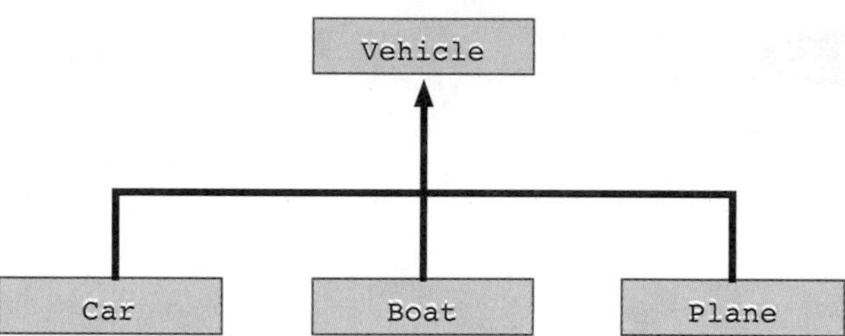

Figure 7.6 A `Vehicle` class hierarchy

For example, we may say that all vehicles have a particular speed. Therefore, we declare a `speed` variable in the `Vehicle` class, and all specific vehicles below it in the hierarchy automatically have that variable via inheritance. Any change we make to the representation of the speed of a vehicle is automatically reflected in all child classes. Similarly, we may declare an abstract method called `fuelConsumption`, whose purpose is to calculate how quickly fuel is being consumed by a particular vehicle. The details of the `fuelConsumption` method must be defined by each type of vehicle, but the `Vehicle` class establishes that all vehicles consume fuel and provide a consistent way to compute that value.

Some concepts don't apply to all vehicles, so we wouldn't represent those concepts at the `Vehicle` level. For instance, we wouldn't include a variable called `numberOfWheels` in the `Vehicle` class, because not all vehicles have wheels. The child classes to which wheels are important can add that concept at the appropriate level in the hierarchy.

There are no restrictions as to where in a class hierarchy an abstract class needs to be defined. For example, an abstract class can be derived from a nonabstract parent, but usually abstract classes are more useful located higher in the class hierarchy.

> **Key Concept**
>
> A class derived from an abstract parent must override all of its parent's abstract methods, or the derived class will also be considered abstract.

Usually, a child of an abstract class will provide a specific definition for an abstract method inherited from its parent. Note that this is just a specific case of overriding a method, giving a different definition than the one the parent provides. If a child of an abstract class does not give a definition for every abstract method that it inherits from its parent, it is also considered to be abstract.

Note that it would be a contradiction for an abstract method to be modified as `final` or `static`. Because a final method cannot be overridden in subclasses, an abstract final method would have no way of being given a definition in subclasses. A static method can be invoked by using the class name without declaring an object of the class. This method of invocation implies that an implementation must exist for the method. Because abstract methods have no implementation, an abstract static method would make no sense.

Choosing which classes and methods to make abstract is an important part of the design process. Such choices should only be made after careful consideration. By using abstract classes wisely, we can create flexible, extensible software designs.

7.4 Polymorphism via Inheritance

In Chapter 5 we examined the ability to use interfaces to create a polymorphic reference. We can also create a polymorphic reference using the inheritance relationships among classes. Recall that a polymorphic reference is one that can refer to different types of objects at different times. The particular code that is executed when a method is invoked through a polymorphic reference depends on the object that is being referred to at that time.

References and Class Hierarchies

In Java, a reference that is declared to refer to an object of a particular class can be used to refer to an object of any class to which it is related by inheritance. For example, if the class `Mammal` is used to derive the class `Horse`, then a `Mammal` reference can be used to refer to an object of class `Horse`. This ability is shown in the code segment below:

```
Mammal animal;
Horse secretariat = new Horse();
animal = secretariat;  // a valid assignment
```

Key Concept

A reference variable can refer to any object created from any class that is related to the reference type by inheritance.

The reverse operation, assigning the `Mammal` object to a `Horse` reference, is also valid, but requires an explicit cast. Assigning a reference in this direction is generally less useful and more likely to cause problems, because although a horse has all the functionality of a mammal (because a horse *is-a* mammal), the reverse is not necessarily true.

This relationship works throughout a class hierarchy. Therefore, an `Object` reference can be used to refer to any object, because ultimately all classes are descendants of the `Object` class. A `Vector` uses polymorphism in that it is designed to hold `Object` references. Therefore, a `Vector` can be used to store any kind of object. In fact, a particular vector can be used to hold several different types of objects at one time, because, in essence, they are all `Object` objects.

The reference variable `animal` can be polymorphic because at any point in time it could refer to a `Mammal` object or a `Horse` object. Suppose that both `Mammal` and `Horse` have a method called `move`. The `Horse` class has overridden the definition of `move` that it inherited from `Mammal`. The following invocation calls the `Mammal` version of `move` if `animal` currently refers to a `Mammal` object, but calls the `Horse` version of `move` if `animal` currently refers to a `Horse` object.

Key Concept

A polymorphic reference uses the type of the object, not the type of the reference, to determine which version of an overridden method to invoke.

```
animal.move();
```

Consider the class hierarchy shown in Figure 7.7. The classes in it represent various types of employees that might be employed at a particular company. Let's explore an example that uses this hierarchy to demonstrate several inheritance issues, including polymorphism.

The `Firm` class, shown in Listing 7.13, contains a `main` driver that creates a `Staff` of employees and invokes the `payday` method to pay them all. The program output includes information about each employee and how much they were paid (if anything).

The `Staff` class (Listing 7.14) maintains an array of objects that represent individual employees of various kinds. Note that the array is declared to hold `StaffMember` references, but it is actually filled with objects created from several other classes, such as `Executive` and `Employee`. These classes are all descendants of the `StaffMember` class, so the assignments are valid.

The `payday` method of the `Staff` class scans through the list of employees, printing their information and invoking their `pay` method to determine how much the employee should be paid. The invocation of the `pay` method is polymorphic because each class has its own version of the `pay` method.

The `StaffMember` class (Listing 7.15) is abstract. It does not represent a particular type of employee, and is not intended to be instantiated. Rather, it

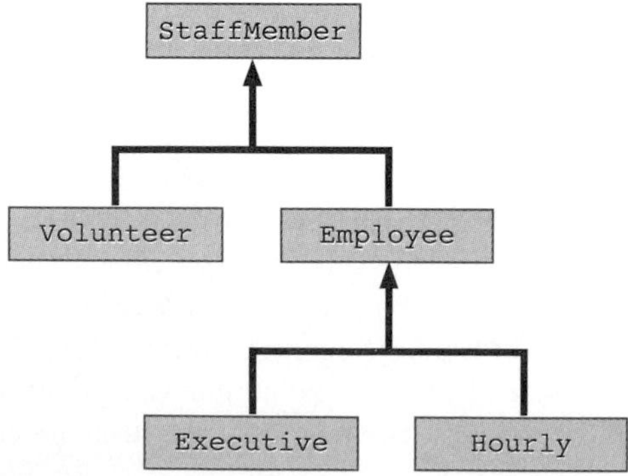

Figure 7.7 A class hierarchy of employees

Listing 7.13

```
//********************************************************************
//  Firm.java       Author: Lewis and Loftus
//
//  Demonstrates polymorphic processing.
//********************************************************************

import Staff;

public class Firm
{
   //-----------------------------------------------------------------
   //  Creates a staff of employees for a firm and pays them.
   //-----------------------------------------------------------------
   public static void main (String[] args)
   {
      Staff personnel = new Staff();

      personnel.payday();
   }
}
```

```
Name: Sam
Address: 123 Main Line
Phone: 555-0469
Social Security Number: 123-45-6789
Paid: 6923.07
-----------------------------------
Name: Carla
Address: 456 Off Line
Phone: 555-0101
Social Security Number: 987-65-4321
Paid: 846.15
-----------------------------------
Name: Woody
Address: 789 Off Rocker
Phone: 555-0000
Social Security Number: 010-20-3040
Paid: 769.23
-----------------------------------
```

Listing 7.13 *(continued)*

```
Name: Diane
Address: 678 Fifth Ave.
Phone: 555-0690
Social Security Number: 958-47-3625
Current hours: 40
Paid: 342.0
-----------------------------------
Name: Norm
Address: 987 Suds Blvd.
Phone: 555-8374
Thanks!
-----------------------------------
Name: Cliff
Address: 321 Duds Lane
Phone: 555-7282
Thanks!
-----------------------------------
```

Listing 7.14

```
//********************************************************************
//  Staff.java       Author: Lewis and Loftus
//
//  Represents the personnel staff of a particular business.
//********************************************************************

import StaffMember;
import Executive;
import Employee;
import Hourly;
import Volunteer;

public class Staff
{
   StaffMember[] staffList;

   //-----------------------------------------------------------------
   //  Sets up the list of staff members.
   //-----------------------------------------------------------------
```

Listing 7.14 ***(continued)***

```
   public Staff ()
   {
      staffList = new StaffMember[6];

      staffList[0] = new Executive ("Sam", "123 Main Line",
         "555-0469", "123-45-6789", 1923.07);

      staffList[1] = new Employee ("Carla", "456 Off Line",
         "555-0101", "987-65-4321", 846.15);
      staffList[2] = new Employee ("Woody", "789 Off Rocker",
         "555-0000", "010-20-3040", 769.23);

      staffList[3] = new Hourly ("Diane", "678 Fifth Ave.",
         "555-0690", "958-47-3625", 8.55);

      staffList[4] = new Volunteer ("Norm", "987 Suds Blvd.",
         "555-8374");
      staffList[5] = new Volunteer ("Cliff", "321 Duds Lane",
         "555-7282");

      ((Executive)staffList[0]).awardBonus (5000.00);

      ((Hourly)staffList[3]).addHours (40);
   }

   //-----------------------------------------------------------------
   //  Pays all staff members.
   //-----------------------------------------------------------------
   public void payday ()
   {
      double amount;

      for (int count=0; count < staffList.length; count++)
      {
         System.out.println (staffList[count]);

         amount = staffList[count].pay();  // polymorphic

         if (amount == 0.0)
            System.out.println ("Thanks!");
         else
            System.out.println ("Paid: " + amount);

         System.out.println ("-----------------------------------");
      }
   }
}
```

Listing 7.15

```
//********************************************************************
//  StaffMember.java       Author: Lewis and Loftus
//
//  Represents a generic staff member.
//********************************************************************

public abstract class StaffMember
{
   protected String name;
   protected String address;
   protected String phone;

   //-----------------------------------------------------------------
   //  Sets up a staff member using the specified information.
   //-----------------------------------------------------------------
   public StaffMember (String eName, String eAddress, String ePhone)
   {
      name = eName;
      address = eAddress;
      phone = ePhone;
   }

   //-----------------------------------------------------------------
   //  Returns a string including the basic employee information.
   //-----------------------------------------------------------------
   public String toString ()
   {
      String result = "Name: " + name + "\n";

      result += "Address: " + address + "\n";
      result += "Phone: " + phone;

      return result;
   }

   //-----------------------------------------------------------------
   //  Derived classes must define the pay method for each employee
   //  type.
   //-----------------------------------------------------------------
   public abstract double pay();
}
```

serves as the ancestor of all employee classes and contains information that applies to all employees. Every employee has a name, address, and phone number, so variables to store these values are declared in the StaffMember class and are inherited by all descendants.

The StaffMember class contains a toString method to return the information managed by the StaffMember class. It also contains an abstract method called pay, which takes no parameters and returns a value of type double. At the generic StaffMember level, it would be inappropriate to give a definition for this method. The descendants of StaffMember, however, each provide their own specific definition for pay. By defining pay abstractly in StaffMember, the payday method of Staff pays all employees, no matter what their type is.

The Volunteer class (Listing 7.16) represents a person that is not paid money for their work. We still want to keep track of their basic information,

Listing 7.16

```
//********************************************************************
//  Volunteer.java       Author: Lewis and Loftus
//
//  Represents a staff member who works as a volunteer.
//********************************************************************

import StaffMember;

public class Volunteer extends StaffMember
{
   //-----------------------------------------------------------------
   //  Sets up a volunteer using the specified information.
   //-----------------------------------------------------------------
   public Volunteer (String eName, String eAddress, String ePhone)
   {
      super (eName, eAddress, ePhone);
   }

   //-----------------------------------------------------------------
   //  Returns a zero pay value for this volunteer.
   //-----------------------------------------------------------------
   public double pay()
   {
      return 0.0;
   }
}
```

which is passed into the constructor of `Volunteer`, which in turn passes it to the `StaffMember` constructor using the `super` reference. The `pay` method of `Volunteer` simply returns a zero pay value. If `pay` had not been overridden, the `Volunteer` class would have been considered abstract and could not have been instantiated.

Note that when a volunteer gets "paid" in the `payday` method of `Staff`, a simple expression of thanks is printed. In all other situations, where the pay value is greater than zero, the payment itself is printed.

The `Employee` class (Listing 7.17) represents an employee that gets paid at a particular rate each pay period. The pay rate, as well as the employee's social security number, is passed along with the other basic information to the `Employee` constructor. The basic information is passed to the constructor of `StaffMember` using the `super` reference.

The `toString` method of `Employee` is overridden to concatenate the additional information that `Employee` manages to the information returned by the parent's version of `toString`, which is called using the `super` reference. The `pay` method of an `Employee` simply returns the pay rate for that employee.

The `Executive` class (Listing 7.18) represents an employee that may earn a bonus in addition to their normal pay rate. The `Executive` class is derived from `Employee` and therefore inherits from both `StaffMember` and `Employee`. The constructor of `Executive` passes along its information to the `Employee` constructor and sets the bonus for the executive to zero.

A bonus is awarded to an executive using the `awardBonus` method. This method is called from the constructor of `Staff` for the only executive that is part of the `personnel` array. Note that the generic `StaffMember` reference must be cast into an `Executive` reference in order to invoke the `awardBonus` method (which doesn't exist for a `StaffMember`).

The `pay` method of an `Executive` is overloaded to first determine the payment as it would for any employee, then adds the bonus. The `pay` method of the `Employee` class is invoked using `super` to obtain the normal payment amount. This technique is better than just using the `payRate` variable because if we choose to change how `Employee` objects get paid, the change will automatically be reflected in `Executive`. After the bonus is awarded, it is reset to zero.

The `Hourly` class (Listing 7.19) represents an employee whose pay rate is applied on an hourly basis. It keeps track of the number of hours worked in the current pay period, which can be modified by calls to the `addHours` method. This method is called from the constructor of `Staff`. The `pay` method of `Hourly` determines the payment based on the number of hours worked, then resets the hours to zero.

Listing 7.17

```
//********************************************************************
//  Employee.java       Author: Lewis and Loftus
//
//  Represents a general paid employee.
//********************************************************************

import StaffMember;

public class Employee extends StaffMember
{
   protected String socialSecurityNumber;
   protected double payRate;

   //-----------------------------------------------------------------
   //  Sets up an employee with the specified information.
   //-----------------------------------------------------------------
   public Employee (String eName, String eAddress, String ePhone,
                    String socSecNumber, double rate)
   {
      super (eName, eAddress, ePhone);

      socialSecurityNumber = socSecNumber;
      payRate = rate;
   }

   //-----------------------------------------------------------------
   //  Returns information about an employee as a string.
   //-----------------------------------------------------------------
   public String toString ()
   {
      String result = super.toString();

      result += "\nSocial Security Number: " + socialSecurityNumber;

      return result;
   }

   //-----------------------------------------------------------------
   //  Returns the pay rate for this employee.
   //-----------------------------------------------------------------
   public double pay ()
   {
      return payRate;
   }
}
```

Listing 7.18

```
//********************************************************************
//  Executive.java       Author: Lewis and Loftus
//
//  Represents an executive staff member who can earn a bonus.
//********************************************************************

import Employee;

public class Executive extends Employee
{
   private double bonus;

   //-----------------------------------------------------------------
   //  Sets up an executive with the specified information.
   //-----------------------------------------------------------------
   public Executive (String eName, String eAddress, String ePhone,
                     String socSecNumber, double rate)
   {
      super (eName, eAddress, ePhone, socSecNumber, rate);

      bonus = 0;  // bonus has yet to be awarded
   }

   //-----------------------------------------------------------------
   //  Awards the specified bonus to this executive.
   //-----------------------------------------------------------------
   public void awardBonus (double execBonus)
   {
      bonus = execBonus;
   }

   //-----------------------------------------------------------------
   //  Computes and returns the pay for an executive, which is the
   //  regular employee payment plus a one-time bonus.
   //-----------------------------------------------------------------
   public double pay ()
   {
      double payment = super.pay() + bonus;

      bonus = 0;

      return payment;
   }
}
```

Listing 7.19

```
//********************************************************************
//  Hourly.java       Author: Lewis and Loftus
//
//  Represents an employee who gets paid by the hour.
//********************************************************************

import Employee;

public class Hourly extends Employee
{
   private int hoursWorked;

   //-----------------------------------------------------------------
   //  Sets up this hourly employee using the specified information.
   //-----------------------------------------------------------------
   public Hourly (String eName, String eAddress, String ePhone,
                  String socSecNumber, double rate)
   {
      super (eName, eAddress, ePhone, socSecNumber, rate);

      hoursWorked = 0;
   }

   //-----------------------------------------------------------------
   //  Adds the specified number of hours to this employee's
   //  accumulated hours.
   //-----------------------------------------------------------------
   public void addHours (int moreHours)
   {
      hoursWorked += moreHours;
   }

   //-----------------------------------------------------------------
   //  Computes and returns the pay for this hourly employee.
   //-----------------------------------------------------------------
   public double pay ()
   {
      double payment = payRate * hoursWorked;

      hoursWorked = 0;

      return payment;
   }
```

Listing 7.19 ***(continued)***

```
   //-----------------------------------------------------------------
   //  Returns information about this hourly employee as a string.
   //-----------------------------------------------------------------
   public String toString ()
   {
      String result = super.toString();

      result += "\nCurrent hours: " + hoursWorked;

      return result;
   }
}
```

7.5 Indirect Use of Noninherited Members

There is a subtle feature of inheritance that is worth noting at this point. The visibility modifiers determine if a variable or method is inherited into a subclass. If a variable or method is inherited, then it can be referenced directly in the subclass by name, as if it were declared locally in the subclass. However, all variables and methods that are defined in a parent class exist for an object of a derived class, even though they can't be referenced directly. They can, however, be referenced indirectly.

Let's look at an example that demonstrates this situation. The program shown in Listing 7.20 contains a `main` method that instantiates a `Pizza` object and invokes a method to determine how many calories the pizza has per serving due to its fat content.

The `FoodItem` class is shown in Listing 7.21 and represents a generic type of food. The constructor of `FoodItem` accepts the number of grams of fat and the number of servings that the food has. The `calories` method returns the number of calories due to fat, which the `caloriesPerServing` method invokes.

The `Pizza` class, shown in Listing 7.22, is derived from `FoodItem`, but adds no special functionality or data. Its constructor calls the constructor of `FoodItem`, assuming that there are eight servings per pizza.

Note that the `Pizza` object called `special` in the `main` method is used to invoke the method `caloriesPerServing`, which is defined as a `public`

Listing 7.20

```
//********************************************************************
//  FoodAnalysis.java       Author: Lewis and Loftus
//
//  Demonstrates indirect referencing through inheritance.
//********************************************************************

import Pizza;

public class FoodAnalysis
{
   //-----------------------------------------------------------------
   //  Instantiates a Pizza object and prints its calories per
   //  serving.
   //-----------------------------------------------------------------
   public static void main (String[] args)
   {
      Pizza special = new Pizza (275);

      System.out.println ("Calories per serving: " +
                          special.caloriesPerServing());
   }
}
```

```
Calories per serving: 309
```

method of `FoodItem` and is therefore inherited by `Pizza`. However, `caloriesPerServing` calls `calories`, which is declared `private`, and is therefore not inherited by `Pizza`. Furthermore, `calories` references the variable `fatGrams` and the constant `CALORIES_PER_GRAM`, which are also declared with `private` visibility.

Even though `Pizza` did not inherit `calories`, `fatGrams`, or `CALORIES_PER_GRAM`, they were available for use when the `Pizza` object needed them. The `Pizza` class cannot refer to them directly by name, because they are not inherited, but they do exist. Note that no `FoodItem` object was ever created, or needed.

Key Concept

All members of a superclass exist for a subclass, but they are not necessarily inherited. Only inherited members can be referenced by name in the subclass.

Figure 7.8 lists each variable and method declared in the `FoodItem` class and indicates whether it exists in or is inherited by the `Pizza` class. Note that every `FoodItem` member exists in the `Pizza` class, no matter how it is declared. The items that are not inherited can only be referenced indirectly.

Listing 7.21

```
//********************************************************************
//  FoodItem.java       Author: Lewis and Loftus
//
//  Demonstrates indirect referencing through inheritance.
//********************************************************************

public class FoodItem
{
   final private int CALORIES_PER_GRAM = 9;
   private int fatGrams;
   protected int servings;

   //-----------------------------------------------------------------
   //  Sets up this food item with the specified number of fat grams
   //  and number of servings.
   //-----------------------------------------------------------------
   public FoodItem (int fatGrams, int servings)
   {
      this.fatGrams = fatGrams;
      this.servings = servings;
   }

   //-----------------------------------------------------------------
   //  Computes and returns the number of calories in this food item
   //  due to fat.
   //-----------------------------------------------------------------
   private int calories ()
   {
      return fatGrams * CALORIES_PER_GRAM;
   }

   //-----------------------------------------------------------------
   //  Computes and returns the number of fat calories per serving.
   //-----------------------------------------------------------------
   public int caloriesPerServing ()
   {
      return (calories() / servings);
   }
}
```

Listing 7.22

```
//********************************************************************
//  Pizza.java       Author: Lewis and Loftus
//
//  Demonstrates indirect referencing through inheritance.
//********************************************************************

import FoodItem;

public class Pizza extends FoodItem
{
   //-----------------------------------------------------------------
   //  Sets up a pizza with the specified amount of fat; assumes
   //  eight servings.
   //-----------------------------------------------------------------
   public Pizza (int fatGrams)
   {
      super (fatGrams, 8);
   }
}
```

Declared in `FoodItem` class	Defined in `Pizza` class	Inherited in `Pizza` class
`CALORIES_PER_GRAM`	yes	no, because the constant is private
`fat`	yes	no, because the variable is private
`servings`	yes	yes, because the variable is protected
`FoodItem`	yes	no, because constructors are not inherited
`calories`	yes	no, because the method is private
`caloriesPerServing`	yes	yes, because the method is public

Figure 7.8 The relationship between `FoodItem` members and the `Pizza` class

7.6 Interface Hierarchies

The concept of inheritance can be applied to interfaces as well as classes. That is, one interface can be derived from another interface. These relationships can form *interface hierarchies,* similar to class hierarchies.

> **Key Concept**
> Inheritance can be applied to interfaces, such that one interface can be derived from another interface.

When a parent interface is used to derive a child interface, the child inherits all abstract methods and constants of the parent. Any class that implements the child interface must implement all of the methods. There are no restrictions on the inheritance because all members of an interface are public.

Class hierarchies and interface hierarchies do not overlap. That is, an interface cannot be used to derive a class, and a class cannot be used to derive an interface. These two constructs interact only when a class is designed to implement a particular interface.

7.7 Inheritance and Graphics

The concept of inheritance affects our use of graphics in various ways. This section explores some of those issues.

Applets Revisited

Recall that to create an applet we define a class that extends the `Applet` class, which is part of the `java.applet` package of the standard class library. This relationship demonstrates a classic use of inheritance, allowing the parent class to shoulder the responsibilities that apply to all of its descendants.

> **Key Concept**
> An applet is a good example of inheritance. The `Applet` parent class handles all common characteristics of applets.

The `Applet` class is already designed to handle all of the details concerning applet creation and execution. For example, an applet program interacts with a browser, can accept parameters thorough HTML code, and is constrained by certain security limitations. The `Applet` class already takes care of these details in a generic way that applies to all applets.

The applet class that we write is free to focus on the purpose of that particular program. In other words, the only issues that we address in our applet code are those that make it different from other applets.

An applet is just one of several graphical user interface (GUI) components that we might use. Later in this chapter we begin to explore some other graphical components. In some cases we use these components just as we use the

`Applet` class: as a base class from which we derive a specific version of the component.

Extending Event Adapter Classes

For event-driven programs, we create listener classes whose job is to acknowledge and respond to a certain set of events. In previous examples we've created the listener classes by implementing a particular listener interface. For instance, to create a class that listens for mouse events, we create a class that implements the `MouseListener` interface. A listener interface often contains event methods that are not important to a particular program, in which case we provided empty definitions just to satisfy the interface requirement.

An alternative technique for creating a listener class is to extend an *event adapter class*. Each listener interface that contains more than one method has a corresponding adapter class that already contains empty definitions for all of the methods in the interface. To create a listener, we derive a new listener class from the appropriate adapter class and override any event methods in which we are interested. Using this technique, we no longer have to provide empty definitions for unused methods.

Key Concept

Listener classes can be created by deriving a new class from an existing event adapter class.

In many situations, it is appropriate and convenient to use an inner class (discussed in Chapter 5) to create a listener from an adapter class. Usually, the inner class is nested within the class that generates the events to which it responds. This relationship hides the listener from other classes and simplifies the communication between the component and the listener.

The program shown in Listing 7.23 is an applet that responds to mouse-click events. Whenever the mouse button is clicked over the applet, a line is drawn from the location of the mouse pointer to the center of the applet (see the accompanying screen shot). The distance that line represents in pixels is displayed.

The class `OffCenterListener` is nested within the definition of the `OffCenter` class. It extends the class called `MouseAdapter`, which is defined in the `java.awt.event` package of the standard class library. The `MouseAdapter` class implements the `MouseListener` interface and contains empty definitions of the mouse-event methods. We override the definition of the `mouseClicked` method to suit our needs.

We now have a choice when it comes to creating event listeners. We can implement an event listener interface, or we can extend an event adapter class. This choice is a design decision that should be considered carefully. The best technique depends on the situation.

Listing 7.23

```
//********************************************************************
//  OffCenter.java       Author: Lewis and Loftus
//
//  Demonstrates the extension of an event adapter class.
//********************************************************************

import java.applet.Applet;
import java.awt.*;
import java.awt.event.*;
import java.text.DecimalFormat;

public class OffCenter extends Applet
{
   private final int APPLET_WIDTH = 200;
   private final int APPLET_HEIGHT = 200;

   private DecimalFormat fmt;
   private Point current;
   private int centerX, centerY;
   private double length;

   //-----------------------------------------------------------------
   //  Sets up the applet, including creating a listener from the
   //  inner class and adding it to the applet.
   //-----------------------------------------------------------------
   public void init()
   {
      addMouseListener (new OffCenterListener());

      centerX = APPLET_WIDTH / 2;
      centerY = APPLET_HEIGHT / 2;

      fmt = new DecimalFormat ("0.##");

      setBackground (Color.yellow);
      setSize (APPLET_WIDTH, APPLET_HEIGHT);
   }
```

Listing 7.23 (continued)

```
   //-----------------------------------------------------------------
   //  Draws a line from the mouse pointer to the center point of
   //  the applet and displays the distance.
   //-----------------------------------------------------------------
   public void paint (Graphics page)
   {
      page.setColor (Color.black);
      if (current != null)
      {
         page.drawLine (current.x, current.y, centerX, centerY);
         page.drawString ("Distance: " + fmt.format(length), 50, 15);
      }
   }

   class OffCenterListener extends MouseAdapter
   {
      //--------------------------------------------------------------
      //  Computes the distance from the mouse pointer to the center
      //  point of the applet.
      //--------------------------------------------------------------
      public void mouseClicked (MouseEvent event)
      {
         current = event.getPoint();
         length = Math.sqrt(Math.pow((current.x-centerX), 2) +
                            Math.pow((current.y-centerY), 2));
         repaint();
      }
   }
}
```

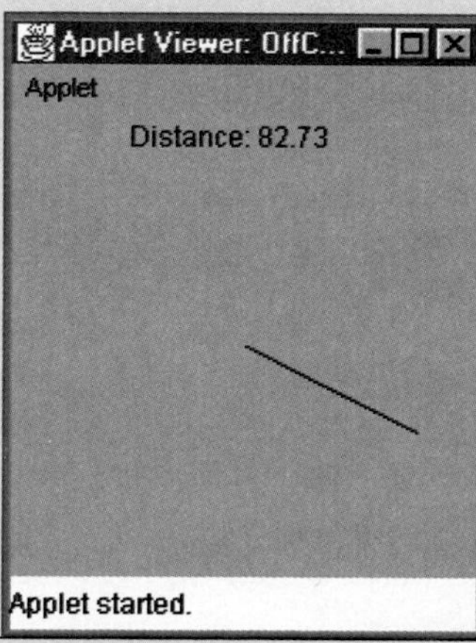

7.8 GUI Components

A *graphical user interface (GUI) component* is an object that represents a visual entity that displays information or allows the user to interact with a program in a certain way. Examples of GUI components include push buttons, text fields, labels, scrollbars, and menus. These components are defined by classes. The components we introduce in this section are part of the `java.awt` package. Another set of components, called Swing components, is introduced in Chapter 9.

Key Concept

A GUI component presents information or allows the user to interact with a program in a certain way.

An applet is also a component. In fact, an applet is a special kind of component called a *container;* it is a component that can hold other components.

Components generate events to which our programs, through listener classes, respond. In previous examples, we've added listeners to an applet in order to capture mouse events that are generated by the applet as the mouse interacts with it.

Key Concept

A GUI component generates events. One or more listeners are added to a particular component to handle events generated by that component.

Each type of component can generate a certain set of events. A push button, for instance, generates an `ActionEvent` whenever it is pushed. A scrollbar generates an `AdjustmentEvent` when its slider is repositioned. Each event has a corresponding listener interface, and many have a corresponding adapter class. Remember that the appropriate listener must be added to the component that generates the event. A component can have multiple listeners. For that matter, one listener can be added to multiple components, if appropriate.

Components take up visual space, and are added to a particular container to be displayed. The order in which components are added, in part, determines how they are displayed on the screen. Many other factors also affect how components appear when displayed. These issues are discussed in Chapter 9.

The program in Listing 7.24 is an applet that converts a Fahrenheit temperature to its equivalent Celsius temperature. The program uses two types of components: labels and text fields. A *label* is a component that displays a line of text in a GUI. It is often used to put a descriptive label on other components or display additional information. The text of a label can be determined under program control, but not by the user. A *text field* is a component that displays a field into which a user can type information. It is a common means to accept input into a GUI program.

The `Fahrenheit` program uses three labels and one text field. The text field is used to obtain the Fahrenheit temperature value from the user. The label called `resultLabel` is used to display the equivalent Celsius temperature. Initially, it displays the string `N/A`, meaning that until the first input is

Listing 7.24

```
//********************************************************************
//  Fahrenheit.java       Author: Lewis and Loftus
//
//  Demonstrates the use of GUI components.
//********************************************************************

import java.applet.Applet;
import java.awt.*;
import java.awt.event.*;

public class Fahrenheit extends Applet implements ActionListener
{
   private int APPLET_WIDTH = 200;
   private int APPLET_HEIGHT = 100;

   private Label inputLabel, outputLabel, resultLabel;
   private TextField fahrenheit;

   //-----------------------------------------------------------------
   //  Sets up the applet with its various components.
   //-----------------------------------------------------------------
   public void init()
   {
      inputLabel = new Label ("Enter Fahrenheit:");
      outputLabel = new Label ("Temperature in Celsius:");
      resultLabel = new Label ("N/A");

      fahrenheit = new TextField (5);
      fahrenheit.addActionListener (this);

      add (inputLabel);
      add (fahrenheit);
      add (outputLabel);
      add (resultLabel);

      setBackground (Color.white);
      setSize (APPLET_WIDTH, APPLET_HEIGHT);
   }
```

Listing 7.24 ***(continued)***

```
   //-----------------------------------------------------------------
   //  Performs the conversion when the Enter key is pressed in
   //  the text field.
   //-----------------------------------------------------------------
   public void actionPerformed (ActionEvent event)
   {
      int fahrenheitTemp, celsiusTemp;

      String text = fahrenheit.getText();

      fahrenheitTemp = Integer.parseInt (text);
      celsiusTemp = (fahrenheitTemp-32) * 5/9;

      resultLabel.setText (Integer.toString (celsiusTemp));
   }
}
```

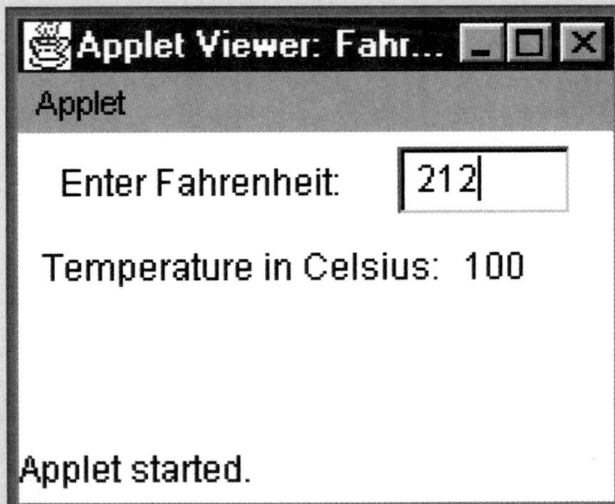

accepted, the output is not applicable. The `Label` constructor accepts the label's string as a parameter. The parameter to the `TextField` constructor is an integer that indicates how many characters the text field should be able to display.

In general, a label does not generate events of interest. A text field generates an `ActionEvent` whenever the Enter key is pressed while typing in the field. We use the applet, which implements the `ActionListener` interface, as the listener for the text field. The `ActionListener` interface contains only one method, called `actionPerformed`, which is automatically called when the user presses the Enter key. Note that the `this` reference is passed to the `addActionListener` method of the text field. Compare this to earlier examples in which the listeners were added to the applet. In the past, the applet generated the events of interest. This time, the text field is generating the only event for which we are listening.

The labels and the text field are added to the applet container by using the applet's `add` method. In previous examples, the applet was the only component we used, so this step is new as well. Components must be added to a container to be displayed. When the container is painted, the components inside the container are painted.

Note the difference between adding a listener to a component and adding a component to a container. One sets up the relationship between a component that will generate an event and the listener object that will handle an event when it occurs. The other sets up the relationship among the visual components that are grouped together in some way.

When the user types in a temperature into the text field and presses Enter, the `actionPerformed` method is called, which accepts an `ActionEvent` object. The `getText` method of the `ActionEvent` object returns the text that was typed into the text field as a string. The program converts that string to an integer and computes the appropriate Celsius temperature. Then we use the `setText` method of the `resultLabel` object to change the output. When the applet is repainted after the event is processed, the new output is displayed.

Consider the difference between using a `Label` component and using the `drawString` method to draw some text. A label is a component that takes up visual space among the other components in a container. The string drawn by `drawString` simply decorates the component on which it is drawn. It would not be taken into account when the components are positioned and displayed.

The `Component` Class Hierarchy

The AWT components are defined as part of a `Component` class hierarchy, shown in part in Figure 7.9. All GUI components are derived from the `Component` class, which defines how all components work in general.

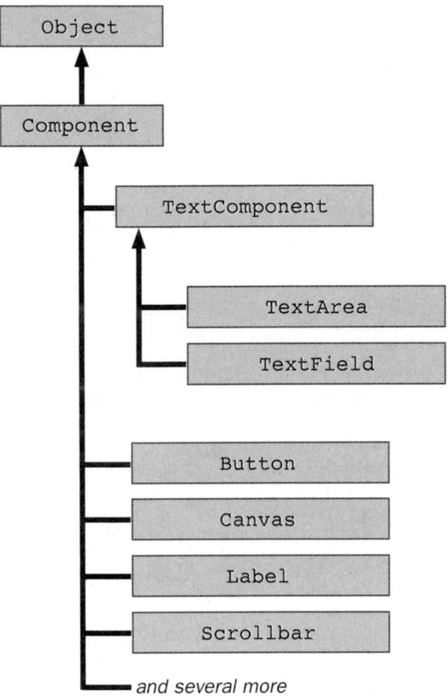

Figure 7.9 Part of the AWT `Component` class hierarchy

The `paint` method, for instance, is defined in the `Component` class. All components inherit the default version of this method, which we have regularly overridden in our applet programs to paint particular shapes.

Let's look at another example that uses GUI components. The `Doodle` program, shown in Listing 7.25, presents an area in which you can draw doodles using the mouse. Each time the user drags the mouse over the doodling area (holding the mouse button down), a line appears as if the user were drawing with a pencil. A push button to the side of the doodling area clears the image so that a new doodle can be started.

The `Doodle` program makes use of a *canvas,* which is a component that serves as an independent drawing surface. The `Canvas` class is designed to be extended into a component that serves a program's particular needs. In our program, we use `Canvas` to derive the class `DoodleCanvas`, which is shown in Listing 7.26.

In the `init` method of the applet class we create the canvas, the button, and a label to serve as an instructive title. We add each of these components to the applet container.

Listing 7.25

```
//********************************************************************
//  Doodle.java       Author: Lewis and Loftus
//
//  Demonstrates the use of GUI components.
//********************************************************************

import DoodleCanvas;

import java.applet.Applet;
import java.awt.*;
import java.awt.event.*;

public class Doodle extends Applet implements ActionListener
{
   private int APPLET_WIDTH = 300;
   private int APPLET_HEIGHT = 250;

   private Label titleLabel;
   private DoodleCanvas canvas;
   private Button clearButton;

   //-----------------------------------------------------------------
   //  Creates the GUI components and adds them to the applet. The
   //  applet serves as the listener for the button.
   //-----------------------------------------------------------------
   public void init ()
   {
      titleLabel = new Label ("Doodle using the mouse.");
      titleLabel.setBackground (Color.cyan);
      add (titleLabel);

      canvas = new DoodleCanvas();
      add (canvas);

      clearButton = new Button("Clear");
      clearButton.addActionListener (this);
      add (clearButton);

      setBackground (Color.cyan);
      setSize (APPLET_WIDTH, APPLET_HEIGHT);
   }
```

Listing 7.25 ***(continued)***

```
   //-----------------------------------------------------------------
   //  Clears the canvas when the clear button is pushed.
   //-----------------------------------------------------------------
   public void actionPerformed (ActionEvent event)
   {
      canvas.clear();
   }
}
```

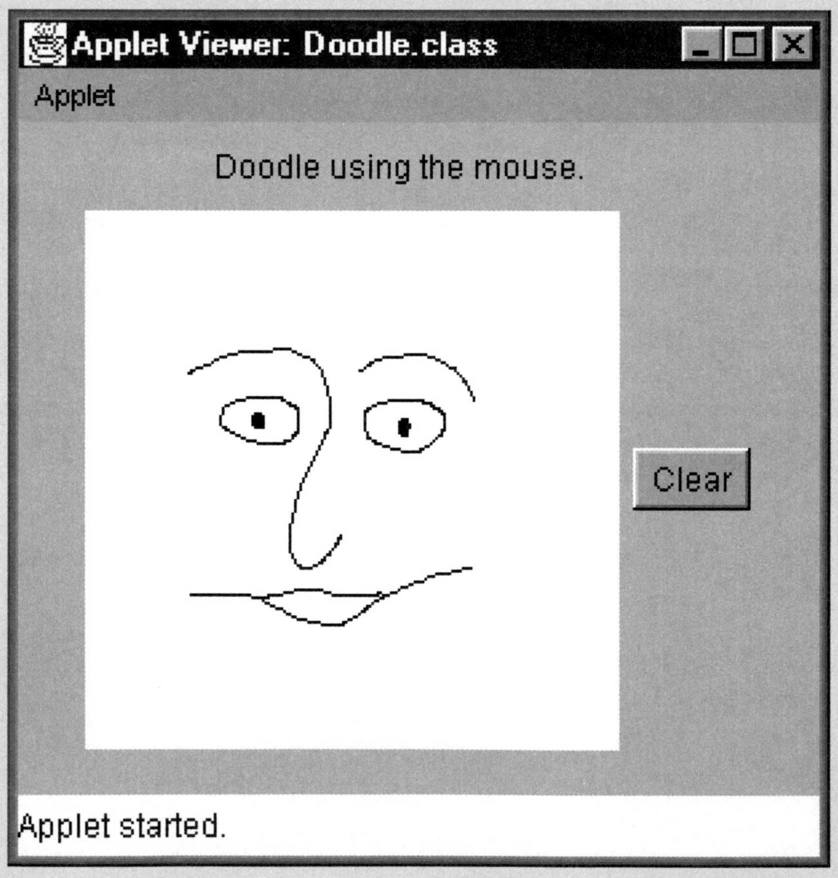

Listing 7.26

```
//********************************************************************
//  DoodleCanvas.java       Author: Lewis and Loftus
//
//  Represents a drawing surface for creating simple doodles.
//********************************************************************

import java.awt.*;
import java.awt.event.*;

class DoodleCanvas extends Canvas implements MouseListener,
                                             MouseMotionListener
{
   private final int CANVAS_WIDTH = 200;
   private final int CANVAS_HEIGHT = 200;

   private int lastX, lastY;

   //-----------------------------------------------------------------
   //  Creates an initially empty canvas.
   //-----------------------------------------------------------------
   public DoodleCanvas ()
   {
      addMouseListener (this);
      addMouseMotionListener (this);

      setBackground (Color.white);
      setSize (CANVAS_WIDTH, CANVAS_HEIGHT);
   }

   //-----------------------------------------------------------------
   //  Determines the initial point for a new doodle line.
   //-----------------------------------------------------------------
   public void mousePressed (MouseEvent event)
   {
      Point first = event.getPoint();
      lastX = first.x;
      lastY = first.y;
   }
```

Listing 7.26 (continued)

```
   //-----------------------------------------------------------------
   //  Draws a line from the last point to the current point.
   //-----------------------------------------------------------------
   public void mouseDragged (MouseEvent event)
   {
      Point current = event.getPoint();

      Graphics page = getGraphics();
      page.drawLine (lastX, lastY, current.x, current.y);

      lastX = current.x;
      lastY = current.y;
   }

   //-----------------------------------------------------------------
   //  Clears the canvas.
   //-----------------------------------------------------------------
   public void clear ()
   {
      Graphics page = getGraphics();
      page.drawRect (0, 0, CANVAS_WIDTH, CANVAS_HEIGHT);
      repaint();
   }

   //-----------------------------------------------------------------
   //  Provides empty definitions for unused event methods.
   //-----------------------------------------------------------------
   public void mouseReleased (MouseEvent event) {}
   public void mouseClicked (MouseEvent event) {}
   public void mouseEntered (MouseEvent event) {}
   public void mouseExited (MouseEvent event) {}
   public void mouseMoved (MouseEvent event) {}
}
```

There are three types of events that this program must capture. One is the action event generated by the push button. The others are mouse and mouse-motion events that we must capture as the user doodles on the canvas. Note that the applet class serves as the listener for the button, but the canvas serves as its own listener for mouse events.

The `actionPerformed` method is invoked in the applet class when the button is pushed, to which we respond by calling the `clear` method of the `DoodleCanvas` class. The `clear` method draws a rectangle over the entire canvas surface, effectively clearing it.

The `mousePressed` and `mouseDragged` methods are invoked when those events occur on the canvas. When the mouse button is first pressed, the location of the mouse pointer is noted. As the mouse is dragged, lines are continually drawn from the last noted location to the current one. This happens sufficiently fast enough so that the lines look like a scribble following the movement of the mouse pointer.

Note that we do not explicitly define the `paint` method for this canvas. In this situation, it was easier to do the drawing in the `mouseDragged` and `clear` methods. We use the `getGraphics` method of the component to obtain a reference to the `Graphics` object that represents the graphics context for this component. It is a reference to the same `Graphics` object that is passed to the `paint` method as a parameter.

Summary of Key Concepts

- Inheritance is the act of deriving a new class from an existing one. It is analogous to creating a new house blueprint from an existing blueprint with similar characteristics.
- A primary purpose of inheritance is to reuse existing software.
- Inherited variables and methods can be used in the derived class as if they had been declared locally.
- You should maintain the is-a relationship between all derived classes in a class hierarchy.
- Visibility modifiers determine which variables and methods are inherited. Protected visibility provides the best encapsulation while still permitting inheritance.
- The parent's constructor can be invoked using the `super` reference.
- A child class can override (redefine) the parent's definition of an inherited method.
- The child of one class can be the parent of one or more other classes, creating a class hierarchy.
- Common features should be located as high in a class hierarchy as is reasonable, maximizing reuse potential and minimizing maintenance efforts.
- All Java classes are derived, directly or indirectly, from the `Object` class.
- The `toString` and `equals` methods are defined in the `Object` class and therefore are inherited by every class in every Java program.
- A new exception is defined by deriving a new class from the `Exception` class or one of its descendants.
- The `throws` clause on a method header must be included for checked exceptions that are not caught and handled in the method.
- An abstract class cannot be instantiated. It represents a concept on which other classes can build their definitions.
- A class derived from an abstract parent must override all of its parent's abstract methods, or the derived class will also be considered abstract.
- A reference variable can refer to any object created from any class that is related to the reference type by inheritance.
- A polymorphic reference uses the type of the object, not the type of the reference, to determine which version of an overridden method to invoke.

- All members of a superclass exist for a subclass, but they are not necessarily inherited. Only inherited members can be referenced by name in the subclass.
- Inheritance can be applied to interfaces, such that one interface can be derived from another interface.
- An applet is a good example of inheritance. The `Applet` parent class handles all common characteristics of applets.
- Listener classes can be created by deriving a new class from an existing event adapter class.
- A GUI component presents information or allows the user to interact with a program in a certain way.
- A GUI component generates events. One or more listeners are added to a particular component to handle events generated by that component.

▶ Self-Review Questions

7.1 Describe the relationship between a parent class and a child class.

7.2 How does inheritance support software reuse?

7.3 What relationship should every class derivation represent?

7.4 Why would a child class override one or more of the methods of its parent class?

7.5 Why is the `super` reference important to a child class?

7.6 How does inheritance support polymorphism?

7.7 How is overriding related to polymorphism?

7.8 What is an interface hierarchy?

7.9 What is an adapter class?

▶ Exercises

7.1 Draw a class hierarchy containing classes that represent different types of clocks. Show the members (variables and method names) for two of these classes.

7.2 Show an alternative hierarchy for the hierarchy in the previous problem. Explain why it may be a better or worse approach than the original.

7.3 Draw and annotate a class hierarchy representing students in a university. Design the pseudocode for a method that can invoke the methods of every object that can be created from the classes. Explain how polymorphism plays a role in this process.

7.4 Experiment with a simple derivation. Put `println` statements in constructors of both the parent and child classes. Do not explicitly call the constructor of the parent in the child. What happens? Why? Change the child's constructor to explicitly call the constructor of the parent. Now what happens?

Programming Projects

7.1 Design and implement a class called `MonetaryCoin` that is derived from the `Coin` class presented in Chapter 4. Store a value in the monetary coin that represents its value. Add a method that returns its value. Create a main driver class to instantiate and compute the sum of several `MonetaryCoin` objects. Demonstrate that a monetary coin inherits its parent's ability to be flipped.

7.2 Design and implement a set of classes that define the employees of a hospital: doctor, nurse, administrator, surgeon, receptionist, janitor, and so on. Include methods in each class that are named according to the services provided by that person and then print an appropriate message. Create a `main` driver class to instantiate and exercise several of the classes.

7.3 Design and implement a set of classes that define various types of reading material: books, novels, magazines, textbooks, and so on. Include data values that describe various attributes of the material such as the number of pages and the names of the primary characters. Include methods that are named appropriately for each class, then print a message. Create a `main` driver class to instantiate and exercise several of the classes.

7.4 Design and implement a class that simulates a VCR remote control. The class should have various methods for interacting with the TV as well as recording and playing tapes. Extend the VCR remote-control class to create a different type of remote control. Add a method to the subclass that provides additional functionality for the remote control. Create a `main` driver class to instantiate several different remote control objects and exercises their methods.

7.5 Design and implement a set of classes that keeps track of various sports statistics. Have each low-level class represent a certain sport. Tailor the services of the classes to the sport in question, and move common attributes to the higher-level classes as appropriate. Create a `main` driver class to instantiate and exercise several of the classes.

7.6 Design and implement a set of classes that keeps track of demographic information about a set of people, such as age, nationality, occupation, income, and so on. Design each class to focus on a particular aspect of data collection. Create a main driver class to instantiate and exercise several of the classes.

7.7 Design and implement an applet that presents a button to the user and displays the number of times the button has been pressed. Use a label to display the output.

7.8 Design and implement an applet that serves as a mortgage calculator. Accept the mortgage amount, the interest rate, and the loan duration (number of years) using three text fields. When the user presses a button, determine and display the total cost of the mortgage and the amount of interest that will be paid.

7.9 Design and implement an applet that produces birthday designs. Accept the user's birth month and day using text fields. When a button is pressed, use a canvas to present a geometric design based on those values. Always produce the same design for a given month and day, but produce a different design for each day of the year. Use various colors and shapes to distinguish the designs.

▶ Answers to Self-Review Questions

7.1 A child class is derived from a parent class using inheritance. The methods and variables of the parent class automatically become a part of the child class, subject to the rules of the visibility modifiers used to declare them.

7.2 Because a new class can be derived from an existing one, the characteristics of the parent class can be reused without the error-prone process of copying and modifying code.

7.3 Any derivation in a class hierarchy should represent an is-a relationship: the child *is-a* more specific version of the parent. If this relationship does not hold, then inheritance is being used improperly.

7.4 A child class may prefer its own definition of a method in favor of the definition provided for it by its parent. In this case, the child overrides (redefines) the parent's definition with its own.

7.5 The `super` reference can be used to call the parent's constructor, which cannot be invoked directly by name. It can also be used to invoke the parent's version of an overridden method.

7.6 Polymorphism is the ability of a reference of one class to refer to an object of another class. In Java, a reference for a parent class can be used to refer to an object of the child class.

7.7 When a child class overrides the definition of a parent's method, two versions of that method exist. If a polymorphic reference is used to invoke the method, the specific version of the method that gets invoked is determined by the type of the object being referred to, not by the type of the reference variable.

7.8 A new interface can be derived from an existing interface using inheritance just as a new class can be derived from an existing class.

7.9 An adapter class is a class that implements a listener interface, providing empty definitions for all of its methods. A listener class can be created by extending the appropriate adapter class and overriding the methods of interest.

8 Exceptions and I/O Streams

This chapter addresses two related topics: exceptions and input/output streams. Exceptions represent problems that occur in software and allow us to handle them appropriately. The ability to handle exceptions is fundamental to being able to perform various I/O operations. Java supports many ways for a program to read information from an external source and to write information to an external destination. The source or destination could be main memory, a file, another program, a network connection, or several other options. The underlying mechanism for accomplishing any I/O operation is called a stream, and there are several classes in the Java standard library that can be used to create and manage streams.

Chapter Objectives

- Examine the `try-catch` statement for handling exceptions.
- Create a new exception.
- Define an I/O stream.
- Explore the classes used to create streams.
- Discuss the standard input and output streams.
- Explain the processing of the `Keyboard` class.
- Determine how to read and write text files.
- Determine how to serialize objects for I/O operations.

8.1 Exceptions

Key Concept

Both errors and exceptions represent unusual or invalid processing, but whereas an exception can be caught and handled, an error should not.

As we've discussed briefly in other parts of the text, problems that arise in a Java program generate exceptions and errors. Recall from Chapter 2 that an exception is an object that defines an unusual or erroneous situation. An exception is thrown by a program or the runtime environment, and can be caught and handled appropriately if desired. An error is similar to an exception, except that an error generally represents an unrecoverable situation, and should not be caught.

Java has a predefined set of exceptions and errors that may occur during the execution of a program. Appendix K contains a list of many of the errors and exceptions defined in the Java standard class library.

We have various options when it comes to dealing with exceptions. A program can be designed to process an exception in one of three ways. It can:

- not handle the exception at all.
- handle the exception where it occurs.
- handle the exception at another point in the program.

We explore each of these approaches in the following sections.

Exception Messages

If an exception is not handled at all by the program, the program will terminate (abnormally) and produce a message that describes what exception occurred and where in the program it was produced. We should always read the exception output carefully because it is often helpful in tracking down the cause of a problem.

Let's look at the output of an exception. An `ArithmeticException` is thrown when an invalid arithmetic operation is attempted, such as dividing by zero. The program shown in Listing 8.1 produces this exception.

Because there is no code in this program to explicitly handle the exception, the program terminates when the exception occurs, printing certain information about the exception that occurred. The first line indicates which exception was thrown and provides some information about why it was thrown. The remaining lines are the *call stack trace,* which indicate where the exception occurred. In this case, there is only one line in the call stack trace, but there may be several depending on where the exception originated in the program. The first line of the trace indicates the method, file, and line number where the exception occurred. The other lines in the trace, if present, indicate the methods that were called to get to the method that produced

Key Concept

The messages printed by a thrown exception indicate the nature of the problem and a call stack trace that shows the methods that were invoked.

Listing 8.1

```
//********************************************************************
//  Zero.java       Author: Lewis and Loftus
//
//  Demonstrates an uncaught exception.
//********************************************************************

public class Zero
{
   //-----------------------------------------------------------------
   //  Deliberately divides by zero to produce an exception.
   //-----------------------------------------------------------------
   public static void main (String[] args)
   {
      int numerator = 10;
      int denominator = 0;

      System.out.println (numerator / denominator);

      System.out.println ("This text will not be printed.");
   }
}
```

```
Exception in thread "main" java.lang.ArithmeticException: / by zero
        at Zero.main(Zero.java:17)
```

the exception. In this program, there is only one method, and it produced the exception; therefore, there is only one line in the trace. Note that the last `println` statement in the program never executes because the exception occurs first.

The call stack trace information is also available by calling several methods of the exception class that is being thrown. The method `getMessage` returns a string explaining the reason the exception was thrown. The method `printStackTrace` prints the call stack trace.

The `try` Statement

Let's now examine how we catch and handle an exception when it is thrown. The *try statement* identifies a block of statements that may throw

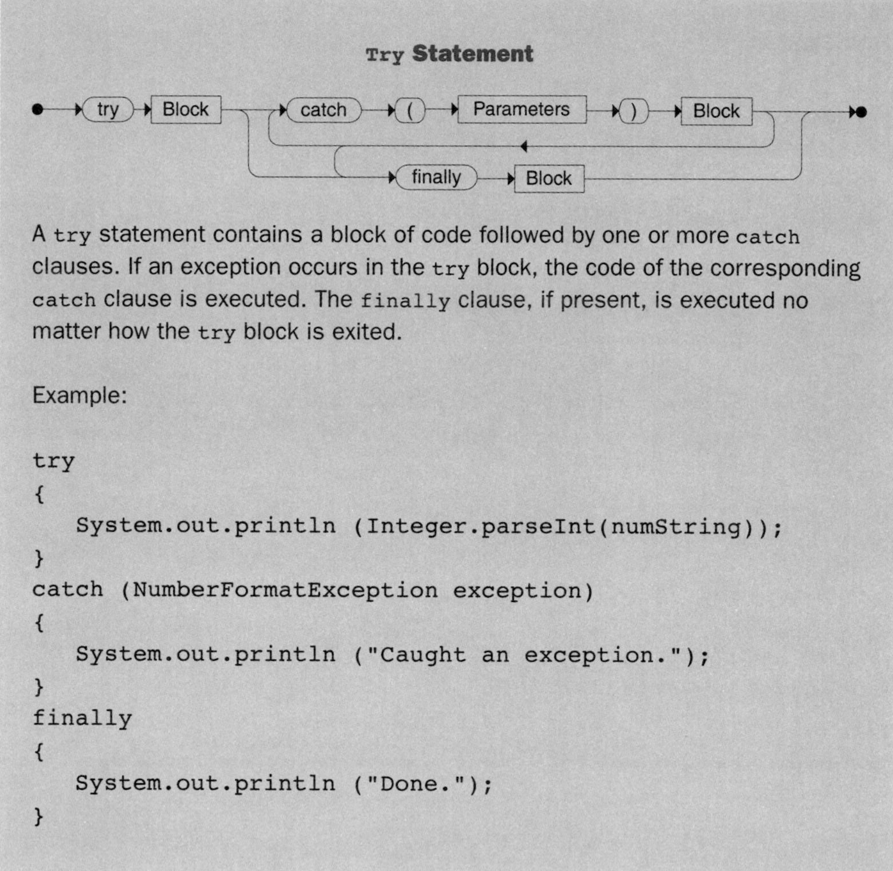

Try Statement

A `try` statement contains a block of code followed by one or more `catch` clauses. If an exception occurs in the `try` block, the code of the corresponding `catch` clause is executed. The `finally` clause, if present, is executed no matter how the `try` block is exited.

Example:

```
try
{
   System.out.println (Integer.parseInt(numString));
}
catch (NumberFormatException exception)
{
   System.out.println ("Caught an exception.");
}
finally
{
   System.out.println ("Done.");
}
```

an exception. A *catch clause,* which follows a `try` block, defines how a particular kind of exception is handled. A `try` block can have several catch clauses associated with it. Each catch clause is called an *exception handler.*

When a `try` statement is executed, the statements in the `try` block are executed. If no exception is thrown during the execution the `try` block, processing continues with the statement following the `try` statement (after all of the `catch` clauses). This situation is the normal execution flow and should occur most of the time.

Key Concept

Each `catch` clause on a `try` statement handles a particular kind of exception that may get thrown from the `try` block.

If an exception is thrown at any point during the execution of the `try` block, control is immediately transferred to the appropriate catch handler. That is, control transfers to the first `catch` clause whose exception class corresponds to the class of the exception that was thrown. After executing the statements in the `catch` clause, control transfers to the statement after the entire `try` statement.

Let's look at an example. Suppose a fictitious company uses codes to represent their various products. A product code includes, among other information, a character in the 10th position that represents the zone from which that product was made and a four-digit integer in positions 4 through 7 that represents the district in which it will be sold. Due to some reorganization, products from zone R are banned from being sold in districts with a designation of 2000 or higher. The program shown in Listing 8.2 reads codes from the user and counts the number of banned codes that are represented.

Listing 8.2

```
//********************************************************************
//  ProductCodes.java       Author: Lewis and Loftus
//
//  Demonstrates the use of a try-catch block.
//********************************************************************

import cs1.Keyboard;

public class ProductCodes
{
   //-----------------------------------------------------------------
   //  Counts the number of product codes that are entered with a
   //  zone of R and and district greater than 2000.
   //-----------------------------------------------------------------
   public static void main (String[] args)
   {
      String code;
      char zone;
      int district, valid = 0, banned = 0;

      System.out.print ("Enter product code (XXX to quit): ");
      code = Keyboard.readString();
```

Listing 8.2 ***(continued)***

```
      while (!code.equals ("XXX"))
      {
         try
         {
            zone = code.charAt(9);
            district = Integer.parseInt(code.substring(3, 7));
            valid++;
            if (zone == 'R' && district > 2000)
               banned++;
         }
         catch (StringIndexOutOfBoundsException exception)
         {
            System.out.println ("Improper code length: " + code);
         }
         catch (NumberFormatException exception)
         {
            System.out.println ("District is not numeric: " + code);
         }

         System.out.print ("Enter product code (XXX to quit): ");
         code = Keyboard.readString();
      }

      System.out.println ("# of valid codes entered: " + valid);
      System.out.println ("# of banned codes entered: " + banned);
   }
}
```

```
Enter product code (XXX to quit): TRV2475A5R-14
Enter product code (XXX to quit): TRD1704A7R-12
Enter product code (XXX to quit): TRL2k74A5R-11
District is not numeric: TRL2k74A5R-11
Enter product code (XXX to quit): TRQ2949A6M-04
Enter product code (XXX to quit): TRV2105A2
Improper code length: TRV2105A2
Enter product code (XXX to quit): TRQ2778A7R-19
Enter product code (XXX to quit): XXX
# of valid codes entered: 4
# of banned codes entered: 2
```

The programming statements in the `try` block attempt to pull out the zone and district information, then determine if it represents a banned code. If there is any problem extracting the zone and district information, the product code is considered to be invalid and will not be processed further. For example, a `StringIndexOutOfBoundsException` could be thrown by either the `charAt` or `substring` methods. Furthermore, a `NumberFormatException` could be thrown by the `parseInt` method if the substring does not contain a valid integer. A particular message is printed depending on which exception was thrown. In either case, since the exception was caught and handled, processing continues normally.

Note that, for each code examined, the integer `valid` is incremented only if no exception is thrown. If an exception is thrown, control transfers immediately to the appropriate `catch` clause. Likewise, the zone and district will be tested by the `if` statement only if no exception was thrown.

The `finally` Clause

A `try` statement can have an optional *`finally` clause*. The `finally` clause defines a section of code that is executed no matter how the `try` block is exited. Most often, a `finally` clause is used to manage resources or to guarantee that particular parts of an algorithm are executed.

If no exception is generated, the statements in the `finally` clause are executed after the `try` block is complete. If an exception is generated in the `try` block, control first transfers to the appropriate `catch` clause. After executing the exception-handling code, control transfers to the `finally` clause and its statements are executed. A `finally` clause, if present, must be listed after all `catch` clauses.

Key Concept

The `finally` clause of a `try` block is executed whether or not the `try` block is exited normally or because of a thrown exception.

Note that a `try` block does not have to have a `catch` clause at all. If there are no `catch` clauses, a `finally` block is used by itself, if that is appropriate for the situation.

Exception Propagation

If an exception is not caught and handled when it occurs, control is immediately returned to the method that invoked the method that produced the exception. We can design our software so that the exception is caught and handled at this outer level. If it isn't caught there, control returns to the method that called it. This process is called *propagating the exception*. This propagation continues until the exception is caught and handled, or until it is passed out of the `main` method, which terminates the program and produces an exception message. To catch an exception at an outer level, the method that produces the exception must be invoked inside a `try` block that has `catch` clauses to handle it.

Key Concept

If an exception is not caught and handled where it occurs, it is propagated to the calling method.

The `Propagation` program shown in Listing 8.3 succinctly demonstrates the process of exception propagation. The `main` method invokes method

Listing 8.3

```
//********************************************************************
//  Propagation.java       Author: Lewis and Loftus
//
//  Demonstrates exception propagation.
//********************************************************************

public class Propagation
{
   //-----------------------------------------------------------------
   //  Invokes the level1 method to begin the exception demonstation.
   //-----------------------------------------------------------------
   static public void main (String[] args)
   {
      ExceptionScope demo = new ExceptionScope();

      System.out.println("Program beginning.");
      demo.level1();
      System.out.println("Program ending.");
   }
}
```

```
Program beginning.
Level 1 beginning.
Level 2 beginning.
Level 3 beginning.

The exception message is: / by zero

The call stack trace:
java.lang.ArithmeticException: / by zero
        at ExceptionScope.level3(ExceptionScope.java:54)
        at ExceptionScope.level2(ExceptionScope.java:41)
        at ExceptionScope.level1(ExceptionScope.java:18)
        at Propagation.main(Propagation.java:17)

Level 1 ending.
Program ending.
```

`level1` in the `ExceptionScope` class (Listing 8.4), which invokes `level2`, which invokes `level3`, which produces an exception. Method `level3` does not catch the exception, so control is transferred back to `level2`. But `level2` does not catch the exception either, so control is transferred back to `level1`. Because the invocation of `level2` is made inside a `try` block (in method `level1`), the exception is caught and handled at that point.

Listing 8.4

```
//********************************************************************
//  ExceptionScope.java       Author: Lewis and Loftus
//
//  Demonstrates exception propagation.
//********************************************************************

public class ExceptionScope
{
   //-----------------------------------------------------------------
   //  Catches and handles the exception that is thrown in level3.
   //-----------------------------------------------------------------
   public void level1()
   {
      System.out.println("Level 1 beginning.");

      try
      {
         level2();
      }
      catch (ArithmeticException problem)
      {
         System.out.println ();
         System.out.println ("The exception message is: " +
                             problem.getMessage());
         System.out.println ();
         System.out.println ("The call stack trace:");
         problem.printStackTrace();
         System.out.println ();
      }

      System.out.println("Level 1 ending.");
   }
```

Listing 8.4 ***(continued)***

```
   //-----------------------------------------------------------------
   //  Serves as an intermediate level.  The exception propagates
   //  through this method back to level1.
   //-----------------------------------------------------------------
   public void level2()
   {
      System.out.println("Level 2 beginning.");
      level3 ();
      System.out.println("Level 2 ending.");
   }

   //-----------------------------------------------------------------
   //  Performs a calculation to produce an exception.  It is not
   //  caught and handled at this level.
   //-----------------------------------------------------------------
   public void level3 ()
   {
      int numerator = 10, denominator = 0;

      System.out.println("Level 3 beginning.");
      int result = numerator / denominator;
      System.out.println("Level 3 ending.");
   }
}
```

Note that the output does not include the messages indicating that the methods `level3` and `level2` were ending. These `println` statements are never executed because an exception occurred and had not yet been caught. However, after method `level1` handles the exception, processing continues normally from that point, printing the messages indicating that method `level1` and the program were ending.

Key Concept

A programmer must carefully consider how exceptions should be handled, if at all, and at what level of the method-calling hierarchy.

Note also that the catch clause that handles the exception uses the `getMessage` and `printStackTrace` methods to output that information. The stack trace shows the methods that were called when the exception occurred.

A programmer must pick the most appropriate level at which to catch and handle an exception. There is no single best answer. It depends on the situation and the design of the system. Sometimes the right approach will be not to catch an exception at all and let the program terminate.

The `Exception` Class Hierarchy

The classes that define various exceptions are related by inheritance, creating a class hierarchy that is shown in part in Figure 8.1.

The `Throwable` class is the parent of both `Error` and `Exception`. Many types of exceptions are derived from the `Exception` class, and these classes also have many children. Though these high level classes are defined in the

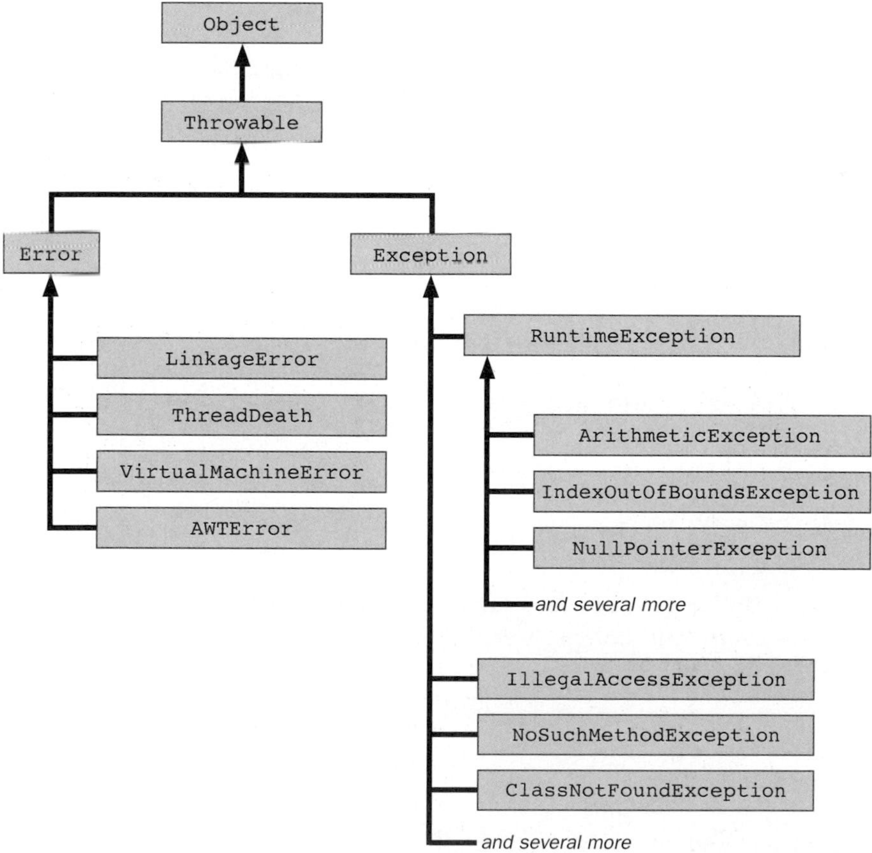

Figure 8.1 Part of the `Error` and `Exception` class hierarchy

java.lang package, many child classes that define specific exceptions are part of several other packages. Inheritance relationships can span package boundaries.

Key Concept

A new exception is defined by deriving a new class from the Exception class or one of its descendants.

We can define our own exceptions by deriving a new class from Exception or one of its descendants. The class we choose as the parent depends on what situation or condition the new exception represents.

The program in Listing 8.5 instantiates an exception object and throws it. The exception is created from the OutOfRangeException class, which is not part of the Java standard class library

Listing 8.5

```
//********************************************************************
//  CreatingExceptions.java       Author: Lewis and Loftus
//
//  Demonstrates the ability to define an exception via inheritance.
//********************************************************************

import OutOfRangeException;
import cs1.Keyboard;

public class CreatingExceptions
{
   //-----------------------------------------------------------------
   //  Creates an exception object and possibly throws it.
   //-----------------------------------------------------------------
   public static void main (String[] args) throws OutOfRangeException
   {
      final int MIN = 25, MAX = 40;

      OutOfRangeException problem =
         new OutOfRangeException ("Input value is out of range.");

      System.out.print ("Enter an integer value between " + MIN +
                        " and " + MAX + ", inclusive: ");
      int value = Keyboard.readInt();

      //  Determines if the exception should be thrown
      if (value < MIN || value > MAX)
         throw problem;

      System.out.println ("End of main method.");  // may never reach
   }
}
```

Listing 8.5 ***(continued)***

```
Enter an integer value between 25 and 40, inclusive: 69
Exception in thread "main" OutOfRangeException:
        Input value is out of range.
        at CreatingExceptions.main(CreatingExceptions.java:20)
```

and is shown in Listing 8.6. This exception represents the situation in which a value is out of a particular valid range.

After reading in an input value, the `main` method evaluates it to see if it is in the valid range. If not, the *throw statement* is executed. A `throw` statement is used to begin exception propagation. Because the `main` method does not catch and handle the exception, the program will terminate if the exception is thrown, printing the message associated with the exception.

We create the `OutOfRangeException` class by extending the `Exception` class. Often, a new exception is nothing more than what you see in this example: an extension of some existing exception class that stores a particular message describing the situation it represents. The important point is that the class

Listing 8.6

```
//********************************************************************
//  OutOfRangeException.java       Author: Lewis and Loftus
//
//  Represents an exceptional condition in which a value is out of
//  some particular range.
//********************************************************************

public class OutOfRangeException extends Exception
{
   //-----------------------------------------------------------------
   //  Sets up the exception object with a particular message.
   //-----------------------------------------------------------------
   OutOfRangeException (String message)
   {
      super (message);
   }
}
```

is ultimately a descendant of `Exception` and `Throwable`, which gives it the ability to be thrown using a `throw` statement.

The type of situation handled by this program, in which a value is out of range, does not need to be represented as an exception. We've previously handled such situations using conditionals or loops. Whether you handle a situation using an exception or whether you take care of it in the normal flow of your program is an important design decision.

Checked and Unchecked Exceptions

Key Concept

The `throws` clause on a method header must be included for checked exceptions that are not caught and handled in the method.

There is one other issue concerning exceptions that we should explore. Some exceptions are checked, while others are unchecked. A *checked exception* must either be caught by a method, or it must be listed in the *`throws` clause* of any method that may throw or propagate it. A `throws` clause is appended to the header of a method definition to formally acknowledge that the method will throw or propagate a particular exception if it occurs. An *unchecked exception* should not be caught, and requires no `throws` clause.

The only unchecked exceptions in Java are objects of type `RuntimeException` or any of its descendents. All other exceptions are considered to be checked exceptions. The `main` method of the `CreatingExceptions` program has a `throws` clause, indicating that it may throw an `OutOfRangeException`. This `throws` clause is required because the `OutOfRangeException` was derived from the `Exception` class, making it a checked exception.

Errors are similar to `RuntimeException` and its descendants, in that they should not be caught and do not require a `throws` clause.

8.2 Input/Output Streams

Key Concept

A stream is a sequential sequence of bytes, which can be used as a source of input or a destination for output.

A *stream* is an ordered sequence of bytes. The term stream comes from the analogy that as we read and write information, the data flows from a source to a destination (or *sink*) as water flows down a stream. The source of the information is like a hose filling the stream, and the destination is like a cave into which the stream flows.

In a program, we treat a stream as either an *input stream,* from which we read information, or as an *output stream,* to which we write information. That is, a program serves either as the hose filling the stream, or as the cave receiving the stream. A program can deal with multiple input and output streams at one time. A particular store of data, such as a file, can either serve as an input stream or an output stream to a program, but cannot be both at the same time.

The `java.io` package of the standard library provides many classes that let us define streams with particular characteristics. Some of the classes deal with files, others with memory, and others with strings. Some classes assume that the data they handle consists of characters, and others assume the data consists of raw bytes of binary information. Some classes provide the means to manipulate the data in the stream in some way, such as buffering the information or numbering it. By combining certain classes in certain ways, we can create objects that represent a stream of information that has exactly the characteristics we want for a particular situation.

The sheer number of classes in the `java.io` package prohibits us from discussing them all in detail. Instead, the goal is to provide an overview of the classes involved, then explore a few specific situations that should prove useful.

Web Bonus

The book's Web site contains discussions and examples of I/O streams in addition to those covered in this chapter.

In addition to dividing the classes in the `java.io` package into input and output streams, they can be subdivided in two other primary ways. First, we can divide the classes by the type of information on which they operate. There are basically two categories of classes in this regard: those that operate on character data and those that operate on byte data. The other way we can divide the classes in the `java.io` package is by the role that they play. Again we have two categories: those that represent a particular type of source or sink for information, such as a file or network connection, and those that provide the means to alter or manage the basic data in the stream. Most of the classes in the `java.io` package fall into one of the subdivisions created by these categories, as shown in Figure 8.2.

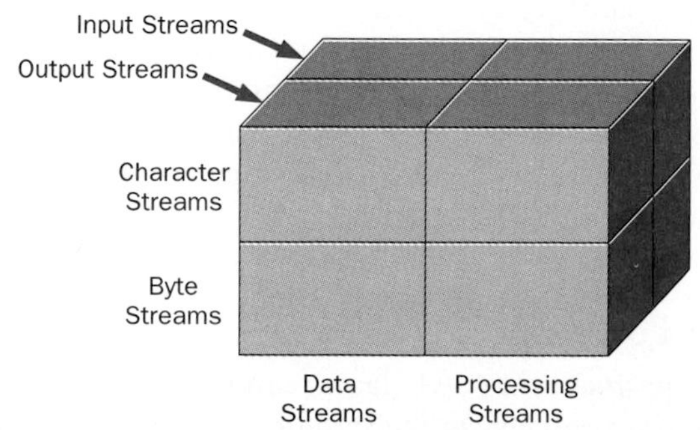

Figure 8.2 Dividing the `java.io` classes into categories

Character Streams vs. Byte Streams

Key Concept

A character stream manages Unicode characters, while a byte stream manages 8-bit bytes.

A *character stream* is designed to manage 16-bit Unicode characters. The stream is nothing more than a long series of characters, though they can be read and written in chunks, such as one line at a time, if we set up the stream with the proper characteristics. A *byte stream*, on the other hand, manages 8-bit bytes of raw binary data. How the bytes are interpreted and used once read depends on the program. Although they can be used to read and write any data, byte streams are typically used to read and write binary data such as sounds and images.

Key Concept

All classes derived from `Reader` and `Writer` represent character streams, and all classes derived from `InputStream` and `OutputStream` represent byte streams.

The classes that manage character streams and byte streams are cleanly divided in the class inheritance hierarchy. The `InputStream` and `OutputStream` classes, and all their descendants represent byte streams, and the `Reader` and `Writer` classes, and all their descendants represent character streams. This relationship is shown in Figure 8.3.

There are some basic similarities between the two class hierarchies. For example, the `Reader` and `InputStream` classes provide similar methods, but for different types of data. They both, for example, provide a basic `read` method. The `read` method of `Reader` reads one character or an array of characters. The `read` method of `InputStream` reads one byte or an array of bytes. Such paired classes are common between the hierarchies, but are not always consistent.

Data Streams vs. Processing Streams

Key Concept

Java I/O classes can also be divided into data streams, which represent a particular source or destination, or processing streams, which perform operations on data in an existing stream.

A *data stream* is a stream that represents a particular source or destination stream, such as a string in memory or a file on disk. A *processing stream* (sometimes called a *filtering stream*) performs some sort of manipulation on the data in a stream. By combining data streams with processing streams, we can create an input or output stream that behaves exactly as we wish.

The classes that represent data streams and processing streams are the same classes that represent character streams and byte streams. It is just another way to categorize them. The data streams and processing streams cut across the class hierarchies, however. That is, all four of the primary class hierarchies in the Java I/O classes can be further subdivided into those that represent data streams, and those that represent processing streams.

The `IOException` Class

Many operations performed by I/O classes can potentially throw an `IOException`. The `IOException` class is the parent of several exception classes that represent problems when trying to perform I/O.

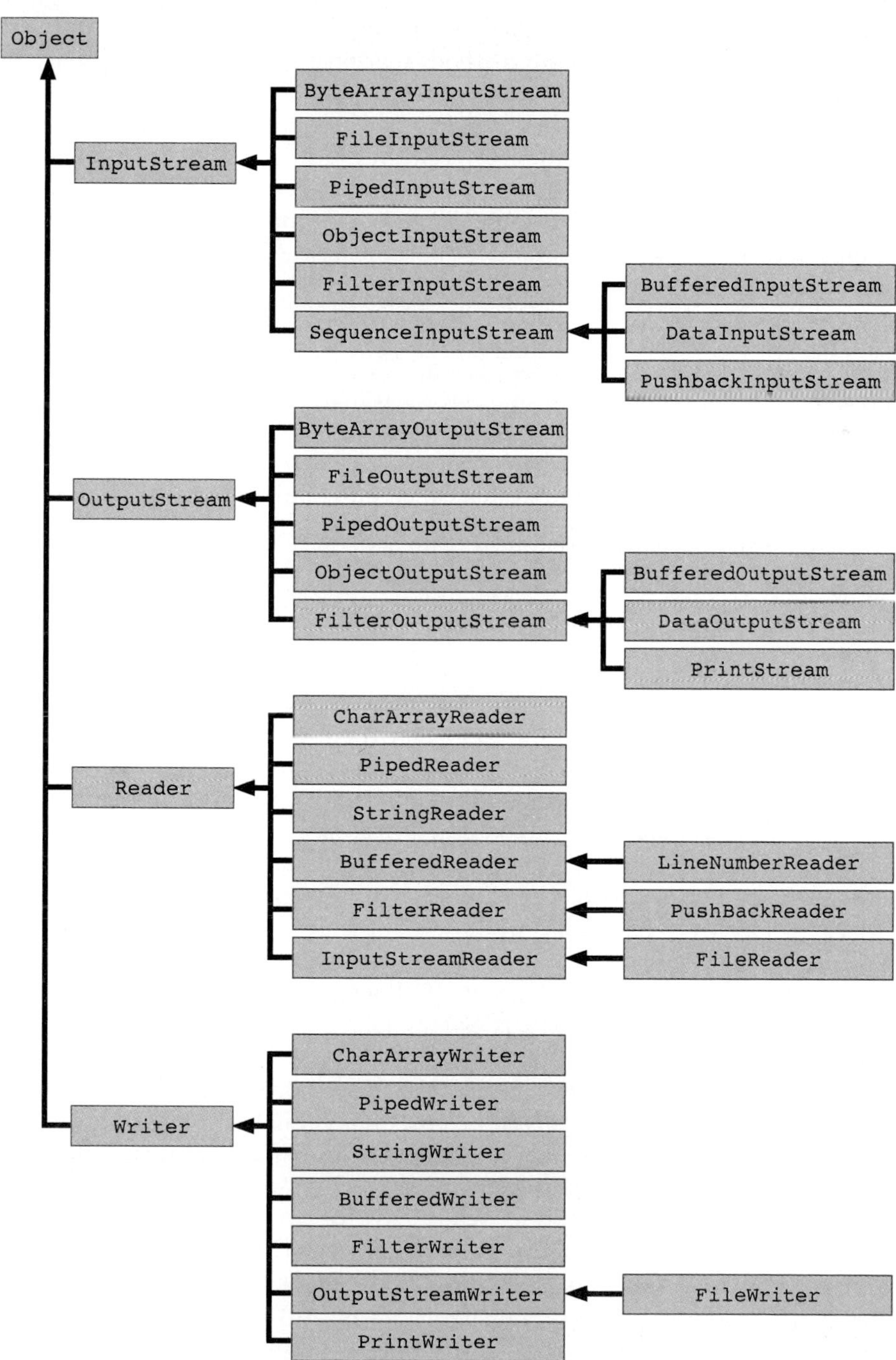

Figure 8.3 The Java I/O class hierarchy

An `IOException` is a checked exception, which means that either the exception must be caught, or all methods that propagate it must declare so in a `throws` clause of the method header.

Because I/O is often dealing with external resources, many problems can arise with programs that attempt to perform I/O operations. For example, a file from which we want to read might not actually be present. Or a data value that we expect to find might not actually be in the input stream. In general, we should try to design our programs to be as robust as possible when dealing with potential problems.

8.3 Standard I/O

There are three streams that are often called the standard I/O streams:

- `System.in`—standard input stream
- `System.out`—standard output stream
- `System.err`—standard error stream

Key Concept

Three variables in the `System` class represent the standard I/O streams.

The `System` class provides methods for examining and using various system-related information. It contains the three object references (`in`, `out`, and `err`) that represent the three standard I/O streams. These references are declared as both `public` and `static`, which allows them to be accessed directly through the `System` class.

These streams usually represent particular default I/O interactions. `System.in` typically maps to keyboard input, while `System.out` and `System.err` typically map to a particular window on the monitor screen. By default, `System.out` and `System.err` write output to the same window (usually the one in which the program was executed), though they could be set up to write to different places. `System.err` is usually where error messages of any kind are sent.

All three of these streams are created and are open by default, and in one sense are ready for use by any Java program. Both `System.out` and `System.err` are declared to be of type `PrintStream`, but `System.in` is declared to be a generic `InputStream` reference.

`PrintStream` objects automatically have `print` and `println` methods defined for them. That makes the `System.out` object useful without any further manipulations. We've used these methods throughout the text to perform simple output. Note that `PrintStream` is technically a byte stream that converts objects and numbers into text for easy output. It is usually used for debugging and simple examples. `PrintStream` does not handle advanced internationalization and error checking, for which the `PrintWriter` class would be a better choice.

The System.in reference is deliberately declared to be a generic InputStream reference so that it is not restricted in its use. That means, however, it must usually be mapped into a stream with more useful characteristics. That is one of the reasons we created the Keyboard class.

The Keyboard Class Revisited

Recall that the Keyboard class was written by the authors of this text to make reading values from the standard input stream easier, especially when we were just getting started and had lots of other issues to worry about. The Keyboard class provides methods such as readInt, readFloat, and readString to obtain a particular type of input value. Now we can peel back the cover of the Keyboard class and discuss its processing.

Key Concept

The Keyboard class, though not part of the standard class library, provides an abstraction for several I/O operations on the standard input stream.

The Keyboard class hides the following I/O operations:

- The declaration of the standard input stream in a useful form
- The handling of any IOException that may be thrown
- The parsing of an input line into separate tokens
- The conversion of an input value to its expected type
- The handling of conversion problems

Because System.in is defined as a reference to a generic InputStream object, it has by default only the basic ability to read byte data. To modify it into a more useful form, the Keyboard class performs the following declaration:

```
InputStreamReader isr = new InputStreamReader (System.in);
BufferedReader stdin = new BufferedReader (isr);
```

The first line creates an InputStreamReader object, which converts the original byte input stream into a character input stream. The second line transforms it into a BufferedReader, which allows us to use the readLine method to get an entire line of character input in one operation.

In the Keyboard class, each invocation of readLine is performed inside a try block, so that an IOException, if it is thrown, can be caught and handled. The readLine method returns a String that includes all information on the input line. If that input line contains multiple values, they must be separated into individual tokens. Recall that the StringTokenizer class performs just that kind of service. The Keyboard class constantly keeps track of the current input line, and uses a StringTokenizer object to pull off the next piece when requested.

On top of all of this, each token as it is pulled from the input line may be needed as a particular primitive type, such as an int. Therefore, each method of the `Keyboard` class performs the proper conversion. For example, the `readInt` method of the `Keyboard` class takes the next token from the input line and calls the `parseInt` method of the `Integer` wrapper class to convert the string to an `int`. Similar processing can be seen in the file I/O examples in the next section.

Web Bonus

The entire source code for the `Keyboard` class is available on the book's Web site for further examination.

8.4 Text Files

Another common programming requirement is to read from and write to files on disk. Information is stored in a file as either byte or character (text) data, and should be read in the same way. This section focuses on text files.

Reading Text Files

The `FileReader` class represents an input file that contains character data. Its constructors set up the relationship between the program and the file, opening a stream from which data can be read. Its abilities to read data are limited to the `read` method, which is inherited from its parent class `InputStreamReader`. If we want to read something other than character arrays, we have to use another input class.

> **Key Concept**
>
> The `FileReader` and `BufferedReader` classes can be used together to create a convenient text file input stream.

As discussed in the previous section, the `BufferedReader` class does not represent any particular data source, but filters data on a given stream by buffering it into more accessible units. In particular, the `BufferedReader` class provides the `readLine` method that allows us to read an entire line of characters in one operation. Recall that the `readLine` method returns a string, which must be processed if individual data values must be extracted from it.

Let's examine a program that reads data from a particular input file and processes it. Suppose a text data file called `inventory.dat` contained the following information:

```
Widget 14 3.35
Spoke 132 0.32
```

```
Wrap 58 1.92
Thing 28 4.17
Brace 25 1.75
Clip 409 0.12
Cog 142 2.08
```

This data represents the inventory of a store. Each line contains an item name, the number of available units, and the price of that item. Each value on a line is separated from the other values by at least one space. The program in Listing 8.7 reads this data file, creates an array of objects based on that data, then prints the information.

Listing 8.7

```
//********************************************************************
//  Inventory.java       Author: Lewis and Loftus
//
//  Demonstrates the use of a character file input stream.
//********************************************************************

import InventoryItem;
import java.util.StringTokenizer;
import java.io.*;

public class Inventory
{
   //-----------------------------------------------------------------
   //  Reads data about a store inventory from an input file,
   //  creating an array of InventoryItem objects, then prints them.
   //-----------------------------------------------------------------
   public static void main (String[] args)
   {
      final int MAX = 100;
      InventoryItem[] items = new InventoryItem[MAX];
      StringTokenizer tokenizer;
      String line, name, file="inventory.dat";
      int units, count = 0;
      float price;
```

Listing 8.7 *(continued)*

```
      try
      {
         FileReader fr = new FileReader (file);
         BufferedReader inFile = new BufferedReader (fr);

         line = inFile.readLine();
         while (line != null)
         {
            tokenizer = new StringTokenizer (line);
            name = tokenizer.nextToken();
            try
            {
               units = Integer.parseInt (tokenizer.nextToken());
               price = Float.parseFloat (tokenizer.nextToken());
               items[count++] = new InventoryItem (name, units, price);
            }
            catch (NumberFormatException exception)
            {
               System.out.println ("Error in input. Line ignored:");
               System.out.println (line);
            }
            line = inFile.readLine();
         }

         inFile.close();

         for (int scan = 0; scan < count; scan++)
            System.out.println (items[scan]);
      }
      catch (FileNotFoundException exception)
      {
         System.out.println ("The file " + file + " was not found.");
      }
      catch (IOException exception)
      {
         System.out.println (exception);
      }
   }
}
```

Listing 8.7 *(continued)*

```
Widget: 14 at 3.35 = 46.9
Spoke:  132 at 0.32 = 42.24
Wrap:   58 at 1.92 = 111.36
Thing:  28 at 4.17 = 116.76
Brace:  25 at 1.75 = 43.75
Clip:   409 at 0.12 = 49.08
Cog:    142 at 2.08 = 295.36
```

The program uses the data it reads from the file to create several `InventoryItem` (see Listing 8.8) objects. The data read from the file is passed to the `InventoryItem` constructor.

Certain parts of the processing in the `Inventory` program are performed within `try` blocks to handle various exceptions that may arise. The declaration of the input file stream is accomplished at the top of the outer `try` block. If the file cannot be located when the `FileReader` constructor is executed, a `FileNotFoundException` is thrown. If at any point during the processing an `IOException` is thrown, it is caught and processing is neatly terminated.

Once the input stream is set up, the program begins to read and process one line of input at a time. The `readLine` method reads an entire line of text until a line terminator character is found. When the end of the file is encountered, `readLine` returns a null reference, which is used as a termination condition for the loop.

Key Concept

The `readLine` method returns null when the end of file is encountered.

Each line is separated into distinct values using a `StringTokenizer` object. First the name of the item is stored. Then the number of units and the unit price are separated and converted into numeric values. A `NumberFormatException` could be thrown if the string does not represent a valid numeric value, so the inner `try` block catches and handles it. If a conversion error is encountered, that input line is ignored, but processing continues.

Note that `BufferedReader` is serving the same purpose in this program as it is in the `Keyboard` class, to buffer input and provide the `readLine` method, even though the actual source of the information is quite different in both cases. This situation illustrates why the designers of the `java.io` package separated the responsibilities the way they did. The Java I/O classes can be combined in many different ways to provide exactly the kind of interaction and character manipulation needed for any particular situation.

Listing 8.8

```
//********************************************************************
//  InventoryItem.java       Author: Lewis and Loftus
//
//  Represents an item in the inventory.
//********************************************************************

import java.text.DecimalFormat;

public class InventoryItem
{
   private String name;
   private int units;    // number of available units of this item
   private float price;  // price per unit of this item
   private DecimalFormat fmt;

   //-----------------------------------------------------------------
   //  Sets up this item with the specified information.
   //-----------------------------------------------------------------
   public InventoryItem (String itemName, int numUnits, float cost)
   {
      name = itemName;
      units = numUnits;
      price = cost;
      fmt = new DecimalFormat ("0.##");
   }

   //-----------------------------------------------------------------
   //  Returns information about this item as a string.
   //-----------------------------------------------------------------
   public String toString()
   {
      return name + ":\t" + units + " at " + price + " = " +
             fmt.format ((units * price));
   }
}
```

Writing Text Files

Writing output to a text file simply requires that we use the appropriate classes to create the output stream, then call the appropriate methods to write the data. As with standard I/O, file output seems to be a little more straightforward than file input.

The `FileWriter` class represents a text output file, but, like `FileReader`, it has minimal method support for manipulating data. The `PrintWriter` class provides `print` and `println` methods, similar to the standard I/O `PrintStream` class.

Suppose we needed to generate a test data file for a program we were writing, but didn't have the real data available. The program shown in Listing 8.9 generates a test file that contains random integer values. The output for `TestData` is also shown.

Although it is not necessary for the program to work, we have added a layer in the file stream configuration to include a `BufferedWriter`. That addition simply gives the stream buffered capabilities, which makes the processing more efficient. While buffering is not crucial in this situation, it is usually a good idea when writing text files.

Note that in the `TestData` program we have eliminated explicit exception handling. That is, if something goes wrong, we simply allow the program to terminate, instead of catching and handling the problem specifically. Because all `IOExceptions` are checked exceptions, we have to include the `throws` clause on the header of the method to indicate that it may be thrown. For each program we have to carefully consider how best to handle the exceptions that may be thrown. That rule is especially true when dealing with I/O, which is fraught with potential problems that cannot necessarily be foreseen.

The `TestData` program uses nested `for` loops to compute a random value and print it to the file. After all values are printed, the file is closed. Output files must be closed explicitly to ensure that the data is retained. In general, it is good practice to explicitly close all file streams when they are no longer needed.

Key Concept

Output file streams must be closed explicitly or they may not correctly retain the data written to them.

The data that is contained in the file `test.dat` after the `TestData` program is run might look like this:

```
85    90    93    15    82    79    52    71    70    98
74    57    41    66    22    16    67    65    24    84
86    61    91    79    18    81    64    41    68    81
98    47    28    40    69    0    85    8    64    4
23    61    27    10    59    89    88    26    24    7
3    89    73    36    54    91    42    73    95    58
19    41    18    14    63    80    96    30    17    28
24    37    0    4    94    23    98    10    78    50
9    28    64    54    59    23    61    15    0    88
51    28    44    48    73    21    1    52    35    38
```

Listing 8.9

```
//********************************************************************
//  TestData.java       Author: Lewis and Loftus
//
//  Demonstrates the use of a character file output stream.
//********************************************************************

import java.io.*;

public class TestData
{
   //-----------------------------------------------------------------
   //  Creates a file of test data that consists of ten lines each
   //  containing ten integer values in the range 0 to 99.
   //-----------------------------------------------------------------
   public static void main (String[] args) throws IOException
   {
      final int MAX = 10;

      int value;
      String file = "test.dat";

      FileWriter fw = new FileWriter (file);
      BufferedWriter bw = new BufferedWriter (fw);
      PrintWriter outFile = new PrintWriter (bw);

      for (int line=1; line <= MAX; line++)
      {
         for (int num=1; num <= MAX; num++)
         {
            value = (int) (Math.random() * 100);
            outFile.print (value + "   ");
         }
         outFile.println ();
      }

      outFile.close();
      System.out.println ("Output file has been created: " + file);
   }
}
```

```
Output file has been created: test.dat
```

8.5 Object Serialization

When a program terminates, the data it was using is destroyed unless a particular effort was made to store it externally. We've seen how we can accomplish that using file I/O to write information to a file in one program and read that information from the file in another. But what happens when we want to store an object, or an array of objects, or some other complex structure? We could write code that stores all the pieces of an object separately, coming up with some representation for it and reconstructing the object when that information is read back in. But the more complex our information, the more difficult and tedious that process becomes.

Persistence is the concept that an object can "live" separate from the executing program that created it. Java contains a mechanism for creating persistent objects, called *object serialization*. An object is serialized by transforming it into a sequence of bytes that represents the object. Later, this representation can be restored to the original object. Once serialized, the object can be stored in a file to be read later, or sent across a network to another computer for further processing.

> **Key Concept**
> Object serialization represents an object as a sequence of bytes that can be stored in a file or transferred to another computer.

In Java, object serialization is accomplished with the help of an interface and two classes. Any object we want to serialize must implement the `Serializable` interface. This interface actually contains no methods; it just serves as a flag to the compiler that objects of this type might be serialized. To serialize an object, we invoke the `writeObject` method of an `ObjectOutputStream`. To deserialize the object, we invoke the `readObject` method of an `ObjectInputStream`. `ObjectOutputStream` and `ObjectInputStream` are processing streams; they must be wrapped around an `OutputStream` or `InputStream` of some kind, respectively. Therefore the actual data streams used by the serialized object can represent files, network communication, or some other type of stream.

For example, suppose we created an object called `myCar` from a class called `Car`. If the `Car` class implements the `Serializable` interface, we can serialize the `myCar` object and, for instance, store it in a file. To do that, we create a `FileOutputStream`, then wrap it in an `ObjectOutputStream`, as follows:

```
FileOuptutStream outFile = new FileOutputStream ("info.dat");
ObjectOutputStream outStream = new ObjectOutputStream (outFile);
```

Then, to serialize the object, we invoke the `writeObject` method:

```
outStream.writeObject (myCar);
```

By invoking the `writeObject` method, the `myCar` object is serialized by the `ObjectOutputStream`, then written to the file represented by the `FileOutputStream`. To reverse the process, we first create the appropriate input stream classes:

```
FileInputStream inFile = new FileInputStream ("info.dat");
ObjectInputStream inStream = new ObjectInputStream (inFile);
```

Then we can invoke the `readObject` method to read the object information from the file and deserialize it. The `readObject` method returns a generic `Object` pointer, so it must be cast into the appropriate class type:

```
Car automobile = (Car) inStream.readObject();
```

The act of serialization automatically takes into account any additional referenced objects. That is, it automatically follows all references contained in the object being serialized and serializes them. So if our `Car` object contains a reference to an `Engine` object, for instance, the `Engine` object would automatically get serialized as part of the act of serializing the car. The `Engine` class must also implement the `Serializable` interface.

Many classes of the Java standard class library implement the `Serializable` interface, so that they can be serialized as needed. The `String` class, for example, implements `Serializable`, so that any class containing references to `String` objects can be serialized without trouble. The `Vector` class also implements the `Serializable` interface, so we can store an entire vector of objects in one operation. Keep in mind that the objects stored in the vector must also implement the `Serializable` interface.

The `transient` Modifier

Sometimes we may prefer to exclude particular information when we serialize an object. For example, we may want to exclude a password so that it is not part of the information that is stored or transferred over the network. The danger is that, even though we declare it with private visibility, once it is serialized it could be read and accessed by some unfriendly source. Another reason we may want to exclude particular information from the serialization process is if it is simply not needed or can easily be reproduced when the object is deserialized. That way the byte stream representing the serialized object does not contain unnecessary information that will increase its size.

The reserved word `transient` can be used to modify the declaration of a variable so that it will not be represented as part of the byte stream when the object it is contained in is serialized. For example, suppose an object contains the following declaration:

```
private transient int password;
```

That variable, when the object in which it is contained is serialized, will not be included in the representation.

Web Bonus

Examples of object serialization, network communication, and other I/O techniques can be found on the book's Web site.

Summary of Key Concepts

- Both errors and exceptions represent unusual or invalid processing, but whereas an exception can be caught and handled, an error should not.
- The messages printed by a thrown exception indicate the nature of the problem and a call stack trace that shows the methods that were invoked.
- Each `catch` clause on a `try` statement handles a particular kind of exception that may get thrown from the `try` block.
- The `finally` clause of a `try` block is executed whether or not the `try` block is exited normally or because of a thrown exception.
- If an exception is not caught and handled where it occurs, it is propagated to the calling method.
- A programmer must carefully consider how exceptions should be handled, if at all, and at what level of the method-calling hierarchy.
- A new exception is defined by deriving a new class from the `Exception` class or one of its descendants.
- The `throws` clause on a method header must be included for checked exceptions that are not caught and handled in the method.
- A stream is a sequential sequence of bytes, which can be used as a source of input or a destination for output.
- A character stream manages Unicode characters, while a byte stream manages 8-bit bytes.
- All classes derived from `Reader` and `Writer` represent character streams, and all classes derived from `InputStream` and `OutputStream` represent byte streams.
- Java I/O classes can also be divided into data streams, which represent a particular source or destination, or processing streams, which perform operations on data in an existing stream.
- Three variables in the `System` class represent the standard I/O streams.
- The `Keyboard` class, though not part of the standard class library, provides an abstraction for several I/O operations on the standard input stream.
- The `FileReader` and `BufferedReader` classes can be used together to create a convenient text file output stream.
- The `readLine` method returns null when the end of file is encountered.
- Output file streams must be explicitly closed or they may not correctly retain the data written to them.
- Object serialization represents an object as a sequence of bytes that can be stored in a file or transferred to another computer.

Self-Review Questions

8.1 What is a stream?

8.2 What is the difference between a character stream and a byte stream?

8.3 What are the standard I/O streams?

8.4 Who wrote the `Keyboard` class? Why?

8.5 What types of processing does the `Keyboard` class hide?

8.6 How is reading and writing files different from reading and writing text using standard I/O?

8.7 How can we detect the end of an input file?

Exercises

8.1 Describe the general purpose of each of the following Java I/O classes. Classify each as character stream or byte stream, and as data stream or processing stream.

a. `InputStreamReader`

b. `Reader`

c. `PrintStream`

d. `FileReader`

8.2 Carefully explain the processing of the `readFloat` method of the `Keyboard` class.

8.3 Determine how, on your system, you can redirect standard input so that, when a program is executed, it takes the input from a file and not from the keyboard. Note that this is not a function of changing the program.

8.4 Similar to the previous exercise, determine how you can redirect standard output on your system so that executing the `System.out.println` method writes its information to a file instead of the default monitor window.

Programming Projects

8.1 Design and implement a program that corresponds to the `Quadratic` example in Chapter 2, without using the `Keyboard` class.

8.2 Design and implement a program that corresponds to the `ExamGrades` example in Chapter 3, without using the `Keyboard` class.

8.3 Design and implement a program to process golf scores. The scores of four golfers are stored in a text file. Each line represents one hole, and the file contains 18 lines. Each line contains five values: par for the hole followed by the number of strokes each golfer used on that hole. Determine the winner and produce a chart showing how well each golfer did (compared to par).

8.4 Design and implement a program to produce a random, but reasonable, test file for the `GolfScores` program described in the previous programming project.

8.5 Design and implement a program that compares two text input files, line by line, for equality. Print any lines that are not equal.

8.6 Design and implement a program that counts the number of punctuation marks in a text input file. Produce a chart that shows how many of each punctuation symbol was found.

8.7 Design and implement a program that helps a hospital analyze the flow of patients into the emergency room. An input file contains integers that represent the number of patients that entered the emergency room during each hour of each day for four weeks. Read the information and store it in a three-dimensional array. Then analyze it to compare the total number of patients per week, per day of the week, and per hour of the day.

8.8 Design and implement a GUI-based application that allows the user to type text into a text area, then when a button is pressed, write the information to a text file.

Answers to Self-Review Questions

8.1 A stream is a sequential series of bytes that serves as a source of input or a destination for output.

8.2 A character stream manages Unicode character data, while a byte stream manages 8-bit bytes.

8.3 The standard I/O streams in Java are `System.in`, the standard input; `System.out`, the standard output stream; and `System.err`, the standard error stream. Usually, standard input comes from the keyboard and standard output and error go to a default window on the monitor screen.

8.4 The `Keyboard` class was written by the authors of the textbook and generally will not be found in a Java development environment. It was written to facilitate reading input from the keyboard.

8.5 The `Keyboard` class hides details of standard input such as stream declaration, error handling, and value conversions.

8.6 All Java I/O operations are similar in that the stream is set up, the data is read or written, and the stream is closed. The primary difference between standard I/O and file I/O are the classes used to create the streams.

8.7 The `readLine` method returns a null reference if an attempt is made to read past the end of the input file.

Graphical User Interfaces

This chapter extends the material that is covered throughout the graphical track of preceding chapters. It explores various aspects of the development of Graphical User Interfaces in Java. In particular, it embraces the Swing components of the Java 2 platform, capitalizing on their advanced capabilities. We explore important GUI issues such as the use of containers and layout managers. We also introduce some additional features that Java provides to enhance the interaction of the user and a program. This entire chapter is part of the Graphics Track used throughout the book.

Chapter Objectives

- Provide a general set of concepts to consider when creating any GUI system.
- Define the concept of a layout manager and explore some in detail.
- Explore particular GUI components in detail.
- Discuss some GUI design guidelines.

9.1 Java GUI Overview

To construct a truly useful graphical user interface in Java, we need to be familiar with the following topic areas. These concepts interact with each other to create an overall presentation to the user. We want to incorporate these issues to create a user interface that is functional, easy to use, and pleasing to the eye.

- Events and Listeners
- Containers
- Components
- Layout Managers
- Special Features

Key Concept

The design and development of a Java GUI involves several interacting concepts.

We have already explored some of these topics briefly in the graphics track of previous chapters. In Chapter 5 and 6 we examined the concept of events and how we use listener objects to handle the events when they occur. We will learn about other events in this chapter.

Containers are special GUI components that contain other components. Containers allow us to organize components in appropriate and efficient ways. As we saw in Chapter 7, an `Applet` is a container to which we can add components to be displayed. In the next section of this chapter we examine containers in more detail.

In Chapter 7 we also introduced the idea of incorporating specific GUI components, such as buttons, into our programs. The few GUI components that we examined in Chapter 7 were from the AWT package. In this chapter, we turn our attention to Swing components, which are more versatile. Section 9.3 discusses several Swing components and demonstrates their use.

Layout managers are objects that specify how components are arranged in a container. There are several specific layout managers provided by the AWT and Swing packages. They are discussed in detail in Section 9.4.

There are a variety of special features that Java provides to create a useful and eye-pleasing GUI. These features are discussed in Section 9.5.

Finally, we conclude this chapter with a short discussion of some general guidelines that we should always follow when creating a user interface. We should never let the technical details of components and layout managers obscure our overall goal of presenting a useful interface for the user.

AWT and Swing

You may recall from earlier discussions that earlier Java platforms exclusively used classes provided by the Abstract Windowing Toolkit package (`java.awt`) to create graphics and graphical user interfaces. With the advent of the Java 2 platform, the Swing classes were introduced. Swing classes expand on the underlying foundation of the AWT.

Many of the Swing classes provide alternative components that are more useful than their corresponding AWT counterpart. For example, Swing's `JButton` class provides more functionality that the AWT `Button` class. In most cases, Swing provides new versions of existing AWT components, and generally uses a class name that appends a `J` to the front. The `JTextArea` class, for example, is the Swing counterpart for the AWT `TextArea` class.

Because Swing classes are generally more useful, we focus on them exclusively in this chapter. However, that does not mean that Swing, in general, has replaced the AWT. Swing technology uses and expands the ideas of the AWT. The AWT classes are not deprecated, and many of them are used by systems in existence today. Swing components rely on many concepts established in the AWT, such as the event classes and the general model we use to listen for events when they occur.

9.2 Containers

As we mentioned earlier, a container is a special component that can hold other components. Containers and their associated layout managers determine how the components are organized and displayed.

The `Applet` class of the `java.applet` package can only contain AWT components. For an applet to display Swing components, it has to be created from the `JApplet` class and the browser that displays the applet must be set up to handle Swing technology. The appletviewer tool will display Swing applets correctly.

In addition to applets, there are several other types of containers in the Java standard class library. Chief among them are frames and panels. A *frame* is a free standing window that can be repositioned anywhere on the screen. A *panel* cannot be displayed on its own and must be added to an existing container. Panels are useful when it comes to organizing groups of components within a larger container. Frames and panels are defined by the Swing classes `JFrame` and `JPanel`, respectively.

Frames and applets are considered to be top-level Swing containers, which internally have a separate component called a *content pane* to which components are added. Components can be added to Swing panels directly.

Graphics in Applications

> **Key Concept**
> Graphics and graphical user interfaces can be accomplished in applications using a container such as a frame.

We've used applets in previous chapters to demonstrate graphics because they were easy to work with and they allowed us to make our programs available across the World Wide Web. However, graphics and applets are not synonymous. Graphics and graphical user interfaces can be performed in applications as well. We just need a container other than an applet to use as a window for our graphical components. Frames are a natural choice for this situation.

The use of a frame requires that we introduce the concept of a *window event*. A window event is represented by a `WindowEvent` object. Window listeners can be extended from the `WindowAdapter` class or they can implement the `WindowListener` interface. There are several window events for which we can listen. For now we will only concern ourselves with the user closing the window, which causes the `windowClosing` method of the listener to be invoked.

Listing 9.1 shows a class that will serve as a generic listener for window closing events. We will use this class in many programs to terminate execution when the main application frame is closed. The call to the `exit` method of the `System` class causes the program to terminate normally.

The program shown in Listing 9.2 demonstrates the creation and display of a frame. The frame is defined by the `FrameDemo` class, shown in Listing 9.3. The `main` method creates a `FrameDemo` object, adds a window listener, then calls the `show` method of the frame to display the frame on the screen. In this example the frame is empty.

The `FrameDemo` class extends `JFrame`. Every `JFrame` object has a *title bar* on which the title of the frame is displayed. The title bar also contains the window closing button (labeled with an X) in the upper right corner. When the

Listing 9.1

```
//********************************************************************
//  GenericWindowListener.java       Author: Lewis and Loftus
//
//  Represents a generic listener for window components.
//********************************************************************

import java.awt.event.*;

public class GenericWindowListener extends WindowAdapter
{
   //-----------------------------------------------------------------
   //  Terminates the program when the window is closed.
   //-----------------------------------------------------------------
   public void windowClosing (WindowEvent event)
   {
      System.exit(0);
   }
}
```

Listing 9.2

```
//********************************************************************
//  ShowFrames.java       Author: Lewis and Loftus
//
//  Demonstrates the use of frames.
//********************************************************************

import FrameDemo;
import GenericWindowListener;
import java.awt.event.*;

public class ShowFrames
{
   //-----------------------------------------------------------------
   //  Creates and displays an empty frame.
   //-----------------------------------------------------------------
   public static void main (String[] args)
   {
      FrameDemo frame = new FrameDemo();
      frame.addWindowListener (new GenericWindowListener());
      frame.show();
   }
}
```

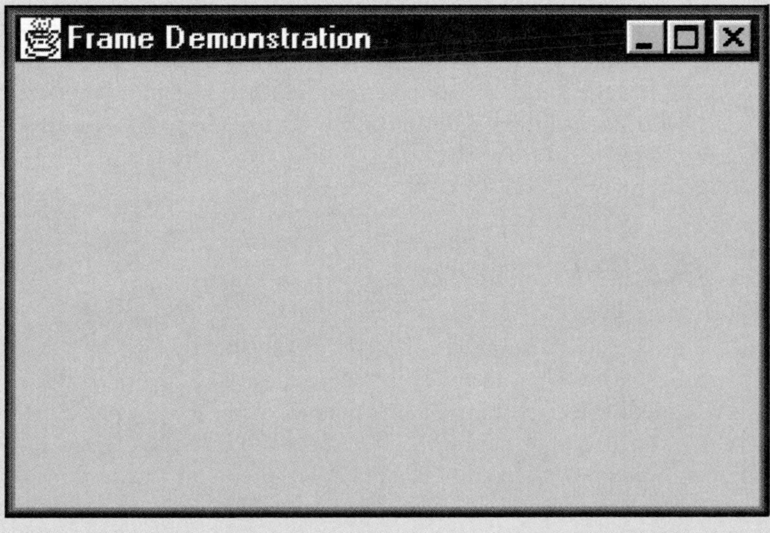

Listing 9.3

```
//********************************************************************
//  FrameDemo.java       Author: Lewis and Loftus
//
//  Demonstrates the use of frames.
//********************************************************************

import javax.swing.JFrame;

public class FrameDemo extends JFrame
{
   //-----------------------------------------------------------------
   //  Sets the title and size of an empty frame.
   //-----------------------------------------------------------------
   public FrameDemo ()
   {
      super ("Frame Demonstration");
      setSize (300, 200);
   }
}
```

user presses that button with the mouse, the frame disappears, the `windowClosing` method of the window listener is called, and the program terminates.

For the `ShowFrames` program, repositioning and closing the main application frame is all we can do. In the next section we explore some more components and add them to frames.

9.3 Components

Figure 9.1 lists some general GUI components. The Java standard library contains classes that allow us to create these and several other components easily. We will focus on components defined in the Swing package.

Each component can have an established *preferred size, minimum size,* and *maximum size.* These sizes are expressed in pixels, and are used by layout managers when determining how to display a set of components.

GUI Component	Description
Label	Displays a line of text.
Text Field	Displays a line of text. It may allow the user to edit its contents, one way to accept typed user input.
Text Area	Displays several lines of text. Like a text field, it may allow editing.
List	Displays a list of selectable items.
Push Button	A single button designed to initiate some action when pushed.
Combo Boxes	A single button that displays a list of choices when pushed. The current choice is shown next to the button.
CheckBox Buttons	A button that can be toggled on or off. Often a group of checkbox buttons are used to define a set of options. Multiple options can be chosen at the same time.
Radio Buttons	A group of buttons that defines a set of options from which a user can choose. Only one option can be selected at any given time.
Scroll Bar	A sliding bar used to indicate a position or a relative value.
Pulldown Menu	A set of options from which a user can choose, located at the top of a window.
Popup Menu	A set of options from which a user can choose, located at a defined location.

Figure 9.1 Some GUI components

Labels and Image Icons

A label, defined by the `JLabel` class, is used to provide information to the user, or decoration to the GUI. It is composed of text, an image, or both. A label is not selectable and does not react to user actions. An image used in a label is defined by an `ImageIcon` object.

The alignment of the text and image within the label can be set explicitly, using the `JLabel` constructor or specific methods for that purpose. Likewise, we can set the position of the text relative to the image.

Key Concept
The alignment of the text and image of a label, as well as their relative positioning, can be explicitly set.

The program shown in Listing 9.4 displays a frame that contains several labels. Each label shows the text and image in different orientations. Keep in mind that a label might be made up of only text or only an image.

The frame is represented by the `LabelDemo` class, shown in Listing 9.5. Its constructor creates three label objects, sets their characteristics, then adds them to the content pane of the frame.

The third parameter to the constructor of a `JLabel` defines the horizontal positioning of the label within the space allowed for the label by the layout

Listing 9.4

```
//********************************************************************
//  ShowLabels.java       Author: Lewis and Loftus
//
//  Demonstrates the use of labels and image icons.
//********************************************************************

import LabelDemo;
import GenericWindowListener;
import java.awt.event.*;

public class ShowLabels
{
   //-----------------------------------------------------------------
   //  Creates and displays the LabelDemo frame.
   //-----------------------------------------------------------------
   public static void main (String[] args)
   {
      LabelDemo frame = new LabelDemo();
      frame.addWindowListener (new GenericWindowListener());
      frame.show();
   }
}
```

Listing 9.5

```
//********************************************************************
//  LabelDemo.java       Author: Lewis and Loftus
//
//  Demonstrates the use of labels and image icons.
//********************************************************************

import java.awt.*;
import javax.swing.*;

public class LabelDemo extends JFrame
{
   private ImageIcon icon;
   private JLabel label1, label2, label3;

   //-----------------------------------------------------------------
   //  Sets up the GUI for this frame using three labels.
   //-----------------------------------------------------------------
   public LabelDemo ()
   {
      super ("Label Demonstration");
      setSize (200, 300);

      icon = new ImageIcon ("devil.gif");

      label1 = new JLabel ("Devil Left", icon, SwingConstants.LEFT);

      label2 = new JLabel ("Devil Right", icon, SwingConstants.LEFT);
      label2.setHorizontalTextPosition (SwingConstants.LEFT);

      label3 = new JLabel ("Devil Above", icon, SwingConstants.LEFT);
      label3.setHorizontalTextPosition (SwingConstants.CENTER);
      label3.setVerticalTextPosition (SwingConstants.BOTTOM);

      Container content = getContentPane();
      content.setLayout (new FlowLayout());
      content.add (label1);
      content.add (label2);
      content.add (label3);
   }
}
```

manager. The `SwingConstants` interface contains several constants used by various Swing components, making it easier to refer to them.

The orientation of the label's text and image is explicitly set using the `setHorizontalTextPosition` and `setVerticalTextPosition` methods. As shown in the case of the first label, the default horizontal position for text is on the right (image on the left), and the default vertical position for text is centered relative to the image.

The content pane of the frame is retrieved using the `getContentPane` method and the labels are added to it. We set the content pane's layout manager to be a `FlowLayout` object, which is described in Section 9.4.

Buttons

There are several types of buttons we may want to use in a GUI. The different types serve particular purposes:

- Push Button—a single button used to initiate some action
- Check Box—a single button that can be toggled on or off, providing a boolean option
- Radio Buttons—a set of buttons that cooperate as a group to provide a set of mutually exclusive options

We've used push buttons many times in previous examples to cause some action to begin processing. A push button is defined by the `JButton` class and generates an `ActionEvent` when pushed. Like a `JLabel`, a `JButton` can be labeled with text, an image, or both.

Check boxes and radio buttons have several similar characteristics. Both are *toggle buttons,* meaning at any time they are either on or off. A visual cue on the button indicates the toggle status. A check box is defined by the `JCheckBox` class, and a radio button is defined by the `JRadioButton` class. Both of these classes are derived from the `JToggleButton` class.

Key Concept

The choice of component, such as check boxes or radio buttons, must be carefully considered based on the type of interaction required.

There are some key differences between check boxes and radio buttons. A check box can be used by itself, to indicate the status of a particular option. A set of check boxes can be used together, but the status of one (on or off) has nothing to do with the status of the others.

A radio button, on the other hand, only makes sense when used in a group of other radio buttons. Only one radio button in a group can be on. When one radio button in the group is toggled on, the radio button that is currently on is toggled off. The `ButtonGroup` class is used to define a set of radio buttons. It is often a good idea to use a border around a set of radio buttons to make it clear which buttons belong to the group.

The `Quotes` program, shown in Listing 9.6, makes use of various button types to determine the characteristics of a string that is displayed. The `QuotesControls` class, shown in Listing 9.7, represents the main application frame.

Listing 9.6

```
//********************************************************************
//  Quotes.java       Author: Lewis and Loftus
//
//  Demonstrates the use of various button types.
//********************************************************************

import QuotesControls;
import GenericWindowListener;
import java.awt.event.*;

public class Quotes
{
   //-----------------------------------------------------------------
   //  Creates and displays the QuotesControls frame.
   //-----------------------------------------------------------------
   public static void main (String[] args)
   {
      QuotesControls frame = new QuotesControls();
      frame.addWindowListener (new GenericWindowListener());
      frame.show();
   }
}
```

Listing 9.7

```
//********************************************************************
//  QuotesControls.java       Author: Lewis and Loftus
//
//  Demonstrates the use of various button types.
//********************************************************************

import javax.swing.*;
import java.awt.*;
import java.awt.event.*;

public class QuotesControls extends JFrame
{
   private String[] text;
   private JLabel quote;

   private JButton uppercase, lowercase;
   private JCheckBox bold, italic;
   private JRadioButton comedy, philosophy, carpentry;
   private ButtonGroup topic;

   private JPanel letters, domain, style, app;

   //-----------------------------------------------------------------
   //  Sets up the GUI for the Quotes program.
   //-----------------------------------------------------------------
   public QuotesControls ()
   {
      super ("Quotes");
      setSize (300, 150);

      text = new String[3];
      text[0] = "Take my wife, please.";
      text[1] = "I think, therefore I am.";
      text[2] = "Measure twice, cut once.";

      quote = new JLabel (text[0], SwingConstants.CENTER);
      quote.setFont (new Font ("Serif", Font.PLAIN, 12));

      uppercase = new JButton ("Uppercase");
      lowercase = new JButton ("Lowercase");
```

Listing 9.7 ***(continued)***

```
      bold = new JCheckBox ("Bold");
      italic = new JCheckBox ("Italic");

      comedy = new JRadioButton ("Comedy", true);
      philosophy = new JRadioButton ("Philosophy", false);
      carpentry = new JRadioButton ("Carpentry", false);

      topic = new ButtonGroup();
      topic.add (comedy);
      topic.add (philosophy);
      topic.add (carpentry);

      QuoteActionListener actionListener = new QuoteActionListener();
      uppercase.addActionListener (actionListener);
      lowercase.addActionListener (actionListener);
      comedy.addActionListener (actionListener);
      philosophy.addActionListener (actionListener);
      carpentry.addActionListener (actionListener);

      QuoteItemListener itemListener = new QuoteItemListener();
      bold.addItemListener (itemListener);
      italic.addItemListener (itemListener);

      // Organize the components
      letters = new JPanel();
      letters.setLayout (new BoxLayout (letters, BoxLayout.Y_AXIS));
      letters.add (uppercase);
      letters.add (lowercase);

      domain = new JPanel();
      domain.setLayout (new BoxLayout (domain, BoxLayout.Y_AXIS));
      domain.add (comedy);
      domain.add (philosophy);
      domain.add (carpentry);

      style = new JPanel();
      style.setLayout (new BoxLayout (style, BoxLayout.Y_AXIS));
      style.add (bold);
      style.add (italic);
```

Listing 9.7 ***(continued)***

```
      app = new JPanel();
      app.setLayout (new BorderLayout(15,10));
      app.add (quote, BorderLayout.NORTH);
      app.add (letters, BorderLayout.WEST);
      app.add (domain, BorderLayout.CENTER);
      app.add (style, BorderLayout.EAST);

      setContentPane (app);
   }

   //*****************************************************************
   //  Inner class to handle the uppercase and lowercase buttons, as
   //  well as the topic buttons.
   //*****************************************************************
   private class QuoteActionListener implements ActionListener
   {
      //--------------------------------------------------------------
      //  Sets the quote to the correct string or the correct case
      //  depending on which button was pressed.
      //--------------------------------------------------------------
      public void actionPerformed (ActionEvent event)
      {
         Object source = event.getSource();

         if (source == uppercase)
            quote.setText (quote.getText().toUpperCase());
         else if (source == lowercase)
            quote.setText (quote.getText().toLowerCase());
         else if (source == comedy)
            quote.setText (text[0]);
         else if (source == philosophy)
            quote.setText (text[1]);
         else  // must be carpentry
            quote.setText (text[2]);
      }
   }
```

Listing 9.7 *(continued)*

```
   //*****************************************************************
   //  Inner class to handle the check boxes for bold and italic.
   //*****************************************************************
   private class QuoteItemListener implements ItemListener
   {
      //--------------------------------------------------------------
      //  Toggles bold or italic as appropriate.
      //--------------------------------------------------------------
      public void itemStateChanged (ItemEvent event)
      {
         Font font = quote.getFont();
         int style = font.getStyle();

         if (event.getSource() == bold)
         {
            if (event.getStateChange() == ItemEvent.SELECTED)
               style += Font.BOLD;
            else
               style -= Font.BOLD;

            quote.setFont (new Font (font.getName(), style, 12));
         }
         else  // must be italic
         {
            if (event.getStateChange() == ItemEvent.SELECTED)
               style += Font.ITALIC;
            else
               style -= Font.ITALIC;

            quote.setFont (new Font (font.getName(), style, 12));
         }
      }
   }
}
```

A set of radio buttons is used to determine which string is printed. Only one of the choices Comedy, Philosophy, or Carpentry is valid at any one time. However, two check boxes are used to determine if the string should be displayed in bold, italic, both, or neither. Because all of these combinations are reasonable, using check boxes is the appropriate GUI choice.

Two push buttons are used to put the string in all uppercase or all lowercase letters. Whenever the topic category is changed, the quote appears in mixed case.

Combo Boxes

A *combo box* allows the user to select one of several options. When the user presses the combo box using the mouse, a list of options is displayed from which the user can choose. The current choice is always displayed in the combo box. A combo box is defined by the `JComboBox` class.

A combo box can be either *editable* or *uneditable*. By default, a combo box is uneditable. Changing the value of an uneditable combo box can only be accomplished by selecting an item from the list. However, if the combo box is editable, the user can type a particular value in the combo box area.

The options in a combo box list can be established in one of two ways. We can create an array of strings and pass them into the constructor of the `JComboBox` class. Alternatively, we can use the `addItem` method to add an item to the combo box after it has been created.

The `JukeBox` program shown in Listing 9.8 demonstrates the use of a combo box. The user chooses a song to play using the combo box, then presses the play button to begin playing the song. The stop button can be pressed at any time to stop the song. Selecting a new song while one is playing will also stop the current song.

The `JukeBoxControls` class, shown in Listing 9.9 represents the frame that contains the juke box controls. The list of songs that are displayed in the combo box is defined in an array of strings. Note that the first entry in the array is an indication that the user should choose a song. This first entry will appear in the combo box by default, and is often used to direct the user. We must take care that the rest of the program does not try to use that option as a valid song.

The array of strings that fill the combo box corresponds to an array of audio clips that are loaded when the program is executed. When the play button is pressed, the current audio clip is played.

Listing 9.8

```
//********************************************************************
//  JukeBox.java       Author: Lewis and Loftus
//
//  Demonstrates the use of a combo box.
//********************************************************************

import JukeBoxControls;
import GenericWindowListener;
import java.awt.event.*;

public class JukeBox
{
   //-----------------------------------------------------------------
   //  Creates and displays the JukeBoxControls frame.
   //-----------------------------------------------------------------
   public static void main (String[] args)
   {
      JukeBoxControls frame = new JukeBoxControls();
      frame.addWindowListener (new GenericWindowListener());
      frame.show();
   }
}
```

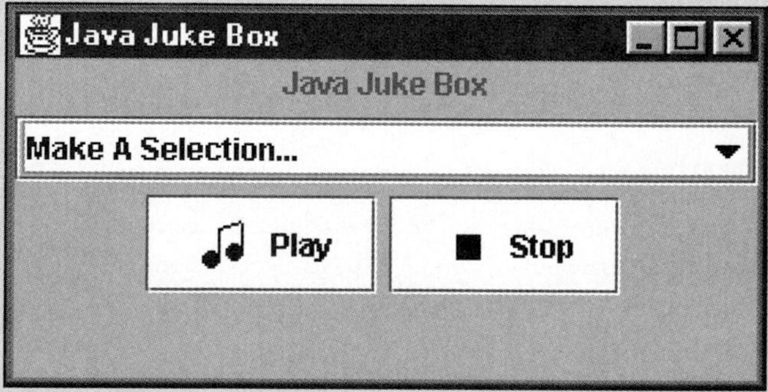

Listing 9.9

```
//********************************************************************
//  JukeBoxControls.java       Author: Lewis and Loftus
//
//  Demonstrates the use of a combo box.
//********************************************************************

import java.awt.*;
import java.awt.event.*;
import java.applet.*;
import javax.swing.*;
import java.net.URL;

public class JukeBoxControls extends JFrame
{
   private JLabel titleLabel;
   private JComboBox musicCombo;
   private JButton stopButton, playButton;
   private JPanel appPanel, buttonPanel;
   private AudioClip[] music;
   private AudioClip current;

   //-----------------------------------------------------------------
   //  Sets up the JukeBox GUI.
   //-----------------------------------------------------------------
   public JukeBoxControls()
   {
      super ("Java Juke Box");
      setSize (300, 200);

      try
      {
         music = new AudioClip[7];
         music[0] = null;  // corresponds to "Make a Selection..."
         music[1] = Applet.newAudioClip (new URL("file", "localhost", "westernBeat.wav"));
         music[2] = Applet.newAudioClip (new URL("file", "localhost", "classical.wav"));
         music[3] = Applet.newAudioClip (new URL("file", "localhost", "jeopardy.au"));
         music[4] = Applet.newAudioClip (new URL("file", "localhost", "newAgeRhythm.wav"));
         music[5] = Applet.newAudioClip (new URL("file", "localhost", "eightiesJam.wav"));
         music[6] = Applet.newAudioClip (new URL("file", "localhost", "hitchcock.wav"));
      }
      catch (Exception exception) {}
```

Listing 9.9 ***(continued)***

```
      titleLabel = new JLabel ("Java Juke Box");
      titleLabel.setAlignmentX (Component.CENTER_ALIGNMENT);

      // Create the list of strings for the combo box options.
      String[] musicNames = {"Make A Selection...", "Western Beat",
               "Classical Melody", "Jeopardy Theme", "New Age Rhythm",
               "Eighties Jam", "Alfred Hitchcock's Theme"};

      musicCombo = new JComboBox (musicNames);
      musicCombo.setAlignmentX (Component.CENTER_ALIGNMENT);

      playButton = new JButton ("Play", new ImageIcon ("play.gif"));
      playButton.setBackground (Color.white);
      stopButton = new JButton ("Stop", new ImageIcon ("stop.gif"));
      stopButton.setBackground (Color.white);

      buttonPanel = new JPanel();
      buttonPanel.setLayout(new BoxLayout(buttonPanel, BoxLayout.X_AXIS));
      buttonPanel.add (playButton);
      buttonPanel.add (Box.createRigidArea (new Dimension(5,0)));
      buttonPanel.add (stopButton);
      buttonPanel.setBackground (Color.cyan);

      appPanel = new JPanel();
      appPanel.setLayout (new BoxLayout(appPanel, BoxLayout.Y_AXIS));
      appPanel.add (titleLabel);
      appPanel.add (Box.createRigidArea (new Dimension(0,5)));
      appPanel.add (musicCombo);
      appPanel.add (Box.createRigidArea (new Dimension(0,5)));
      appPanel.add (buttonPanel);
      appPanel.setBackground (Color.cyan);

      setContentPane (appPanel);

      musicCombo.addActionListener (new JukeBoxListener());
      stopButton.addActionListener (new JukeBoxListener());
      playButton.addActionListener (new JukeBoxListener());

      current = null;
   }
```

Listing 9.9 *(continued)*

```
   //*****************************************************************
   //  An inner class to handle the various events of the juke box.
   //*****************************************************************
   private class JukeBoxListener implements ActionListener
   {
      //--------------------------------------------------------------
      //  Handles the play and stop buttons and the combo box.
      //--------------------------------------------------------------
      public void actionPerformed (ActionEvent event)
      {
         if (current != null)  // stop current clip no matter what
            current.stop();

         Object source = event.getSource();
         if (source == playButton)
         {
            if (current != null)
               current.play();
         }
         else if (source == musicCombo)
            current = music[musicCombo.getSelectedIndex()];
      }
   }
}
```

The juke box components are organized using several `JPanel` objects. One primary `JPanel` object, called `appPanel`, is set as the content pane of the frame.

The book's Web site contains more details and examples of Java Swing components

9.4 Layout Managers

A *layout manager* is an object that governs how components are arranged in a container. It determines the size and position of each component, and may take many factors into account to do so. Every component has a default layout manager, although we can replace it if we prefer another one.

Key Concept

Layout managers determine the size and position of components in a container.

A component's layout manager is consulted whenever the container might need to change its visual appearance. When a container is resized, for example, the layout manager is consulted to determine how all of the components in the container should now appear. Every time a component is added to a container, the layout manager determines how it affects all of the existing components.

The predefined layout managers provided by the Java class libraries include:

- Flow Layout
- Border Layout
- Box Layout
- Card Layout
- Grid Layout
- GridBag Layout
- Overlay Layout

Each layout manager has its own particular properties and rules governing the layout of components. For some layout managers, the order in which you add the components affects their positioning, while in others you have more specific control. Some layout managers take a component's preferred size or alignment into account, while others don't. To develop good graphical interfaces in Java, it is important to become familiar with the idiosyncrasies of various layout managers.

Key Concept

Some layout managers take into account component features such as maximum size, and others do not.

Choosing layout managers goes hand-in-hand with organizing the component hierarchy using containers. Each container can have a unique layout manager. Many combinations are possible, and there is not necessarily a single best option. As always, we should be guided by the desired goal to design a system that is easily understood and maintainable.

To change a container's layout manager, we can use the `setLayout` method. For example:

```
JPanel panel = new JPanel();
panel.setLayout (new BorderLayout());
```

Flow Layout

Flow layout is one of the most simple layout managers to use. The `JPanel` class uses flow layout by default.

Flow layout puts as many components on a row as possible, at their preferred size. When a component cannot fit on a row, it is put on the next row. As many rows are added as needed to fit all components that have been added to the container. Figure 9.2 depicts a container governed by a Flow Layout manager.

Within each row, components are either centered, left-aligned, or right-aligned. The alignment for a given flow layout is determined when the layout manager is created. The alignment defaults to center. The horizontal and vertical gap size between components can also be specified when the layout manager is created. Alignment and gap size can also be set using appropriate methods.

Border Layout

A *border layout* has five areas to which components can be added: North, South, East, West, and Center. The areas have a particular positional relationship to each other, as shown in Figure 9.3.

The four outer areas become as big as needed in order to accommodate the component that they contain. If no components are added to the North, South, East, or West areas, then those areas do not take up any room in the overall layout. The Center area expands to fill any available space.

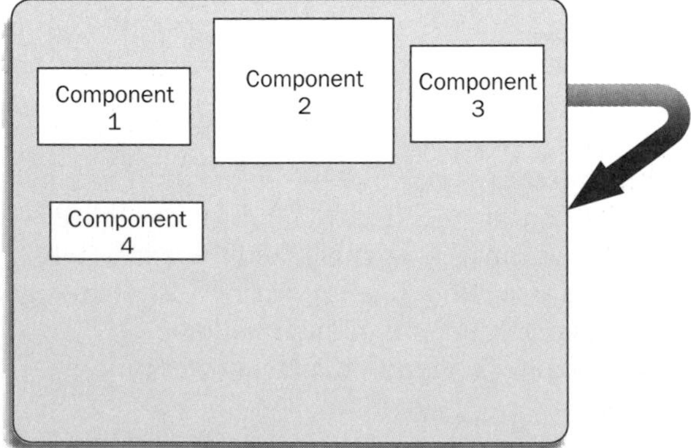

Figure 9.2 Flow layout puts as many components on one row as possible

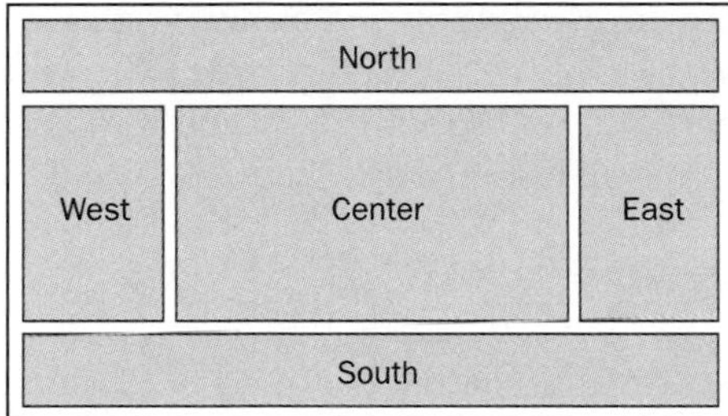

Figure 9.3 Border layout organizes components in five areas

A particular container may only use a few areas, as needed. For example, a container may be well organized by using only the Center, South, and West areas. This versatility makes border layout a very useful layout manager.

> **Key Concept**
> Not all areas of a border layout need to be used. The other areas fill the space to compensate.

The add method for a container governed by a border layout takes as its first parameter the component to be added, and takes a second parameter that indicates the area to which it is added. The area is specified using constants defined in the `BorderLayout` class. For example:

```
add (component1, BorderLayout.CENTER);
add (component2, BorderLayout.EAST);
```

Note that each area only displays one component. That is, only one component should be added to each area of a given border layout. A common error is to add two components to a particular area of a border layout, in which case the first component added is replaced by the second and only the second is seen when the container is displayed.

To add multiple components to an area within a border layout, we rely on the component hierarchy. First add the components to another container, such as a `JPanel`, then add the panel to the area.

Box Layout

The `FlowLayout` and `BorderLayout` classes are an original part of the AWT graphics library. The `BoxLayout` class is a relatively new addition to the set of layout managers, introduced with the Swing library. It is a fairly simple layout manager, but can be used to create interesting component organizations that would earlier have only been accomplished with a `GridBagLayout` manager, which is far more complex.

> **Key Concept**
> Box layout provides the ability to create component designs that previously required more complex layout managers.

A box layout organizes components either vertically or horizontally, in one row or one column, as shown in Figure 9.4. When the `BoxLayout` object is created, we specify that it will either follow the X axis (horizontal) or the Y axis (vertical), using constants defined in the `BoxLayout` class. For example:

```
new BoxLayout (component, BoxLayout.X_AXIS);
```

Unlike other layout managers, the constructor of a `BoxLayout` takes as its first parameter the component that it will govern. Therefore, a new `BoxLayout` object must be created for each component.

Components in containers governed by a box layout are organized (top to bottom or left to right) in the order in which they are added to the container.

There is a special container defined by the class `Box`, which has `BoxLayout` as its default. `Box` is not derived from `JComponent`, as are other Swing components, and therefore lacks certain features, such as having borders. Occasionally, though, a `Box` may be an appropriate choice, rather than creating another component, such as a `JPanel`, and applying a `BoxLayout`.

Recall that `FlowLayout` and `BorderLayout` allow us to specify the horizontal and vertical gap among all components. The gap in these layout managers has to be the same among all components in the container. In a `BoxLayout`, we don't specify a general gap size; instead, we can add invisible components of varying sizes to create the look that we desire.

Whether or not we are using a `Box` object, the `Box` class can be used to create invisible components. Two types of invisible components are *rigid areas,* which are a fixed-size space, and *glue,* which specifies where excess space in a layout should go. A rigid area is created using the `createRigidArea` method of the `Box` class, and takes a `Dimension` object as a parameter to

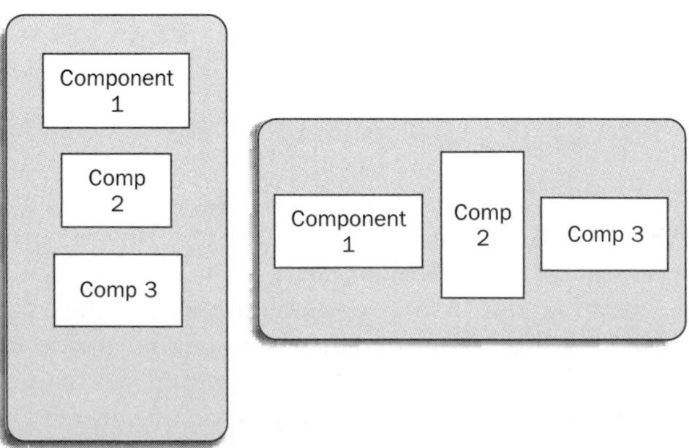

Figure 9.4 Box layout organizes components either vertically or horizontally

define the size of the invisible area. Glue is created using the methods `createHorizontalGlue` or `createVerticalGlue`, as appropriate.

Once created, these invisible components are added to the container like any other. For example:

```
panel.add (component1);
panel.add (Box.createHorizontalGlue());
panel.add (component2);
```

9.5 Special Features

There are a variety of features provided by the Java graphic libraries that don't fall into other categories. Swing components, in particular, provide features such as:

- Tool Tips—a short description that pops up when the mouse cursor rests on the component for a moment
- Borders—graphical edges around components in various designs
- Mnemonics—keyboard shortcuts for activating graphical objects, such as buttons

Any Swing component can be assigned a *tool tip*, which is a short line of text that will appear when the mouse cursor is rested momentarily on top of the component. Tool tips are usually used to inform the user about the component, such as the purpose of a particular button. A tool tip can be assigned using the `setToolTipText` method of a Swing component:

```
JButton button = new JButton ("Compute");
button.setToolTipText ("Calculates the area under the curve.");
```

Swing also provides the ability to put a *border* around any component. A border is not a component itself, but defines how the edge of any component should be drawn. A border provides visual cues as to how GUI components are organized, and can be used to give titles to components.

Predefined borders in the Java class library include:

- Line border
- Etched border
- Bevel border (raised or lowered)
- Titled border
- Matte border
- Empty border

An empty border is used to create a visually pleasing space around a component. A matte border uses an image as a template for the border. Two borders can be combined into a *compound border.*

The `BorderFactory` class is useful in creating borders for components. Once created, a border is applied to a component using the `setBorder` method. For example:

```
JPanel panel = new JPanel();
panel.setBorder (BorderFactory.createLineBorder (Color.black));
```

Key Concept

A mnemonic provides a keyboard alternative to pushing a button.

A *mnemonic* is a character that allows the user to push a button or make a menu choice using the keyboard in addition to using the mouse. When a mnemonic has been defined for a button, for instance, the user can hold down the ALT key and press the mnemonic character to activate the button. It works the same as if the mouse was used to press the button.

A mnemonic character should be chosen from the label on a button or menu item. Once the mnemonic has been established using the `setMnemonic` method, the character in the label will appear underlined to indicate that it can be used as a shortcut. If a letter is chosen that is not in the label, nothing will be underlined and the user won't know how to use the shortcut. Here is an example of setting a mnemonic:

```
JButton button = new JButton ("Calculate");
button.setMnemonic ('C');
```

9.6 GUI Design

Knowing the details of components and layout managers gives us the tools to put graphical interfaces together, but we must guide that knowledge with some fundamental ideas that lead to a system that really solves the user's problem. This section discusses some guidelines that apply in almost all situations.

- Know the user

The designer of a system needs to truly understand the needs and operations of the user in order to develop an interface that will serve that user well. Keep in mind that, to the user, the interface *is* the software. It is the only way in which the user interacts with the system. As such, the interface must address the user's needs.

- Prevent user errors

Whenever possible, we should design our interfaces so that the user can make as few mistakes as possible. For instance, if an input value must be one of a set of particular values, a combo box would probably be a better choice than a text field, which would allow the user to type invalid values. Once again, the choice of components is fundamental.

- Optimize user abilities

Not all users are alike. Some are more adept at using GUI components than others. We should not design to the lowest common denominator. Provide mnemonic shortcuts whenever reasonable. Don't make a user move through five screens to get to a particular piece of information.

- Be consistent

This guideline is important when dealing with large systems or multiple systems in a common environment. Users get familiar with a particular organization or color scheme, and these should not be changed arbitrarily.

Summary of Key Concepts

- The design and development of a Java GUI involves several interacting concepts.
- Graphics and graphical user interfaces can be accomplished in applications using a container such as a frame.
- Layout managers determine the size and position of components in a container.
- Some layout managers take into account component features such as maximum size, and others do not.
- A mnemonic provides a keyboard alternative to pushing a button.
- Not all areas of a border layout need to be used. The other areas fill the space to compensate.
- Box layout provides the ability to create component designs that previously required more complex layout managers.
- The alignment of the text and image of a label, as well as their relative positioning, can be explicitly set.
- The choice of component, such as check boxes or radio buttons, must be carefully considered based on the type of interaction required.

Self-Review Questions

9.1 Name the various issues that must be taken into account when designing a Java GUI.

9.2 What is a layout manager?

9.3 How does the Flow Layout manager work?

9.4 Why are there so many GUI components?

9.5 What's the difference between a check box and a radio button?

9.6 What is a combo box?

Exercises

9.1 Explain the relationship between a container and a layout manager.

9.2 Draw the component hierarchy for the Quotes applet.

9.3 Draw the component hierarchy for the Juke Box applet.

9.4 Explain how the component hierarchy is different from the inheritance hierarchy.

9.5 Change the layout manager of the Quotes applet and document the effects. Try a variety of options.

9.6 Compare and contrast a label and a text field.

9.7 Compare and contrast a text field and a text area.

Programming Projects

9.1 Design and implement a new version of the `Doodle` program from Chapter 7 such that only Swing components are used. Remember that there is no corresponding Swing component for the AWT `Canvas` class, because any Swing component can be drawn upon.

9.2 Design and implement a GUI application that displays a traffic light. Use a push button to change the state of the light.

9.3 Modify the Quotes example in this chapter to allow the user to change the size of the displayed text. Use an editable combo box to set the size.

9.4 Design and implement an application that displays a photo album. Allow the user to select (using FileChooser) the directory in which the images are contained. Load the images and display them one at a time. Use buttons to select the directory of images and to move between images. Use a combo box to choose and move directly to a particular picture.

9.5 Design and implement an applet that serves as a pizza ordering system. Display prices. Capture information about quantity, size, and toppings. Display the cost of the order as information is gathered.

9.6 Design and implement an application that simulates a delicatessen order system. Allow the user to construct various kinds of deli sandwiches, with various contents and condiments. Determine quantities and display prices. Use appropriate components to capture and display the information. Display the cost of the order as information is gathered.

9.7 Design and implement an applet that displays various weather information: wind speed, humidity, etc. Create an object that simulates a sensor and produces random values (in reasonable ranges) for the weather features. Poll the sensor on a regular basis and update the weather display appropriately.

9.8 Design and implement an applet that draws the graph of the equation $ax^2 + bx + c$, where the values of a, b, and c are set using three sliders.

9.9 Design and implement an application that performs flashcard testing of simple mathematical problems. Allow the user to pick the category. Repetitively display a problem and get the user's answer. Indicate if the user's answer is right or wrong for each problem, and display an ongoing score.

▶ Answers to Self-Review Questions

9.1 A Java GUI must use components that provide specific types of interaction with the user. These components generate events that must be handled by event listeners. Components are organized using containers, forming a component hierarchy. The way a set of components appear when displayed depends on the layout manager that governs the container. All of these features interact and have an effect on the GUI presentation.

9.2 A layout manager is an object that determines the size and position of each component that is added to a container.

9.3 Flow layout attempts to put as many components on a row as possible. Multiple rows are created as needed.

9.4 There are so many GUI components because there are many ways in which we want to interact with the user. We must choose our components carefully to ensure the best interaction.

9.5 A check box is independent of any other components and simply indicates a boolean condition that is toggled either on or off. A radio button is used in a group with other radio buttons such that only one is toggled on at any time.

9.6 A combo box is a component that allows the user to choose from a set of options in a pull-down list. An editable combo box also allows the user to enter a specific value.

10 Software Engineering

The quality of software is only as good as the process used to create it. In Chapter 3, we introduced four basic activities that are a part of any software development effort: requirements, design, implementation, and testing. These basic steps have served us well as we developed small programs using new techniques. To successfully develop larger systems, however, we must refine these activities into a well-defined process that can be applied repeatedly and consistently. This chapter explores models for developing software, and defines an evolutionary approach that specifically takes object-oriented issues into account. This approach is illustrated using an extended example that synthesizes many of the programming concepts explored thus far in the book.

Chapter Objectives

- Explore several different software development models.
- Explain the life cycle of a software system and its implications for software development.
- Contrast linear and iterative development approaches.
- Discuss prototypes and their various uses.
- Explore the goals and techniques of testing.
- Define an evolutionary approach to object-oriented design and implementation.
- Demonstrate evolutionary development using a nontrivial example.

10.1 Software Development Models

A program goes through many phases from its initial conception to its ultimate demise. This sequence is often called the *life cycle* of the program. Too often programmers focus so much on the particular issues involved in getting a program to run, they ignore other important characteristics. Developing high-quality programs requires an appreciation for many issues, and those issues must be taken into account in the day-to-day activities of a programmer. These issues are explored as we discuss the software life cycle and software development models.

Software Life Cycle

The life cycle of a program is shown in Figure 10.1. All programs go through three fundamental stages: development, use, and maintenance. Initially, the idea for a program is conceived by a software developer or by a user who has a particular need. The new program is created in the *development* stage. At some point the new program is considered to be complete and is turned over to the users. The version of the program that is made available to the users is often called an initial *release* of the program.

Almost certainly, users will discover problems with the program. They also often have suggestions for new features that they would like to see added to the program in order to make it more useful. The defects and ideas for new features are conveyed back to the developer, and the program undergoes maintenance.

Key Concept

Maintaining software is the process of modifying a program in order to enhance it or fix problems.

Software maintenance is the process of modifying a program in order to enhance it or fix problems. The changes are made to a copy of the program, so the user can still use the current release while the program is being maintained. When the changes are seri-

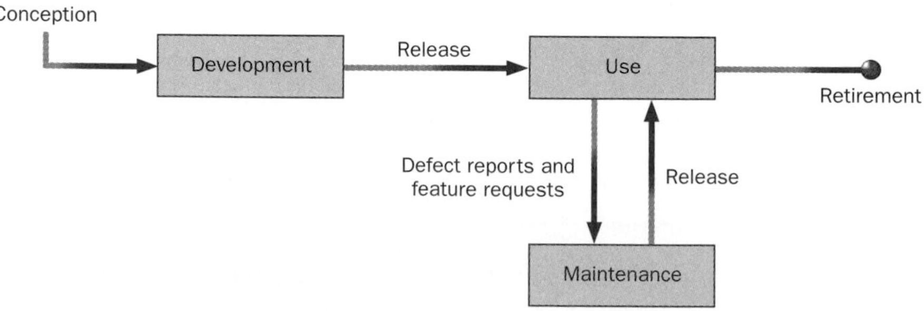

Figure 10.1 The life cycle of a program

ous enough or numerous enough, a new version of the program is released for use. A program might be maintained many times over, resulting in several releases.

For a variety of reasons, a developer may decide that it is no longer worth the effort to maintain an existing program and therefore releases no further versions of it. Eventually, a program will outlive its usefulness, and users will abandon it or seek another solution. This eventual demise is sometimes referred to as the program's *retirement* from active use.

The duration of a program's life cycle varies greatly depending on the purpose of the program, how useful it is, and how well it is constructed. The time taken for the development portion of a program can vary from a few weeks to several years. Likewise, a program may be used and maintained for many years.

One important aspect of software development is based in the relationship between development efforts and maintenance efforts. Figure 10.2 shows a typical ratio of development effort to maintenance effort. This may seem contrary to intuition because it seems that the initial development of a program is where the real work is done, but it turns out that isn't true. Much more effort is expended overall to enhance and fix an existing system than to develop it originally.

Maintenance tasks require more effort for various reasons. One reason is that the original developers are rarely the same people as the ones who maintain it. Often a significant amount of time goes by between the initial development and the maintenance tasks, and personnel responsibilities have changed. Therefore, the effort involved in a maintenance task, such as fixing a defect, depends on the ability of a new developer to understand the program, determine what the cause of the problem is, and correct it.

Key Concept

The maintainers of a program are often not the program's original developers, so maintainers must be able to understand a program that they didn't design.

The ability to read and understand a program depends on how well it is designed, implemented, and documented. It depends on how classes are

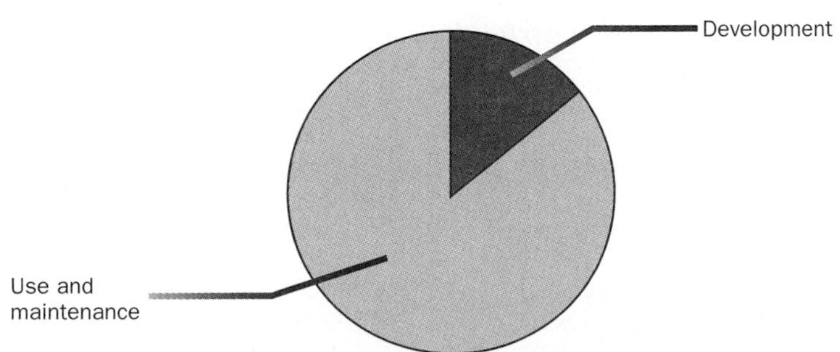

Figure 10.2 A typical ratio of development effort to maintenance effort

derived and how objects are used. It depends on how elegantly methods accomplish their goals and on how closely coding guidelines are followed. In short, the ability to read and understand a program depends on the effort put into the initial development process.

When requirements are not clearly established, and when designs are not thought out carefully, the software created can be unnecessarily complex and difficult to understand. The more complex a program is, the easier it is to introduce errors during development, and the more difficult it is to remove these errors when they are found. The earlier the problems are discovered, the easier and less costly they are to correct.

Key Concept

Rushing through the development stage often leads to significant increases in the effort expended during maintenance.

Writing a program without a careful design is as absurd as building a house without creating a blueprint. The builder may actually create some kind of structure, even one that looks good on a superficial examination. However, it is likely that the structure will fail to meet the safety requirements of the local building code, and it will not stand up to severe weather nearly as well as a house that has been carefully designed. Likewise, a program that is created in an ad hoc fashion, with little or no attention to requirements or design, is likely to contain many defects and will not perform well when used.

The relationship between development effort and maintenance effort is not linear. Small changes in the development effort can greatly reduce the effort necessary during maintenance. The bars in Figure 10.3 show relationships between the development effort and the effort required for maintenance tasks. The bottom bar shows that if a small increase in effort is expended during development, significantly higher savings in maintenance effort can be gained. The effort put into the development stage is an investment that will reduce the overall effort required throughout the life cycle of the program. A good programmer has the long-term effects in mind while performing short-term activities.

In some ways, this issue is a question of maturity. An experienced software developer realizes the advantages of certain development activities. It is somewhat analogous to dental care. To many children, brushing teeth is often a chore that they try to avoid. To an adult, brushing is simply part of a daily routine, necessary for a lifetime of healthy teeth. Similarly, the mature software developer realizes that even small, unobtrusive activities can have a dra-

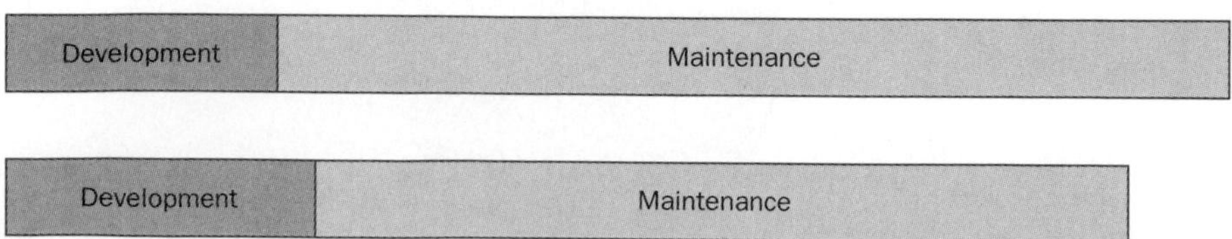

Figure 10.3 Development effort relative to maintenance effort

matic effect over the life of the program, even if the results are not immediately apparent.

Therefore, the goal of writing software is not to minimize the amount of time it takes to develop a program, but to minimize the overall amount of effort required to create and maintain a useful program. A working program is not necessarily a good program. With this goal in mind, the development process should be well defined and rigorously followed.

Key Concept

A working program is not necessarily a good program. Our goal should be to develop software that minimizes the efforts to create and maintain a program.

Development Process Models

Too often, programmers follow the build-and-fix approach depicted in Figure 10.4. In it, a programmer creates an initial version of a program, then continually modifies it until it has reached some level of acceptance. The testing activities to discover errors are not systematic or carefully planned, and therefore problems often go undiscovered. The programmer is simply reacting to problems, as opposed to creating something worthy in the first place. Therefore, the so-called build-and-fix model is not really a development model at all.

A program produced using the build-and-fix approach is a product of ad hoc, reckless activities. Although some problems might have been eliminated during the development, the overall quality of the product has never been addressed. Defects that still exist will be difficult to isolate and correct. Enhancements to the program will also be challenging because the system was never designed well in the first place.

Key Concept

A program produced using the build-and-fix approach is the result of ad hoc, reckless activities.

As discussed in Chapter 3, the following activities need to be specifically addressed during development: establishing requirements, creating a design, implementing the design, and testing the implementation. Many attempts have been made to incorporate these activities into a precise development strategy. One of the first development process models was offered in the early 1970s. It is called the *waterfall model* and is depicted in Figure 10.5.

The waterfall model is linear, with one stage followed directly by the next. In fact, the name of the waterfall model comes from the implication that information is flowing in one direction from stage to stage until the final release is

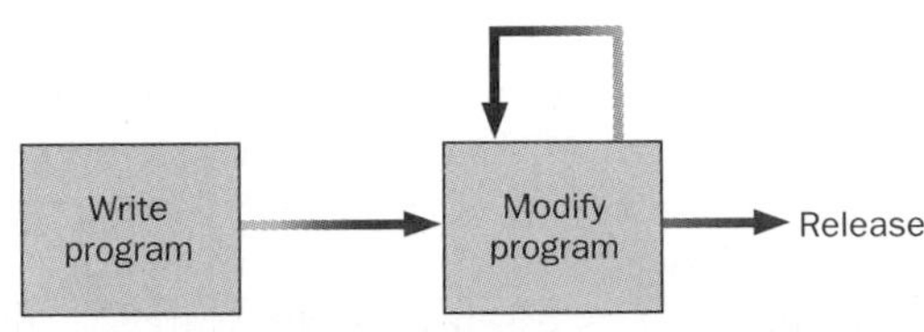

Figure 10.4 The build-and-fix approach

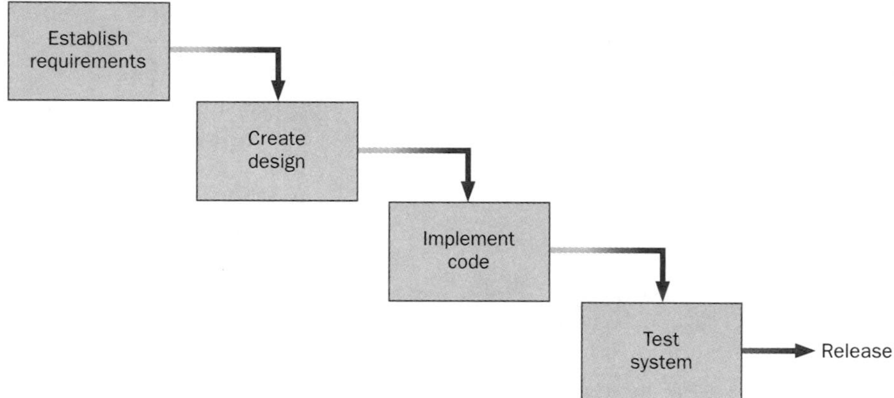

Figure 10.5 The waterfall model

created. It does not allow for an earlier stage to be revisited after a new stage is begun.

It would be nice if all of the requirements of a program were completely specified and analyzed before the design activities are started. Likewise, it would be nice to have all of the design decisions made before the implementation begins. Unfortunately, it almost never works out that cleanly. No matter how carefully the requirements are established, or how thoroughly the design is analyzed, it is impossible to predict the future, and there will always come a time when the developer realizes an earlier decision was in error.

Furthermore, since stages are not revisited in the waterfall model, a tremendous effort needs to go into each stage to ensure its completeness. However, sometimes proceeding to later stages is an efficient way to discover the issues that have not been addressed in the earlier stages.

Therefore, a realistic model must take into account that the development activities are somewhat overlapping. However, we must be careful not to degenerate into a build-and-fix approach. We need a flexible development model with interacting activities, while still maintaining rigorous attention to each stage, ensuring the quality of the overall product.

Iterative Processes

An *iterative process* is one that allows a software developer to cycle through the different development activities. Earlier stages can be revisited, formally, allowing proper changes to be made when needed. Figure 10.6 shows an initial version of an iterative process.

The process in Figure 10.6 is essentially the waterfall model with backtracking. That is, when new information is uncovered that changes the

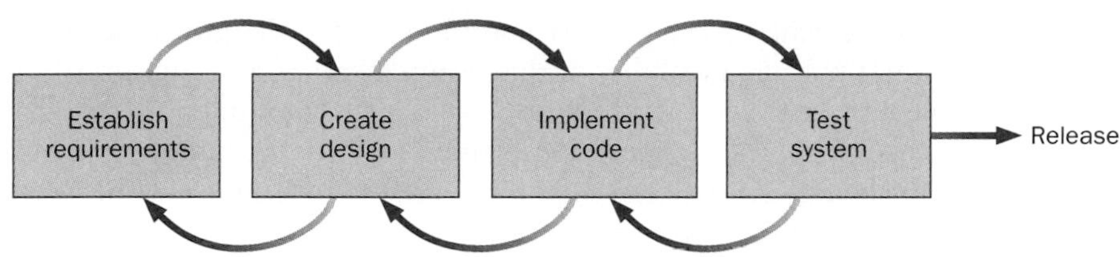

Figure 10.6 An iterative process

requirements or design, we have a way to formally go back and modify the affected stages. The appropriate documents are updated to reflect the new decisions.

The danger of backtracking is that the developer might rely on it too much. This model is not intended to reduce the amount of effort that goes into developing the initial requirements prior to starting on the design. Likewise, the design of a program should still be well established before beginning implementation. The backtracking activity should be used primarily to correct problems uncovered in later stages.

Any realistic development model will include the concept of revisiting previous activities. It will also include prototyping and formal test strategies, as discussed in the next sections.

10.2 Prototypes

A *prototype* is a program or representation that is created to explore a particular concept. Sometimes a programmer simply doesn't know how to accomplish a particular task, or whether a certain requirement is feasible, or if the user interface is acceptable to the client. Prototypes can be used to explore all of these issues, instead of proceeding on an assumption that may later prove unwise.

Key Concept

A prototype can be used to explore the feasibility of a decision instead of proceeding on an assumption that may later prove unwise.

For example, a programmer might have had no experience using a particular set of classes provided by a library. Before committing to its use, the programmer may produce a small program that exercises the classes in order to establish that they are a viable choice for use in the design, providing the functionality needed in an acceptable manner. If they prove unreasonable, the design could then take into account that new classes must be developed from scratch.

Another prototype might be created to test the feasibility of a requirement that states that the program should perform a certain task and print the results within one second. The prototype would focus exclusively on the ability to satisfy that requirement. If it can be accomplished, the design can proceed with confidence; if not, the feasibility of the requirements can be questioned. It is better to question requirements early because any changes might have a significant impact on the entire system. For example, if the task in question cannot be accomplished in the required time frame, the user interface would have to be modified to produce special status messages.

Yet another prototype might be created to show a simplified version of the user interface. The developer and the client can then discuss the interaction between the user and the program to see if it is acceptable. Keep in mind that this prototype need not be a program. A set of diagrams that show the layout of buttons and other components may be enough to explore the issues involved.

A prototype can often pinpoint problems that lists of requirements might obscure or miss altogether. It can be used to reject certain design or implementation decisions before they become a problem, and it can clarify the user's intentions. It is not uncommon, after a system has been fully developed, for a user to make a statement such as: "I know that's what I said I wanted, but that's not what I meant."

Throw-away Prototypes

Usually, a prototype is a "quick and dirty" test of an idea or concept. They are created with little regard to software engineering principles. They are created to validate an idea or approach, not as an element of the final system. This type of prototype is sometimes called a *throw-away prototype* because once it has been written and served its purpose, it is discarded.

A throw-away prototype has its benefits; it takes relatively little effort to develop it because good design and coding techniques are not a priority. It serves an invaluable service by helping us avoid improper and costly decisions.

The problem with a throw-away prototype is that programmers sometimes feel like they're wasting the effort it took to create it and want to incorporate the prototype into their final system. The solution to this problem is to realize that the prototype has served its purpose, and that its inclusion at this point could cause more problems than it solves. We should take what we learn from a throw-away prototype and incorporate that knowledge into a sound design. The code itself is irrelevant.

10.3 Testing

The term testing can be applied in many ways to software development. Testing certainly includes its traditional definition: the act of running a completed program with various inputs to discover problems. But it also includes any evaluation that is performed by human or machine to assess the quality of the developing system. These evaluations should occur long before a single line of code is written.

Before moving on to the next stage of the development process, the results of the current stage should be evaluated. Prior to moving on to creating a design, the requirements should be carefully evaluated to ensure that they are complete, consistent, and unambiguous. Prior to implementation, the design should be evaluated to make sure that each requirement is adequately addressed.

Walkthroughs

One technique used to evaluate design or code is called a *walkthrough,* which is a meeting in which several people carefully review a design document or section of code. The participants discuss its merits and problems, and create a list of issues that must be addressed. The goal of a walkthrough is to identify problems, not to solve them, which usually takes much more time.

Key Concept

A design or code walkthrough is a meeting in which several people review and critique a software design or implementation.

A design walkthrough should determine whether the requirements are addressed, as well as assessing the way the system is decomposed into classes and objects. A code walkthrough should determine how faithfully the implementation represents the design, and identify any specific problems that would cause the implementation to fail in its responsibilities.

Defect Testing

The goal of most testing efforts is to find errors and is generally called *defect testing.* With that goal in mind, a good test is one that uncovers a problem in a program. This might seem strange because we ultimately don't want to have problems in our system. But keep in mind that errors almost certainly exist, and our testing efforts should make every attempt to find them. We want to increase the reliability of our program by finding and fixing the errors that exist, rather than letting the user discover them.

Key Concept

The goal of testing is to find errors; therefore, a good test is one that uncovers a problem in a program.

It is possible to prove that a program is correct, but that technique is incredibly complex for large systems, and errors can always be made in the proof. Therefore, we generally rely on testing to determine the quality of a program. We run specific tests in an attempt to find problems. As more tests are run and fewer errors are found, our confidence in a program increases.

A *test case* is a set of inputs, user actions, or other initial conditions, and the expected output. A test case should be appropriately documented so that it can be repeated. Developers often create a complete *test suite,* which is a set of test cases that cover all aspects of the system.

Key Concept

Because programs operate on a large number of possible inputs, it is not feasible to create test cases for all possible input or user actions.

Because programs operate on a large number of possible inputs, it is not feasible to create test cases for all possible input or user actions. For example, to exhaustively test a single integer parameter would require billions of test cases, one case for every possible value the parameter might hold. Many of these test cases end up being so similar that they are not actually testing anything different about the program, and they are therefore a wasted effort. Therefore, we want to choose our test cases carefully. To that end, let's examine two defect testing approaches: black box and white box.

As the name implies, *black-box testing* treats the thing being tested as a black box. That is, test cases are developed without regard to the internal workings. Black-box tests are based on inputs and outputs. An entire program can be tested using a black-box technique, in which case the inputs are the user-provided information and user actions such as button pushes. A single class can also be tested using a black-box technique, which focuses on the system interface (its public methods) of the class. Certain parameters are passed in producing certain results. Often black-box test cases are derived directly from the requirements of the system, or from the stated purpose of a method.

The input data for a black-box test case are often selected by defining equivalence categories. An *equivalence category* is a collection of inputs that are expected to produce similar outputs. Generally, if a method will work for one value in the equivalence class, we have every reason to believe it will work for the others. For example, the input to a method that computes the square root of a number can be divided into two equivalence categories: positive integers and negative integers. For this method, positive integers will produce valid output, and negative integers will not.

Equivalence categories have defined boundaries. Because all values of an equivalence category essentially test the same features of a program, there is only a need for one or two test cases inside the equivalence boundary. However, the boundary itself should be tested exhaustively. For an integer boundary, an exhaustive test would use the exact value of the boundary, the boundary −1, and the boundary +1. Test cases should be defined that use these cases, plus one or two cases within the boundary.

Consider a method whose purpose is to validate that particular integer value is in the range 0 and 99, inclusive. Black-box testing would dictate that we use test values that surround and fall on the boundaries, as well as general values from the equivalence categories. Therefore, a set of black-box test cases for this situation might be: −500, −1, 0, 1, 50, 98, 99, 100, and 500. For each test case, the expected output should be established prior to running the test. For this simplistic example, this might seem like more effort than necessary, but the same technique can be applied to more complicated situations with success.

White-box testing, also known as *glass-box testing,* exercises the internal structure and implementation of a method. A white-box test case is based on the internal workings of a method. The goal is to ensure that every part of a program is executed at least once. This testing is done by mapping the different possible paths through the code and ensuring that the input associated with the test cases causes every path to be executed. This type of testing is often called *statement coverage.*

Paths through code are controlled by various control flow statements that use conditional expressions, such as an `if` statement. In order to get every path through the program executed at least once, the input data values for the test cases need to control the values for the conditional expressions. The input data of one or more test cases should cause the condition of an `if` statement to evaluate to `true` in at least one case and to `false` in at least one case. Covering both true and false values in the `if` statement will guarantee that both the paths through the `if` statement will be executed. Similar situations can be created for loops and other constructs.

10.4 Evolutionary Development

Let's examine a realistic development model that specifically takes object-oriented issues into account. The model is shown in Figure 10.7.

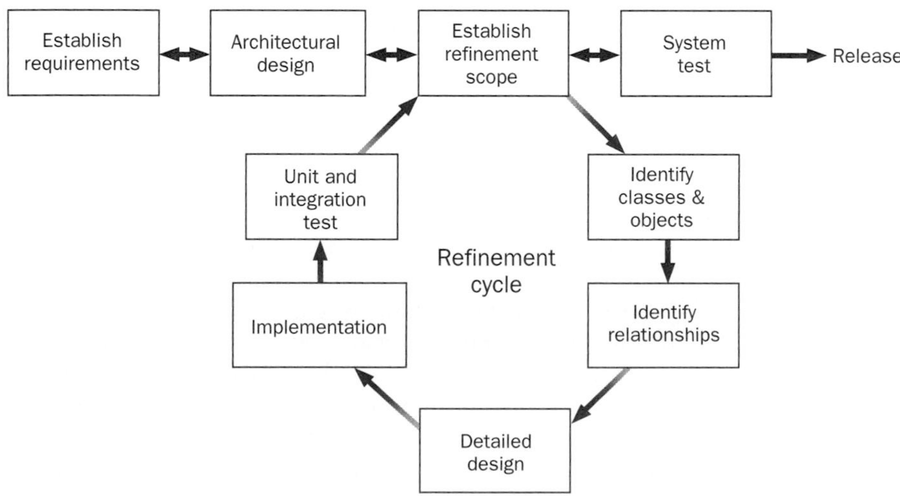

Figure 10.7 An object-oriented software development process

Key Concept

A refinement focuses on a single aspect of a program, such as the user interface or a particular algorithm.

A key part of this model is the *refinement cycle*. Each refinement focuses on fleshing out one aspect of the overall system. Part of a refinement can also be devoted to addressing problems that were established during the testing of a previous refinement. The system evolves rather than being created in one large effort. Therefore, not only is this process iterative, it is *evolutionary*.

The refinement cycle is performed many times, until all parts of a program are completed and tested. At this point the entire system is tested and the software is released to the user. Usually, the iterations continue until the program is considered to be "good enough" for release. What "good enough" means is different for every situation and depends in part on the user's expectations.

Key Concept

An architectural design establishes the general structure of a system, whereas a detailed design focuses on specific methods and algorithms.

In this model, design activity is divided into multiple steps. An *architectural design* (also called a high-level design) establishes the general structure and responsibilities of system elements; it is done at the beginning of the software development process. The refinement stages include various design issues, including identifying the classes and objects needed in the refinement, as well as the relationships between them. The refinement cycle also includes a *detailed design* stage, which focuses on specific issues such as the methods and algorithms used in a particular class.

Because the design stages are broken up, the interactions between design and implementation are better controlled and focused. Each refinement concentrates on one aspect of a program, such as designing the user interface, and the design steps in the refinement are focused on only that aspect. This reduces the overall level of complexity the design needs to address during each refinement.

By following these smaller design efforts with their implementation, the consequences of design decisions are known at a more appropriate time, soon after the design of that refinement is completed, but before the entire design is completed. In this way, the information uncovered during implementation can affect changes in the design of the current refinement and all future refinements. Also, by defining refinements that are independent of each other, several refinements can be done at the same time by different implementation teams.

Key Concept

Object-oriented programming is particularly well suited for the refinement process because it supports many types of abstraction, such as modularity and encapsulation.

Object-oriented programming is particularly well suited for this approach, since it supports many types of abstraction. These abstraction techniques make it possible for the design and implementation to work hand-in-hand. By using techniques such as encapsulation to isolate what has not yet been specified by a refinement, an implementation for a refinement can be completed and tested.

The following sections describe the details of each step in the refinement cycle.

Establish Refinement Scope

Refinement scope is the set of issues that are addressed in a particular refinement. The scope can be very broad, addressing a large portion of a program, or it might be focused on a particular detail of the program. Typical refinements might include the following:

- Create the user interface for a program.
- Flesh out the algorithm for a portion of a program.
- Create the output results of a program.
- Develop a class library to be used in writing other parts of the program.
- Flesh out a particular requirement or feature of a program.

The scope of a particular refinement is a tradeoff between the resources available and the complexity of the program. If there are many programmers that will be writing and designing a particular program, the scope of one refinement can be larger than if there is only one programmer. In addition, if the area of the refinement is particularly complex, then a refinement might focus on only one small aspect of the system, allowing for many refinement cycles to complete that part of the program.

Key Concept

The scope of a refinement is a tradeoff between the resources available to write the program and the complexity of the program.

Refinements allow a programmer to focus on specific issues without having to embrace the entire system at once. Careful separation of refinement responsibilities can significantly improve the overall development effort. After the scope of the refinement has been established and documented, the design process can begin.

Identifying Classes and Objects

At this stage, our goal is to identify all the known requirements related to the current refinement and associate them with some part of the software. It is usually easier to brainstorm about some of the objects we need, then generalize to determine the classes from which they will be instantiated. Keep in mind that although an object tends to represent nouns, it does not have to represent something tangible. An error is a perfectly good object, even though we can't touch it.

Candidates for objects can come in a variety of categories. The following list shows some categories you should consider when attempting to identify objects in which we are interested. Examples of each category are shown in parentheses.

- physical things (ball, book, car)
- people (student, clerk, author)
- places (room, school, airport)
- containers of things (cash register, bookcase, cabinet)

- occurrences (sale, meeting, accident)
- information stores (catalog, ledger, event log)

Key Concept

One way to identify objects is to consider various object categories; another is to examine the noun phrases of the requirements document.

Some of these categories overlap, which is fine. We're not trying to categorize the objects at this point; we're trying to use categories to uncover the need to represent the object. Any means that we can use to discover them is helpful.

Another technique for identifying objects is to review the requirements document, highlighting the noun phrases. Each of these phrases could indicate an object or class that we may want to represent.

Don't hesitate to write down anything that may be a candidate object. It is better to identify more objects than we need than to forget a crucial one. We can always discard it later.

Once we have the objects identified, we need to consider the classes that are used to define them. Often, the classes for some objects will be obvious. In other cases, however, some thought needs to be put into the best way to represent them. For example, we may initially assume that a `Student` class is sufficient to represent the students in our system, only to discover after some thought that we'd be better off with two separate classes to distinguish graduate students from undergraduate students.

Identifying Relationships

Once a basic set of classes and objects is identified, we should identify the way in which each class relates to the others. There are three primary relationships to consider:

- inheritance (is-a)
- composition (has-a)
- general association (uses)

The inheritance relationship is discussed in detail in Chapter 7. Sometimes a proper inheritance relationship is difficult to see. In particular, consider the common characteristics of certain objects. That may lead to the creation of a new class whose sole purpose is to serve as the parent of the others, gathering common data and methods in one place.

The composition (or aggregation) relationship is discussed in Chapter 5. Some objects contain references to other objects, and therefore one object can be thought of as part of another. Sometimes the cardinality of the relationship should be noted, indicating the numeric relationship between the objects. For example, a car has between one and four passengers.

Most other relationships can be generally described as one object using another in some sense. It is often worth noting such relationships if only to document what the roles of certain objects are. The objects of these classes will often provide services for each other. That is, one will likely invoke one or more methods of the other.

All of these relationships can be described in class diagrams. We've used class diagrams in other chapters only for showing inheritance relationships, but with some modified notation we can indicate the other relationships as well.

The notation we use to draw class diagrams is called the *Unified Modeling Language*, or UML. It is a popular notation for visualizing object-oriented systems. Class diagrams are just one of several diagram types that UML uses to capture and convey software design decisions, but the other diagrams are beyond the scope of this textbook.

Web Bonus

The textbook's Web site contains more information about UML notation.

The class diagram shown in Figure 10.8 illustrates the three types of relationships. Inheritance is shown with the arrowhead pointing to the base class. Composition is shown using a diamond on the end that represents the composite and a straight line at the end that represents the part. A general association is a simple straight line that is usually labeled to give an indication of the type of relationship.

Note that the classes in a class diagram can be divided into three sections. The first section shows the name of the class, the second lists some of the data attributes of the class, and the third lists some methods of the class. These sections may or may not be included at the designer's discretion.

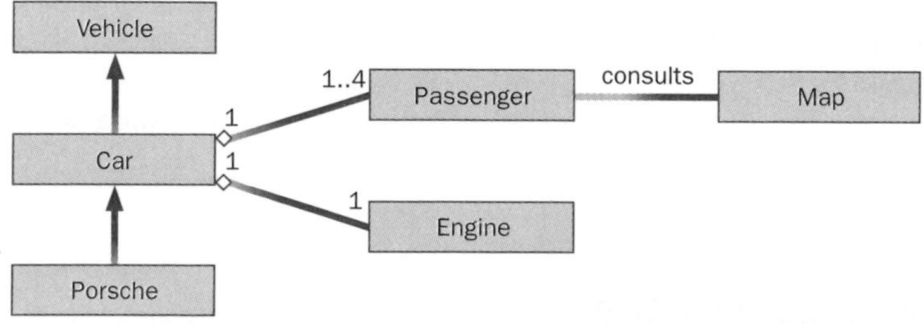

Figure 10.8 A class diagram showing various relationships between classes

Detailed Design

Once we have an understanding of how the program will work with respect to classes and objects, we need to flesh out the smaller details. All of the methods of a class need to be identified. These include all the methods necessary to satisfy the assumptions of any previous refinement phases. Though we are primarily concerned with public methods, we can also identify methods that will be used to support the others.

We must determine the data that each class and object will contain, and the manner by which that data will be modified. That includes the manner in which the data will be given an initial value and any methods that will set the value. It is not imperative that every piece of data be painstakingly identified at this stage, but the key elements should be.

Finally, the algorithms of any methods that perform unusual or crucial tasks should be carefully thought out and documented. Pseudocode is often a good choice for capturing these design decisions.

Implementation

The implementation should be a concrete representation of the design. If we've done a good job with previous steps, the implementation of the classes should come together nicely. Any important decisions should have been made earlier. Of course, this isn't always the case, and some problems will arise. Care should be taken to follow all coding guidelines and to produce readable, clear source code.

If serious problems are discovered during implementation, the impact on the overall system should be considered. The appropriate decision at this point may be to resolve the issue in a future refinement.

Often during a refinement a program will need to use a class, method, or object that is not part of the current refinement. Because we need to test the current refinement, we often use a *stub* object or method as a placeholder. A stub provides enough information for the rest of the refinement code to work. It is replaced in a future refinement with a fully implemented version.

For example, perhaps the system design includes an input routine that will display a dialog box, then accept and validate some user input. The current refinement calls the method, but it has not yet been created. For testing purposes, it can be temporarily replaced with a stub method that simply returns a particular integer value.

We should try to avoid defining our refinements so that such dependencies exist. However, other more important issues sometimes require that we deal with these situations.

Unit and Integration Testing

Until now, we've primarily concentrated on testing an entire program. For smaller programs, that may be sufficient. As our programs grow, it is important to focus on specific pieces, and the nuances involved in making those pieces interact.

Once the classes for a particular refinement are written, they must be tested. Initially, the individual pieces that were created should be tested separately. A test that specifically targets one particular piece of a system, such as a class or method, is called a *unit test*.

Eventually, the classes of the refinement are integrated together, and eventually the entire refinement is integrated with previous refinements. Integrating one piece of code with another will often uncover errors, even if the code seemed to work correctly as individual pieces. Separate testing efforts should be used to specifically explore the interaction between the integrated elements. Such a test is called an *integration test*. Full system testing is really just the ultimate integration test.

10.5 The `PaintBox` Project

Let's examine a larger software development project than any other described in this book. As we explore this program, we will walk through most of the steps described in the evolutionary development model that are described in previous sections of this chapter.

The program will allow the user to create drawings with various shapes and colors. You have probably seen and used similar programs. This type of project encompasses a variety of issues that are commonly found in large-scale software development, and provides a good basis for exploring our development model. We will call this the `PaintBox` project.

Suppose the client provides the following set of initial requirements. The program will:

- Present a graphical user interface that is primarily mouse-driven for all user actions.
- Allow the user to draw lines, ovals, circles, rectangles, and squares.
- Allow the user to change the drawing color.
- Display the current drawing color.
- Allow the user to fill a shape, except for a line, with a color.
- Allow the user to select a shape in order to move it or modify its dimensions or color.
- Allow the user to cut, copy, and paste individual shapes in a drawing.
- Allow the user to save a drawing in a file and load a previously stored drawing from a file for further editing.
- Allow the user to begin a new drawing at any time.
- Perform checks to ensure that the user does not lose unsaved changes to a drawing.

After examining these general requirements for a while, we might sit down with the client and discuss some of the details to ensure that there are no misunderstandings. We might create a new requirements document that gets much more specific about issues.

During these interactions with the client, we might create a sketch, such as the one shown in Figure 10.9, of a user interface for the system. This sketch serves as a basic prototype of the interface, and gives us something to refer to in our discussions with the client. For other systems there may be many such sketches for each screen of the program.

The interface sketch shows a main drawing area where the user will create a drawing. The left edge contains a set of buttons used to select various tools, such as the oval tool to draw an oval or circle, the color tool to change the current drawing color, and a select tool to select a previously drawn shape in order to modify or move it. Two menu headings are shown along the top edge. The File menu will contain operations to begin a new drawing, save a drawing, and exit the program. The Edit menu will contain editing operations such as cut, copy, and paste.

As a result of the discussions with the client, several additional issues are established:

- There is no need to have separate user interactions for a circle or square because they are subsets of ovals and rectangles.

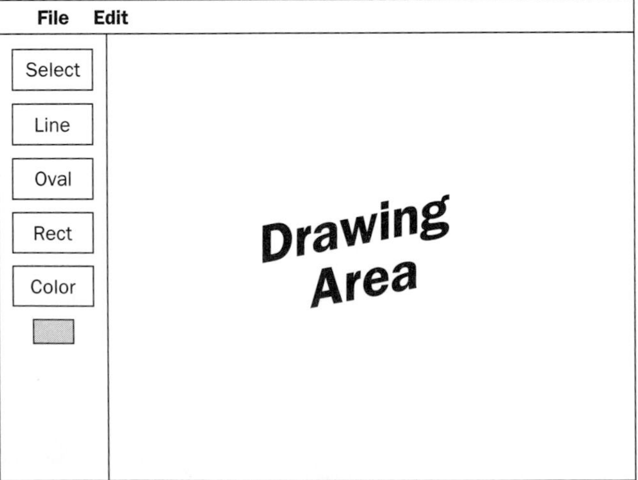

Figure 10.9 A sketch of the user interface for the `PaintBox` program

- The client has decided that the user should also have the ability to create polyline shapes.
- The buttons used to select drawing tools should have icons instead of words.
- The option to save a drawing under a particular name should be provided (the traditional "save as" operation).
- Traditional keyboard shortcuts for operations such as cut, copy, and paste will be included.

After we have clarified the requirements with the client, we can begin to think about some of the elements of the architectural design of the system. For example, many of the classes needed for the user interface can come from the Java standard class library in the AWT and Swing packages. It also seems reasonable that a separate class could be used to represent each shape type and each individually drawn shape should be an instantiation of the appropriate shape class.

The process of defining an architectural design could take a while, and the key is to make the most important and fundamental decisions that will affect the entire system, without skipping ahead to decisions that are better left to individual refinements of the system.

The evolution of the `PaintBox` project could be broken down into the following refinement steps:

- Establish the basic user interface.
- Allow the user to draw basic shapes and change the drawing color.
- Allow the user to select, move, and fill shapes.
- Allow the user to cut, copy, and paste shapes.
- Allow the user to edit the dimensions of shapes.
- Allow the user to save and reload drawings.

These refinements could have been broken down further. For example, one refinement could have been devoted to the ability to draw one particular type of shape. The level of refinement, just like many other decisions when developing a software system, is a judgment call. The developer must decide what is best in any particular situation.

The user interface refinement seems like a logical first step because all other activity relies on it. Most of the classes used for the interface will come from predefined libraries. We will use Swing technology whenever reasonable. For example, we can use a `JPanel` for the overall interface space, as well as separate `JPanel` objects to organize the button tools and the drawing area. The `JButton` class will serve well for the buttons, and classes such as `JMenuBar` and `JMenuItem` will serve for the menus.

The detailed design and implementation for the interface refinement might develop similarly to other graphical projects we've seen in this book. We can create listener objects and methods as appropriate, but not concern ourselves with their inner workings at this time. We can modify the details of the user interface until it appears just the way we'd like it.

At the end of the interface refinement, we are left with a completely implemented program that only presents the user interface. The buttons do not do anything when pushed, and the menu items do nothing when selected. We have no way of creating a drawing yet. What we do have, however, is a complete entity that has been debugged and tested to the level of this refinement. We may show it to the client at this point and get further input. Any changes that result from these discussions can be incorporated into future refinements.

For space reasons, the code for the various `PaintBox` refinements are not presented in the text. The fully implemented interface refinement, as well as the next one we will discuss (drawing basic shapes), can be downloaded from the book's web site. The other refinements are left as projects.

Web Bonus

The program code for the `PaintBox` project can be obtained from the textbook's web site.

The next refinement to address is almost certainly the ability to draw basic shapes, because all other operations use drawn shapes in one way or another. In this refinement we can therefore focus on putting most of the processing power behind the buttons that draw shapes and specify color.

Most of the objects and classes that we will use in this refinement are not predefined, as they were in the interface refinement. We need to come up with a way to represent the shapes. We can consider using the `Rectangle` class from the Java standard library, but on further investigation we realize that its role is not really consistent with our goals.

Let's begin by imagining one class per shape type: `Line`, `Oval`, `Rect`, and `Poly`. Remember that circles and squares will just be specific instances of the `Oval` and `Rect` classes. We can envision that each shape class will have a `draw` method that knows how to draw that kind of shape on the screen. Then we consider the kind of information that each one needs to store to be able to

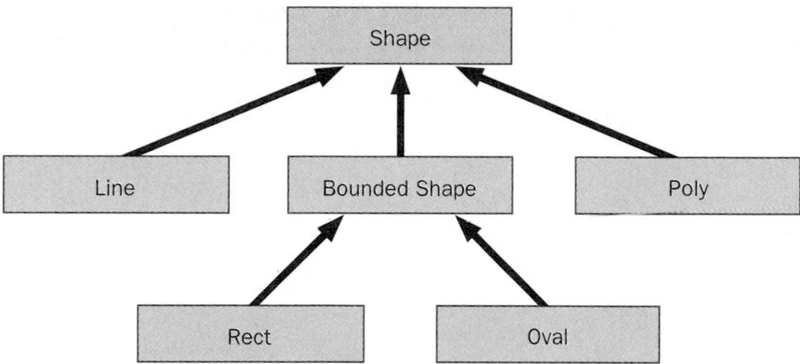

Figure 10.10 The inheritance hierarchy of the shape classes in the `PaintBox` program

draw itself. That might lead to the realization that `Oval` and `Rect` objects have some common characteristics, such as their need to be defined by a bounded rectangle, which is quite different from the information needed for lines and polylines. After some consideration, we could end up with a tentative class hierarchy as shown in Figure 10.10.

The `Shape` class can serve as the ancestor of all drawn shapes, though we never intend to actually instantiate it. Therefore, it should probably be an `abstract` class. In fact, if we define an `abstract` method called `draw` in `Shape` that all of its children implement, we could capitalize on polymorphism to perform the drawing of the shapes in the drawing area. The `BoundedShape` class represents the parent of any shape that is defined by a bounding rectangle. It will also be abstract.

Selecting a current color can be relegated to the `ColorChooser` component provided by the Swing package. The color button will bring up the `ColorChooser` dialog box and respond accordingly to the user's selection.

Multiple shapes will accumulate on the drawing surface. We could define a class to serve as a collection of the drawn shape objects. It could use a Vector to keep track of the list of shapes. Whenever the drawing area needs to be refreshed, we can iterate through the vector of shapes and draw each one in turn.

Figure 10.11 shows the `PaintBox` program after the interface and shapes refinements have been completed. Once again, we could visit the client to see how the evolution of the system meets with their satisfaction.

The refinements of the `PaintBox` program continue until all requirement issues and problems have been addressed. This type of evolutionary development is crucial for medium and large-scale development efforts.

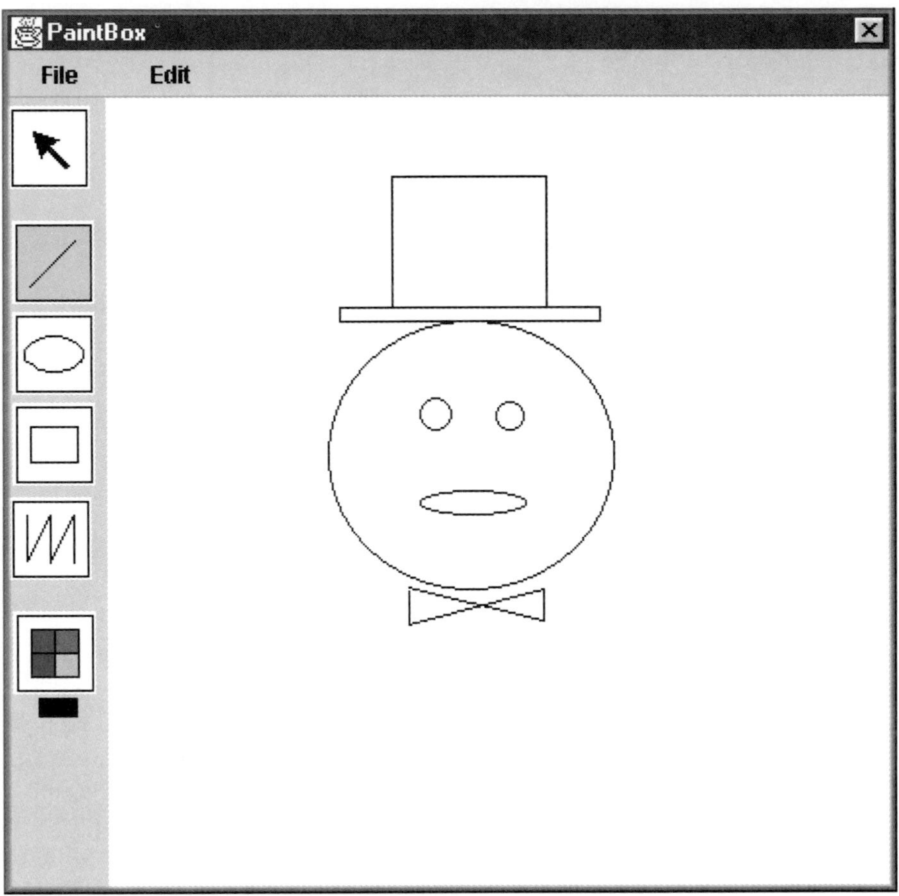

Figure 10.11 The `PaintBox` program after the interface and shapes refinements

Summary of Key Concepts

- Maintaining software is the process of modifying a program in order to enhance it or fix problems.
- The maintainers of a program are often not the program's original developers, so maintainers must be able to understand a program that they didn't design.
- Rushing through the development stage often leads to significant increases in the effort expended during maintenance.
- A working program is not necessarily a good program. Our goal should be to develop software that minimizes the efforts to create and maintain a program.
- A program produced using the build-and-fix approach is the result of ad hoc, reckless activities.
- A prototype can be used to explore the feasibility of a decision, instead of proceeding on an assumption that may later prove unwise.
- A design or code walkthrough is a meeting in which several people review and critique a software design or implementation.
- The goal of testing is to find errors; therefore, a good test is one that uncovers a problem in a program.
- Because programs operate on a large number of possible inputs, it is not feasible to create test cases for all possible input or user actions.
- A refinement focuses on a single aspect of a program, such as the user interface or a particular algorithm.
- An architectural design establishes the general structure of a system, whereas a detailed design focuses on specific methods and algorithms.
- Object-oriented programming is particularly well suited for the refinement process because it supports many types of abstraction, such as modularity and encapsulation.
- The scope of a refinement is a tradeoff between the resources available to write the program and the complexity of the program.
- One way to identify objects is to consider various object categories; another is to examine the noun phrases of the requirements document.

▶ Self-Review Questions

10.1 What is the relationship between development effort and maintenance effort?

10.2 Describe the build-and-fix approach to software development.

10.3 What is the main problem with the waterfall model?

10.4 What is a prototype?

10.5 What is a code walkthrough?

10.6 How is white-box testing different from black-box testing?

10.7 What is evolutionary software development?

10.8 What is a program refinement?

▶ Exercises

10.1 Consider the development of a software program to perform library book management. The system should be able to catalog all books, record books being borrowed and returned, and associated fines related to books returned late.

a. Identify several possible refinements, such as book borrowing, for the system.

b. Identify several objects and classes for the book-borrowing refinement.

c. Identify possible relationships between classes and objects in the book-borrowing refinement.

d. Draw a class diagram showing a class hierarchy and use relationships.

10.2 Consider the development of a software program to manage a household budget. The system should be able to:

a. Identify several possible refinements, such as the user interface, for the system.

b. Identify several objects and classes for the user-interface refinement.

c. Identify possible relationships between classes and objects in the user-interface refinement.

d. Draw a class diagram showing a class hierarchy and use relationships.

10.3 Consider the development of a software program to simulate an airport. The system should be able to simulate takeoffs and landings of planes on different runways, simulate an air traffic controller's screen, and allow an operator to control the takeoff, landing, and flying attributes of planes (such as course and speed).

a. Identify several possible refinements, such as plane simulation, for the system.

b. Identify several objects and classes for the plane-simulation refinement.

c. Identify possible relationships between classes and objects in the plane-simulation refinement.

d. Draw a class diagram showing a class hierarchy and use relationships.

Programming Projects

10.1 Develop the `PaintBox` refinement to select, move, and fill a previously drawn shape. The move should be accomplished using a mouse drag that shows an outline of the shape as it moves to a new position.

10.2 Develop the `PaintBox` refinement to allow the user to cut, copy, and paste shapes. These operations should be available through the Edit menu as well as by using the traditional keyboard shortcuts. Pasted shapes should appear in the middle of the drawing space.

10.3 Develop the `PaintBox` refinement to edit the dimensions of a selected shape. The currently selected shape should display box handles that assist in the modification of the shape.

10.4 Develop the `PaintBox` refinement to allow the user to save the current drawing, load a previously saved drawing, and save the current drawing under a particular file name. These operations should be available through the File menu.

Answers to Self-Review Questions

10.1 Much more effort is traditionally put into maintenance tasks than development. Small, fundamental improvements in development efforts can greatly reduce the overall maintenance effort.

10.2 The build-and-fix approach is the ad hoc process of creating software without attention to important efforts such as requirements and design, then modifying the software until it reaches some minimal level of acceptance. It is not really a development methodology at all.

10.3 The traditional waterfall model assumes that development activities fundamentally progress in a linear fashion. The truth is that medium and large-scale systems cannot be developed that way, and should be created using a model that allows the system to evolve in stages.

10.4 A prototype is a program, drawing, or mockup of some kind that allows the developer to explore an idea before committing to it in the developing system.

10.5 A code walkthrough is a meeting in which developers carefully go over parts of a software system to discuss its implementation and search for problems.

10.6 White-box testing focuses on the internal details of a module (such as a method) to ensure that the logic of the module is thoroughly tested. Black-box testing focuses on different categories of input to see its effect on the output.

10.7 Evolutionary software development is a controlled iterative process that creates a program as a series of well-defined refinements. Evolutionary development acknowledges our limited ability to plan all details of the program design and implementation initially.

10.8 Each refinement in an iterative development process focuses on one particular aspect of a software system. For example, one refinement may be to develop the user interface. A refinement allows a programmer to target a particular task while keeping the overall architectural design in mind.

11 Recursion

Recursion is a powerful programming technique that provides elegant solutions to certain problems. This chapter serves as an introduction to recursive processing. It contains an explanation of the basic concept underlying recursion, then explores the use of recursion in programming. Several specific problems are solved using recursion, demonstrating its versatility, simplicity, and elegance.

Chapter Objectives

- Explain the underlying concepts of recursion.
- Examine recursive methods and unravel their processing steps.
- Define infinite recursion and discuss the ways to avoid it.
- Explain when recursion should be used and when it should not.
- Demonstrate the use of recursion to solve problems.

11.1 Recursive Thinking

Key Concept

Recursion is a programming technique in which a method calls itself. The key to being able to program recursively is to be able to think recursively.

We've seen many times in previous examples that one method can call another method to accomplish a goal. What we haven't seen yet, however, is that a method can call itself. *Recursion* is a programming technique in which a method calls itself in order to fulfill its purpose. But before we get into the details of how we use recursion in a program, we need to explore the general concept of recursion first. The ability to think recursively is essential to being able to use recursion as a programming technique.

In general, recursion is the process of defining something in terms of itself. For example, consider the following definition of the word decoration:

```
decoration: any ornament or adornment used to decorate
            something
```

The word decorate is used to define the word decoration. You may recall your grade school teacher telling you to avoid such recursive definitions when explaining the meaning of the word. However, in many situations, recursion is a simple and appropriate way to express an idea or definition. For example, suppose we wanted to formally define a list of one or more numbers, separated by commas. Such a list can be defined recursively as either a number or as a number followed by a comma followed by a list. This definition can be expressed as follows:

```
A List is a:      number
or a:             number  comma  List
```

This recursive definition of `List` defines each of the following lists of numbers:

```
24, 88, 40, 37
96, 43
14, 64, 21, 69, 32, 93, 47, 81, 28, 45, 81, 52, 69
70
```

No matter how long a list is, the recursive definition describes it. A list of one element, such as in the last example, never follows the recursive part of the definition (the part which refers to itself). For any list longer than one element, the recursive part is followed as many times as necessary, until the last element is reached. Figure 11.1 shows how one particular list of numbers corresponds to the recursive definition of `List`.

```
LIST:   number comma LIST

          24     ,   88, 40, 37

                     number comma LIST

                       88     ,  40, 37

                                 number comma LIST

                                 40       ,   37

                                              number

                                                37
```

Figure 11.1 Tracing the recursive definition of a *List*

Infinite Recursion

Note that the definition of *List* contains one option that is recursive, and one option that is not. The part of the definition that is not recursive is called the *base case.* If all options had a recursive element, then the recursion would never end. For example, if the definition of a list was simply "a number followed by a comma followed by a list," then no list could ever end. This problem is called *infinite recursion.* It is similar to an infinite loop, except that the "loop" occurs in the definition itself.

Key Concept

Any recursive definition must have a nonrecursive part, called the base case, which permits the recursion to eventually end.

As in the infinite loop problem, a programmer must be careful to design algorithms so that they avoid infinite recursion. Any recursive definition must have a base case that does not result in following a recursive option. The base case of the *List* definition is a single number that is not followed by a comma. In other words, when the last number in the list is reached, the base case option terminates the recursive path.

Recursion in Math

Mathematical formulas are often expressed recursively. For example, the definition of $N!$ (pronounced N factorial) is defined for any positive integer N as the product of all integers between 1 and N inclusive. Therefore:

```
3!  =  3*2*1  =  6
```

and

```
5!  =  5*4*3*2*1  =  120.
```

The definition of $N!$ can be expressed recursively as:

```
1! = 1
N! = N * (N-1)!
```

Key Concept

Mathematical problems and formulas are often expressed recursively.

The base case of this definition is 1!, which is defined to be 1. All other values of $N!$ are defined recursively as N times the value $(N - 1)!$. Therefore 50! is equal to 50 $*$ 49!. And 49! is equal to 49 $*$ 48!. And 48! is equal to 48 $*$ 47!. This process continues until you get to the base case of 1. Because $N!$ is defined for only positive integers, this definition is complete and will always conclude with the base case.

The next section describes how recursion is accomplished in programs.

11.2 Recursive Programming

Let's use a simple mathematical operation to demonstrate the concepts of recursive programming. Consider the process of summing the values between 1 and N inclusive, where N is any positive integer. The sum of the values from 1 to N can be expressed as N plus the sum of the other $N - 1$ values. That sum can be expressed similarly, and so on, as shown in Figure 11.2.

For example, the sum of the values between 1 and 20 is equal to 20 plus the sum of the values between 1 and 19. Continuing this idea, the sum of the values between 1 and 19 is equal to 19 plus the sum of the values between 1 and 18. This may sound like a funny way to think about this problem, but it is a simple example that can be used to demonstrate how recursion is programmed.

In Java, as in many other programming languages, a method can call itself. Each call to the method creates a new environment in which to work.

$$\begin{aligned}\sum_{i=1}^{N} i &= N + \sum_{i=1}^{N-1} i = N + N-1 + \sum_{i=1}^{N-2} i \\ &= N + N-1 + N-2 + \sum_{i=1}^{N-3} i \\ &\;\;\vdots \\ &= N + N-1 + N-2 + \cdots + 2 + 1\end{aligned}$$

Figure 11.2 The sum of the numbers 1 through N, defined recursively

All local variables and parameters are newly defined with their own unique data space every time the method is called. Each parameter is given an initial value based on the new call. Each time a method terminates, processing returns to the method that called it (which may be an earlier invocation of the same method). These rules are no different than those governing any "regular" method invocation.

Key Concept

Each recursive call to a method creates new local variables and parameters.

A recursive solution to the summation problem is defined by the following recursive method called sum:

```
// This method returns the sum of 1 to N
public int sum (int N)
{
   int result;
   if (N == 1)
      result = 1;
   else
      result = N + sum (N-1);
   return result;
}
```

Note that this method essentially embodies our recursive definition that the sum of the numbers between 1 and N is equal to N plus the sum of the numbers between 1 and $N - 1$. The call to sum is recursive because sum calls itself. The parameter passed to sum is decremented each time sum is called, until it reaches the base case of 1.

Suppose the main method calls sum, passing it an initial value of 1, which is stored in the parameter N. Since N is equal to 1, the result of 1 is returned to main and no recursion occurs.

Now let's trace the execution of the sum method when it is passed an initial value of 2. Since N does not equal 1, sum is called again with an argument of N-1, or 1. This is a new call to the method sum, with a new parameter N and a new local variable result. Since this N is equal to 1 in this invocation, the result of 1 is returned without further recursive calls. Control returns to the first version of sum that was invoked. The return value of 1 is added to the initial value of N in that call to sum, which is 2. Therefore, result is assigned the value 3, which is returned to the main method. The method called from main correctly calculates the sum of the integers from 1 to 2, and returns the result of 3.

Key Concept

A careful trace of recursive processing can provide insight into the way it is used to solve a problem.

The base case in the summation example is when N equals 1, at which point no further recursive calls are made. The recursion begins to fold back into the earlier versions of the sum method, returning the appropriate value each time. Each return value contributes to the computation of the sum at the

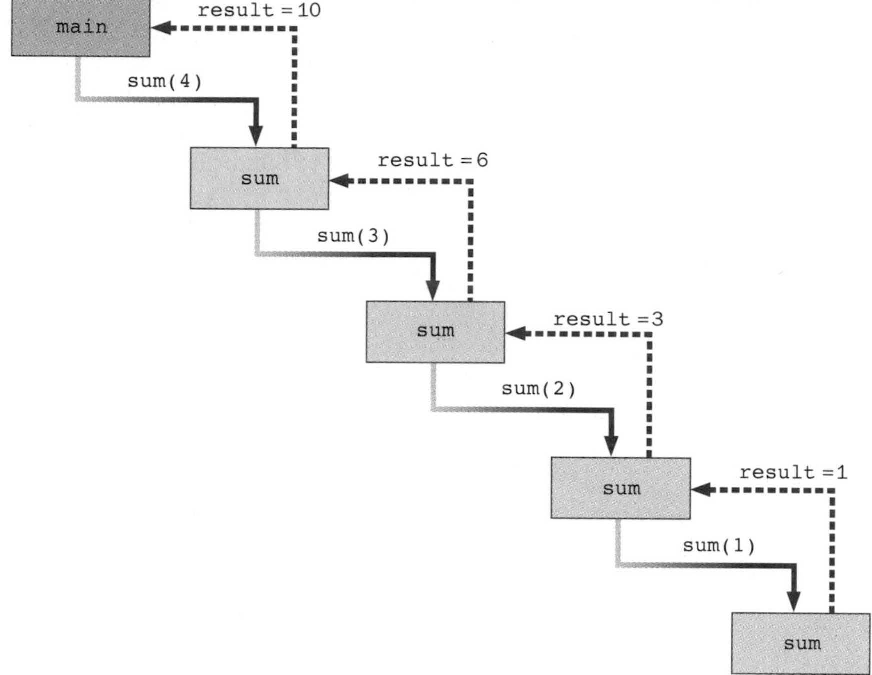

Figure 11.3 Recursive calls to the sum method

higher level. Without the base case, infinite recursion would result. Each call to a method requires additional memory space, therefore infinite recursion often results in a run-time error indicating that memory has been exhausted.

Trace the `sum` function with different initial values of `N` until this processing becomes familiar. Figure 11.3 illustrates the recursive calls when `main` invokes `sum` to determine the sum of the integers from 1 to 4. Each box represents a copy of the method as it is invoked. Invocations are shown as solid lines, and returns as dotted lines. The return value `result` is shown at each step. The recursive path is followed completely until the base case is reached; then the calls begin to return their result up through the chain.

Recursion vs. Iteration

Of course, there is a nonrecursive solution to the summation problem we just explored. One way to compute the sum of the numbers between 1 and N inclusive in an iterative manner is as follows:

```
sum = 0;
for (int number = 1; number <= N; number++)
    sum += number;
```

This solution is certainly more straightforward than the recursive version. We used the summation problem to demonstrate recursion because it is simple, not because you would use recursion to solve it under normal conditions. Recursion has the overhead of multiple method invocations and, in this case, presents a more complicated solution than its iterative counterpart.

Key Concept

Recursion is the most elegant and appropriate way to solve some problems, but for others it is less intuitive than an iterative solution.

A programmer must decide when to use recursion and when not to use it. Determining which approach is best depends on the problem being solved. All problems can be solved in an iterative manner, but in some cases the iterative version is much more complicated. Recursion, for some problems, allows us to create relatively short, elegant solutions.

Direct vs. Indirect Recursion

Direct recursion occurs when a method invokes itself, such as when `sum` calls `sum`. *Indirect recursion* occurs when a method invokes another method, eventually resulting in the original method being invoked again. For example, if method `m1` invokes method `m2`, and `m2` invokes method `m1`, we can say that `m1` is indirectly recursive. The amount of indirection could be several levels deep, as when `m1` invokes `m2`, which invokes `m3`, which invokes `m4`, which invokes `m1`. Figure 11.4 depicts a situation with indirect recursion. Method invocations are shown with solid lines, and returns are shown with dotted lines. The entire invocation path is followed, then the recursion unravels following the return path.

Indirect recursion requires all of the same attention to base cases that direct recursion requires. Furthermore, indirect recursion can be more difficult to trace because of the intervening method calls. Therefore, extra care is warranted when designing or evaluating indirectly recursive methods. Ensure that the indirection is truly necessary and clearly explained in documentation.

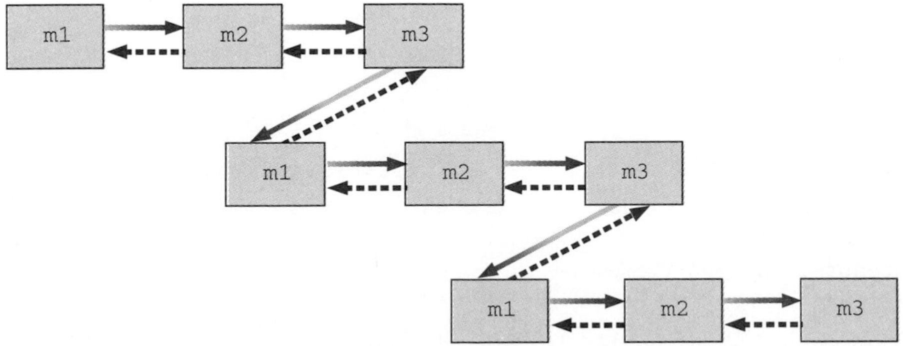

Figure 11.4 Indirect recursion

11.3 Using Recursion

Each of the following sections describes a particular recursive problem. For each one, we examine exactly how recursion plays a role in the solution and how the base case is used to terminate the recursion. Consider how complicated a nonrecursive solution for each problem would be.

Traversing a Maze

Solving a maze involves a great deal of trial and error: following a path, backtracking when you cannot go farther, and trying other options. Such activities often are handled nicely using recursion. The program shown in Listing 11.1 creates a `Maze` object and attempts to traverse it.

The `Maze` class, shown in Listing 11.2, uses a two-dimensional array of integers to represent the maze. Initially, a 1 indicates a clear path, and a 0 indicates a blocked path. As the maze is solved, these array elements are changed to other values to indicate attempted and successful paths through the maze.

The only valid moves through the maze are in the four primary directions: up, down, right, and left. No diagonal moves are allowed. The goal is to start in the upper-left corner of the maze (0, 0) and find a path that reaches the bottom-right corner. In this example, the maze is 8 rows by 13 columns, although the code is designed to handle a maze of any size.

The recursive method in the `Maze` class is called `traverse`. It returns a boolean value that indicates whether a solution was found. First the method determines if a move to that row and column is valid. A move is considered valid if it stays within the grid boundary and if the grid contains a 1 in that location, indicating that a move in that direction is not blocked. The initial call to `traverse` passes in the upper-left location (0, 0).

If the move is valid, the grid entry is changed from a 1 to a 3, marking this location as visited so that later we don't retrace our steps. Then the `traverse` method determines if the maze has been completed by having

Listing 11.1

```
//********************************************************************
//  MazeSearch.java       Author: Lewis and Loftus
//
//  Demonstrates recursion.
//********************************************************************
```

Listing 11.1 (*continued*)

```
import Maze;

public class MazeSearch
{
   //-----------------------------------------------------------------
   //  Creates a new maze, prints its original form, attempts to
   //  solve it, and prints out its final form.
   //-----------------------------------------------------------------
   public static void main (String[] args)
   {
      Maze labyrinth = new Maze();

      System.out.println (labyrinth);

      if (labyrinth.traverse (0, 0))
         System.out.println ("The maze was successfully traversed!");
      else
         System.out.println ("There is no possible path.");

      System.out.println (labyrinth);
   }
}
```

```
1110110001111
1011101111001
0000101010100
1110111010111
1010000111001
1011111101111
1000000000000
1111111111111

The maze was successfully traversed!

7770110001111
3077707771001
0000707070300
7770777070333
7070000773003
7077777703333
7000000000000
7777777777777
```

Listing 11.2

```
//********************************************************************
//  Maze.java       Author: Lewis and Loftus
//
//  Represents a maze of characters. The goal is to get from the
//  top left corner to the bottom right, following a path of 1s.
//********************************************************************

public class Maze
{
   private final int TRIED = 3;
   private final int PATH = 7;

   private int[][] grid = { {1,1,1,0,1,1,0,0,0,1,1,1,1},
                            {1,0,1,1,1,0,1,1,1,1,0,0,1},
                            {0,0,0,0,1,0,1,0,1,0,1,0,0},
                            {1,1,1,0,1,1,1,0,1,0,1,1,1},
                            {1,0,1,0,0,0,0,1,1,1,0,0,1},
                            {1,0,1,1,1,1,1,1,0,1,1,1,1},
                            {1,0,0,0,0,0,0,0,0,0,0,0,0},
                            {1,1,1,1,1,1,1,1,1,1,1,1,1} };

   //-----------------------------------------------------------------
   //  Attempts to recursively traverse the maze.  It inserts special
   //  characters indicating locations that have been tried and that
   //  eventually become part of the solution.
   //-----------------------------------------------------------------
   public boolean traverse (int row, int column)
   {
      boolean done = false;

      if (valid (row, column))
      {
         grid[row][column] = TRIED;  // this cell has been tried

         if (row == grid.length-1 && column == grid[0].length-1)
            done = true;  // the maze is solved
         else
```

Listing 11.2 ***(continued)***

```
      {
         done = traverse (row+1, column);     // down
         if (!done)
            done = traverse (row, column+1);  // right
         if (!done)
            done = traverse (row-1, column);  // up
         if (!done)
            done = traverse (row, column-1);  // left
      }

      if (done)  // this location is part of the final path
         grid[row][column] = PATH;
   }

   return done;
}

//-----------------------------------------------------------------
//  Determines if a specific location is valid.
//-----------------------------------------------------------------
private boolean valid (int row, int column)
{
   boolean result = false;

   // Check if cell is in the bounds of the matrix
   if (row >= 0 && row < grid.length &&
       column >= 0 && column < grid[row].length)

      //  Check if cell is not blocked and not previously tried
      if (grid[row][column] == 1)
         result = true;

   return result;
}
```

Listing 11.2 (*continued*)

```
   //-----------------------------------------------------------------
   //  Returns the maze as a string.
   //-----------------------------------------------------------------
   public String toString ()
   {
      String result = "\n";

      for (int row=0; row < grid.length; row++)
      {
         for (int column=0; column < grid[row].length; column++)
            result += grid[row][column] + "";
         result += "\n";
      }

      return result;
   }
}
```

reached the bottom-right location. Therefore, there are actually three possibilities of the base case for this problem that will terminate a recursive path:

- An invalid move because the move is out of bounds
- An invalid move because the move has been tried before
- A move that arrives at the final location

If the current location is not the bottom-right corner, we search for a solution in each of the primary directions, if necessary. First, we look down by recursively calling the `traverse` method and passing in the new location. The logic of the `traverse` method starts all over again using this new position. A solution is either ultimately found by starting down from the current location, or it's not found. If it's not found, we try moving right. If that fails, we try up. Finally, if no other direction has yielded a correct path, we try left. If no direction from the current location yields a correct solution, then there is no path from this location, and `traverse` returns false.

If a solution was found from the current location, then the grid entry is changed to a 7. Therefore, when the final maze is printed, the zeros still indicate a blocked path, a 1 indicates an open path that was never tried, a 3 indicates a path that was tried but failed to yield a correct solution, and a 7 indicates a part of the final solution of the maze.

Note that there are several opportunities for recursion in each call to the `traverse` method. Any or all of them might be followed, depending on the maze configuration. Carefully trace the execution of this code while following the maze array to see how the recursion solves the problem.

The Towers of Hanoi

The *Towers of Hanoi* puzzle was invented in the 1880s by Edouard Lucas, a French mathematician. It has become a favorite among computer scientists because its solution is an excellent demonstration of recursive elegance.

The puzzle is made up of three upright pegs and a set of disks with holes in the middle so that they slide onto the pegs. Each disk has a different diameter. Initially, all of the disks are stacked on one peg in order of size such that the largest disk is on the bottom, as shown in Figure 11.5.

The goal of the puzzle is to move all of the disks from their original (first) peg to the destination (third) peg. We can use the "extra" peg as a temporary place to put disks, but we must obey the following two rules:

- We can only move one disk at a time.
- We cannot move a larger disk on top of a smaller disk.

These rules imply that we must move smaller disks "out of the way" in order to move a larger disk from one peg to another. Figure 11.6 shows the step-by-step solution for the Towers of Hanoi puzzle using three disks. In order to ultimately move all three disks from the first peg to the third peg, we first have to get to the point where the smaller two disks are out of the way on the second peg so that the largest disk can be moved from the first peg to the third peg.

The first three moves shown in Figure 11.6 can be thought of as "moving the smaller disks out of the way." The fourth move puts the largest disk in its final place. Then the last three moves put the smaller disks to their final place on top of the largest one.

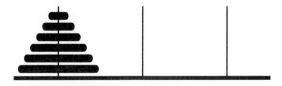

Figure 11.5 The Towers of Hanoi puzzle

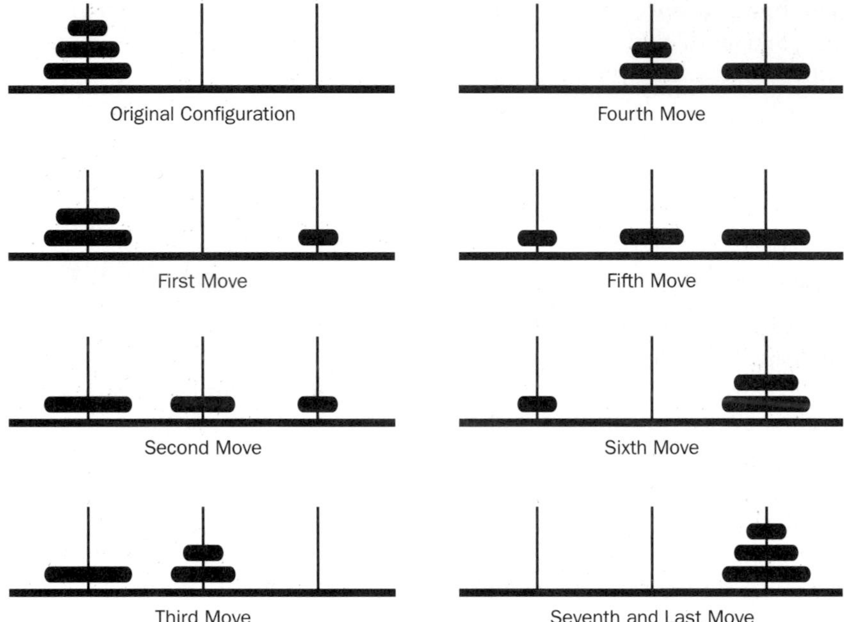

Figure 11.6 A solution to the three-disk Towers of Hanoi puzzle

Let's use this idea to form a general strategy. To move a stack of N disks from the original peg to the destination peg:

- Move the topmost $N - 1$ disks from the original peg to the extra peg.
- Move the largest disk from the original peg to the destination peg.
- Move the $N - 1$ disks from the extra peg to the destination peg.

This strategy lends itself to a recursive solution. The step to move the $N - 1$ disks out of the way is the same problem all over again: moving a stack of disks. For this subtask, though, there is one less disk, and our destination peg is what we were originally calling the extra peg. An analogous situation occurs after we've moved the largest disk, and we have to move the original $N - 1$ disks again.

The base case for this problem occurs when we want to move a "stack" that consists of only one disk. That step can be accomplished directly without recursion.

The program in Listing 11.3 creates a `TowersOfHanoi` object and invokes its `solve` method. The output is a step-by-step list of instructions that describe how the disks should be moved to solve the puzzle. This example uses four disks, which is specified by a parameter to the `TowersOfHanoi` constructor.

Listing 11.3

```
//********************************************************************
//  SolveTowers.java       Author: Lewis and Loftus
//
//  Demonstrates recursion.
//********************************************************************

import TowersOfHanoi;

public class SolveTowers
{
   //-----------------------------------------------------------------
   //  Creates a TowersOfHanoi puzzle and solves it.
   //-----------------------------------------------------------------
   public static void main (String[] args)
   {
      TowersOfHanoi towers = new TowersOfHanoi (4);

      towers.solve();
   }
}
```

```
Move one disk from 1 to 2
Move one disk from 1 to 3
Move one disk from 2 to 3
Move one disk from 1 to 2
Move one disk from 3 to 1
Move one disk from 3 to 2
Move one disk from 1 to 2
Move one disk from 1 to 3
Move one disk from 2 to 3
Move one disk from 2 to 1
Move one disk from 3 to 1
Move one disk from 2 to 3
Move one disk from 1 to 2
Move one disk from 1 to 3
Move one disk from 2 to 3
```

The `TowersOfHanoi` class, shown in Listing 11.4, uses the `solve` method to make an initial call to `moveTower`, the recursive method. The initial call indicates that all of the disks should be moved from peg 1 to peg 3, using peg 2 as the extra position.

The `moveTower` method first considers the base case (a "stack" of one disk). When that occurs, it calls the `moveOneDisk` method that prints a single line describing that particular move. If the stack contains more than one disk, we call `moveTower` again to get the $N - 1$ disks out of the way, then move the largest disk, then move the $N - 1$ disks to their final destination with yet another call to `moveTower`.

Note that the parameters to `moveTower` describing the pegs are switched around as needed to move the partial stacks. This code follows our general

Listing 11.4

```
//********************************************************************
//  TowersOfHanoi.java       Author: Lewis and Loftus
//
//  Represents the classic Towers of Hanoi puzzle.
//********************************************************************

public class TowersOfHanoi
{
   private int totalDisks;

   //-----------------------------------------------------------------
   //  Sets up the puzzle with the specified number of disks.
   //-----------------------------------------------------------------
   public TowersOfHanoi (int disks)
   {
      totalDisks = disks;
   }

   //-----------------------------------------------------------------
   //  Performs the initial call to moveTower to solve the puzzle.
   //-----------------------------------------------------------------
   public void solve ()
   {
      moveTower (totalDisks, 1, 3, 2);
   }
```

Listing 11.4 ***(continued)***

```
   //-----------------------------------------------------------------
   //  Moves the specified number of disks from one tower to another
   //  by moving a subtower of n-1 disks out of the way, moving one
   //  disk, then moving the subtower back. Base case of 1 disk.
   //-----------------------------------------------------------------
   private void moveTower (int numDisks, int start, int end, int temp)
   {
      if (numDisks == 1)
         moveOneDisk (start, end);
      else
      {
         moveTower (numDisks-1, start, temp, end);
         moveOneDisk (start, end);
         moveTower (numDisks-1, temp, end, start);
      }
   }

   //-----------------------------------------------------------------
   //  Prints instructions to move one disk from the specified start
   //  tower to the specified end tower.
   //-----------------------------------------------------------------
   private void moveOneDisk (int start, int end)
   {
      System.out.println ("Move one disk from " + start + " to " +
                          end);
   }
}
```

strategy, and uses the `moveTower` method to move all partial stacks. Trace the code carefully for a stack of three disks to understand the processing. Compare the processing steps to Figure 11.6.

Contrary to its short and elegant implementation, the solution to the Towers of Hanoi puzzle is terribly inefficient. To solve the puzzle with a stack of N disks, we have to make $2^N - 1$ individual disk moves. This situation is an example of *exponential complexity*. As the number of disks increases, the number of required moves increases exponentially.

Key Concept

The Towers of Hanoi solution has exponential complexity, which is very inefficient. Yet the implementation of the solution is incredibly short and elegant.

Legend has it that priests of Brahma are working on this puzzle in a temple at the center of the world. They are using 64 gold disks, moving them between pegs of pure diamond. The downside is that when the priests finish the puzzle, the world will end. The upside is that even if they move one disk every second of every day, it will take them over 584 billion years to complete it. That's with a puzzle of only 64 disks! It is certainly an indication of just how inefficient exponential algorithm complexity is.

11.4 Recursion in Graphics

The concept of recursion has several uses in the world of graphics and images. The following section explores some graphics-based recursion examples.

Mirrored Pictures

Carefully examine the screen shot for the `MirroredPictures` applet, shown in Listing 11.5. There are actually three unique images among the menagerie. The entire area is divided into four equal quadrants. A picture of the world (with a circle indicating the Himalayan mountain region) is shown in the bottom-right quadrant. The bottom-left quadrant contains a picture of Mt. Everest. In the top-right quadrant is a picture of a mountain goat.

The interesting part of the picture is the top-left quadrant. It contains a copy of the entire collage, including itself. In this smaller version you can see the three simple pictures in their three quadrants. And again, in the top-left corner, the picture is repeated (including itself). This repetition continues for several levels. It is similar to the effect you can create when looking at a mirror in the reflection of another mirror.

This visual effect is created quite easily using recursion. The applet's `init` method initially loads the three images. Then the `paint` method invokes the `drawPictures` method, which accepts a parameter that defines the size of the area in which pictures are displayed. It draws the three images using the `drawImage` method, with parameters that scale the picture to the right size and location. Then the `drawPictures` method is called recursively to draw the upper-left quadrant.

On each invocation, if the drawing area is large enough, the `drawPictures` method is invoked again, using a smaller drawing area. Eventually, the drawing area becomes so small that the recursive call is not performed. Note that `drawPictures` assumes the origin <0, 0> coordinate as the relative location of the new images, no matter what their size is.

The base case of the recursion in this problem specifies a minimum size for the drawing area. Because the size is decreased each time, eventually the base

Listing 11.5

```
//********************************************************************
//  MirroredPictures.java       Author: Lewis and Loftus
//
//  Demonstrates the use of recursion.
//********************************************************************

import java.applet.Applet;
import java.awt.*;

public class MirroredPictures extends Applet
{
   private final int APPLET_WIDTH = 320;
   private final int APPLET_HEIGHT = 320;
   private final int MIN = 20;  // smallest picture size

   private Image world, everest, goat;

   //-----------------------------------------------------------------
   //  Loads the images.
   //-----------------------------------------------------------------
   public void init()
   {
      world = getImage (getDocumentBase(), "world.gif");
      everest = getImage (getDocumentBase(), "everest.gif");
      goat = getImage (getDocumentBase(), "goat.gif");

      setSize (APPLET_WIDTH, APPLET_HEIGHT);
   }

   //-----------------------------------------------------------------
   //  Draws the three images, then calls itself recursively.
   //-----------------------------------------------------------------
   public void drawPictures (int size, Graphics page)
   {
      page.drawImage (everest, 0, size/2, size/2, size/2, this);
      page.drawImage (goat, size/2, 0, size/2, size/2, this);
      page.drawImage (world, size/2, size/2, size/2, size/2, this);

      if (size > MIN)
         drawPictures (size/2, page);
   }
```

Listing 11.5 (*continued*)

```
   //-----------------------------------------------------------------
   //  Performs the initial call to the drawPictures method.
   //-----------------------------------------------------------------
   public void paint (Graphics page)
   {
      drawPictures (APPLET_WIDTH, page);
   }
}
```

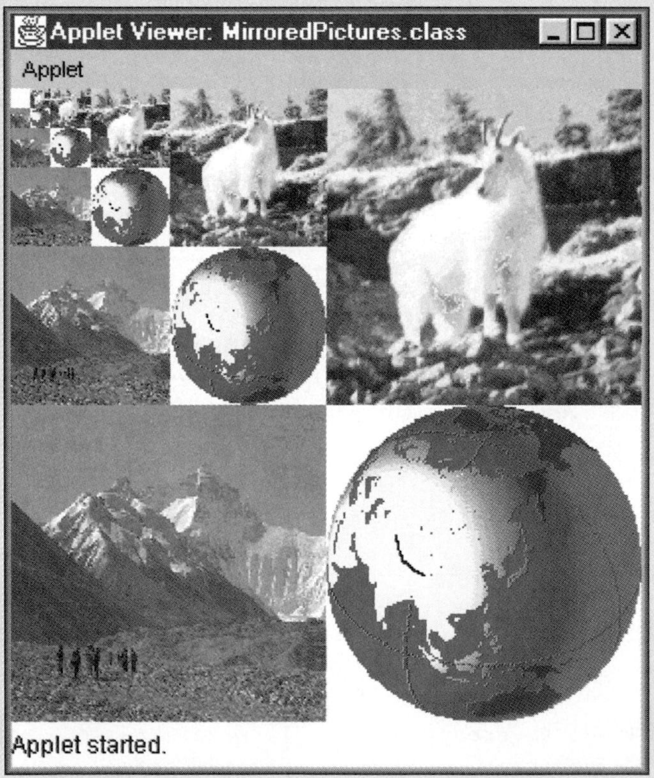

case is reached and the recursion stops. This is the reason that the upper-right corner is empty in the smallest version of the collage.

Fractals

A *fractal* is a geometric shape made up of the same pattern repeated at different scales and orientations. Interest in fractals has grown immensely in recent years, largely due to Benoit Mandelbrot, a Polish mathematician born in 1924. He demonstrated that fractals occur in many places in mathematics and nature. Computers have made fractals much easier to generate and research. Lately, the bright, interesting images that can be created with fractals seem to be considered as much an art form as a mathematical interest.

One particular example of a fractal is called the *Koch snowflake*, named after Helge von Koch, a Swedish mathematician. It begins with an equilateral triangle, which is considered to be the Koch fractal of order 0. Koch fractals of higher orders are constructed by repeatedly modifying all of the line segments in the shape.

To create the next higher order Koch fractal, each line segment in the shape is modified by replacing its middle third with a sharp protrusion made of two line segments, each having the same length as the replaced part. Relative to the entire shape, the protrusion on any line segment always points outward. Several orders of Koch fractals are shown in Figure 11.7. As the order increases, the shape begins to look like a snowflake.

The applet shown in Listing 11.6 draws a Koch snowflake of several different orders. The buttons at the top of the applet allow the user to increase and decrease the order of the fractal. Each time a button is pressed, the fractal image is redrawn. The applet serves as the listener for the buttons.

The fractal image is drawn on a canvas defined by the `KochPanel` class, shown in Listing 11.7. The `paintComponent` method makes the initial calls to the recursive method `drawFractal`. The three calls to `drawFractal` represent the original three sides of the equilateral triangle that make up a Koch fractal of order 0.

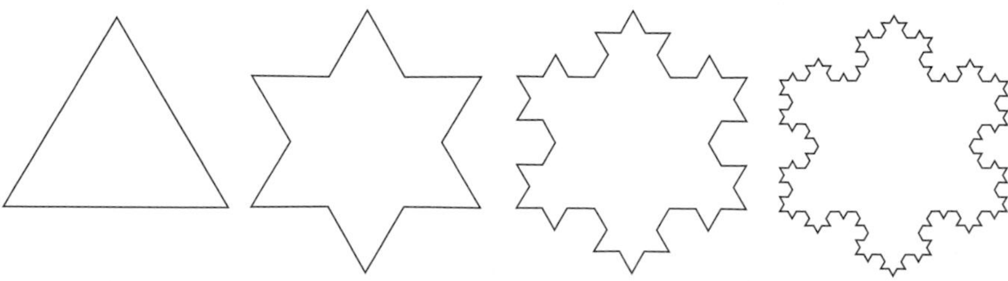

Figure 11.7 Several orders of the Koch snowflake

Listing 11.6

```
//********************************************************************
//  KochSnowflake.java       Author: Lewis and Loftus
//
//  Demonstrates the use of recursion.
//********************************************************************

import KochPanel;
import java.applet.Applet;
import java.awt.*;
import java.awt.event.*;
import javax.swing.*;

public class KochSnowflake extends JApplet implements ActionListener
{
   private final int APPLET_WIDTH = 400;
   private final int APPLET_HEIGHT = 440;

   private final int MIN = 1, MAX = 9;

   private JButton increase, decrease;
   private JLabel titleLabel, orderLabel;
   private KochPanel drawing;
   private JPanel appletPanel, tools;

   //-----------------------------------------------------------------
   //  Sets up the components for the applet.
   //-----------------------------------------------------------------
   public void init()
   {
      tools = new JPanel ();
      tools.setLayout (new BoxLayout(tools, BoxLayout.X_AXIS));
      tools.setBackground (Color.yellow);
      tools.setOpaque (true);

      titleLabel = new JLabel ("The Koch Snowflake");
      titleLabel.setForeground (Color.black);

      increase = new JButton (new ImageIcon ("increase.gif"));
      increase.setPressedIcon (new ImageIcon ("increasePressed.gif"));
      increase.setMargin (new Insets (0, 0, 0, 0));
      increase.addActionListener (this);
```

Listing 11.6 (*continued*)

```
      decrease = new JButton (new ImageIcon ("decrease.gif"));
      decrease.setPressedIcon (new ImageIcon ("decreasePressed.gif"));
      decrease.setMargin (new Insets (0, 0, 0, 0));
      decrease.addActionListener (this);

      orderLabel = new JLabel ("Order: 1");
      orderLabel.setForeground (Color.black);

      tools.add (titleLabel);
      tools.add (Box.createHorizontalStrut (20));
      tools.add (decrease);
      tools.add (increase);
      tools.add (Box.createHorizontalStrut (20));
      tools.add (orderLabel);

      drawing = new KochPanel (1);

      appletPanel = new JPanel();
      appletPanel.add (tools);
      appletPanel.add (drawing);

      getContentPane().add (appletPanel);

      setSize (APPLET_WIDTH, APPLET_HEIGHT);
   }

   //-----------------------------------------------------------------
   //  Determines which button was pushed, and sets the new order
   //  if it is in range.
   //-----------------------------------------------------------------
   public void actionPerformed (ActionEvent event)
   {
      int order = drawing.getOrder();

      if (event.getSource() == increase)
         order++;
      else
         order--;
```

Listing 11.6 (*continued*)

```
        if (order >= MIN && order <= MAX)
        {
           orderLabel.setText ("Order: " + order);
           drawing.setOrder (order);
           repaint();
        }
    }
}
```

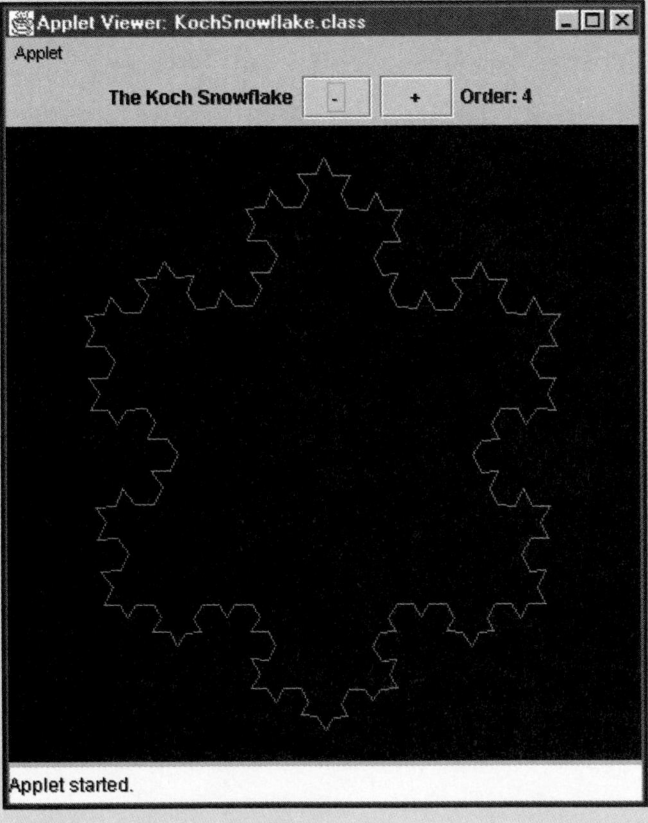

Listing 11.7

```
//********************************************************************
//  KochPanel.java       Author: Lewis and Loftus
//
//  Represents a drawing surface on which to paint a Koch Snowflake.
//********************************************************************

import java.awt.*;
import javax.swing.JPanel;

public class KochPanel extends JPanel
{
   private final int PANEL_WIDTH = 400;
   private final int PANEL_HEIGHT = 400;

   private final double SQ = Math.sqrt(3.0) / 6;

   private final int TOPX = 200, TOPY = 20;
   private final int LEFTX = 60, LEFTY = 300;
   private final int RIGHTX = 340, RIGHTY = 300;

   private int current; //current order

   //-----------------------------------------------------------------
   //  Sets the initial fractal order to the value specified.
   //-----------------------------------------------------------------
   public KochPanel (int currentOrder)
   {
      current = currentOrder;
      setBackground (Color.black);
      setPreferredSize (new Dimension(PANEL_WIDTH, PANEL_HEIGHT));
   }
```

Listing 11.7 ***(continued)***

```
   //-----------------------------------------------------------------
   //  Draws the fractal recursively. Base case is an order of 1 for
   //  which a simple straight line is drawn. Otherwise three
   //  intermediate points are computed, and each line segment is
   //  drawn as a fractal.
   //-----------------------------------------------------------------
   public void drawFractal (int order, int x1, int y1, int x5, int y5,
                            Graphics page)
   {
      int deltaX, deltaY, x2, y2, x3, y3, x4, y4;

      if (order == 1)
         page.drawLine (x1, y1, x5, y5);
      else
      {
         deltaX = x5 - x1;  // distance between end points
         deltaY = y5 - y1;

         x2 = x1 + deltaX / 3;  // one third
         y2 = y1 + deltaY / 3;

         x3 = (int) ((x1+x5)/2 + SQ * (y1-y5));  // tip of projection
         y3 = (int) ((y1+y5)/2 + SQ * (x5-x1));

         x4 = x1 + deltaX * 2/3;  // two thirds
         y4 = y1 + deltaY * 2/3;

         drawFractal (order-1, x1, y1, x2, y2, page);
         drawFractal (order-1, x2, y2, x3, y3, page);
         drawFractal (order-1, x3, y3, x4, y4, page);
         drawFractal (order-1, x4, y4, x5, y5, page);
      }
   }
```

Listing 11.7 ***(continued)***

```
   //-----------------------------------------------------------------
   //  Performs the initial calls to the drawFractal method.
   //-----------------------------------------------------------------
   public void paintComponent (Graphics page)
   {
      super.paintComponent (page);

      page.setColor (Color.green);

      drawFractal (current, TOPX, TOPY, LEFTX, LEFTY, page);
      drawFractal (current, LEFTX, LEFTY, RIGHTX, RIGHTY, page);
      drawFractal (current, RIGHTX, RIGHTY, TOPX, TOPY, page);
   }

   //-----------------------------------------------------------------
   //  Sets the fractal order to the value specified.
   //-----------------------------------------------------------------
   public void setOrder (int order)
   {
      current = order;
   }

   //-----------------------------------------------------------------
   //  Returns the current order.
   //-----------------------------------------------------------------
   public int getOrder ()
   {
      return current;
   }
}
```

The variable `current` represents the order of the fractal to be drawn. Each recursive call to `drawFractal` decrements the order by 1. The base case of the recursion occurs when the order of the fractal is 1, which results in a simple line segment between the coordinates specified by the parameters.

If the order of the fractal is higher than 1, three additional points are computed. In conjunction with the parameters, these points form the four line segments of the modified fractal. The transformation is shown in Figure 11.8.

The calculations to determine the three new points actually have nothing to do with the recursive technique used to draw the fractal. If desired, they can be taken at face value. Based on the position of the two end points of the original line segment, a point one-third of the way and a point two-thirds of the way between them are computed. The calculation of $<x_3, y_3>$, the point at the tip of the protrusion, is more convoluted and uses a simplifying constant that incorporates multiple geometric relationships.

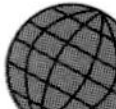

Web Bonus

The textbook's Web site contains a discussion of the geometry involved in the Koch fractal transformation, as well as additional fractal images.

An interesting mathematical feature of a Koch snowflake is that it has an infinite perimeter, but a finite area. As the order of the fractal increases, the perimeter grows exponentially larger, with a mathematical limit of infinity. However, a rectangle large enough to surround the first order fractal for the Koch snowflake is large enough to contain all higher-order fractals. The shape is restricted forever in area, but its perimeter gets infinitely longer.

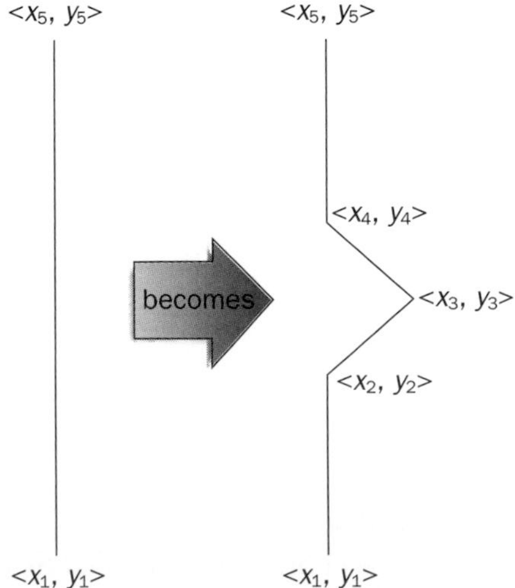

Figure 11.8 The transformation of each line segment of a `Koch snowflake`

Summary of Key Concepts

- Recursion is a programming technique in which a method calls itself. The key to being able to program recursively is to be able to think recursively.
- Any recursive definition must have a nonrecursive part, called the base case, which permits the recursion to eventually end.
- Mathematical problems and formulas are often expressed recursively.
- Each recursive call to a method creates new local variables and parameters.
- A careful trace of recursive processing can provide insight into the way it is used to solve a problem.
- Recursion is the most elegant and appropriate way to solve some problems, but for others it is less intuitive than an iterative solution.
- The Towers of Hanoi solution has exponential complexity, which is very inefficient. Yet the implementation of the solution is incredibly short and elegant.

▶ Self-Review Questions

11.1 What is recursion?

11.2 What is infinite recursion?

11.3 When is a base case needed for recursive processing?

11.4 Is recursion necessary?

11.5 When should recursion be avoided?

11.6 What is indirect recursion?

11.7 Explain the general approach to solving the Towers of Hanoi puzzle. How does it relate to recursion?

11.8 What is a fractal? What does it have to do with recursion?

▶ Exercises

11.1 Write a recursive definition of a valid Java identifier (see Chapter 2).

11.2 Write a recursive definition of x^y (x raised to the power y), where x and y are integers and $y > 0$.

11.3 Write a recursive definition of $i * j$ (integer multiplication), where $i > 0$. Define the multiplication process in terms of integer addition.

11.4 Write a recursive definition of the Fibonacci numbers. The Fibonacci numbers are a sequence of integers, each of which is the sum of the previous two numbers. The first two numbers in the sequence are 0 and 1. Explain why you would not normally use recursion to solve this problem.

11.5 Modify the method that calculates the sum of the integers between 1 and *N* shown in this chapter. Have the new version match the following recursive definition: The sum of 1 to *N* is the sum of 1 to (*N*/2) plus the sum of (*N*/2 + 1) to *N*. Trace your solution using an *N* of 7.

11.6 Write a recursive method that returns the value of *N*! (*N* factorial) using the definition given in this chapter. Explain why you would not normally use recursion to solve this problem.

11.7 Write a recursive method to reverse a string. Explain why you would not normally use recursion to solve this problem.

11.8 Design a new maze for the `MazeSearch` program in this chapter and rerun the program. Explain the processing in terms of your new maze, giving examples of a path that was tried but failed, a path that was never tried, and the ultimate solution.

11.9 Annotate the lines of output of the `SolveTowers` program in this chapter to show the recursive steps.

11.10 Produce a chart showing the number of moves required to solve the Towers of Hanoi puzzle using the following number of disks: 2, 3, 4, 5, 6, 7, 8, 9, 10, 15, 20, and 25.

11.11 How many line segments are used to construct a Koch snowflake of order *N*? Produce a chart showing the number of line segments that make up a Koch snowflake for orders 1 through 9.

Programming Projects

11.1 Design and implement a recursive version of the `PalindromeTester` program from Chapter 3.

11.2 Design and implement a program that implements Euclid's algorithm for finding the greatest common divisor of two positive integers. The greatest common divisor is the largest integer that divides both values without producing a remainder. An iterative version of this method was part of the `Rational` class presented in Chapter 4. In a class called `DivisorCalc`, define a `static` method called `gcd` that accepts two integers, `num1` and `num2`. Create a `main` driver to test your implementation. The recursive algorithm is defined as follows:

- `gcd (num1, num2) is num2 if num2 <= num1 and num2 divides num1`
- `gcd (num1, num2) is gcd (num2, num1) if num1 < num2`
- `gcd (num1, num2) is gcd (num2, num1%num2) otherwise`

11.3 Modify the `Maze` class so that it prints out the path of the final solution as it is discovered without storing it.

11.4 Modify the `MirroredPictures` program so that the repeated images appear in the lower-right quadrant.

11.5 Design and implement a recursive program that solves the Nonattacking Queens problem: Determine how eight queens can be positioned on an eight-by-eight chessboard so that none of them are in the same row, column, or diagonal as any other queen. There are no other chess pieces on the board.

11.6 In the language of an alien race, all words take the form of Blurbs. A Blurb is a Whoozit followed by one or more Whatzits. A Whoozit is the character 'x' followed by zero or more 'y's. A Whatzit is a 'q' followed by either a 'z' or a 'd', followed by a Whoozit. Design and implement a recursive program that generates random Blurbs in this alien language.

11.7 Design and implement a recursive program to determine if a string is a valid Blurb as defined in the previous problem.

11.8 Design and implement an applet that generalizes the `KochSnowflake` program. Allow the user to choose a fractal design from a menu item. Also allow the user to pick the background and drawing colors. The buttons to increase and decrease the order of the fractal will apply to whichever fractal design is chosen. In addition to the Koch snowflake, include a *C-curve fractal* whose order 1 is a straight line. Each successive order is created by replacing all line segments by two line segments, both half of the size of the original, and which meet at a right angle. Specifically, a C-curve of order N from $<x_1, y_1>$ to $<x_3, y_3>$ is replaced by two C-curves from $<x_1, y_1>$ to $<x_2, y_2>$ and from $<x_2, y_2>$ to $<x_3, y_3>$ where:

```
x2 = (x1 + x3 + y1 - y3) / 2;
y2 = (x3 + y1 + y3 - x1) / 2;
```

11.9 Design and implement a graphic version of the Towers of Hanoi puzzle. Allow the user to set the number of disks used in the puzzle. The user should be able to interact with the puzzle in two main ways. The user can move the disks from one peg to another using the mouse, in which case the program should ensure that each move is legal. The user can also watch a solution take place as an animation, with pause/resume buttons.

Answers to Self-Review Questions

11.1 Recursion is a programming technique in which a method calls itself, solving a smaller version of the problem each time, until the terminating condition is reached.

11.2 Infinite recursion occurs when there is no base case that serves as a terminating condition, or when the base case is improperly specified. The recursive path is followed forever. In a recursive program, infinite recursion will often result in an error that indicates that available memory has been exhausted.

11.3 A base case is always required to terminate recursion and begin the process of returning through the calling hierarchy. Without the base case, infinite recursion would result.

11.4 Recursion is not necessary. Every recursive algorithm can be written in an iterative manner. However, some problem solutions are much more elegant and straightforward when written recursively.

11.5 Avoid recursion when the iterative solution is simpler and more easily understood. Recursion has the overhead of multiple method calls and is not always intuitive.

11.6 Indirect recursion occurs when a method calls another method, which calls another method, and so on until one of the called methods invokes the original. Indirect recursion is usually more difficult to trace than direct recursion, in which a method calls itself.

11.7 The Towers of Hanoi puzzle of N disks is solved by moving $N - 1$ disks out of the way onto an extra peg, moving the largest disk to its destination, then moving the $N - 1$ disks from the extra peg to the destination. This solution is inherently recursive because to move the substack of $N - 1$ disks, we can use the same process.

11.8 A fractal is a geometric shape that is composed of multiple versions of the same shape at different scales and different angles of orientation. Recursion can be used to draw the repetitive shapes over and over again.

12 Data Structures

Advanced problem solving often requires advanced techniques for organizing and managing information. The term data structures refers to the various ways information can be organized and used. Many data structures have been developed over the years, and some of them have become classics. A data structure can often be implemented in a variety of ways. This chapter explains how data structures can be implemented using references to link one object to another. It also serves as an introduction to some specific data structures.

Chapter Objectives

- Explore the concept of a collection.
- Examine the difference between static and dynamic implementations.
- Define and use dynamically linked lists.
- Define queue and stack data structures.
- Introduce the predefined collection classes in the Java standard class library.

12.1 Collections

A *collection* is an object that serves as a repository for other objects. It is a generic term that can be applied to many situations, but we usually use it when discussing an object whose specific role is to provide services to add, remove, and otherwise manage the elements that are contained within. For example, the `Vector` class (discussed in Chapter 6) represents a collection. It provides methods to add elements to the end of a vector or to a particular location in the vector based on an index value. It provides methods to remove specific elements as needed.

Some collections maintain their elements in a specific order, while others do not. Some collections are *homogeneous,* meaning that they can contain all of the same type of object; other collections are *heterogeneous,* which means they can contain objects of various types. A `Vector` is heterogeneous because it can hold an object of any type. Its heterogeneous nature comes from the fact that a `Vector` stores references to `Object` objects, which means it can store any object because of inheritance and polymorphism (as discussed in Chapter 7).

Separating Interface from Implementation

A crucial aspect of collections is that they can be implemented in a variety of ways. That is, the underlying *data structure* that stores the objects could be implemented using various techniques. The `Vector` class from the Java standard library, for instance, is implemented using an array. All operations on a vector are accomplished by invoking methods that perform the appropriate operations on the underlying array.

An *abstract data type* (ADT) is a collection of data and the particular operations that are allowed on that data. An ADT is considered abstract because the operations you perform on it are separated from the underlying implementation. A `Vector` is an abstract data type, because its interface (the operations we perform on it) is separated from the implementation.

Key Concept

An abstract data type hides the implementation of a data structure behind a well-defined interface. This characteristic makes objects a perfect way to define ADTs.

Objects are perfectly suited for defining ADTs since an object, by definition, has a well-defined interface whose implementation is hidden in the class. The data that is represented, and the operations that manage the data, are encapsulated together inside the object. An encapsulated ADT is more reusable and reliable, since its interaction with the rest of the system is controlled.

12.2 Implementing Data Structures

Using an array is only one way in which a `Vector` could be implemented. Arrays are limited in one sense because they have a fixed size throughout their existence. Sometimes we don't know how big to make an array because we don't know how much information we will store. The `Vector` class handles this by creating a larger array and copying everything over whenever necessary. This is not necessarily an efficient implementation.

A *dynamic data structure* is implemented using links. Using references as links between objects, we can create whatever types of structures are most appropriate for the situation. If implemented carefully, they can be quite efficient to search and modify. Structures created this way are considered to be dynamic, since their size is determined dynamically, as they are used, and not by their declaration.

Key Concept

A fixed data structure has a fixed size for the duration of its existence, whereas a dynamic data structure grows and shrinks as needed.

Dynamic Structures

Recall from Chapter 4 that all objects are created dynamically using the `new` operator. A variable used to keep track of an object is actually a reference to the object. Recall that a declaration such as:

```
Book myBook = new Book ("The Cuckoo's Egg");
```

actually accomplishes two things: it declares `myBook` to be a reference to a `Book` object, and it instantiates an object of class `Book`. Now consider an object that contains a reference to another object of the same type. For example:

```
class Node
{
   int info;
   Node next;
}
```

Two objects of this class can be instantiated and chained together by having the `next` reference of one `Node` object refer to the other. The second object's `next` reference can refer to a third `Node` object, and so on, creating a *linked list*. The first node in the list could be referenced using a separate variable. The last node in the list would have a `next` reference that is `null`, indicating the end of the list. This situation is pictured in Figure 12.1. For this example, the information stored in each `Node` class is a simple integer, but keep in mind that we could define a class to contain any amount of information of any type.

Key Concept

A dynamically linked list is managed by storing and updating references to objects.

A Dynamically Linked List

The program in Listing 12.1 sets up a list of `Book` objects, then prints the list. The list of books is encapsulated inside the `BookList` class, shown in Listing 12.2, and is maintained as a dynamically linked list.

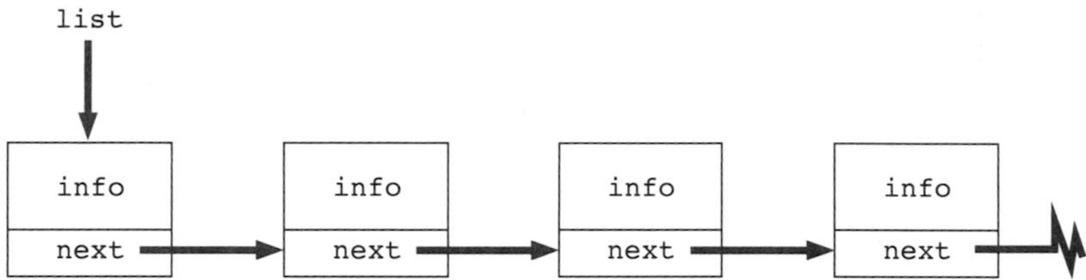

Figure 12.1 A linked list

Listing 12.1

```
//********************************************************************
//  Library.java       Author: Lewis and Loftus
//
//  Driver to exercise the BookList collection.
//********************************************************************

import BookList;
import Book;

public class Library
{
   //-----------------------------------------------------------------
   //  Creates a BookList object, adds several books to the list,
   //  then prints them.
   //-----------------------------------------------------------------
   public static void main (String[] args)
   {
      BookList books = new BookList();

      books.add (new Book("The Hitchhiker's Guide to the Galaxy"));
      books.add (new Book("Jonathan Livingston Seagull"));
      books.add (new Book("A Tale of Two Cities"));
      books.add (new Book("Java Software Solutions"));

      System.out.println (books);
   }
}
```

```
The Hitchhiker's Guide to the Galaxy
Jonathan Livingston Seagull
A Tale of Two Cities
Java Software Solutions
```

Listing 12.2

```
//********************************************************************
//  BookList.java       Author: Lewis and Loftus
//
//  Represents a collection of books.
//********************************************************************

import Book;

public class BookList
{
   private BookNode list;

   //-----------------------------------------------------------------
   //  Sets up an initially empty list of books.
   //-----------------------------------------------------------------
   BookList()
   {
      list = null;
   }

   //-----------------------------------------------------------------
   //  Creates a new Book object and adds it to the end of
   //  the linked list.
   //-----------------------------------------------------------------
   public void add (Book newBook)
   {

      BookNode node = new BookNode (newBook);
      BookNode current;

      if (list == null)
         list = node;
      else
      {
         current = list;
         while (current.next != null)
            current = current.next;
         current.next = node;
      }
   }
```

Listing 12.2 *(continued)*

```
   //-----------------------------------------------------------------
   //  Returns this list of books as a string.
   //-----------------------------------------------------------------
   public String toString ()
   {
      String result = "";

      BookNode current = list;

      while (current != null)
      {
         result += current.book.toString() + "\n";
         current = current.next;
      }

      return result;
   }

   //*****************************************************************
   //  An inner class that represents a node in the book list. The
   //  public variables are accessed by the BookList class.
   //*****************************************************************
   private class BookNode
   {
      public Book book;
      public BookNode next;

      //--------------------------------------------------------------
      //  Sets up the node
      //--------------------------------------------------------------
      public BookNode (Book theBook)
      {
         book = theBook;
         next = null;
      }
   }
}
```

The book list is embodied inside the `BookList` class. From outside of the class, it is not known how the list is implemented, nor is it really important. The `BookList` class provides a set of methods that allow the user to maintain the list of books. That set of methods, specifically `add` and `toString`, define the operations to the `BookList` ADT.

The `BookList` class uses an inner class called `BookNode` to represent a node on the linked list. It contains references to one book, and a reference to the next node in the list. Because `BookNode` is an inner class, it is reasonable to allow the data values in the class to be public. Therefore the code in the `BookList` class refers to those data values directly.

The `Book` class, shown in Listing 12.3, is well encapsulated, with all data declared as private and methods provided to accomplish any updates necessary. Because we use a separate class to represent a node in the list, the `Book`

Listing 12.3

```
//********************************************************************
//  Book.java       Author: Lewis and Loftus
//
//  Represents a single book.
//********************************************************************

public class Book
{
   private String title;

   //-----------------------------------------------------------------
   //  Sets up the new book with its title.
   //-----------------------------------------------------------------
   public Book (String newTitle)
   {
      title = newTitle;
   }

   //-----------------------------------------------------------------
   //  Returns this book as a string.
   //-----------------------------------------------------------------
   public String toString ()
   {
      return title;
   }
}
```

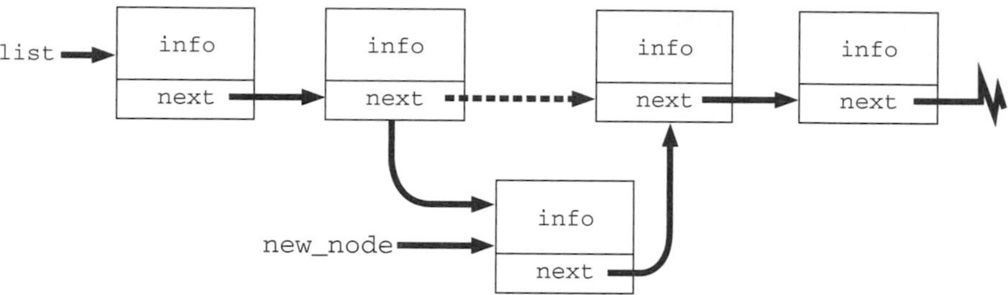

Figure 12.2 Inserting a node into the middle of a list

class itself does not have to contain a link to the next `Book` in the list. That allows the `Book` class to be free of any issues regarding its containment in a list.

> **Key Concept**
>
> A versatile list ADT contains insert and delete operations, which can be implemented by carefully manipulating object references.

Other methods could be included in the `BookList` ADT. The `add` method provided always adds a new book to the end of the list. Another method called `insert` could be defined to add a node anywhere in the list (to keep it sorted, for instance). A parameter to `insert` could indicate the value of the node after which the new node should be inserted. The picture in Figure 12.2 shows how the references would be updated to insert a new node.

Another operation that would be helpful in the list ADT would be a `delete` method, to remove a particular node. Recall that by removing all references to an object, it becomes a candidate for garbage collection. Figure 12.3 shows the way references would be updated to delete a node from a list. Care must be taken to accomplish the modifications to the references in the proper order to ensure that other nodes are not lost and that references continue to refer to valid, appropriate nodes in the list.

Other Dynamic List Implementations

Many variations on list implementations can be used, depending on the specific needs of the program being designed. For example, in some situations it may make your processing easier to implement a *doubly linked list* in which each node has not only a reference to the next node in the list, but also

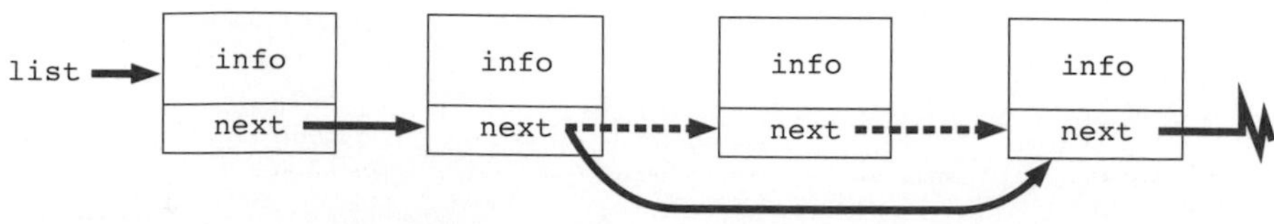

Figure 12.3 Deleting a node from a list

another reference to the previous node in the list. Our generic `Node` class might be declared as follows:

```
class Node
{
   int info;
   Node next, prev;
}
```

A doubly linked list is pictured in Figure 12.4. Note that, like a single linked list, the `next` reference of the last node is null. Similarly, the previous node of the first node is null, since there is no node that comes before the first one. This type of structure makes it easy to move back and forth between nodes in the list, but it is somewhat more trouble to set up and modify.

Key Concept

There are many variations on the implementation of dynamic linked lists.

Another implementation of a linked list could include a header node for the list that has a reference to the front of the list and another to the rear. A rear reference makes it easier to add new nodes to the end of the list. The header node could contain other information, such as a count of the number of nodes currently in the list. The declaration of the header node would be similar to the following:

```
class ListHeader
{
   int count;
   Node front, rear;
}
```

Note that the header node is not of the same class as the `Node` class to which it refers. A linked list that is implemented using a header node is pictured in Figure 12.5.

Other linked list implementations could be created. For instance, the use of a header can be combined with a doubly linked list, or the list could be maintained in sorted order. The implementation should cater to the type of processing that is necessary. Some extra effort to maintain a more complex data structure may be worthwhile if it makes common operations on the structure more efficient.

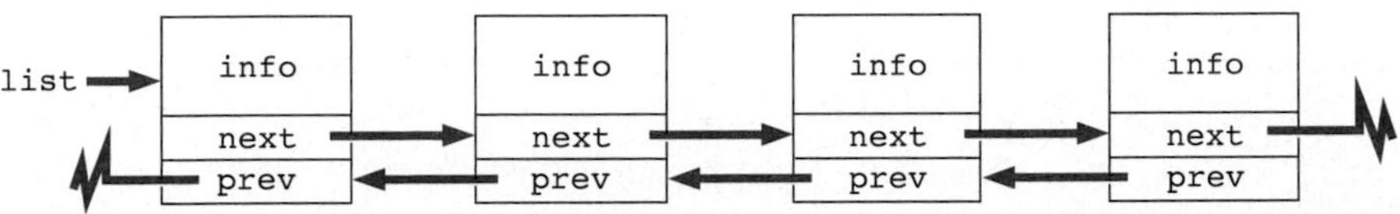

Figure 12.4 A doubly linked list

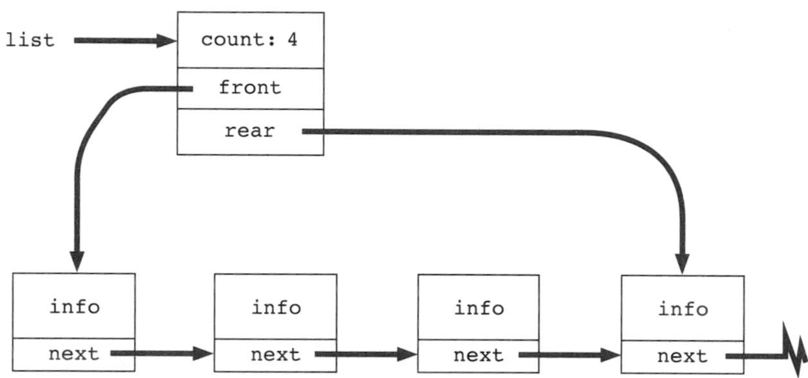

Figure 12.5 A list with front and rear references

12.3 Classic Data Structures

Some data structures have become classic in that they represent important generic situations that commonly occur in computing. We will examine two classic data structures: queues and stacks.

Queues

A *queue* is similar to a list, except that it has restrictions on the way you put items on and take items off. Specifically, a queue uses *first-in, first-out* (FIFO) processing. That is, the first item put on the list is the first item that comes off the list. Think about a line of people waiting at a bank. You enter the queue at the back, and work your way to the front. Eventually you come off of the front of the line to be processed (served by the teller). Figure 12.6 depicts the FIFO processing of a queue.

Key Concept

A queue is a linear data structure that manages data in a first-in, first-out manner.

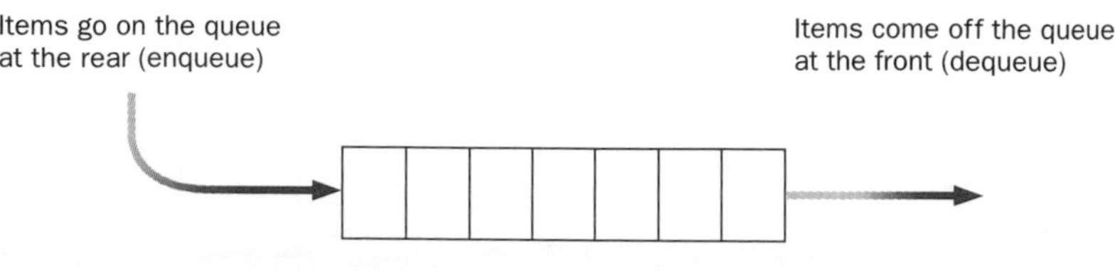

Figure 12.6 A queue, with FIFO processing

A queue data structure typically has the following operations:

- enqueue—adds an item to the rear of the queue
- dequeue—removes an item from the front of the queue
- empty—returns true if the queue is empty

Stacks

A *stack* is similar to a queue except that its elements go on and come off at the same end. The last item to go on a stack is the first item to come off, like a stack of trays in a cafeteria. A stack processes information in a *last-in, first-out* (LIFO) manner, as shown in Figure 12.7.

Key Concept

A stack is a linear data structure that manages data in a last-in, first-out manner.

A typical stack ADT contains the following operations:

- push—pushes an item onto the top of the stack
- pop—removes an item from the top of the stack
- peek—retrieves the top item of the stack without removing it
- empty—returns true if the stack is empty

The `java.util` package of the API contains a class called `Stack` that implements a stack data structure. It contains methods that correspond to the standard stack operations, plus a method that searches for a particular object in the stack.

The `Stack` class is derived from `Vector`. The search method returns an integer corresponding to the position in the stack of the particular object. This type of searching is not usually considered to be part of the classic stack ADT.

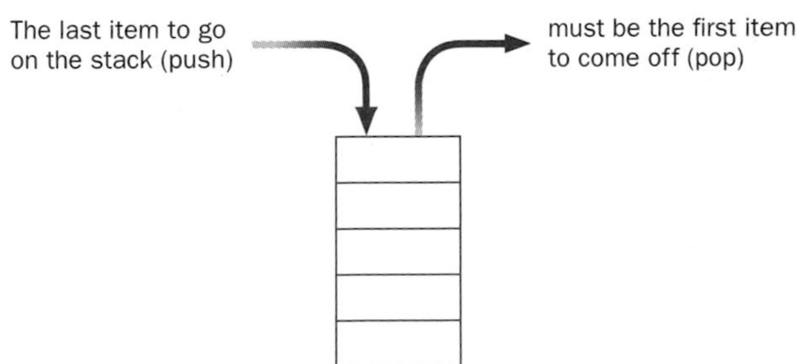

Figure 12.7 A stack, with LIFO processing

Like `Vector` operations, the `Stack` operations operate on the `Object` class. Since all objects are derived from the `Object` class, any object can be pushed onto a stack. If primitive types are to be stored, they must be converted to objects using the corresponding wrapper class. Unlike the `Stack` class, there is no `Queue` class defined in the Java API.

Example: Message Decoding

The program in Listing 12.4 accepts a string of characters that it interprets as a secret message. The program decodes the message and prints it. A coded

Listing 12.4

```
//********************************************************************
//  Decode.java        Author: Lewis and Loftus
//
//  Demonstrates the use of the Stack class.
//********************************************************************

import java.util.Stack;
import cs1.Keyboard;

public class Decode
{
   //-----------------------------------------------------------------
   //  Decodes a message by reversing each word in a string.
   //-----------------------------------------------------------------
   public static void main (String[] args)
   {
      Stack word = new Stack();
      String message;
      int index = 0;

      System.out.println ("Enter the coded message:");
      message = Keyboard.readString();
      System.out.println ("The decoded message is:");
```

Listing 12.4 (continued)

```
      while (index < message.length())
      {
         // Push word onto stack
         while (index < message.length() && message.charAt(index) != ' ')
         {
            word.push (new Character(message.charAt(index)));
            index++;
         }

         // Print word in reverse
         while (!word.empty())
            System.out.print (((Character)word.pop()).charValue());
         System.out.print (" ");
         index++;
      }

      System.out.println();
   }
}
```

```
Enter the coded message:
artxE eseehc esaelp
The decoded message is:
Extra cheese please
```

message has each individual word in the message reversed. Words in the message are separated by a single space. The program uses the `Stack` class to push the characters of each word on the stack. When an entire word has been read, it is popped off the stack in reverse order and printed.

12.4 Collection Classes

The Java 2 platform contains several classes that represent collections of one type or another. The class names generally indicate both the collection type and the underlying implementation. For example, the `LinkedList` class represents a list collection with a dynamically linked internal implementation. There is also an `ArrayList` class that represents a list, but uses an array for its underlying implementation scheme. The `Vector` class is carried over from previous Java incarnations.

Several interfaces are used to define the collection operations themselves. The interfaces include `List`, `Set`, `SortedSet`, `Map`, and `SortedMap`. A `Set` is consistent with its normal interpretation as a collection of elements without duplicates. A `Map` is a group of elements that can be referenced by a key value.

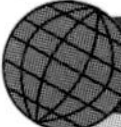

Web Bonus

The textbook's Web site contains detailed discussions of the predefined collection classes.

Summary of Key Concepts

- A static data structure has a fixed size for the duration of its existence, whereas a dynamic data structure grows and shrinks as needed.
- A dynamically linked list is managed by storing and updating references to objects.
- An abstract data type hides the implementation of a data structure behind a well-defined interface. This characteristic makes objects a perfect way to define ADTs.
- A versatile list ADT contains insert and delete operations, which can be implemented by carefully manipulating object references.
- There are many variations on the implementation of dynamic linked lists.
- A queue is a linear data structure that manages data in a first-in, first-out manner.
- A stack is a linear data structure that manages data in a last-in, first-out manner.

Self-Review Questions

12.1 What is a dynamic structure?

12.2 Why are objects a good choice for implementing an abstract data type?

12.3 What is a doubly linked list?

12.4 What is a header node for a linked list?

12.5 How is a queue different from a list?

12.6 What is a stack?

12.7 What is the `Stack` class?

Exercises

12.1 Suppose `current` is a reference to a `Node` object and that it currently refers to a specific node in a linked list. List, in pseudocode, the steps that would delete the node following `current` from the list. Carefully consider the cases in which `current` is referring to the first and last nodes in the list.

12.2 Modify your answer to the previous problem assuming that the list was set up as a doubly linked list, with next and prev references.

12.3 Suppose `current` and `newNode` are references to `Node` objects. Assume `current` currently refers to a specific node in a linked list and `newNode` refers to an unattached `Node` object. List, in pseudocode, the steps that would insert `newNode` behind `current` in the list. Carefully consider the cases in which `current` is referring to the first and last nodes in the list.

12.4 Modify your answer to the previous problem assuming that the list was set up as a doubly linked list, with next and prev references.

12.5 Show the contents of a queue after the following operations are performed. Assume the queue is initially empty. Does it matter how the dequeue operations are intermixed with the enqueue operations? Does it matter how the enqueue operations are intermixed among themselves? Explain.

enqueue (45);
enqueue (12);
enqueue (28);
dequeue();
dequeue();
enqueue (69);
enqueue (27);
enqueue (99);
dequeue();
enqueue (24);
enqueue (85);
enqueue (16);
dequeue();

12.6 Show the contents of a stack after the following operations are performed. Assume the stack is initially empty. Does it matter how the pop operations are intermixed with the push operations? Does it matter how the push operations are intermixed among themselves? Explain.

push (45);
push (12);
push (28);
pop();

pop();
push (69);
push (27);
push (99);
pop();
push (24);
push (85);
push (16);
pop();

Programming Projects

12.1 Consistent with the example from Chapter 6, design and implement an application that maintains a linked list of objects instantiated from a class called CD, where each node represents a compact disk in an audio collection. In each node, keep track of the title of the CD, the artist's name, and the number of tracks on the CD. In a class called `Tunes`, define a main method that adds various CDs to the collection. Print the list when complete.

12.2 Modify the `Library` program presented in this chapter by adding delete and insert operations into the `BookList` class. The insert method should be based on a compare method in the `Book` class that determines if one book title comes before another alphabetically. In the `main` method, exercise various insertion and deletion operations. Print the book list when complete.

12.3 Design and implement a version of selection sort (from Chapter 6) that operates on a linked list of nodes that each contain an integer.

12.4 Design and implement a version of insertion sort (from Chapter 6) that operates on a linked list of nodes that each contain an integer.

12.5 Design and implement an application that simulates the customers waiting in line at a bank. Use a queue data structure to represent the line. As customers arrive at the bank, customer objects are put on the end of the line with an enqueue operation. When the teller is ready to service another customer, the customer object is taken off the queue with a dequeue operation. Print a message each time an operation occurs during the simulation.

12.6 We are familiar with *infix expressions,* in which an operator is positioned between its two operands. A *postfix expression* puts the operators after its operands. Keep in mind that an operand could be the result of another operation. This eliminates the need for parentheses to force precedence. For example, the infix expression

(5 + 2) * (8 - 5)

is equivalent to the following postfix expression

5 2 + 8 5 - *

The evaluation of a postfix expression is fairly easy when you use a stack. As you progress through a postfix expression from left to right, you encounter operands and operators. If you encounter an operand, push it on the stack. If you encounter an operator, pop two operands off the stack, perform the operation, and push the result back on the stack. When you have processed the entire expression, there will be one value on the stack, which is the result of the entire expression.

Design and implement an application that evaluates a postfix expression that operates on integer operands using the arithmetic operators +, -, *, /, and %. You may want to use a `StringTokenizer` object to assist in the parsing of the expression.

▶ Answers to Self-Review Questions

12.1 A dynamic data structure is one constructed using references to link various objects together into a particular organization to facilitate its use. It is dynamic because it can grow and shrink dynamically as needed. New objects can be created and added to the structure, or obsolete objects can be removed from the structure, by adjusting references between objects in the structure.

12.2 An abstract data type is a collection of data and the operations that can be performed on that data. An object is essentially the same thing, in that we encapsulate related variables and methods in an object. Therefore an object is an appropriate way to represent an ADT.

12.3 Each node in a doubly linked list has references to both the node that comes before it in the list and the node that comes after it in the list. This organization allows for easy movement forward and backward in the list.

12.4 A header node for a linked list is a special node that holds information about the list, such as references to the front and rear of the list and an integer to keep track of how many nodes are currently in the list.

12.5 A queue is a linear data structure, like a list, but it has more constraints concerning its use. A general list can be modified by inserting or deleting nodes anywhere in the list, but a queue only adds nodes to one end (enqueue) and takes them off of the other (dequeue). The difference is largely conceptual, determined by the purpose of the structure for a given situation.

12.6 A stack is a linear data structure that adds (pushes) and removes (pops) nodes from one end. It manages information using a last-in, first-out (LIFO) approach.

12.7 The `Stack` class is defined in the `java.util` package of the Java standard class library. It implements a generic stack ADT. The `Stack` class stores `Object` references, so the stack can be used to store any kind of object.

Appendix A

Glossary

abstract—A `Java` reserved word that serves as a modifier for classes, interfaces, and methods. An `abstract` class cannot be instantiated, and is used to specify bodiless abstract methods that are given definitions by derived classes. Interfaces are inherently `abstract`.

abstract class—See abstract.

abstract data type—A collection of data and the operations that are defined on that data. An abstract data type might be implemented in a variety of ways, but the interface operations are consistent. Abbreviated ADT.

abstract method—See abstract.

abstraction—The concept of hiding details. If the right details are hidden at the right times, abstraction can significantly help control complexity and focus attention on appropriate issues.

Abstract Windowing Toolkit—The package in the Java API (`java.awt`) that contains classes related to graphics and graphical user interfaces. Abbreviated AWT.

access—The ability to reference a variable or invoke a method from outside the class in which it is declared. Controlled by the visibility modifier used to declare the variable or method. Also called scope or level of encapsulation. See also: visibility modifier.

access modifier—See visibility modifier.

actual parameter—The value passed to a method as a parameter. See also: formal parameter.

address—(1) A numeric value that uniquely identifies a particular memory location in a computer's main memory. (2) A designation that uniquely identifies a computer among all others on a network.

aggregate object—An object that contains variables that are references to other objects.

algorithm—A step-by-step process for solving a problem. A program is based on one or more algorithms.

alias—A reference to an object that is currently also referred to by another reference. Each reference is an alias of the other.

analog—A representation that is in direct proportion to the source of the information. See also: digital.

applet—A Java program that is linked into an HTML document, then retrieved and executed using a Web browser, as opposed to a stand-alone Java application.

appletviewer—A software tool that interprets and displays Java applets through links in HTML documents. Part of the Java Development Kit (JDK).

API—See Application Programming Interface.

application—(1) A generic term for any program. (2) A Java program that can be run without the use of a Web browser, as opposed to a Java applet.

Application Programming Interface—A set of classes that defines services for a programmer. Not part of the language itself, but often relied upon to perform even basic tasks. Abbreviated API. See also: class library.

arc angle—When defining an arc, the radial distance that defines the arc's length. See also: start angle.

architectural design—A high-level design that identifies the large portions of a software system and key data structures. See also: detailed design.

architecture—See computer architecture.

architecture neutral—Not specific to any particular hardware platform. Java code is considered to be architecture neutral since it is compiled into bytecode, then interpreted on any machine with a Java interpreter.

arithmetic operator—An operator that performs a basic arithmetic computation, such as addition or multiplication.

arithmetic promotion—The act of promoting the type of a numeric operand to be consistent with the other operand.

array—A programming language construct used to store an ordered list of primitive values or objects. Each element in the array is referenced using a numerical index from 0 to $N - 1$, where N is the size of the array.

ASCII—A popular character set used by many programming languages. ASCII stands for American Standard Code for Information Interchange. It is a subset of the Unicode character set, which is used by Java.

assembly language—A low-level language that uses mnemonics to represent program commands.

assignment conversion—Some data types can be converted to another in an assignment statement. See widening conversion.

assignment operator—An operator that results in an assignment to a variable. The = operator performs basic assignment. Many additional assignment operators perform additional operations prior to the assignment, such as the *= operator.

association—See operator association.

AWT—See Abstract Windowing Toolkit.

background color—The color of the background on an applet or HTML page. See also: foreground color.

Backus-Naur Form—A notation for representing language syntax using a formal grammar. Abbreviated BNF.

base—The numerical value on which a particular number system is based. It determines the number of digits available in that number system and the place value of each digit in a number. See also: binary, octal, decimal, hexadecimal, place value.

base 2—See binary.

base 8—See octal.

base 10—See decimal.

base 16—See hexadecimal.

base case—The situation that terminates recursive processing, allowing the active recursive methods to begin returning to their point of invocation.

base class—See superclass.

behavior—The functional characteristics of an object, defined by its methods. See also: state, identity.

binary—The base-2 number system. Modern computer systems store information as strings of binary digits.

binary operator—An operator that uses two operands.

binary search—A searching algorithm that requires that the list be sorted. It repetitively compares the "middle" element of the list to the target value, narrowing the scope of the search each time. See also: linear search.

binary string—A series of binary digits (bits).

binding—The process of associating an identifier with the construct that it represents. For example, the process of binding a method name to the specific definition that it invokes.

bit—A binary digit, either 0 or 1.

bit shifting—The act of shifting the bits of a data value to the left or right, losing bits on one end and inserting new bits on the other.

bits per second—A measurement rate for data transfer devices. Abbreviated bps.

bitwise operator—An operator that manipulates individual bits of a value, either by calculation or shifting.

black-box testing—Producing and evaluating test cases based on the input and expected output of a software component. The test cases focus on covering the equivalence categories and boundary values of the input. See also: white-box testing.

block—A group of programming statements and declarations delimited by braces (`{}`).

BNF—See Backus-Naur Form.

boolean—A Java reserved word representing a logical primitive data type that can only take the values `true` or `false`.

boolean expression—An expression that evaluates to a true or false result, primarily used as conditions in selection and repetition statements.

boolean operator—Any of the bitwise operators AND (`&`), OR (`|`), or XOR (`^`) when applied to `boolean` operands. The results are equivalent to their logical counterparts, except that boolean operators are not short-circuited.

bounding rectangle—A rectangle that delineates a region in which an oval or arc is defined.

boundary values—The input values corresponding to the edges of equivalence categories. Used in black-box testing.

bounds checking—The process of determining if an array index is in bounds, given the size of the array. Java performs automatic bounds checking.

break—A Java reserved word used to interrupt the flow of control by breaking out of the current loop or `switch` statement.

browser—Software that retrieves HTML documents across network connections and formats them for viewing. A browser is the primary vehicle for accessing the World Wide Web. See also: Netscape Navigator.

bug—A slang term for a defect or error in a computer program.

build-and-fix approach—An approach to software development in which a program is created without any significant planning or design, then modified until it reaches some level of acceptance. It is a prevalent, but unwise, approach.

bus—A group of wires in the computer that carry data between components such as the CPU and main memory.

byte—(1) A unit of binary storage equal to eight bits. (2) A Java reserved word that represents a primitive integer type, stored using eight bits in two's complement format.

bytecode—The low-level format into which the Java compiler translates Java source code. The bytecodes are interpreted and executed by the Java interpreter, perhaps after transportation over the Internet.

byvalue—A Java reserved word that is not currently used. It may be used in the future to specify parameters that are passed by value into methods.

capacity—See storage capacity.

case—(1) A Java reserved word that is used to identify each unique option in a `switch` statement. (2) The orientation of an alphabetic character (uppercase or lowercase).

case sensitive—Differentiating between the uppercase and lowercase versions of an alphabetic letter. Java is case sensitive; therefore the identifier `total` and the identifier `Total` are considered to be different identifiers.

cast—(1) A Java reserved word that is not currently used. (2) A Java operation expressed using a type or class name in parentheses to explicitly convert and return a value of one data type into another.

catch—A Java reserved word that is used to specify an exception handler, defined after a try block.

CD ROM—An optical secondary memory medium that stores binary information in a manner similar to a musical compact disc.

central processing unit—The hardware component that controls the main activity of a computer, including the flow of information and the execution of commands.

char—A Java reserved word that represents the primitive character type. All Java characters are members of the Unicode character set and are stored using 16 bits.

character set—An ordered list of characters, such as the ASCII or Unicode character sets. Each character corresponds to a specific, unique numeric value within a given character set. A programming language adopts a particular character set to use for character representation and management.

character string—A series of ordered characters. Represented in Java using the `String` class and string literals such as `"hello"`.

checked exception—A Java exception that must be either caught or explicitly thrown to the calling method. See also: unchecked exception.

child class—See subclass.

class—(1) A Java reserved word used to define a class. (2) The blueprint of an object. The model that defines the variables and methods an object will contain when instantiated.

class diagram—A diagram that shows the relationships between classes, including inheritance and use relationships.

class hierarchy—The treelike structure created when classes are derived from other classes through inheritance.

class library—A set of classes that define useful services for a programmer. See also: Application Programmer Interface.

class method—A method that can be invoked using only the class name. An instantiated object is not required, as it is with instance methods. Defined in a Java program by using the `static` reserved word.

CLASSPATH—An operating system setting that determines where the Java interpreter searches for class files.

class variable—A variable that is shared among all objects of a class. It can also be referenced through the class name, without instantiating any object of that class. Defined in a Java program by using the `static` reserved word.

client-server model—A manner in which to construct a software design based on objects (clients) making use of the services provided by other objects (servers).

coding guidelines—A series of conventions that describe how programs should be constructed. They make programs easier to read, exchange, and integrate. Sometimes referred to as coding standards, especially when they are enforced.

coding standard—See coding guidelines.

cohesion—The strength of the relationship among the parts within a software component. See also: coupling.

collision—The process of two hash values producing the same hash code. See also: hashing, hash code.

command-line arguments—The values that follow the program name on the command line. Accessed within a Java program through the `String` array parameter to the `main` method.

comment—A programming language construct that allows a programmer to embed human-readable annotations into the source code. See also: documentation.

compiler—A program that translates code from one language to equivalent code in another language. The Java compiler translates Java source code into Java bytecode. See also: interpreter.

compile-time error—Any error that occurs during the compilation process, often indicating that a program does not conform to the language syntax or that an operation was attempted on an inappropriate data type. See also: syntax error, logical error, run-time error.

component—Any portion of a software system that performs a specific task, transforming input to output. See also: GUI component.

component hierarchy—The relationships among graphical components of a user interface. See also: container.

computer architecture—The structure and interaction of the hardware components of a computer.

concatenation—See string concatenation.

condition—A `boolean` expression used to determine if the body of a selection or repetition statement should be executed.

conditional coverage—A strategy used in white box testing in which all conditions in a program are executed, producing both `true` and `false` results. See also: statement coverage.

conditional operator—A Java ternary operator that evaluates one of two expressions based on a condition.

conditional statement—See selection statement.

const—A Java reserved word that is not currently used.

constant—An identifier that contains a value that cannot be modified. Used to make code more readable and to facilitate changes. Defined in Java using the `final` modifier.

constructor—A special method in a class that is invoked when an object is instantiated from the class. Used to initialize the object.

container—A Java GUI component that can contain other components. See also: component hierarchy.

control characters—See nonprintable characters.

controller—Hardware devices that control the interaction between a computer system and a particular kind of peripheral.

coupling—The strength of the relationship between two software components. See also: cohesion.

CPU—See central processing unit.

data structure—Any programming construct, either defined in the language or by a programmer, used to organize data into a format to facilitate access and processing. Arrays, linked lists, and stacks can all be considered data structures.

data type—The designation that specifies the set of values (which may be infinite). For example, each variable has a data type that specifies the kinds of values that can be stored in it.

data transfer device—A hardware component that allows information to be sent between computers, such as a modem.

debugger—A software tool that allows a programmer to step through an executing program and examine the value of variables at any point. See also: jdb.

decimal—The base-10 number system, which humans use in everyday life. See also: binary.

default—A Java reserved word that is used to indicate the default case of a `switch` statement, used if no other cases match.

default visibility—The level of access designated when no explicit visibility modifier is used to declare a class, interface, method, or variable. Sometimes referred to as package visibility. Classes and interfaces declared with default visibility can be used within their package. A method or variable declared with default visibility is inherited and accessible by all subclasses in the same package.

defect testing—Testing designed to uncover errors in a program.

defined—Existing for use in a derived class, even if it can only be accessed indirectly. See also: inheritance.

delimiter—Any symbol or word used to set the boundaries of a programming language construct, such as the braces (`{}`) used to define a Java block.

derived class—See subclass.

design—(1) The plan for implementing a program, which includes a specification of the classes and objects used and an expression of the important program algorithms. (2) The process of creating a program design.

desk check—A type of review in which a developer carefully examines a design or program to find errors.

detailed design—(1) The low-level algorithmic steps of a method. (2) The development stage at which low-level algorithmic steps are determined.

development stage—The software life-cycle stage in which a software system is first created, preceding use, maintenance, and eventual retirement.

digital—A representation that breaks information down into pieces, which are in turn represented as numbers. All modern computer systems are digital.

digitize—The act of converting an analog representation into a digital one by breaking it down into pieces.

dimension—The number of index levels of a particular array.

direct recursion—The process of a method invoking itself. See also: indirect recursion.

do—A Java reserved word that represents a repetition construct. A `do` statement is executed one or more times. See also: while, for.

documentation—Supplemental information about a program, including comments in a program's source code and printed reports such as a user's guide.

domain name—The portion of an Internet address that specifies the organization to which the computer belongs.

Domain Name System—Software that translates an Internet address into an IP address using a domain server. Abbreviated DNS.

domain server—A file server that maintains a list of Internet Addresses and their corresponding IP addresses.

double—A Java reserved word that represents a primitive floating point numeric type, stored using 64 bits in IEEE 754 format.

doubly linked list—A linked list with two references in each node: one that refers to the next node in the list and one that refers to the previous node in the list.

dynamic binding—The process of associating an identifier with its definition during run time. See also: binding.

dynamic data structure—A set of objects that are linked using references, which can be modified as needed during program execution.

editor—A software tool that allows the user to enter and store a file of characters on a computer. Often used by programmers to enter the source code of a program.

efficiency—The characteristic of an algorithm that specifies the required number of a particular operation in order to complete its task. For example, the efficiency of a sort can be measured by the number of comparisons required to sort a list. See also: order.

else—A Java reserved word that designates the portion of code in an `if` statement that will be executed if the condition is false.

encapsulation—The characteristic of an object that limits access to the variables and methods contained in it. All interaction with an object occurs through a well-defined interface that supports a modular design.

equality operator—One of two Java operators that returns a boolean result based on whether two values are equal (`==`) or not equal (`!=`).

equivalence category—A range of functionally equivalent input values as specified by the requirements of the software component. Used when developing black-box test cases.

error—(1) Any defect in a design or program. (2) An object that can be thrown and processed by special `catch` blocks, though usually errors should not be caught. See also: compile-time error, syntax error, logical error, run-time error, exception.

escape sequence—In Java, a sequence of characters beginning with the backslash character (\), used to indicate a special situation when printing values. For example, the escape sequence `\t` specifies that a horizontal tab should be printed.

exception—(1) A situation that arises during program execution that is erroneous or out of the ordinary. (2) An object that can be thrown and processed by special `catch` blocks. See also: error.

exponent—The portion of a floating point value's internal representation that specifies how far the decimal point is shifted. See also: mantissa.

expression—A combination of operators and operands that produce a result.

extends—A Java reserved word used to specify the parent class in the definition of a child class.

event—(1) A user action, such as a mouse click or key press. (2) An object that represents a user action, to which the program can respond. See also: event-driven programming.

event-driven programming—An approach to software development in which the program is designed to acknowledge that an event has occurred and act accordingly. See also: event.

false—A Java reserved word that serves as one of the two boolean literals (`true` and `false`).

fetch-decode-execute—The cycle through which the CPU continually obtains instructions from main memory and executes them.

FIFO—See first-in, first-out.

file server—A computer in a network, usually with a large secondary storage capacity, which is dedicated to storing software that are needed by many network users.

final—A Java reserved word that serves as a modifier for classes, methods, and variables. A `final` class cannot be used to derive a new class. A `final` method cannot be overridden. A `final` variable is a constant.

finalize—A Java method defined in the `Object` class that can be overridden in any other class. It is called after the object becomes a candidate for garbage collection and before it is destroyed. It can be used to perform "clean-up" activity that is not performed automatically by the garbage collector.

finalizer method—A Java method, called `finalize`, that is called before an object is destroyed. See also: finalize.

finally—A Java reserved word that designates a block of code to be executed when an exception is thrown, after any appropriate catch handler is processed.

first-in, first-out—A data management technique in which the first value that is stored in a data structure is the first value that comes out. Abbreviated FIFO. See also: queue, LIFO.

float—A Java reserved word that represents a primitive floating point numeric type, stored using 32 bits in IEEE 754 format.

flushing—The process of forcing the contents of the output buffer to be displayed on the output device.

font—A specification that defines the distinct look of a character when it is printed or drawn.

for—A Java reserved word that represents a repetition construct. A `for` statement is executed zero or more times, and is usually used when a precise number of iterations is known.

foreground color—The color in which any current drawing will be rendered. See also: background color.

formal parameter—An identifier that serves as a parameter name in a method. It receives its initial value from the actual parameter passed to it. See also: actual parameter.

fourth-generation language—A high-level language that provides built-in functionality beyond that of traditional high-level languages, such as automatic report generation or database management.

function—A named group of declarations and programming statements that can be invoked (executed) when needed. A function that is part of a class is called a method. Java has no functions because all code is part of a class.

future—A Java reserved word that is not currently used.

garbage—(1) An unspecified or uninitialized value in a memory location. (2) An object that cannot be accessed anymore because all references to it have been lost.

garbage collection—The process of reclaiming unneeded, dynamically allocated, memory. Java performs automatic garbage collection of objects that no longer have any valid references to them.

generic—A Java reserved word that is not currently used.

gigabyte—A unit of binary storage, equal to 2^{30} (approximately 1 billion) bytes. Abbreviated GB.

goto—(1) A Java reserved word that is not currently used. (2) An unconditional branch.

grammar—A representation of language syntax that specifies how reserved words, symbols, and identifiers can be combined into valid programs.

graphical user interface—Software that provides the means to interact with a program or operating system by making use of graphical images and point-and-click mechanisms such as buttons and scroll bars. Abbreviated GUI.

graphics context—The drawing surface and related coordinate system on which a drawing is rendered or GUI components placed.

GUI component—A visual element, such as a button or slide bar, that are used to make up a graphical user interface (GUI).

hardware—The tangible components of a computer system, such as the keyboard, monitor, and circuit boards.

hashing—A technique for storing items so that they can be found efficiently. Items are stored in a hash table at a position specified by a calculated hash code. See also: hash method.

hash code—An integer value calculated from any given data value or object, used to determine where a value should be stored in a hash table. Also called a hash value. See also: hashing.

hash method—A method that calculates a hash code from a data value or object. The same data value or object will always produce the same hash code. Also called a hash function. See also: hashing.

hash table—A data structure in which values are stored for efficient retrieval. See also: hashing.

hexadecimal—The base-16 number system, often used as an abbreviated representation of binary strings.

hierarchy—An organizational technique in which items are layered or grouped to reduce complexity.

high-level language—A programming language in which each statement represents many machine-level instructions.

HTML—See HyperText Markup Language.

hybrid object-oriented language—A programming language that can be used to implement a program in a procedural manner or an object-oriented manner, at the programmer's discretion. See also: pure object-oriented language.

hypermedia—The concept of hypertext extended to include other media types such as graphics, audio, video, and programs.

hypertext—A document representation that allows a user to easily navigate through it in other than a linear fashion. Links to other parts of the document are embedded at the appropriate places to allow the user to jump from one part of the document to another. See also: hypermedia.

HyperText Markup Language—The notation used to define Web pages. Abbreviated HTML. See also: World Wide Web, browser.

identifier—Any name that a programmer makes up to use in a program, such as a class name or variable name.

identity—The designation of an object, which, in Java, is an object's reference name. See also: state, behavior.

IEEE 754—A standard for representing floating point values. Used by Java to represent `float` and `double` data types.

if—A Java reserved word that specifies a simple conditional construct. See also: else.

immutable—The characteristic of something that does not change. For example, the contents of a Java character string are immutable once it has been defined.

implementation—(1) The process of translating a design into source code. (2) The source code that defines a method, class, abstract data type, or other programming entity.

implements—A Java reserved word that is used in a class declaration to specify that the class implements the methods specified in a particular interface.

import—A Java reserved word that is used to specify the packages and classes that are used in a particular Java source code file.

index—The integer value used to specify a particular element in an array.

index operator—The brackets ([ ]) in which an array index is specified.

indirect recursion—The process of a method invoking another method, which eventually results in the original method being invoked again. See also: direct recursion.

infinite loop—A loop that does not terminate because the condition controlling the loop never becomes false.

infinite recursion—A recursive series of invocations that does not terminate because the base case is never reached.

infix expression—An expression in which the operators are positioned between the operands on which they work. See also: postfix expression.

inheritance—The ability to derive a new class from an existing one. Inherited variables and methods of the original (parent) class are available in the new (child) class as if they were declared locally.

initialize—To give an initial value to a variable.

initializer list—A comma-separated list of values, delimited by braces ({ }), used to initialize and specify the size of an array.

inline documentation—Comments that are included in the source code of a program.

inner—A Java reserved word that is not currently used.

input / output devices—Hardware components that allow the human user to interact with the computer, such as a keyboard, mouse, and monitor.

input / output buffer—A storage location for data on its way from the user to the computer (input buffer) or from the computer to the user (output buffer).

insertion sort—A sorting algorithm in which each value, one at a time, is inserted into a sorted subset of the entire list. See also: selection sort.

inspection—See walkthrough.

instance—An object, created from a class. Multiple objects can be instantiated from a single class.

instanceof—A Java reserved word that is also an operator, used to determine the class or type of a variable.

instance method—A method that must be invoked through a particular instance of a class, as opposed to a class method.

instance variable—A variable that must be referenced through a particular instance of a class, as opposed to a class variable.

instantiation—The act of creating an object from a class.

int—A Java reserved word that represents a primitive integer type, stored using 32 bits in two's complement format.

integration test—The process of testing software components that are made up of other interacting components. Stresses the communication between components rather than the functionality of individual components.

interface—(1) A Java reserved word that is used to define a set of bodiless methods that will be implemented by particular classes. (2) The set of messages to which an object responds, defined by the methods that can be invoked from outside of the object. (3) The techniques through which a human user interacts with a program, often graphically. See also: graphical user interface.

interpreter—A program that translates and executes code on a particular machine. The Java interpreter translates and executes Java bytecode. See also: compiler.

Internet—The most pervasive wide-area network in the world; it has become the primary vehicle for computer-to-computer communication.

Internet address—A designation that uniquely identifies a particular computer or device on the Internet.

Internet Naming Authority—The governing body that approves all Internet addresses.

invocation—See method invocation.

IP address—A series of several integer values, separated by periods (.), that uniquely identifies a particular computer or device on the Internet. Each Internet address has a corresponding IP address.

I/O devices—See input / output devices.

is-a relationship—The relationship created through properly derived classes via inheritance. The subclass *is-a* more specific version of the superclass.

ISO-Latin-1—A 128 character extension to the ASCII character set defined by the International Standards Organization. The characters correspond to the numeric values 128 through 255 in both ASCII and Unicode.

iteration—(1) One execution of the body of a repetition statement. (2) One pass through a cyclic process, such as an iterative development process.

iteration statement—See repetition statement.

iterative development process—A step-by-step approach for creating software, which contains a series of stages that are performed repetitively.

Java—The programming language used throughout this text to demonstrate software development concepts. Described by its developers as object-oriented, robust, secure, architecture neutral, portable, high-performance, interpreted, threaded, and dynamic.

Java API—See Application Programmer Interface.

Java Development Kit—A collection of software tools available free from Sun Microsystems, the creators of the Java programming language. Abbreviated JDK.

java—The Java command-line interpreter, which translates and executes Java bytecode. Part of the Java Development Kit (JDK).

javac—The Java command-line compiler, which translates Java source code into Java bytecode. Part of the Java Development Kit (JDK).

javadoc—A software tool that creates external documentation in HTML format about the contents and structure of a Java software system. Part of the Java Development Kit (JDK).

javah—A software tool that generates C header and source files, used for implementing `native` methods. Part of the Java Development Kit (JDK).

javap—A software tool that disassembles a Java class file, containing unreadable bytecode, into a human-readable version. Part of the Java Development Kit (JDK).

Java Virtual Machine—The underlying software system through which Java bytecode is executed.

jdb—The Java command-line debugger. Part of the Java Development Kit (JDK).

JDK—See Java Development Kit.

JVM—See Java Virtual Machine.

kilobyte—A unit of binary storage, equal to 2^{10}, or 1024 bytes. Abbreviated K or KB.

label—An identifier in Java used to specify a particular line of code. The `break` and `continue` statements can jump to a specific, labeled line in the program.

LAN—See local-area network.

last-in, first-out—A data management technique in which the last value that is stored in a data structure is the first value that comes out. Abbreviated LIFO. See also: stack, FIFO.

layout manager—An object that specifies the presentation of GUI components.

life cycle—The stages through which a software product is developed and used.

LIFO—See last-in, first-out.

linear search—A search algorithm in which each item in the list is compared to the target value until the target is found or the list is exhausted. See also: binary search.

link—(1) A designation in a hypertext document that "jumps" to a new document (or to a new part of the same document) when followed. (2) A connection between two items in a dynamically linked structure, represented as an object reference.

linked list—A dynamic data structure in which objects are linked using references.

literal—A primitive value used explicitly in a program, such as the numeric literal 147 or the string literal `"hello"`.

local-area network—A computer network designed to span short distances and connect a relatively small number of computers. Abbreviated LAN. See also: wide-area network.

local variable—A variable defined within a method, which does not exist except during the execution of the method.

logical error—A problem stemming from inappropriate processing in the code. It does not cause an abnormal termination of the program, but produces incorrect results. See also: compile-time error, syntax error, run-time error.

logical line of code—A logical programming statement in a source code program, which may extend over multiple physical lines. See also: physical line of code.

logical operator—One of the operators that perform a logical NOT (`!`), AND (`&&`), or OR (`||`), returning a boolean result. The logical operators are short-circuited, meaning that if their left operand is sufficient to determine the result, the right operand is not evaluated.

long—A Java reserved word that represents a primitive integer type, stored using 64 bits in two's complement format.

loop—See repetition statement.

loop control variable—A variable whose value specifically determines how many times a loop body is executed.

low-level language—Either machine language or assembly language, which are not as convenient to construct software in as high-level languages are.

machine language—The native language of a particular CPU. Any software that runs on a particular CPU must be translated into its machine language.

main memory—The volatile hardware storage device where programs and data are held when they are actively needed by the CPU. See also: secondary memory.

maintenance—(1) The process of fixing errors in or making enhancements to a released software product. (2) The software life cycle phase in which the software is in use and changes are made to it as needed.

mantissa—The portion of a floating point value's internal representation that specifies the magnitude of the number. See also: exponent.

megabyte—A unit of binary storage, equal to 2^{20} (approximately 1 million) bytes. Abbreviated MB.

member—A variable or method in an object or class.

memory—Hardware devices that store programs and data. See also: main memory, secondary memory.

memory location—An individual, addressable cell inside main memory into which data can be stored.

memory management—The process of controlling dynamically allocated portions of main memory, especially the act of returning allocated memory when it is no longer required. See also: garbage collection.

method—A named group of declarations and programming statements that can be invoked (executed) when needed. A method is part of a class.

method definition—The specification of the code that gets executed when the method is invoked. The definition includes declarations of local variables and formal parameters.

method invocation—A line of code that causes a method to be executed. It specifies any values that are passed to the method as parameters.

method call conversion—The automatic widening conversion that can occur when a value of one type is passed to a formal parameter of another type.

method overloading—See overloading.

mnemonic—A word or identifier that specifies a command or data value in an assembly language.

modal—Having multiple modes (such as a dialog box).

modem—A data transfer device that allows information to be sent along a telephone line.

modifier—A designation used in a Java declaration that specifies particular characteristics to the construct being declared.

monitor—The screen in the computer system that serves as an output device.

multidimensional array—An array that uses more than one index to specify a value stored in it.

multiple inheritance—Deriving a class from more than one parent, inheriting methods and variables from each. Not supported in Java.

NaN—An abbreviation that stands for "not a number," which is the designation for an inappropriate or undefined numeric value.

narrowing conversion—A conversion between two values of different but compatible data types. Narrowing conversions could lose information because the converted type usually has an internal representation smaller than the original storage space. See also: widening conversion.

native—A Java reserved word that serves as a modifier for methods. A native method is implemented in another programming language.

natural language—A language that humans use to communicate, such as English or French.

negative infinity—A special floating point value that represents the "lowest possible" value. See also: positive infinity.

nested if statement—An `if` statement that has as its body another `if` statement.

Netscape Navigator—A popular World Wide Web browser.

network—Two or more computers connected together so that they can exchange data and share resources.

network address—See address.

new—A Java reserved word that is also an operator, used to instantiate an object from a class.

newline character—A nonprintable character that indicates the end of a line.

nonprintable characters—Any character, such as escape or newline, that does not have a symbolic representation that can be displayed on a monitor or printed by a printer. See also: printable characters.

nonvolatile—The characteristic of a memory device that retains its stored information even after the power supply is turned off. Secondary memory devices are nonvolatile. See also: volatile.

null—A Java reserved word that is a reference literal, used to indicate that a reference does not currently refer to any object.

number system—A set of values and operations defined by a particular base value that determines the number of digits available and the place value of each digit.

object—(1) The primary software construct in the object-oriented paradigm. (2) An encapsulated collection of data variables and methods. (3) An instance of a class.

object-oriented programming—An approach to software design and implementation that is centered around objects and classes. See also: procedural programming.

octal—The base-8 number system, sometimes used to abbreviate binary strings. See also: hexadecimal.

off-by-one error—An error caused by a calculation or condition being off by one, such as when a loop is set up to access one too many array elements.

operand—A value on which an operator performs its function. For example, in the expression 5 + 2, the values 5 and 2 are operands.

operating system—The collection of programs that provide the primary user interface to a computer and manage its resources, such as memory and the CPU.

operator—(1) A Java reserved word that is not currently used. (2) A symbol that represents a particular operation in a programming language, such as the addition operator (+).

operator association—The order in which operators within the same precedence level are evaluated, either right to left or left to right. See also: operator precedence.

operator overloading—Assigning additional meaning to an operator. Operator overloading is not supported in Java, though method overloading is.

operator precedence—The order in which operators are evaluated in an expression as specified by a well-defined hierarchy.

order—The dominant term in an equation that specifies the efficiency of an algorithm. For example: selection sort is of order *n*2.

outer—A Java reserved word that is not currently used.

overflow—A problem that occurs when a data value grows too large for its storage size, which can result in inaccurate arithmetic processing. See also: underflow.

overloading—Assigning additional meaning to a programming language construct, such as a method or operator. Method overloading is supported by Java, but operator overloading is not.

overriding—The process of modifying the definition of an inherited method to suit the purposes of the subclass. See also: shadowing variables.

package—A Java reserved word that is used to specify a group of related classes.

package visibility—See default visibility.

parameter—(1) A value passed from a method invocation to its definition. (2) The identifier in a method definition that accepts the value passed to it when the method is invoked. See also: actual parameter, formal parameter.

parameter list—The list of actual or formal parameters to a method.

parent class—See superclass.

pass by reference—The process of passing a reference to a value into a method as the parameter. In Java, all objects are managed using references, so an object's formal parameter is an alias to the original. See also: pass by value.

pass by value—The process of making a copy of a value and passing the copy into a method. Therefore, any change made to the value inside the method is not reflected in the original value. All Java primitive types are passed by value.

peripheral—Any hardware device other than the CPU or main memory.

persistence—The ability of an object to stay in existence after the executing program that creates it terminates. Java currently has no built-in mechanisms to support object persistence.

physical line of code—A line in a source code file, terminated by a newline or similar character. See also: logical line of code.

pixel—A picture element. A digitized picture is made up of many pixels.

place value—The value of each digit position in a number, which determines the overall contribution of that digit to the value. See also: number system.

pointer—A variable that can hold a memory address. Instead of pointers, Java uses references, which provide essentially the same functionality as pointers but without the complications.

point-to-point connection—The link between two networked devices that are connected directly by a wire.

polymorphism—An object-oriented technique by which a reference that is used to invoke a method can result in different methods being invoked at different times. A Java reference can point to any type of object in its inheritance ancestry, and all Java method invocations are polymorphic in that they invoke the method of the object type, not the reference type.

portability—The ability of a program to be moved from one hardware platform to another without having to change it. Because Java bytecode is not related to any particular hardware environment, Java programs are considered portable. See also: architecture neutral.

positive infinity—A special floating point value that represents the "highest possible" value. See also: negative infinity.

postfix expression—An expression in which an operator is positioned after the operands on which it works. See also: infix expression.

postfix operator—In Java, an operator that is positioned behind its single operand, whose evaluation yields the value prior to the operation being performed. Both the increment (++) and decrement (--) operators can be applied postfix. See also: prefix operator.

precedence—See operator precedence.

prefix operator—In Java, an operator that is positioned in front of its single operand, whose evaluation yields the value after the operation has been performed. Both the increment (++) and decrement (--) operators can be applied prefix. See also: postfix operator.

primitive data type—A data type that is predefined in a programming language.

printable characters—Any character that has a symbolic representation that can be displayed on a monitor or printed by a printer. See also: nonprintable characters.

private—A Java reserved word that serves as a visibility modifier for methods and variables. Private methods and variables are not inherited by subclasses, and can only be accessed in the class in which they are declared.

procedural programming—An approach to software design and implementation that is centered around procedures (or functions) and their interaction. See also: object-oriented programming.

program—A series of instructions executed by hardware, one after another.

Program Design Language—A language in which a program's design and algorithms are expressed. Abbreviated PDL. See also: pseudocode.

programming language—A specification of the syntax and semantics of the statements used to create a program.

programming language statement—An individual instruction in a given programming language.

prompt—A message or symbol used to request information from the user.

protected—A Java reserved word that serves as a visibility modifier for methods and variables. Protected methods and variables are inherited by all subclasses and are accessible from all classes in the same package.

prototype—A program used to explore an idea or prove the feasibility of a particular approach.

pseudocode—Structured and abbreviated natural language used to express the algorithmic steps of a program. See also: Program Design Language.

pseudo–random number—A value generated by software that performs extensive calculations based on an initial seed value. The result is not truly random, because it is based on a calculation, but it is usually random enough for most purposes.

public—A Java reserved word that serves as a visibility modifier for classes, interfaces, methods, and variables. A public class or interface can be used anywhere. A public method or variable is inherited by all subclasses, and is accessible anywhere.

pure object-oriented language—A programming language that enforces, to some degree, software development using an object-oriented approach. See also: hybrid object-oriented language.

queue—An abstract data type that manages information in a first-in, first-out manner.

RAM—See random access memory.

random access device—A memory device whose information can be directly accessed. See also: random access memory, sequential access device.

random access memory—A term basically interchangeable with main memory. Should probably be called read-write memory, to distinguish it from read-only memory. Abbreviated RAM.

random number generator—Software that produces a pseudo–random number, generated by calculations based on a seed value.

read-only memory—Any memory device whose stored information is stored permanently when the device is created. It can be read from, but not written to. Abbreviated ROM.

recursion—The process of a method invoking itself, either directly or indirectly.

reference—A variable that holds the address of an object. In Java, a reference can be used to interact with an object, but its address cannot be accessed, set, or operated on directly.

refinement—One iteration of a cyclic development cycle in which a particular aspect of the system, such as the user interface or a particular algorithm, is addressed.

relational operator—One of several operators that determine the ordering relationship between two values: less than (<), less than or equal to (<=), greater than (>), and greater than or equal to (>=). See also: equality operator.

release—A version of a software product that is made available to the customer.

register—A small area of storage in the central processing unit (CPU) of the computer.

repetition statement—A programming construct that allows a set of statements to be executed repetitively as long as a particular condition is true. The body of the repetition statement should eventually make the condition false. Also called an iteration statement or loop. See also: while, do, for.

requirements—(1) The specification of what a program must and must not do. (2) An early phase of the software development process in which the program requirements are established.

reserved word—A word that has special meaning in a programming language, and cannot be used for any other purpose.

rest—A Java reserved word that is not currently used.

retirement—The phase of a program's life cycle in which the program is taken out of active use.

return—A Java reserved word that causes the flow of program execution to return from a method to the point of invocation.

return type—The type of value returned from a method, specified before the method name in the method declaration. Could be void, which indicates that no value is returned.

reuse—Using existing software components to create new ones.

review—The process of critically examining a design or program to discover errors. There are many types of reviews. See also: desk check, walkthrough.

RGB value—A collection of three values that define a color. Each value represents the contribution of the primary colors red, green, and blue.

ROM—See read-only memory.

run-time error—A problem that occurs during program execution that causes the program to terminate abnormally. See also: compile-time error, syntax error, logical error.

scope—See access.

searching—The process of determining the location of a target value within a list of values. See also: linear search, binary search.

secondary memory—Hardware storage devices, such as magnetic disks or tapes, which store information in a relatively permanent manner. See also: main memory.

seed value—A value used by a random number generator as a base for the calculations that produce a pseudo-random number.

selection sort—A sorting algorithm in which each value, one at a time, is placed in its final, sorted position. See also: insertion sort.

selection statement—A programming construct that allows a set of statements to be executed if a particular condition is true. See also: if, switch.

semantics—The interpretation of a program or programming construct.

sentinel value—A specific value used to indicate a special condition, such as the end of input.

service methods—Methods in an object that are declared with public visibility and define a service that the object's client can invoke.

shadowing variables—The process of defining a variable in a subclass that supersedes an inherited version.

short—A Java reserved word that represents a primitive integer type, stored using 16 bits in two's complement format.

sibling—Two items in a tree or hierarchy, such as a class inheritance hierarchy, that have the same parent.

sign bit—A bit in a numeric value that represents the sign (positive or negative) of that value.

signed numeric value—A value that stores a sign (positive or negative). All Java numeric values are signed. A Java character is stored as an unsigned value.

signature—The number, types, and order of the parameters of a method. Overloaded methods must each have a unique signature.

software—Programs and data. The intangible components of a computer system.

software component—See component.

software engineering—The discipline within computer science that addresses the process of developing high-quality software within practical constraints.

sorting—The process of putting a list of values into a well-defined order. See also: selection sort, insertion sort.

stack—An abstract data type that manages data in a last-in, first-out manner.

start angle—When defining an arc, the angle at which the arc begins. See also: arc angle.

state—The state of being of an object, defined by the values of its data. See also: behavior, identity.

statement—See programming language statement.

statement coverage—A strategy used in white-box testing in which all statements in a program are executed. See also: condition coverage.

static—A Java reserved word that serves as a modifier for methods and variables. A static method is also called a class method, and can be referenced without an instance of the class. A static variable is also called a class variable and is common to all instances of the class.

static data structure—A data structure that has a fixed size and cannot grow and shrink as needed. See also: dynamic data structure.

storage capacity—The total number of bytes that can be stored in a particular memory device.

stream—A source of input or a destination for output.

string—See character string.

string concatenation—The process of attaching the beginning of one character string to the end of another, resulting in one longer string.

strongly typed language—A programming language in which each variable is associated with a particular data type for the duration of its existence. Variables are not allowed to take on values or be used in operations that are inconsistent with their type.

structured programming—An approach to program development in which each software component has one entry and exit point and in which the flow of control does not cross unnecessarily.

stub—A method that simulates the functionality of a particular software component. Often used during unit testing.

subclass—A class derived from another class via inheritance. Also called a derived class or child class. See also: superclass.

subscript—See index.

super—A Java reserved word that is a reference to the parent class of the object making the reference. Often used to invoke a parent's constructor.

superclass—The class from which another class is derived via inheritance. Also called a base class or parent class. See also: subclass.

super reference—See super.

support methods—Methods in an object that are not intended for use outside the class. They provide support functionality for service methods. As such, they are usually not declared with public visibility.

swapping—The process of exchanging the values of two variables.

switch—A Java reserved word that specifies a compound conditional construct.

synchronization—The process of ensuring that data shared among multiple threads cannot be accessed by more than one thread at a time. See also: synchronized.

synchronized—A Java reserved word that serves as a modifier for methods. Separate threads of a process can execute concurrently in a method, unless the method is synchronized, making it a mutually exclusive resource. Methods that access shared data should be synchronized.

syntax rules—The set of specifications that govern how the elements of a programming language can be put together to form valid statements.

syntax error—An error produced by the compiler because a program did not conform to the syntax of the programming language. Syntax errors are a subset of compile-time errors. See also: syntax rules, compile-time error, logical error, run-time error.

target value—The value that is sought when performing a search on a collection of data.

TCP/IP—The Transmission Control Protocol / Internet Protocol. Software that controls the movement of messages across the Internet.

terabyte—A unit of binary storage, equal to 2^{40} (approximately 1 trillion) bytes. Abbreviated TB.

termination—The point at which a program stops executing.

ternary operator—An operator that uses three operands.

test case—A set of input values and user actions, along with a specification of the expected output, used to find errors in a system.

testing—(1) The process of running a program with various test cases in order to discover problems. (2) The process of critically evaluating a design or program.

this—A Java reserved word that is a reference to the object executing the code making the reference. A reference to the current object is implicitly passed to all methods.

thread—An independent process executing within a program. A Java program can have multiple threads running in a program at one time.

throw—A Java reserved word that is used to start an exception propagation.

throws—A Java reserved word that specifies that a method may throw a particular type of exception.

token—A portion of a string defined by a set of delimiters.

transient—A Java reserved word that serves as a modifier of variables to indicate that they do not contribute to the object's persistent state, and therefore do not need to be saved.

true—A Java reserved word that serves as one of the two boolean literals (`true` and `false`).

truth table—A complete enumeration of all permutations of values involved in a boolean expression, and the computed result.

try—A Java reserved word that is used to define the context in which certain exceptions will be handled if they are thrown.

two's complement—A technique for representing numeric binary data. Used by all Java integer primitive types (`byte`, `short`, `int`, `long`).

type—See data type.

unary operator—An operator that uses only one operand.

unchecked exception—A Java exception that does not need to be caught or dealt with if the programmer so chooses.

underflow—A problem that occurs when a floating point value becomes too small for its storage size, which can result in inaccurate arithmetic processing. See also: overflow.

Unicode—The international character set used to define valid Java characters. Each character is represented using a 16-bit unsigned numeric value.

uniform resource locator—A designation for a resource that can be located through a World Wide Web browser. Abbreviated URL.

unit test—The process of testing an individual software component. May require the creation of stub modules to simulate other system components.

URL—See uniform resource locator.

unsigned numeric value—A value that does not store a sign (positive or negative). The bit usually reserved to represent the sign is included in the value, doubling the magnitude of the number that can be stored. Java characters are stored as unsigned numeric values, but there are no primitive numeric types that are unsigned.

use relationship—A relationship between two classes, often shown in a class diagram, that establishes that one class uses another in some way, such as relying on its services.

user interface—The manner in which the user interacts with a software system, which is often graphical. See also: graphical user interface.

var—A Java reserved word that is not currently used.

variable—An identifier in a program that represents a memory location in which a data value is stored.

visibility modifier—A Java modifier that defines the scope in which a construct can be accessed. The Java visibility modifiers are public, protected, private, and default (no modifier used).

void—A Java reserved word that can be used as a return value for a method, indicating that no value is returned.

volatile—(1) A Java reserved word that serves as a modifier for variables. A volatile variable might be changed asynchronously and therefore indicates that the compiler should not attempt optimizations on it. (2) The characteristic of a memory device that loses stored information when the power supply is interrupted. Main memory is a volatile storage device. See also: nonvolatile.

von Neumann architecture—The computer architecture named after John von Neumann, in which programs and data are stored together in the same memory devices.

walkthrough—A form of review in which a group of developers, managers, and quality assurance personnel examine a design or program in order to find errors. Sometimes referred to as an inspection. See also: desk check.

WAN—See wide-area network.

waterfall model—One of the earliest software development process models. It defines a basically linear interaction between the requirements, design, implementation, and testing stages.

Web—See World Wide Web.

while—A Java reserved word that represents a repetition construct. A `while` statement is executed zero or more times. See also: do, for.

white-box testing—Producing and evaluating test cases based on the interior logic of a software component. The test cases focus on stressing decision points and ensuring coverage. See also: condition coverage, statement coverage, black-box testing.

white space—Spaces, tabs, and blank lines that are used to set off sections of source code to make programs more readable.

wide-area network—A computer network that connects two or more LANs, usually across long geographic distances. Abbreviated WAN. See also: local-area network.

widening conversion—A conversion between two values of different but compatible data types. Widening conversions usually maintain the data value intact because the converted type has an internal representation equal to or larger than the original storage space. See also: narrowing conversion.

word—A unit of binary storage. The size of a word varies by computer, usually two, four, or eight bytes. The word size indicates the amount of information that can be moved through the machine at one time.

World Wide Web—Software that makes the exchange of information across a network easier by providing a common user interface for multiple types of information. Web browsers are used to retrieve and format HTML documents. Abbreviated WWW or Web.

wrapper class—A class designed to store a primitive type in an object. Usually used when an object reference is needed and a primitive type would not suffice.

WWW—See World Wide Web.

XOR mode—A Java graphics mode that defines a reversible operation between colors. It can be used to make overlapping shapes distinct and to erase shapes by redrawing them in the same position.

Appendix B

Number Systems

This appendix contains a detailed introduction to number systems and their underlying characteristics. The particular focus is on the binary number system, its use with computers, and its similarities to other number systems. This introduction also covers conversions between bases.

In our everyday lives, we use the *decimal number system* to represent values, count, and perform arithmetic. The decimal system is also referred to as the *base-10* number system. We use 10 digits (0 through 9) to represent values in the decimal system.

Computers use the *binary number system* to store and manage information. The binary system, also called the *base-2* number system, only has two digits (0 and 1). Each 0 and 1 is called a *bit,* short for binary digit. A series of bits is called a *binary string.*

There is nothing particularly special about either the binary or decimal systems. Long ago, humans adopted the decimal number system probably because we have 10 fingers on our hands. If humans had 12 fingers, we would probably be using a base-12 number system regularly and find it as easy to deal with as we do the decimal system now. It all depends on what you get used to. As you explore the binary system, it will become more familiar and natural.

Binary is used for computer processing because the devices used to manage and store information are less expensive and more reliable if they only have to represent two possible values. Computers have been made that use the decimal system; they just are not as convenient.

There are an infinite number of number systems, and they all follow the same basic rules. You already know how the binary number system works, but you just might not be aware that you do. It all goes back to the basic rules of arithmetic.

Place Value

In decimal, we represent the values of 0 through 9 using only one digit. To represent any value higher than 9, we must use more than one digit. The position of each digit has a *place value* that indicates the amount it contributes to the overall value. In decimal, we refer to the one's column, the ten's column, the hundred's column, and so on forever.

Each place value is determined by the *base* of the number system, raised to increasing powers as we move from right to left. In the decimal number system, the place value of the digit furthest to the right is 10^0, or 1. The place value of the next digit is 10^1, or 10. The place value of the third digit from the right is 10^2, or 100. And so on. Figure B.1 shows how each digit in a decimal number contributes to the value.

The binary system works the same way, except that we exhaust the available digits much sooner. We can represent 0 and 1 with a single bit, but to represent any value higher than one, we must use multiple bits.

The place values in binary are determined by increasing powers of the base as we move right to left, just as they are in the decimal system. But in binary, the base value is 2. Therefore the place value of the bit furthest to the right is 2^0, or 1. The place value of the next bit is 2^1, or 2. The place value of the third bit from the right is 2^2, or 4, and so on. Figure B.2 shows a binary number and its place values.

The number 1101 is a valid binary number, but it is also a valid decimal number as well. Sometimes to make it clear which number system is being used, the base value is appended as a subscript to the end of a number. Therefore you can distinguish between 1101_2, which is equivalent to 13 in decimal, and 1101_{10} (one thousand, one hundred and one), which in binary is represented as 10001001101_2.

A number system with base *N* has *N* digits (0 through $N - 1$). As we have seen, the decimal system has 10 digits (0 through 9), and the binary system

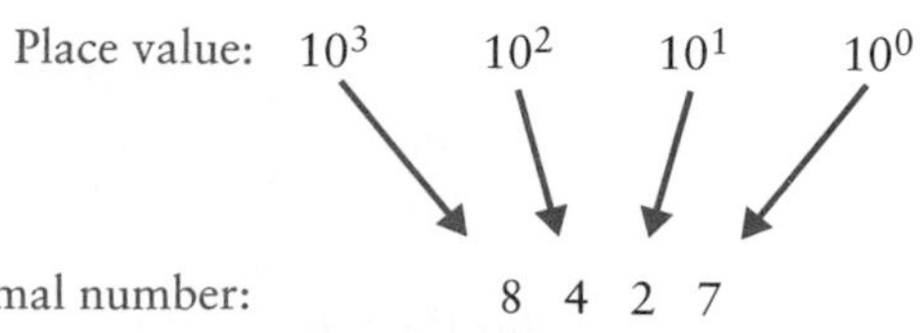

Decimal number:

Decimal number: $8 * 10^3 + 4 * 10^2 + 2 * 10^1 + 7 * 10^0 =$

$8 * 1000 + 4 * 100 + 2 * 10 + 7 * 1 = 8427$

Figure B.1 Place values in the decimal system

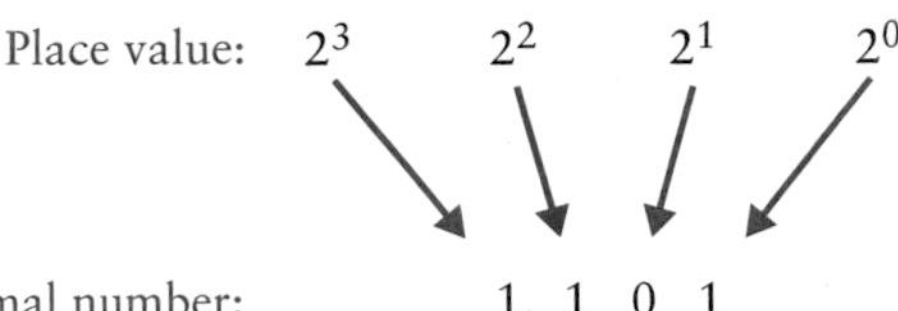

Decimal number: 1 1 0 1

Decimal number: $1 * 2^3 + 1 * 2^2 + 0 * 2^1 + 1 * 2^0 =$

$1 * 8 + 1 * 4 + 0 * 2 + 1 * 1 = 13$

Figure B.2 Place values in the binary system

has two digits (0 and 1). They all work the same way. For instance, the base-5 number system has five digits (0 to 4).

Note that, in any number system, the place value of the digit furthest to the right is 1, since any base raised to the zero power is 1. Also notice that the value 10, which we refer to as "ten" in the decimal system, always represents the base value in any number system. In base 10, 10 is one ten and zero ones. In base 2, 10 is one two and zero ones. In base 5, 10 is one five and zero ones.

Bases Higher than 10

Since all number systems with base *N* have *N* digits, then base 16 has 16 digits. But what are they? We are used to the digits 0 through 9, but in bases higher than 10, we need a single digit, a single symbol, that represents the decimal value 10. In fact, in *base 16,* which is also called *hexadecimal,* we need digits that represent the decimal values 10 through 15.

For number systems higher than 10, we use alphabetic characters as single digits for values greater than 9. The hexadecimal digits are 0 through F, where 0 through 9 represent the first 10 digits, and A represents the decimal value 10, B represents 11, C represents 12, D represents 13, E represents 14, and F represents 15.

Therefore the number 2A8E is a valid hexadecimal number. The place values are determined as they are for decimal and binary, using increasing powers of the base. So in hexadecimal, the place values are powers of 16. Figure B.3 shows how the place values of the hexadecimal number 2A8E contribute to the overall value.

All number systems with bases greater than 10 use letters as digits. For example, base 12 has the digits 0 through B and base 19 has the digits 0 through I. But beyond having a different set of digits and a different base, the rules governing each number system are the same.

Keep in mind that when we change number systems, we are simply changing the way we represent values, not the values themselves. If you have 18_{10}

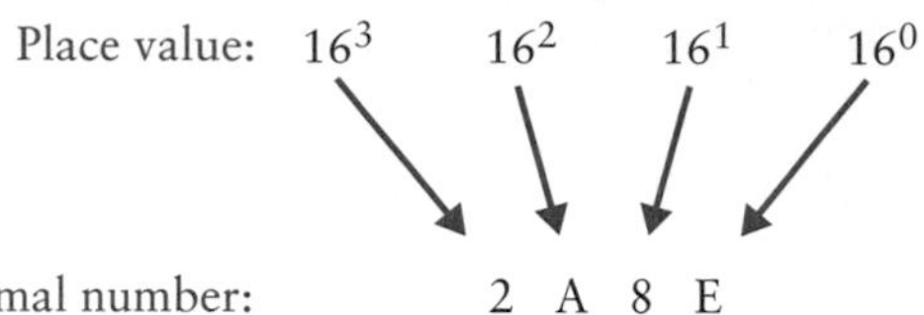

Hexadecimal number: 2 A 8 E

Decimal number: $2 * 16^3 + 10 * 16^2 + 8 * 16^1 + 14 * 16^0 =$

$2 * 4096 + 10 * 256 + 8 * 16 + 14 * 1 = 10894$

Figure B.3 Place values in the hexadecimal system

pencils, it may be written as 10010 in binary or as 12 in hexadecimal, but it is still the same number of pencils.

Figure B.4 shows the representations of the decimal values 0 through 20 in several bases, including *base 8,* which is also called *octal.* Note that the larger the base, the higher the value that can be represented in a single digit.

Conversions

We've already seen how a number in another base is converted to decimal by determining the place value of each digit and computing the result. This process can be used to convert any number in any base to its equivalent value in base 10.

Now let's reverse the process, converting a base-10 value to another base. First, find the highest place value in the new number system that is less than or equal to the original value. Then divide the original number by that place value to determine the digit that belongs in that position. The remainder is the value that must be represented in the remaining digit positions. Continue this process, position by position, until the entire value is represented.

For example, the process of converting the decimal value 180 into binary is shown in Figure B.5. The highest place value in binary that is less than or equal to 180 is 128 (or 2^7), which is the eighth bit position from the right. Dividing 180 by 128 yields 1 with 52 remaining. Therefore, the first bit is 1, and the decimal value 52 must be represented in the remaining seven bits. Dividing 52 by 64, which is the next place value (2^6), yields 0 with 52 remaining. So the second bit is 0. Dividing 52 by 32 yields 1 with 20 remaining. So the third bit is 1 and the remaining five bits must represent the value 20. Dividing 20 by 16 yields 1 with 4 remaining. Dividing 4 by 8 yields 0 with 4 remaining. Dividing 4 by 4 yields 0 with 0 remaining.

Since the number has been completely represented, the rest of the bits are zero. Therefore, 180_{10} is equivalent to 10110100 in binary. This can be con-

Binary (base 2)	Octal (base 8)	Decimal (base 10)	Hexadecimal (base 16)
0	0	0	0
1	1	1	1
10	2	2	2
11	3	3	3
100	4	4	4
101	5	5	5
110	6	6	6
111	7	7	7
1000	10	8	8
1001	11	9	9
1010	12	10	A
1011	13	11	B
1100	14	12	C
1101	15	13	D
1110	16	14	E
1111	17	15	F
10000	20	16	10
10001	21	17	11
10010	22	18	12
10011	23	19	13
10100	24	20	14

Figure B.4 Counting in various number systems

firmed by converting the new binary number back to decimal to make sure we get the original value.

This process works to convert any decimal value to any target base. For each target base, the place values and possible digits change. If you start with the correct place value, each division operation will yield a valid digit in the new base.

In the example in Figure B.5, the only digits that could have resulted from each division operation would have been 1 or 0, since we were converting to binary. However, when we are converting to other bases, any valid digit in the

Place value	Number	Digit
128	180	1
64	52	0
32	52	1
16	20	1
8	4	0
4	4	1
2	0	0
1	0	0

$180_{10} = 10110100_2$

Figure B.5 Converting a decimal value into binary

new base could result. For example, Figure B.6 shows the process of converting the decimal value 1967 into hexadecimal.

The place value of 256, which is 16^2, is the highest place value less than or equal to the original number, since the next highest place value is 16^3 or 4096. Dividing 1967 by 256 yields 7 with 175 remaining. Dividing 175 by 16 yields 10 with 15 remaining. Remember that 10 in decimal can be represented as the single digit A in hexadecimal. The 15 remaining can be represented as the digit F. Therefore 1967_{10} is equivalent to 7AF in hexadecimal.

Shortcut Conversions

We have established techniques for converting any value in any base to its equivalent representation in base 10, and from base 10 to any other base. Therefore, you can now convert a number in any base to any other base by

Place value	Number	Digit
256	1967	7
16	175	A
1	15	F

$1967_{10} = 7AF_{16}$

Figure B.6 Converting a decimal value into hexidecimal

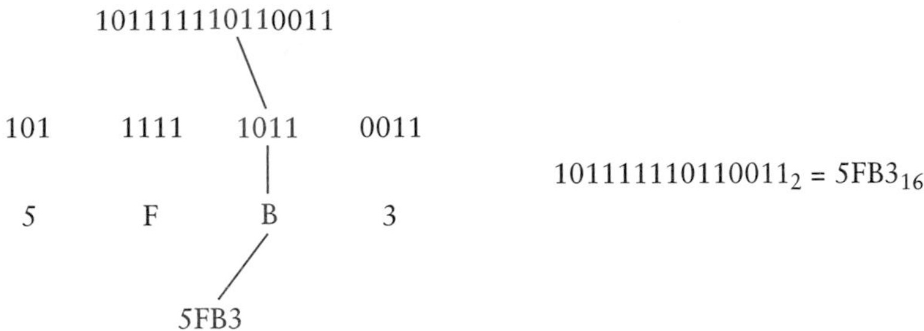

Figure B.7 Shortcut conversion from binary to hexadecimal

going through base 10. However, an interesting relationship exists between the bases that are powers of 2, such as binary, octal, and hexadecimal, that allows very quick conversions between them.

To convert from binary to hexadecimal, for instance, you can simply group the bits of the original value into groups of four, starting from the right, then convert each group of four into a single hexadecimal digit. The example in Figure B.7 demonstrates this process.

To go from hexadecimal to binary, we reverse this process, and expand each hexadecimal digit into four binary digits. Note that you may have to add leading zeros to the binary version of each expanded hexadecimal digit if necessary to make four binary digits. Figure B.8 shows the conversion of the hexadecimal value 40C6 to binary.

Why do we section the bits into groups of four when converting from binary to hexadecimal? The shortcut conversions work between binary and any base that is a power of 2. We section the bits into groups of that power. Since $2^4 = 16$, we section the bits in groups of four.

Converting from binary to octal is the same process, except that the bits are sectioned into groups of three, since $2^3 = 8$. Likewise, when converting from octal to binary we expand each octal digit into three bits.

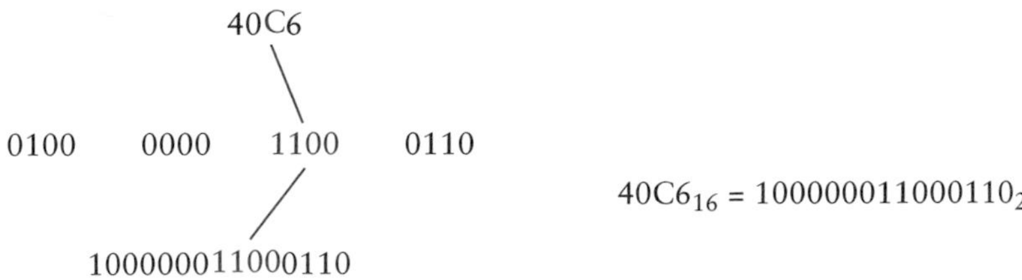

Figure B.8 Shortcut conversion from hexadecimal to binary

To convert between, say, hexadecimal and octal is now a process of doing two shortcut conversions. First convert from hexadecimal to binary, then take that result and perform a shortcut conversion from binary to octal.

By the way, these types of shortcut conversions can be performed between any base *B* and any base that is a power of *B*. For example, conversions between base 3 and base 9 can be accomplished using the shortcut grouping technique, sectioning or expanding digits into groups of two, since $3^2 = 9$.

Appendix C

The Unicode Character Set

The Java programming language uses the Unicode character set for managing text. A character set is simply an ordered list of characters, each corresponding to a particular numeric value. Unicode is an international character set that contains letters, symbols, and ideograms for languages all over the world. Each character is represented as a 16-bit unsigned numeric value. Unicode, therefore, can support over 65 thousand unique characters. Only about half of those values have characters assigned to them at this point. The Unicode character set continues to be refined as characters from various languages are included.

Many programming languages still use the ASCII character set. ASCII stands for the American Standard Code for Information Interchange. The 8-bit extended ASCII set is quite small, so the developers of Java opted to use Unicode in order to support international users. However, ASCII is essentially a subset of Unicode, including corresponding numeric values, so programmers used to ASCII should have no problems with Unicode.

Figure C.1 shows a list of commonly used characters and their Unicode numeric values. These characters also happen to be ASCII characters.

All of the characters in Figure C.1 are called *printable characters,* since they have a symbolic representation that can be displayed on a monitor or printed by a printer. Other characters are called *nonprintable characters* because they have no such symbolic representation. Note that the space character (numeric value 32) is considered to be a printable character, even though no symbol is printed when it is displayed. Nonprintable characters are sometimes called *control characters,* since many of them can be generated by holding down the control key on a keyboard and pressing another key.

The Unicode characters with numeric values 0 through 31 are nonprintable characters. Also, the delete character, with numeric value 127, is a nonprintable character. All of these characters are also ASCII characters as well.

Value	Char	Value	Char	Value	Char	Value	Char	Value	Char
32	*space*	51	3	70	F	89	Y	108	l
33	!	52	4	71	G	90	Z	109	m
34	"	53	5	72	H	91	[	110	n
35	#	54	6	73	I	92	\	111	o
36	$	55	7	74	J	93	]	112	p
37	%	56	8	75	K	94	^	113	q
38	&	57	9	76	L	95	–	114	r
39	'	58	:	77	M	96	'	115	s
40	(	59	;	78	N	97	a	116	t
41	)	60	<	79	O	98	b	117	u
42	*	61	+	80	P	99	c	118	v
43	+	62	>	81	Q	100	d	119	w
44	'	63	?	82	R	101	e	120	x
45	–	64	@	83	S	102	f	121	y
46	.	65	A	84	T	103	g	122	z
47	/	66	B	85	U	104	h	123	{
48	0	67	C	86	V	105	i	124	|
49	1	68	D	87	W	106	j	125	}
50	2	69	E	88	X	107	k	126	~

Figure C.1 A small portion of the Unicode character set

Many of them have fairly common and well-defined uses, while others are more general. The table in Figure C.2 lists a small sample of the nonprintable characters.

Nonprintable characters are used in many situations to represent special conditions. For example, certain nonprintable characters can be stored in a text document to indicate, among other things, the beginning of a new line. An editor will process these characters by starting the text that follows it on a new line, instead of printing a symbol to the screen. Various types of computer systems use different nonprintable characters to represent particular conditions.

Except for having no visible representation, nonprintable characters are essentially equivalent to printable characters. They can be stored in a Java character variable and be part of a character string. They are stored using 16

Value	Character
0	*null*
7	*bell*
8	*backspace*
9	*tab*
10	*line feed*
12	*form feed*
13	*carriage return*
27	*escape*
127	*delete*

Figure C.2 Some nonprintable characters in the Unicode character set

bits, can be converted to their numeric value, and can be compared using relational operators.

The first 128 characters of the Unicode character set correspond to the common ASCII character set. The first 256 characters correspond to the ISO-Latin-1 extended ASCII character set. Many operating systems and Web browsers will handle these characters, but may not be able to print the other Unicode characters.

Appendix D

Java Operators

Java operators are evaluated according to the precedence hierarchy shown in Figure D.1. Operators at low precedence levels are evaluated before operators at higher levels. Operators within the same precedence level are evaluated according to the specified association, either right to left (R to L) or left to right (L to R). Operators in the same precedence level are not listed in any particular order.

The order of operator evaluation can always be forced by the use of parentheses. It is often a good idea to use parentheses even when they are not required to make it explicitly clear how an expression is evaluated.

Precedence Level	Operator	Operation	Associates

1	`[]`
	`.`
	(parameters)
	`++`
	`--`
		array indexing
		object member reference
		parameter evaluation and method invocation
		postfix increment
		postfix decrement
			L to R

2	`++`
	`--`
	`+`
	`-`
	`~`
	`!`
		prefix increment
		prefix decrement
		unary plus
		unary minus
		bitwise NOT
		logical NOT
			R to L

3	`new` *(type)*	object instantiation cast	R to L

Figure D.1 Java operator precedence

<table>
<tr><th>Precedence Level</th><th>Operator</th><th>Operation</th><th>Associates</th></tr>
<tr><td>4</td><td>*
/
%</td><td>multiplication
division
remainder</td><td>L to R</td></tr>
<tr><td>5</td><td>+
+
-</td><td>addition
string concatenation
subtraction</td><td>L to R</td></tr>
<tr><td>6</td><td><<
>>
>>></td><td>left shift
right shift with sign
right shift with zero</td><td></td></tr>
<tr><td>7</td><td><
<=
>
>=
instanceof</td><td>less than
less than or equal
greater than
greater than or equal
type comparison</td><td>L to R</td></tr>
<tr><td>8</td><td>==
!=</td><td>equal
not equal</td><td>L to R</td></tr>
<tr><td>9</td><td>&
&</td><td>bitwise AND
boolean AND</td><td>L to R</td></tr>
<tr><td>10</td><td>^
^</td><td>bitwise XOR
boolean XOR</td><td>L to R</td></tr>
<tr><td>11</td><td>|
|</td><td>bitwise OR
boolean OR</td><td>L to R</td></tr>
<tr><td>12</td><td>&&</td><td>logical AND</td><td>L to R</td></tr>
<tr><td>13</td><td>||</td><td>logical OR</td><td>L to R</td></tr>
<tr><td>14</td><td>?:</td><td>conditional operator</td><td>R to L</td></tr>
<tr><td>15</td><td>=
+=
+=
-=
*=
/=
%=
<<=
>>=
>>>=
&=
&=
^=
^=
|=
|=</td><td>assignment
addition, then assignment
string concatenation, then assignment
subtraction, then assignment
multiplication, then assignment
division, then assignment
remainder, then assignment
left shift, then assignment
right shift (sign), then assignment
right shift (zero), then assignment
bitwise AND, then assignment
boolean AND, then assignment
bitwise XOR, then assignment
boolean XOR, then assignment
bitwise OR, then assignment
boolean OR, then assignment</td><td>R to L</td></tr>
</table>

Figure D.1 *(continued)*

For some operators, the operand types determine which operation is carried out. For instance, if the + operator is used on two strings, string concatenation is performed, but if it is applied to two numeric types, they are added in the arithmetic sense. If only one of the operands is a string, the other is converted to a string, and string concatenation is performed. Similarly, the operators `&`, `^`, and `|` perform bitwise operations on numeric operands, but boolean operations on boolean operands. Appendix E describes the bitwise and boolean operators in more detail.

The boolean operators `&` and `|` differ from the logical operators `&&` and `||` in a subtle way. The logical operators are "short-circuited" in that if the result of an expression can be determined by evaluating only the left operand, then the right operand is not evaluated. The boolean versions always evaluate both sides of the expression. There is no logical operator that performs an exclusive OR (XOR) operation

Appendix E

Java Bitwise Operators

This appendix contains a discussion of the Java *bitwise operators,* which operate on individual bits within a primitive value. They are only defined for integers and characters. They are unique among all Java operators because they let us work at the lowest level of binary storage. Figure E.1 lists the Java bitwise operators.

Three of the bitwise operators are similar to the logical operators `!`, `&&`, and `||`. The bitwise NOT, AND, and OR operations work basically the same way as their logical counterparts, except they work on individual bits of a value. The rules are essentially the same. Figure E.2 shows the results of bitwise operators on all combinations of two bits. Compare this chart to the truth tables for the logical operators in Chapter 5 to see the similarities.

The bitwise operators include the XOR operator, which stands for *exclusive OR*. The logical `||` operator is an *inclusive OR* operation, which means

Operator	Description
~	bitwise NOT
&	bitwise AND
|	bitwise OR
^	bitwise XOR
<<	left shift
>>	right shift with sign
>>>	right shift with zero fill

Figure E.1 Java bitwise operators

a	b	~ a	a & b	a | b	a ^ b
0	0	1	0	0	0
0	1	1	0	1	1
1	0	0	0	1	1
1	1	0	1	1	0

Figure E.2 Bitwise operators on individual bits

it returns true if both operands are true. The | bitwise operator is also inclusive, and yields a 1 if both corresponding bits are 1. However, the exclusive OR operator (^) yields a 0 if both operands are 1. There is no logical exclusive OR operator in Java.

When the bitwise operators are applied to integer values, the operation is performed individually on each bit in the value. For example, suppose the integer variable `number` is declared to be of type `byte` and currently holds the value 45. Stored as an 8-bit byte, it is represented in binary as `00101101`. When the bitwise complement operator (~) is applied to `number`, each bit in the value is inverted, yielding `11010010`. Since integers are stored using two's complement representation, the value represented is now negative, specifically 246.

Similarly, for all bitwise operators, the operations are applied bit-by-bit, which is where the term bitwise comes from. For binary operators (with two operands), the operations are applied to corresponding bits in each operand. For example, assume `num1` and `num2` are `byte` integers, and `num1` holds the value 45, and `num2` holds the value 14. Figure E.3 shows the results of several bitwise operations.

The operators `&`, `|`, and `^` can also be applied to boolean values, and they have basically the same meaning as their logical counterparts. When used with boolean values, they are called *boolean operators*. However, unlike the operators `&&` and `||`, which are "short-circuited," the boolean operators are not. Both sides of the expression are evaluated every time.

num1 & num2	num1 | num2	num1 ^ num2
00101101 & 00001110 = 00001100	00101101 | 00001110 = 00101111	00101101 ^ 00001110 = 00100011

Figure E.3 Java bitwise operators

Like the other bitwise operators, the three bitwise shift operators manipulate the individual bits of an integer value. They all take two operands. The left operand is the value whose bits are shifted, and the right operand specifies how many positions they should move. Prior to performing a shift, `byte` and `short` values are promoted to `int` for all shift operators. Furthermore, if either of the operands is `long`, then the other operand is promoted to `long`. For readability, we only use 16 bits in the examples in this section, but the concepts are the same when carried out to 32- or 64-bit strings.

When bits are shifted, some bits are lost off one end, and others need to be filled in on the other. The *left shift* operator (<<) shifts bits to the left, filling the right bits with zeros. For example, if the integer variable `number` currently has the value 13, then the statement

```
number = number << 2;
```

stores the value 52 into `number`. Initially, `number` contains the bit string `0000000000001101`. When shifted to the left, the value becomes `0000000000110100`, or 52. Notice that for each position shifted to the left, the original value is multiplied by 2.

The sign bit of a number is shifted along with all of the others. Therefore, the sign of the value could change if enough bits are shifted to change the sign bit. For example, the value 28 is stored in binary two's complement form as `1111111111111000`. When shifted left two positions, it becomes `1111111111100000`, which is 232. However, if enough positions are shifted, a negative number can become positive, and vice versa.

There are two forms of the right shift operator: one that preserves the sign of the original value (>>) and one that fills the leftmost bits with zeros (>>>).

Let's examine two examples of the *right-shift-with-sign-fill* operator. If the `int` variable `number` currently has the value 39, then the expression `(number >> 2)` results in the value 9. The original bit string stored in `number` is `0000000000100111`, and the result of a right shift two positions is `0000000000001001`. The leftmost sign bit, which in this case is a zero, is used to fill from the left.

If `number` has an original value of 216, or `1111111111110000`, then the right shift (with sign fill) expression `(number >> 3)` results in the binary string `1111111111111110`, or 22. The leftmost sign bit is a 1 in this case, and is used to fill in the new left bits, maintaining the sign.

If maintaining the sign is not desirable, the *right-shift-with-zero-fill* operator (>>>) can be used. It operates similarly to the >> operator, but fills with zero no matter what the sign of the original value is.

Appendix F
Java Modifiers

This appendix summarizes the modifiers that give particular characteristics to Java classes, interfaces, methods, and variables. For discussion purposes, the set of all Java modifiers are divided into two groups: visibility modifiers and all others.

Java Visibility Modifiers

The table in Figure F.1 describes the effect of Java visibility modifiers on various constructs. Some relationships are not applicable (N/A). For instance, a class cannot be declared with protected visibility. Note that each visibility modifier operates in the same way on classes and interfaces and in the same way on methods and variables.

Default visibility means that no visibility modifier was explicitly used. Default visibility is sometimes called *package visibility,* but you cannot use the

Modifier	Classes and interfaces	Methods and variables
default (*no modifier*)	Visible in its package.	Inherited by any subclass in the same package as its class. Accessible by any class in the same package as its class.
`public`	Visible anywhere.	Inherited by all subclasses of its class. Accessible anywhere.
`protected`	N/A	Inherited by all subclasses of its class. Accessible by any class in the same package as its class.
`private`	N/A	Not inherited by any subclass. Not accessible by any other class.

Figure F.1 Java visibility modifiers

reserved word `package` as a modifier. Classes and interfaces can only have default or public visibility; this visibility determines whether a class or interface can be referenced outside of its package.

When applied to methods and variables, the visibility modifiers dictate two specific characteristics:

- *Inheritance,* which determines whether a method or variable can be referenced in a subclass as if it were declared locally.
- *Access,* or the degree of encapsulation, which determines the scope in which a method or variable can be directly referenced. All methods and variables are accessible in the class in which they are declared.

Public methods and variables are inherited by all subclasses and can be accessed by anyone. *Private* methods and variables are not inherited by any subclasses and can only be accessed inside the class in which they are declared.

Protected visibility and default visibility (no modifier) vary in subtle ways. Note that a subclass of a parent may or may not be in the same package as the parent, and that not all classes in a package are related by inheritance.

Protected methods and variables are inherited by all subclasses, whether or not they are in the same package as the parent. Access to protected methods and variables is given to any class in the same package as the class in which they are declared. Therefore, a subclass in a different package will inherit them, but it cannot directly reference them in an instance of the parent. Furthermore, a class can directly access a protected method or variable that is declared in another class in the same package, whether or not the two classes are related by inheritance.

A method or variable with *default visibility* is inherited only by subclasses that are in the same package as the class in which the method or variable is declared. A method or variable with default visibility can be accessed by any class in the same package, whether they are related by inheritance or not.

All methods and variables declared in a parent class exist for all subclasses, but are not necessarily inherited by them. For example, when a child class is instantiated, memory space is reserved for a private variable of the parent class. However, that child class cannot refer to that variable by name since the variable was not inherited. The child class can, however, call an inherited method that references that variable. Similarly, an inherited method can invoke a method that the child class cannot call explicitly. For this reason, inheritance is carefully defined using the words "as if it were declared locally." Noninherited methods and variables can still be referenced indirectly.

A Visibility Example

Consider the situation depicted in the Figure F.2. Class `P` is the parent class that is used to derive child classes `C1` and `C2`. Class `C1` is in the same package as `P`, but `C2` is not. Class `P` contains four methods, each with different visibility modifiers. One object has been instantiated from each of these classes.

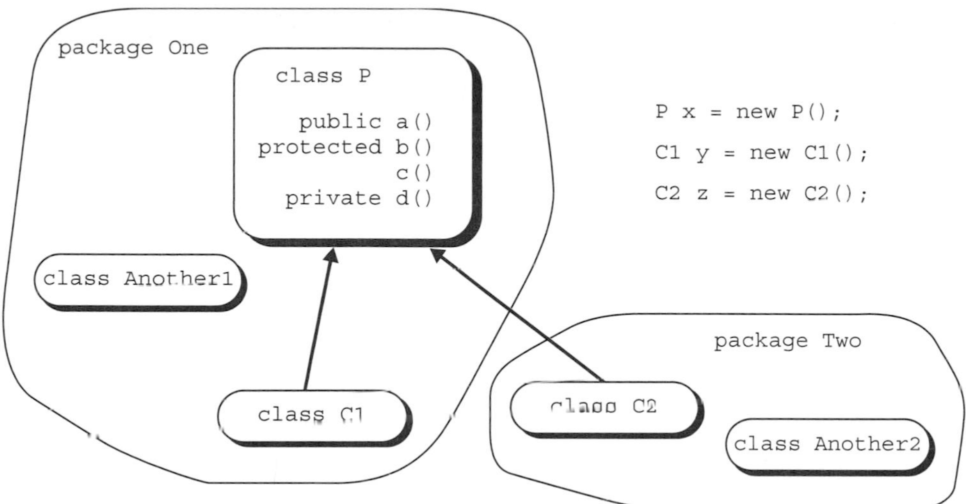

Figure F.2 A situation demonstrating Java visibility modifiers

The `public` method `a()` has been inherited by `C1` and `C2`, and any code with access to object `x` can invoke `x.a()`. The `private` method `d()` is not inherited by `C1` or `C2`, so objects `y` and `z` have no such method available to them. Furthermore, `d()` is fully encapsulated and can only be invoked from within object `x`.

`Protected` method `b()` is inherited by both `C1` and `C2`. A method in `y` could invoke `x.b()`, but a method in `z` could not. Furthermore, an object of any class in package `One` could invoke `x.b()`, even those that are not related to class `P` by inheritance, such as an object created from class `Another1`.

Method `c()` has default visibility, since no visibility modifier was used to declare it. Class `C1` inherits `c()`, but `C2` does not. Therefore object `y` can refer to the method `c()` as if it were declared locally, but object `z` cannot. Object `y` can invoke `x.c()`, as can an object instantiated from any class in package `One`, such as `Another1`. Object `z` cannot invoke `x.c()`.

These rules generalize in the same way for variables. The visibility rules may appear complicated initially, but they can be mastered with a little effort.

Other Java Modifiers

Figure F.3 summarizes the rest of the Java modifiers, which address a variety of issues. Furthermore, any given modifier has a different effect on classes, interfaces, methods, and variables. Some modifiers cannot be used with certain constructs, and therefore are listed as not applicable (N/A).

Modifier	Class	Interface	Method	Variable
`abstract`	The class may contain abstract methods. It cannot be instantiated.	All interfaces are inherently abstract. The modifier is optional.	No method body is defined. The method requires implementation when inherited.	N/A
`final`	The class cannot be used to drive new classes.	N/A	The method cannot be overridden.	The variable is a constant, whose value cannot be changed once initially set.
`native`	N/A	N/A	No method body is necessary since implementation is in another language.	N/A
`static`	N/A	N/A	Defines a class method. It does not require an instantiated object to be invoked. It cannot reference non-static methods or variables. It is implicitly final.	Defines a class variable. It does not require an instantiated object to be referenced. It is shared (common memory space) among all instances of the class.
`synchronized`	N/A	N/A	The execution of the method is mutually exclusive among all threads.	N/A
`transient`	N/A	N/A	N/A	The variable will not be serialized.
`volatile`	N/A	N/A	N/A	The variable is changed asynchronously. The compiler should not perform optimizations onit.

Figure F.3 The rest of the Java modifiers

The `transient` modifier is used to indicate data that need not be stored in a persistent (serialized) object. That is, when an object is written to a serialized stream, the object representation will include all data that is not specified as transient. See Chapter 8 for a more detailed description.

Appendix G

Java Coding Guidelines

This appendix contains a series of guidelines that describe how to organize and format Java source code. They are designed to make programs easier to read and maintain. Some guidelines can be attributed to personal preferences and could be modified. But it is important to have some standard set of practices that make sense and to follow them carefully. The guidelines presented here are followed in the example code throughout the text and are consistent with the Java naming conventions.

Consistency is half of the battle. If you follow the same rules throughout a program, and follow them from one program to another, you make the effort of reading and understanding your code easier for yourself and others. It is not unusual for a programmer to develop some software that seems straightforward at the time, only to revisit it months later and have difficulty remembering how it works. If you follow consistent development guidelines, you reduce this problem considerably.

When an organization adopts a coding standard, it is easier for people to work together. A software product is often created by a team of cooperating developers, each responsible for a piece of the system. If they all follow the same development guidelines, they facilitate the process of integrating the separate pieces into one cohesive entity.

You may have to make tradeoffs between some guidelines. For example, you may be asked to make all of your identifiers easy to read, yet keep them to a reasonably short length. Use common sense on a case-by-case basis to embrace the spirit of all guidelines as much as possible.

You may opt, or be asked, to follow this set of guidelines as presented. If changes or additions are made, make sure they are clear and that they represent a conscious effort to use good programming practices. Most of these issues are discussed further in appropriate areas of the text, but are presented succinctly here, without elaboration.

I Design Guidelines

A. Design Preparation

1. The ultimate guideline is to develop a clean design. Think before you start coding. A working program is not necessarily a good program.
2. Express and document your design with consistent, clear notation.

B. Structured Programming

1. Do not use the `continue` statement.
2. Only use the `break` statement to terminate cases of a `switch` statement.
3. Have only one `return` statement in a method, as the last line, unless it unnecessarily complicates the method.

C. Classes and Packages

1. Do not have additional methods in the class that contains the `main` method.
2. Define the class that contains the `main` method at the top of the file it is in, followed by other classes if appropriate.
3. If only one class is used from an imported package, import that class by name. If two or more are imported, use the `*` symbol.

D. Modifiers

1. Do not declare variables with `public` visibility.
2. Do not use modifiers inside an interface.
3. Always use the most appropriate modifiers for each situation. For example, if a variable is used as a constant, explicitly declare it as a constant using the `final` modifier.

E. Exceptions

1. Use exception handling only for truly exceptional conditions such as terminating errors, or for significantly unusual or important situations.
2. Do not use exceptions to disguise or hide inappropriate processing.
3. Handle each exception at the appropriate level of design.

F. Miscellaneous

1. Use constants instead of literals in almost all situations.
2. Design methods so that they perform one logical function. As such, the length of a method will tend to be no longer than 50 lines of code, and usually much shorter.
3. Keep the physical lines of a source code file to less than 80 characters in length.

4. Extend a logical line of code over two or more physical lines only when necessary. Divide the line at a logical place.

II Style Guidelines

A. Identifier Naming

1. Give identifiers semantic meaning. Example: Do not use single letter names such as `a` or `i`, unless the single letter has semantic meaning.
2. Make identifiers easy to read. Example: Use `currentValue` instead of `curval`.
3. Keep identifiers to a reasonably short length.
4. Use the underscore character to separate words of a constant.

B. Identifier Case

1. Use UPPERCASE for constants.
2. Use Title Case for class, package, and interface names.
3. Use lowercase for variable and method names, except for the first letter of each word other than the first word. Example: `minTaxRate`. Note that all reserved words must be lowercase.

C. Indentation

1. Indent the code in any block three spaces.
2. If the body of a loop, `if` statement, or `else` clause is a single statement (not a block), indent the statement three spaces on its own line.
3. Put the left brace (`{`) starting each new block on a new line. Line up the terminating right brace (`}`) with the opening left brace. Example:

```
while (value < 25)
{
   value += 5;
   System.out.println ("The value is " + value);
}
```

4. In a `switch` statement, indent each `case` label three spaces. Indent all code associated with a `case` three additional spaces.

D. Spacing

1. Carefully use white space to draw attention to appropriate features of a program.
2. Put one space after each comma in a parameter list.
3. Put one space on either side of a binary operator.

4. Do not put spaces immediately after a left parenthesis or before a right parenthesis.
5. Do not put spaces before a semicolon.
6. Put one space before a left parenthesis, except before an empty parameter list.
7. When declaring arrays, associate the brackets with the element type, as opposed to the array name, so that it applies to all variables on that line. Example:

```
int[30] list1, list2;
```

8. When referring to the type of an array, do not put any spaces between the element type and the square brackets, such as `int[]`.

E. Messages and Prompts

1. Do not condescend.
2. Do not attempt to be humorous.
3. Be informative, but succinct.
4. Define specific input options in prompts when appropriate.
5. Specify default selections in prompts when appropriate.

F. Output

1. Label all output clearly.
2. Present information to the user in a consistent manner.

III Documentation Guidelines

A. The Reader

1. Write all documentation as if the reader is computer literate and basically familiar with the Java language.
2. Assume the reader knows almost nothing about what the program is supposed to do.
3. Remember that a section of code that seems intuitive to you when you write it might not seem so to another reader or to yourself later. Document accordingly.

B. Content

1. Make sure comments are accurate.
2. Keep comments updated as changes are made to the code.
3. Be concise but thorough.

C. Header Blocks

1. Every source code file should contain a header block of documentation providing basic information about the contents and the author.
2. Each class and interface, and each method in a class, should have a small header block that describes its role.
3. Each header block of documentation should have a distinct delimiter on the top and bottom so that the reader can visually scan from one construct to the next easily. Example:

```
//*****************************************************
//              header block
//*****************************************************
```

D. In-Line Comments

1. Use in-line documentation as appropriate to clearly describe interesting processing.
2. Put a comment on the same line with code only if the comment applies to one line of code and can fit conveniently on that line. Otherwise, put the comment on a separate line above the line or section of code to which it applies.

E. Miscellaneous

1. Avoid the use of the `/* */` style of comment, except to conform to the javadoc (`/** */`) commenting convention.
2. Don't wait until a program is finished to insert documentation. As pieces of your system are completed, comment appropriately.

Appendix H
Review Checklist

This appendix contains a checklist of issues that should be addressed during a design or code review. A *review* is a careful critique of the design or code after it has been completed. A review can take many forms. In a *desk check* a programmer reviews his or her own work. In a *walkthrough* or *inspection* a group of people meet to examine and discuss the product. No matter what form a review takes, using a checklist ensures that particular issues important to creating high-quality software are not overlooked.

Reviews involve reading through a program or design to check that objects and classes are well designed, that algorithms are implemented correctly, that code is commented properly, and that other quality attributes of the software are ensured. When a review is conducted as a walkthrough, the participants usually include the author of the code, the designer (if a separate person), one or more additional software engineers, and a person that understands the system requirements. Other people that might attend a walkthrough include managers and quality control personnel.

During a walkthrough many problems usually come to light. Errors in implementation and misunderstandings about requirements are discovered. Careful notes must be taken so that these issues can be addressed. The goal is not necessarily to solve the problems in the meeting, but at least to note them for later consideration. Many walkthroughs have been sidetracked by participants following tangents concerning one particular problem.

Walkthroughs on large software projects are an absolute necessity. Unfortunately, on small software projects walkthroughs are often overlooked or dismissed as nonessential. The same benefits that occur in reviews of a large software project also occur on smaller projects. They should never be considered unnecessary. There is considerable evidence that as much as 70 percent of the errors in a program can be identified during a careful walkthrough.

Before a walkthrough can begin, the people involved must be prepared. The software or design must be complete and ready for review. The relevant documentation, such as design documents and requirements, must be gathered. The appropriate people to attend the walkthrough must be identified and given the documentation. By the time the meeting takes place, the participants should have reviewed all of the provided materials and prepared constructive comments and suggestions. An unsuccessful walkthrough is usually the result of a lack of preparation.

During the walkthrough, the author often initially presents a brief overview of the software or design. The author may ask the others in the meeting to concentrate on particular areas of concern. A specific person is usually designated as a recorder to capture the major questions or problems that come up. The author and reviewers then step through the code or design in detail, bringing up concerns and identifying problems at the appropriate time. After a walkthrough, the problems and corrective actions noted during the meeting should be summarized and presented to the author of the code or design so that they can be addressed.

The following checklist contains specific issues that should be covered in a review, whether conducted by yourself or in a meeting. A checklist makes the review process systematic and prevents important issues from being overlooked. Depending on your knowledge of software development and Java constructs, some of the checklist issues may not be clear. Initially, focus on those issues that you understand and incorporate others as they become familiar.

This checklist can be augmented with other issues. Don't hesitate to add particular topics that address your own common programming and design challenges.

Review Checklist

General Issues

- ❑ Is the design or code complete?
- ❑ Can any algorithms be simplified?
- ❑ Does the program work for all valid input?
- ❑ Does the program handle invalid input appropriately?
- ❑ Does the program do everything it is supposed to?
- ❑ Does the program operate under all constraints that were established?
- ❑ Is the API being used to its fullest extent?
- ❑ Have resources (such as books and the Web) been checked for published sources of required algorithms?

Design Issues

- ❑ Are classes designed to encapsulate specific implementation decisions?
- ❑ Are classes designed to maximize reuse?

- ❑ Is the design modular to facilitate the inclusion of new algorithms or components?
- ❑ Does each inheritance derivation represent an appropriate "*is-a*" relationship?
- ❑ Is the class hierarchy appropriate for the problem being solved?
- ❑ Are abstract classes used to enhance the design of the class hierarchy?
- ❑ Are interfaces used properly in the design to maximize consistency among classes?
- ❑ Are classes grouped appropriately into packages?
- ❑ Are exceptions only used for handling erroneous conditions or truly unusual processing?
- ❑ Are threads used appropriately to minimize user response time?

Implementation Issues

- ❑ Are all coding standards followed?
- ❑ Are all comments complete and accurate?
- ❑ Are all variables initialized before they are used?
- ❑ Are constants used to make the code more readable and facilitate modifications?
- ❑ Are all identifiers named so that their role is clear?
- ❑ Do all loops terminate?
- ❑ Do all array indexes stay within bounds?
- ❑ Do all method arguments match their parameters appropriately?
- ❑ Are modifications to parameters in methods consistent with how those parameters are passed?
- ❑ Do all overriding methods have the same signature as the parent's method?
- ❑ Are all appropriate "clean-up" activities performed, such as files being closed?
- ❑ Is the implementation consistent with the design?

Appendix I

Comparing Java to C++

The designers of Java based much of its syntax on the programming languages C and C++ so that developers who know those languages would feel comfortable using Java. However, Java should not be thought of as a revision of C++. There are many critical differences between them.

In fact, Java has integrated the best characteristics of several programming languages. At the heart of Java are important tenents of program design and implementation that are fundamentally distinct from the approach of C++. However, because of the similar syntax, and the popularity of C++, comparisons between these two languages are inevitable.

This appendix compares and contrasts Java and C++. It is a focussed summary of the primary similarities and differences, intended for developers with experience using C++.

Primitive Types

There are several important differences between Java and C++ concerning primitive data types and their use. These differences are summarized in Figure I.1.

Each variable in a Java program is either associated with a primitive type (`boolean`, `char`, `byte`, `short`, `int`, `long`, `float`, or `double`) or it is a reference to an object. C++ has various primitive types, plus structs, unions, enums, arrays, and pointers. C++ pointers might or might not refer to objects.

C++ structs are subsumed by Java objects. Java does not currently have an enumerated type. The concept of unions to save memory space was considered unnecessary by Java designers. All Java primitives are signed and have a consistent size no matter what platform is used, enhancing portability.

All Java implementations are based on the international Unicode character set, while most C++ implementations use ASCII (American Standard Code

Java	C++
Two type categories.	Various type categories.
All nonprimitive types are objects.	Separate types for structs, unions, enums, and arrays.
All numeric types are signed.	Signed and unsigned numeric types.
All primitive types are a fixed size for all platforms.	Primitive type size varies by platform.
16-bit Unicode characters.	8-bit ASCII characters.
Boolean data type primitive.	No explicit boolean data type.
Conditions must be boolean expressions.	integer results are interpreted as boolean conditions.
Variables are automatically initialized.	No automatic initialization of variables.

Figure I.1 Java versus C++: Primitive types

for Information Interchange). However, since ASCII is essentially a subset of Unicode, this distinction is transparent for programmers used to using ASCII. Unicode characters can be used in identifiers and literals in a Java program.

The `boolean` type in Java cannot be cast to any other type, and vice versa. Java integers cannot be used as logical conditions. In C++ there is no boolean type and integers must be used for decision making.

No Java variables can contain garbage, since they are set to a default value if not initialized when created. However, Java compilers may warn against the use of variables before their value has been explicitly set, whether intentional or not.

Pointers and Data Structures

The absence of pointers in Java is a key difference between the two languages. The differences concerning the use of pointers, references, and basic data structures are summarized in Figure I.2.

Java uses references that provide the functionality and versatility of pointers without their involved syntax and dangerous characteristics. Linked data structures are accomplished with references as you would with pointers in C++, but in Java it is impossible to get a segmentation fault since a reference can only refer to an object, not an arbitrary memory location.

Arrays and character strings are objects in Java, with appropriate support methods. String concatenation is a built-in operation in the Java language, and array bounds checking is automatic.

Multidimensional arrays in Java are actually arrays of arrays, in which each array is a distinct object. Therefore, for example, each row in a two-dimensional array can have a different number of elements. The length of each

Java	C++
References, with no explicit pointer manipulation and no pointer arithmetic.	Pointers, with derefernciing (* or ->) and address (&) operators.
Array references are not translated to pointer arithmetic.	Array references translate to ponter arithmetic.
Arrays automatically check index limits.	No automatic array bounds checking.
Array lengths in multidimensional arrays can vary from one element to the next one dimension.	Array lengths in multidimensional arrays are all the same size in a given dimension, fixed by the declaration.
Strings are objects.	Strings are null-terminated character arrays.
Built-in string concatenation operator (+).	String concatenation through a library function.
Use string concatenation operator for long string literals.	Use line continuation (\) for long string literals.
No `typedef`.	`typedef` to define types.

Figure I.2 Java versus C++: Pointers and data structures

array is determined when each array object is instantiated, not when the initial declaration is made.

Defining explicit type names is not necessary in either Java or C++ since the declaration of larger structures, such as classes, implicitly defines a type name. C++ includes the `typedef` operation for compatibility with C.

Object-Oriented Programming

Both languages are object-oriented, but have significantly different philosophies and techniques, as summarized in Figure I.3.

C++ supports the object-oriented approach, but it doesn't enforce it. Since C++ is essentially a superset of C, which is a procedural language, a program written in C++ could be a *hybrid* mix of procedural and object-oriented techniques. Java is a *pure* object-oriented language since it enforces the object-oriented approach. As such, all functions in Java are methods, defined inside a class.

Several constructs and techniques that are a part of C++ are not included in Java, mainly to keep the complexity of the language down. These include multiple inheritance, parameterized types, and operator overloading. However, Java has the ability to define a formal interface specification, which gives the most important characteristics of multiple inheritance to Java programs. Both languages support method overloading.

In C++, a method must be explicitly declared as virtual in order to allow run-time dynamic binding of a method invocation to the appropriate definition. In Java, all methods are handled consistently and are dynamically bound, except for methods that are defined with the `final` modifier.

Java	C++
Pure object-oriented language.	Hybrid between procedural and object-oriented.
All functions (methods) are part of a class.	Can have stand-alone functions.
No multiple inheritance.	Multiple inheritance.
Formal interface specifications.	No formal interface specifications.
No parameterized type.	Templates as a parameterized type.
No operator overloading.	Operator overloading.
All methods (except final methods) are dynamically bound.	Virtual functions are dynamically bound.

Figure I.3 Java versus C++: Object-oriented programming

Special Characteristics

Some of the most highly promoted aspects of Java concern its relationship to the Web and other special characteristics that distinguish it from C++. These differences are summarized in Figure I.4.

Links to Java applets can be embedded in HTML documents, then retrieved and executed using Web browsers. The Java API has specific support for network communication.

A C++ programmer must perform explicit dynamic memory management, releasing objects and other dynamically allocated data space when it is no longer needed. In Java, garbage collection is automatic. An object in a Java program is marked as a candidate for garbage collection after the last reference to it is removed. Therefore, Java does not support destructors, though there is the ability to define a `finalize` method for other cleanup activity.

Java	C++
Specifically attuned to network and Web processing.	No relationship to networks or the Web.
Automatic garbage collection.	No automatic garbage collection.
Combination of compiled and interpreted.	Compiled.
Slower execution when interpreted.	Fast execution.
Architecture neutral.	Architecture specific.
Supports multithreading.	No multithreading.
Automatic generation of documentation in HTML format.	No automatic documentation generation.

Figure I.4 Java versus C++: Special characteristics

Java source code is compiled into bytecode, a low-level representation that is not tied to any particular processor. The bytecode can then be executed on any platform that has a Java interpreter. Java is therefore considered to be architecture-neutral.

When interpreted, Java programs have a slower execution speed, but because they are already compiled to a low-level representation, the interpretation overhead is not problematic for many applications. C++ compilers are specific to each type of processor.

The Java language supports multiple threads of execution, with synchronization mechanisms. It also has a special comment syntax, which can be used to generate external documentation in HTML format about the contents and structure of a Java system.

General Programming Issues

There are several specific differences between Java and C++ that affect basic programming practices. They are summarized in Figure I.5.

Java	C++
Method bodies must be defined inside the class to which they belong.	Method bodies must be defined inside the class to which they belong.
No forward referencing required.	Explicit forward referencing required.
No preprocessor.	Heavy reliance on preprocessor.
No comma operator.	Comma operator.
No variable-length parameter lists.	Variable-length parameter lists.
No optional method parameters.	Optional function parameters.
No `const` reference parameters.	`const` reference parameters.
No `goto` statement.	`goto` statement.
Labels on `break` and `continue`.	No labels on `break` and `continue`.
Command-line arguments do not include the program name.	Command-line arguments do not include the program name.
Main method cannot return a value.	Main function can return a value.
No global variables.	Global variables.
Character escape sequences can appear in a program.	Character escape sequences must appear in a string or character literal.
Cannot mask identifiers through scope.	Can mask identifiers through scope.

Figure I.5 Java versus C++: General programming issues

Java does not support variable-length parameter lists for methods. It also does not allow parameters to be given a default value which essentially makes them optional during invocation.

Java has no comma operator, though its `for` loop syntactically allows multiple initializations and increments using the comma symbol. Java does not allow variables to be declared with global scope. In C++, you must use an explicit forward reference (function prototype) to inform the compiler that a function will be used prior to its definition, but in Java no such forward referencing is needed.

Java does not rely on a preprocessor. Most of the functionality that is provided by the C++ preprocessor is defined in the Java language itself.

There is no `goto` statement in Java, though `goto` is included in the Java reserved words. Java allows statements to be labeled, and the `break` and `continue` statements can jump to specific labeled points in the code.

Finally, in Java, an identifier name cannot be masked by another declaration and scope, as it can in C++. For example, the following code segment is valid in C++, but causes a compile-time error in Java:

```
{
int x = 12;
    {
        int x = 25;     // same variable name with
                        // distinct memory space
    }
}
```

Appendix J

An HTML Tutorial

This appendix contains a brief tutorial covering the HyperText Markup Language (HTML) and the creation of basic Web pages. HTML files contain instructions that describe how text, images, and multimedia are displayed by Web browsing software. Two of the more popular Web browsers are Internet Explorer by Microsoft and Navigator by Netscape.

HTML files can be created using a simple text editor. They contain the text to be displayed and *tags* that describe the layout, style, and other features of a document. Tags suggest how the browser program should display the document, but each browser interprets the meaning of a tag in its own way. Furthermore, although all browsers recognize a common set of tags, a particular browser may also recognize additional tags that others do not. Therefore what you see when you view a particular HTML document with one browser might be different than what you see when viewed with another.

In this appendix, we describe the most popular HTML tags. However, if you plan to create advanced Web pages, you may want to use additional sources covering all aspects of HTML. Many Web sites contain detailed information on specific HTML constructs. In fact, one of the best ways to learn HTML is to find interesting Web pages, and use your Web browser to view the HTML source for that document.

Basic HTML Documents

There are two basic sections to every HTML file. The first section is the head of the document, which contains a description of the document, including its title. The second section is the body of the document, which contains the information to be displayed, such as text, images, and links to other documents. The following is an example of a basic HTML document for a local student activities group:

```
<HTML>
   <HEAD>
      <TITLE>Students in Action</TITLE>
   </HEAD>
   <BODY>
      Students in Action is dedicated to help our local
      community by using the volunteer effort of college
      students.  This semester our planned actions are:
      to help a local food drive for flood victims in
      the Midwest, to visit local adult care centers, and
      teach Java to grade school students.
      Our group is active, energetic, and always in need of
      donations of equipment, effort, or money.  We are
      always willing to help staff and plan community
      events.
      As always, our president (at x222) is eager and
      willing to answer questions and hear suggestions on
      how we can be more active in our community.
   </BODY>
</HTML>
```

The words such as `HEAD`, `TITLE`, and `BODY` are called elements. Tags are specified using an element enclosed in angle brackets (< >). Tags are often used in pairs, called a start tag and an end tag. These tags delimit, or mark, a particular region of text. Generally, the start tag uses the element name, such as `<HEAD>`, and the end tag uses a slash (/) followed by the element name, such as `</HEAD>`.

Everything between `<HEAD>` and `</HEAD>` is considered to be the introduction of the document. In this case, it contains one line that defines the title of the document. The text between `<TITLE>` and `</TITLE>` appears in the title bar of the Web browser when the document is displayed.

Everything between `<BODY>` and `</BODY>` is considered to be the body of the document. In this case, the body contains several paragraphs of text that will be displayed in the browser window. The text in an HTML document can be in any form convenient for its author. Browsers only pay attention to tags. Therefore, it does not matter how white space is used to separate words or lines between tags. Browsers will reformat the text to be displayed appropriately for the width and height of the browser window, independent of how the document is written. Figure J.1 shows this Web page as displayed in a browser. Figure J.2 shows the same Web page, but in a differently shaped

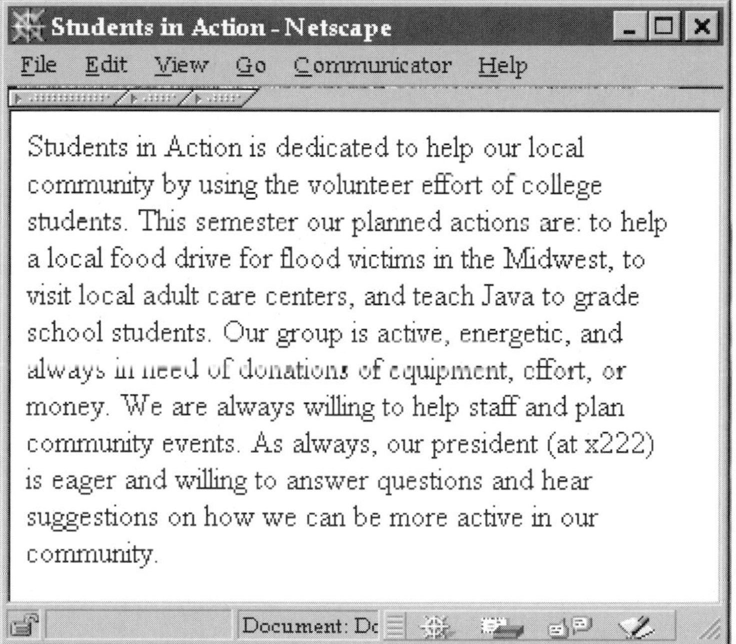

Figure J.1 Initial Web page for Students in Action

browser window. Notice how the text is reformed because of the browser's width and height.

Formatting Text

There are many tags that can be used to aid browsers with formatting text. Notice in Figures J.1 and J.2 that the blank spaces in the paragraphs were ignored when the text was displayed. For browsers to understand how to format text, each part of the text must be marked up with tags. To indicate to the browser what paragraphs are in the text, the `P` element should be used. The following is a marked up version of the Students in Action Web page, so that the original paragraphs are reflected in what a browser presents, as shown in Figure J.3.

```
<HTML>
   <HEAD>
      <TITLE>Students in Action</TITLE>
```

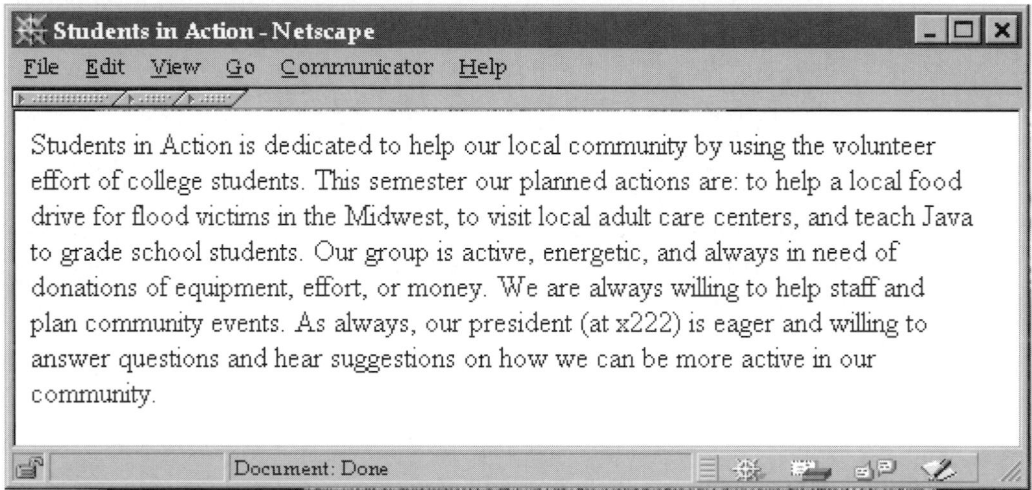

Figure J.2 Initial Web page for Students in Action reformatted

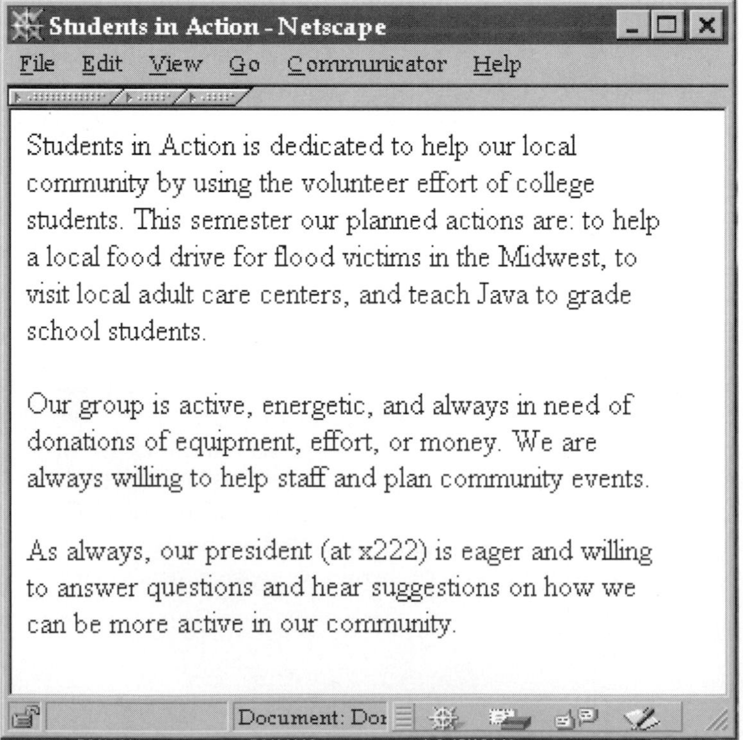

Figure J.3 Paragraph-formatted Web page

```
    </HEAD>
    <BODY>
       <P>Students in Action is dedicated to help our
       local community by using the volunteer effort of
       college students.  This semester our planned actions
       are: to help a local food drive for flood victims
       in the Midwest, to visit local adult care centers,
       and teach Java to grade school students.</P>
       <P>Our group is active, energetic, and always in
       need of donations of equipment, effort, or money.
       We are always willing to help staff and plan
       community events.</P>
       <P>As always, our president (at x222) is eager and
       willing to answer questions and hear suggestions on
       how we can be more active in our community.</P>
    </BODY>
</HTML>
```

Figure J.3 is a snapshot showing the effects of the <P> tag used in the text. Notice the <P> is not displayed by the browser, but instead a single blank line has been inserted.

Besides the P element there are many other elements that can be used to change the format of the text. The table in Fig. J.4 shows some elements and their effect on the text associated with a tag.

B, I, and U are popular elements that control the style of the font presented. They work similarly to how a word processor allows text to be bold, italic, or underlined. For example, the following HTML lines:

```
<P><B>I'd buy that for a dollar</B></P>
<P><I>May the force be with you</I></P>
<P><I><B>I'll be back</B></I></P>
```

would be displayed by a browser as:

I'd buy that for a dollar
May the force be with you
I'll be back

Many elements can be nested to produce a combination of effects. Notice the use of I and B on the last line of the previous example. Usually, it is considered good practice to unnest tags in the same order as they were nested. This practice makes it easier to modify the HTML later. The rest of the elements

Element	Effect or Purpose
U	Underline
B	Boldface
I	Italics
STRONG	Strong type, often rendered using boldface
EM	Emphasis, often rendered using italics
STRIKE	A line drawn through the text
TT	typewriter typeface
CODE	Code listings
KBD	Keyboard input
VAR	Variables or arguments to commands
BIG	A larger point size than the current font
SMALL	A smaller point size than the current font
SUB	Subscript
SUP	Superscript
CITE	Citation of reference documents
BLINK	blinks on and off

Figure J.4 Some HTML text elements

described in Figure J.4 also change characteristics of the font displayed by the browser.

There are several other elements similar to the `P` element that can be used to change the layout of the text. The `<CENTER>` and `</CENTER>` tags indicate that the browser should center the text associated with the tag. The `<BR>` tag forces a line break in the text. The `<HR>` tag tells the browser to include a horizontal rule in the document. The horizontal rule is often used to separate sections of a document visually. Note that the `HR` and `BR` elements do not have associated ending tags, because they do not affect text directly. The `<NOBR>` and `</NOBR>` tags indicate that the browser should not insert line breaks anywhere when displaying the text associated with the tags. The `<Q>` tag is used within a line of text to quote a few words. Text associated with the `Q` element is displayed within single quotes. The `<BQ>` tag can be used to quote a block of text, such as a paragraph.

In addition to marking up portions of the document to be displayed in a particular way, HTML header tags can provide an overall hierarchical structure to the document. Headers are used to indicate different sections of a document. HTML provides six heading levels: `<H1>`, `<H2>`, `<H3>`, `<H4>`, `<H5>`, and `<H6>`. The `<H1>` heading tag is the highest heading level and `<H6>` is the lowest. An `H1` element can be thought of as marking a chapter of a book. An `H2` element can be thought of as marking a section of a chapter. An `H3` element is associated with a subsection, and the other headers follow suit. Generally, headings are displayed by most browsers as bold text, and usually are larger in size (compared to the rest of the "normal" text in the document). For example, consider the following HTML document:

```
<HTML>
    <HEAD>
        <TITLE>Header Example</TITLE>
    </HEAD>
    <BODY>
        <H1> 1. Heading One
        <H2> 2. Heading Two
        <H3> 3. Heading Three
        <H4> 4. Heading Four
        <H5> 5. Heading Five
        <H6> 6. Heading Six
    </BODY>
</HTML>
```

The display of this page is shown in Figure J.5.

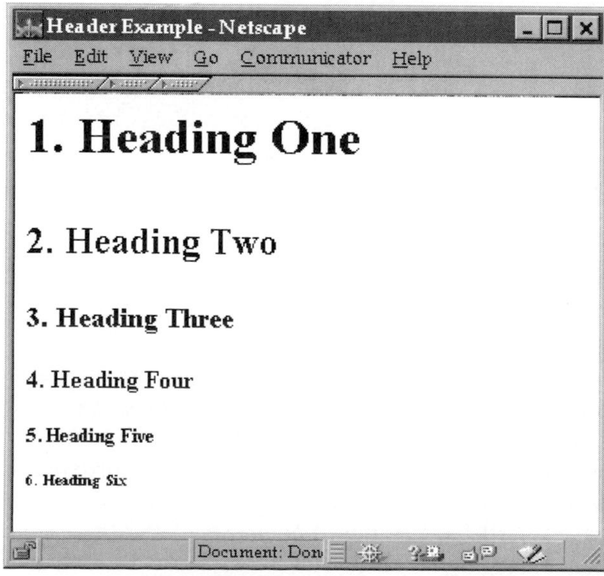

Figure J.5 Header example

There are several reasons to use headers in your web pages. The first is that headers make a document easier to read. They provide a visual cue to a reader of the different sections of your text. These cues enable a reader to easily identify and skip to the appropriate section of a web page. The second reason is that Web search engines often catalog the text associated with headers in a document. Therefore, using a good heading for a section of a document may help others find your page on the Internet. Generally, documents should contain no more than three levels of headings.

The following HTML is the Students in Action Web page marked up with a header and some font styles.

```
<HTML>
   <HEAD>
      <TITLE>Students in Action</TITLE>
   </HEAD>
   <BODY>
      <CENTER><H1>Students in Action</H1></CENTER>
      <CENTER><I>Dedicated to help our local community
      by using the volunteer effort of college
      students.</I></CENTER>
      <P>This semester our planned actions are: to help a
      local food drive for flood victims in the Midwest,
      to visit local adult care centers, and teach Java
      to grade school students.</P>
      <P>Our group is active, energetic, and always in
      need of donations of equipment, effort, or money.
      We are always willing to help staff and plan
      community events.</P>

      <P>As always, our president (at x222) is eager and
      willing to answer questions and hear suggestions on
      how we can be more active in our community.</P>

   </BODY>
</HTML>
```

The display of this page can be seen in Figure J.6.

Besides headers, there are several other ways to structure a Web document including frames, tables, and lists. Frames and tables are more complicated than the tags we have seen so far, and are beyond the scope of this tutorial. HTML has two types of lists: an ordered list and an unordered list. Creating a list requires two parts to be identified using tags. The first is the entire list. For an ordered list, place the `<OL>` tag at the start of the list, and `</OL>` at the

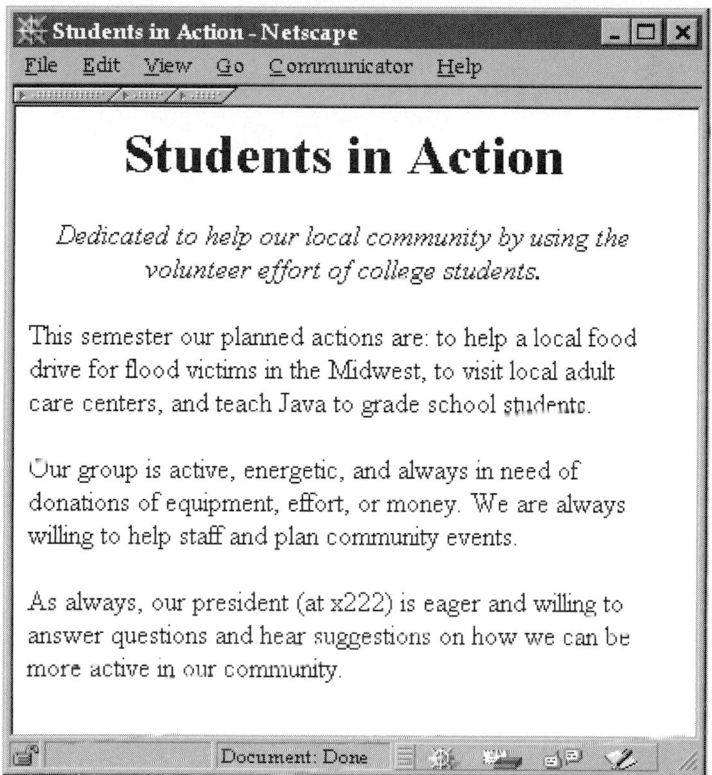

Figure J.6 Header, centering, and font changes for Web page

end of the list, and then surround each item in the list with `<LI>` and `</LI>`. For example, the following HTML defines one list with three items:

```
<OL>
   <LI>I'd buy that for a dollar</LI>
   <LI>May the force be with you</LI>
   <LI>I'll be back</LI>
</OL>
```

This text will be formatted in browsers as:

1. I'd buy that for a dollar
2. May the force be with you
3. I'll be back

Notice that the browser will automatically count and sequence the list items for you. Lists can also be nested within lists. Consider the following HTML code:

```
<OL>
    <LI>First Item in first list</LI>
    <OL>
        <LI>First Item in first sublist</LI>
        <LI>Second Item in first sublist</LI>
    </OL>
    <LI>Second Item in first list</LI>
    <OL>
        <LI>First Item in second sublist</LI>
        <LI>Second Item in second sublist</LI>
    <OL>
</OL>
```

This text will be formatted similar to the following:

1. First Item in first list
   1. First Item in first sublist
   2. Second Item in first sublist
2. Second Item in first list
   1. First Item in second sublist
   2. Second Item in second sublist

An unordered list is very similar to an ordered list. Unordered lists use the `UL` element instead of the `OL` element that ordered lists use. Unordered lists are usually displayed with a bullet symbol to the left of the list item. Some browsers may use a different symbol, and there are tag attributes that you can specify that will let you use images as the list item symbol.

The following uses an unordered list to represent the various activities that the Students in Action have planned for this semester. In addition, we added horizontal rules to offset the `H1` element in the document.

```
<HTML>
    <HEAD>
        <TITLE>Students in Action</TITLE>
    </HEAD>
    <BODY>
        <HR>
```

```
        <CENTER><H1>Students in Action</H1></CENTER>

        <HR>

        <CENTER><I>Dedicated to help our local community
        by using the volunteer effort of college
        students.</I></CENTER>

        <HR>

        <P>This semester our planned actions are:</P>

        <UL>
           <LI> to help a local food drive for flood
           victims in the Midwest</LI>
           <LI> to visit local adult care centers</LI>
           <LI> to teach Java to grade school students</LI>
        </UL>

        <P>Our group is active, energetic, and always in
        need of donations of equipment, effort, or money.
        We are always willing to help staff and plan
        community events.</P>

        <P>As always, our president (at x222) is eager and
        willing to answer questions and hear suggestions on
        how we can be more active in our community.</P>

    </BODY>
</HTML>
```

The display of this document can be seen in Figure J.7.

As you can see from Figure J.7, although the content of the Web page has not changed since Figure J.1, the presentation has changed dramatically.

Links

The World Wide Web would not be a Web without links between documents. A link connects one document to another. The destination of the link can be a local file or a remote file hosted on another computer. Links are displayed in a number of different ways, but the most popular and recognizable is blue text that is underlined. In most browsers, when you move your pointing device (mouse, or other device) over a link in a graphical browser, the destination of

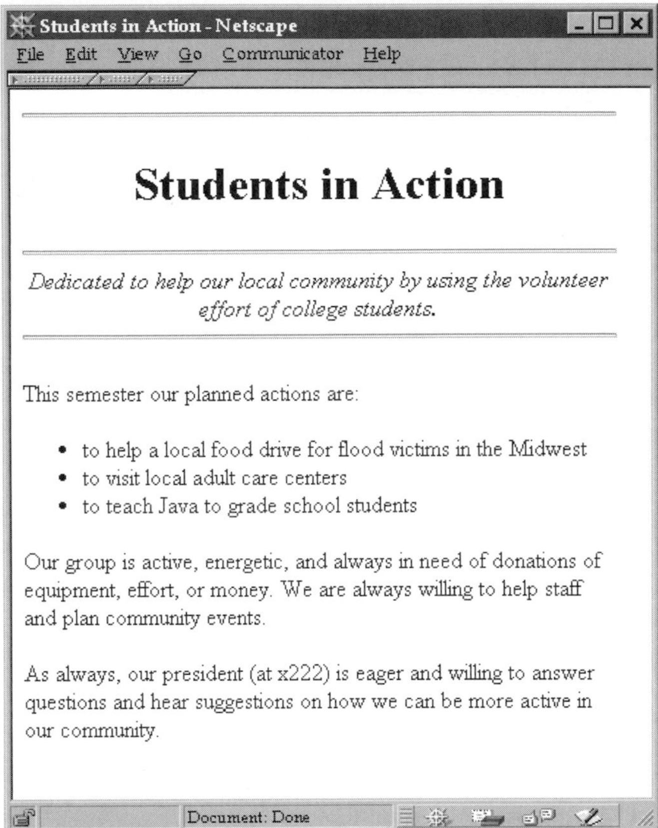

Figure J.7 Lists and lines added to Web page

the link is displayed somewhere on the screen. The most popular browsers display the destination link on the bottom of the display window.

The link tag, <A>, takes one attribute that defines its destination. Inside the link tags (also known as anchor tags) the URL of a new document is specified. For example, the following HTML creates two links

```
<A HREF="http://www.csc.vill.edu/~lewis">Dr. Lewis' Home Page
      Link</A>
<A HREF="http://www.yahoo.com">Yahoo Internet Search Link</A>
```

The text associated with the <A> and </A> tags is what the browser will usually display as underlined blue text. No checking is done on the validity of the destination until the user selects (or clicks on) the link. Therefore, when one writes a Web page, all links should be tested (i.e., clicked on or exercised). Following the selection of a link by a user, the browser will attempt to load the contents of the destination. When a successful connection is made to the destination link (either as a remote computer, or another file on your own computer), the browser will display the contents of the destination page.

Links are very useful for breaking up a document based on content. Links have been the driving force of the popularity of HTML and the World Wide Web because they allow users to read documents located on computers throughout the world. The following HTML has five example links in it. The first three represent links to local documents that describe more detail about the Students in Action projects and are located on the same server. The fourth link represents an absolute URL, which can refer to any document in the World Wide Web. The fifth link is a mailto link. This is a special type of link that allows users to send mail by clicking on the link. In the following case, the mail would be sent to `president@breakaway.com`.

```
<HTML>
   <HEAD>
      <TITLE>Students in Action</TITLE>
   </HEAD>
   <BODY>
      <HR>

      <CENTER><H1>Students in Action</H1></CENTER>

      <HR>

      <CENTER><I>Dedicated to help our local community
      by using the volunteer effort of college
      students.</I></CENTER>

      <HR>

      <P>This semester our planned actions are:</P>

      <UL>
         <LI> to <A HREF="food.html">help a local food drive</A>
              for flood victims in the Midwest</LI>
         <LI> to <A HREF="adult.html">visit local adult care
              centers</A></LI>
         <LI> to <A HREF="grade.html">teach Java to grade
              school students</A></LI>
      </UL>

      <P>Our group is active, energetic, and always in
      need of donations of equipment, effort, or money.
      We are always willing to help staff and plan
      community events.</P>
```

```
        <P>As always, our <A HREF="mailto:president@breakaway.com">
        president</A> (at x222) is eager and willing to answer
        questions and hear suggestions on how we can be more
        active in our community.</P>

        <P>Visit our <A HREF="http://www.vill.edu">University Home
        Page</A>.</P>

    </BODY>
</HTML>
```

Figure J.8 shows how this page will be displayed by a browser.

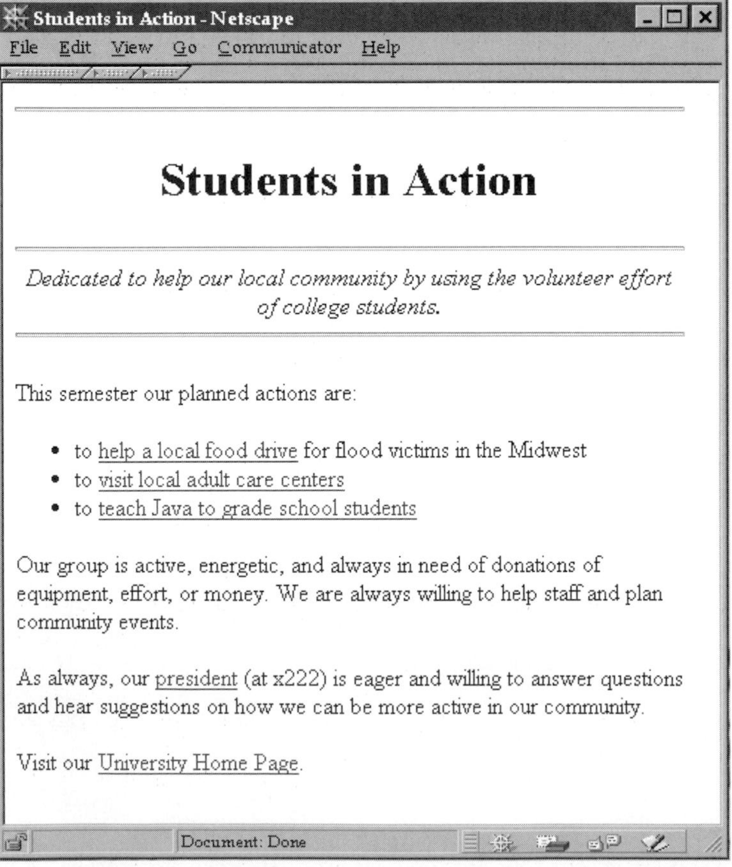

Figure J.8 Links added to Web page

Color and Images

Some of the most popular browsers (Netscape Navigator and Microsoft Internet Explorer) have introduced common extension attributes to the <BODY> tag to allow a background color or images for the document to be specified. Background images or color can dramatically improve the aesthetic appearance on a color capable display.

The first attribute is the BGCOLOR attribute. This attribute is used to set the background color of the entire document. For example, the following text will set the background color to red in an HTML document:

```
<BODY BGCOLOR=RED>
```

There are two basic methods for defining a color in HTML. The first, as seen in the previous example, uses a standard color name. Note that the display of HTML code is solely under the control of a browser; therefore these names are not truly standard, but are common color names that most browsers support. Be sure to check all browsers your users may have, to see what specific color names are accepted before choosing an appropriate color. A few de facto standard names for colors that are accepted by both Netscape and Microsoft's browsers are black, blue, gray, green, navy, purple, red, yellow, and white. The second method of choosing a color is to change the color name to an RGB value. An RGB value is a sequence of three numbers that represents the amount of red, green, and blue that will be used to create the color. The numbers represent the various strength of the colors involved (0=off, 255=full on). The combination of three values produce a specific color. The RGB values are represented as three pairs of hex characters preceded by a number sign (#) and surrounded by double quotes. For example, to represent the color in which red is 50, green is 150, and blue is 255, the <BODY> tag would look like the following:

```
<BODY BGCOLOR="#3296FF">
```

There are many good shareware programs available on the Internet that will help you determine the RGB values for a particular color.

In addition to setting the background to a single color, it is also possible to tile the background with a particular image. Most graphical browsers have implemented an extension to the <BODY> tag that will take a GIF or JPEG image and repeat it both horizontally and vertically (i.e., tiling) to create a background pattern. Some images can be fairly simple, like a single color image. Others can be more complex, representing a repeating pattern (e.g., bathroom tiles, or a stone mosaic). To use an image as a background use the BACKGROUND attribute in the <BODY> tag and follow it with the name of the image file in quotes. For example, the piece of HTML code below uses the `STONE.GIF` image as a tiling background image.

```
<BODY BACKGROUND="STONE.GIF">
```

Care should be given to the type of image, and strength of its colors. Many times, using an interesting image can make the document's text difficult to read. There are many pages on the World-Wide Web that have free images that you can copy and use as backgrounds.

Graphic images can be included in an HTML document in other ways as well. Most of the popular browsers can show both GIF and JPEG image formats. To include an image use the `<IMG>` tag. The `SRC` attribute of the `<IMG>` tag can be used to describe the URL of the graphic image file. For example, the following HTML fragment will include an image called `new.gif`:

```
<IMG SRC="new.gif">
```

The following HTML code is the Students in Action Web page modified to use an image as a banner that introduces the organization, and a new image to draw attention to a portion of the page that may have changed recently.

```
<HTML>
   <HEAD>
      <TITLE>Students in Action</TITLE>
   </HEAD>
   <BODY>
      <HR>

      <CENTER><IMG SRC="SIA.gif"></CENTER>

      <HR>

      <CENTER><I>Dedicated to help our local community
      by using the volunteer effort of college
      students.</I></CENTER>

      <HR>

      <P>This semester our planned actions are:</P>

      <UL>
         <LI> to <A HREF="food.html">help a local food drive</A>
              for flood victims in the Midwest</LI>
         <LI> to <A HREF="adult.html">visit local adult care
```

```
            centers</A></LI>
        <LI> to <A HREF="grade.html">teach Java to grade
            school students</A> <IMG SRC="new.gif"></LI>
    </UL>

    <P>Our group is active, energetic, and always in
    need of donations of equipment, effort, or money.
    We are always willing to help staff and plan
    community events.</P>

    <P>As always, our <A HREF="mailto:president@wpllabs.com">
    president</A> (at x222) is eager and willing to answer
    questions and hear suggestions on how we can be more
    active in our community.</P>

    <P>Visit our <A HREF="http://www.vill.edu">University Home
    Page</A>.</P>

  </BODY>
</HTML>
```

Figure J.9 shows how this page is displayed by a browser.

Applets

The <APPLET> tag is used to execute an applet in a document. The <APPLET> tag has many possible attributes. Its only required attribute is the CODE attribute. The CODE attribute names the class file of the applet that should execute in the document. The browser will load that applet's class file from the same URL as the document that contains the <APPLET> tag. For example, to execute the Marquee applet, the following HTML fragment is used:

```
<APPLET code=Marquee WIDTH=100 HEIGHT=50>
</APPLET>
```

A browser displaying this HTML code will load the Marquee.class file into the browser and execute it. Attributes for the <APPLET> tag include:

- HEIGHT—used to define the space in pixels reserved for the display height of the applet
- WIDTH—used to define the space in pixels reserved for the display width of the applet
- CODEBASE—used to define an alternate URL for the location of the class file

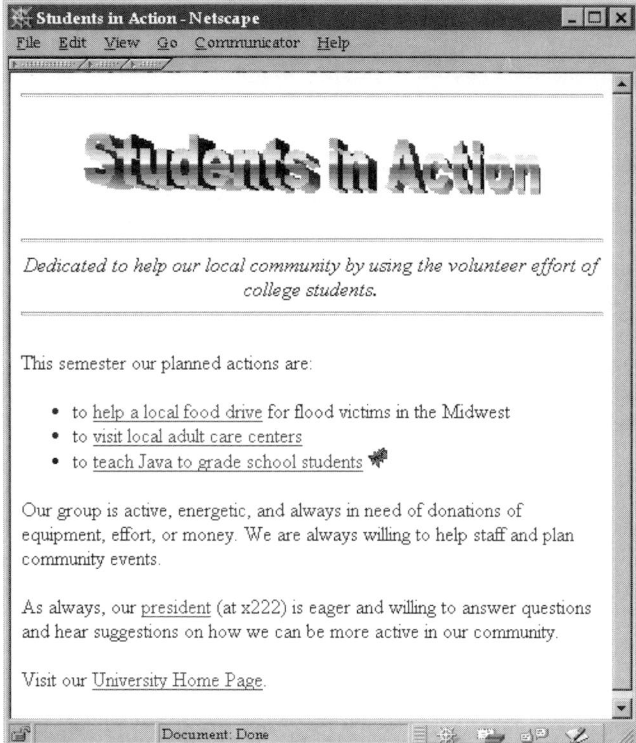

Figure J.9 Images added to Web page

In this example, we will reserve 50 pixels for the height, and 100 pixels for the width. In the code fragment below, we also reset the location of the class code to another site.

```
<APPLET CODE=Marquee WIDTH=100 HEIGHT=50
   CODEBASE="http://www.javasite.com/applets2use">
</APPLET>
```

When inserted between the `<APPLET>` and `</APPLET>` tags, the `<PARAM>` tag allows you to pass parameters to the Java applet at run time. The `<PARAM>` tag has two required attributes that allow it to pass information to the applet program. The attributes are `NAME` and `VALUE`. By defining a `NAME` and `VALUE` pair, the applet can use and decipher the information it is passed at run time. The following example sends two parameters, a state and city, to the `Map` applet:

```
<APPLET CODE=Map WIDTH=100 HEIGHT=5
   CODEBASE="http://www.javasite.com/applets2use">
```

```
    <PARAM NAME="state" VALUE="pennsylvania">
    <PARAM NAME="city" VALUE="philadelphia">

</APPLET>
```

The following HTML code is the Students in Action Web page, with an applet added that scrolls a message across the document as the page is browsed.

```
<HTML>
   <HEAD>
      <TITLE>Students in Action</TITLE>
   </HEAD>
   <BODY BGCOLOR="WHITE" TEXT="BLACK">
      <HR>

      <CENTER><IMG SRC="SIA.gif"></CENTER>

      <HR>

      <CENTER><I>Dedicated to help our local community
      by using the volunteer effort of college
      students.</I></CENTER>

      <HR>

      <P>This semester our planned actions are:</P>

      <UL>
         <LI> to <A HREF="food.html">help a local food drive</A>
              for flood victims in the Midwest</LI>
         <LI> to <A HREF="adult.html">visit local adult care
              centers</A></LI>
         <LI> to <A HREF="grade.html">teach Java to grade
              school students</A> <IMG SRC="new.gif"></LI>
      </UL>

      <P>Our group is active, energetic, and always in
      need of donations of equipment, effort, or money.
      We are always willing to help staff and plan
      community events.</P>

      <P>As always, our <A HREF="mailto:loftus@wpllabs.com">
      president</A> (at x222) is eager and willing to answer
```

```
        questions and hear suggestions on how we can be more
        active in our community.</P>

        <APPLET CODE="Marquee.class" WIDTH=500 HEIGHT=50>
           <PARAM NAME=text
              VALUE="Join us for our Spring picnic in April!">
           <PARAM NAME=delay       VALUE="100">
           <PARAM NAME=bgcolor     VALUE="255255255">
           <PARAM NAME=fgcolor     VALUE="000000128">
        </APPLET>

        <P>Visit our <A HREF="http://www.vill.edu">University Home
        Page</A>.</P>

     </BODY>
  </HTML>
```

Figure J.10 shows how this page is displayed in a browser.

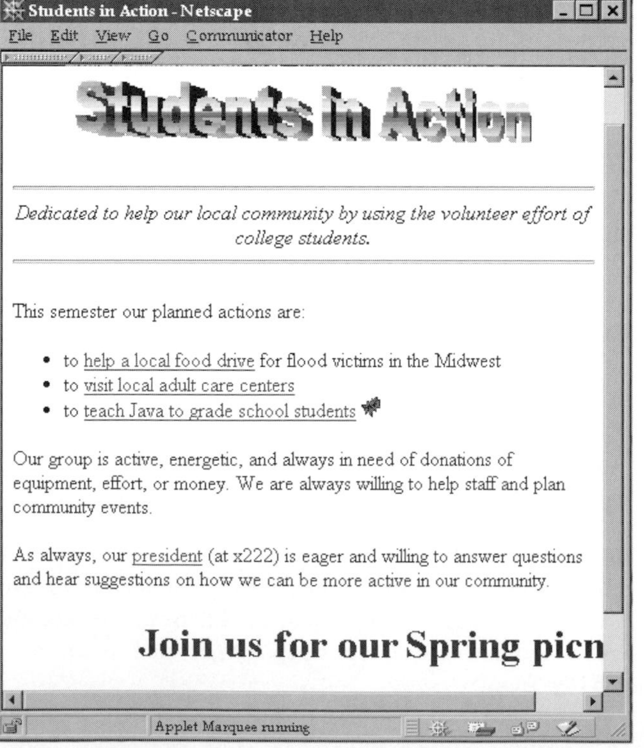

Figure J.10 Applets added to Web page

Appendix K

Java Exceptions and Errors

This appendix contains a list of run-time *exceptions* and *errors* produced by the Java language and the classes of the standard Java library. It is not an exhaustive list, but does contain most of the exceptions and errors that arise in programs within the scope of this text.

Both exceptions and errors indicate that a problem has occurred while a program was executing. Exceptions can be caught and handled under programmer control using the Java `try-catch` statements. Errors represent more serious problems and generally should not be caught. Some exceptions and errors indicate the same type of problem, such as `NoSuchMethodException` and `NoSuchMethodError`. In these cases, the particular situation in which the problem arises determines whether an exception or an error is thrown.

Exceptions

`AccessControlException (java.security)`
Requested access to a critical system resource is denied.

`ArithmeticException (java.lang)`
An illegal arithmetic operation was attempted, such as dividing by zero.

`ArrayIndexOutOfBoundsException (java.lang)`
An index into an array object is out of range.

`ArrayStoreException (java.lang)`
An attempt was made to assign a value to an array element of an incompatible type.

`AWTException (java.awt)`
A general exception indicating that some problem has occurred in a class of the `java.awt` package.

`BindException (java.net)`
A socket could not be bound to a local address and port.

`ClassCastException (java.lang)`
An attempt was made to cast an object reference to an incompatible type.

`ClassNotFoundException (java.lang)`
A specific class or interface could not be found.

`CloneNotSupportedException (java.lang)`
An attempt was made to clone an object instantiated from a class that does not implement the `Cloneable` interface.

`EmptyStackException (java.util)`
An attempt was made to reference an element from an empty stack.

`EOFException (java.io)`
The end of file has been encountered before normal completion of an input operation.

`Exception (java.lang)`
The root of the exception hierarchy.

`FileNotFoundException (java.io)`
A specified file name could not be found.

`GeneralSecurityException (java.security)`
The root of all security exceptions.

`IllegalAccessException (java.lang)`
The currently executing method does not have access to the definition of a class that it is attempting to load.

`IllegalArgumentException (java.lang)`
An invalid or inappropriate argument was passed to a method.

`IllegalComponentStateException (java.awt)`
An operation was attempted on a component that was in an inappropriate state.

`IllegalMonitorStateException (java.lang)`
A thread attempted to notify or wait on another thread that is waiting on an object that it has not locked.

`IllegalStateException (java.lang)`
A method was invoked from an improper state.

`IllegalThreadStateException (java.lang)`
An operation was attempted on a thread that was not in an appropriate state for that operation to succeed.

`IndexOutOfBoundsException (java.lang)`
An index into an object such as an array, string, or vector was out of range. The invalid index could be part of a subrange, specified by a start and end point or a start point and a length.

`InstantiationException (java.lang)`
A class could not be instantiated using the `newInstance` method of class `Class` because it is abstract, or an array, or an interface.

`InterruptedException (java.lang)`
While one thread was waiting, another thread interrupted it using the `interrupt` method of the `Thread` class.

`InterruptedIOException (java.io)`
While one thread was waiting for the completion of an I/O operation, another thread interrupted it using the `interrupt` method of the `Thread` class.

`InvalidClassException (java.io)`
The serialization runtime has detected a problem with a class.

`InvalidParameterException (java.security)`
An invalid parameter has been passed to a method.

`IOException (java.io)`
A requested I/O operation could not be completed normally.

`JarException (java.util.jar)`
A problem occurred while reading from or writing to a JAR file.

`MalformedURLException (java.net)`
A specified URL does not have an appropriate format or used an unknown protocol.

`NegativeArraySizeException (java.lang)`
An attempt was made to instantiate an array that has a negative length.

`NoRouteToHostException (java.net)`
A path could not be found when attempting to connect a socket to a remote address and port.

`NoSuchElementException (java.util)`
An attempt was made to access an element of an empty vector.

`NoSuchFieldException (java.lang)`
An attempt was made to access a nonexistent field.

`NoSuchMethodException (java.lang)`
A specified method could not be found.

`NullPointerException (java.lang)`
A null reference was used where an object reference was needed.

`NumberFormatException (java.lang)`
An operation was attempted using a number in an illegal format.

`ParseException (java.text)`
A string could not be parsed according to the specified format.

`ProtocolException (java.net)`
Some aspect of a network communication protocol was not executed correctly.

`RuntimeException (java.lang)`
The superclass of all unchecked runtime exceptions.

`SecurityException (java.lang)`
An operation was attempted which violates some kind of security measure.

`SocketException (java.net)`
An operation using a socket could not be completed normally.

`StringIndexOutOfBoundsException (java.lang)`
An index into a `String` or `StringBuffer` object is out of range.

`TooManyListenersException (java.util)`
An event source has registered too many listeners.

`UTFDataFormatException (java.io)`
An attempt was made to convert a string to or from UTF-8 format, but the string was too long or the data were not in valid UTF-8 format.

`UnknownHostException (java.net)`
A specified network host name could not be resolved into a network address.

`UnknownServiceException (java.net)`
An attempt was made to request a service that the current network connection does not support.

Errors

`AbstractMethodError (java.lang)`
An attempt was made to invoke an `abstract` method.

`AWTError (java.awt)`
A general error indicating that a serious problem has occurred in a class of the `java.awt` package.

`ClassCircularityError (java.lang)`
A circular dependency was found while performing class initialization.

`ClassFormatError (java.lang)`
The format of the bytecode in a class file is invalid.

`Error (java.lang)`
The root of the error hierarchy.

`ExceptionInInitializerError (java.lang)`
An exception has occurred in a static initializer.

`IllegalAccessError (java.lang)`
An attempt was made to reference a class, method, or variable that was not accessible.

`IncompatibleClassChangeError (java.lang)`
An illegal operation was attempted on a class.

`InstantiationError (java.lang)`
An attempt was made to instantiate an abstract class or an interface.

`InternalError (java.lang)`
An error occurred in the Java interpreter.

`LinkageError (java.lang)`
An error occurred while attempting to link classes or resolve dependencies between classes.

`NoClassDefFoundError (java.lang)`
The definition of a specified class could not be found.

`NoSuchFieldError (java.lang)`
A specified field could not be found.

`NoSuchMethodError (java.lang)`
A specified method could not be found.

`OutOfMemoryError (java.lang)`
The interpreter has run out of memory and cannot reclaim more through garbage collection.

`StackOverflowError (java.lang)`
A stack overflow has occurred in the Java interpreter.

`ThreadDeath (java.lang)`
The `stop` method of a thread has caused a thread (but not the interpreter) to terminate. No error message is printed.

`UnknownError (java.lang)`
An error has occurred in the Java Virtual Machine (JVM).

`UnsatisfiedLinkError (java.lang)`
All of the links in a loaded class could not be resolved.

`VerifyError (java.lang)`
A class failed the bytecode verification procedures.

`VirtualMachineError (java.lang)`
The superclass of several errors relating to the Java Virtual Machine (JVM).

Appendix L

Java Syntax

Compilation Unit

Package Declaration

Import Declaration

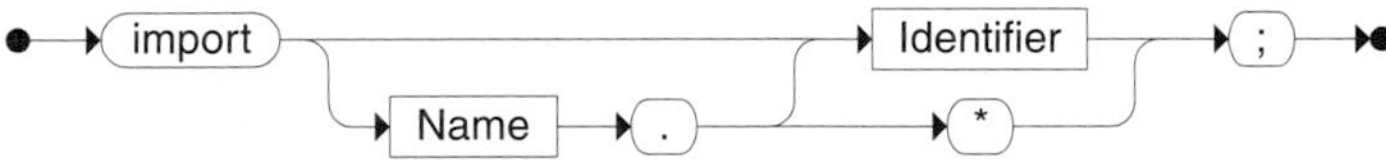

Type Declaration

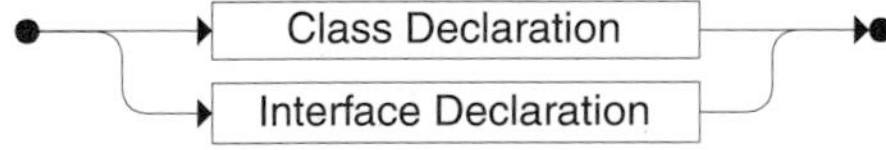

Class Declaration

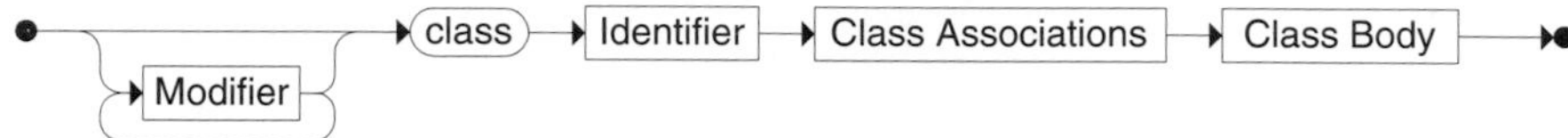

Class Associations

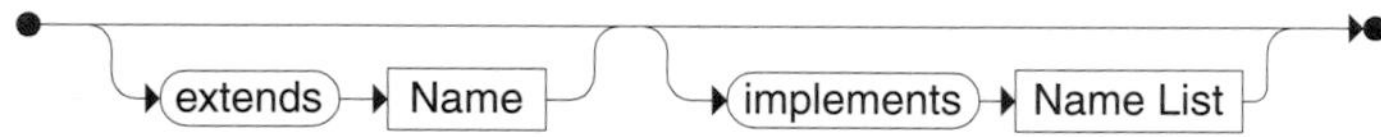

Class Body

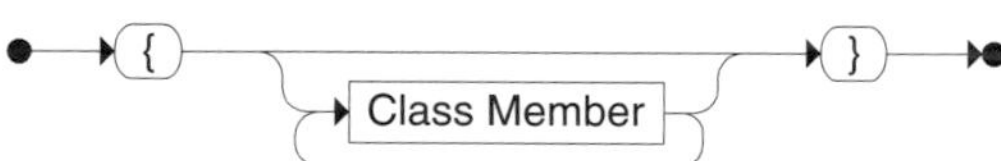

Class Member

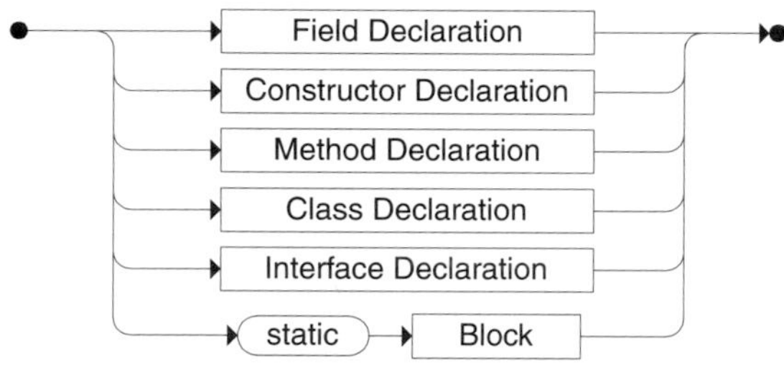

Interface Declaration

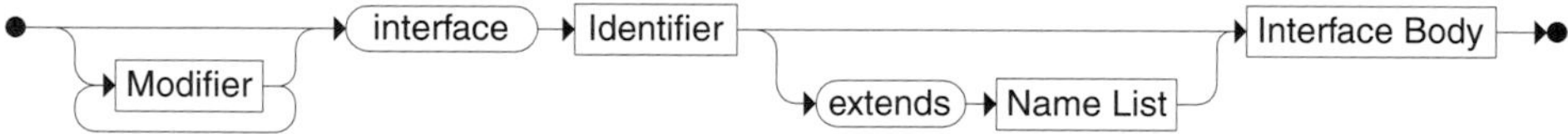

Interface Body

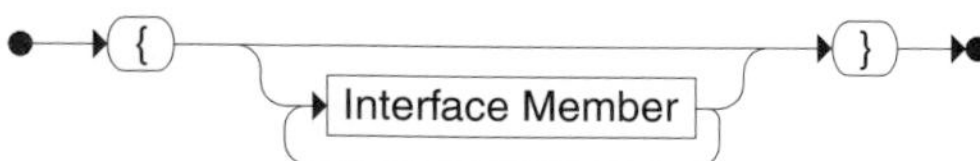

Interface Member

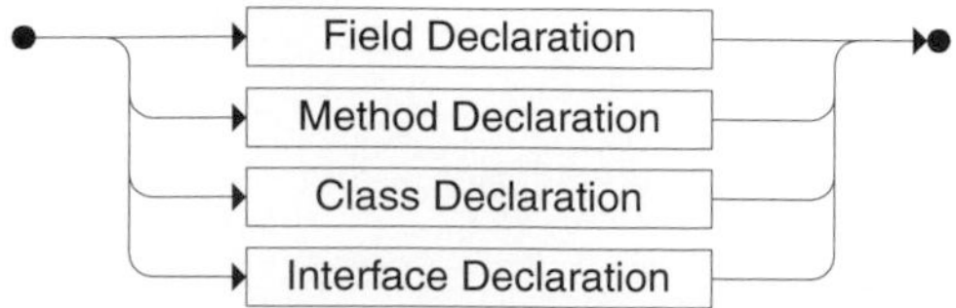

Field Declaration

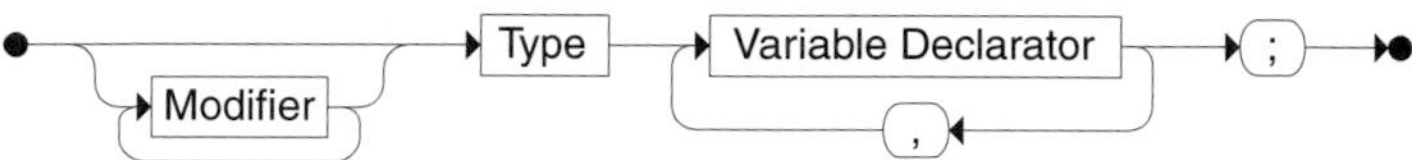

Variable Declarator

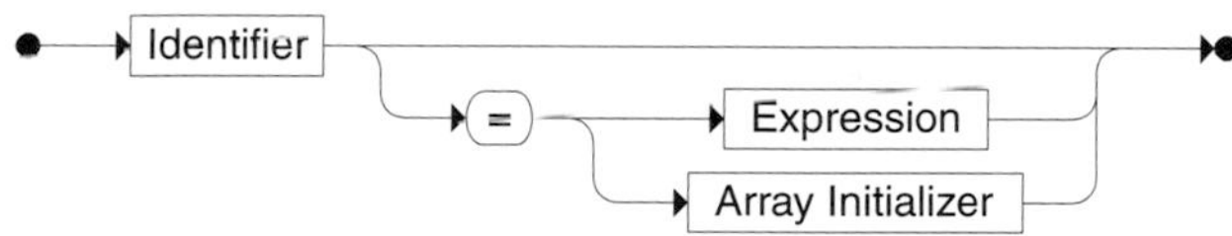

Type

Modifier

Primitive Type

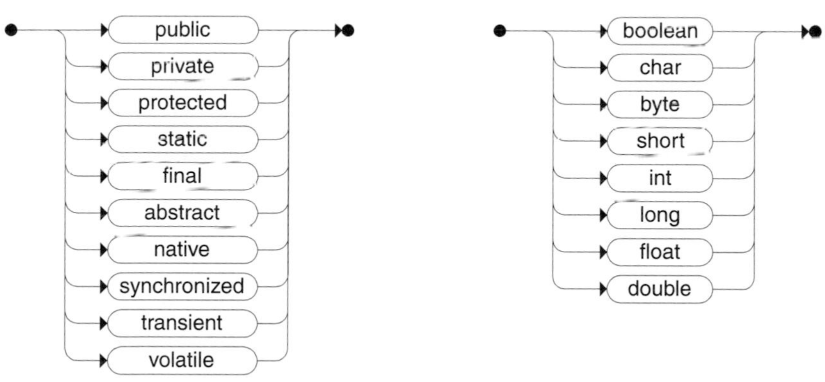

Array Initializer

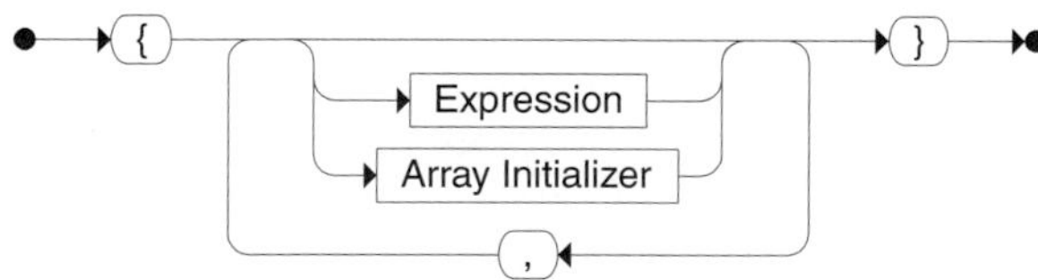

Name

Name List

Method Declaration

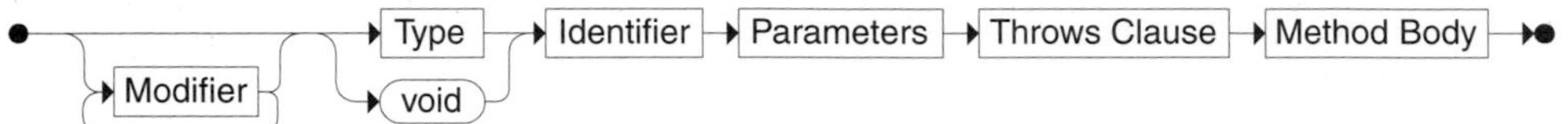

Parameters

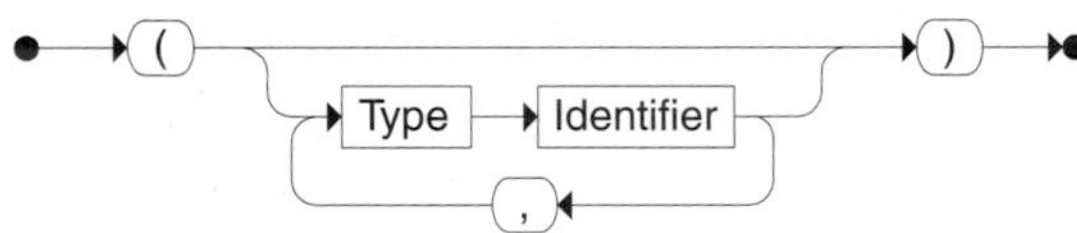

Throws Clause

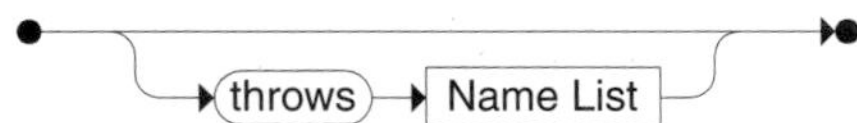

Method Body

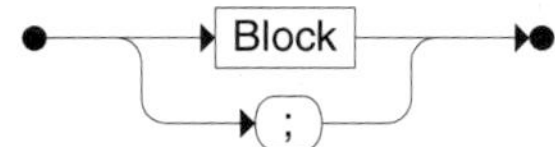

Constructor Declaration

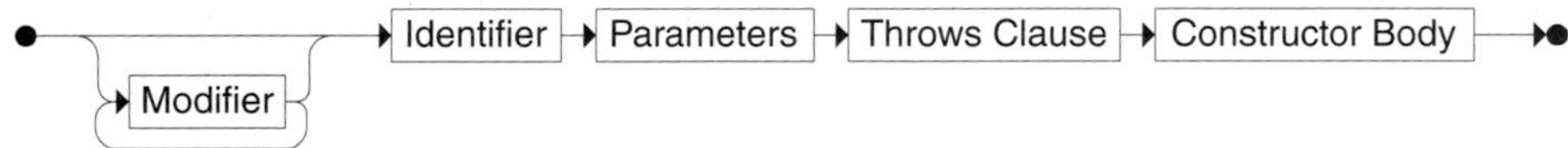

Constructor Body

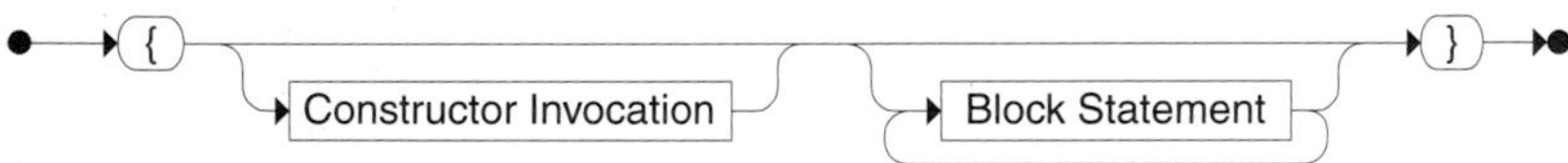

Constructor Invocation

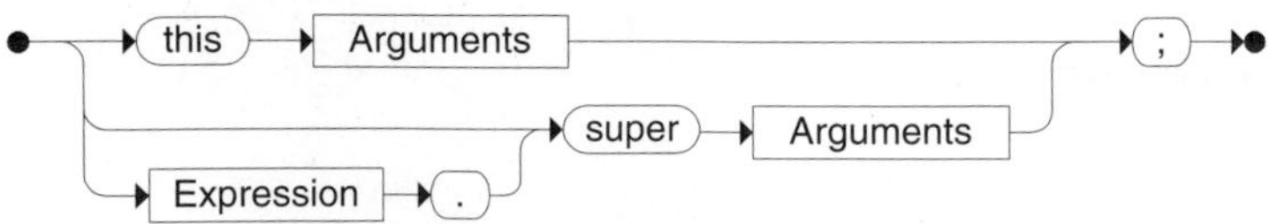

Block

Block Statement

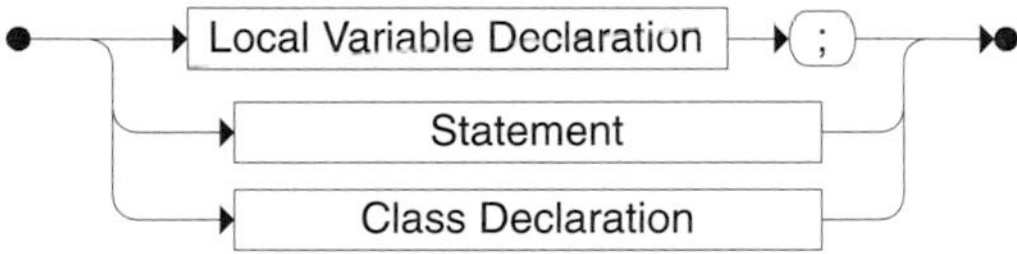

Local Variable Declaration

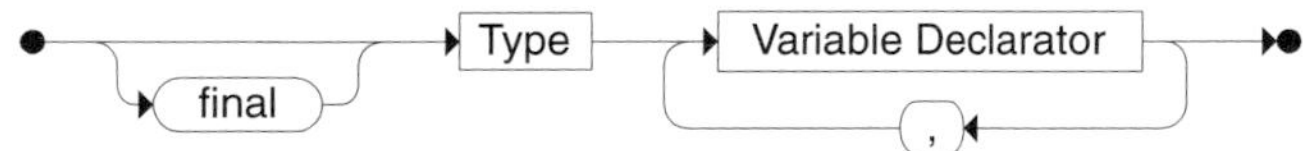

Statement

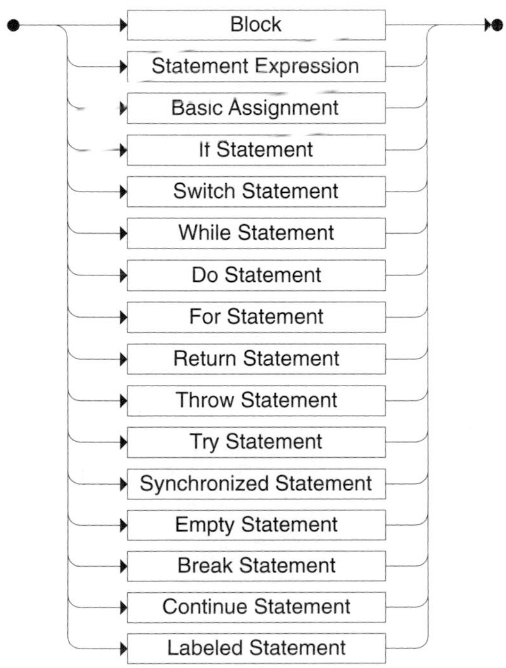

If Statement

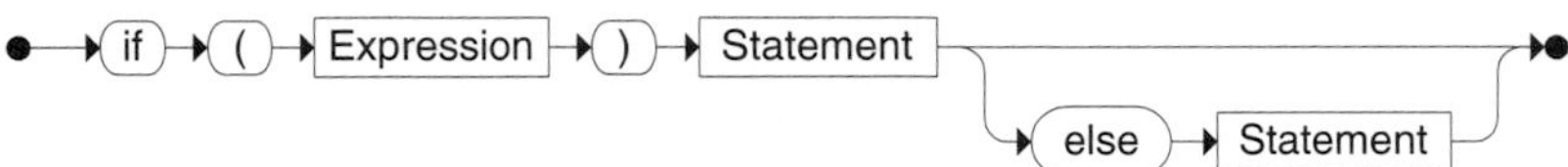

Switch Statement

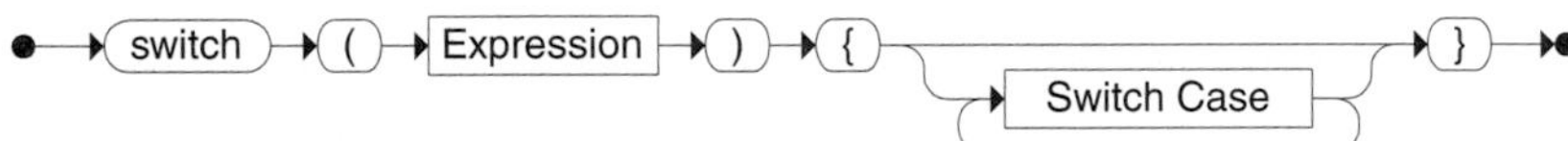

Switch Case

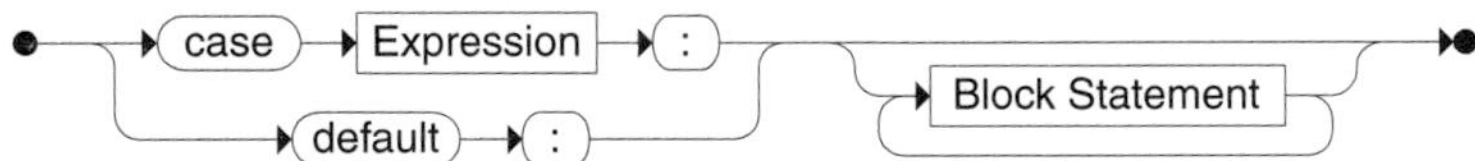

While Statement

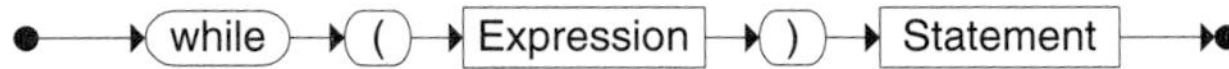

Do Statement

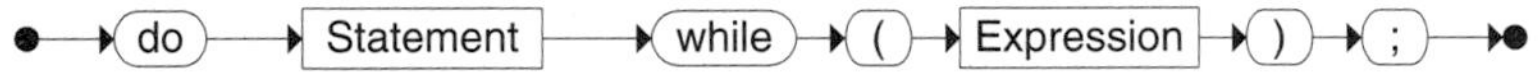

For Statement

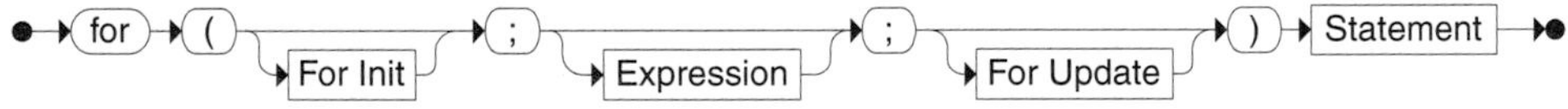

For Init

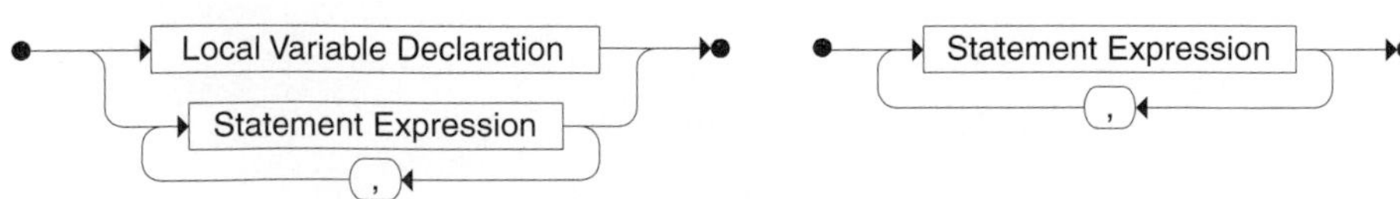

For Update

Basic Assignment

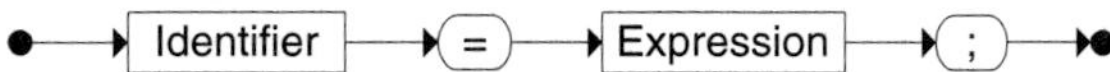

Return Statement

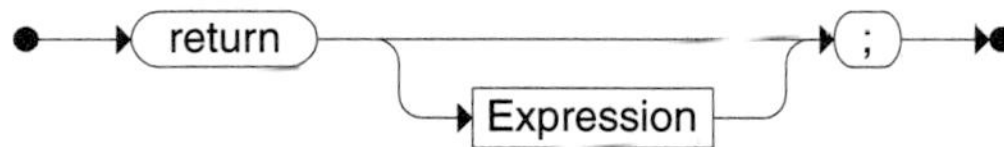

Throw Statement

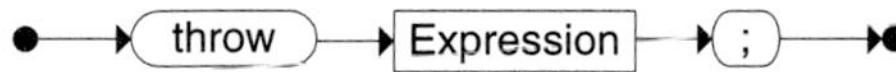

Try Statement

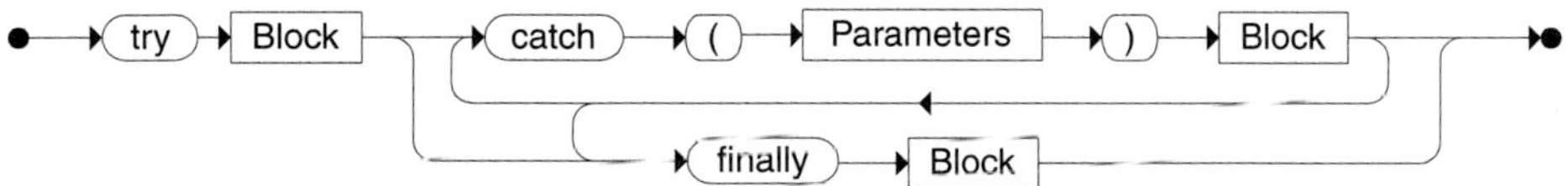

Synchronized Statement

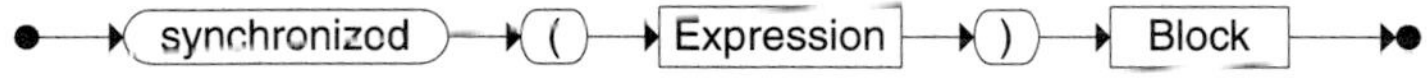

Empty Statement

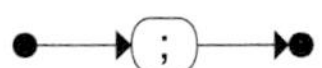

Break Statement

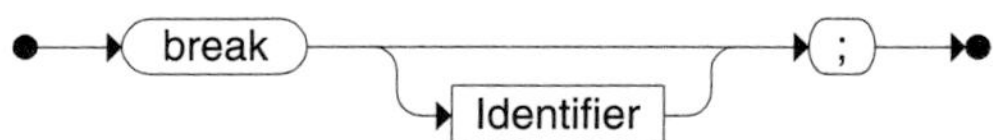

Continue Statement

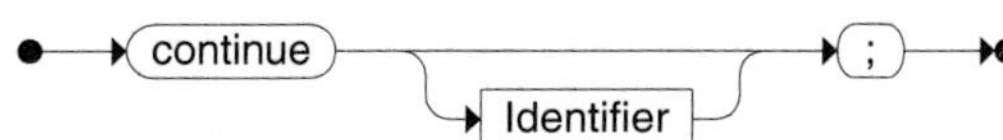

Labeled Statement

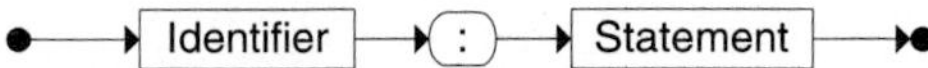

Expression

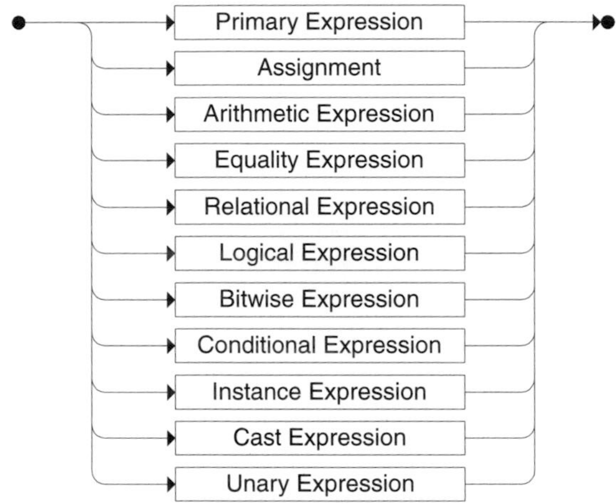

Primary Expression

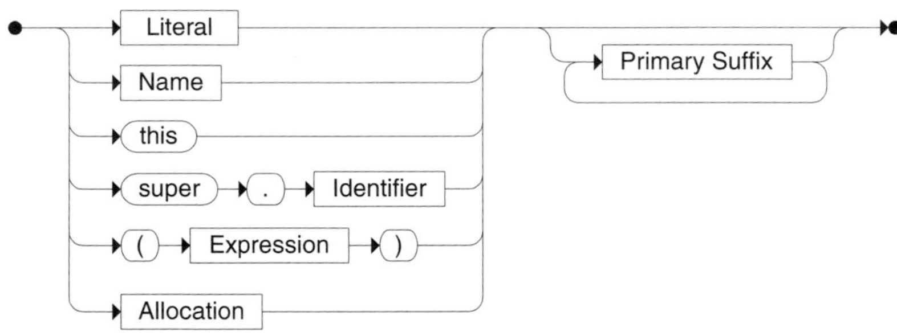

Primary Suffix

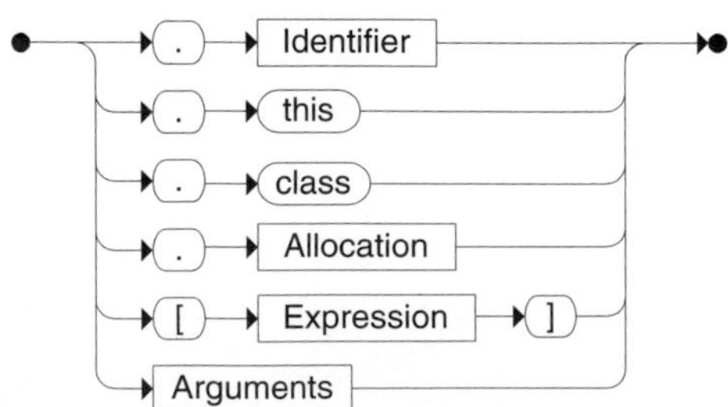

Arguments

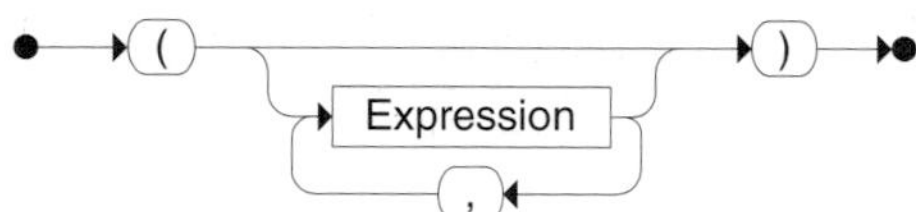

Allocation

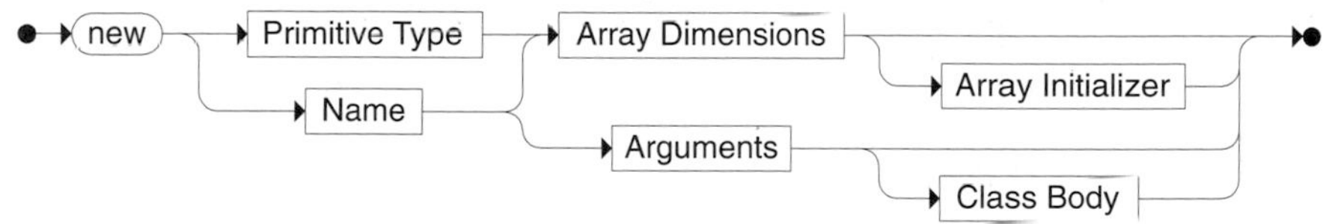

Array Dimensions

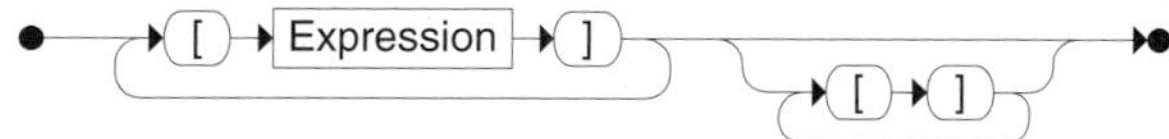

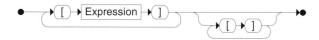

Statement Expression

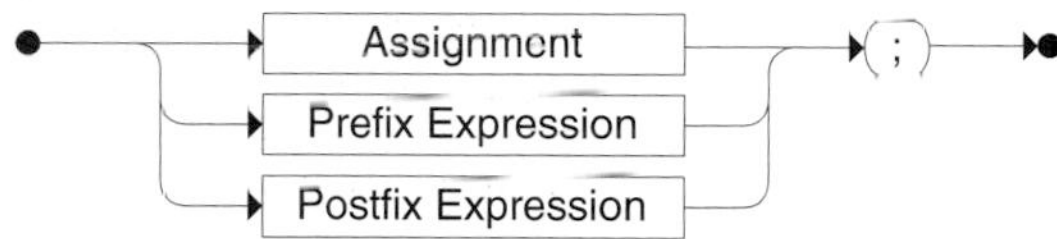

Assignment

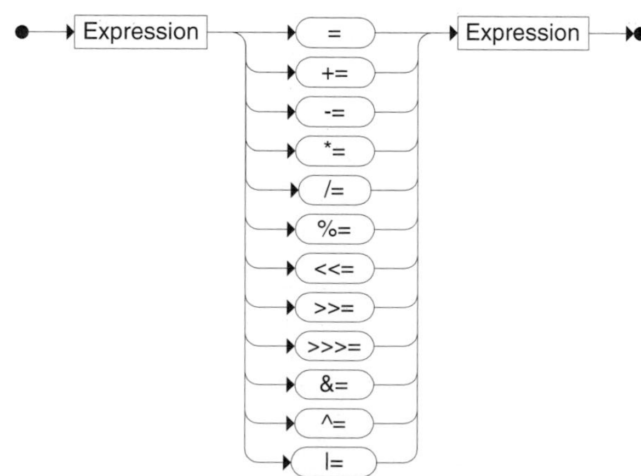

Arithmetic Expression

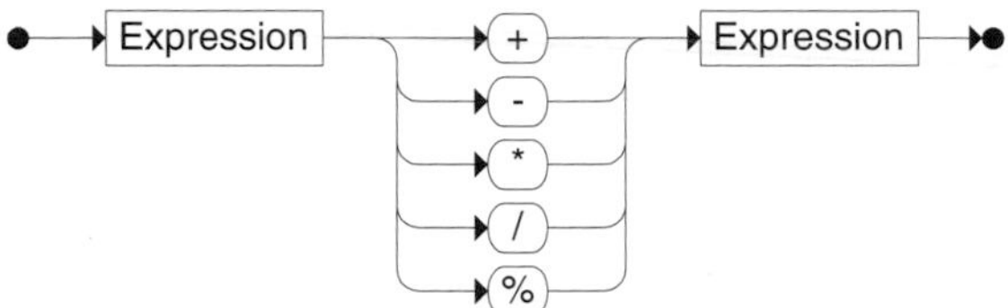

Equality Expression

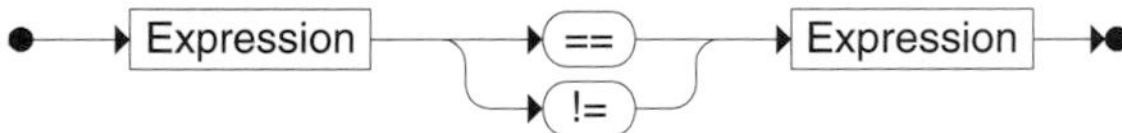

Relational Expression

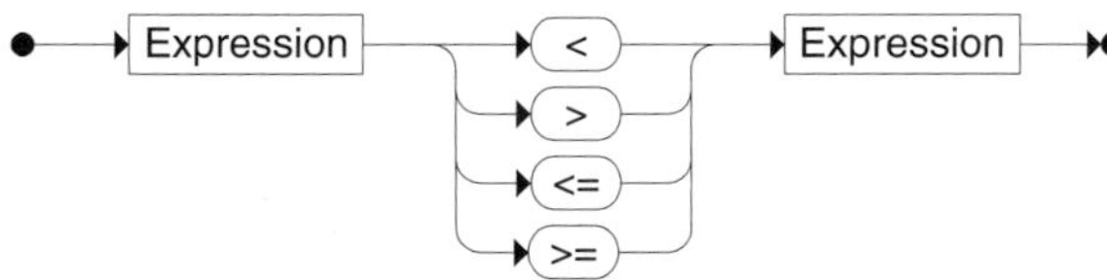

Logical Expression

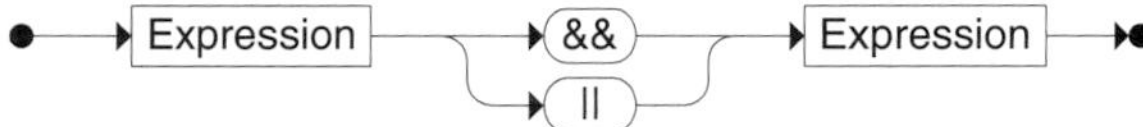

Bitwise Expression

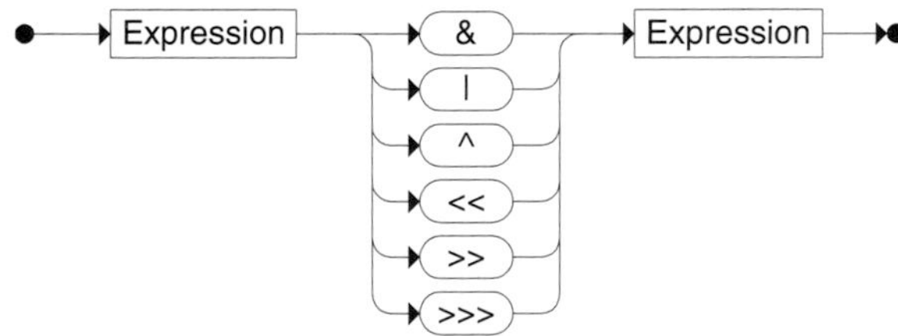

Conditional Expression

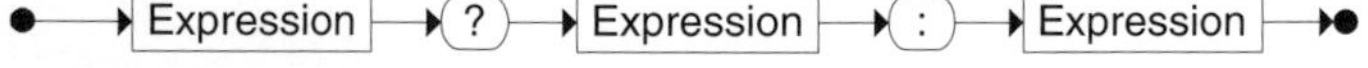

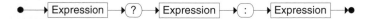

Instance Expression

Cast Expression

Unary Expression

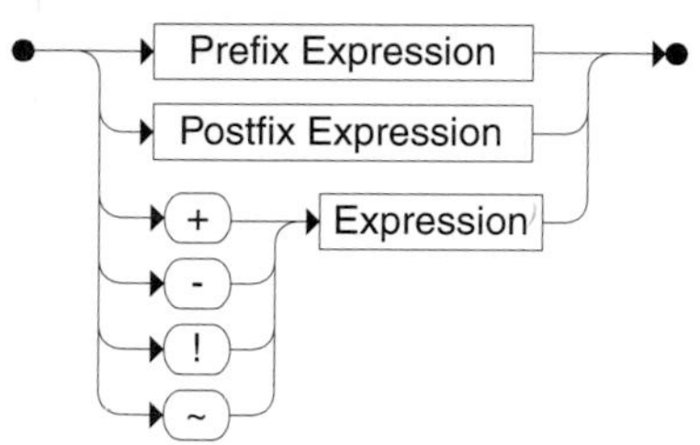

Prefix Expression

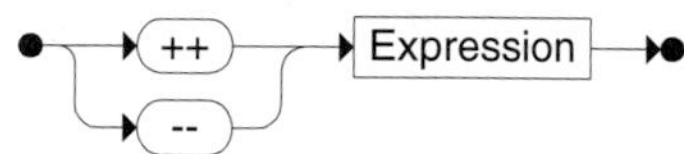

Postfix Expression

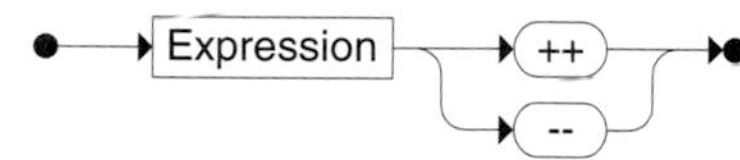

Literal

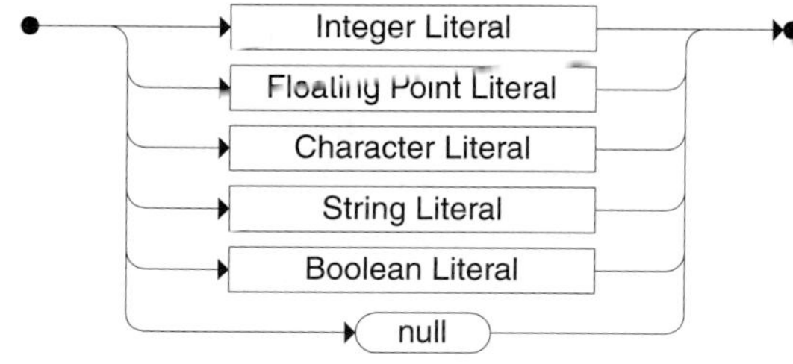

Integer Literal

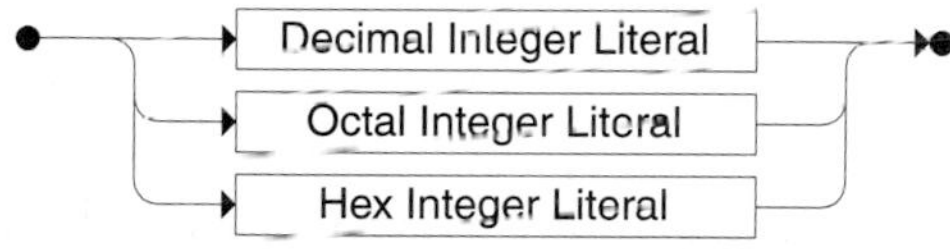

Decimal Integer Literal

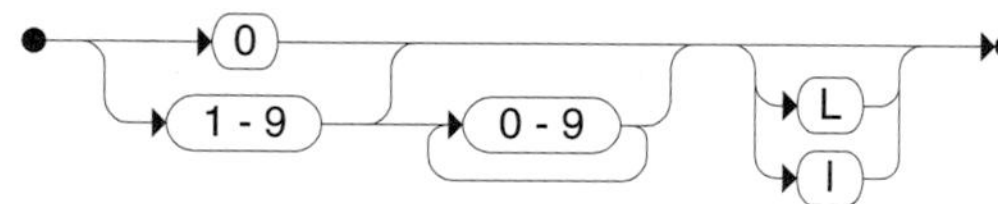

Octal Integer Literal

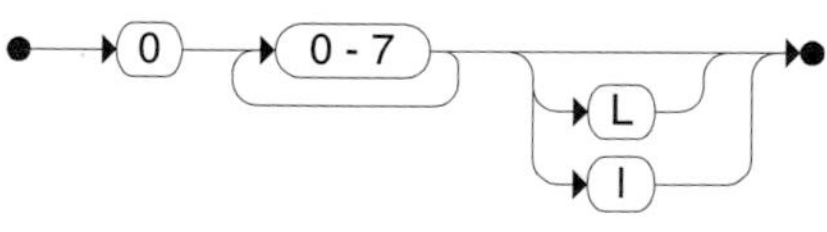

Hex Digit

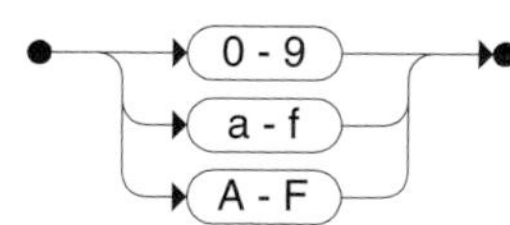

Hex Integer Literal

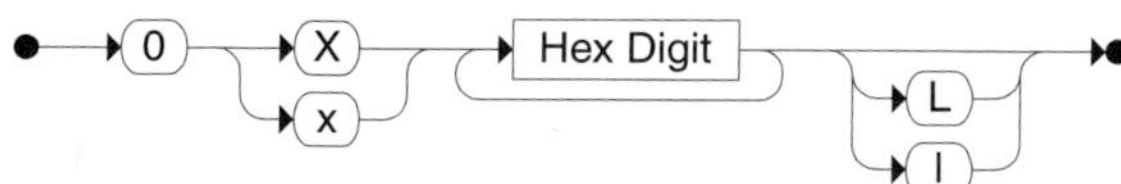

Floating Point Literal

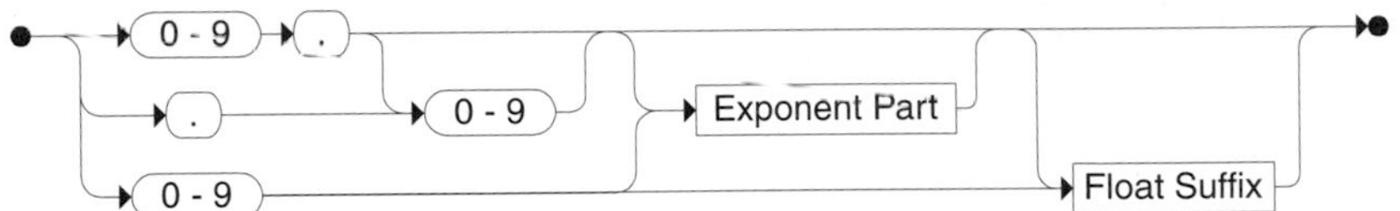

Exponent Part

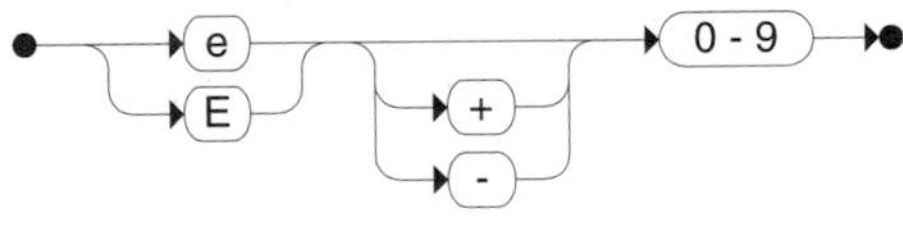

Float Suffix

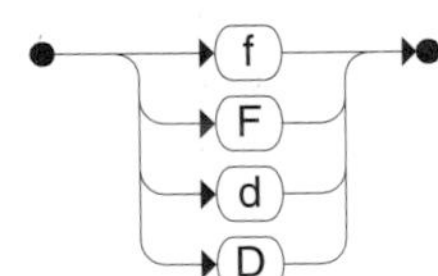

Character Literal

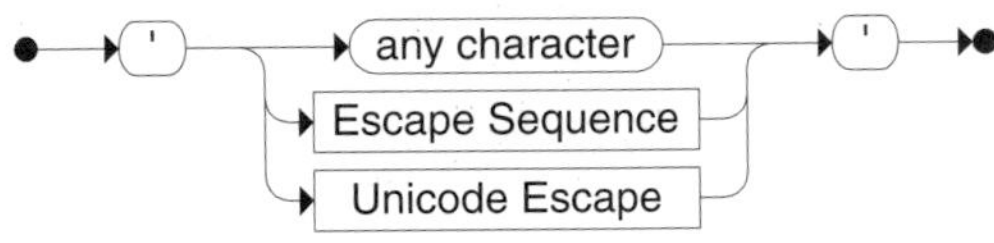

Boolean Literal

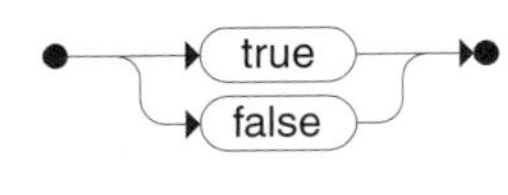

String Literal

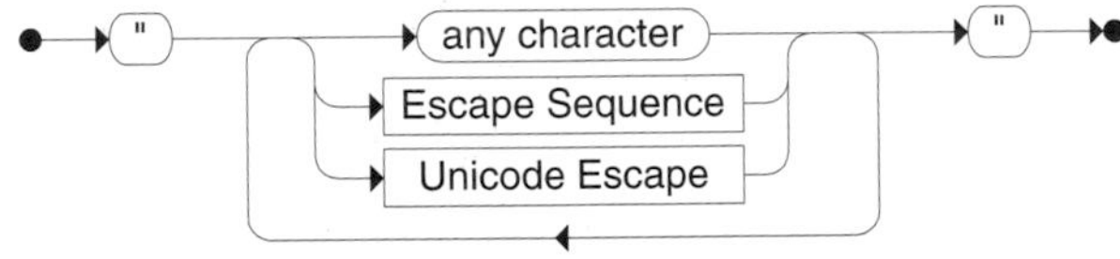

Unicode Escape

Escape Sequence

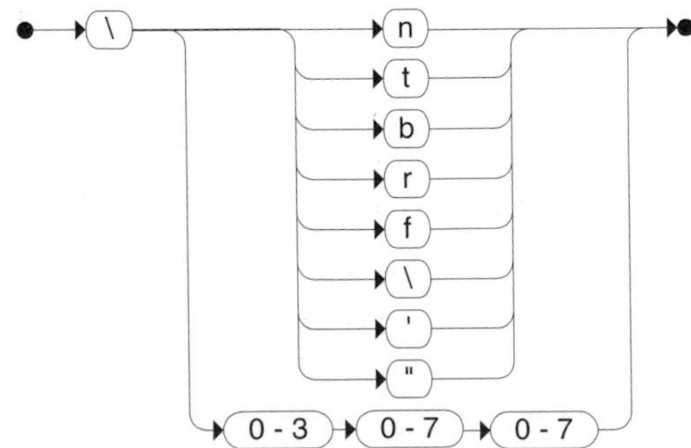

Identifier

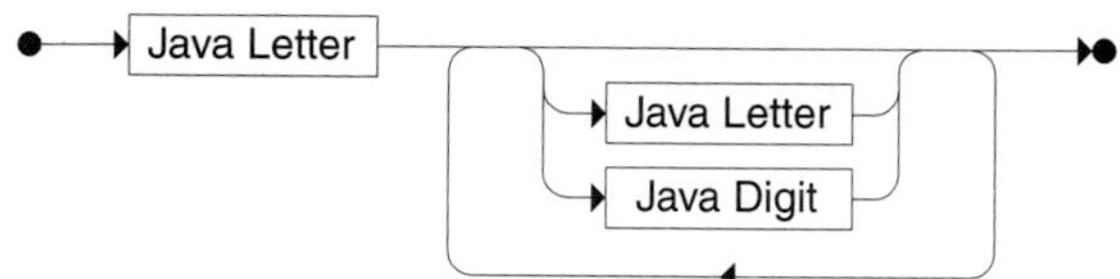

Java Letter

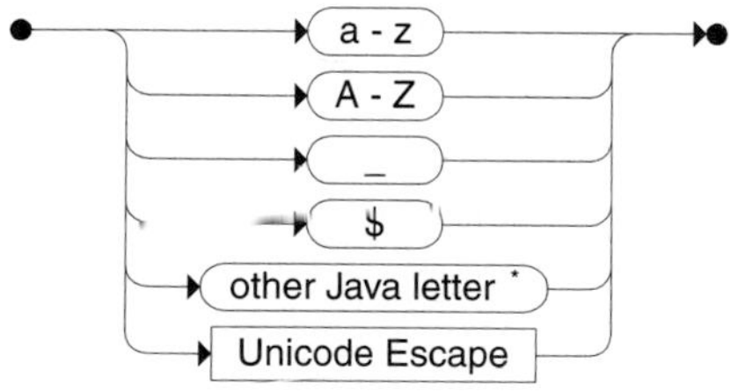

Java Digit

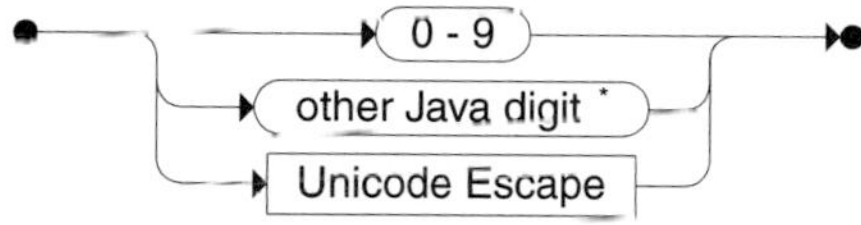

Appendix M

The Java Class Library

This appendix is a reference for many of the classes in the Java standard class library. We list the variables, constants, constructors, and methods of each class. Items within a class are grouped according to their purpose. The classes are listed in alphabetical order. The package each class is contained in is given in parentheses after the class name.

ActionEvent (`java.awt.event`)

A public class, derived from AWTEvent, that represents an AWT action event (from a component such as a Button, List, MenuItem or TextField).

Variables and Constants

`public static final int ALT_MASK`
`public static final int CTRL_MASK`
`public static final int META_MASK`
`public static final int SHIFT_MASK`

Constant values which represent masks for the Alt, Control, Meta, and Shift keys being pressed during an action event.

`public static final int ACTION_FIRST`
`public static final int ACTION_LAST`

Constant values that represent the index of the first and last action event ids.

`public static final int ACTION_PERFORMED`

A constant value that represents an action performed AWT event type.

Constructors

`public ActionEvent(Object src, int type, String cmd)`

`public ActionEvent(Object src, int type, String cmd, int keys)`

Creates a new instance of an `ActionEvent` from the specified source object, event type, and command string. Additionally, a mask value can be set that defines the types of keys depressed during the event.

Methods

`public String getActionCommand()`

Returns the command string associated with this action.

`public int getModifiers()`

Returns the mask of the modifiers (special keys) depressed during this event.

`public String paramString()`

Returns a string containing the parameters of this `ActionEvent`.

AdjustmentEvent (`java.awt.event`)

A public class, derived from AWTEvent, that represents an AWT adjustment event (from a component such as a Scrollbar or ScrollPane).

Variables and Constructs

`public static final int ADJUSTMENT_FIRST`
`public static final int ADJUSTMENT_LAST`

Constant values that represent the index of the first and last adjustment event ids.

`public static final int ADJUSTMENT_VALUE_CHANGED`

A constant value that represents an adjustment value change event.

`public static final int BLOCK_DECREMENT`
`public static final int BLOCK_INCREMENT`

Constant values that represent block decrement and increment events.

`public static final int TRACK`

A constant value which represents an absolute tracking adjustment event.

`public static final int UNIT_DECREMENT`
`public static final int UNIT_INCREMENT`

Constant values which represent unit decrement and increment events.

Constructors

`public AdjustmentEvent(Adjustable source, int id, int type, int val)`

Creates a new instance of an `AdjustmentEvent` from a specified `source` and having a specified `id`, `type`, and `value`.

Methods

`public Adjustable getAdjustable()`
Returns the adjustable object that originated this AWT `AdjustmentEvent`.

`public int getAdjustmentType()`
Returns the type of adjustment for this event.

`public int getValue()`
Returns the current value of this `AdjustmentEvent`.

`public String paramString()`
Returns a string containing the parameters of this event.

Applet (`java.applet`)

A public class, derived from `Panel`, that is intended to be used as a program running inside a Web page.

Constructors

`public Applet()`
Creates a new instance of an applet for inclusion on a Web page.

Methods

`public void destroy()`
Destroys the applet and all of its resources. This method contains no functionality and should be overridden by subclasses.

`public AppletContext getAppletContext()`
Returns this applet's context (the environment in which it is running).

`public String getAppletInfo()`
Returns a string representation of information regarding this applet. This method contains no functionality and should be overridden by subclasses.

`public AudioClip getAudioClip(URL audio)`
`public AudioClip getAudioClip(URL base, String filename)`
Returns the `AudioClip` requested. The location of the audio clip can be given by the `base` URL and the `filename` relative to that `base`.

`public URL getCodeBase()`
`public URL getDocumentBase()`
`public Locale getLocale()`
Returns the URL of this applet, the document that contains this applet, or the locale of this applet.

`public Image getImage(URL image)`

`public Image getImage(URL base, String filename)`

Returns the image requested. The location of the image can be given by the `base` URL and the `filename` relative to that `base`.

`public String getParameter(String param)`

`public String[][] getParameterInfo()`

Returns the value of the specified parameter for this applet. An array of string elements containing information about each parameter for this applet can also be obtained. Each element of the returned array should be comprised of three strings (parameter name, type, and description). This method contains no functionality and should be overridden by subclasses.

`public void init()`

This method provides initialization functionality to the applet prior to the first time that the applet is started. It is automatically called by the browser or the `appletviewer` program. This method contains no functionality and should be overridden by subclasses.

`public boolean isActive()`

Returns a true value if this applet is currently active. An applet is considered active just prior to execution of its `start` method and is no longer active just after execution of its `stop` method.

`public void play(URL source)`

`public void play(URL base, String filename)`

Plays the audio clip located at `source`. The location of the audio clip can be given as a `base` URL and the `filename` relative to that `base`.

`public void resize(Dimension dim)`

`public void resize(int w, int h)`

Resizes this applet according to the specified dimension.

`public final void setStub(AppletStub stub)`

Sets the interface between this applet and the browser or appletviewer program.

`public void showStatus(String message)`

Prints the specified `message` in the browser's status window.

`public void start()`

This method generally contains functionality relevant to the starting of this applet. It is called after the applet has been initialized (with the `init` method) and every time the applet is reloaded in the browser or `appletviewer` program. This method contains no functionality and should be overridden by subclasses.

`public void stop()`

This method generally contains functionality relevant to the stopping of this applet. It is called by the browser (when the containing Web page is replaced) or appletviewer program. This method contains no functionality and should be overridden by subclasses.

AWTEvent (`java.awt`)

A public class, derived from `EventObject`, that is the root class for all of the AWT event classes.

Variables and Constants

`public final static long ACTION_EVENT_MASK`
`public final static long ADJUSTMENT_EVENT_MASK`
`public final static long COMPONENT_EVENT_MASK`
`public final static long CONTAINER_EVENT_MASK`
`public final static long FOCUS_EVENT_MASK`
`public final static long ITEM_EVENT_MASK`
`public final static long KEY_EVENT_MASK`
`public final static long MOUSE_EVENT_MASK`
`public final static long MOUSE_MOTION_EVENT_MASK`
`public final static long TEXT_EVENT_MASK`
`public final static long WINDOW_EVENT_MASK`

Constant values representing the AWT event masks for various events.

`protected boolean consumed`

A variable representing the state of the event. A true value means that it has not been sent to the appropriate peer, false indicates that it has.

`protected int id`

The numeric identification for this event.

Constructors

`public AWTEvent(Event evt)`

Creates a new `AWTEvent` from the specified event.

`public AWTEvent(Object src, int type)`

Creates a new `AWTEvent` from a specified source, and having a defined type.

Methods

`protected void consume()`

Targets this `AWTEvent` to be sent to the appropriate peer.

`public int getID()`

Returns this event's type.

`protected boolean isConsumed()`

Returns a true value if this `AWTEvent` has been sent to the appropriate peer.

`public String paramString()`

Returns the parameter string for this `AWTEvent`.

`public String toString()`

Returns a string representation of this AWTEvent.

BigDecimal (`java.math`)

A public class, derived from `Number`, which can be used to represent a decimal number with a definable precision.

Variables and Constants

`ROUND_CEILING`

A constant that represents a rounding mode in which the value of the `BigDecimal` is rounded up (away from zero) if the number is positive, and down (closer to zero) if the number is negative.

`ROUND_DOWN`

A constant that represents a rounding mode in which the value of the `BigDecimal` is rounded closer to zero (decreasing a positive number and increasing a negative number).

`ROUND_FLOOR`

A constant that represents a rounding mode in which the value of the `BigDecimal` is rounded down (closer to zero) if the number is positive, and up (away from zero) if the number is negative.

`ROUND_HALF_DOWN`

A constant that represents a rounding mode in which the value of the `BigDecimal` is rounded as in `ROUND_UP` if the fraction of the number is greater than 0.5 and as `ROUND_DOWN` in all other cases.

`ROUND_HALF_EVEN`

A constant that represents a rounding mode in which the value of the `BigDecimal` is rounded as in `ROUND_HALF_UP` if the number to the left of the decimal is odd and as `ROUND_HALF_DOWN` when the number is even.

`ROUND_HALF_UP`

A constant that represents a rounding mode in which the value of the `BigDecimal` is rounded as in `ROUND_UP` if the fraction of the number is greater than or equal to 0.5 and as in `ROUND_DOWN` in all other cases.

`ROUND_UNNECESSARY`

A constant that represents a rounding mode in which the value of the `BigDecimal` is not rounded (if possible) and an exact result be returned.

`ROUND_UP`

A constant that represents a rounding mode in which the value of the `BigDecimal` is rounded away from zero (increasing a positive number, and decreasing a negative number).

Constructors

```
public BigDecimal(BigInteger arg)
public BigDecimal(BigInteger arg, int scale) throws NumberFormatException
public BigDecimal(double arg) throws NumberFormatException
public BigDecimal(String arg) throws NumberFormatException
```

Creates an instance of a BigDecimal from `arg`. The string argument may contain a preceding minus sign indicating a negative number. The resulting `BigDecimal`'s scale will be the number of integers to the right of the decimal point in the string, a specified value, or 0 (zero) if none are present.

Methods

`public double doubleValue()`
`public float floatValue()`
`public int intValue()`
`public long longValue()`
`public BigInteger toBigInteger()`
`public String toString()`

Converts this `BigDecimal` to either a Java primitive type or a `BigInteger`.

`public BigDecimal abs()`

Returns the absolute value of this `BigDecimal` with the same scale as this `BigDecimal`.

`public BigDecimal add(BigDecimal arg)`
`public BigDecimal subtract(BigDecimal arg)`

Returns the result of `arg` added to or subtracted from this `BigDecimal`, with the resulting scale equal to the larger of the two `BigDecimal`'s scales.

`public int compareTo(BigDecimal arg)`

This method compares this `BigDecimal` to `arg` and will return a -1 if this `BigDecimal` is less than `arg`, 0 if equal to `arg` or a 1 if greater than `arg`. If the values of the two `BigDecimals` are identical and the scales are different, they are considered equal.

`public BigDecimal divide(BigDecimal arg, int mode) throws ArithmeticException, IllegalArgumentException`
`public BigDecimal divide(BigDecimal arg, int scale, int mode) throws ArithmeticException, IllegalArgumentException`

Returns the result of this `BigDecimal` divided by `arg`. If required the rounding `mode` is used. The resulting `BigDecimal`'s scale is identical to this `BigDecimal`'s scale or a specified value.

`public boolean equals(Object arg)`

Returns a true value if this `BigDecimal`'s value and scale are equal to `arg's` value and scale.

`public int hashCode()`

Returns the hash code of this `BigDecimal`.

`public BigDecimal max(BigDecimal arg)`
`public BigDecimal min(BigDecimal arg)`

Returns the greater or lesser of this `BigDecimal` and `arg`.

`public BigDecimal movePointLeft(int num)`
`public BigDecimal movePointRight(int num)`

Returns this `BigDecimal` with the decimal point moved `num` positions.

`public BigDecimal multiply(BigDecimal arg)`

Returns the result of this `BigDecimal` multiplied with the value of `arg`. The scale of the resulting `BigDecimal` is the result of the addition of the two `BigDecimal`'s scales.

`public BigDecimal negate()`

Returns the negation of this `BigDecimal`'s value with the same scale.

`public int scale()`

Returns the scale of this `BigDecimal`.

`public BigDecimal setScale(int val) throws ArithmeticException, IllegalArgumentException`

`public BigDecimal setScale(int val, int mode) throws ArithmeticException, IllegalArgumentException`

Returns a `BigDecimal` whose value is the same as this `BigDecimal`'s and has a new scale specified by `val`. If rounding is necessary, a rounding `mode` can be specified.

`public int signum()`

Returns a -1 if this `BigDecimal` is negative, 0 if zero, and 1 if positive.

`public static BigDecimal valueOf(long value)`

`public static BigDecimal valueOf(long value, int scale) throws NumberFormatException`

Returns a `BigDecimal` with a defined `value`. The scale of the returned number is specified or it defaults to 0 (zero).

BigInteger (`java.math`)

A public class, derived from `Number`, that can be used to represent an integer in a two's complement format of any precision.

Constructors

`public BigInteger(byte[] arg) throws NumberFormatException`

`public BigInteger(int signum, byte[] magnitude) throws NumberFormatException`

Creates an instance of a `BigInteger` from the specified byte array. The sign of the number can be placed in `signum` (where -1 is negative, 0 is zero, and 1 is positive).

`public BigInteger(String arg) throws NumberFormatException`

`public BigInteger(String arg, int radix) throws NumberFormatException`

Creates an instance of a `BigInteger` from the string `arg`, which can contain decimal numbers preceded by an optional minus sign. The argument `radix` specifies the base of the `arg` value.

`public BigInteger(int size, Random rand) throws IllegalArgumentException`

`public BigInteger(int size, int prob, Random rand)`

Creates a (generally) prime instance of a `BigInteger` from a random integer, `rand`, of a specified length, `size`. The certainty parameter (`prob`) represents the amount of probability that the generated number is a prime. The probability is generated as 1 - (.5 ** `prob`).

Methods

`public double doubleValue()`

`public float floatValue()`

`public int intValue()`

`public long longValue()`
`public String toString()`
`public String toString(int base)`

Converts this `BigDecimal` to either a Java primitive type or a `BigInteger`. The `base` can specify the radix of the number value returned.

`public BigInteger abs()`

Returns the absolute value of this `BigInteger`.

`public BigInteger add(BigInteger arg) throws ArithmeticException`
`public BigInteger subtract(BigInteger arg)`

Adds the argument to, or subtracts `arg` from this `BigInteger` and returns the result.

`public BigInteger and(BigInteger arg)`
`public BigInteger andNot(BigInteger arg)`
`public BigInteger not()`
`public BigInteger or(BigInteger arg)`
`public BigInteger xor(BigInteger arg)`

Returns the result of a logical operation of this `BigInteger` and the value of `arg`. The `not` method returns the logical not of this `BigInteger`.

`public int bitCount()`

Returns the number of bits from this `BigInteger` that are different from the sign bit.

`public int bitLength()`

Returns the number of bits from this `BigInteger`, excluding the sign bit.

`public BigInteger clearBit(int index) throws ArithmeticException`

Returns the modified representation of this `BigInteger` with the bit at position `index` cleared.

`public int compareTo(BigInteger arg)`

Compares this `BigInteger` to the parameter `arg`. If this `BigInteger` is less than `arg`, a -1 is returned, if equal to `arg` a 0 (zero) is returned, and if greater than `arg`, a 1 is returned.

`public BigInteger divide(BigInteger arg) throws ArithmeticException`
`public BigInteger[] divideAndRemainder(BigInteger arg) throws ArithmeticException`

Returns the result of this `BigInteger` divided by `arg`. The `divideAndRemainder` method returns as the first element ([0]) the quotient, and the second element ([1]) the remainder.

`public boolean equals(Object arg)`

Returns a true value if this `BigInteger` is equal to the parameter `arg`.

`public BigInteger flipBit(int index) throws ArithmeticException`

Returns the modified representation of this `BigInteger` with the bit at position `index` flipped.

`public BigInteger gcd(BigInteger arg)`

Returns the greatest common denominator of the absolute value of this `BigInteger` and the absolute value of the parameter `arg`.

`public int getLowestSetBit()`

Returns the index of the rightmost bit that is equal to one from this `BigInteger`.

`public int hashCode()`

Returns the hash code of this `BigInteger`.

`public boolean isProbablePrime(int prob)`
Returns a true value if this `BigInteger` is probably a prime number. The parameter `prob` represents the certainty of the decision, calculated as 1 - (.5**`prob`).

`public BigInteger max(BigInteger arg)`
`public BigInteger min(BigInteger arg)`
Returns the larger or smaller of this `BigInteger` or `arg`.

`public BigInteger mod(BigInteger arg)`
`public BigInteger modInverse(BigInteger arg) throws ArithmeticException`
`public BigInteger modPow(BigInteger exp, BigInteger arg)`
Returns the result of this `BigInteger` mod `arg`. The `modInverse` returns the modular multiplicative inverse. `modPow` returns the result of this (`BigInteger` ** `exp`) mod `arg`.

`public BigInteger multiply(BigInteger arg)`
Returns the result of this `BigInteger` multiplied by `arg`.

`public BigInteger negate()`
Returns this `BigInteger` negated (this `BigInteger` * -1).

`public BigInteger pow(int exp) throws ArithmeticException`
Returns the result of this `BigInteger` ** `exp`.

`public BigInteger remainder(BigInteger arg) throws ArithmeticException`
Returns the result of this `BigInteger` mod `arg`.

`public BigInteger setBit(int index) throws ArithmeticException`
Returns the result of this `BigInteger` with the bit at the specified `index` set.

`public BigInteger shiftLeft(int num)`
`public BigInteger shiftRight(int num)`
Returns the result of this `BigInteger` shifted `num` bits.

`public int signum()`
Returns a -1 if the value of this `BigInteger` is negative, 0 if zero, and 1 if positive.

`public boolean testBit(int index) throws ArithmeticException`
Returns a true value if the bit at the specified `index` is set.

`public byte[] toByteArray()`
Returns the two's complement of this `BigInteger` in an array of bytes.

`public static BigInteger valueOf(long arg)`
Returns a `BigInteger` from the value of `arg`.

BitSet (`java.util`)

A public final class, derived from `Object` and implementing `Cloneable` and `Serializable`, that allows for the manipulation of a vectored array of bits.

Constructors

`public BitSet()`
`public BitSet(int size)`
Creates a new instance of a bit sequence of `size` bits (the default is 64). Each of the initial bits are set to false.

Methods

`public void and(BitSet arg)`
`public void or(BitSet arg)`
`public void xor(BitSet arg)`
Places all of the bits from both this BitSet AND/OR/XORed with the bits of `arg` into this `BitSet`.

`public void clear(int index)`
`public void set(int index)`
Clears or sets the bit (sets it to false) at location `index`.

`public Object clone()`
Returns a clone of this `BitSet`.

`public boolean equals(Object arg)`
Returns a true if `arg` is not null and all bits are equal to this `BitSet`.

`public boolean get(int index)`
Returns the boolean value of the bit at location `index`.

`public int hashCode()`
Returns the hash code of this `BitSet`.

`public int size()`
Returns the size of this `BitSet`.

`public String toString()`
Returns a string representation of this `BitSet` in set notation (i.e., {1, 2, 5})

Boolean (`java.lang`)

A public final class, derived from `Object` and implementing `Serializable`, that contains boolean logic operations, constants, and methods as a wrapper around the Java primitive type `boolean`.

Variables and Constants

`public final static Boolean TRUE`
`public final static Boolean FALSE`
Boolean constant values of true or false.

`public final static Class TYPE`
The `Boolean` constant value of the boolean type class.

Constructors

```
public Boolean(boolean arg)
public Boolean(String arg)
```

Creates an instance of the `Boolean` class from the parameter `arg`.

Methods

`public boolean booleanValue()`

The boolean value of the current object.

`public boolean equals(Object arg)`

Returns the result of an equality comparison against `arg`. Here `arg` must be a boolean object with the same value as this `Boolean` for a resulting true value.

`public static boolean getBoolean(String str)`

Returns a boolean representation of the system property named in `str`.

`public int hashCode()`

Returns the hash code for this object.

`public String toString()`

Returns the string representation of the state of the current object (i.e., “true” or “false”).

`public static Boolean valueOf(String str)`

Returns a new Boolean initialized to the value of `str`.

BorderLayout (`java.awt`)

A public class, derived from `Object` and implementing `LayoutManager2` and `Serializable`, that lays out a container using five distinct areas (North, South, East, West, and Center).

Variables and Constants

```
public final static String CENTER
public final static String EAST
public final static String NORTH
public final static String SOUTH
public final static String WEST
```

Constant values indicating areas of the border layout manager.

Constructors

```
public BorderLayout()
public BorderLayout(int hgap, int vgap)
```

Creates a new instance of a `BorderLayout`. If no initial horizontal and vertical gaps are specified, they default to zero.

Methods

`public void addLayoutComponent(Component item, Object constraints)`
`public void removeLayoutComponent(Component item)`
Adds or removes a component to this layout manager. When adding a component, it is possible to restrict the component to the specified constraints.

`public int getHgap()`
`public int getVgap()`
Returns the horizontal or vertical gap of components laid out by this layout manager.

`public float getLayoutAlignmentX(Container parent)`
`public float getLayoutAlignmentY(Container parent)`
Returns the horizontal or vertical alignment value of the specified container.

`public void invalidateLayout(Container cont)`
Forces this layout manager to discard any cached layout information about the specified container.

`public void layoutContainer(Container cont)`
Lays out the specified container with this layout manager.

`public Dimension maximumLayoutSize(Container cont)`
`public Dimension minimumLayoutSize(Container cont)`
`public Dimension preferredLayoutSize(Container cont)`
Returns the maximum, minimum or preferred size of the specified container when laid out by this layout manager.

`public void setHgap(int hgap)`
`public void setVgap(int vgap)`
Sets the horizontal or vertical gap in pixels of components laid out by this layout manager.

`public String toString()`
Returns a string representation of this layout manager.

BufferedReader (`java.io`)

A public class, derived from `Reader`, that provides a buffered stream of character-based input.

Constructors

`public BufferedReader(Reader rdr)`
`public BufferedReader(Reader rdr, int size)`
Creates a `BufferedReader` from the specified `Reader`, by using a specified size (in characters). The default size is 8192 characters.

Methods

`public void close() throws IOException`
Closes this `BufferedReader`.

`public void mark(int readAheadLimit) throws IOException`
Sets a mark in the stream where attempts to reset this `BufferedReader` will return to. The `readAheadLimit` determines how far ahead the stream can be read before the mark expires.

`public boolean markSupported()`
An overridden method from `Reader` that determines if this stream supports the setting of a mark.

`public int read() throws IOException`
`public String readLine() throws IOException`
Reads a single character or an entire line from this `BufferedReader` stream. The character is returned as an `int`, the line as a string. A line of text is considered to be a series of characters ending in a carriage return (`\r`), a line feed (`\n`), or a carriage return followed by a line (`\r\n`).

`public int read(char[] dest, int offset, int size) throws IOException`
Reads `size` characters from this `BufferedReader` stream. Reading will skip `offset` characters into the current location in the stream, and place them in the destination array. This method will return the number of characters read from the stream or a -1 if the end of the stream was reached.

`public boolean ready() throws IOException`
Returns a true value if this `BufferedReader` is capable of being read from. This state can only be true if the buffer is not empty.

`public void reset() throws IOException`
Resets this `BufferedReader` to the last mark.

`public long skip(long num) throws IOException`
Skips forward `num` characters in the stream and returns the actual number of characters skipped.

Button (`java.awt`)

A public class, derived from `Component`, that creates a graphical button that a user can push to initiate an action.

Constructors

`public Button()`
`public Button(String str)`
Creates a new instance of a button with a label of `str` (or none, in the case of the first constructor).

Methods

`public void addActionListener(ActionListener listener)`

`public void removeActionListener(ActionListener listener)`
Adds or removes the specified action `listener` to this button.

`public void addNotify()`
Creates this button's peer.

`public String getActionCommand()`
`public void setActionCommand(String str)`
Returns or sets the name of the command initiated by this button.

`public String getLabel()`
`public void setLabel(String str)`
Returns or sets the label of this button.

`protected String paramString()`
Returns a string containing the parameters of this button.

`protected void processActionEvent(ActionEvent event)`
Handles an AWT `event` for this button, sending it to a registered listener.

`protected void processEvent(AWTEvent event)`
Processes an AWT `event` for this button, sending it to the `processAWTEvent` method if it is an AWT event, otherwise forwarding it to the superclass' `processAWTEvent` method.

Byte (`java.lang`)

A public final class, derived from `Number`, that contains byte logic operations, constants, and methods as a wrapper around the Java primitive type `byte`.

Variables and Constants

`public final static byte MAX_VALUE`
`public final static byte MIN_VALUE`
A constant value that holds the maximum (127) and minimum (-128) values a byte can contain.

`public final static Class TYPE`
The `Byte` constant value of the byte type class.

Constructors

`public Byte(byte arg)`
`public Byte(String arg) throws NumberFormatException`
Creates a new instance of a `Byte` from `arg`.

Methods

`public byte byteValue()`
`public double doubleValue()`

`public float floatValue()`
`public int intValue()`
`public long longValue()`
`public short shortValue()`

Returns the value of this `Byte` as a Java primitive type.

`public static Byte decode(String str) throws NumberFormatException`

Returns the given string (`str`) as a `Byte`. The parameter string may be encoded as an octal, hexadecimal, or binary number.

`public boolean equals(Object arg)`

Returns a true value if this `Byte` is equal to the parameter object `arg`.

`public int hashCode()`

Returns the hash code of this `Byte`.

`public static byte parseByte(String str) throws NumberFormatException`
`public static byte parseByte(String str, int base) throws NumberFormatException`

Returns the value of the parsed string (`str`) as a byte. The radix of the string can be specified in `base`.

`public String toString()`
`public static String toString(byte prim)`

Returns a string representation of this `Byte` or the specified primitive byte (`prim`), whose radix is assumed to be 10.

`public static Byte valueOf(String str) throws NumberFormatException`
`public static Byte valueOf(String str, int base) throws NumberFormatException`

Returns a `Byte` object whose initial value is the result of the parsed parameter (`str`). The parameter is assumed to be the text representation of a byte and its radix 10 (unless specified in `base`).

Calendar (`java.util`)

A public abstract class, derived from `Object` and implementing `Cloneable` and `Serializable`, that allows for the manipulation of a `Date` object.

Variables and Constants

`public static final int AM`
`public static final int PM`

Constant values that represent ante and post meridian.

`public static final int ERA`
`public static final int YEAR`
`public static final int MONTH`
`public static final int WEEK_OF_YEAR`
`public static final int WEEK_OF_MONTH`
`public static final int DATE`

```
public static final int DAY_OF_MONTH
public static final int DAY_OF_YEAR
public static final int DAY_OF_WEEK
public static final int DAY_OF_WEEK_IN_MONTH
public static final int AM_PM
public static final int HOUR
public static final int HOUR_OF_DAY
public static final int MINUTE
public static final int SECOND
public static final int MILLISECOND
public static final int ZONE_OFFSET
public static final int DST_OFFSET
```

Constant values that represent the index to the field where particular data is stored representing an instance of time (to millisecond precision). The combination of all of these fields yields a full representation of a moment of time with respect to a particular calendar (i.e., `GregorianCalendar`).

```
public static final int JANUARY
public static final int FEBRUARY
public static final int MARCH
public static final int APRIL
public static final int MAY
public static final int JUNE
public static final int JULY
public static final int AUGUST
public static final int SEPTEMBER
public static final int OCTOBER
public static final int NOVEMBER
public static final int DECEMBER
public static final int UNDECIMBER
```

Constant values representing various calendar months. `UNDECIMBER` represents the 13th month of a Gregorian calendar (lunar month).

```
public static final int SUNDAY
public static final int MONDAY
public static final int TUESDAY
public static final int WEDNESDAY
public static final int THURSDAY
public static final int FRIDAY
public static final int SATURDAY
```

Constant values representing the days of a week.

```
protected boolean areFieldsSet
```

A boolean flag that indicates if the time fields have been set for this `Calendar`.

```
public static final int FIELD_COUNT
```

A constant value that represents the number of date/time fields stored by a `Calendar`.

`protected int fields[]`
The integer array that contains the values that make up the information about this `Calendar`.

`protected boolean isSet[]`
The boolean array that contains status values used to indicate if a corresponding time field has been set.

`protected boolean isTimeSet`
A boolean flag field that is used to indicate if the time is set for this `Calendar`.

`protected long time`
A `long int` field that contains the time set for this `Calendar`.

Methods

`public abstract void add(int field, int val)`
Adds (or subtracts in the case of a negative `val`) an amount of days or time from the specified `field`.

`public abstract boolean after(Object arg)`
`public abstract boolean before(Object arg)`
Returns a true value if this `Calendar` date is after or before the date specified by `arg`.

`public final void clear()`
`public final void clear(int field)`
Clears the value from the specified time `field` from this `Calendar`. The `clear` method will clear all of the values from this `Calendar`.

`public Object clone()`
Returns a clone of this `Calendar`.

`protected void complete()`
Attempts to complete any empty date/time fields by calling the `completeTime()` and `completeFields()` methods of this `Calendar`.

`protected abstract void computeFields()`
`protected abstract void computeTime()`
Computes the values of the time fields based on the currently set time (`computeFields()`) or computes the time based on the currently set time fields (`computeTime()`) for this `Calendar`.

`public abstract boolean equals(Object arg)`
Returns a true value if this `Calendar` is equal to the value of `arg`.

`public final int get(int fld)`
Returns the value of the specified time field from this `Calendar`.

`public static synchronized Locale[] getAvailableLocales()`
Returns the list of locales that are available.

`public int getFirstDayOfWeek()`
`public void setFirstDayOfWeek(int val)`
Returns or sets the first day of the week to `val` for this `Calendar`.

`public abstract int getGreatestMinimum(int fld)`
Returns the largest allowable minimum value for the specified field.

`public static synchronized Calendar getInstance()`
`public static synchronized Calendar getInstance(Locale locale)`
`public static synchronized Calendar getInstance(TimeZone tz)`
`public static synchronized Calendar getInstance(TimeZone tz, Locale locale)`

Returns an instance of a `Calendar` based on the default time zone and locale, or from a specified time zone and/or locale.

`public abstract int getLeastMaximum(int fld)`

Returns the smallest allowable maximum value for the specified field.

`public abstract int getMaximum(int fld)`
`public abstract int getMinimum(int fld)`

Returns the largest or smallest allowable value for the specified field.

`public int getMinimalDaysInFirstWeek()`
`public void setMinimalDaysInFirstWeek(int val)`

Returns or sets the smallest allowable number of days in the first week of the year, based on the locale.

`public final Date getTime()`
`public final void setTime(Date dt)`

Returns or sets the time for this `Calendar`.

`protected long getTimeInMillis()`
`protected void setTimeInMillis(long ms)`

Returns or sets the time in milliseconds for this `Calendar`.

`public TimeZone getTimeZone()`
`public void setTimeZone(TimeZone val)`

Returns or sets the time zone for this `Calendar`.

`protected final int internalGet(int fld)`

An internal method used to obtain field values to be used by subclasses of `Calendar`.

`public boolean isLenient()`
`public void setLenient(boolean flag)`

Returns or sets the flag indicating leniency for date/time input.

`public final boolean isSet(int fld)`

Returns a true value if a value is set for the specified field.

`public abstract void roll(int fld, boolean direction)`

Adds one single unit of time to the specified date/time field. A true value specified for `direction` increases the field's value, false decreases it.

`public final void set(int fld, int val)`

Sets a single specified field to a value.

`public final void set(int year, int month, int date)`
`public final void set(int year, int month, int date, int hour, int min)`
`public final void set(int year, int month, int date, int hour, int min, int sec)`

Sets the year, month, date, hour, minute, and seconds of the time fields for this `Calendar`.

Canvas (`java.awt`)

A public class, derived from `Component`, that creates a graphical drawing canvas.

Constructors

`public Canvas()`

Creates a new instance of a canvas.

Methods

`public void addNotify()`

Creates this canvas' peer.

`public void paint(Graphics gc)`

Repaints this canvas with the graphics context `gc`.

CardLayout (`java.awt`)

A public class, derived from `Object` and implementing `LayoutManager2` and `Serializable`, that lays out components in a series of separate cards, only one of which is visible at any time. The visibility of the cards can be changed, essentially providing the ability to sequence through the cards.

Constructors

`public CardLayout()`
`public CardLayout(int hg, int vg)`

Creates a new instance of a card layout with a specified horizontal and vertical gap (or no gap in the case of the first constructor).

Methods

`public void addLayoutComponent(Component item, Object constr)`
`public void removeLayoutComponent(Component item)`

Adds or removes a component to this layout manager. While adding, it is possible to restrict the component to the specified constraints (`constr`).

`public void first(Container cont)`
`public void last(Container cont)`

Moves to the first or last card in the layout. `cont` is the container that is laid out by this layout manager.

`public int getHgap()`
`public int getVgap()`

Returns the horizontal or vertical gap between the components laid out by this layout manager.

`public float getLayoutAlignmentX(Container parent)`

`public float getLayoutAlignmentY(Container parent)`
Returns the horizontal or vertical alignment value of the specified container.

`public void invalidateLayout(Container cont)`
Forces this layout manager to discard any cached layout information about the specified container.

`public void layoutContainer(Container cont)`
Lays out the specified container with this layout manager.

`public Dimension maximumLayoutSize(Container cont)`
`public Dimension minimumLayoutSize(Container cont)`
`public Dimension preferredLayoutSize(Container cont)`
Returns the maximum, minimum or preferred size of the specified container when laid out by this layout manager.

`public void next(Container cont)`
`public void previous(Container cont)`
Cycles to the next or previous card. `cont` is container that is laid out by this layout manager.

`public void setHgap(int hg)`
`public void setVgap(int vg)`
Sets the horizontal or vertical gap in pixels of components laid out by this layout manager.

`public void show(Container cont, String str)`
Cycles to the card the contains the component with the name `str`. When found, the specified container is laid out with this layout manager.

`public String toString()`
Returns a string representation of this layout manager.

Character (java.lang)

A public class, derived from `Object` and implementing `Serializable`, that contains character constants and methods to convert and identify characters.

Variables and Constants

```
public final static byte COMBINING_SPACING_MARK
public final static byte CONNECTOR_PUNCTUATION
public final static byte CONTROL
public final static byte CURRENCY_SYMBOL
public final static byte DASH_PUNCTUATION
public final static byte DECIMAL_DIGIT_NUMBER
public final static byte ENCLOSING_MARK
public final static byte END_PUNCTUATION
public final static byte FORMAT
public final static byte LETTER_NUMBER
public final static byte LINE_SEPARATOR
public final static byte LOWERCASE_LETTER
```

```
public final static byte MATH_SYMBOL
public final static byte MODIFIER_LETTER
public final static byte MODIFIER_SYMBOL
public final static byte NON_SPACING_MARK
public final static byte OTHER_LETTER
public final static byte OTHER_NUMBER
public final static byte OTHER_PUNCTUATION
public final static byte OTHER_SYMBOL
public final static byte PARAGRAPH_SEPARATOR
public final static byte PRIVATE_USE
public final static byte SPACE_SEPARATOR
public final static byte START_PUNCTUATION
public final static byte SURROGATE
public final static byte TITLECASE_LETTER
public final static byte UNASSIGNED
public final static byte UPPERCASE_LETTER
```

Constant values representing various character symbols and types.

`public final static int MAX_RADIX`

A constant value that represents the largest possible value of a radix (base).

`public final static char MAX_VALUE`

A constant value that represents the largest possible value of a character in Java = `\uffff'`.

`public final static int MIN_RADIX`

A constant value that represents that smallest possible value of a radix (base).

`public final static char MIN_VALUE`

A constant value that represents the smallest possible value of a character in Java = `\u0000'`.

`public final static Class TYPE`

The `Character` constant value of the character type class.

Constructors

`public Character(char prim)`

Creates an instance of the `Character` class from the primitive parameter `prim`.

Methods

`public char charValue()`

Returns the value of this `Character` as a primitive character.

`public static int digit(char c, int base)`
`public static char forDigit(int c, int base)`

Returns the numeric value or the character depiction of the parameter `c` in radix `base`.

`public boolean equals(Object arg)`

Returns a true value if this `Character` is equal to the parameter `arg`.

`public static int getNumericValue(char c)`

Returns the Unicode representation of the character parameter (`c`) as a nonnegative integer. If the character has no numeric representation, a -1 is returned. If the character cannot be represented as a nonnegative number, -2 will be returned.

`public static int getType(char c)`

Returns an integer value that represents the type of character the parameter `c` is.

`public int hashCode()`

Returns a hash code for this `Character`.

`public static boolean isDefined(char c)`
`public static boolean isISOControl(char c)`

Returns a true value if the parameter `c` has a defined meaning in Unicode or is an ISO control character.

`public static boolean isIdentifierIgnorable(char c)`

Returns a true value if the parameter `c` is a character that can be ignored in a Java identifier (such as control characters).

`public static boolean isJavaIdentifierPart(char c)`
`public static boolean isJavaIdentifierStart(char c)`

Returns a true value if the parameter `c` can be used in a valid Java identifier in any but the leading character. `isJavaIdentifierStart` returns a true value if the parameter `c` can be used as the leading character in a valid Java identifier.

`public static boolean isDigit(char c)`
`public static boolean isLetter(char c)`
`public static boolean isLetterOrDigit(char c)`
`public static boolean isLowerCase(char c)`
`public static boolean isSpaceChar(char c)`
`public static boolean isTitleCase(char c)`
`public static boolean isUnicodeIdentifierPart(char c)`
`public static boolean isWhitespace(char c)`
`public static boolean isUnicodeIdentifierStart(char c)`
`public static boolean isUpperCase(char c)`

Returns a true value if the parameter `c` is a digit; letter; letter or a digit; lowercase character; space character; titlecase character; can be used in a valid Unicode identifier in any but the leading character; a white space character; can be used as the leading character in a valid Unicode identifier or an uppercase character (respectively).

`public static char toLowerCase(char c)`
`public String toString()`
`public static char toTitleCase(char c)`
`public static char toUpperCase(char c)`

Returns a lowercase character, string representation, titlecase, or uppercase character of the parameter `c`.

Checkbox (`java.awt`)

A public class, derived from `Component` and implementing `ItemSelectable`, that creates a graphical box with an "on" and "off" state that the user can toggle with a mouse click.

Constructors

`public Checkbox()`
`public Checkbox(String str)`
`public Checkbox(String str, boolean toggle)`

Creates a new instance of a checkbox (possibly with a label of `str`), to the value of `toggle` (or false by default), and not a member of a checkbox group.

`public Checkbox(String str, CheckboxGroup grp, boolean toggle)`
`public Checkbox(String str, boolean toggle, CheckboxGroup grp)`

Creates a new instance of a checkbox with a label (`str`), belonging to a checkbox group and having an initial state of `toggle`.

Methods

`public void addItemListener(ItemListener listener)`
`public void removeItemListener(ItemListener listener)`

Adds or removes the specified `listener` to this checkbox.

`public void addNotify()`

Creates this checkbox's peer.

`public CheckboxGroup getCheckboxGroup()`
`public void setCheckboxGroup(CheckboxGroup cg)`

Returns or sets the group of this checkbox.

`public String getLabel()`
`public void setLabel(String str)`

Returns or sets the label of this checkbox.

`public Object[] getSelectedObjects()`

Returns an array of size 1 containing the label of the checkbox if it is selected, otherwise a null is returned.

`public boolean getState()`
`public void setState(boolean toggle)`

Returns or sets the state of this checkbox.

`protected String paramString()`

Returns a string containing this checkbox's parameters.

`protected void processEvent(AWTEvent event)`

Processes an `AWTEvent` for this checkbox, sending it to the `processItemEvent` method if it is an `ItemEvent`; otherwise, it forwards the event to the superclass' `processEvent` method.

`protected void processItemEvent(ItemEvent event)`

Handles an `ItemEvent` for this checkbox, sending it to a registered `ItemListener`.

CheckboxGroup (java.awt)

A public class, derived from `Object` and implementing `Serializable`, that manages a list of checkboxes, allowing only one to be "on" at any time.

Constructors

`public CheckboxGroup()`
Creates a new checkbox group.

Methods

`public Checkbox getSelectedCheckbox()`
Returns the currently selected checkbox.

`public synchronized void setSelectedCheckbox(Checkbox checkbox)`
Selects the specified `checkbox` in this checkbox group.

`public String toString()`
Returns a string representation of this checkbox group.

CheckboxMenuItem (java.awt)

A public class, derived from `MenuItem` and implementing `Serializable`, that creates a menu item that has a part of its label as a checkbox. The user can change the start of the checkbox by clicking on the box.

Constructors

`public CheckboxMenuItem()`
`public CheckboxMenuItem(String str)`
`public CheckboxMenuItem(String str, boolean toggle)`
Creates a new instance of a checkbox menu item with a label of `str` (or none by default), and initially set to `toggle` (or false by default).

Methods

`public void addItemListener(ItemListener listener)`
`public void removeItemListener(ItemListener listener)`
Adds or removes the specified `listener` to this checkbox menu item.

`public void addNotify()`
Creates this checkbox menu item's peer.

`public synchronized Object[] getSelectedObjects()`
Returns an array of size 1 containing the checkbox item if it is checked to a true value; otherwise, a null is returned.

`public boolean getState()`
`public void setState(boolean toggle)`

Returns or sets the current state of this checkbox menu item.

`public String paramString()`

Returns a string containing the parameters for this checkbox menu item.

`protected void processEvent(AWTEvent event)`

Processes an AWT event for this checkbox menu item, sending it to the `processItemEvent` method if it is an `ItemEvent`; otherwise, it forwards the event to the superclass' `processEvent` method.

`protected void processItemEvent(ItemEvent event)`

Handles an `ItemEvent` for this checkbox menu item, sending it to a registered `ItemListener`.

Choice (`java.awt`)

A public class, derived from `Component` and implementing `ItemSelectable`, that creates and manages a graphical list of items from which the user can choose.

Constructors

`public Choice()`

Creates a new instance of a choice menu with no items in it.

Methods

`public synchronized void add(String str) throws NullPointerException`
`public void addItem(String str) throws NullPointerException`

Adds the specified item to this choice menu.

`public void addItemListener(ItemListener listener)`
`public void removeItemListener(ItemListener listener)`

Adds or removes the specified `listener` to this choice menu.

`public void addNotify()`

Creates this choice menu's peer.

`public String getItem(int index)`

Returns the label of the item at position `index`.

`public int getItemCount()`

Returns the number of items in this choice menu.

`public int getSelectedIndex()`
`public String getSelectedItem()`

Returns the index or the label of the currently selected item in this choice menu.

`public synchronized Object[] getSelectedObjects()`

Returns an array of size 1 containing the currently selected item from this choice menu.

`public synchronized void insert(String str, int idx) throws IllegalArgumentException`
`public synchronized void remove(int idx)`
`public synchronized void remove(String str)`

Inserts or removes the item `str` in this choice menu at the specified index (`idx`).

`protected String paramString()`

Returns a string containing the parameters for this choice menu.

`protected void processEvent(AWTEvent event)`

Processes an `AWTEvent` for this choice menu, sending it to the `processItemEvent` method (if the event is an `ItemEvent`); otherwise, the event is sent to the superclass' `processEvent` method.

`protected void processItemEvent(ItemEvent event)`

Handles an `ItemEvent` for this choice menu, sending it to a registered listener.

`public void select(int pos) throws IllegalArgumentException`

Selects the item at position `pos` in this choice menu.

`public synchronized void removeAll()`

Removes all of the items from the choice menu.

`public synchronized void select(int idx)`
`public void select(String str)`

Selects this item with the specified label or at a specific index in this choice menu.

ChoiceFormat (`java.text`)

A public class, derived from `NumberFormat`, that facilitates the formatting of values based on a range of numbers.

Constructors

`public ChoiceFormat(String str)`

Creates a new instance of a `ChoiceFormat` from the specified string pattern.

`public ChoiceFormat(double[] lims, String[] formats)`

Creates a new instance of a `ChoiceFormat` from the specified range of double limits, and a set of string formats that correspond to a limit.

Methods

`public void applyPattern(String str)`

Sets the pattern for this `ChoiceFormat`.

`public Object clone()`

Returns a copy of this `ChoiceFormat`.

`public boolean equals(Object arg)`

Returns a true value if this `ChoiceFormat` is equal to `arg`.

`public StringBuffer format(double num, StringBuffer dest, FieldPosition pos)`
`public StringBuffer format(long num, StringBuffer dest, FieldPosition pos)`

Formats the specified long or double number, starting at position pos, placing the result in the destination buffer. This method returns the value of the buffer.

`public Object[] getFormats()`
`public double[] getLimits()`

Returns the set of formats and limits for this `ChoiceFormat`.

`public int hashCode()`

Returns the hash code for this `ChoiceFormat`.

`public static final double nextDouble(double num)`

Returns the smallest double value greater than the specified number.

`public static double nextDouble(double num, boolean toggle)`

Returns the smallest double value larger than the specified number.

`public Number parse(String str, ParsePosition pos)`

Parses the source string, starting at position pos, and returns a long (if possible) or double value corresponding to the string.

`public static final double previousDouble(double num)`

Returns the largest double value less than the specified number.

`public void setChoices(double[] lims, String[] formats)`

Sets the limits and formats for this `ChoiceFormat`.

`public String toPattern()`

Returns the pattern of this `ChoiceFormat`.

Class (`java.lang`)

A public final class, derived from `Object` and implementing `Serializable`, that describes both interfaces and classes in the currently running Java program.

Methods

`public static Class forName(String class) throws ClassNotFoundException`

Returns a `Class` object that corresponds with the named `class`. The name of the specified class must be a fully qualified class name (as in `java.io.Reader`).

`public Class[] getClasses()`
`public Class[] getDeclaredClasses() throws SecurityException`

Returns an array of `Classes` that contains all of the interfaces and classes that are members of this `Class` (excluding superclasses). `getClasses` returns only the list of public interfaces and classes.

`public ClassLoader getClassLoader()`

Returns the `ClassLoader` for this `Class`.

public Class getComponentType()
Returns the Component type of the array that is represented by this Class.

public Constructor getConstructor(Class[] types) throws NoSuchMethodException, SecurityException

public Constructor[] getConstructors() throws SecurityException
Returns the Constructor object or an array containing the public constructors for this class. The signature of the public constructor that is returned must match exactly the types and sequence of the parameters specified by the types array.

public Constructor getDeclaredConstructor(Class[] types) throws NoSuchMethodException, SecurityException

public Constructor[] getDeclaredConstructors() throws SecurityException
Returns the Constructor object or an array containing the constructors for this class. The signature of the public constructor that is returned must match exactly the types and sequence of the parameters specified by the types array parameter.

public Field getDeclaredField(String field) throws NoSuchFieldException, SecurityException

public Field[] getDeclaredFields() throws SecurityException
Returns the Field object or an array containing all of the fields for the specified matching field name for this Class.

public Method getDeclaredMethod(String method, Class[] types) throws NoSuchMethodException, SecurityException

public Method[] getDeclaredMethods() throws SecurityException
Returns a Method object or an array containing all of the methods for the specified method of this Class. The requested method's parameter list must match identically the types and sequence of the elements of the types array.

public Class getDeclaringClass()
Returns the declaring class of this Class, provided that this Class is a member of another class.

public Field getField(String field) throws NoSuchFieldException, SecurityException

public Field[] getFields() throws SecurityException
Returns a Field object or an array containing all of the fields of a specified matching field name for this Class.

public Class[] getInterfaces()
Returns an array containing all of the interfaces of this Class.

public Method getMethod(String method, Class[] types) throws NoSuchMethodException, SecurityException

public Method[] getMethods() throws SecurityException
Returns a Method object or an array containing all of the public methods for the specified public method of this Class. The requested method's parameter list must match identically the types and sequence of the elements of the types array.

public int getModifiers()
Returns the encoded integer visibility modifiers for this Class. The values can be decoded using the Modifier class.

`public String getName()`

Returns the string representation of the name of the type that this `Class` represents.

`public URL getResource(String arg)`

Returns a URL representing the system resource for the class loader of this `Class`.

`public InputStream getResourceAsStream(String arg)`

Returns an input stream representing the `named` system resource from the class loader of this `Class`.

`public Object[] getSigners()`

Returns an array of `Objects` that contains the signers of this `Class`.

`public Class getSuperclass()`

Returns the superclass of this `Class`, or null if this `Class` is an interface or of type `Object`.

`public boolean isArray()`

Returns a true value if this `Class` represents an array type.

`public boolean isAssignableFrom(Class other)`

Returns a true value if this `Class` is the same as a superclass or superinterface of the `other` class.

`public boolean isInstance(Object target)`

Returns a true value if the specified `target` object is an instance of this `Class`.

`public boolean isInterface()`
`public boolean isPrimitive()`

Returns a true value if this `Class` represents an interface class or a primitive type in Java.

`public Object newInstance() throws InstantiationException, IllegalAccessException`

Creates a new instance of this `Class`.

`public String toString()`

Returns a string representation of this `Class` in the form of the word class or interface, followed by the fully qualified name of this `Class`.

Color (`java.awt`)

A public final class, derived from `Object` and implementing `Serializable`, that is used to represent colors. A color is defined by three components, red, blue, and green, that each have a value ranging from 0 to 255.

Variables and Constants

```
public final static Color black
public final static Color blue
public final static Color cyan
public final static Color darkGray
public final static Color gray
public final static Color green
```

```
public final static Color lightGray
public final static Color magenta
public final static Color orange
public final static Color pink
public final static Color red
public final static Color white
public final static Color yellow
```

A constant value that describes the colors black (0, 0, 0), blue (0, 0, 255), cyan (0, 255, 255), darkGray (64, 64, 64), gray (128, 128, 128), green (0, 255, 0), lightGray (192, 192, 192), magenta (255, 0, 255), orange (255, 200, 0), pink (255, 175, 175), red (255, 0, 0), white (255, 255, 255) and yellow (255, 255, 0) as a set of RGB values.

Constructors

```
public Color(float r, float g, float b)
public Color(int rgb)
public Color(int r, int g, int b)
```

Creates a new instance of the color described by the `rgb` value. When passed as a single integer value, the red component is represented in bits 16 to 23, green in 15 to 8, and blue in 0 to 7.

Methods

```
public Color brighter()
public Color darker()
```

Returns a brighter or darker version of this color.

```
public static Color decode(String str) throws NumberFormatException
```

Returns the color specified by `str`.

```
public boolean equals(Object arg)
```

Returns a true value if this color is equal to `arg`.

```
public int getBlue()
public int getGreen()
public int getRed()
```

Returns the blue, green, or red component value for this color.

```
public static Color getColor(String str)
public static Color getColor(String str, Color default)
public static Color getColor(String str, int default)
```

Returns the color represented in the string `str` (where its value is an integer). If the value is not determined, the color `default` is returned.

```
public static Color getHSBColor(float h, float s, float b)
```

Returns a color specified by the Hue-Saturation-Brightness model for colors, where `h` is the hue, `s` is the saturation, and `b` is the brightness of the desired color.

```
public int getRGB()
```

Returns an integer representation of the RGB value for this color.

`public int hashCode()`

Returns the hash code for this color.

`public static int HSBtoRGB(float hue, float saturation, float brightness)`

Converts a `hue`, `saturation`, and `brightness` representation of a color to a RGB value.

`public static float[] RGBtoHSB(int r, int g, int b, float[] hsbvals)`

Converts a RGB representation of a color to a HSB value, placing the converted values into the `hsbvals` array. The RGB value is represented via a red (`r`), green (`g`), and blue (`b`) value.

`public String toString()`

Returns a string representation of this color.

Component (`java.awt`)

A public abstract class, derived from `Object` and implementing `ImageObserver`, `MenuContainer`, and `Serializable`, that is the superclass to every AWT item that is represented on screen with a specific size and position.

Variables and Constants

`public final static float BOTTOM_ALIGNMENT`
`public final static float LEFT_ALIGNMENT`
`public final static float RIGHT_ALIGNMENT`
`public final static float TOP_ALIGNMENT`

Constant values that represent specified alignments within the component.

`protected Locale locale`

Holds the locale for this component.

Constructors

`protected Component()`

Creates a new instance of a component.

Methods

`public synchronized void add(PopupMenu popmenu)`
`public synchronized void remove(MenuComponent popmenu)`

Adds or removes the specified popup menu to this component.

`public synchronized void addComponentListener(ComponentListener listener)`
`public synchronized void addFocusListener(FocusListener listener)`
`public synchronized void addKeyListener(KeyListener listener)`
`public synchronized void addMouseListener(MouseListener listener)`
`public synchronized void addMouseMotionListener(MouseMotionListener listener)`
`public synchronized void removeComponentListener(ComponentListener listener)`
`public synchronized void removeFocusListener(FocusListener listener)`

`public synchronized void removeKeyListener(KeyListener listener)`
`public synchronized void removeMouseListener(MouseListener listener)`
`public synchronized void removeMouseMotionListener(MouseMotionListener listener)`

Adds or removes the specified `listener` to this component.

`public void addNotify()`
`public void removeNotify()`

Notifies the component that a peer must be created or destroyed.

`public int checkImage(Image img, ImageObserver obs)`
`public int checkImage(Image img, int width, int height, ImageObserver obs)`

Returns the status of the construction of a scaled image `img`. The image created can be scaled to a `width` and `height`. The image `obs` will be informed of the status of the image.

`public boolean contains(int x, int y)`
`public boolean contains(Point pt)`

Returns a true value if this component contains the specified position.

`public Image createImage(ImageProducer prod)`
`public Image createImage(int width, int height)`

Returns a new image created from `prod`. The second method creates another image which is generally offscreen (having `width` and `height`), used for double-buffering drawings.

`protected final void disableEvents(long mask)`
`protected final void enableEvents(long mask)`

Disables or enables all events specified by the `mask` for this component.

`public final void dispatchEvent(AWTEvent event)`

Dispatches an `AWTEvent` to this component or one of its subcomponents.

`public void doLayout()`

Lays out this component.

`public float getAlignmentX()`
`public float getAlignmentY()`

Returns the horizontal or vertical alignment for this component.

`public Color getBackground()`
`public Color getForeground()`
`public void setBackground(Color clr)`
`public void setForeground(Color clr)`

Returns or sets the background or foreground color for this component.

`public Rectangle getBounds()`
`public void setBounds(int x, int y, int width, int height)`

Returns or sets the bounds of this component. Setting the bounds resizes and reshapes this component to the bounding box of <x, y> to <x+width, y+height>.

`public ColorModel getColorModel()`

Returns the color model of this component.

`public Component getComponentAt(int x, int y)`
`public Component getComponentAt(Point pt)`

Returns the component located at the specified point.

`public Cursor getCursor()`
`public synchronized void setCursor(Cursor csr)`
Returns or sets the cursor set for this component.

`public Font getFont()`
`public void setFont(Font ft)`
Returns or sets the font of this component.

`public FontMetrics getFontMetrics(Font ft)`
Returns the font metrics of the specified font.

`public Graphics getGraphics()`
Returns the graphics context for this component.

`public Locale getLocale()`
`public void setLocale(Locale locale)`
Returns or sets the locale for this component.

`public Point getLocation()`
`public Point getLocationOnScreen()`
Returns the location of this component relative to the containing or screen space.

`public Dimension getMaximumSize()`
`public Dimension getMinimumSize()`
`public Dimension getPreferredSize()`
Returns the maximum, minimum or preferred size of this component.

`public String getName()`
`public void setName(String str)`
Returns or sets the name of this component.

`public Container getParent()`
Returns the parent container of this component.

`public Dimension getSize()`
`public void setSize(Dimension dim)`
`public void setSize(int width, int height)`
Returns the size of or resizes this component to the specified dimension(s).

`public Toolkit getToolkit()`
Returns the toolkit of this component.

`public final Object getTreeLock()`
Returns the AWT object that is used as the base of the component tree and layout operations for this component.

`public boolean imageUpdate(Image src, int flags, int x, int y, int width, int height)`
Draws more of an image (`src`) as its information becomes available. The exact value of the `x`, `y`, `width`, and `height` variables is dependent on the value of the `flags` variable.

`public void invalidate()`
Forces this component to be laid out again by making it "invalid."

`public boolean isEnabled()`

`public void setEnabled(boolean toggle)`

Returns or sets the enabled state of this component.

`public boolean isFocusTraversable()`

Returns a true value if this component can be traversed using Tab or Shift-Tab sequences.

`public boolean isShowing()`
`public boolean isValid()`

Returns a true value if this component is visible on screen or does not need to be laid out (valid).

`public boolean isVisible()`
`public void setVisible(boolean toggle)`

Returns or sets the state of this component's visibility.

`public void list()`
`public void list(PrintStream outstrm)`
`public void list(PrintStream outstrm, int spc)`
`public void list(PrintWriter outstrm)`
`public void list(PrintWriter outstrm, int spc)`

Prints a listing of this component's parameters to the print writer stream `outstrm` (default of `System.out`), indenting `spc` spaces (default of 0).

`public void paint(Graphics gc)`
`public void print(Graphics gc)`

Paints or prints this component with the graphics context `gc`.

`public void paintAll(Graphics gc)`
`public void printAll(Graphics gc)`

Paints or prints this component and all of its subcomponents with the graphics context `gc`.

`protected String paramString()`

Returns a string describing the parameters of this component.

`public boolean prepareImage(Image src, ImageObserver obs)`
`public prepareImage(Image src, int width, int height, ImageObserver obs)`

Downloads the `src` for display. The image can be scaled to a `width` and `height`. The `obs` is informed of the status of the image.

`protected void processComponentEvent(ComponentEvent event)`
`protected void processFocusEvent(FocusEvent event)`
`protected void processKeyEvent(KeyEvent event)`
`protected void processMouseEvent(MouseEvent event)`
`protected void processMouseMotionEvent(MouseEvent event)`

Processes the specified event for this component, sending the event to a registered event listener.

`protected void processEvent(AWTEvent event)`

Processes an AWT event for this component, sending it to the appropriate processing routine (i.e., `processComponentEvent` method) for further handling.

`public void repaint()`
`public void repaint(int x, int y, int width, int height)`

Repaints a rectangular portion of this component from <x, y> to <x+width, y+height>.

`public void repaint(long msec)`

`public void repaint(long msec, int x, int y, int width, int height)`
Repaints a rectangular portion of this component from `<x, y>` to `<x+width, y+height>` after a delay of `msec` milliseconds.

`public void requestFocus()`
Requests that this component get the input focus.

`public void setLocation(int x, int y)`
`public void setLocation(Point pt)`
Moves this component to the specified point in the containing space.

`public String toString()`
Returns a string representation of this component.

`public void transferFocus()`
Transfers focus from this component to the next component.

`public void update(Graphics gc)`
Updates this component using graphics context `gc`.

`public void validate()`
Validates this component if needed.

ComponentAdapter (`java.awt.event`)

A public abstract class, derived from `Object` and implementing `ComponentListener`, that permits a derived class to override the predefined no-op component events.

Constructors

`public ComponentAdapter()`
Creates a new instance of a `ComponentAdapter`.

Methods

`public void componentHidden(ComponentEvent event)`
`public void componentMoved(ComponentEvent event)`
`public void componentResized(ComponentEvent event)`
`public void componentShown(ComponentEvent event)`
Empty methods that should be overridden in order to implement event handling for AWT components.

ComponentEvent (`java.awt.event`)

A public class, derived from `AWTEvent`, that represents an AWT component event.

Variables and Constants

```
public static final int COMPONENT_FIRST
public static final int COMPONENT_LAST
```

Constant values that represent the index of the first and last component event ids.

```
public static final int COMPONENT_MOVED
public static final int COMPONENT_RESIZED
public static final int COMPONENT_SHOWN
public static final int COMPONENT_HIDDEN
```

Constant values that represent AWT component event ids.

Constructors

```
public ComponentEvent(Component src, int type)
```

Creates a new instance of a `ComponentEvent` from the specified source and of a specific type.

Methods

```
public Component getComponent()
```

Returns the AWT component that triggered this event.

```
public String paramString()
```

Returns a string containing the parameters of this event.

Container (`java.awt`)

A public abstract class, derived from `Component`, that is the superclass to any AWT component that can contain one or more AWT components.

Constructors

```
protected Container()
```

Creates a new instance of a container.

Methods

```
public Component add(Component item)
public Component add(Component item, int idx)
public void add(Component item, Object constr)
public void add(Component item, Object constr, int idx)
public Component add(String str, Component item)
```

Adds component `item` to this container at index `idx` (or to the end by default). The new item can have constraints (`constr`) applied to it. A string name can be associated with the added component in the case of the last constructor.

```
public void addContainerListener(ContainerListener listener)
```

`public void removeContainerListener(ContainerListener listener)`

Adds or removes the specified `listener` to this container.

`protected void addImpl(Component item, Object constr, int idx)`

Adds component `item` to this container at index `idx`, and passes the constraints for the new item (`constr`) to the layout manager for this container.

`public void addNotify()`
`public void removeNotify()`

Creates or destroys this container's peer.

`public void doLayout()`

Lays out the components of this container.

`public float getAlignmentX()`
`public float getAlignmentY()`

Returns the horizontal or vertical alignment value of this container.

`public Component getComponent(int idx) throws ArrayIndexOutOfBoundsException`
`public Component getComponentAt(int x, int y)`
`public Component getComponentAt(Point pt)`

Returns the component that is located at the specified point or index.

`public int getComponentCount()`

Returns the number of components in this container.

`public Component[] getComponents()`

Returns an array of all of the components in this container.

`public Insets getInsets()`

Returns the insets of this container.

`public LayoutManager getLayout()`
`public void setLayout(LayoutManager layout)`

Returns or sets the layout manager of this container.

`public Dimension getMaximumSize()`
`public Dimension getMinimumSize()`
`public Dimension getPreferredSize()`

Returns the maximum, minimum, or preferred size of this container.

`public void invalidate()`

Marks the layout of this container as invalid, forcing the need to lay out the components again.

`public boolean isAncestorOf(Component comp)`

Returns a true value if the specified component (`comp`) is contained in the component hierarchy of this container.

`public void list(PrintStream outstream, int spaces)`
`public void list(PrintWriter outstream, int spaces)`

Prints a listing of all of the components of this container to print stream `outstream`, indented a specified number of `spaces` (default of 0).

`public void paint(Graphics gwin)`

`public void print(Graphics gwin)`
Paints or prints this container with graphics context `gwin`.

`public void paintComponents(Graphics gwin)`
`public void printComponents(Graphics gwin)`
Repaints or prints all of the components in this container with graphics context `gwin`.

`protected String paramString()`
Returns a string representation of this container's parameters.

`protected void processContainerEvent(ContainerEvent event)`
Processes any container `event`, passing the event to a registered container listener.

`protected void processEvent(AWTEvent event)`
Handles any `AWTEvent`, invoking `processContainerEvent` for container events, and passing the event to the superclass' `processEvent` otherwise.

`public void remove(Component comp)`
`public void remove(int idx)`
Removes the specified component (or the component at the specified index) from this container.

`public void removeAll()`
Removes all components from this container.

`public void validate()`
Validates this container and all of the subcomponents in it.

`protected void validateTree()`
Validates this container and all subcontainers in it.

ContainerAdapter (`java.awt.event`)

A public abstract class, derived from `Object` and implementing `ContainerListener`, that permits a derived class to override the predefined no-op container events.

Constructors

`public ContainerAdapter()`
Creates a new instance of a `ContainerAdapter`.

Methods

`public void componentAdded(ContainerEvent event)`
`public void componentRemoved(ContainerEvent event)`
Empty methods that should be overridden in order to implement event handling for AWT containers.

ContainerEvent (`java.awt.event`)

A public class, derived from `ComponentEvent`, that describes a particular AWT container event.

Variables and Constants

`public static final int COMPONENT_ADDED`
`public static final int COMPONENT_REMOVED`
Constant values that represent various container events (a component being added or removed to this container).

`public static final int CONTAINER_FIRST`
`public static final int CONTAINER_LAST`
Constant values that represent the index of the first and last component event ids.

Constructors

`public ContainerEvent(Component src, int type, Component comp)`
Creates a new instance of a `ContainerEvent` with a specified source component, event type and a defined component (which is being added or removed).

Methods

`public Component getChild()`
Returns the child component that was added or removed, triggering this event.

`public Container getContainer()`
Returns the container in which this event was triggered.

`public String paramString()`
Returns a string containing the parameters of this `ComponentEvent`.

ContentHandler (`java.net`)

A public abstract class, derived from `Object`, that is the superclass to URL-handling classes. Its purpose is to return an object as the target of a URL.

Constructors

`public ContentHandler()`
Creates a new instance of a `ContentHandler`.

Methods

`public abstract Object getContent(URLConnection src) throws IOException`

Retrieves the content at `src` and returns it as an `Object`. This abstract method is overridden by subclasses.

Cursor (java.awt)

A public class, derived from `Object` and implementing `Serializable`, that represents the different states and images of the mouse cursor in a graphical application or applet.

Variables and Constants

```
public final static int CROSSHAIR_CURSOR
public final static int DEFAULT_CURSOR
public final static int E_RESIZE_CURSOR
public final static int HAND_CURSOR
public final static int MOVE_CURSOR
public final static int N_RESIZE_CURSOR
public final static int NE_RESIZE_CURSOR
public final static int NW_RESIZE_CURSOR
public final static int S_RESIZE_CURSOR
public final static int SE_RESIZE_CURSOR
public final static int SW_RESIZE_CURSOR
public final static int TEXT_CURSOR
public final static int W_RESIZE_CURSOR
public final static int WAIT_CURSOR
```

Constant values that represent various cursors.

`protected static Cursor predefined[]`

An array used to hold the cursors as they are defined and implemented.

Constructors

`public Cursor(int cursortype)`

Creates a new instance of a cursor of the specified type (`cursortype`).

Methods

`public static Cursor getDefaultCursor()`

Returns the default cursor.

`public static Cursor getPredefinedCursor(int cursortype)`

Returns the cursor of the specified type (`cursortype`).

`public int getType()`
Returns the type of this cursor.

Date (`java.util`)

A public class, derived from `Object` and implementing `Serializable` and `Cloneable`, that creates and manipulates a single moment of time.

Constructors

`public Date()`
`public Date(long date)`
Creates a new instance of a `Date` from a specified `date` (time in milliseconds since midnight, January 1, 1970 GMT) or by using the current time.

Methods

`public boolean after(Date arg)`
`public boolean before(Date arg)`
Returns a true value if this `Date` is after/before the date specified in `arg`.

`public boolean equals(Object arg)`
Returns a true value if this `Date` is equal to `arg`.

`public long getTime()`
`public void setTime(long tm)`
Returns or sets the time specified by this `Date`. The time is represented as a long integer equal to the number of seconds since midnight, January 1, 1970 UTC.

`public int hashCode()`
Returns the hash code for this `Date`.

`public String toString()`
Returns a string representation of this `Date`.

DateFormat (`java.text`)

A public abstract class, derived from `Cloneable`, that is used to convert date/time objects to locale-specific strings, and vice versa.

Variables and Constants

`public static final int DEFAULT`
`public static final int FULL`
`public static final int LONG`

```
public static final int MEDIUM
public static final int SHORT
```
Constant values that represent formatting styles.

```
public static final int AM_PM_FIELD
public static final int DATE_FIELD
public static final int DAY_OF_WEEK_FIELD
public static final int DAY_OF_WEEK_IN_MONTH_FIELD
public static final int DAY_OF_YEAR_FIELD
public static final int ERA_FIELD
public static final int HOUR0_FIELD
public static final int HOUR1_FIELD
public static final int HOUR_OF_DAY0_FIELD
public static final int HOUR_OF_DAY1_FIELD
public static final int MILLISECOND_FIELD
public static final int MINUTE_FIELD
public static final int MONTH_FIELD
public static final int SECOND_FIELD
public static final int TIMEZONE_FIELD
public static final int WEEK_OF_MONTH_FIELD
public static final int WEEK_OF_YEAR_FIELD
public static final int YEAR_FIELD
```
Constant values that represent various fields for date/time formatting.

`protected Calendar calendar`

Holds the calendar that this `DateFormat` uses to produce its date/time formatting.

`protected NumberFormat numberFormat`

Holds the number format that this `DateFormat` uses to produce its number formatting.

Constructors

`protected DateFormat()`

Creates a new instance of a `DateFormat`.

Methods

`public Object clone()`

Returns a copy of this `DateFormat`.

`public boolean equals(Object arg)`

Returns a true value is this `DateFormat` is equal to `arg`.

`public final String format(Date src)`

Formats the specified `Date` object into a string.

`public abstract StringBuffer format(Date src, StringBuffer dest, FieldPosition pos)` `public final StringBuffer format(Object src, StringBuffer dest, FieldPosition pos)`

Formats the source object into the specified destination, starting at field `pos`. This method returns the same value as the destination buffer.

`public static Locale[] getAvailableLocales()`

Returns the set of available locales for this `DateFormat`.

`public Calendar getCalendar()`
`public void setCalendar(Calendar cal)`

Returns or sets the calendar associated with this `DateFormat`.

`public static final DateFormat getDateInstance()`
`public static final DateFormat getDateInstance(int style)`
`public static final DateFormat getDateInstance(int style, Locale locale)`

Returns the `DateFormat` for the specified or default locale (using the default or specified date formatting style).

`public static final DateFormat getDateTimeInstance()`
`public static final DateFormat getDateTimeInstance(int dstyle, int tstyle)`
`public static final DateFormat getDateTimeInstance(int dstyle, int tstyle, Locale locale)`

Returns the `DateFormat` for the specified or default locale (using the default or specified date and time formatting styles).

`public static final DateFormat getInstance()`

Returns the `DateFormat` for the default locale using the short formatting style.

`public NumberFormat getNumberFormat()`
`public void setNumberFormat(NumberFormat format)`

Returns or sets the `NumberFormat` for this `DateFormat`.

`public static final DateFormat getTimeInstance()`
`public static final DateFormat getTimeInstance(int style)`
`public static final DateFormat getTimeInstance(int style, Locale locale)`

Returns the `DateFormat` for the specified or default locale (using the default or specified time formatting style).

`public TimeZone getTimeZone()`
`public void setTimeZone(TimeZone tz)`

Returns or sets the time zone for this `DateFormat`.

`public int hashCode()`

Returns the hash code for this `DateFormat`.

`public boolean isLenient()`
`public void setLenient(boolean lenient)`

Returns or sets the state of the leniency for this `DateFormat`.

`public Date parse(String src) throws ParseException`

Parses the specified source to a `Date` object.

`public abstract Date parse(String src, ParsePosition pos)`

`public Object parseObject(String src, ParsePosition pos)`

Parses the specified source string to a `Date` or `Object`, starting at the specified position.

DateFormatSymbols (`java.text`)

A public class, derived from `Object` and implementing `Serializable` and `Cloneable`, that contains functionality for formatting both date and time values. This class is usually utilized as part of a `DateFormat` class (or subclass).

Constructors

`public DateFormatSymbols()`
`public DateFormatSymbols(Locale locale)`

Creates a new instance of DateFormatSymbols using the specified or default locale.

Methods

`public Object clone()`

Returns a clone of this `DateFormatSymbols`.

`public boolean equals(Object arg)`

Returns a true value if this `DateFormatSymbols` is equal to `arg`.

`public String[] getAmPmStrings()`
`public void setAmPmStrings(String[] newstr)`

Returns or sets the AM/PM strings for this set of symbols.

`public String[] getEras()`
`public void setEras(String[] newstr)`

Returns or sets the eras for this set of symbols.

`public String getLocalPatternChars()`
`public void setLocalPatternChars(String newchars)`

Returns or sets the local pattern characters for date and time for this set of symbols.

`public String[] getMonths()`
`public void setMonths(String[] newmon)`

Returns or sets the full names of months for this set of symbols.

`public String[] getShortMonths()`
`public void setShortMonths(String[] newmon)`

Returns or sets the short names of months for this set of symbols.

`public String[] getShortWeekdays()`
`public void setShortWeekdays(String[] newdays)`

Returns or sets the short names of weekdays for this set of symbols.

`public String[] getWeekdays()`

`public void setWeekdays(String[] newdays)`

Returns or sets the full names of weekdays for this set of symbols.

`public String[][] getZoneStrings()`
`public void setZoneStrings(String[][] newzone)`

Returns or sets the time zone strings for this set of symbols.

`public int hashCode()`

Returns the hash code for this set of symbols.

DecimalFormat (`java.text`)

A public class, derived from `NumberFormat`, that is used to format decimal numbers to locale-based strings, and vice versa.

Constructors

`public DecimalFormat()`
`public DecimalFormat(String str)`
`public DecimalFormat(String str, DecimalFormatSymbols sym)`

Creates a new instance of a `DecimalFormat` from the specified or default pattern, specified or default symbols and using the default locale.

Methods

`public void applyLocalizedPattern(String str)`
`public String toLocalizedPattern()`

Sets or returns the pattern of this `DecimalFormat`. The specified pattern is in a locale-specific format.

`public void applyPattern(String str)`
`public String toPattern()`

Sets or returns the pattern of this `DecimalFormat`.

`public Object clone()`

Returns a copy of this `DecimalFormat`.

`public boolean equals(Object arg)`

Returns a true value if this `DecimalFormat` is equal to `arg`.

`public StringBuffer format(double num, StringBuffer dest, FieldPosition pos)`
`public StringBuffer format(long num, StringBuffer dest, FieldPosition pos)`

Formats the specified Java primitive type starting at `pos`, according to this `DecimalFormat`, placing the resulting string in the specified destination buffer. This method returns the value of the string buffer.

`public DecimalFormatSymbols getDecimalFormatSymbols()`
`public void setDecimalFormatSymbols(DecimalFormatSymbols symbols)`

Returns or sets the decimal number format symbols for this `DecimalFormat`.

`public int getGroupingSize()`
`public void setGroupingSize(int val)`
Returns or sets the size of groupings for this `DecimalFormat`.

`public int getMultiplier()`
`public void setMultiplier(int val)`
Returns or sets the value of the multiplier for use in percent calculations.

`public String getNegativePrefix()`
`public void setNegativePrefix(String val)`
Returns or sets the prefix for negative numbers for this `DecimalFormat`.

`public String getNegativeSuffix()`
`public void setNegativeSuffix(String val)`
Returns or sets the suffix for negative numbers for this `DecimalFormat`.

`public String getPositivePrefix()`
`public void setPositivePrefix(String val)`
Returns or sets the prefix for positive numbers for this `DecimalFormat`.

`public String getPositiveSuffix()`
`public void setPositiveSuffix(String val)`
Returns or sets the suffix for positive numbers for this `DecimalFormat`.

`public int hashCode()`
Returns the hash code for this `DecimalFormat`.

`public boolean isDecimalSeparatorAlwaysShown()`
`public void setDecimalSeparatorAlwaysShown(boolean toggle)`
Returns or sets the state value that allows/prevents the display of the decimal point when formatting integers.

`public Number parse(String src, ParsePosition pos)`
Parses the specified string as a long (if possible) or double, starting a position `pos`, and returns a `Number`.

DecimalFormatSymbols (`java.text`)

A public class, derived from `Object` and implementing `Serializable` and `Cloneable`, that contains functionality for formatting decimal values. This class is usually utilized as part of a `DecimalFormat` class (or subclass).

Constructors

`public DecimalFormatSymbols()`
`public DecimalFormatSymbols(Locale locale)`
Creates a new instance of `DecimalFormatSymbols` using the specified or default locale.

Methods

`public Object clone()`

Returns a clone of this `DecimalFormatSymbols`.

`public boolean equals(Object arg)`

Returns a true value if this `DecimalFormatSymbols is equal to arg`.

`public char getDecimalSeparator()`
`public void setDecimalSeparator(char separator)`

Returns or sets the character used to separate decimal numbers in this set of symbols.

`public char getDigit()`
`public void setDigit(char num)`

Returns or sets the character used as a digit placeholder in a pattern for this set of symbols.

`public char getGroupingSeparator()`
`public void setGroupingSeparator(char separator)`

Returns or sets the character used to separate groups of thousands for this set of symbols.

`public String getInfinity()`
`public void setInfinity(String str)`

Returns or sets the string used to represent the value of infinity for this set of symbols.

`public char getMinusSign()`
`public void setMinusSign(char minus)`

Returns or sets the character used to represent the minus sign for this set of symbols.

`public String getNaN()`
`public void setNaN(String str)`

Returns or sets the character used to represent a NAN value for this set of symbols.

`public char getPatternSeparator()`
`public void setPatternSeparator(char separator)`

Returns or sets the character used to separate positive and negative numbers in a pattern from this set of symbols.

`public char getPercent()`
`public void setPercent(char percent)`

Returns or sets the character used as a percent sign for this set of symbols.

`public char getPerMill()`
`public void setPerMill(char perMill)`

Returns or sets the character used as a mille percent sign for this set of symbols.

`public char getZeroDigit()`
`public void setZeroDigit(char zero)`

Returns or sets the character used to represent zero for this set of symbols.

`public int hashCode()`

Returns the hash code for this set of symbols.

Dialog (`java.awt`)

A public class, derived from `Window`, that creates a graphical window that requests input from the user.

Constructors

`public Dialog(Frame pframe)`
`public Dialog(Frame pframe, boolean toggle)`
`public Dialog(Frame pframe, String str)`
`public Dialog(Frame pframe, String str, boolean toggle)`
Creates a new instance of a dialog window with a parent frame (`pframe`) and an initial title (`str`). The resulting dialog window can be made modal by setting `toggle` (default is false, not modal).

Methods

`public void addNotify()`
Creates this dialog's peer.

`public String getTitle()`
`public void setTitle(String str)`
Returns or sets the title of this dialog.

`public boolean isModal()`
`public void setModal(boolean toggle)`
Returns or sets the modal state for this dialog.

`public boolean isResizable()`
`public void setResizable(boolean toggle)`
Returns or sets the resizable state for this dialog.

`protected String paramString()`
Returns a string containing the parameters of this dialog.

`public void show()`
Makes this dialog window visible and places it on top of any other window currently displayed.

Dictionary (`java.util`)

A public abstract class, derived from `Object`, that associates keys with elements.

Constructors

`public Dictionary()`
Creates a new instance of a `Dictionary`.

Methods

`public abstract Enumeration elements()`
Returns an enumerated list of the elements of this `Dictionary`.

`public abstract Object get(Object idx)`
`public abstract Object put(Object idx, Object val) throws NullPointerException`
`public abstract Object remove(Object idx)`
Returns, inserts or removes an element, `val`, into the `Dictionary` with a key value of `idx`.

`public abstract boolean isEmpty()`
Returns a true value if this `Dictionary` contains no elements or keys.

`public abstract Enumeration keys()`
Returns an enumerated list of keys of this `Dictionary`.

`public abstract int size()`
Returns the number of elements in the `Dictionary`.

Dimension (`java.awt`)

A public class, derived from `Object` and implementing `Serializable`, that is used to encapsulate an object's dimensions (height and width).

Variables and Constants

`public int height`
`public int width`
Variables which contain the height and width of an object.

Constructors

`public Dimension()`
`public Dimension(Dimension dim)`
`public Dimension(int width, int height)`
Creates a new instance of a dimension from specified dimensions (or 0 width and 0 height by default).

Methods

`public boolean equals(Object arg)`
Returns a true value if this dimension is equal to `arg`.

`public Dimension getSize()`
`public void setSize(Dimension dim)`
`public void setSize(int width, int height)`
Returns or sets the size of this dimension.

`public String toString()`
Returns the string representation of this dimension.

Double (`java.lang`)

A public final class, derived from `Number`, that contains floating point math operations, constants, methods to compute minimum and maximum numbers, and string manipulation routines related to the `double` primitive type.

Variables and Constants

`public final static double MAX_VALUE`
`public final static double MIN_VALUE`
Constant values that contain the maximum (1.79769313486231570e+
308d) and minimum (4.94065645841246544e2324d) possible values of an integer in Java.

`public final static double NaN`
A constant value that contains the representation of the Not-A-Number double (0.0d).

`public final static double NEGATIVE_INFINITY`
`public final static double POSITIVE_INFINITY`
Constant values that contain the negative (-1.0d / 0.0d) and positive (1.0d / 0.0d) infinity double.

`public final static Class TYPE`
A constant value of the `Double` type class.

Constructors

`public Double(double arg)`
`public Double(String arg) throws NumberFormatException`
Creates an instance of the `Double` class from the parameter `arg`.

Methods

`public byte byteValue()`
`public double doubleValue()`
`public float floatValue()`
`public int intValue()`
`public long longValue()`
`public short shortValue()`
Returns the value of the current object as a Java primitive type.

`public static long doubleToLongBits(double num)`
`public static double longBitsToDouble(long num)`
Returns a long bit stream or a double representation of parameter `num`. Bit 63 of the returned `long` is the sign bit, bits 52 to 62 are the exponent, and bits 0 to 51 are the mantissa.

`public boolean equals(Object param)`
Returns a true value if this `Double` is equal to the specified parameter (`param`).

`public int hashCode()`
Returns a hash code for this `Double`.

`public boolean isInfinite()`
`public static boolean isInfinite(double num)`
Returns true if the current object or `num` is positive or negative infinity, false in all other cases.

`public boolean isNaN()`
`public static boolean isNaN(double num)`
Returns true if the current object or `num` is Not-A-Number, false in all other cases.

`public static double parseDouble(String str) throws NumberFormatException`
Returns the double value represented by `str`.

`public String toString()`
`public static String toString(double num)`
Returns the string representation of the current object or `num` in base 10 (decimal).

`public static Double valueOf(String str) throws NumberFormatException`
Returns a `Double` initialized to the value of `str`.

Error (`java.lang`)

A public class, derived from `Throwable`, that is used to signify program-terminating errors that should not be caught.

Constructors

`public Error()`
`public Error(String str)`
Creates a new instance of an error. A message can be provided via `str`.

Event (`java.awt`)

A public class, derived from `Object`, that represents event obtained from a graphical user interface.

Variables and Constants

`public final static int ACTION_EVENT`
A constant that represents the user desires an action.

`public final static int ALT_MASK`
`public final static int CTRL_MASK`
`public final static int META_MASK`

`public final static int SHIFT_MASK`

Constant values which represent the mask for Alt, Control, Meta, and Shift keys modifying events.

`public Object arg`

An optional argument used by some events.

```
public final static int BACK_SPACE
public final static int CAPS_LOCK
public final static int DELETE
public final static int DOWN
public final static int END
public final static int ENTER
public final static int ESCAPE
public final static int F1
public final static int F2
public final static int F3
public final static int F4
public final static int F5
public final static int F6
public final static int F7
public final static int F8
public final static int F9
public final static int F10
public final static int F11
public final static int F12
public final static int HOME
public final static int INSERT
public final static int LEFT
public final static int NUM_LOCK
public final static int PAUSE
public final static int PGDN
public final static int PGUP
public final static int PRINT_SCREEN
public final static int RIGHT
public final static int SCROLL_LOCK
public final static int TAB
public final static int UP
```

Constant values that represent keyboard keys.

`public int clickCount`

The number of consecutive clicks during a MOUSE_DOWN event.

`public Event evt`

The next event to take place, as in a linked list.

`public final static int GOT_FOCUS`

An id field constant that represents when an AWT component gets the focus.

`public int id`

The numeric identification for this event.

`public int key`

The keyboard key that was pressed during this event.

`public final static int KEY_ACTION`
`public final static int KEY_ACTION_RELEASE`

Constant values that represent when the user presses or releases a function key.

`public final static int KEY_PRESS`
`public final static int KEY_RELEASE`

Constant values that represent when the user presses or releases a keyboard key.

`public final static int LIST_DESELECT`
`public final static int LIST_SELECT`

Constant values that represent when the user deselects or selects a list item.

`public final static int LOAD_FILE`
`public final static int SAVE_FILE`

Constant values that represent when a file load or save event occurs.

`public final static int LOST_FOCUS`

An id field constant that represents when an AWT component loses the focus.

`public int modifiers`

Value of any key modifiers for this event.

`public final static int MOUSE_DOWN`
`public final static int MOUSE_DRAG`
`public final static int MOUSE_ENTER`
`public final static int MOUSE_EXIT`
`public final static int MOUSE_MOVE`
`public final static int MOUSE_UP`

Constant values that represent mouse events.

`public final static int SCROLL_ABSOLUTE`

An id field constant that represents when the user has moved the bubble in a scrollbar.

`public final static int SCROLL_BEGIN`
`public final static int SCROLL_END`

Constant values that represent the scroll begin or ending event.

`public final static int SCROLL_LINE_DOWN`
`public final static int SCROLL_LINE_UP`

Constant values that represent when the user has clicked in the line down or up area of the scrollbar.

`public final static int SCROLL_PAGE_DOWN`
`public final static int SCROLL_PAGE_UP`

Constant values that represent when the user has clicked in the page down or up area of the scrollbar.

`public Object target`

The object that this event was created from or took place over.

`public long when`

The time stamp of this event. Represented as the number of milliseconds since midnight, January 1, 1970 UTC.

`public final static int WINDOW_DEICONIFY`
`public final static int WINDOW_DESTROY`
`public final static int WINDOW_EXPOSE`
`public final static int WINDOW_ICONIFY`
`public final static int WINDOW_MOVED`

Constant values that represent various window events.

`public int x`
`public int y`

The horizontal or vertical coordinate location of this event.

Constructors

`public Event(Object obj, int id, Object arg)`
`public Event(Object obj, long ts, int id, int x, int y, int key, int state)`
`public Event(Object obj, long ts, int id, int x, int y, int key, int state, Object arg)`

Creates a new instance of an event with an initial target Object (`obj`), `id`, `x` location, `y` location, `key`, modifier `state`, time stamp (`ts`), and argument (`arg`).

Methods

`public boolean controlDown()`
`public boolean metaDown()`
`public boolean shiftDown()`

Returns a true value if the Control, Meta, or Shift key is down for this event.

`protected String paramString()`

Returns the parameter string for this event.

`public String toString()`

Returns a string representation of this event.

`public void translate(int xval, int yval)`

Translates this event, modifying the `x` and `y` coordinates for this event by adjusting the `x` location by `xval` and the `y` location by `yval`.

EventQueue (`java.awt`)

A public class, derived from `Object`, that represents an event queue.

Constructors

`public EventQueue()`

Creates a new instance of an `EventQueue`.

Methods

`public synchronized AWTEvent getNextEvent() throws InterruptedException`

Removes the next event from the queue and returns it to the calling method. If the queue is currently empty, this method will block until an event arrives.

`public synchronized AWTEvent peekEvent()`
`public synchronized AWTEvent peekEvent(int type)`

Returns the next event if any, of the specified `type` from this queue but does not remove it.

`public synchronized void postEvent(AWTEvent event)`

Places a Java 1.0 AWT event at the end of this queue.

Exception (`java.lang`)

A public class, derived from `Throwable`, that catches conditions that are thrown by methods.

Constructors

`public Exception()`
`public Exception(String str)`

Creates a new instance of an exception. A message can be provided via `str`.

FieldPosition (`java.text`)

A public class, derived from `Object`, that is used to identify specific fields in formatted output. This class is generally used by the `Format` class (and subclasses).

Constructors

`public FieldPosition(int field)`

Creates a new instance of a `FieldPosition` from the specified field.

Methods

`public int getBeginIndex()`
`public int getEndIndex()`

Returns the beginning or ending character index for this field.

`public int getField()`

Returns the identifier value for this field.

FileDialog (`java.awt`)

A public class, derived from `Dialog`, that creates a graphical window from which the user can select a file.

Variables and Constants

`public final static int LOAD`
`public final static int SAVE`

Constant values that specify that this file dialog is intended for loading or saving a file.

Constructors

`public FileDialog(Frame prt)`
`public FileDialog(Frame prt, String str)`
`public FileDialog(Frame prt, String str, int lsmode)`

Creates a new instance of a file dialog with a specified parent frame, an initial title (`str`) and an initial mode (LOAD (default) or SAVE).

Methods

`public void addNotify()`

Creates this file dialog's peer.

`public String getDirectory()`
`public void setDirectory(String str)`

Returns or sets the directory currently displayed by this file dialog.

`public String getFile()`
`public void setFile(String str)`

Returns or sets the name of the file currently selected in this file dialog.

`public FilenameFilter getFilenameFilter()`
`public void setFilenameFilter(FilenameFilter fltr)`

Returns or sets the current value of this file dialog's file filter.

`public int getMode()`
`public void setMode(int md)`

Returns or sets the current mode of this file dialog.

`protected String paramString()`

Returns a string containing the parameters of this file dialog.

Float (`java.lang`)

A public final class, derived from `Number`, that contains floating point math operations, constants, methods to compute minimum and maximum numbers, and string manipulation routines related to the primitive `float` type.

Variables and Constants

`public final static float MAX_VALUE`
`public final static float MIN_VALUE`

Constant values that contain the maximum possible value (3.40282346638528860e+38f) or the minimum possible value (1.40129846432481707e245f) of a float in Java.

`public final static float NaN`

A constant value that contains the representation of the Not-A-Number float (0.0f).

`public final static float NEGATIVE_INFINITY`
`public final static float POSITIVE_INFINITY`

Constant values that contain the representation of the negative (-1.0f / 0.0f) or positive (1.0f / 0.0f) infinity float.

`public final static Class TYPE`

The `Float` constant value of the float type class.

Constructors

`public Float(double arg)`
`public Float(float arg) throws NumberFormatException`
`public Float(String arg)`

Creates an instance of the Float class from the parameter `arg`.

Methods

`public byte byteValue()`
`public float floatValue()`
`public double doubleValue()`
`public int intValue()`
`public long longValue()`
`public short shortValue()`

Returns the value of the current object as a Java primitive type.

`public boolean equals(Object arg)`

Returns the result of an equality comparison against `arg`.

`public static int floatToIntBits(float num)`
`public static float intBitsToFloat(int num)`

Returns the bit stream or float equivalent of the parameter `num` as an `int`. Bit 31 of the `int` returned value is the sign bit, bits 23 to 30 are the exponent, while bits 0 to 22 are the mantissa.

`public int hashCode()`
Returns a hash code for this object.

`public boolean isInfinite()`
`public static boolean isInfinite(float num)`
Returns true if the current object or `num` is positive or negative infinity, false in all other cases.

`public boolean isNaN()`
`public static boolean isNaN(float num)`
Returns true if the current object or `num` is Not-A-Number, false in all other cases.

`public static float parseFloat(String str) throws NumberFormatException`
Returns the float value represented by `str`.

`public String toString()`
`public static String toString(float num)`
Returns the string representation of the current object or `num`.

`public static Float valueOf(String str) throws NumberFormatException`
Returns a `Float` initialized to the value of `str`.

FlowLayout (`java.awt`)

A public class, derived from `Object` implementing `LayoutManager` and `Serializable`, that lays out components in a sequential horizontal order using their preferred size.

Variables and Constants

`public final static int CENTER`
`public final static int LEFT`
`public final static int RIGHT`
Constant values indicating areas of the flow layout manager.

Constructors

`public FlowLayout()`
`public FlowLayout(int al)`
`public FlowLayout(int al, int hg, int vg)`
Creates a new instance of a flow layout and gives it `al` alignment (default of centered) with a `vg` vertical and `hg` horizontal gap (default of 0).

Methods

`public void addLayoutComponent(String str, Component cpnt)`
`public void removeLayoutComponent(Component cpnt)`
Adds or removes a component to/from this layout manager. When adding a component, a name may be specified.

`public int getAlignment()`

`public void setAlignment(int alg)`
Returns or sets the alignment value for this layout manager.

`public int getHgap()`
`public int getVgap()`
Returns the value of the horizontal or vertical gap between components laid out by this layout manager.

`public void layoutContainer(Container cont)`
Lays out the specified container with this layout manager.

`public Dimension minimumLayoutSize(Container cont)`
`public Dimension preferredLayoutSize(Container cont)`
Returns the minimum or preferred size of the specified container when laid out by this layout manager.

`public void setHgap(int hg)`
`public void setVgap(int vg)`
Sets the horizontal or vertical gap for this layout manager.

`public String toString()`
Returns a string representation of this layout manager.

FocusAdapter (`java.awt.event`)

A public abstract class, derived from `Object` and implementing `FocusListener`, that permits derived classes to override the predefined no-op focus events.

Constructors

`public FocusAdapter()`
Creates a new instance of a `FocusAdapter`.

Methods

`public void focusGained(FocusEvent event)`
`public void focusLost(FocusEvent event)`
Empty methods that should be overridden in order to implement event handling for AWT focus-based events.

FocusEvent (`java.awt.event`)

A public class, derived from `ComponentEvent`, that describes a particular AWT focus event.

Variables and Constants

`public static final int FOCUS_FIRST`
`public static final int FOCUS_LAST`

Constant values that represent the index of the first and last focus event ids.

`public static final int FOCUS_GAINED`
`public static final int FOCUS_LOST`

Constant values that represent the gain and loss of focus events.

Constructors

`public FocusEvent(Component src, int type)`
`public FocusEvent(Component src, int type, boolean toggle)`

Creates a new instance of a `FocusEvent` from the specified source, having a defined event type and toggling this event as a temporary change of focus (false by default).

Methods

`public boolean isTemporary()`

Returns the status value of the temporary focus toggle.

`public String paramString()`

Returns a string containing the parameters of this `FocusEvent`.

Font (`java.awt`)

A public class, derived from `Object` and implementing `Serializable`, that represents a GUI font.

Variables and Constants

`public final static int BOLD`
`public final static int ITALIC`
`public final static int PLAIN`

Constant values that indicate the style of the font.

`protected String name`

The name of the font.

`protected int size`

The size of the font in pixels.

`protected int style`

The style of the font.

Constructors

`public Font(String str, int st, int sz)`
Creates a new font with an initial name (`str`), style (`st`), and size (`sz`).

Methods

`public static Font decode(String arg)`
Returns the requested font from a specified string.

`public boolean equals(Object obj)`
Returns a true value if this font is equal to `obj`.

`public String getFamily()`
Returns the name of the family this font belongs to.

`public static Font getFont(String str)`
`public static Font getFont(String str, Font ft)`
Returns the font named `str`. If the font cannot be located, the second method returns `ft` as the default.

`public String getName()`
Returns the name of this font.

`public FontPeer getPeer()`
Returns the peer of this font.

`public int getSize()`
`public int getStyle()`
Returns the size or style of this font.

`public int hashCode()`
Returns the hash code for this font.

`public boolean isBold()`
`public boolean isItalic()`
`public boolean isPlain()`
Returns a true value if this font is bolded, italicized, or plain.

`public String toString()`
Returns a string representation of this font.

FontMetrics (`java.awt`)

A public class, derived from `Object` and implementing `Serializable`, that provides detailed information about a particular font.

Variables and Constants

`protected Font font`
The font upon which the metrics are generated.

Constructors

`protected FontMetrics(Font f)`
Creates a new instance of metrics from a given font `f`.

Methods

`public int bytesWidth(byte[] src, int offset, int size)`
`public int charsWidth(char[] src, int offset, int size)`
Returns the advance width for displaying the subarray of `src`, starting at index `offset`, and having a length of `size`.

`public int charWidth(char c)`
`public int charWidth(int c)`
Returns the advance width of the character `c` for the font in this font metric.

`public int getAscent()`
`public int getDescent()`
Returns the amount of ascent or descent for the font in this font metric.

`public Font getFont()`
Returns the font in this font metric.

`public int getHeight()`
Returns the standard height of the font in this font metric.

`public int getLeading()`
Returns the standard leading of the font in this font metric.

`public int getMaxAdvance()`
Returns the maximum amount of advance for the font in this font metric.

`public int getMaxAscent()`
`public int getMaxDescent()`
Returns the maximum amount of ascent or descent for the font in this font metric.

`public int[] getWidths()`
Returns an `int` array containing the advance widths of the first 256 characters of the font.

`public int stringWidth(String str)`
Returns the advance width of the string `str` as represented by the font in this font metric.

`public String toString()`
Returns a string representation of the font metrics.

Format (`java.text`)

A public abstract class, derived from `Object` and implementing `Cloneable` and `Serializable`, which is used to format locale-based values into Strings, and vice versa.

Constructors

`public Format()`
Creates a new instance of a `Format`.

Methods

`public Object clone()`
Returns a copy of this `Format`.

`public final String format(Object arg)`
Returns a formatted string from `arg`.

`public abstract StringBuffer format(Object arg, StringBuffer dest, FieldPosition pos)`
Formats the specified argument (starting at field `pos`) into a string, and appends it to the specified `StringBuffer`. This method returns the same value as the destination buffer.

`public Object parseObject(String src) throws ParseException`
Parses the specified source string into a formatted object.

`public abstract Object parseObject(String src, ParsePosition pos)`
Parses the specified source string into a formatted object starting at the specified `ParsePosition`.

Frame (`java.awt`)

A public class, derived from `Window` and implementing `MenuContainer`, that creates a graphical window with a border and a title bar. A frame may also contain a menu bar.

Variables and Constants

```
public final static int CROSSHAIR_CURSOR
public final static int DEFAULT_CURSOR
public final static int E_RESIZE_CURSOR
public final static int HAND_CURSOR
public final static int MOVE_CURSOR
public final static int N_RESIZE_CURSOR
public final static int NE_RESIZE_CURSOR
public final static int NW_RESIZE_CURSOR
public final static int S_RESIZE_CURSOR
public final static int SE_RESIZE_CURSOR
public final static int SW_RESIZE_CURSOR
public final static int TEXT_CURSOR
public final static int W_RESIZE_CURSOR
public final static int WAIT_CURSOR
```

Constant values that define a frame cursor.

Constructors

`public Frame()`
`public Frame(String str)`
Creates a new instance of a frame with a title of `str` (or no title present).

Methods

`public void addNotify()`
Creates this frame's peer.

`public void dispose()`
Removes this frame and all resources associated with it.

`public Image getIconImage()`
`public void setIconImage(Image img)`
Returns or sets the icon image for this frame.

`public MenuBar getMenuBar()`
`public void setMenuBar(MenuBar bar)`
Returns or sets the menu bar for this frame.

`public String getTitle()`
`public void setTitle(String str)`
Returns or sets the title for this frame.

`public boolean isResizable()`
`public void setResizable(boolean toggle)`
Returns or sets the state of the resizability of this frame.

`protected String paramString()`
Returns a string containing the parameters for this frame.

`public void remove(MenuComponent mc)`
Removes the specified menu component from this frame.

Graphics (`java.awt`)

A public abstract class, derived from `Object`, that provides many useful drawing methods and tools for the manipulation of graphics. A `Graphics` object defines a context in which the user draws.

Constructors

`protected Graphics()`
Creates a new `Graphics` instance. This constructor cannot be called directly.

Methods

public abstract void clearRect(int x, int y, int width, int height)

Draws a rectangle (with no fill pattern) in the current background color at position <x, y>, and having a width and height.

public abstract void clipRect(int x, int y, int width, int height)

Sets a clipping rectangle at position <x, y> and having a width and height.

public abstract void copyArea(int x, int y, int width, int height, int newx, int newy)

Copies a graphic rectangular area at position <x, y> and having a width and height, to position newx and newy.

public abstract Graphics create()

public Graphics create(int x, int y, int width, int height)

Returns a copy of this graphics context from position <x, y>, and having a width and height. In the case of the first method, the entire area is copied.

public abstract void dispose()

Disposes this graphics context.

public void draw3DRect(int x, int y, int width, int height, boolean toggle)

Draws a 3D rectangle at position <x, y> and having a width and height. If toggle is true, the rectangle will appear raised; otherwise, it will appear indented.

public abstract void drawArc(int x, int y, int width, int height, int sAngle, int aAngle)

Draws an arc with a starting position <x, y> and having a width and height. The start angle (sAngle) and arc angle (aAngle) are both measured in degrees and describe the starting and ending angle of the arc.

public void drawBytes(byte[] src, int index, int ln, int x, int y)

public void drawChars(char[] src, int index, int ln, int x, int y)

Draw ln bytes or characters of array src (starting at the offset index) at position <x, y>.

public abstract boolean drawImage(Image src, int x, int y, Color bgc, ImageObserver obsv)

public abstract boolean drawImage(Image src, int x, int y, ImageObserver obsv)

Draws a graphic image (src) at position <x, y>. Any transparent color pixels are drawn as bgc, and the obsv monitors the progress of the image.

public abstract boolean drawImage(Image src, int x, int y, int width, int height, Color bgc, ImageObserver obsv)

public abstract boolean drawImage(Image src, int x, int y, int width, int height, ImageObserver obsv)

Draws a graphic image (src) at position <x, y> and having a width and height. Any transparent color pixels are drawn as bgc, and the obsv monitors the progress of the image.

public abstract boolean drawImage(Image src, int xsrc1, int ysrc1, int xsrc1, int ysrc2, int xdest1, int ydest1, int xdest1, int ydest2, Color bgc, ImageObserver obsv)

public abstract boolean drawImage(Image src, int xsrc1, int ysrc1, int xsrc1, int ysrc2, int xdest1, int ydest1, int xdest1, int ydest2, ImageObserver obsv)

Draws a graphic image (src) from the area defined by the bounding rectangle <xsrc1, ysrc1> to <xsrc2, ysrc2> in the area defined by the bounding rectangle <xdest1, ydest1> to <xdest2, ydest2>. Any transparent color pixels are drawn as bgc, and the obsv monitors the progress of the image.

public abstract void drawLine(int xsrc, int ysrc, int xdest, int ydest)

Draws a line from position <xsrc, ysrc> to <xdest, ydest>.

public abstract void drawOval(int xsrc, int ysrc, int width, int height)

Draws an oval starting at position <xsrc, ysrc> and having a width and height.

public abstract void drawPolygon(int[] x, int[] y, int num)
public void drawPolygon(Polygon poly)

Draws a polygon constructed from poly or an array of x points, y points and a number of points in the polygon (num).

public void drawRect(int xsrc, int ysrc, int width, int height)
public abstract void drawRoundRect(int xsrc, int ysrc, int width, int height, int awd, int aht)

Draws a rectangle with or without rounded corners at position <xsrc, ysrc> and having a width and height. The shape of the rounded corners are determined by the width of the arc (awd) and the height of the arc (aht).

public abstract void drawString(String str, int x, int y)

Draws the string str at position <x, y> in this Graphic's current font and color.

public void fill3DRect(int x, int y, int width, int height, boolean toggle)

Draws a filled 3D rectangle at position <x, y> and having a width and height. The rectangle is filled with this Graphic's current color, and if toggle is true, the rectangle is drawn raised. (Otherwise it is drawn indented.)

public abstract void fillArc(int x, int y, int width, int height, int sAngle, int aAngle)

Draws a filled arc at position <x, y> and having a width and height. The arc has a starting angle of sAngle and an ending angle of aAngle.

public abstract void fillOval(int x, int y, int width, int height)

Draws a filled oval at position <x, y> and having a width and height.

public abstract void fillPolygon(int[] x, int[] y, int num)
public void fillPolygon(Polygon poly)

Draws a filled polygon defined by poly or the arrays x, y and the number of points in the polygon, num.

public abstract void fillRect(int x, int y, int width, int height)
public abstract void fillRoundRect(int x, int y, int width, int height, int aWidth, int aHeight)

Draws a filled rectangle with or without rounded corners at position <x, y> and having a width and height. The shape of the rounded corners are determined by the width of the arc (aWidth) and the height of the arc (aHeight).

`public void finalize()`

Disposes of the current graphics context.

`public abstract Shape getClip()`

Returns a shape object of the current clipping area for this graphics context.

`public abstract Rectangle getClipBounds()`

Returns a rectangle describing the bounds of the current clipping area for this graphics context.

`public abstract Color getColor()`
`public abstract void setColor(Color clr)`

Returns or sets the current color for this graphics context.

`public abstract Font getFont()`
`public abstract void setFont(Font ft)`

Returns or sets the current font of this graphics context.

`public FontMetrics getFontMetrics()`
`public abstract FontMetrics getFontMetrics(Font fn)`

Returns the font metrics associated with this graphics context or font `fn`.

`public abstract void setClip(int x, int y, int width, int height)`
`public abstract void setClip(Shape shp)`

Sets the clipping area for this graphics context to be at position <x, y> and having a `width` and `height` or to be of a specified shape (`shp`).

`public abstract void setPaintMode()`

Sets the current graphics context's paint mode to overwrite any subsequent destinations with the current color.

`public abstract void setXORMode(Color clr)`

Sets the current graphics context's paint mode to overwrite any subsequent destinations with the alternating current color and `clr` color.

`public String toString()`

Returns a string representation of this graphics context.

`public abstract void translate(int x, int y)`

Modifies the origin of this graphics context to be relocated to <x, y>.

GregorianCalendar (`java.util`)

A public class, derived from `Calendar`, that represents the standard world Gregorian calendar.

Variables and Constants

`AD`
`BC`

Constant values representing periods of an era.

Constructors

`public GregorianCalendar()`
`public GregorianCalendar(Locale locale)`
`public GregorianCalendar(TimeZone zone)`
`public GregorianCalendar(TimeZone zone, Locale locale)`

Creates a new `GregorianCalendar` from the current time in the specified time zone (or the default) and the specified locale (or the default).

`public GregorianCalendar(int year, int month, int date)`
`public GregorianCalendar(int year, int month, int date, int hour, int min)`
`public GregorianCalendar(int year, int month, int date, int hour, int min, int sec)`

Creates a new `GregorianCalendar`, setting the year, month, date, hour, minute, and seconds of the time fields.

Methods

`public void add(int field, int val)`

Adds (or subtracts in the case of a negative `val`) an amount of days or time from the specified `field`.

`public boolean after(Object arg)`
`public boolean before(Object arg)`

Returns a true value if this `GregorianCalendar` date is after or before the date specified by `arg`.

`public Object clone()`

Returns a clone of this `GregorianCalendar`.

`protected void computeFields()`
`protected void computeTime()`

Computes the values of the time fields based on the currently set time (`computeFields()`) or computes the time based on the currently set time fields (`computeTime()`) for this `GregorianCalendar`.

`public boolean equals(Object arg)`

Returns a true value if this `GregorianCalendar` is equal to the value of `arg`.

`public int getGreatestMinimum(int fld)`
`public int getLeastMaximum(int fld)`

Returns the largest allowable minimum or smallest allowable maximum value for the specified field.

`public final Date getGregorianChange()`
`public void setGregorianChange(Date dt)`

Returns or sets the date of the change from Julian to Gregorian calendars for this calendar. The default value is October 15, 1582 (midnight local time).

`public int getMaximum(int fld)`
`public int getMinimum(int fld)`

Returns the largest or smallest allowable value for the specified field.

`public synchronized int hashCode()`

Returns the hash code for this `GregorianCalendar`.

`public boolean isLeapYear(int year)`

Returns a true value if the specified year is a leap year.

`public void roll(int fld, boolean direction)`

Adds one single unit of time to the specified date/time field. A true value specified for `direction` increases the field's value, false decreases it.

GridBagConstraints (`java.awt`)

A public class, derived from `Object` and implementing `Cloneable`, that specifies the layout constraints for each component laid out with a `GridBagLayout`.

Variables and Constants

`public int anchor`

Determines where to place a component that is smaller in size than its display area in the gridbag.

`public final static int BOTH`
`public final static int HORIZONTAL`
`public final static int NONE`
`public final static int VERTICAL`

Constant values that indicate the direction(s) that the component should grow.

`public final static int CENTER`
`public final static int EAST`
`public final static int NORTH`
`public final static int NORTHEAST`
`public final static int NORTHWEST`
`public final static int SOUTH`
`public final static int SOUTHEAST`
`public final static int SOUTHWEST`
`public final static int WEST`

Constant values that indicate where the component should be placed in its display area.

`public int fill`

Determines how to resize a component that is smaller than its display area in the gridbag.

`public int gridheight`
`public int gridwidth`

Specifies the number of vertical and horizontal cells the component shall occupy.

`public int gridx`
`public int gridy`

Describes horizontal and vertical cell locations (indices) in the gridbag, where `gridx=0` is the left-most cell and `gridy=0` is the topmost cell.

`public Insets insets`

Defines the amount of space (in pixels) around the component in its display area.

`public int ipadx`
`public int ipady`

Defines the amount of space (in pixels) to add to the minimum horizontal and vertical size of the component.

`public final static int RELATIVE`

A constant that specifies that this component is the next to last item in its gridbag row or that it should be placed next to the last item added to the gridbag.

`public final static int REMAINDER`

A constant that specifies that this component is the last item in its gridbag row.

`public double weightx`
`public double weighty`

Specifies the weight of horizontal and vertical growth of this component relative to other components during a resizing event. A larger value indicates a higher percentage of growth for this component.

Constructors

`public GridBagConstraints()`

Creates a new instance of `GridBagConstraints`.

Methods

`public Object clone()`

Creates a copy of these gridbag constraints.

GridBagLayout (java.awt)

A public class, derived from `Object` and implementing `Serializable` and `LayoutManager`, that creates a gridlike area for component layout. Unlike `GridLayout`, `GridBagLayout` does not force the components to be the same size or to be constrained to one cell.

Variables and Constants

`public double columnWeights[]`
`public int columnWidths[]`

Holds the weights and widths of each column of this `GridBagLayout`.

`protected Hashtable comptable`

A hashtable of the components managed by this layout manager.

`protected GridBagConstraints defaultConstraints`

Holds the default constraints for any component laid out by this layout manager.

`protected GridBagLayoutInfo layoutInfo`
Holds specific layout information (such as the list of components or the constraints of this manager) for this `GridBagLayout`.

`protected final static int MAXGRIDSIZE`
A constant value that contains the maximum (512) number of grid cells that can be laid out by this `GridBagLayout`.

`protected final static int MINSIZE`
A constant value that contains the minimum (1) number of cells contained within this `GridBagLayout`.

`protected final static int PREFERREDSIZE`
A constant value that contains the preferred (2) number of cells contained within this `GridBagLayout`.

`public int rowHeights[]`
`public double rowWeights[]`
Holds the heights and weights of each row of this `GridBagLayout`.

Constructors

`public GridBagLayout()`
Creates a new instance of a `GridBagLayout`.

Methods

`public void addLayoutComponent(Component item, Object constraints)`
Adds the component `item` to this layout manager using the specified constraints on the item.

`public void addLayoutComponent(String str, Component item)`
Adds the component `item` to this layout manager and names it `str`.

`protected void AdjustForGravity(GridBagConstraints constraints, Rectangle rect)`
Sets the characteristics of `rect` based on the specified constraints.

`protected void ArrangeGrid(Container parent)`
Arranges the entire grid on the parent.

`public GridBagConstraints getConstraints(Component item)`
Returns a copy of the constraints for the `item` component.

`public float getLayoutAlignmentX(Container parent)`
`public float getLayoutAlignmentY(Container parent)`
Returns the horizontal and vertical alignment values for the specified container.

`public int[][] getLayoutDimensions()`
Returns a two-dimensional array in which the zero index of the first dimension holds the minimum width of each column and the one index of the first dimension holds the minimum height of each column.

`protected GridBagLayoutInfo GetLayoutInfo(Container parent, int sizeflag)`
Computes and returns a `GridBagLayoutInfo` object for components associated with the specified parent container.

`public Point getLayoutOrigin()`

Returns this layout's point of origin.

`public double[][] getLayoutWeights()`

Returns a two-dimensional array in which the zero index of the first dimension holds the weight in the *x* direction of each column and the one index of the first dimension holds the weight in the *y* direction of each column.

`protected Dimension GetMinSize(Container parent, GridBagLayoutInfo info)`

Returns the minimum size for the specified parent container based on laying out the container using the specified `GridBagLayoutInfo`.

`public void invalidateLayout(Container cont)`

Forces this layout manager to discard any cached layout information about the specified container.

`public void layoutContainer(Container cont)`

Lays out the specified container with this layout manager.

`public Point location(int x, int y)`

Returns the upper right corner of the cell in this `GridBagLayout` with dimensions greater than the specified <`x, y`> coordinate.

`protected GridBagConstraints lookupConstraints(Component item)`

Returns the actual constraints for the specified component.

`public Dimension maximumLayoutSize(Container cont)`
`public Dimension minimumLayoutSize(Container cont)`
`public Dimension preferredLayoutSize(Container cont)`

Returns the maximum, minimum, or preferred size of the specified container when laid out by this layout manager.

`public void removeLayoutComponent(Component comp)`

Removes the specified component from this layout manager.

`public void setConstraints(Component item, GridBagConstraints constraints)`

Sets the `constraints` for the `item` component in this layout manager.

`public String toString()`

Returns a string representation of this layout manager.

GridLayout (`java.awt`)

A public class, derived from `Object` and implementing `Serializable` and `LayoutManager`, that creates a grid area of equal sized rectangles to lay out components in.

Constructors

`public GridLayout()`

`public GridLayout(int r, int c)`

Creates a new instance of a `GridLayout` with a dimension of `r` rows and `c` columns (default of 1 by any).

`public GridLayout(int r, int c, int hg, int vg)`

Creates a new instance of a `GridLayout` with a dimension of `r` rows and `c` columns. The grid cells have a `hg` pixel horizontal gap and a `vg` pixel vertical gap.

Methods

`public void addLayoutComponent(String str, Component comp)`
`public void removeLayoutComponent(Component comp)`

Adds or removes the specified component. When adding, the component can be given a name (`str`).

`public int getColumns()`
`public void setColumns(int val)`

Returns or sets the number of columns of this layout manager.

`public int getHgap()`
`public int getVgap()`

Returns the value of the horizontal or vertical gap for this layout manager.

`public int getRows()`
`public void setRows(int val)`

Returns or sets the number of rows of this layout manager.

`public void layoutContainer(Container cont)`

Lays out the specified container with this layout manager.

`public Dimension minimumLayoutSize(Container cont)`
`public Dimension preferredLayoutSize(Container cont)`

Returns the minimum or preferred size of the specified container when laid out with this layout manager.

`public void setHgap(int val)`
`public void setVgap(int val)`

Sets the horizontal or vertical gap for this layout manager to `val`.

`public String toString()`

Returns a string representation of this layout manager.

Hashtable (java.util)

A public class, derived from `Dictionary` and implementing `Serializable` and `Cloneable`, that allows for the storing of objects that have a relationship with a key. You can then use this key to access the object stored.

Constructors

```
public Hashtable()
public Hashtable(int size)
public Hashtable(int size, float load) throws IllegalArgumentException
```

Creates a new instance of a hashtable, setting the initial capacity (or using the default size of 101) and a load factor (default of 0.75). The initial capacity sets the number of objects the table can store, and the load factor value is the percentage filled the table may become before being resized.

Methods

```
public void clear()
```

Removes all keys and elements from this `Hashtable`.

```
public Object clone()
```

Returns a clone of this `Hashtable` (the keys and values are not cloned).

```
public boolean contains(Object arg) throws NullPointerException
```

Returns a true value if this `Hashtable` contains a key that is related to the element `arg`.

```
public boolean containsKey(Object obj)
```

Returns a true value if this `Hashtable` contains an entry for the key at `obj`.

```
public Enumeration elements()
public Enumeration keys()
```

Returns an enumerated list of all of the elements or keys of this `Hashtable`.

```
public Object get(Object obj)
public Object put(Object obj, Object arg) throws NullPointerException
public Object remove(Object obj)
```

Returns, inserts or removes the element `arg` that corresponds to the key `obj`.

```
public boolean isEmpty()
```

Returns a true value if the `Hashtable` is empty.

```
protected void rehash()
```

Resizes this `Hashtable`. The method is invoked automatically when the number of keys exceeds the capacity and load factor.

```
public int size()
```

Returns the number of elements in this `Hashtable`.

```
public String toString()
```

Returns a string representation of this `Hashtable`'s key-element pairings.

HttpURLConnection (`java.net`)

A public class, derived from `URLConnection`, that supports HTTP–protocol-based exchanges.

Variables and Constants

```
public final static int HTTP_ACCEPTED
public final static int HTTP_BAD_GATEWAY
public final static int HTTP_BAD_METHOD
public final static int HTTP_BAD_REQUEST
public final static int HTTP_CLIENT_TIMEOUT
public final static int HTTP_CONFLICT
public final static int HTTP_CREATED
public final static int HTTP_ENTITY_TOO_LARGE
public final static int HTTP_FORBIDDEN
public final static int HTTP_GATEWAY_TIMEOUT
public final static int HTTP_GONE
public final static int HTTP_INTERNAL_ERROR
public final static int HTTP_INTERNAL_ERROR
public final static int HTTP_MOVED_PERM
public final static int HTTP_MOVED_TEMP
public final static int HTTP_MULT_CHOICE
public final static int HTTP_NO_CONTENT
public final static int HTTP_NOT_ACCEPTABLE
public final static int HTTP_NOT_AUTHORITATIVE
public final static int HTTP_NOT_FOUND
public final static int HTTP_NOT_MODIFIED
public final static int HTTP_OK
public final static int HTTP_PARTIAL
public final static int HTTP_PAYMENT_REQUIRED
public final static int HTTP_PRECON_FAILED
public final static int HTTP_PROXY_AUTH
public final static int HTTP_REQ_TOO_LONG
public final static int HTTP_RESET
public final static int HTTP_SEE_OTHER
public final static int HTTP_SERVER_ERROR
public final static int HTTP_UNAUTHORIZED
public final static int HTTP_UNAVAILABLE
public final static int HTTP_UNSUPPORTED_TYPE
public final static int HTTP_USE_PROXY
public final static int HTTP_VERSION
```

A constant that represents an HTTP v1.1 response code (for example: `HTTP_NOT_FOUND=404`).

`protected String method`
Contains the method of the URL request for this HttpURLConnection.
`responseCode`
Contains the HTTP response code for last exchange.
`responseMessage`
Contains the HTTP response message for last exchange.

Constructors

`protected HttpURLConnection(URL src)`
Creates an instance of an `HttpURLConnection` to the specified URL (`src`).

Methods

`public abstract void disconnect()`
Disconnects the connection to the URL.
`public static boolean getFollowRedirects()`
`public static void setFollowRedirects(boolean follow)`
Returns or sets the state if this `HttpURLConnection` will follow HTTP redirects.
`public String getRequestMethod()`
`public void setRequestMethod(String method) throws ProtocolException`
Returns or sets the current request method for this `HttpURLConnection`.
`public int getResponseCode() throws IOException`
`public String getResponseMessage() throws IOException`
Returns the last HTTP response code or message for this `HttpURLConnection`.
`public abstract boolean usingProxy()`
Returns a true value if this `HttpURLConnection` is passing through a proxy.

Image (`java.awt`)

A public abstract class, derived from `Object`, that is used to manage graphic images.

Variables and Constants

`public final static int SCALE_AREA_AVERAGING`
`public final static int SCALE_DEFAULT`
`public final static int SCALE_FAST`
`public final static int SCALE_REPLICATE`
`public final static int SCALE_SMOOTH`
Constant values used to indicate specific scaling algorithms.

`public final static Object UndefinedProperty`
A constant value that is returned whenever an undefined property for an image is attempted to be obtained.

Constructors

`public Image()`
Creates a new instance of an image.

Methods

`public abstract void flush()`
Frees the cache memory containing this image.

`public abstract Graphics getGraphics()`
Returns a newly created graphics context for drawing off-screen images.

`public abstract int getHeight(ImageObserver obs)`
`public abstract int getWidth(ImageObserver obs)`
Returns the height or width of this image. If the height is not known, a -1 is returned and the `obs` is informed later.

`public abstract Object getProperty(String property, ImageObserver obs)`
Returns the value of the `property` for this image. If the value is not known, a null is returned and `obs` is informed later.

`public Image getScaledInstance(int width, int height, int algo)`
Returns a scaled version of this image. The new image is scaled to `width` pixels by `height` pixels using the specified scaling algorithm (`algo`). If either of the new width or height values are -1, then the new image will maintain the aspect ratios of the old image.

`public abstract ImageProducer getSource()`
Returns the source image producer for this image.

InetAddress (`java.net`)

A public final class, derived from `Object` implementing `Serializable`, that is used to represent and manipulate Internet addresses.

Methods

`public boolean equals(Object arg)`
Returns a true value if this address is equal to `arg`.

`public byte[] getAddress()`
`public String getHostAddress()`

`public String getHostName()`
Returns the IP or hostname address of this `InetAddress`. The IP address can be returned as an array of bytes or a string of the form "153.104.7.168".

`public static InetAddress[] getAllByName(String hostname) throws UnknownHostException`

`public static InetAddress getByName(String hostname) throws UnknownHostException`
Returns an array of all given addresses for the specified `hostname`. The given `hostname` can be specified as either an IP address (e.g., 153.104.7.168) or a name (e.g., matisse.vill.edu). The `getByName` method will only return one address.

`public static InetAddress getLocalHost() throws UnknownHostException`
Returns the `InetAddress` for the local machine.

`public int hashCode()`
Returns the hash code for this `InetAddress`.

`public boolean isMulticastAddress()`
Returns a true value if this `InetAddress` is a multicast address.

`public String toString()`
Returns the string representation of this `InetAddress` in IP format.

InputEvent (`java.awt.event`)

A public abstract class, derived from `ComponentEvent`, that describes a particular AWT input event.

Variables and Constants

`public static final int ALT_MASK`
`public static final int BUTTON1_MASK`
`public static final int BUTTON2_MASK`
`public static final int BUTTON3_MASK`
`public static final int CTRL_MASK`
`public static final int META_MASK`
`public static final int SHIFT_MASK`
Constant values which represent various keyboard and mouse masks.

Methods

`public void consume()`
Consumes this event, preventing it from being passed to its peer component.

`public int getModifiers()`
Returns the modifiers for this event.

`public long getWhen()`
Returns the timestamp of this event.

`public boolean isConsumed()`

Returns a true value if this event is consumed.

`public boolean isAltDown()`
`public boolean isControlDown()`
`public boolean isMetaDown()`
`public boolean isShiftDown()`

Returns a true value if the Alt, Control, Meta, or Shift key is depressed during this event.

InputStream (`java.io`)

A public abstract class, derived from `Object`, that is the parent class of any type of input stream that reads bytes.

Constructors

`public InputStream()`

Generally called only by subclasses, this constructor creates a new instance of an `InputStream`.

Methods

`public int available() throws IOException`

Returns the number of available bytes that can be read. This method returns a 0 (zero) value and should be overridden by a subclass implementation.

`public void close() throws IOException`

Closes the input stream. This method has no functionality and should be overridden by a subclass implementation.

`public void mark(int size)`

Sets a mark in the input stream, allowing a rereading of the stream data to occur if the reset method is invoked. The `size` parameter indicates how many bytes may be read following the mark being set, before the mark is considered invalid.

`public boolean markSupported()`

Returns a true value if this `InputStream` object supports the mark and reset methods. This method always returns a false value and should be overridden by a subclass implementation.

`public abstract int read() throws IOException`

Reads the next byte of data from this `InputStream` and returns it as an `int`. This method has no functionality and should be implemented in a subclass. Execution of this method will block until data is available to be read, the end of the input stream occurs, or an exception is thrown.

`public int read(byte[] dest) throws IOException`
`public int read(byte[] dest, int offset, int size) throws IOException`

Reads from this InputStream into the array `dest`, and returns the number of bytes read. `size` specifies the maximum number of bytes read from this InputStream into the array `dest[]` starting at index `offset`. This method returns the actual number of bytes read or -1, indicating that the end of the stream was reached. To read `size` bytes and throw them away, call this method with `dest[]` set to null.

`public synchronized void reset() throws IOException`

Resets the read point of this `InputStream` to the location of the last mark set.

`public long skip(long offset) throws IOException`

Skips over `offset` bytes from this `InputStream`. Returns the actual number of bytes skipped, as it is possible to skip over less than `offset` bytes.

InputStreamReader (`java.io`)

A public class, derived from `Reader`, that is an input stream of characters.

Constructors

`public InputStreamReader(InputStream input)`

`public InputStreamReader(InputStream input, String encoding) throws 2UnsupportedEncodingException`

Creates an instance of `InputStreamReader` from the `InputStream input` with a specified `encoding`.

Methods

`public void close() throws IOException`

Closes this `InputStreamReader`.

`public String getEncoding()`

Returns the string representation of this `InputStreamReader`'s encoding.

`public int read() throws IOException`

Reads a single character from this `InputStreamReader`. The character read is returned as an `int`, or a -1 is returned if the end of this `InputStreamReader` was encountered.

`public int read(char[] dest, int offset, int size) throws IOException`

Reads no more than `size` bytes from this `InputStreamReader` into the array `dest[]` starting at index `offset`. This method returns the actual number of bytes read or -1, indicating that the end of the stream was reached. To read `size` bytes and throw them away, call this method with `dest[]` set to null.

`public boolean ready() throws IOException`

Returns a true value if this `InputStreamReader` is capable of being read from. This state can only be true if the buffer is not empty.

Insets (`java.awt`)

A public class, derived from `Object` and implementing `Serializable` and `Cloneable`, that specify the margins of a container.

Variables and Constants

`public int bottom`
`public int left`
`public int right`
`public int top`
Contains the value of the inset for a particular margin.

Constructors

`public Insets(int t, int l, int b, int r)`
Creates an instance of insets with initial top (`t`), bottom (`b`), left (`l`) and right (`r`) inset values.

Methods

`public Object clone()`
Creates a copy of this group of inset values.
`public boolean equals(Object arg)`
Returns a true value if this inset is equal to the object `arg`.
`public String toString()`
Returns a string representation of this group of inset values.

Integer (`java.lang`)

A public final class, derived from `Number`, that contains integer math operations, constants, methods to compute minimum and maximum numbers, and string manipulation routines related to the primitive `int` type.

Variables and Constants

`public final static int MAX_VALUE`
`public final static int MIN_VALUE`
Constant values that contain the maximum possible value (2147483647) or minimum possible value (-2147483648) of an integer in Java.
`public final static Class TYPE`
The `Integer` constant value of the integer type class.

Constructors

```
public Integer(int num)
public Integer(String num) throws NumberFormatException
```

Creates an instance of the `Integer` class from the parameter num.

Methods

```
public byte byteValue()
public double doubleValue()
public float floatValue()
public int intValue()
public long longValue()
public short shortValue()
```

Returns the value of this integer as a Java primitive type.

```
public static Integer decode(String str) throws NumberFormatException
```

Decodes the given string (`str`) and returns it as an `Integer`. The decode method can handle octal, hexadecimal, and decimal input values.

```
public boolean equals(Object num)
```

Returns the result of an equality comparison against num.

```
public static Integer getInteger(String str)
public static Integer getInteger(String str, int num)
public static Integer getInteger(String str, Integer num)
```

Returns an `Integer` representation of the system property named in `str`. If there is no property corresponding to num, or the format of its value is incorrect, then the default num is returned as an `Integer` object.

```
public int hashCode()
```

Returns a hash code for this object.

```
public static int parseInt(String str) throws NumberFormatException
public static int parseInt(String str, int base) throws NumberFormatException
```

Evaluates the string `str` and returns the `int` equivalent in radix `base`.

```
public static String toBinaryString(int num)
public static String toHexString(int num)
public static String toOctalString(int num)
```

Returns the string representation of parameter num in base 2 (binary), 8 (octal), or 16 (hexadecimal).

```
public String toString()
public static String toString(int num)
public static String toString(int num, int base)
```

Returns the string representation of this integer or num. The radix of num can be specified in `base`.

```
public static Integer valueOf(String str) throws NumberFormatException
public static Integer valueOf(String str, int base) throws NumberFormatException
```

Returns an `Integer` initialized to the value of `str` in radix `base`.

ItemEvent (`java.awt.event`)

A public class, derived from `AWTEvent`, that represents an AWT item event (from a component such as a Checkbox, `CheckboxMenuItem`, `Choice`, or `List`).

Variables and Constants

`public static final int DESELECTED`
`public static final int SELECTED`
Constant values representing the deselection or selection of an AWT item component.
`public static final int ITEM_FIRST`
`public static final int ITEM_LAST`
Constant values that represent the index of the first and last item event ids.
`public static final int ITEM_STATE_CHANGED`
A constant value that represents the event of the change of state for an AWT item.

Constructors

`public ItemEvent(ItemSelectable src, int type, Object obj, int change)`
Creates a new instance of an `ItemEvent` from the specified source, having a specific `type`, item `object`, and state `change`.

Methods

`public Object getItem()`
Returns the specific item that triggered this event.
`public ItemSelectable getItemSelectable()`
Returns the `ItemSelectable` object that triggered this event.
`public int getStateChange()`
Returns the state change type (deselection or selection) that triggered this event.
`public String paramString()`
Returns a parameter string containing the values of the parameters for this event.

KeyAdapter (`java.awt.event`)

A public abstract class, derived from `Object` and implementing `KeyListener`, that permits derived classes to override the predefined no-op keyboard events.

Constructors

`public KeyAdapter()`
Creates a new instance of a `KeyAdapter`.

Methods

```
public void keyPressed(KeyEvent event)
public void keyReleased(KeyEvent event)
public void keyTyped(KeyEvent event)
```

Empty methods that should be overridden in order to implement event handling for keyboard events.

KeyEvent (`java.awt.event`)

A public class, derived from `InputEvent`, that represents an AWT keyboard event.

Variables and Constants

```
public static final int VK_0
public static final int VK_1
public static final int VK_2
public static final int VK_3
public static final int VK_4
public static final int VK_5
public static final int VK_6
public static final int VK_7
public static final int VK_8
public static final int VK_9
```

Constant values that represent the keyboard keys 0–9.

```
public static final int KEY_FIRST
public static final int KEY_LAST
```

Constant values that represent the index of the first and last key event ids.

```
public static final int KEY_PRESSED
public static final int KEY_RELEASED
public static final int KEY_TYPED
```

Constant values that represent the ids of a key being pressed, released, or typed.

```
public static final char CHAR_UNDEFINED
```

A constant value that represents an event of a key press or release that does not correspond to a Unicode character.

```
public static final int VK_LEFT
public static final int VK_RIGHT
public static final int VK_UP
public static final int VK_DOWN
public static final int VK_HOME
public static final int VK_END
public static final int VK_PAGE_UP
```

```
public static final int VK_PAGE_DOWN
```
Constant values that represent various keyboard directional keys.

```
public static final int VK_INSERT
public static final int VK_DELETE
```
Constant values that represent various keyboard editing control keys.

```
public static final int VK_NUMPAD0
public static final int VK_NUMPAD1
public static final int VK_NUMPAD2
public static final int VK_NUMPAD3
public static final int VK_NUMPAD4
public static final int VK_NUMPAD5
public static final int VK_NUMPAD6
public static final int VK_NUMPAD7
public static final int VK_NUMPAD8
public static final int VK_NUMPAD9
public static final int VK_ADD
public static final int VK_SUBTRACT
public static final int VK_MULTIPLY
public static final int VK_DIVIDE
public static final int VK_ENTER
public static final int VK_DECIMAL
```
Constant values that represent various keyboard number pad keys.

```
public static final int VK_PERIOD
public static final int VK_EQUALS
public static final int VK_OPEN_BRACKET
public static final int VK_CLOSE_BRACKET
public static final int VK_BACK_SLASH
public static final int VK_SLASH
public static final int VK_COMMA
public static final int VK_SEMICOLON
public static final int VK_SPACE
public static final int VK_BACK_SPACE
public static final int VK_QUOTE
public static final int VK_BACK_QUOTE
public static final int VK_TAB
public static final int VK_SLASH
```
Constant values that represent various keyboard character keys.

```
public static final int VK_PAUSE
public static final int VK_PRINTSCREEN
public static final int VK_SHIFT
public static final int VK_HELP
public static final int VK_CONTROL
public static final int VK_ALT
```

```
public static final int VK_ESCAPE
public static final int VK_META
public static final int VK_ACCEPT
public static final int VK_CANCEL
public static final int VK_CLEAR
public static final int VK_CONVERT
public static final int VK_NONCONVERT
public static final int VK_MODECHANGE
public static final int VK_SEPARATER
public static final int VK_KANA
public static final int VK_KANJI
public static final int VK_FINAL
```

Constant values that represent various keyboard command and control keys.

```
public static final int VK_UNDEFINED
```

A constant value for `KEY_TYPED` events for which there is no defined key value.

```
public static final int VK_F1
public static final int VK_F2
public static final int VK_F3
public static final int VK_F4
public static final int VK_F5
public static final int VK_F6
public static final int VK_F7
public static final int VK_F8
public static final int VK_F9
public static final int VK_F10
public static final int VK_F11
public static final int VK_F12
```

Constant values that represent the keyboard keys F1–F12.

```
public static final int VK_CAPS_LOCK
public static final int VK_NUM_LOCK
public static final int VK_SCROLL_LOCK
```

Constant values that represent various keyboard control keys.

```
public static final int VK_A
public static final int VK_B
public static final int VK_C
public static final int VK_D
public static final int VK_E
public static final int VK_F
public static final int VK_G
public static final int VK_H
public static final int VK_I
public static final int VK_J
public static final int VK_K
```

```
public static final int VK_L
public static final int VK_M
public static final int VK_N
public static final int VK_O
public static final int VK_P
public static final int VK_Q
public static final int VK_R
public static final int VK_S
public static final int VK_T
public static final int VK_U
public static final int VK_V
public static final int VK_W
public static final int VK_X
public static final int VK_Y
public static final int VK_Z
```

Constant values that represent the keyboard keys A–Z.

Constructors

```
public KeyEvent(Component src, int id, long when, int modifiers, int keyCode)
public KeyEvent(Component src, int id, long when, int modifiers, int keyCode,
    char keyChar)
```

Creates a new instance of a `KeyEvent` from the specified source, having a specific type (`id`), time stamp, modifiers, key code, and/or key character.

Methods

```
public char getKeyChar()
public void setKeyChar(char character)
```

Returns or sets the character associated with this `KeyEvent`. For events that have no corresponding character, a `CHAR_UNDEFINED` is returned.

```
public int getKeyCode()
public void setKeyCode(int code)
```

Returns or sets the code associated with this `KeyEvent`. For events that have no corresponding code, a `VK_UNDEFINED` is returned.

```
public static String getKeyModifiersText(int mods)
public static String getKeyText(int keyCode)
```

Returns a string representation of the `KeyEvent` modifiers key code (i.e., "Meta+Shift" or "F1").

```
public boolean isActionKey()
```

Returns a true value if this event is from an action key.

```
public String paramString()
```

Returns a string representation of the parameters of this event.

```
public void setModifiers(int mods)
```

Sets the key event modifiers for this event.

Label (java.awt)

A public class, derived from Component, that places a text string in a container.

Variables and Constants

public final static int CENTER
public final static int LEFT
public final static int RIGHT
Constant values that indicate the alignment of the label's text.

Constructors

public Label()
public Label(String str)
public Label(String str, int align)
Creates a new label with the text string str, with align justification (default is LEFT).

Methods

public void addNotify()
Creates this label's peer.

public int getAlignment()
public void setAlignment(int align) throws IllegalArgumentException
Returns or sets the alignment of this label.

public String getText()
public void setText(String str)
Returns or sets the text string of this label.

protected String paramString()
Returns a string containing this label's parameters.

List (java.awt)

A public class, derived from Component, that graphically shows a group of items from which the user can select one or more.

Constructors

public List()
public List(int num)
public List(int num, boolean toggle)
Creates a new list with an initial number of visible rows of data (default is 0). If toggle is true, then more than one item from the list can be selected at a time.

Methods

`public void addItem(String str)`
`public void addItem(String str, int idx)`

Adds an item with the label `str` to the list in position `idx` (or the bottom as the default).

`public void addActionListener(ActionListener listener)`
`public void removeActionListener(ActionListener listener)`

Adds or removes the specified action `listener` from this list.

`public void addItemListener(ItemListener listener)`
`public void removeItemListener(ItemListener listener)`

Adds or removes the specified item `listener` to this list.

`public void addItem(String str)`
`public synchronized void addItem(String str, int idx)`

Adds an item with the label `str` to the list in position `idx` (or the bottom as the default).

`public void addNotify()`
`public void removeNotify()`

Creates or removes this list's peer.

`public void delItem(int idx)`

Removes an item from index `idx`.

`public void deselect(int idx)`
`public void select(int idx)`

Deselects or selects the item at `idx`.

`public String getItem(int idx)`

Returns the label for the item at `idx`

`public int getItemCount()`

Returns the number of items in this list.

`public synchronized String[] getItems()`

Returns an array of the items in this list.

`public Dimension getMinimumSize()`
`public Dimension getMinimumSize(int num)`
`public Dimension getPreferredSize()`
`public Dimension getPreferredSize(int num)`

Returns the minimum or preferred size of this list. If a new number of rows is specified, the minimum/preferred size for the change is returned.

`public int getRows()`

Returns the current number of visible rows in this list.

`public int getSelectedIndex()`
`public int[] getSelectedIndexes()`

Returns the index(s) of the currently selected item.

`public String getSelectedItem()`
`public String[] getSelectedItems()`

Returns the string label of the currently selected item(s) from this list.

`public Object[] getSelectedObjects()`
Returns an array of objects of the currently selected items from this list.

`public int getVisibleIndex()`
Returns the index of the last item made visible by the `makeVisible` method.

`public boolean isIndexSelected(int idx)`
Returns a true value if the item at position `idx` is currently selected.

`public boolean isMultipleMode()`
Returns a true value if this list is allowed to have more than one item selected at a time.

`public void makeVisible(int idx)`
Scrolls the list so the item at position `idx` is visible.

`protected String paramString()`
Returns a string value of the parameters of this list.

`protected void processActionEvent(ActionEvent event)`
Handles any action `event` for this list by passing it to a registered action listener.

`protected void processEvent(AWTEvent event)`
Processes an incoming `event` for this list, passing it to `procesActionEvent` if it is an action event, or to `processItemEvent` if it is an item event; otherwise, the specified event is passed to the superclass' `processEvent` method.

`protected void processItemEvent(ItemEvent event)`
Handles any item `event` for this list by passing them to a registered item listener.

`public synchronized void remove(int idx)`
`public synchronized void remove(String str)`
Removes the item at a specified index or the first occurrence of item `str` from this list.

`public synchronized void removeAll()`
Removes all items from this list.

`public void replaceItem(String str, int idx)`
Changes the value of the label for the item at position `idx` to `str`.

`public synchronized void setMultipleMode(boolean toggle)`
If `toggle` is set to true, this list will allow for multiple selections at one time.

Locale (`java.util`)

A public class, derived from `Object` and implementing `Serializable` and `Cloneable`, that represents geographic-specific or political-specific information.

Variables and Constants

`public static final Locale CANADA`
`public static final Locale CANADA_FRENCH`
`public static final Locale CHINA`

```
public static final Locale FRANCE
public static final Locale GERMANY
public static final Locale ITALY
public static final Locale JAPAN
public static final Locale KOREA
public static final Locale PRC
public static final Locale TAIWAN
public static final Locale UK
public static final Locale US
```

Constant values that represent locales based on countries.

```
public static final Locale CHINESE
public static final Locale ENGLISH
public static final Locale FRENCH
public static final Locale GERMAN
public static final Locale ITALIAN
public static final Locale JAPANESE
public static final Locale KOREAN
public static final Locale SIMPLIFIED_CHINESE
public static final Locale TRADITIONAL_CHINESE
```

Constant values that represent locales based on languages.

Constructors

```
public Locale(String lang, String country)
public Locale(String lang, String country, String var)
```

Creates a new locale from the specified two character ISO codes for a language and country. A computer and browser variant of a locale can also be included. These usually take the form of WIN for Windows or MAC for Macintosh.

Methods

```
public Object clone()
```

Returns a copy of this locale.

```
public boolean equals(Object arg)
```

Returns a true value if this locale is equal to `arg`.

```
public String getCountry()
public String getLanguage()
public String getVariant()
```

Returns the character code for the name of this locale's country, language or variant.

```
public static synchronized Locale getDefault()
public static synchronized void setDefault(Locale locale)
```

Returns or sets the default locale.

```
public final String getDisplayCountry()
```

public String getDisplayCountry(Locale displaylocale)

Returns the display version of the country name for this locale in either the specified or default locales.

public final String getDisplayLanguage()

public String getDisplayLanguage(Locale displaylocale)

Returns the display version of the language name for this locale in either the specified or default locales.

public final String getDisplayName()

public String getDisplayName(Locale displaylocale)

Returns the display version of the name for this locale in either the specified or default locales.

public final String getDisplayVariant()

public String getDisplayVariant(Locale displaylocale)

Returns the display version of the variant for this locale in either the specified or default locales.

public String getISO3Country() throws MissingResourceException

public String getISO3Language() throws MissingResourceException

Returns the three-character ISO abbreviation for the country or language for this locale.

hashCode()

Returns the hash code for this locale.

toString()

Returns a string representation of this locale.

Long (java.lang)

A public final class, derived from Number, that contains long integer math operations, constants, methods to compute minimum and maximum numbers, and string manipulation routines related to the primitive long type.

Variables and Constants

public final static long MAX_VALUE

public final static long MIN_VALUE

Constant values that contain the maximum possible value (9223372036854775807L) or minimum possible value (29223372036854775808L) of a long in Java.

public final static Class TYPE

The Integer constant value of the integer type class.

Constructors

public Long(long num)

public Long(String num) throws NumberFormatException

Creates an instance of the Long class from the parameter num.

Methods

```
public byte byteValue()
public double doubleValue()
public float floatValue()
public int intValue()
public long longValue()
public short shortValue()
```

Returns the value of this `Long` as a Java primitive type.

```
public boolean equals(Object arg)
```

Returns the result of the equality comparison between this `Long` and the parameter `arg`.

```
public static Long getLong(String prop)
public static Long getLong(String prop, long num)
public static Long getLong(String prop, long num)
```

Returns a `Long` representation of the system property named in `prop`. If there is no property corresponding to `prop`, or the format of its value is incorrect, then the default `num` is returned.

```
public int hashCode()
```

Returns a hash code for this `Long`.

```
public static Long parseLong(String str) throws NumberFormatException
public static Long parseLong(String str, int base) throws NumberFormatException
```

Evaluates the string `str` and returns the long equivalent in radix `base`.

```
public static String toBinaryString(long num)
public static String toHexString(long num)
public static String toOctalString(long num)
```

Returns the string representation of parameter `num` in base 2 (binary), 8 (octal), or 16 (hexadecimal).

```
public String toString()
public static String toString(long num)
public static String toString(long num, int base)
```

Returns the string representation of this `long` or `num` in base 10 (decimal). The radix of the returned number can also be specified in `base`.

```
public static Long valueOf(String str) throws NumberFormatException
public static Long valueOf(String str, int base) throws NumberFormatException
```

Returns a `Long` initialized to the value of `str` in radix `base`.

Math (`java.lang`)

A public final class, derived from `Object`, that contains integer and floating point constants, and methods to perform various math operations, compute minimum and maximum numbers, and generate random numbers.

Variables and Constants

```
public final static double E
public final static double PI
```

Constant values that contain the natural base of logarithms (2.7182818284590452354) and the ratio of the circumference of a circle to its diameter (3.14159265358979323846).

Methods

```
public static double abs(double num)
public static float abs(float num)
public static int abs(int num)
public static long abs(long num)
```

Returns the absolute value of the specified parameter.

```
public static double acos(double num)
public static double asin(double num)
public static double atan(double num)
```

Returns the arc cosine, arc sine, or arc tangent of parameter `num` as a double.

```
public static double atan2(double x, double y)
```

Returns the component θ of the polar coordinate $\{r,\theta\}$ that corresponds to the cartesian coordinate <x, y>.

```
public static double ceil(double num)
```

Returns the smallest integer value that is not less than the argument `num`.

```
public static double cos(double angle)
public static double sin(double angle)
public static double tan(double angle)
```

Returns the cosine, sine, or tangent of parameter `angle` measured in radians.

```
public static double exp(double num)
```

Returns *e* to the `num`, where *e* is the base of natural logarithms.

```
public static double floor(double num)
```

Returns a double that is the largest integer value that is not greater than the parameter `num`.

```
public static double IEEEremainder(double arg1, double arg2)
```

Returns the mathematical remainder between `arg1` and `arg2` as defined by IEEE 754.

```
public static double log(double num) throws ArithmeticException
```

Returns the natural logarithm of parameter `num`.

```
public static double max(double num1, double num2)
public static float max(float num1, float num2)
public static int max(int num1, int num2)
public static long max(long num1, long num2)
```

Returns the larger of parameters `num1` and `num2`.

```
public static double min(double num1, double num2)
public static float min(float num1, float num2)
public static int min(int num1, int num2)
```

`public static long min(long num1, long num2)`
Returns the minimum value of parameters `num1` and `num2`.

`public static double pow(double num1, double num2) throws ArithmeticException`
Returns the result of `num1` to `num2`.

`public static double random()`
Returns a random number between 0.0 and 1.0.

`public static double rint(double num)`
Returns the closest integer to parameter `num`.

`public static long round(double num)`
`public static int round(float num)`
Returns the closest `long` or `int` to parameter `num`.

`public static double sqrt(double num) throws ArithmeticException`
Returns the square root of parameter `num`.

Menu (java.awt)

A public class, derived from `MenuItem` and implementing `MenuContainer`, that contains a selection of items that "pop-down," from which the user can choose one.

Constructors

`public Menu()`
`public Menu(String lbl)`
`public Menu(String lbl, boolean toggle)`
Creates a new instance of a menu with a label (or none if not specified). If `toggle` is true, then the menu can be "torn" from the menu bar, staying on the screen after the menu is no longer selected.

Methods

`public MenuItem add(MenuItem item)`
`public void add(String lbl)`
Adds an item with a label (`lbl`) to this menu. If the item is a `MenuItem`, the added menu item is returned.

`public void addNotify()`
`public void removeNotify()`
Creates or removes the menu's peer.

`public void addSeparator()`
`public void insertSeparator(int idx)`
Adds a separator line to the end, or inserts it at the specified index, of this menu.

`public MenuItem getItem(int num)`
Returns the menu item at position `num` from this menu.

`public int getItemCount()`
Returns the number of items in this menu.

`public synchronized void insert(MenuItem item, int idx)`
`public void insert(String lbl, int idx)`
Inserts an item into this list at the specified index. The inserted item can have a string label of `lbl`.

`public boolean isTearOff()`
Returns true if this menu can be torn off.

`public String paramString()`
Returns the parameter string for this menu.

`public void remove(int idx)`
`public void remove(MenuComponent item)`
Removes the specified menu item from this menu.

`public synchronized void removeAll()`
Removes all of the menu items from this menu.

MenuBar (`java.awt`)

A public class, derived from `MenuComponent` and implementing `MenuContainer`, that creates graphical menu regions that are bound to frames and allow graphical menus to be attached.

Constructors

`public MenuBar()`
Creates a new instance of a menu bar.

Methods

`public Menu add(Menu arg)`
Adds menu `arg` to this menu bar.

`public void addNotify()`
`public void removeNotify()`
Creates or destroys this menu bar's peer.

`public void deleteShortcut(MenuShortcut shortcut)`
Removes the specified menu `shortcut` from this menu bar.

`public Menu getHelpMenu()`
`public void setHelpMenu(Menu helpmenu)`
Returns or sets the menu designated as the help menu for this menu bar.

`public Menu getMenu(int idx)`
Returns the menu indexed at position `idx` on this menu bar.

`public int getMenuCount()`
Returns the number of menus attached to this menu bar.

`public MenuItem getShortcutMenuItem(MenuShortcut shortcut)`

Returns the menu item that is associated with the specified menu `shortcut`, or null if none exists.

`public void remove(int idx)`
`public void remove(MenuComponent comp)`

Removes the specified menu component or item at index `idx` from this menu.

`public synchronized Enumeration shortcuts()`

Returns an enumerated list of all of the menu shortcuts from this menu bar.

MenuComponent (`java.awt`)

A public abstract class, derived from `Object` and implementing `Serializable`, that is the superclass to all menu component classes.

Constructors

`public MenuComponent()`

Creates a new instance of a menu component.

Methods

`public final void dispatchEvent(AWTEvent evt)`

Sends the specified event (`evt`) to this menu component or one of its submenu component objects.

`public Font getFont()`
`public void setFont(Font fnt)`

Returns or sets the font for this menu component.

`public String getName()`
`public void setName(String str)`

Returns or sets the name of this menu component.

`public MenuContainer getParent()`

Returns this menu component's parent container.

`protected String paramString()`

Overridden by subclasses, this method returns a string containing the parameters for this menu component.

`public boolean postEvent(Event arg)`

Posts event `arg` to this menu component.

`protected void processEvent(AWTEvent evt)`

An abstract method used to process incoming events (`evt`) from this menu component.

`public void removeNotify()`

Removes this menu component's peer.

`public String toString()`

Returns a string representation of this menu component.

MenuItem (`java.awt`)

A public class, derived from `MenuComponent`, that represents a single choice in a menu.

Constructors

```
public MenuItem()
public MenuItem(String str)
public MenuItem(String str, MenuShortcut shortcut)
```

Creates a new instance of a menu item. Item can have both a label and a shortcut associated with it.

Methods

```
public void addActionListener(ActionListener listener)
public void removeActionListener(ActionListener listener)
```

Adds or removes the specified `listener` to this menu item.

```
public void addNotify()
```

Creates this menu item's peer.

```
public void deleteShortcut()
```

Removes the shortcut associated with this menu item.

```
protected final void disableEvents(long mask)
protected final void enableEvents(long mask)
```

Disables or enables events from the specified `mask` from being handled by this menu item.

```
public String getActionCommand()
public void setActionCommand(String command)
```

Returns or sets the name of the command that results from selection of this menu item.

```
public String getLabel()
public synchronized void setLabel(String str)
```

Returns or sets the label of this menu item.

```
public MenuShortcut getShortcut()
public void setShortcut(MenuShortcut shortcut)
```

Returns or sets the menu shortcut associated with this menu item.

```
public boolean isEnabled()
public synchronized void setEnabled(boolean toggle)
```

Returns or sets the current enabled state for this menu item.

```
public String paramString()
```

Returns the string parameter of this menu item.

```
protected void processActionEvent(ActionEvent evt)
```

Handles any action events (`evt`) for this menu item, sending them to a registered listener.

`protected void processEvent(AWTEvent evt)`

Handles any events (`evt`) on this menu item, sending all action events to this menu item's `processActionEvent` method.

MenuShortcut (`java.awt`)

A public class, derived from `Object` and implementing `Serializable`, that is a combination of keyboard actions that yield a menu item selection.

Constructors

`public MenuShortcut(int value)`
`public MenuShortcut(int value, boolean toggle)`

Creates an instance of a menu shortcut using the specified key code `value`. If `toggle` is true, then the Shift key must be depressed in order for this shortcut to function.

Methods

`public boolean equals(MenuShortcut arg)`

Returns a true value if this menu shortcut is equal to the specified shortcut.

`public int getKey()`

Returns the key code value for this menu shortcut.

`protected String paramString()`

Returns the parameter string for this menu shortcut.

`public String toString()`

Returns a string representation of this menu shortcut.

`public boolean usesShiftModifier()`

Returns a true value if this menu shortcut requires the use of a shift key.

MessageFormat (`java.text`)

A public class, derived from `Format`, that is used to build formatted message strings.

Constructors

`public MessageFormat(String str)`

Creates a new instance of a `MessageFormat` from the specified string pattern.

Methods

`public void applyPattern(String str)`

`public String toPattern()`

Sets and returns the pattern for this `MessageFormat`.

`public Object clone()`

Returns a copy of this `MessageFormat`.

`public boolean equals(Object arg)`

Returns a true value if this `MessageFormat` is equal to `arg`.

`public final StringBuffer format(Object src, StringBuffer dest, FieldPosition ignore)`

`public final StringBuffer format(Object[] src, StringBuffer dest, FieldPosition ignore)`

Formats the specified source object with this `MessageFormat`, placing the result in `dest`. This method returns the value of the destination buffer.

`public static String format(String str, Object[] args)`

Formats the given string applying specified arguments. This method allows for message formatting with the creation of a `MessageFormat`.

`public Format[] getFormats()`

`public void setFormats(Format[] newFormats)`

Returns and sets the formats for this `MessageFormat`.

`public Locale getLocale()`

`public void setLocale(Locale locale)`

Returns and sets the locale for this `MessageFormat`.

`public int hashCode()`

Returns the hash code for this `MessageFormat`.

`public Object[] parse(String src) throws ParseException`

`public Object[] parse(String src, ParsePosition pos)`

Parses the string source (starting at position pos, or 0 by default), returning its objects.

`public Object parseObject(String src, ParsePosition pos)`

Parses the string source (starting at position pos, or 0 by default), returning one object.

`public void setFormat(int var, Format fmt)`

Sets an individual format at index `var`.

MouseAdapter (`java.awt.event`)

A public abstract class, derived from `Object` and implementing `MouseListener`, that permits derived classes to override the predefined no-op mouse events.

Constructors

`public MouseAdapter()`

Creates a new instance of a `MouseAdapter`.

Methods

```
public void mouseClicked(MouseEvent event)
public void mouseEntered(MouseEvent event)
public void mouseExited(MouseEvent event)
public void mousePressed(MouseEvent event)
public void mouseReleased(MouseEvent event)
```

Empty methods which should be overridden in order to implement event handling for mouse events.

MouseEvent (`java.awt.event`)

A public class, derived from `InputEvent`, that represents events triggered by the mouse.

Variables and Constants

```
public static final int MOUSE_CLICKED
public static final int MOUSE_DRAGGED
public static final int MOUSE_ENTERED
public static final int MOUSE_EXITED
public static final int MOUSE_MOVED
public static final int MOUSE_PRESSED
public static final int MOUSE_RELEASED
```

Constant variables that represent a variety of mouse events.

```
public static final int MOUSE_FIRST
public static final int MOUSE_LAST
```

Constant values that represent the index of the first and last mouse event ids.

Constructors

```
public MouseEvent(Component src, int type, long timestamp, int mods, int x, int
    y, int clickCount, boolean popupTrigger)
```

Creates a new instance of a `MouseEvent` from a given source, with a specified type, timestamp, keyboard modifiers, x and y locations, number of clicks and a state value, if this event triggers a popup menu.

Methods

```
public int getClickCount()
```

Returns the number of mouse clicks in this event.

```
public Point getPoint()
```

Returns the point location of this event, relative to the source component's space.

```
public int getX()
```

`public int getY()`

Returns the *x* or *y* location of this event, relative to the source component's space.

`public boolean isPopupTrigger()`

Returns a true value if this event is a trigger for popup-menus.

`public String paramString()`

Returns a string representation of the parameters of this `MouseEvent`.

`public synchronized void translatePoint(int xoffset, int yoffset)`

Offsets the *x* and *y* locations of this event by the specified amounts.

MouseMotionAdapter (`java.awt.event`)

A public abstract class, derived from `Object` and implementing `MouseMotionListener`, that permits a derived class to override the predefined no-op mouse motion events.

Constructors

`public MouseMotionAdapter()`

Creates a new instance of a `MouseMotionAdapter`.

Methods

`public void mouseDragged(MouseEvent event)`
`public void mouseMoved(MouseEvent event)`

Empty methods that should be overridden in order to implement event handling for mouse motion events.

Number (`java.lang`)

A public abstract class, derived from `Object` and implementing `Serializable`, that is the parent class to the wrapper classes `Byte`, `Double`, `Integer`, `Float`, `Long` and `Short`.

Constructors

`public Number()`

Creates a new instance of a `Number`.

Methods

`public byte byteValue()`
`public abstract double doubleValue()`
`public abstract float floatValue()`

```
public abstract int intValue()
public abstract long longValue()
public short shortValue()
```
Returns the value of this `Number` as a Java primitive type.

NumberFormat (java.text)

A public abstract class, derived from `Format` and implementing `Cloneable`, that is used to convert number objects to locale-specific strings, and vice versa.

Variables and Constants

```
public static final int FRACTION_FIELD
public static final int INTEGER_FIELD
```
Constant values that indicate field locations in a `NumberFormat`.

Constructors

```
public NumberFormat()
```
Creates a new instance of a `NumberFormat`.

Methods

```
public Object clone()
```
Returns a copy of this `NumberFormat`.

```
public boolean equals(Object arg)
```
Returns a true value if this `NumberFormat` is equal to `arg`.

```
public final String format(double num)
public final String format(long num)
```
Formats the specified Java primitive type according to this `NumberFormat`, returning a string.

```
public abstract StringBuffer format(double num, StringBuffer dest,FieldPosition
    pos)
public abstract StringBuffer format(long num, StringBuffer dest, FieldPosition
    pos)
public final StringBuffer format(Object num, StringBuffer dest, FieldPosition
    pos)
```
Formats the specified Java primitive type (or object) starting at `pos`, according to this `NumberFormat`, placing the resulting string in the specified destination buffer. This method returns the value of the string buffer.

```
public static Locale[] getAvailableLocales()
```
Returns the available locales.

```
public static final NumberFormat getCurrencyInstance()
```

`public static NumberFormat getCurrencyInstance(Locale locale)`

Returns the `NumberFormat` for currency for the default or specified locale.

`public static final NumberFormat getInstance()`
`public static NumberFormat getInstance(Locale locale)`

Returns the default number format for the default or specified locale.

`public int getMaximumFractionDigits()`
`public void setMaximumFractionDigits(int val)`

Returns or sets the maximum number of fractional digits allowed in this `NumberFormat`.

`public int getMaximumIntegerDigits()`
`public void setMaximumIntegerDigits(int val)`

Returns or sets the maximum number of integer digits allowed in this `NumberFormat`.

`public int getMinimumFractionDigits()`
`public void setMinimumFractionDigits(int val)`

Returns or sets the minimum number of fractional digits allowed in this `NumberFormat`.

`public int getMinimumIntegerDigits()`
`public void setMinimumIntegerDigits(int val)`

Returns or sets the minimum number of integer digits allowed in this `NumberFormat`.

`public static final NumberFormat getNumberInstance()`
`public static NumberFormat getNumberInstance(Locale locale)`

Returns the `NumberFormat` for numbers for the default or specified locale.

`public static final NumberFormat getPercentInstance()`
`public static NumberFormat getPercentInstance(Locale locale)`

Returns the `NumberFormat` for percentages for the default or specified locale.

`public int hashCode()`

Returns the hash code for this `NumberFormat`.

`public boolean isGroupingUsed()`
`public void setGroupingUsed(boolean toggle)`

Returns or sets the toggle flag for the use of the grouping indicator by this `NumberFormat`.

`public boolean isParseIntegerOnly()`
`public void setParseIntegerOnly(boolean toggle)`

Returns or sets the toggle flag for the use of parsing numbers as integers only by this `NumberFormat`.

`public Number parse(String str) throws ParseException`

Parses the specified string as a number.

`public abstract Number parse(String str, ParsePosition pos)`
`public final Object parseObject(String str, ParsePosition pos)`

Parses the specified string as a long (if possible) or double, starting a position pos. Returns a number or an object.

Object (`java.lang`)

A public class that is the root of the hierarchy tree for all classes in Java.

Constructors

`public Object()`
Creates a new instance of the object class.

Methods

`protected Object clone() throws OutOfMemoryError, CloneNotSupportedException`
Returns an exact copy of the current object.

`public boolean equals(Object arg)`
Returns a true value if the current object is equal to `arg`.

`protected void finalize() throws Throwable`
The finalize method contains code that is called as the object is being destroyed.

`public final Class getClass()`
Returns the class of the current object.

`public int hashCode()`
Returns a hash code for the current object.

`public final void notify() throws IllegalMonitorStateException`
`public final void notifyAll() throws IllegalMonitorStateException`
Informs a paused thread that it may resume execution. `notifyAll` informs all paused threads.

`public String toString()`
Returns a string representation of the current object.

`public final void wait() throws IllegalMonitorStateException, InterruptedException`

`public final void wait(long msec) throws IllegalMonitorStateException, InterruptedException`

`public final void wait(long msec, int nsec) throws IllegalMonitorStateException, InterruptedException, IllegalArgumentException`
Causes a thread to suspend execution for `msec` milliseconds and `nsec` nanoseconds. The `wait()` method (without parameters) causes a thread to suspend execution until further notice.

PaintEvent (`java.awt.event`)

A public class, derived from `ComponentEvent`, that describes a particular AWT paint event.

Variables and Constants

`public static final int PAINT`

public static final int UPDATE
Constant values representing the paint and update event types.

public static final int PAINT_FIRST
public static final int PAINT_LAST
Constant values that represent the index of the first and last paint event ids.

Constructors

public PaintEvent(Component src, int type, Rectangle rect)
Creates a new instance of a PaintEvent from a specified source component, having an event type and a defined rectangular region to update.

Methods

public Rectangle getUpdateRect()
public void setUpdateRect(Rectangle rect)
Returns or sets the rectangular region that is updated as a result of this PaintEvent.

public String paramString()
Returns a string containing the parameters of this PaintEvent.

Panel (java.awt)

A public class, derived from Container, that allocates space in which you can place other components and containers.

Constructors

public Panel()
public Panel(LayoutManager mgr)
Creates a new instance of a panel with the specified layout manager or uses FlowLayout as the default.

Methods

public void addNotify()
Creates this panel's peer.

ParsePosition (java.text)

A public class, derived from Object, that is used to track the position of the index during parsing. This class is generally used by the Format class (and its subclasses).

Constructors

```
public ParsePosition(int index)
```

Creates a new instance of a `ParsePosition` from the specified index.

Methods

```
public int getIndex()
public void setIndex(int num)
```

Returns or sets the parse position.

Point (`java.awt`)

A public class, derived from `Object` and implementing `Serializable`, that defines and manipulates a location on a two-dimensional coordinate system.

Variables and Constants

```
public int x
public int y
```

The `x` and `y` locations of this point.

Constructors

```
public Point()
public Point(Point pt)
public Point(int x, int y)
```

Creates a new instance of a `Point` from the specified coordinates, the specified point, or using <0, 0> by default.

Methods

```
public boolean equals(Object arg)
```

Returns a true value if this point is identical to `arg`.

```
public Point getLocation()
public void move(int x, int y)
public void setLocation(Point pt)
public void setLocation(int x, int y)
```

Returns or relocates the position of this point.

```
public int hashCode()
```

Returns the hash code of this point.

```
public String toString()
```

Returns a string representation of this point.

`public void translate(int xoffset, int yoffset)`
Relocates this point to `<x+xoffset, y+yoffset>`.

Polygon (`java.awt`)

A public class, derived from `Object` and implementing `Shape` and `Serializable`, that maintains a list of points that define a polygon shape.

Variables and Constants

`protected Rectangle bounds`
The bounds of this polygon.

`public int npoints`
The total number of points of this polygon.

`public int xpoints[]`
`public int ypoints[]`
The arrays of `x` and `y` locations for the points of this polygon.

Constructors

`public Polygon()`
`public Polygon(int[] x, int[] y, int np)`
Creates a new instance of a polygon, initially defined by the arrays of `x` and `y` locations `<x, y>` and comprised of `np` points. The default constructor creates a new polygon that contains no points.

Methods

`public void addPoint(int newx, int newy)`
Adds the point located at `<newx, newy>` to this polygon.

`public boolean contains(int x, int y)`
`public boolean contains(Point pt)`
Returns a true value if this polygon contains the specified point.

`public Rectangle getBounds()`
Returns the bonds of this polygon.

`public void translate(int xoffset, int yoffset)`
Relocates all of the `x` and `y` points of this polygon by `xoffset` and `yoffset`.

PopupMenu (`java.awt`)

A public class, derived from `Menu`, that can produce a menu inside a component.

Constructors

`public PopupMenu()`
`public PopupMenu(String lbl)`
Creates a new instance of a popup menu with the specified label (or having no label in the case of the first constructor).

Methods

`public synchronized void addNotify()`
Creates this popup menu's peer.

`public void show(Component source, int x, int y)`
Displays the popup menu at the position <`x, y`> relative to the specified component.

PrintStream (`java.io`)

A public class, derived from `FilterOutputStream`, that provides methods to print data types in a format other than byte-based.

Constructors

`public PrintStream(OutputStream out)`
`public PrintStream(OutputStream out, boolean autoflush)`
Creates a new instance of a `PrintStream` on `out`. If the `autoflush` value is set to true, then the output buffer is flushed at every occurrence of a newline.

Methods

`public boolean checkError()`
Flushes this print stream's buffer and returns a true value if an error occurred.

`public void close()`
Closes this print stream.

`public void flush()`
Flushes this print stream's buffer.

`public void print(boolean b)`
`public void print(char c)`
`public void print(char[] s)`

```
public void print(double d)
public void print(float f)
public void print(int i)
public void print(long l)
public void print(Object obj)
public void print(String s)
public void println()
public void println(boolean b)
public void println(char c)
public void println(char[] s)
public void println(double d)
public void println(float f)
public void println(int i)
public void println(long l)
public void println(Object obj)
public void println(String s)
```

Prints the specified Java primitive type, Object, or blank line to this print stream. When using a character, only the lower byte is printed.

```
public void write(int b)
public void write(byte[] b, int off, int len)
```

Writes a byte or `len` bytes from the array `b`, starting at index `off` to this print stream.

Random (`java.util`)

A public class, derived from `Object` and implementing `Serializable`, that produces sequences of pseudo-random numbers.

Constructors

```
public Random()
public Random(long rnd)
```

Creates a new instance of a random class using the value of `rnd` as the random number seed. When the default constructor is used, the current time in milliseconds is the seed.

Methods

```
protected int next(int b)
```

Returns the next random number (from the specified number of bits).

```
public void nextBytes(byte[] b)
```

Generates an array of random bytes as defined by `b[]`.

```
public double nextDouble()
public float nextFloat()
```

Returns a random number between 0.0 and 1.0 in the specified primitive type.

`public int nextInt()`
`public long nextLong()`
Returns a random integer value from all possible int or long values (positive and negative).

`public double nextGaussian()`
Returns a Gaussian double random number with a mean value of 0.0 and a standard deviation of 1.0.

`public void setSeed(long rnd)`
Sets the seeds for this random number generator to `rnd`.

Rectangle (`java.awt`)

A public class, derived from `Object` and implementing `Shape` and `Serializable`, that represents a rectangular shape that is described by an `x` and `y` location, and a width and height.

Variables and Constants

`public int height`
`public int width`
The height and width of this rectangle.

`public int x`
`public int y`
The `x` and `y` locations of the upper-left corner of this rectangle.

Constructors

`public Rectangle()`
`public Rectangle(Dimension dim)`
`public Rectangle(Point pt)`
Creates a new instance of a `Rectangle` with an initial location of the corresponding values of `pt` or `dim`, with a height of 0 and width of 0. If neither `pt` or `dim` are specified, then the initial location is <0, 0> and the height and width are set to 0.

`public Rectangle(Rectangle rect)`
`public Rectangle(Point pt, Dimension dim)`
Creates a new instance of a `Rectangle` with initial location and size values the same as corresponding values in `rect`, or with an initial location of the corresponding values of `pt`, and with a width and height corresponding to the values of `dim`.

`public Rectangle(int width, int height)`
`public Rectangle(int x, int y, int width, int height)`
Creates a new instance of a `Rectangle` with an initial location of <`x, y`> (or <0, 0> by default), and with a `height` and `width`.

Methods

`public void add(int x, int y)`
`public void add(Point point)`
`public void add(Rectangle rect)`

Adds the specified point in space, defined by coordinates, a point, or the initial location of the specified `Rectangle`, to this `Rectangle`. This method may expand the `Rectangle` (if the point lies outside) or reduce the `Rectangle` (if the point lies inside).

`public boolean contains(int x, int y)`
`public boolean contains(Point pt)`

Returns a true value if this `Rectangle` contains the specified point.

`public boolean equals(Object rect2)`

Returns a true value if this `Rectangle` and the rectangle `rect2` are identical.

`public Rectangle getBounds()`

Returns the bounds of this `Rectangle`.

`public Point getLocation()`
`public Dimension getSize()`

Returns the location or size of this `Rectangle`.

`public void grow(int width, int height)`

Increases this `Rectangle` by `height` and `width` pixels.

`public int hashCode()`

Returns the hash code for this `Rectangle`.

`public Rectangle intersection(Rectangle rect2)`

Returns the intersection of this `Rectangle` and the specified rectangle (`rect2`).

`public boolean intersects(Rectangle rect2)`

Returns a true value if this `Rectangle` intersects `rect2`.

`public boolean isEmpty()`

Returns a true value if this `Rectangle` is empty (height and width <= 0).

`public void setBounds(int x, int y, int width, int height)`
`public void setBounds(Rectangle rect)`

Resets the `x` and `y` locations, width and height of this `rectangle` to the respective values of `rect` or the specified values of `x, y, width`, and `height`.

`public void setLocation(int x, int y)`
`public void setLocation(Point pt)`

Resets the location of this `Rectangle` to the specified point.

`public void setSize(Dimension dim)`
`public void setSize(int width, int height)`

Resets the size to `width` and `height`, or the corresponding values of `dim`.

`public String toString()`

Returns a string representation of this `Rectangle`.

`public void translate(int width, int height)`

Adds the specified `width` and `height` to this `Rectangle`'s width and height values.

`public Rectangle union(Rectangle rect2)`

Returns the union of this `Rectangle` and `rect2`.

Scrollbar (`java.awt`)

A public class, derived from `Component` and implementing `Adjustable`, that creates a graphical representation of a range of values which the user can set.

Variables and Constants

`public final static int HORIZONTAL`
`public final static int VERTICAL`

Constant values representing the orientation of a horizontal or vertical scrollbar.

Constructors

`public Scrollbar()`
`public Scrollbar(int direction) throws IllegalArgumentException`
`public Scrollbar(int direction, int val, int size, int min, int max)`

Creates a new scrollbar in the specified `direction` that ranges from `min` to `max`. The initial value is set to `val`, and the size of the bubble is set to `size`. If the default constructor is used, a vertical scrollbar is created. The first and second constructors use initial values of 0, 10, 0, 100 for the initial value, size of the bubble, min, and max values, respectively.

Methods

`public void addAdjustmentListener(AdjustmentListener listener)`
`public void removeAdjustmentListener(AdjustmentListener listener)`

Adds or removes the specified `listener` to this scrollbar.

`public void addNotify()`

Creates this scrollbar's peer.

`public int getBlockIncrement()`
`public synchronized void setBlockIncrement(int val)`

Returns or sets the amount of the increment when the user pushes the increment/decrement device of this scrollbar.

`public int getMaximum()`
`public int getMinimum()`

Returns the maximum or minimum value of this scrollbar.

`public int getOrientation()`

`public synchronized void setOrientation(int direction)`

Returns or sets the orientation of this scrollbar.

`public int getUnitIncrement()`
`public synchronized void setUnitIncrement(int num)`

Returns or sets the unit increment for this scrollbar.

`public int getValue()`

Returns the current value of this scrollbar.

`public int getVisibleAmount()`
`public synchronized void setVisibleAmount(int bubble)`

Returns or sets the visible amount of this scrollbar.

`protected String paramString()`

Returns a string representation of this scrollbar's parameters.

`protected void processAdjustmentEvent(AdjustmentEvent event)`

Handles the adjustment event for this scrollbar, sending it to the appropriate registered listener.

`protected void processEvent(AWTEvent event)`

Processes all events for this scrollbar, passing them to the `processAdjustmentEvent` if they apply, otherwise the event is passed to the superclass' `processEvent` method.

`public synchronized void setMaximum(int num)`
`public synchronized void setMinimum(int num)`

Sets the maximum or minimum value for this scrollbar to `num`.

`public void setValue(int num)`

Sets this scrollbar's value to `num`.

`public void setValues(int num, int size, int min, int max)`

Sets the value (`num`), bubble `size`, `min`, and `max` values of this scrollbar.

ScrollPane (`java.awt`)

A public class, derived from `Container`, that creates a graphical pane area which can contain a single GUI component. The pane of the area can contain scrollbars for easier viewing of the component.

Variables and Constants

`public final static int SCROLLBARS_ALWAYS`
`public final static int SCROLLBARS_AS_NEEDED`
`public final static int SCROLLBARS_NEVER`

Constant values indicating the policy for the creation of scrollbars at instantiation of this scroll pane.

Constructors

`public ScrollPane()`
`public ScrollPane(int policy)`

Creates a new instance of a scroll pane, using the specified `policy` (or the default of `SCROLLBARS_AS_NEEDED`, in the case of the default constructor) for the creation of scrollbars.

Methods

`protected final void addImpl(Component obj, Object constraints, int index)`

Adds the specified component object to this scroll pane at `index`. The `constraints` parameter is not presently used.

`public void addNotify()`

Creates the peer for this scroll pane.

`public void doLayout()`

Lays out this scroll pane by resizing the component to the preferred size.

`public Adjustable getHAdjustable()`
`public Adjustable getVAdjustable()`

Returns the state of the horizontal or vertical scrollbar if it exists; otherwise, it returns a null.

`public int getHScrollbarHeight()`
`public int getVScrollbarWidth()`

Returns the height in pixels of the horizontal scrollbar or the width in pixels of the vertical scrollbar (even if they are not created).

`public int getScrollbarDisplayPolicy()`

Returns the creation and display policy for the scrollbars of this scroll pane.

`public Point getScrollPosition()`

Returns the `x` and `y` coordinate of the embedded component that is aligned with the upper right corner of the scroll pane's view window.

`public Dimension getViewportSize()`

Returns the current size in pixels of this scroll pane's view window.

`public String paramString()`

Returns a string representation of the parameters of this scroll pane.

`public void printComponents(Graphics dest)`

Prints the component of this scroll pane on the specified graphics destination (`dest`).

`public final void setLayout(LayoutManager manager)`

Sets the layout manager for this scroll pane to `manager`.

`public void setScrollPosition(int xpos, int ypos)`
`public void setScrollPosition(Point dest)`

Scrolls the embedded component to the specified position.

ServerSocket (java.net)

A public final class, derived from `Object`, that represents a socket which listens for connection requests, receives data, and potentially returns a result to the requestor.

Constructors

`public ServerSocket(int num) throws IOException`
`public ServerSocket(int num, int queue) throws IOException`
`public ServerSocket(int num, int queue, InetAddress addr) throws IOException`

Creates a new instance of a `ServerSocket` on local port `num` (a value of 0 means connect to any free port), setting an incoming queue length for the socket (default is 50 connections), bound to the local machine `addr`.

Methods

`public Socket accept() throws IOException`

Accept an incoming request on this socket.

`public void close() throws IOException`

Closes this server socket.

`public InetAddress getInetAddress()`

Returns the Internet address for the machine this socket has connected to. If no connection yet exists, a null value is returned.

`public int getLocalPort()`

Returns the number of the local port this socket is bound to.

`public synchronized int getSoTimeout() throws IOException`
`public synchronized void setSoTimeout(int num) throws SocketException`

Returns or sets the timeout value for this socket in milliseconds.

`protected final void implAccept(Socket arg) throws IOException`

This method is provided so that subclasses of `ServerSocket` can override the accept method.

`public static void setSocketFactory(SocketImplFactory sif) throws IOException, SocketException`

Sets the `ServerSocket` implementation factory for this `ServerSocket` to the specified value.

`public String toString()`

Returns a string representation for this socket.

Short (java.lang)

A public class, derived from `Number`, that contains integer math operations, constants, methods to compute minimum and maximum numbers, and string manipulation routines related to the primitive `short` type.

Variables and Constants

```
public final static short MAX_VALUE
public final static short MIN_VALUE
```

A constant value that contains the maximum possible value (32767) or minimum possible value (-32768) of an integer in Java.

```
public final static Class TYPE
```

The `Short` constant value of the short type class.

Constructors

```
public Short(short num)
public Short(String num) throws NumberFormatException
```

Creates a new instance of a `Short` from the specified `num`.

Methods

```
public byte byteValue()
public double doubleValue()
public float floatValue()
public int intValue()
public long longValue()
public short shortValue()
```

Returns the value of this `Short` as a Java primitive type.

```
public static Short decode(String str) throws NumberFormatException
```

Returns the short representation of the coded argument (`str`). The argument can be coded in decimal, hexadecimal or octal formats.

```
public boolean equals(Object arg)
```

Returns a true value if this `Short` is equal to the parameter `arg`.

```
public int hashCode()
```

Returns the hash code for this `Short`.

```
public static short parseShort(String str) throws NumberFormatException
public static short parseShort(String str, int base) throws NumberFormatException
```

Returns the string argument (`str`) as a short in base 10. The radix of the returned number can be specified in `base`.

```
public static String toString(short num)
```

```
public String toString()
```
Returns a string representation of this `Short` or num.

```
public static Short valueOf(String str) throws NumberFormatException
public static Short valueOf(String str, int base) throws NumberFormatException
```
Returns an instance of a new `Short` object initialized to the value specified in `str`. The radix of the returned number can be specified in `base`.

SimpleDateFormat (java.text)

A public class, derived from `DateFormat`, that allows for the parsing of dates to locale-based strings, and vice versa.

Constructors

```
public SimpleDateFormat()
public SimpleDateFormat(String str)
public SimpleDateFormat(String str, Locale locale)
```
Creates a new instance of a `SimpleDateFormat` using the specified or default pattern and the specified or default locale.

```
public SimpleDateFormat(String str, DateFormatSymbols format)
```
Creates a new instance of a `SimpleDateFormat` using the specified pattern and format data.

Methods

```
public void applyLocalizedPattern(String str)
public String toLocalizedPattern()
```
Sets or returns the locale-based string that describes this `SimpleDateFormat`.

```
public void applyPattern(String str)
public String toPattern()
```
Sets or returns the non-locale-based string that describes this SimpleDateFormat.

```
public Object clone()
```
Returns a copy of this `SimpleDateFormat`.

```
public boolean equals(Object arg)
```
Returns a true value if this `SimpleDateFormat` is equal to `arg`.

```
public StringBuffer format(Date date, StringBuffer dest, FieldPosition pos)
```
Formats the specified string, starting at field pos, placing the result in the specified destination buffer. This method returns the value of the buffer.

```
public DateFormatSymbols getDateFormatSymbols()
public void setDateFormatSymbols(DateFormatSymbols symbols)
```
Returns or sets the date/time formatting symbols for this `SimpleDateFormat`.

`public int hashCode()`

Returns the hash code for this `SimpleDateFormat`.

`public Date parse(String str, ParsePosition pos)`

Parses the specified string, starting at position `pos`, and returns a `Date object`.

SimpleTimeZone (`java.util`)

A public class, derived from `TimeZone`, that represents a time zone in a Gregorian calendar.

Constructors

`public SimpleTimeZone(int offset, String id)`

`public SimpleTimeZone(int offset, String id, int stMonth, int stNthDayWeekIn-Month, int stDayOfWeek, int stTime, int endMonth, int endNthDayWeekInMonth, int endDayOfWeek, int endTime)`

Creates a new `SimpleTimeZone` from an offset from GMT and a time zone id. ID should be obtained from the `TimeZone.getAvailableIDs` method. You can also define the starting and ending times for daylight savings time. Each period has a starting and ending month (`stMonth`, `endMonth`), day of the week in a month (`stNthDayWeekInMonth`, `endNthDayWeekInMonth`), day of the week (`stDayOfWeek`, `endDayOfWeek`), and time (`stTime`, `endTime`).

Methods

`public Object clone()`

Returns a copy of this `SimpleTimeZone`.

`public boolean equals(Object arg)`

Returns a true value if this `SimpleTimeZone` is equal to `arg`.

`public int getOffset(int era, int year, int month, int day, int dayOfWeek, int millisec)`

Returns the offset from the Greenwich Mean Time (GMT), taking into account daylight savings time.

`public int getRawOffset()`

`public void setRawOffset(int millisec)`

Returns or sets the offset from Greenwich Mean Time (GMT) for this `SimpleTimeZone`. These methods do not take daylight savings time into account.

`public synchronized int hashCode()`

Returns the hash code for this `SimpleTimeZone`.

`public boolean inDaylightTime(Date dt)`

Returns a true value if the specified date falls within Daylight Savings Time.

`public void setEndRule(int month, int dyWkInMo, int dyWk, int tm)` `public void setStartRule(int month, int dyWkInMo, int dyWk, int tm)`

Sets the starting and ending times for Daylight Savings Time for this `SimpleTimeZone` to a specified month, day of a week in a month, day of a week, and time (in milliseconds).

`public void setStartYear(int year)`

Sets the Daylight Savings starting year for this `SimpleTimeZone`.

`public boolean useDaylightTime()`

Returns a true value if this `SimpleTimeZone` uses Daylight Savings Time.

Socket (`java.net`)

A public final class, derived from `Object`, that defines a client-side socket.

Constructors

`protected Socket()`

`protected Socket(SocketImpl implementation) throws SocketException`

Creates a new instance of a socket, (not connected to any machine). A socket implementation can be specified or a default one is utilized.

`public Socket(InetAddress dest, int num) throws IOException`

`public Socket(InetAddress dest, int num, InetAddress local, int lnum) throws IOException`

`public Socket(String dest, int num) throws IOException`

`public Socket(String dest, int num, InetAddress local, int lnum) throws IOException`

Creates a new instance of a socket to a destination at port `num`. The socket can be connected to the local machine (`local`) on a local port (`lnum`).

Methods

`public void close() throws IOException`

Closes this socket.

`public InetAddress getInetAddress()`

Returns the Internet address this socket is connected to.

`public InputStream getInputStream() throws IOException`

Returns the input stream this socket utilizes for reading.

`public InetAddress getLocalAddress()`

Returns the local host this socket is bound to.

`public int getLocalPort()`

Returns the local port this socket is using for its connection.

`public OutputStream getOutputStream() throws IOException`

Returns the output stream this socket uses for writing.

`public int getPort()`
Returns the port number the socket is connected to on the destination machine.

`public int getSoLinger() throws SocketException`
`public void setSoLinger(boolean toggle, int num) throws SocketException`
Returns or sets the socket linger time in milliseconds.

`public synchronized int getSoTimeout() throws SocketException`
`public synchronized void setSoTimeout(int num) throws SocketException`
Returns or sets the socket timeout value in milliseconds.

`public boolean getTcpNoDelay() throws SocketException`
`public void setTcpNoDelay(boolean toggle) throws SocketException`
Returns or sets a true value if the `TCP_NODELAY` is set for this socket.

`public static void setSocketImplFactory(SocketImplFactory arg) throws IOException, SocketException`
Sets the socket implementation factory for this socket to `arg`.

`public String toString()`
Returns a string representation of this socket.

Stack (`java.util`)

A public class, derived from `Vector`, that represents a last-in-first-out stack.

Constructors

`public Stack()`
Creates a new instance of an empty stack.

Methods

`public boolean empty()`
Returns a true value if this stack contains no elements.

`public Object peek() throws EmptyStackException`
Returns the item on the top of the stack, but does not remove it.

`public Object pop() throws EmptyStackException`
`public Object push(Object obj)`
Returns and removes the item on the top of the stack (`pop`) or pushes a new item onto the stack (`push`).

`public int search(Object obj)`
Returns the relative position of item `obj` from the top of the stack, or -1 if the item is not in this stack.

String (java.lang)

A public final class, derived from Object and implementing Serializable, that contains methods for creating and parsing strings. Because the contents of a string cannot be modified, many of the methods return a new string.

Constructors

```
public String()
public String(byte[] arg)
public String(byte[] arg, int index, int count)
public String(byte[] arg, String code) throws UnsupportedEncodingException
public String(byte[] arg, int index, int count, String code) throws Unsupporte-
    dEncodingException
```

Creates a new instance of the String class from the array arg. The parameter index indicates which element of arg is the first character of the resulting string, and the parameter count is the number of characters to add to the new string. The String() method creates a new string of no characters. The characters are converted using code encoding format.

```
public String(char[] chars)
public String(char[] chars, int index, int count) throws StringIndexOutOfBound-
    sException
```

Creates an instance of the String class from the array chars. The parameter index indicates which element of chars is the first character of the resulting string, and the parameter count is the number of characters to add to the new string.

```
public String(String str)
public String(StringBuffer str)
```

Creates an instance of the String class from the parameter str.

Methods

```
public char charAt(int idx) throws StringIndexOutOfBoundsException
```

Returns the character at index idx in the current object. The first character of the source string is at index 0.

```
public int compareTo(String str)
```

Compares the current object to str. If both strings are equal, 0 (zero) is returned. If the current string is lexicographically less than the argument, an int less than zero is returned. If the current string is lexicographically greater than the argument, an int greater than zero is returned.

```
public String concat(String source)
```

Returns the product of the concatenation of argument source to the end of the current object.

```
public static String copyValueOf(char[] arg)
public static String copyValueOf(char[] arg, int index, int count)
```

Returns a new String that contains the characters of arg, beginning at index index, and of length count.

`public boolean endsWith(String suff)`

Returns true if the current object ends with the specified suffix.

`public boolean equals(Object arg)`
`public boolean equalsIgnoreCase(String arg)`

Returns true if the current object is equal to `arg`. `arg` must not be null, and must be of exact length and content as the current object. `equalsIgnoreCase` disregards the case of the characters.

`public byte[] getBytes()`
`public byte[] getBytes(String enc) throws UnsupportedEncodingException`

Returns the contents of the current object in an array of bytes decoded with `enc`. When a decoding format is not present, the platform default it used.

`public void getChars(int start, int end, char[] dest, int destStart)`

Copies the contents of the current object starting at index `start` and ending at `end` into the character array `dest` starting at index `destStart`.

`public int hashCode()`

Returns the hash code of the current object.

`public int indexOf(char c)`
`public int indexOf(char c, int index)`

Returns the index of the first occurrence of the character `c` in the current object, no less than `index` (default of 0). Returns a -1 if there is no such occurrence.

`public int indexOf(String str)`
`public int indexOf(String str, int index)`

Returns the index of the first occurrence of the string `str` in the current object, no less than `index` (default of 0). Returns a -1 if there is no such occurrence.

`public String intern()`

Creates a new canonical string with identical content to this string.

`public int lastIndexOf(char c)`
`public int lastIndexOf(char c, int index)`

Returns the index of the last occurrence of the character `c` in the current object, no less than `index` (default of 0). Returns a -1 if there is no such occurrence.

`public int lastIndexOf(String str)`
`public int lastIndexOf(String str, int index)`

Returns the index of the last occurrence of the string `str` in the current object, no less than `index` (default of 0). Returns a -1 if there is no such occurrence.

`public int length()`

Returns the integer length of the current object.

`public boolean regionMatches(boolean case, int cindex, String str, int strindex, int size)`
`public boolean regionMatches(int cindex, String str, int strindex, int size)`

Returns a true result if the subregion of parameter `str` starting at index `strindex` and having length `size`, is identical to a substring of the current object starting at index `cindex` and having the same length. If `case` is true, then character case is ignored during the comparisons.

`public String replace(char oldC, char newC)`

Returns a new string with all occurrences of the `oldC` replaced with the `newC`.

`public boolean startsWith(String str)`
`public boolean startsWith(String str, int index)`

Returns a true if the current object starts with the string `str` at location `index` (default of 0).

`public String substring(int startindex) throws StringIndexOutOfBoundsException`
`public String substring(int startindex, int lastindex) throws StringIndexOutOfBoundsException`

Returns the substring of the current object starting with `startindex` and ending with `lastindex-1` (or the last index of the string in the case of the first method).

`public char[] toCharArray()`
`public String toString()`

Returns the current object as an array of characters or a string. Is present due to the automatic use of the `toString` method in output routines.

`public String toLowerCase()`
`public String toLowerCase(Locale loc)`

Returns the current object with each character in lower case, taking into account variations of the specified locale (`loc`).

`public String toUpperCase()`
`public String toUpperCase(Locale loc)`

Returns the current object with each character in uppercase, taking into account variations of the specified locale (`loc`).

`public String trim()`

Returns the current object with leading and trailing white space removed.

`public static String valueOf(boolean arg)`
`public static String valueOf(char arg)`
`public static String valueOf(char[] arg)`
`public static String valueOf(char[] arg, int index, int size)`
`public static String valueOf(double arg)`
`public static String valueOf(float arg)`
`public static String valueOf(int arg)`
`public static String valueOf(long arg)`
`public static String valueOf(Object arg)`

Returns a string representation of the parameter `arg`. A starting `index` and specified `size` are permitted.

StringBuffer (`java.lang`)

A public class, derived from `Object` and implementing `Serializable`, that contains methods for creating, parsing and modifying string buffers. Unlike a `String`, the content and length of a `StringBuffer` can be changed dynamically.

Constructors

`public StringBuffer()`
`public StringBuffer(int size) throws NegativeArraySizeException`

Creates an instance of the `StringBuffer` class that is empty but has an initial capacity of `size` characters (16 by default).

`public StringBuffer(String arg)`

Creates an instance of the `StringBuffer` class from the string `arg`.

Methods

`public StringBuffer append(boolean arg)`
`public StringBuffer append(char arg)`
`public StringBuffer append(char[] arg)`
`public StringBuffer append(char[] arg, int index, int size)`
`public StringBuffer append(double arg)`
`public StringBuffer append(float arg)`
`public StringBuffer append(int arg)`
`public StringBuffer append(long arg)`
`public StringBuffer append(Object arg)`
`public StringBuffer append(String arg)`

Returns the current object with the `String` parameter `arg` appended to the end. A substring of a character array can be appended by specifying an `index` and `size`.

`public int capacity()`

Returns the capacity of this `StringBuffer`.

`public char charAt(int idx) throws StringIndexOutOfBoundsException`

Returns the character at the specified index of this `StringBuffer`.

`public void ensureCapacity(int min)`

Sets the minimum capacity of this `StringBuffer` to be no less than `min`. The new capacity set by this method may actually be greater than `min`.

`public void getChars(int start, int end, char[] dest, int destindex) throws StringIndexOutOfBoundsException`

Copies the characters at index `start` to `end` from this `StringBuffer` to `dest`, starting at index `destindex`.

`public StringBuffer insert(int index, boolean arg) throws StringIndexOutOfBoundsException`

public StringBuffer insert(int index, char arg) throws StringIndexOutOfBoundsException
public StringBuffer insert(int index, char[] arg) throws StringIndexOutOfBoundsException
public StringBuffer insert(int index, double arg) throws StringIndexOutOfBoundsException
public StringBuffer insert(int index, float arg) throws StringIndexOutOfBoundsException
public StringBuffer insert(int index, int arg) throws StringIndexOutOfBoundsException
public StringBuffer insert(int index, long arg) throws StringIndexOutOfBoundsException
public StringBuffer insert(int index, Object arg) throws StringIndexOutOfBoundsException
public StringBuffer insert(int index, String arg) throws StringIndexOutOfBoundsException

Inserts the string representation of parameter `arg` into this `StringBuffer` at index `index`. Characters to the right of the specified index of this `StringBuffer` are shifted to the right.

public int length()

Returns the length of this `StringBuffer`.

public StringBuffer reverse()

Returns the value of this `StringBuffer` with the order of the characters reversed.

public void setCharAt(int idx, char c)

Sets the character at the specified index to `c`.

public void setLength(int size) throws StringIndexOutOfBoundsException

Truncates this `StringBuffer`, if needed, to the new length of `size`.

public String toString()

Returns the `String` representation of this `StringBuffer`.

StringTokenizer (java.util)

A public class, derived from `Object` and implementing `Enumeration`, that manipulates string values into tokens separated by delimiter characters.

Constructors

public StringTokenizer(String arg)
public StringTokenizer(String arg, String delims)

`public StringTokenizer(String arg, String delims, boolean tokens)`

Creates a new instance of a `StringTokenizer` with the string initialized to `arg`, and utilizing the specified delimiters or the defaults

(`" \t\n\r"`: a space, tab, newline, and carriage return). If `tokens` is true, the delimiters are treated as words within the string and are subject to being returned as tokens.

Methods

`public int countTokens()`

Returns the number of tokens present in this string tokenizer.

`public boolean hasMoreElements()`
`public boolean hasMoreTokens()`

Returns a true value if there are more tokens to be returned by this string tokenizer. `hasMoreElements()` is identical to `hasMoreTokens()` and is implemented to complete the implementation of the `Enumerated` interface.

`public Object nextElement() throws NoSuchElementException`
`public String nextToken() throws NoSuchElementException`
`public String nextToken(String delims) throws NoSuchElementException`

Returns the next token in the string. `nextElement()` is identical to `nextToken()` and is implemented to complete the implementation of the `Enumerated` interface. New delimiters can be specified in the last method, and stay in effect until changed.

System (`java.lang`)

A public final class, derived from `Object`, that contains the standard input, output, and error streams, as well as various system related methods.

Variables and Constants

`public static PrintStream err`
`public static InputStream in`
`public static PrintStream out`

Constant values that are the standard error output stream (stderr), standard input stream (stdin), and the standard output stream (stdout).

Methods

`public static void arraycopy(Object source, int`
srcindex, Object dest, int destindex, int size) throws ArrayIndexOutOfBoundsException, ArrayStoreException

Copies a subarray of `size` objects from `source`, starting at index `srcindex`, to `dest` starting at `destindex`.

`public static long currentTimeMillis()`

Returns the current system in milliseconds from midnight, January 1st, 1970 UTC.

`public static void exit(int num) throws SecurityException`

Exits the program with the status code of `num`.

`public static void gc()`

Executes the `gc` method of the `Runtime` class, which attempts to garbage collect any unused objects, freeing system memory.

`public static Properties getProperties() throws SecurityException`

`public static void setProperties(Properties newprops) throws SecurityException`

Returns or sets the current system properties.

`public static String getProperty(String name) throws SecurityException`

`public static String getProperty(String name, String default) throws SecurityException`

Returns the system property for `name`, or returns the value `default` as a default result if no such `name` exists.

`public static SecurityManager getSecurityManager()`

`public static void setSecurityManager(SecurityManager mgr) throws SecurityException`

Returns or sets the security manager for the current application. If no security manager has been initialized, then a null value is returned by the `get` method.

`public static int identityHashCode(Object arg)`

Returns the hash code for the specified object. This will return the default hash code, in the event that the object's `hashCode` method has been overridden.

`public static void load(String name) throws UnsatisfiedLinkError, SecurityException`

Loads `name` as a dynamic library.

`public static void loadLibrary(String name) throws UnsatisfiedLinkError, SecurityException`

Loads `name` as a system library.

`public static void runFinalization()`

Requests that the Java Virtual Machine execute the finalize method on any outstanding objects.

`public static void runFinalizersOnExit(boolean toggle)`

Allows the execution of the finalizer methods for all objects, when `toggle` is true.

`public static void setErr(PrintStream strm)`

`public static void setIn(InputStream strm)`

`public static void setOut(PrintStream strm)`

Reassigns the error stream, input stream, or output stream to `strm`.

SystemColor (java.awt)

A public final class, derived from `Color` and implementing `Serializable`, that represents the current window system color for the current system. If the user changes the window system colors for this system and the window system can update the new color selection, these color values will change as well.

Variables and Constants

`public final static int ACTIVE_CAPTION`

Constant index to the active caption color in the system color array.

`public final static int ACTIVE_CAPTION_BORDER`
`public final static int ACTIVE_CAPTION_TEXT`

Constant indices to the active caption border and text colors in the system color array.

`public final static int CONTROL`

Constant index to the control color in the system color array.

`public final static int CONTROL_DK_SHADOW`
`public final static int CONTROL_SHADOW`

Constant indices to the control shadow and control dark shadow colors in the system color array.

`public final static int CONTROL_HIGHLIGHT`
`public final static int CONTROL_LT_HIGHLIGHT`

Constant indices to the control highlight and light highlight colors in the system color array.

`public final static int CONTROL_TEXT`

Constant index to the control text color in the system color array.

`public final static int DESKTOP`

Constant index to the desktop color in the system color array.

`public final static int INACTIVE_CAPTION`

Constant index to the inactive caption color in the system color array.

`public final static int INACTIVE_CAPTION_BORDER`
`public final static int INACTIVE_CAPTION_TEXT`

Constant indices to the inactive caption border and text colors in the system color array.

`public final static int INFO`

Constant index to the information (help) text background color in the system color array.

`public final static int INFO_TEXT`
`public final static int MENU_TEXT`

Constant indices to the information (help) and menu text colors in the system color array.

`public final static int NUM_COLORS`

Constant value that holds the number of colors in the system color array.

`public final static int SCROLLBAR`

Constant index to the scrollbar background color in the system color array.

`public final static int TEXT`

Constant index to the background color of text components in the system color array.

`public final static int TEXT_HIGHLIGHT`
`public final static int TEXT_HIGHLIGHT_TEXT`

Constant indices to the background and text colors for highlighted text in the system color array.

`public final static int TEXT_INACTIVE_TEXT`

Constant index to the inactive text color in the system color array.

`public final static int TEXT_TEXT`

Constant index to the color of text components in the system color array.

`public final static int WINDOW`

Constant index to the background color of windows in the system color array.

`public final static int WINDOW_BORDER`
`public final static int WINDOW_TEXT`

Constant indices to the border and text colors of windows in the system color array.

`public final static SystemColor activeCaption`

The system's background color for window border captions.

`public final static SystemColor activeCaptionBorder`
`public final static SystemColor activeCaptionText`

The system's border and text colors for window border captions.

`public final static SystemColor control`

The system's color for window control objects.

`public final static SystemColor controlDkShadow`
`public final static SystemColor controlShadow`

The system's dark shadow and regular shadow colors for control objects.

`public final static SystemColor controlHighlight`
`public final static SystemColor controlLtHighlight`

The system's highlight and light highlight colors for control objects.

`public final static SystemColor controlText`

The system's text color for control objects.

`public final static SystemColor desktop`

The system's color of the desktop background.

`public final static SystemColor inactiveCaption`

The system's background color for inactive caption areas of window borders.

`public final static SystemColor inactiveCaptionBorder`
`public final static SystemColor inactiveCaptionText`

The system's border and text colors for inactive caption areas of window borders.

`public final static SystemColor info`

The system's background color for information (help) text.

`public final static SystemColor infoText`

The system's text color for information (help) text.

`public final static SystemColor menu`
The system's background color for menus.

`public final static SystemColor menuText`
The system's text color for menus.

`public final static SystemColor scrollbar`
The system's background color for scrollbars.

`public final static SystemColor text`
The system's color for text components.

`public final static SystemColor textHighlight`
The system's background color for highlighted text.

`public final static SystemColor textHighlightText`
`public final static SystemColor textInactiveText`
The system's text color for highlighted and inactive text.

`public final static SystemColor textText`
The system's text color for text components.

`public final static SystemColor window`
The system's background color for windows.

`public final static SystemColor windowBorder`
`public final static SystemColor windowText`
The system's border and text colors for windows.

Methods

`public int getRGB()`
Returns the RGB values of this `SystemColor`'s symbolic color.

`public String toString()`
Returns a string representation of this `SystemColor`'s values.

TextArea (`java.awt`)

A public class, derived from `TextComponent`, that provides a graphical multiline area for displaying text.

Variables and Constants

`public final static int SCROLLBARS_BOTH`
`public final static int SCROLLBARS_HORIZONTAL_ONLY`
`public final static int SCROLLBARS_NONE`
`public final static int SCROLLBARS_VERTICAL_ONLY`
Constant values indicating the creation policy of scrollbars for this text area during instantiation.

Constructors

`public TextArea()`
`public TextArea(int r, int c)`
`public TextArea(String str)`
`public TextArea(String str, int r, int c)`
`public TextArea(String str, int r, int c, int sb)`

Creates a new instance of a text area from the string `str`, of the size `r` rows by `c` columns and creating scrollbars according to the direction of the value of `sb` (scrollbar visibility constant). Default values for these constructors include 0 rows and columns, and `SCROLLBARS_BOTH` for the scrollbar creation policy.

Methods

`public void addNotify()`

Creates this text area's peer.

`public void append(String str)`

Appends the specified string to the text area.

`public int getColumns()`
`public void setColumns(int num)`

Returns or sets the number of columns in this text area.

`public Dimension getMinimumSize()`
`public Dimension getPreferredSize()`

Returns the minimum and preferred size of this text area.

`public Dimension getMinimumSize(int r, int c)`
`public Dimension getPreferredSize(int r, int c)`

Returns the minimum and preferred size of this text area, sized to `r` rows and `c` columns.

`public void getRows()`
`public void setRows(int num)`

Sets the number of rows for this text area to `num`.

`public int getScrollbarVisibility()`

Returns the scrollbar visibility status, corresponding to this scrollbar's constant values.

`public void insert(String src, int index)`

Inserts the string `src` into this text area at position `index`.

`protected String paramString()`

Return a string containing the parameters of this text area.

`public synchronized void replaceRange(String newtxt, int begin, int end)`

Replaces the current text from position `begin` to `end` with `newtxt`.

TextComponent (`java.awt`)

A public class, derived from `Component`, that allows for the editing of text in a window toolkit component.

Variables and Constants

`protected transient TextListener textListener`

The current text listener for this text component.

Methods

`public void addTextListener(TextListener listener)`
`public void removeTextListener(TextListener listener)`

Adds or removes the specified `listener` to this text component.

`public int getCaretPosition()`
`public void setCaretPosition(int pos)`

Returns or sets the position of the insertion caret for this text component.

`public synchronized String getSelectedText()`

Returns a string containing the entire text in this text component.

`public synchronized String getText()`
`public synchronized void setText(String str)`

Returns or sets the text contained in this text component.

`public synchronized int getSelectionEnd()`
`public synchronized int getSelectionStart()`

Returns the index of the starting or ending of the current selection from this text component.

`public boolean isEditable()`
`public synchronized void setEditable(boolean toggle)`

Returns or sets the status variable that indicates if this text component can be edited by the user.

`protected String paramString()`

Returns the string representation of the parameters for this text component.

`protected void processEvent(AWTEvent event)`

Handles the specified `event`, passing it to the `processTextEvent` method if `event` is a `TextEvent`; otherwise, this method passes the `event` to the parent's `processEvent method`.

`protected void processTextEvent(TextEvent event)`

Processes this text event, sending it to the appropriate registered listener.

`public void removeNotify()`

Removes the peer for this text component.

`public synchronized void select(int start, int end)`

Selects the text in this text component, starting at index position `start`, and ending at index position `end`.

`public synchronized void selectAll()`
Selects all of the text from this text component.

`public synchronized void setSelectionEnd(int pos)`
`public synchronized void setSelectionStart(int pos)`
Sets the starting or ending position of the selection area in this text component to index position `pos`.

TextEvent (`java.awt.event`)

A public class, derived from `AWTEvent`, that describes a particular AWT text-based event.

Variables and Constants

`public static final int TEXT_FIRST`
`public static final int TEXT_LAST`
Constant values that represent the index of the first and last text event ids.

`public static final int TEXT_VALUE_CHANGED`
A constant value that represents the event of a text component's text value changing.

Constructors

`public TextEvent(Object src, int type)`
Creates a new instance of a `TextEvent` from a specified source object and having a defined event type.

Methods

`public String paramString()`
Returns a string containing the parameters of this `TextEvent`.

TextField (`java.awt`)

A public class, derived from `TextComponent`, that provides a graphical single line of text that can be edited by the user.

Constructors

`public TextField()`
`public TextField(int num)`
`public TextField(String str)`

`public TextField(String str, int num)`

Creates a new instance of a text field from the specified string, `num` columns wide. The first constructor creates a text field with no string present, and 0 columns wide. The third constructor sizes the field based on the number of characters in the string.

Methods

`public void addActionListener(ActionListener listener)`
`public void removeActionListener(ActionListener listener)`

Adds or removes the specified `listener` to this text field.

`public void addNotify()`

Creates this text field's peer.

`public boolean echoCharIsSet()`

Returns a true value if the echo character for this text field is set.

`public int getColumns()`
`public void setColumns(int num)`

Returns or sets the number of columns for this text field.

`public char getEchoChar()`
`public void setEchoChar(char c)`

Returns or sets the current echo character for this text field.

`public Dimension getMinimumSize()`
`public Dimension getPreferredSize()`

Returns the minimum or preferred size needed to display this text field.

`public Dimension getMinimumSize(int num)`
`public Dimension getPreferredSize(int num)`

Returns the minimum or preferred size needed to display this text field of `num` columns.

`protected String paramString()`

Returns a string containing this text field's parameters.

`protected void processActionEvent(ActionEvent event)`

Handles the specified `event` for this text field, sending it to any registered listener.

`protected void processEvent(AWTEvent event)`

Handles any `event` on this text field, passing to the `processActionEvent` method if it is an action event. Otherwise, the event is passed to the parent's `processEvent method`.

Thread (`java.lang`)

A public class, derived from `Object` and implementing `Runnable`, that handles the implementation and management of Java execution threads.

Variables and Constants

`public final static int MAX_PRIORITY`
`public final static int MIN_PRIORITY`
`public final static int NORM_PRIORITY`

Constant values that contain the maximum (10), minimum (1), and normal (6) priority values a thread can have.

Constructors

`public Thread()`

Creates a new instance of a thread.

`public Thread(Runnable arg)`

Creates a new instance of a thread. `arg` specifies which object's run method is invoked to start the thread.

`public Thread(String str)`
`public Thread(Runnable arg, String str)`

Creates a new instance of a thread, named `str`. `arg` specifies which object's run method is invoked to start the thread.

`public Thread(ThreadGroup tgrp, String str) throws SecurityException`
`public Thread(ThreadGroup tgrp, Runnable arg) throws SecurityException`
`public Thread(ThreadGroup tgrp, Runnable arg, String str) throws SecurityException`

Creates a new instance of a thread, named `str` and belonging to thread group `tgrp`. The `arg` parameter specifies which object's `run` method is invoked to start the thread.

Methods

`public static int activeCount()`

Returns the number of active threads in this thread's group.

`public void checkAccess() throws SecurityException`

Validates that the current executing thread has permission to modify this thread.

`public static Thread currentThread()`

Returns the currently executing thread.

`public void destroy()`

Destroys this thread.

`public static void dumpStack()`

Dumps a trace of the stack for the current thread.

`public static int enumerate(Thread[] dest)`

Copies each of the members of this thread's group into the thread array `dest`.

`public final String getName()`
`public final int getPriority()`
`public final ThreadGroup getThreadGroup()`

Returns the name, priority, or thread group of this thread.

`public void interrupt()`

Interrupts this thread's execution.

`public static boolean interrupted()`

Returns a true value if the current thread's execution has been interrupted.

`public final boolean isAlive()`
`public boolean isInterrupted()`

Returns a true value if this thread's execution is alive or has been interrupted.

`public final boolean isDaemon()`

Returns a true value if this thread is a daemon thread.

`public final void join() throws InterruptedException`
`public final void join(long msec) throws InterruptedException`
`public final void join(long msec, int nsec) throws InterruptedException`

Waits up to `msec` milliseconds and `nsec` nanoseconds for this thread to die. The `join()` method waits forever for this thread to die.

`public void run()`

Method containing the main body of the executing thread code. Run methods can run concurrently with other thread run methods.

`public final void setDaemon(boolean flag) throws IllegalThreadStateException`

Sets this thread as a daemon thread, if `flag` is true.

`public final void setName(String str) throws SecurityException`
`public final void setPriority(int val) throws SecurityException`

Sets the name of this thread to `str` or the priority to `val`.

`public static void sleep(long msec) throws InterruptedException`
`public static void sleep(long msec, int nsec) throws InterruptedException`

Causes the current thread to sleep for `msec` milliseconds and `nsec` nanoseconds.

`public void start() throws IllegalThreadStateException`

Start this thread's execution, calling this thread's run method.

`public String toString()`

Returns a string representation of this thread.

`public static void yield()`

Causes the currently executing thread to pause in execution, allowing other threads to run.

Throwable (`java.lang`)

A public class, derived from `Object` and implementing `Serializable`, that is the superclass of all of the errors and exceptions thrown.

Constructors

`public Throwable()`

`public Throwable(String str)`
Creates a new instance of a throwable object with the specified message (`str`) or none present.

Methods

`public Throwable fillInStackTrace()`
Fills in the executable stack trace for this throwable object.

`public String getLocalizedMessage()`
Returns a locale specific description of this object. Locale specific messages should override this method; otherwise, the same message that the `getMessage` method produces will be returned.

`public String getMessage()`
Returns the detail message for this throwable.

`public void printStackTrace()`
`public void printStackTrace(PrintStream stream)`
`public void printStackTrace(PrintWriter stream)`
Prints the stack trace for this throwable to the standard error stream or to the specified `stream`.

`public String toString()`
Returns a string representation of this throwable object.

TimeZone (`java.util`)

A public abstract class, derived from `Object` and implementing `Serializable` and `Cloneable`, that represents an amount of time offset from GMT that results in local time. Functionality is provided to allow for Daylight Savings Time within a time zone.

Methods

`clone()`
Returns a copy of this `TimeZone`.

`public static synchronized String[] getAvailableIDs()`
`public static synchronized String[] getAvailableIDs(int offset)`
Returns a list of all of the supported time zone ids, or only those for a specified time zone offset.

`public static synchronized TimeZone getDefault()`
`public static synchronized void setDefault(TimeZone tz)`
Returns or sets the default time zone.

`public String getID()`
Returns the id of this time zone.

`public abstract int getOffset(int era, int year, int month, int day, int dayOf-Week, int milliseconds)`
Returns the offset from the Greenwich Mean Time (GMT), taking into account daylight savings time.

`public abstract int getRawOffset()`
`public abstract void setRawOffset(int millisec)`
Returns or sets the offset from Greenwich Mean Time (GMT) for this `SimpleTimeZone`. These methods do not take daylight savings time into account.

`public static synchronized TimeZone getTimeZone(String id)`
Returns the time zone corresponding to the specified id value.

`public abstract boolean inDaylightTime(Date dt)`
Returns a true result if the specified date falls within the Daylight Savings Time for this `TimeZone`.

`public void setID(String id)`
Sets the id value of this `TimeZone`.

`public abstract boolean useDaylightTime()`
Returns a true value if this `TimeZone` uses Daylight Savings Time.

Toolkit (`java.awt`)

A public class, derived from `Object`, that is used to tie abstract window classes provided in the AWT to their native implementation on a destination system.

Constructors

`public Toolkit()`
Creates an instance of a toolkit.

Methods

`public abstract void beep()`
Plays a beep, created by the audio device.

`public abstract int checkImage(Image img, int width, int height, ImageObserver obs)`
Returns the status of an image (`img`) that is being loaded by the specified observer (`obs`) at a `width` and `height` on the screen.

`protected abstract ButtonPeer createButton(Button arg)`
`protected abstract CanvasPeer createCanvas(Canvas arg)`
`protected abstract CheckboxPeer createCheckbox(Checkbox arg)`
`protected abstract CheckboxMenuItemPeer createCheckboxMenuItem(CheckboxMenuItem arg)`
`protected abstract ChoicePeer createChoice(Choice arg)`
`protected LightweightPeer createComponent(Component arg)`
`protected abstract DialogPeer createDialog(Dialog arg)`
`protected abstract FileDialogPeer createFileDialog(FileDialog arg)`
`protected abstract FramePeer createFrame(Frame arg)`
`protected abstract LabelPeer createLabel(Label arg)`

```
protected abstract ListPeer createList(List arg)
protected abstract MenuPeer createMenu(Menu arg)
protected abstract MenuBarPeer createMenuBar(MenuBar arg)
protected abstract MenuItemPeer createMenuItem(MenuItem arg)
protected abstract PanelPeer createPanel(Panel arg)
protected abstract PopupMenuPeer createPopupMenu(PopupMenu arg)
protected abstract ScrollbarPeer createScrollbar(Scrollbar arg)
protected abstract ScrollPanePeer createScrollPane(ScrollPane arg)
protected abstract TextAreaPeer createTextArea(TextArea arg)
protected abstract TextFieldPeer createTextField(TextField arg)
protected abstract WindowPeer createWindow(Window arg)
```

Creates a new AWT component and returns its peer.

```
public Image createImage(byte[] image)
public abstract Image createImage(byte[] image, int index, int size)
public abstract Image createImage(ImageProducer prod)
```

Creates a new image from the specified array of bytes or image producer. The second method allows for an offset from the start of the array as well as the number of bytes to use from the array.

```
public abstract ColorModel getColorModel()
```

Returns the color model provided from this toolkit.

```
public static synchronized Toolkit getDefaultToolkit() throws AWTError
```

Returns the default toolkit.

```
public abstract String[] getFontList()
```

Returns the list of available fonts provided from this toolkit.

URL (`java.net`)

A public final class, derived from `Object` and implementing `Serializable`, that represents a Web Uniform Resource Locator (URL).

Constructors

```
public URL(String arg) throws MalformedURLException
public URL(URL url, String type) throws MalformedURLException
```

Creates a URL instance from a string argument, or by parsing a `type` (http, gopher, ftp) and the remaining base.

```
public URL(String proto, String source, int num, String doc) throws Malforme-
    dURLException
public URL(String proto, String source, String doc) throws MalformedURLException
```

Creates a URL instance using a defined protocol (`proto`), `source` system, destination port `num`, and document (`doc`).

Methods

`public boolean equals(Object obj)`
Returns a true value if this URL is equal in all respects (protocol, source, port, and document) to `obj`.

`public final Object getContent() throws IOException`
Returns the retrieved contents as an `Object`.

`public String getFile()`
`public String getRef()`
Returns the name of the file (document) or its anchor this URL will attempt to retrieve.

`public String getHost()`
`public int getPort()`
Returns the name of the host (source) or the port this URL will attempt to connect to.

`public String getProtocol()`
Returns the protocol this URL will use in retrieving the data.

`public int hashCode()`
Returns the hash code for this URL.

`public URLConnection openConnection() throws IOException`
`public final InputStream openStream() throws IOException`
Returns a connection to this URL and returns the connection or a stream.

`public boolean sameFile(URL arg)`
Returns a true value if this URL retrieves the same file as the `arg` URL.

`protected void set(String proto, String source, int num, String doc, String anchor)`
Sets the protocol (`proto`), `source`, port `num`, file (`doc`) and reference (`anchor`) for this URL.

`public static void setURLStreamHandlerFactory(URLStreamHandlerFactory fac) throws Error`
Sets the URL `StreamHandlerFactory` for this application to `fac`.

`public String toExternalForm()`
`public String toString()`
Returns a string representation of this URL.

URLConnection (`java.net`)

A public abstract class, derived from `Object`, that is the superclass to any class that establishes a connection between a specified URL and an application.

Variables and Constants

`protected boolean allowUserInteraction`
When true, allows for user interaction with some types of URLs (such as password dialogs).

`protected boolean connected`

Holds the status of the current connection.

`protected boolean doInput`
`protected boolean doOutput`

When true, signifies that this URL is used for reading and writing.

`protected long ifModifiedSince`

Holds a time value used in determining if a URL's object should be fetched if it has been modified more recently than this time.

`public static FileNameMap fileNameMap`

Holds the file name mapping of a file name to a MIME type for this URLConnection.

`protected URL url`

The remote file or object this connection will communicate with.

`protected boolean useCaches`

When true, allows the protocol to use cached information, if possible.

Constructors

`protected URLConnection(URL arg)`

Creates a new `URLConnection` to `arg`.

Methods

`public abstract void connect() throws IOException`

Opens a connection to this URL.

`public boolean getAllowUserInteraction()`
`public void setAllowUserInteraction(boolean flag)`

Returns or sets the state of the `allowUserInteraction` field.

`public Object getContent() throws IOException, UnknownServiceException`
`public String getContentEncoding()`
`public int getContentLength()`
`public String getContentType()`
`public URL getURL()`

Returns the document encoding value, content, length, type, or URL for this `URLConnection`.

`public long getDate()`
`public long getExpiration()`
`public long getLastModified()`

Returns the date field or expiration time from the header of this `URLConnection`. `getLastModified` returns the number of seconds since midnight, January 1, 1970 UTC that the URL content for this URLConnection was last modified.

`public static boolean getDefaultAllowUserInteraction()`
`public static void setDefaultAllowUserInteraction(boolean flag)`

Returns or sets the default value of the `allowUserInteraction` field.

`public static String getDefaultRequestProperty(String prop)` `public static void setDefaultRequestProperty(String prop, String val)`

Returns or sets the default request property, named `prop`, for this URLConnection.

`public boolean getDefaultUseCaches()`

`public void setDefaultUseCaches(boolean flag)`

Returns or sets the default value of the `useCaches` field.

`public boolean getDoInput()`

`public boolean getDoOutput()`

`public void setDoInput(boolean flag)`

`public void setDoOutput(boolean flag)`

Returns or sets a true value if this connection is used for reading input or writing output.

`public String getHeaderField(int num)`

`public String getHeaderField(String key)`

Returns the numth header field or the value that corresponds to `key` of the URL.

`public long getHeaderFieldDate(String key, long default)`

`public int getHeaderFieldInt(String key, int default)`

`public String getHeaderFieldKey(int num)`

Returns the value of the header field named `key`, or the `default` if there is no such field. The key can also be specified as an index number.

`public long getIfModifiedSince()`

`public void setIfModifiedSince(long since)`

Returns or sets the value of the `ifModifiedSince` field.

`public InputStream getInputStream() throws UnknownServiceException`

`public OutputStream getOutputStream() throws IOException, UnknownServiceException`

Returns the input or output stream for this `URLConnection`.

`public String getRequestProperty(String prop)`

`public void setRequestProperty(String prop, String val)`

Returns or sets the value of the request property, `prop`, for this `URLConnection`.

`public boolean getUseCaches()`

`public void setUseCaches(boolean flag)`

Returns or sets the value of the `useCaches` field of this `URLConnection`.

`protected static String guessContentTypeFromName(String name)`

`protected static String guessContentTypeFromStream(InputStream strm) throws IOException`

Returns a guess of the type of content from a data stream or a name.

`public static void setContentHandlerFactory(ContentHandlerFactory arg) throws Error`

Sets the `ContentHandlerFactory` for this application to `arg`.

`public String toString()`

Returns a string representation of this `URLConnection`.

URLEncoder (`java.net`)

A public class, derived from `Object`, that converts a string to a MIME format.

Methods

`public static String encode(String str)`

Encodes the string `str` into MIME “x-www-form-urlencoded” format.

URLStreamHandler (`java.net`)

A public abstract class, derived from `Object`, that is the superclass for all stream-based protocol handling classes.

Constructors

`public URLStreamHandler()`

Creates a new instance of a `URLStreamHandler`.

Methods

`protected abstract URLConnection openConnection(URL dest) throws IOException`

Opens a connection to the specified URL.

`protected void parseURL(URL url, String src, int init, int end)`

Parses the string representation of a URL (`url`), starting at index position `init` and ending at index `end`, into `dest`.

`protected void setURL(URL url, String prot, String src, int num, String doc, String anchor)`

Sets the URL (`url`) fields to `prot` (name of the protocol), `src` (name of the remote machine), `num` (port number of connection on remote machine), `doc` (object to retrieve), and `anchor` (anchor reference).

`protected String toExternalForm(URL url)`

Returns a string representation of the specified URL.

Vector (`java.util`)

A public class, derived from `Object` and implementing `Serializable` and `Cloneable`, that manages an array of objects. Elements can be added or removed from this list and the size of the list can change dynamically.

Variables and Constants

`protected int capacityIncrement`

The amount of element spaces to be added to the vector each time that an increase must occur. A `capacityIncrement` of 0 indicates that the list will double in size at every resizing.

`protected int elementCount`
`protected Object elementData[]`

The number of elements and the array containing the elements currently in this `Vector`.

Constructors

`public Vector()`
`public Vector(int size)`
`public Vector(int size, int incr)`

Creates a new instance of a vector with an initial size of `size` (or using the default of 10). An initial `capacityIncrement` can also be specified.

Methods

`public final void addElement(Object arg)`
`public final void insertElementAt(Object arg, int index) throws ArrayIndexOutOfBoundsException`

Adds element `arg` to the end of this `Vector` or at a specific `index`. The capacity of the vector is adjusted if needed.

`public final int capacity()`
`public final void ensureCapacity(int size)`

Returns the current capacity of this `Vector`, or ensures that it can contain at least `size` elements

`public Object clone()`

Returns the clone of this `Vector`.

`public final boolean contains(Object arg)`

Returns a true value if this Vector contains object `arg`.

`public final void copyInto(Object[] dest)`

Copies each of the elements of this `Vector` into the array `dest`.

`public final Object elementAt(int index) throws ArrayIndexOutOfBoundsException`

Returns the element at location `index` from this `Vector`.

`public final Enumeration elements()`

Returns an `Enumeration` of the elements in this `Vector`.

`public final Object firstElement() throws NoSuchElementException`

```
public final Object lastElement() throws NoSuchElementException
```
Returns the first or last element in this `Vector`.

```
public final int indexOf(Object arg)
public final int indexOf(Object arg, int index)
```
Returns the index of the first occurrence of element `arg`, starting at `index`. A -1 value is returned if the element is not found.

```
public final boolean isEmpty()
```
Returns a true value if this `Vector` contains no elements.

```
public final int lastIndexOf(Object arg)
public final int lastIndexOf(Object arg, int index)
```
Returns the first index that object `arg` occurs at in this `Vector`, starting a backwards search at the specified index. If the object is not located, a -1 is returned.

```
public final void removeAllElements()
public final boolean removeElement(Object arg)
public final void removeElementAt(int index) throws ArrayIndexOutOfBoundsExcep-
    tion
```
Removes element `arg` and returns a true value. If the object requested is not located, a false value is returned. An element can also be removed at a specific `index` value, or all elements can be removed.

```
public final void setElementAt(Object arg, int index) throws ArrayIndexOutOf-
    BoundsException
```
Sets the element at the specified `index` equal to object `arg`.

```
public final void setSize(int size)
```
Sets the size of this `Vector` to `size`.

```
public final int size()
```
Returns the number of elements in this `Vector`.

```
public final String toString()
```
Returns a string representation of this `Vector`.

```
public final void trimToSize()
```
Reduces the size of this `Vector` to contain all of the elements present.

Void (`java.lang`)

An uninstantiable class that acts as a placeholder for the primitive `void` type in the `Class` object.

Variables and Constants

```
public final static Class TYPE
```
The `Void` constant value of the void type class.

Window (`java.awt`)

A public class, derived from `Container`, that creates a graphical area that has no borders or menus and can be used to contain AWT components.

Constructors

`public Window(Frame frm)`

Creates a new instance of a window that has a parent frame (`frm`). The window is initially not visible.

Methods

`public void addNotify()`

Creates this window's peer.

`public synchronized void addWindowListener(WindowListener listener)`
`public synchronized void removeWindowListener(WindowListener listener)`

Removes or adds the specified window listener (`listener`) for this window.

`public void dispose()`

Removes this window and deletes any resources used by this window.

`public Component getFocusOwner()`

Returns the component from this active window that currently has the focus.

`public Locale getLocale()`

Returns the locale for this window.

`public Toolkit getToolkit()`

Returns the toolkit for this window.

`public final String getWarningString()`

Returns the warning string for this window.

`public boolean isShowing()`

Returns a true value if this window is currently visible on the screen.

`public void pack()`

Causes all of the components of this window to be laid out according to their preferred size.

`protected void processEvent(AWTEvent event)`

Processes the specified event for this window. If the event is a `WindowEvent`, then this method calls the process `WindowEvent` method of this window, otherwise it will call the parent class' `processEvent` method.

`protected void processWindowEvent(WindowEvent event)`

Handles any `WindowEvent` (`event`) generated on this window, and passes them to a registered listener for that event.

`public void show()`

Makes this window visible to the user and brings it to the front (on top of other windows).

`public void toBack()`

void toFront()

Sends this window to the back or front of other windows currently displayed on the screen.

WindowAdapter (java.awt.event)

A public abstract class, derived from Object and implementing WindowListener, that permits a derived class to override the predefined no-op AWT window events.

Constructors

public WindowAdapter()

Creates a new instance of a WindowAdapter.

Methods

```
public void windowActivated(WindowEvent event)
public void windowClosed(WindowEvent event)
public void windowClosing(WindowEvent event)
public void windowDeactivated(WindowEvent event)
public void windowDeiconified(WindowEvent event)
public void windowIconified(WindowEvent event)
public void windowOpened(WindowEvent event)
```

Empty methods that should be overridden in order to implement event handling for window events.

WindowEvent (java.awt.event)

A public class, derived from ComponentEvent, that describes a particular AWT window-based event.

Variables and Constants

```
public static final int WINDOW_ACTIVATED
public static final int WINDOW_CLOSED
public static final int WINDOW_CLOSING
public static final int WINDOW_DEACTIVATED
public static final int WINDOW_DEICONIFIED
public static final int WINDOW_FIRST
public static final int WINDOW_ICONIFIED
public static final int WINDOW_LAST
```

`public static final int WINDOW_OPENED`

Constant values which represent a variety of window event types.

Constructors

`public WindowEvent(Window src, int type)`

Creates a new instance of a `WindowEvent` from a specified source window and having a specific event type.

Methods

`public Window getWindow()`

Returns the source window that this event was triggered in.

`public String paramString()`

Returns a string containing the parameters for this `WindowEvent`.

Index

B

C

F

G

H

I

M

N

O

P

Q

R

S

T

U

V

Sun Microsystems, Inc.
Binary Code License Agreement

READ THE TERMS OF THIS AGREEMENT AND ANY PROVIDED SUPPLEMENTAL LICENSE TERMS (COLLECTIVELY "AGREEMENT") CAREFULLY BEFORE OPENING THE SOFTWARE MEDIA PACKAGE. BY OPENING THE SOFTWARE MEDIA PACKAGE, YOU AGREE TO THE TERMS OF THIS AGREEMENT. IF YOU ARE ACCESSING THE SOFTWARE ELECTRONICALLY, INDICATE YOUR ACCEPTANCE OF THESE TERMS BY SELECTING THE "ACCEPT" BUTTON AT THE END OF THIS AGREEMENT. IF YOU DO NOT AGREE TO ALL THESE TERMS, PROMPTLY RETURN THE UNUSED SOFTWARE TO YOUR PLACE OF PURCHASE FOR A REFUND OR, IF THE SOFTWARE IS ACCESSED ELECTRONICALLY, SELECT THE "DECLINE" BUTTON AT THE END OF THIS AGREEMENT.

1. **LICENSE TO USE.** Sun grants you a non-exclusive and non-transferable license for the internal use only of the accompanying software and documentation and any error corrections provided by Sun (collectively "Software"), by the number of users and the class of computer hardware for which the corresponding fee has been paid.

2. **RESTRICTIONS** Software is confidential and copyrighted. Title to Software and all associated intellectual property rights is retained by Sun and/or its licensors. Except as specifically authorized in any Supplemental License Terms, you may not make copies of Software, other than a single copy of Software for archival purposes. Unless enforcement is prohibited by applicable law, you may not modify, decompile, or reverse engineer Software. You acknowledge that Software is not designed, licensed or intended for use in the design, construction, operation or maintenance of any nuclear facility. Sun disclaims any express or implied warranty of fitness for such uses. No right, title or interest in or to any trademark, service mark, logo or trade name of Sun or its licensors is granted under this Agreement."

3. **LIMITED WARRANTY.** Sun warrants to you that for a period of ninety (90) days from the date of purchase, as evidenced by a copy of the receipt, the media on which Software is furnished (if any) will be free of defects in materials and workmanship under normal use. Except for the foregoing, Software is provided "AS IS". Your exclusive remedy and Sun's entire liability under this limited warranty will be at Sun's option to replace Software media or refund the fee paid for Software.

4. **DISCLAIMER OF WARRANTY.** UNLESS SPECIFIED IN THIS AGREEMENT, ALL EXPRESS OR IMPLIED CONDITIONS, REPRESENTATIONS AND WARRANTIES, INCLUDING ANY IMPLIED WARRANTY OF MERCHANTABILITY, FITNESS FOR A PARTICULAR PURPOSE OR NON-INFRINGEMENT ARE DISCLAIMED, EXCEPT TO THE EXTENT THAT THESE DISCLAIMERS ARE HELD TO BE LEGALLY INVALID.

5. **LIMITATION OF LIABILITY.** TO THE EXTENT NOT PROHIBITED BY LAW, IN NO EVENT WILL SUN OR ITS LICENSORS BE LIABLE FOR ANY LOST REVENUE, PROFIT OR DATA, OR FOR SPECIAL, INDIRECT, CONSEQUENTIAL, INCIDENTAL OR PUNITIVE DAMAGES, HOWEVER CAUSED REGARDLESS OF THE THEORY OF LIABILITY, ARISING OUT OF OR RELATED TO THE USE OF OR INABILITY TO USE SOFTWARE, EVEN IF SUN HAS BEEN ADVISED OF THE POSSIBILITY OF SUCH DAMAGES. In no event will Sun's liability to you, whether in contract, tort (including negligence), or otherwise, exceed the amount paid by you for Software under this Agreement. The foregoing limitations will apply even if the above stated warranty fails of its essential purpose.

6. **Termination.** This Agreement is effective until terminated. You may terminate this Agreement at any time by destroying all copies of Software. This Agreement will terminate immediately without notice from Sun

if you fail to comply with any provision of this Agreement. Upon Termination, you must destroy all copies of Software.

7. **Export Regulations.** All Software and technical data delivered under this Agreement are subject to US export control laws and may be subject to export or import regulations in other countries. You agree to comply strictly with all such laws and regulations and acknowledge that you have the responsibility to obtain such licenses to export, re-export, or import as may be required after delivery to you.

8. **U.S. Government Restricted Rights.** If Software is being acquired by or on behalf of the U.S. Government or by a U.S. Government prime contractor or subcontractor (at any tier), then the Government's rights in Software and accompanying documentation will be only as set forth in this Agreement; this is in accordance with 48 CFR 227.7201 through 227.7202-4 (for Department of Defense (DOD) acquisitions) and with 48 CFR 2.101 and 12.212 (for non-DOD acquisitions).

9. **Governing Law.** Any action related to this Agreement will be governed by California law and controlling U.S. federal law. No choice of law rules of any jurisdiction will apply.

10. **Severability.** If any provision of this Agreement is held to be unenforceable, this Agreement will remain in effect with the provision omitted, unless omission would frustrate the intent of the parties, in which case this Agreement will immediately terminate.

11. **Integration.** This Agreement is the entire agreement between you and Sun relating to its subject matter. It supersedes all prior or contemporaneous oral or written communications, proposals, representations and warranties and prevails over any conflicting or additional terms of any quote, order, acknowledgment, or other communication between the parties relating to its subject matter during the term of this Agreement. No modification of this Agreement will be binding, unless in writing and signed by an authorized representative of each party.

For inquiries please contact: Sun Microsystems, Inc. 901 San Antonio Road, Palo Alto, California 94303

JAVA(TM) DEVELOPMENT TOOLS
FORTE(TM) FOR JAVA(TM), COMMUNITY EDITION, VERSION 1.0
SUPPLEMENTAL LICENSE TERMS

These supplemental license terms ("Supplement") add to or modify the terms of the Binary Code License Agreement (collectively, the "Agreement"). Capitalized terms not defined in this Supplement shall have the same meanings ascribed to them in the Agreement. These Supplemental terms shall supersede any inconsistent or conflicting terms in the Agreement, or in any license contained within the Software.

1. **Internal Use and Development License Grant.** Subject to the terms and conditions of this Agreement, including but not limited to Section 3 (Java Technology Restrictions) of this Supplement, Sun grants you a non-exclusive, non-transferable, limited license to reproduce internally and use internally the binary form of the Software for the sole purpose of designing, developing and testing your Java(TM) applets and applications intended to run on a compatible Java environment (the "Programs").

2. **License to Distribute.** Subject to the terms and conditions of this Agreement, including but not limited to Section 3 (Java Technology Restrictions) of this Supplement, Sun grants you a non-exclusive, non-transferable, limited license to reproduce and distribute the binary form of the Software, to third party end users, either separately or bundled with Programs provided that you: (i) distribute the Software complete and unmodified; (ii) do not distribute additional software intended to supersede any component(s) of the Software; (iii) do not remove or alter any proprietary legends or notices contained in or on the Software;

and (iv) only distribute the Software pursuant to a license agreement that protects Sun's interests consistent with the terms contained in this Agreement, and (v) agree to defend and indemnify Sun and its licensors from and against any damages, costs, liabilities, settlement amounts and/or expenses (including attorneys' fees) incurred in connection with any claim, lawsuit or action by any third party that arises or results from the use or distribution of any and all Programs and/or Software.

3. **Java Technology Restrictions.** (i) You may not modify the Java Platform Interface ("JPI", identified as classes contained within the "java" package or any subpackages of the "java" package), by creating additional classes within the JPI or otherwise causing the addition to or modification of the classes in the JPI. (ii) In the event that you create an additional class and associated API(s) which (a) extends the functionality of a Java Platform; and, (b) is exposed to third party software developers for the purpose of developing additional software which invokes such additional API, you must promptly publish broadly an accurate specification for such API for free use by all developers. (iii) You may not create, or authorize your licensees to create additional classes, interfaces, or subpackages that are in any way identified as "java", "javax" or "sun" or similar as specified by Sun in any class file naming convention designation. Refer to the Java Runtime Environment Version 1.3 binary code license (http ://java.sun.com/products/jdk/1.3/jre/index.html) for the availability of runtime code that may be distributed with Java applets and applications.

5. **Trademarks and Logos.** You acknowledge and agree as between you and Sun that Sun owns the Java trademark and all Java-related trademarks, service marks, logos and other brand designations including the Coffee Cup logo and Duke logo ("Java Marks"), and you agree to comply with the Sun Trademark and Logo Usage Requirements currently located at http://www.sun.com/policies/trademarks. Any use you make of the Java Marks inures to Sun's benefit.

6. **Source Code.** Software may contain source code that is provided solely for reference purposes pursuant to the terms of this Agreement. Source code may not be redistributed.

JAVA™ 2 SOFTWARE DEVELOPMENT KIT STANDARD EDITION VERSION 1.3 SUPPLEMENTAL LICENSE TERMS

These supplemental license terms ("Supplemental Terms") add to or modify the terms of the Binary Code License Agreement (collectively, the "Agreement"). Capitalized terms not defined in these Supplemental Terms shall have the same meanings ascribed to them in the Agreement. These Supplemental Terms shall supersede any inconsistent or conflicting terms in the Agreement, or in any license contained within the Software.

1. **Internal Use and Development License Grant.** Subject to the terms and conditions of this Agreement, including, but not limited to, Section 2 (Redistributables) and Section 4 (Java Technology Restrictions) of these Supplemental Terms, Sun grants you a non-exclusive, non-transferable, limited license to reproduce the Software for internal use only for the sole purpose of development of your Java™ applet and application ("Program"), provided that you do not redistribute the Software in whole or in part, either separately or included with any Program.

2. **Redistributables.** In addition to the license granted in Paragraph 1 above, Sun grants you a non-exclusive, non-transferable, limited license to reproduce and distribute, only as part of your separate copy of JAVA(™) 2 RUNTIME ENVIRONMENT STANDARD EDITION VERSION 1.3 software, those files specifically identified as redistributable in the JAVA(™) 2 RUNTIME ENVIRONMENT STANDARD EDITION VERSION 1.3 "README" file (the "Redistributables") provided that: (a) you distribute the Redistributables complete and unmodified (unless otherwise specified in the applicable README file),

and only bundled as part of the Java™ applets and applications that you develop (the "Programs:); (b) you do not distribute additional software intended to supersede any component(s) of the Redistributables; (c) you do not remove or alter any proprietary legends or notices contained in or on the Redistributables; (d) you only distribute the Redistributables pursuant to a license agreement that protects Sun's interests consistent with the terms contained in the Agreement, and (e) you agree to defend and indemnify Sun and its licensors from and against any damages, costs, liabilities, settlement amounts and/or expenses (including attorneys' fees) incurred in connection with any claim, lawsuit or action by any third party that arises or results from the use or distribution of any and all Programs and/or Software.

3. **Separate Distribution License Required.** You understand and agree that you must first obtain a separate license from Sun prior to reproducing or modifying any portion of the Software other than as provided with respect to Redistributables in Paragraph 2 above.

4. **Java Technology Restrictions.** You may not modify the Java Platform Interface ("JPI", identified as classes contained within the "java" package or any subpackages of the "java" package), by creating additional classes within the JPI or otherwise causing the addition to or modification of the classes in the JPI. In the event that you create an additional class and associated API(s) which (i) extends the functionality of a Java environment, and (ii) is exposed to third party software developers for the purpose of developing additional software which invokes such additional API, you must promptly publish broadly an accurate specification for such API for free use by all developers. You may not create, or authorize your licensees to create additional classes, interfaces, or subpackages that are in any way identified as "java", "javax", "sun" or similar convention as specified by Sun in any class file naming convention. Refer to the appropriate version of the Java Runtime Environment binary code license (currently located at http://www.java.sun.com/jdk/index.html) for the availability of runtime code which may be distributed with Java applets and applications.

5. **Trademarks and Logos.** You acknowledge and agree as between you and Sun that Sun owns the Java trademark and all Java-related trademarks, service marks, logos and other brand designations including the Coffee Cup logo and Duke logo ("Java Marks"), and you agree to comply with the Sun Trademark and Logo Usage Requirements currently located at http://www.sun.com/policies/trademarks. Any use you make of the Java Marks inures to Sun's benefit.

6. **Source Code.** Software may contain source code that is provided solely for reference purposes pursuant to the terms of this Agreement.

7. **Termination.** Sun may terminate this Agreement immediately should any Software become, or in Sun's opinion be likely to become, the subject of a claim of infringement of a patent, trade secret, copyright or other intellectual property right.